Memory Dump Analysis Anthology
Volume 1

Collector's Revised Edition

Dmitry Vostokov
Software Diagnostics Institute

OpenTask

Published by OpenTask, Republic of Ireland

OpenTask books are available through booksellers and distributors worldwide. For further information or comments, send requests to press@opentask.com.

A CIP catalog record for this book is available from the British Library.

ISBN-13: 978-1912636211 (Paperback)
ISBN-13: 978-1906717018 (Hardback)

Revision 4.11 (May 2025)

Dedicated to the memory of my mother.

[This page is intentionally left blank]

Summary of Contents

[This page is intentionally left blank]

Contents

[This page is intentionally left blank]

Preface

This reference volume consists of revised, edited, cross-referenced, and thematically organized articles from Software Diagnostics Institute (DumpAnalysis.org) and Software Diagnostics Library (former Crash Dump Analysis blog, DumpAnalysis.org/blog) written in August 2006 - December 2007. This major revision updates tool information and links with ones relevant for Windows 10 and removes obsolete references. Some articles are preserved for historical reasons. The output of a few WinDbg commands was updated to reflect the debugger engine changes. Most of the content, especially memory analysis pattern language, is still relevant today and for the foreseeable future.

We hope this reference is useful for:

- Software engineers developing and maintaining products on Windows platforms.
- Technical support, escalation, and site reliability engineers dealing with complex software issues.
- Quality assurance engineers testing software on Windows platforms.
- Security and vulnerability researchers, reverse engineers, malware and memory forensics analysts.

If you encounter any error, please send me a personal message using this contact e-mail:

dmitry.vostokov@dumpanalysis.org

Alternatively, via Twitter @DumpAnalysis

Facebook page and group:

http://www.facebook.com/DumpAnalysis
http://www.facebook.com/groups/dumpanalysis

[This page is intentionally left blank]

Acknowledgments

First, special thanks to Julio Rodriguez, who opened to me the world of technical support and escalation engineering.

Thousands of people reviewed DumpAnalysis.org blog content, and I would like to thank all of them, including the following individuals for providing their comments, suggestions, and encouragement:

Francisco Alves
Andrei Belogortseff
Tate Calhoun
Jeff Curless
Volker von Einem
Michelle Griffin
Da-Chang Guan
Laurent Falguiere
Roberto Farah
Mario Hewardt
Ken Johnson
Lalit Kaushal
Heejune Kim
Martin Kulov
Kiran Kumar
Marc Kilduff
John Lambert
Taehwa Lee
Ivan Lorente
Fatima Mansour
Ramzy Mansour
Thomas Monahan
Mikhail Naganov
Toby Opferman
Alexey Pakhunov
Victor Pendlebury
Kapildev Ramlal
Jerome Reid
Tal Rosen
Nicolas Ruff
Marc Sherman
Konstantin Tchebotarev
Serhat Toktamisoglu
Hugh Tonks
Nicholas Vasile

Thanks to Tony Donegan, for the front cover design.

Special thanks to Igor Dzyubenko, who suggested corrections and improvements for the previous revision.

[This page is intentionally left blank]

About the Author

Dmitry Vostokov is an internationally recognized expert, speaker, educator, scientist, inventor, and author. He founded the pattern-oriented software diagnostics, forensics, and prognostics discipline (Systematic Software Diagnostics) and Software Diagnostics Institute (DA+TA: DumpAnalysis.org + TraceAnalysis.org). Vostokov has also authored over 50 books on software diagnostics, anomaly detection and analysis, software and memory forensics, root cause analysis and problem solving, memory dump analysis, debugging, software trace and log analysis, reverse engineering, and malware analysis. He has over 30 years of experience in software architecture, design, development, and maintenance in various industries, including leadership, technical, and people management roles. Dmitry founded OpenTask Iterative and Incremental Publishing (OpenTask.com) and Software Diagnostics Technology and Services (former Memory Dump Analysis Services) PatternDiagnostics.com. In his spare time, he explores Software Narratology and Quantum Software Diagnostics. His interest areas are theoretical software diagnostics and its mathematical and computer science foundations, application of formal logic, semiotics, artificial intelligence, machine learning, and data mining to diagnostics and anomaly detection, software diagnostics engineering and diagnostics-driven development, diagnostics workflow and interaction. Recent interest areas also include functional programming, cloud native computing, monitoring, observability, visualization, security, automation, applications of category theory to software diagnostics, development and big data, and diagnostics of artificial intelligence.

[This page is intentionally left blank]

PART 1: Crash Dumps for Beginners

Crash Dumps Depicted

There is much confusion among Windows users about different dump types. Windows has three major dump types, not including various mini-dumps: complete, kernel, and user. A long time ago, I created a hand-crafted picture showing how various parts of computer memory are saved in a dump:

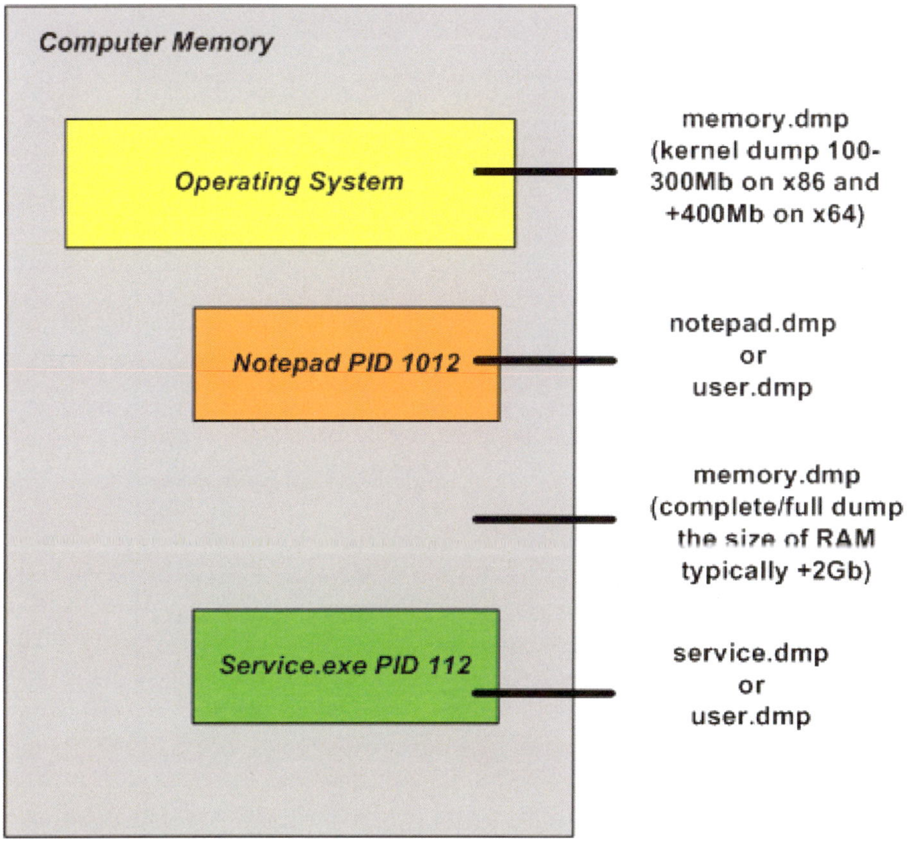

Right Crash Dumps

How do we make sure our customers got the right crash dumps? If the dump type is not what we asked for, what recommendations do we need to provide for further customer actions? Troubled with such questions during my first years in Citrix technical support I developed a lightweight Explorer extension and a command-line version of a dump checking tool called Citrix DumpCheck:

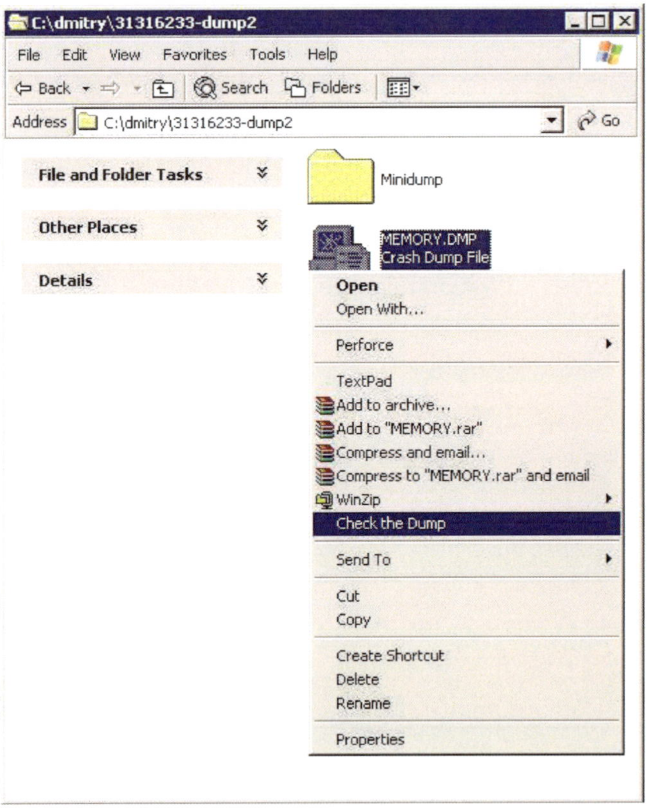

It did necessary validity checks and showed the dump type, for example:

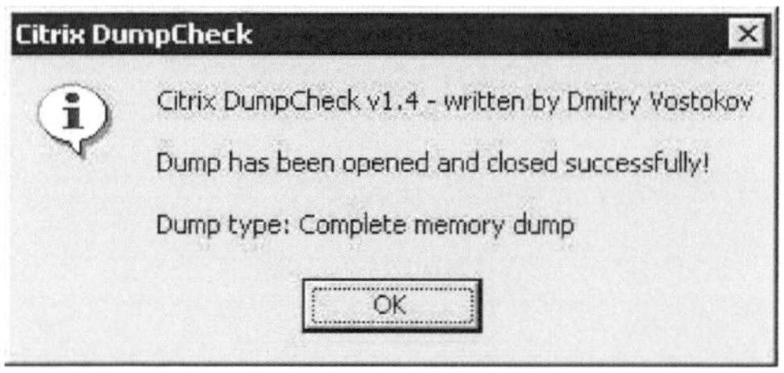

For small minidump type (64Kb), the tool would have suggested changing settings in Control Panel.

For convenience, I reprint **FAQ** from the tool article which is no longer accessible at the time of this revision (various links are omitted for the same reason):

Q. Is it possible to show more information like process name in a user dump or whether full page heap was enabled?

A. Indeed, it is possible to include. However, it requires access to OS symbol files during runtime, and most customers don't have them installed or downloaded from the Microsoft symbol server. So the design decision was not to include these checks in version 1.x.

Q. The customer doesn't want to modify the environment by installing the extension. Is there any command-line version of this tool?

A. Yes, there is.

Q. Does this extension work in 64-bit Windows?

A. No, but we can use the command-line equivalent shown in answer to the previous question.

Crashes Explained

Now I'll try to explain crashes, dumps, and postmortem debuggers.

Sometimes, a computer (CPU, Central Processing Unit) cannot perform its job because the instruction it gets to do some calculation, read or write data is wrong. Imagine a situation when we get an address to deliver a message to, and we find that it doesn't exist. The following idealized picture shows this situation (if memory locations, addresses, are indexed from 0 then -1 is the wrong address):

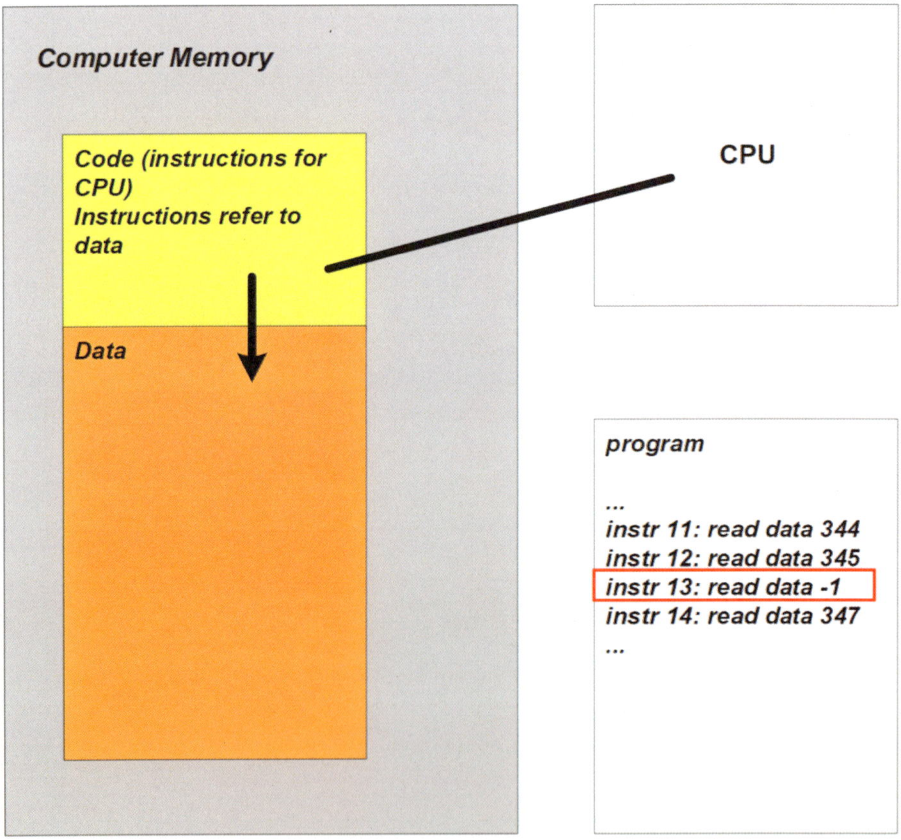

When referencing an invalid address, CPU executes the special sequence of actions (called a trap) that ultimately leads to saving memory so we can later examine its contents and find out which instruction was invalid. If a crash happens inside the Windows operating system, you see a bluescreen. Then kernel memory or full computer physical memory is saved in a file called either kernel or complete memory dump, respectively. If we have a crash in a running application or service, then its memory contents are saved in a file called a user dump, also called a postmortem dump, and we call a program which saves it a postmortem debugger. There can be several such programs, and the one which is specified in the registry to be executed whenever a crash happens in a running application or service is called a default postmortem debugger. The following picture illustrates this on which the spooler service, spoolsv.exe, was crashed by a faulty printer driver:

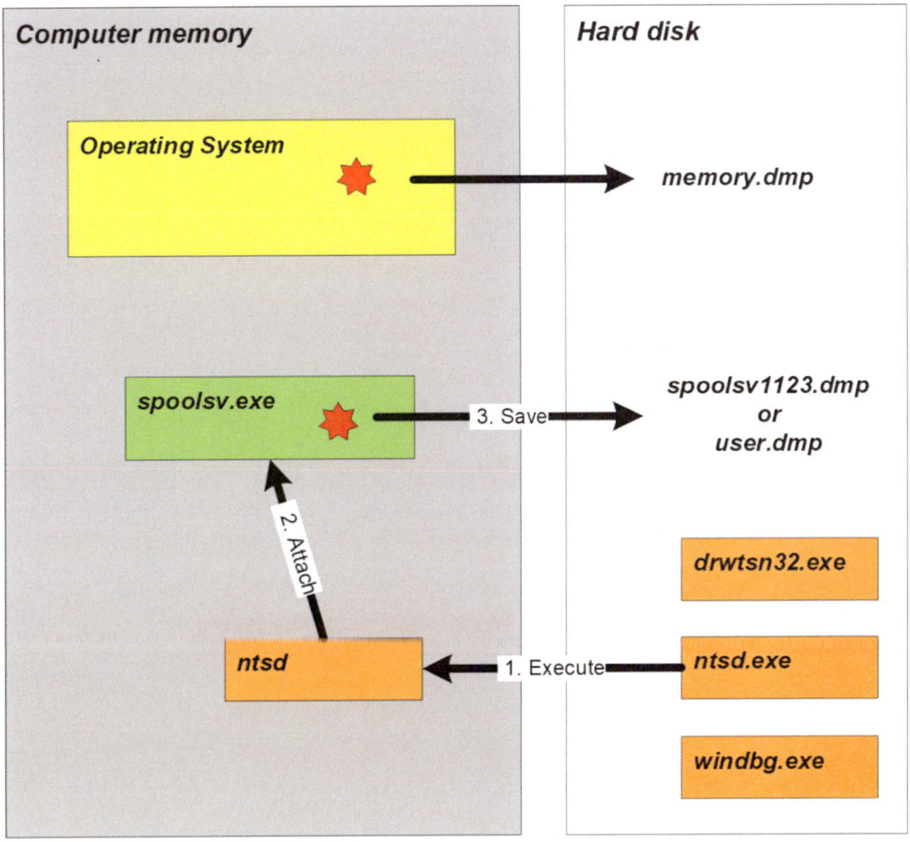

By default, a postmortem debugger on Windows versions before Vista was Dr. Watson (*drwtsn32.exe*). Sometimes it didn't work in a terminal services environment and had other limitations, so we always recommended configuring NTSD (*ntsd.exe*).

Now, at the time of this revision, the **LocalDumps** registry key is the preferred way to capture crash dumps automatically in Windows 10. See the following article for further details: https://docs.microsoft.com/en-us/windows/win32/wer/collecting-user-mode-dumps.

I prefer to call both user and kernel/complete memory dumps postmortem (not only user dumps) because they are saved after an application, service, or system is already dead (crash or fatal error had already happened). It distinguishes them from live memory dumps (snapshots) manually saved whenever we want them.

Hangs Explained

Another category of problems happens very often where we also need a dump for analysis: hangs. There is some confusion in understanding the difference between these two categories: crash and hang. Although sometimes a hang is a direct consequence of a crash, most of the time hangs happen independently. They also manifest themselves differently. Let's look at the application (process) crashes and hangs first. When a crash happens, an application process often disappears. When a hang happens an application process is still in memory: we can see it in Task Manager, for example, but it doesn't respond to user commands or any other requests like pinging a TCP/IP port. If we have a crash in OS, then the most visible manifestation is a bluescreen or reboot. If we have a hang, then everything freezes.

Application or system hangs because, from the high level of view, the interaction between applications and OS components (modules) is done via messages. One component sends a message to another and waits for a response. Some components are critical, for example, a registry. The following hand-made picture depicts widespread system hang situations when the Registry component stops responding. Then every running application process stops responding if its execution path depends on registry access.

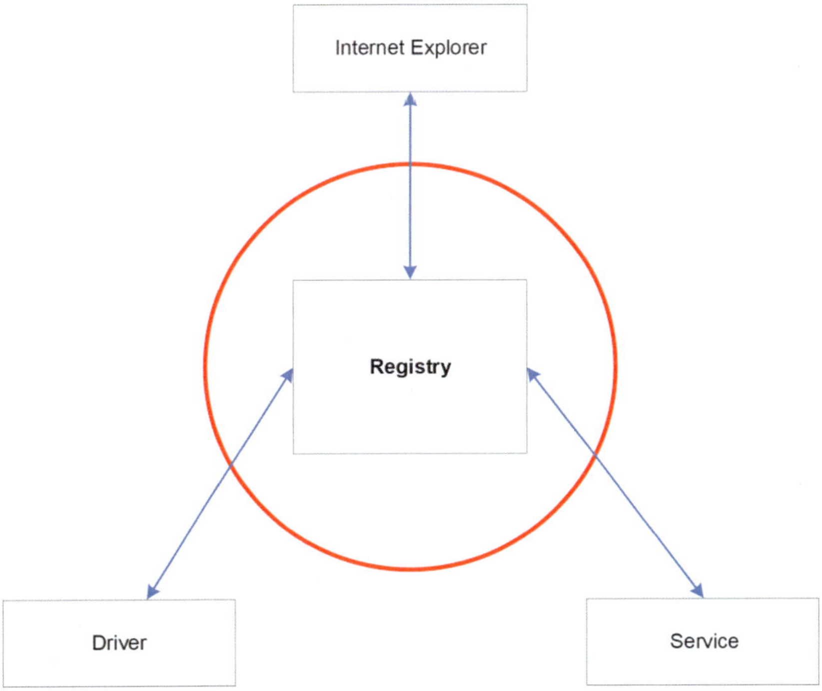

The common reason for a hang is the so-called **deadlock** when two running applications, their execution paths, or threads are waiting for each other. Here is an analogy with a blocked road:

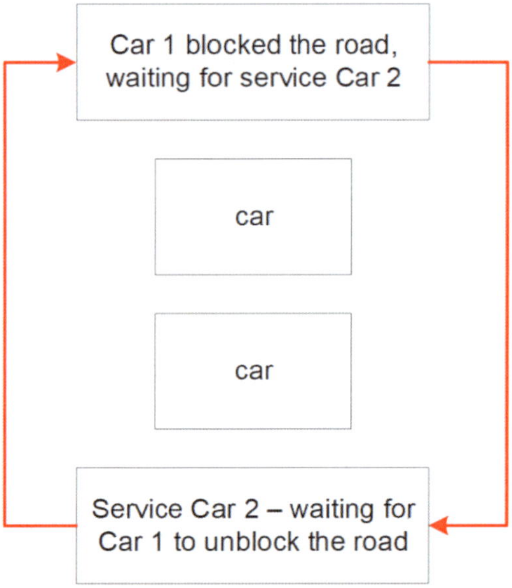

To see what's inside a process or OS, which caused a hang, we need a memory dump. Usually, it is called a crash dump, too. Because to get it, the usual method is to make some sort of a trap that causes an application or OS to crash and to save the dump. I prefer to call such crash dumps just memory dumps to avoid confusion.

Some FAQ:

Q. How can we get a memory dump if our application or service hangs?

A. It is possible to do using various methods:

- by using NTSD command-line options (NTSD was always present in a pre-Vista system)

- **Preferred:** by using ProcDump (https://docs.microsoft.com/en-us/sysinternals/downloads/procdump) or Task Manager (previously we used *userdump.exe*, https://support.microsoft.com/en-ie/help/241215/how-to-use-the-userdump-exe-tool-to-create-a-dump-file)

- by attaching and saving the dump interactively via NTSD or WinDbg
- by using ADPlus in a hang mode (https://support.microsoft.com/en-ie/help/286350/how-to-use-adplus-vbs-to-troubleshoot-hangs-and-crashes)

Q. How can we get a memory dump if our system hangs?

A. Two standard methods are:

- manually via keyboard (https://docs.microsoft.com/en-us/windows-hardware/drivers/debugger/forcing-a-system-crash-from-the-keyboard)
- by using a tool that forces a system crash such as NotMyFault if some user session is alive (https://docs.microsoft.com/en-us/sysinternals/downloads/notmyfault)

For most system hangs, choosing the Kernel memory dump option in *Control Panel\System and Security\System\Advanced system settings\Start-up and Recovery* applet is sufficient. Kernel memory dumps are smaller and less susceptible to corruption or truncation due to small page file size. If you discover that you need to peer inside running user applications, then you can always ask for another complete memory dump when the problem happens again.

Symbol Files Explained

Symbol files are usually called PDB files because they have .PDB extension although the older ones can have .DBG extension. PDB files are needed to read dump files properly. Without PDB files, the dump file data is just a collection of numbers, the contents of memory, without any meaning. PDB files help tools like WinDbg to interpret the data and present it in a human-readable format.

Roughly speaking, PDB files contain associations between numbers and their meanings expressed in short text strings:

```
Dump data (memory contents)

...
...
...
773f8ea4 0012f9f4 6be82f08
00000000 7e4188da 00000000
0012fa80 7fffffff 000003e8
00406258 00000000 00000001
00da00ab 00aa00f3 00dc0000
...
...
...
```

```
comctl32.pdb

...
773f8ea4 Button_WndProc
...
```

```
ProductA.pdb

...
0012f9f4 ProcessPayment
...
```

```
imgutil.pdb

...
6be82f08 DrawImage
...
```

Because these associations are changed when we have a fix or service pack on a computer, and we have a crash dump from it, we need newer PDB files that correspond to updated components such as DLLs or drivers.

A long time ago, we had to download symbol files manually from Microsoft or get them from CDs. Now Microsoft has its dedicated internet symbol server, and WinDbg can download PDB files automatically. However, in some cases, we may need to specify the

Microsoft symbol server location in *File\Symbol File Path...* dialog and check Reload checkbox. The location is usually (check http://windbg.org):

```
srv*c:\mss*http://msdl.microsoft.com/download/symbols
```

If we don't remember the location when we run WinDbg for the first time or on a new computer, we can enter **.symfix** command to set Microsoft symbol server path automatically and specify the location where to download symbol files. We can check our current symbol search path by using **.sympath** command and then reload symbols by entering **.reload** command:

```
0:000> .symfix

0:000> .sympath
Symbol search path is: srv*
Expanded Symbol search path is:
cache*;SRV*https://msdl.microsoft.com/download/symbols

************* Path validation summary **************
Response                         Time (ms)     Location
Deferred                                       srv*

0:000> .symfix c:\mss

0:000> .sympath
Symbol search path is: c:\mss
Expanded Symbol search path is: c:\mss

************* Path validation summary **************
Response                         Time (ms)     Location
OK                                             c:\mss

0:000> .reload
```

Crashes and Hangs Differentiated

In the articles, **Crashes Explained** (page 28) and **Hangs Explained** (page 31), I highlighted the difference between crashes and hangs. In this part, I elaborate on terminology a bit further. First of all, we have to unify them as manifestations of a functional failure. Considering a computer as a system of components having certain functions, we shall subdivide failures into system and component failures. Of course, systems themselves may be components in some larger hierarchy, like in the case of virtualization. Application and service process failures fall under component failures category. Bluescreen and server freezes fall under the system failures category. Now it is obvious why most computer users confuse crashes and hangs. They are just failures, and often, the distinction between them is blurred from the user perspective.

Software developers tend to make a sharp distinction between crashes and hangs because they consider a situation when a computer accesses an invalid memory location or executes an invalid instruction as a crash. However, after such a situation, a computer system may or may not terminate that application or service.

Therefore, I propose to consider crashes as situations when a system or component is not observed anymore. For example, a running application or service disappears from Task Manager, the computer system shows bluescreen or reboots. In hang situations, we can observe the existence of a failed component in Task Manager, or a computer system doesn't reboot automatically and shows some screen image different from BSOD or panic message. The so-called sluggish behavior or long response time can also be considered as hang situations.

Here is a simple rough diagram I devised to illuminate the proposed terminological difference:

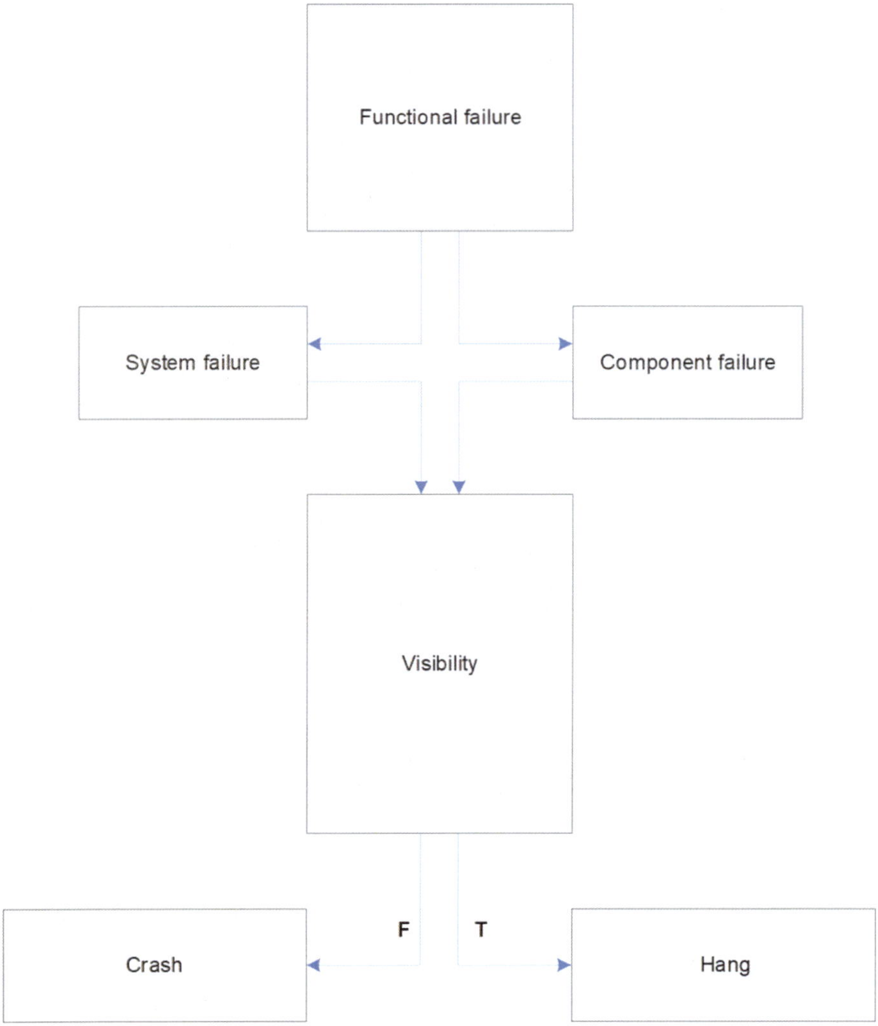

Based on the clarification above, the task of collecting memory or crash dumps is much more straightforward and transparent.

In the case of a system crash or hang, we need to set-up correct crash dump options in *Advanced System Settings* in *Control Panel* and check page file size in case of the complete memory dump option. A system crash saves the dump automatically. For a system hang, we need to actively trigger crash dump saving procedure using either standard keyboard method, NotMyFault tool, or live system debugging.

In the case of an application crash, we need to set-up the *LocalDumps* registry key or a postmortem debugger, get WER report or attach a debugger to a component and wait for a failure to happen. In the case of a hang, we save a memory dump manually either by using process dumpers like *procmon.exe*, Task Manager, or attaching a debugger.

Links to some dump collection techniques can be found in the previous **Crashes Explained** and **Hangs Explained** articles.

Proactive Crash Dumps

In **Crashes and Hangs Differentiated** article (page 36), I introduced apparent separation between crashes and hangs and outlined memory dump capturing methods for each category. However, looking from the users' point of view, we need to tell them what the best way is to capture a dump based on observations they have and their failure level, system, or component. The latter failure type usually happens with user applications and services.

For user applications, the best way is to get a memory dump proactively or put in other words, manually and do not rely on a postmortem debugger that may not be set up correctly on a problem server in one hundred server farm. When an error message box appears with a message that an application stopped working or that it has encountered an application error, then we can use process dumpers like *procdump.exe*.

Suppose we have the following error message when TestWER application crashes in Windows 10 (the same technique applies to earlier OS too):

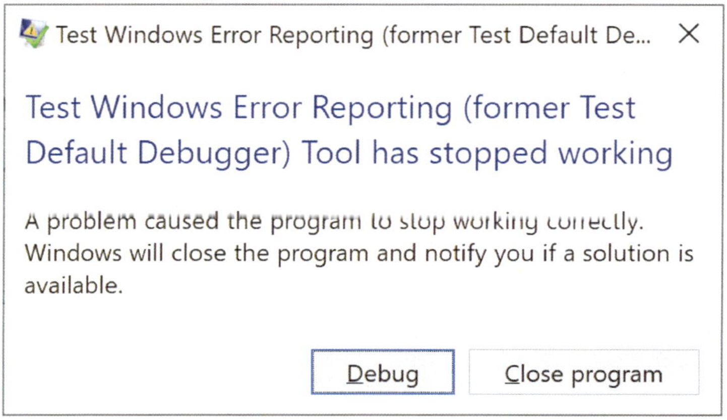

Then we can dump the process while it displays the problem message if we know its process ID:

```
c:\Tools\Procdump>procdump -ma 30888

ProcDump v9.0 - Sysinternals process dump utility
Copyright (C) 2009-2017 Mark Russinovich and Andrew Richards
Sysinternals - www.sysinternals.com

[08:02:57] Dump 1 initiated: c:\Tools\Procdump\TestWER64.exe_200327_080257.dmp
[08:02:57] Dump 1 writing: Estimated dump file size is 78 MB.
[08:02:57] Dump 1 complete: 78 MB written in 0.2 seconds
[08:02:57] Dump count reached.


c:\Tools\Procdump>
```

Starting from Windows Vista, this can be done even more quickly by dumping the process from Task Manager directly:

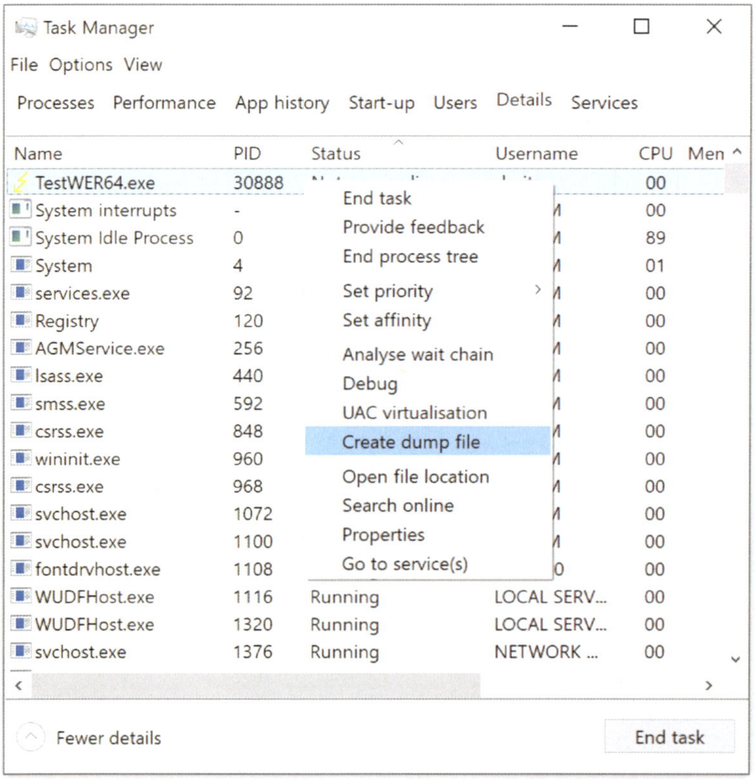

If we choose to Create Dump File we see this message box:

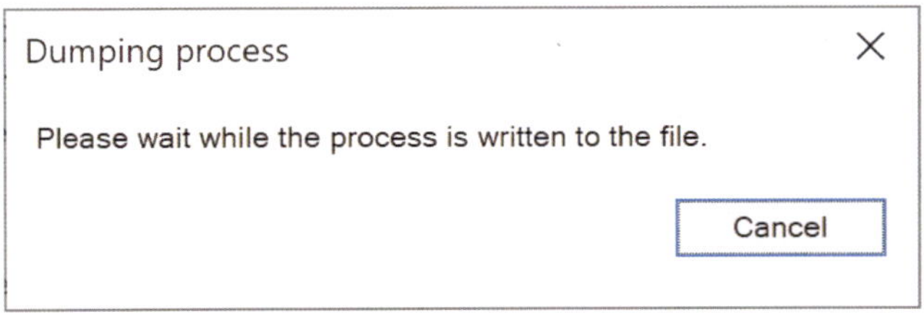

The process dump is saved to a user location for temporary files:

Although the application above is the native Windows application, the same method applies for .NET applications. For example, TestWER.NET application shows the unhandled exception message when we click on *Crash Me* button, and we can dump the process manually while it displays that message:

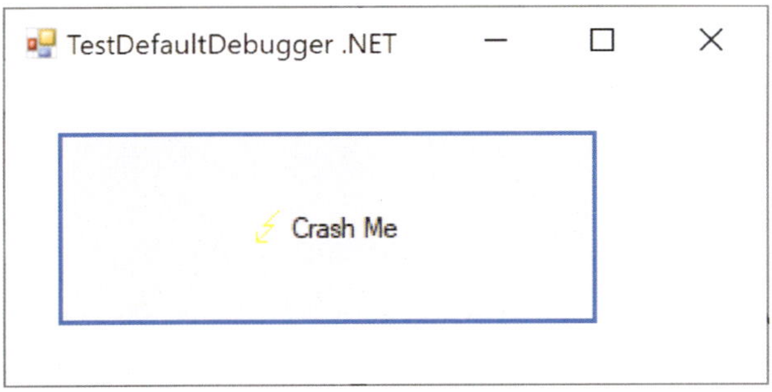

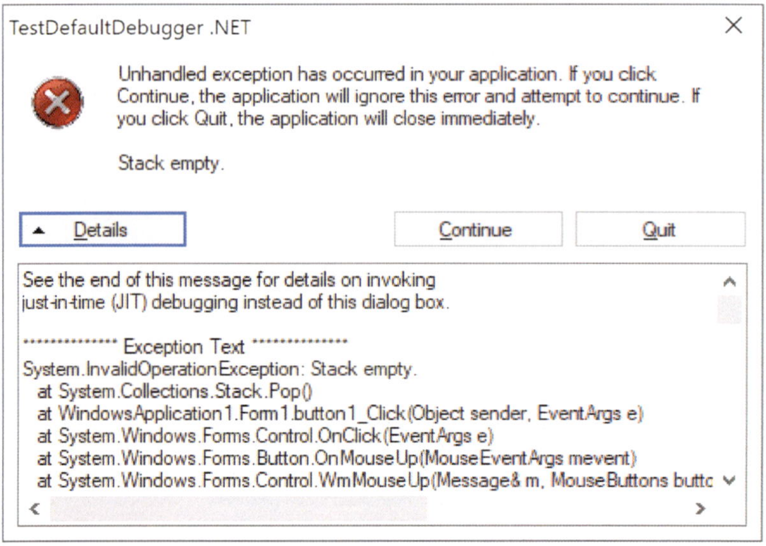

Although, if we choose *Close* or *Quit* in error message boxes, both applications disappear from Task Manager, and, therefore, are considered crashes under the new refined terminology, they are considered application hangs at the time when they show their stop messages. This is why we use manual process dumpers.

PART 2: Professional Crash Dump Analysis

Minidump Analysis

Scripts and WinDbg Commands

Small Memory Dumps, also referred to as minidumps because they are stored in *%SystemRoot% \ Minidump* folder, contain only bugcheck information, kernel mode stack data, and the list of loaded drivers. They can be used to transmit system crash information to a vendor or 3rd-party for an automated crash dump analysis. Another use is to keep the system crash history. In this part, I discuss the scripting approach to extract information from all minidumps stored in a particular system. The script processes all minidump files and creates text log files containing the following information:

1. Crash dump name and type.
2. OS information, crash time, and system uptime.
3. Processor context (**r**) and verbose stack trace (**kv**) before applying **!analyze -v**. It is useful sometimes when WinDbg reconstructs a different stack trace after changing a processor context to the execution context at the time of a trap, exception, or fault.
4. The output of **!analyze -v** command.
5. Processor context (**r**) and verbose stack trace (**kv**) after **!analyze -v** command.
6. Code disassembly for the current execution pointer (RIP for x64 or EIP for x86). It includes forward (**u**) and backward (**ub**) disassembly, and we also try to disassemble the whole function (**uf**), which should succeed if we have symbolic information.
7. Raw stack dump with symbol information (**dps**).
8. The same raw stack data but interpreted as pointers to Unicode zero-terminated strings (**dpu**). Some pointers on the stack might point to local string buffers located in the same stack region. It can be a slow operation, and WinDbg may temporarily hang.
9. The same raw stack data but interpreted as pointers to ASCII zero-terminated strings (**dpa**). It can be a slow operation too, and WinDbg may temporarily hang.
10. Verbose information about loaded drivers (**lmv**).
11. CPU, machine ID, machine-specific registers, and verbose SMBIOS information like motherboard and devices (**!sysinfo**).

Here is a listing of our WinDbg script:

```
$$
$$ MiniDmp2Txt: Dump information from minidump into log
$$
.logopen /d /u
.echo "command> ||"
||
.echo "command> vertarget"
vertarget
.echo "command> r (before analysis)"
r
.echo "command> kv (before analysis)"
kv 100
.echo "command> !analyze -v"
!analyze -v
.echo "command> r"
r
.echo "command> kv"
kv 100
.echo "command> ub rip"
ub rip
.echo "command> u rip"
u rip
.echo "command> uf rip"
uf rip
.echo "command> dps rsp-3000 rsp+3000"
dps rsp-3000 rsp+3000
.echo "command> dpu rsp-3000 rsp+3000"
dpu esp-3000 rsp+3000
.echo "command> dpa rsp-3000 rsp+3000"
dpa rsp-3000 rsp+3000
.echo "command> lmv"
lmv
.echo "command> !sysinfo cpuinfo"
!sysinfo cpuinfo
.echo "command> !sysinfo cpuspeed"
!sysinfo cpuspeed
.echo "command> !sysinfo cpumicrocode"
!sysinfo cpumicrocode
.echo "command> !sysinfo gbl"
!sysinfo gbl
.echo "command> !sysinfo machineid"
!sysinfo machineid
.echo "command> !sysinfo registers"
!sysinfo registers
.echo "command> !sysinfo smbios -v"
!sysinfo smbios -v
.logclose
$$
$$ MiniDmp2Txt: End of File
$$
```

To run WinDbg automatically against each minidump file (.dmp) we can use the following VB script (in the past, we also needed to customize the symbol search path after **-y** parameter to point to our symbol folders):

```
'
' MiniDumps2Txt.vbs
'
Set fso = CreateObject("Scripting.FileSystemObject")
Set Folder = fso.GetFolder(".")
Set Files = Folder.Files
Set WshShell = CreateObject("WScript.Shell")
For Each File In Files
  If Mid(File.Name,Len(File.Name)-3,4) = ".dmp" Then
    Set oExec = WshShell.Exec("C:\Program Files (x86)\Windows
Kits\10\Debuggers\x64\WinDbg.exe -z " + File.Name + " -c
""$$><c:\MemoryDumps\MiniDmp2Txt.txt;q"" -Q -QS -QY -QSY")
    Do While oExec.Status = 0
      WScript.Sleep 1000
    Loop
  End If
Next
'
' MiniDumps2Txt.vbs: End of File
'
```

We can also use *kd.exe* instead of WinDbg, but its window is hidden if we use the same VB script. Also the modified script can be used for user dumps with some commands removed such as **!sysinfo**.

Component Identification

Now I show how to find a 3rd-party driver that might have been responsible for a system crash and verify that WinDbg reports that driver correctly.

For example, one of the log files shows the following output from **!analyze -v** WinDbg command:

```
command> !analyze -v
*************************************************************
*                                                           *
*                    Bugcheck Analysis                      *
*                                                           *
*************************************************************

BAD_POOL_CALLER (c2)
The current thread is making a bad pool request. Typically this is at a
bad IRQL level or double freeing the same allocation, etc.
Arguments:
Arg1: 00000047, Attempt to free a non-allocated nonpaged pool address
Arg2: 85083000, Starting address
Arg3: 00005083, physical page frame
Arg4: 000bfff9, highest physical page frame

Debugging Details:
------------------
BUGCHECK_STR:  0xc2_47

CUSTOMER_CRASH_COUNT:  2

DEFAULT_BUCKET_ID:  DRIVER_FAULT_SERVER_MINIDUMP

PROCESS_NAME:  3rdPartyAntivirus.exe

CURRENT_IRQL:  0

LAST_CONTROL_TRANSFER:  from 8054d2eb to 805435b9

STACK_TEXT:
b325db68 8054d2eb 000000c2 00000047 85083000 nt!KeBugCheckEx+0x19
b325db94 805689c2 85083000 00080000 85083000
nt!MmGetSizeOfBigPoolAllocation+0x1cb
b325dbe4 f77c8098 00000000 00000000 00000004 nt!ExFreePoolWithTag+0x1d0
WARNING: Stack unwind information not available. Following frames may be
wrong.
b325dc24 f77c8234 8599d4e0 8599d4e0 88cecf38 3rdPartyAVDrv+0x1098
b325dc3c 804f04f3 871d2cf0 00004808 8743b6a0 3rdPartyAVDrv+0x1234
b325dc4c 80585208 8599d550 872c8028 8599d4e0 nt!IofCallDriver+0x3f
```

```
b325dc60 80585fe6 871d2cf0 8599d4f0 872c8028
nt!IopSynchronousServiceTail+0x6f
b325dd00 80586028 00000468 00000614 00000000 nt!IopXxxControlFile+0x607
b325dd34 804dfd24 00000468 00000614 00000000 nt!NtDeviceIoControlFile+0x28
b325dd34 7ffe0304 00000468 00000614 00000000 nt!KiSystemService+0xd0
0087b6c0 00000000 00000000 00000000 00000000
SharedUserData!SystemCallStub+0x4


STACK_COMMAND:  kb

FOLLOWUP_IP:
3rdPartyAVDrv+1098
f77c8098 ??              ???

SYMBOL_STACK_INDEX:  3

SYMBOL_NAME:  3rdPartyAVDrv+1098

FOLLOWUP_NAME:  MachineOwner

MODULE_NAME: 3rdPartyAVDrv

IMAGE_NAME:  3rdPartyAVDrv.sys

DEBUG_FLR_IMAGE_TIMESTAMP:  410752c5

FAILURE_BUCKET_ID:  0xc2_47_3rdPartyAVDrv+1098

BUCKET_ID:  0xc2_47_3rdPartyAVDrv+1098

Followup: MachineOwner
---------
```

MODULE_NAME and IMAGE_NAME fields report 3rd-party antivirus driver *3rdPartyAVDrv.sys* as responsible for BSOD. However, the top lines from STACK_TEXT field report **nt** module, Windows kernel, and system. We can get information about all loaded drivers from the output of **lmv** command:

```
command> lmv
start    end        module name
804de000 80744000   nt        # (pdb
symbols)          c:\...\ntkrnlmp.pdb\...\ntkrnlmp.pdb
    Loaded symbol image file: ntkrnlmp.exe
    Mapped memory image file: c:\...\ntkrnlmp.exe\...\ntkrnlmp.exe
    Image path: ntkrnlmp.exe
    Image name: ntkrnlmp.exe
    Timestamp:        Tue Mar 25 08:39:34 2003 (3E8015C6)
```

```
    CheckSum:           00254553
    ImageSize:          00266000
    File version:       5.2.3790.0
    Product version:    5.2.3790.0
    File flags:         0 (Mask 3F)
    File OS:            40004 NT Win32
    File type:          1.0 App
    File date:          00000000.00000000
    Translations:       0415.04b0
    CompanyName:        Microsoft Corporation
    ProductName:        Microsoft® Windows® Operating System
    InternalName:       ntkrnlmp.exe
    OriginalFilename: ntkrnlmp.exe
    ProductVersion:     5.2.3790.0
    FileVersion:        5.2.3790.0 (srv03_rtm.030324-2048)
    FileDescription:    NT Kernel & System
    LegalCopyright:     © Microsoft Corporation. All rights reserved.
...
...
...
f77c7000 f77cf000   3rdPartyAVDrv 3rdPartyAVDrv.sys
    Loaded symbol image file: 3rdPartyAVDrv.sys
    Symbol file: 3rdPartyAVDrv.sys
    Image path: 3rdPartyAVDrv.sys
    Timestamp:          Wed Jul 28 07:15:21 2004 (410752C5)
    CheckSum:           00011518
    ImageSize:          00008000
    Translations:       0000.04b0 0000.04e0 0409.04b0 0409.04e0
...
...
...
```

Why does WinDbg skip Microsoft modules and point to the 3rd-party one? Because, when WinDbg encounters a non-Microsoft driver, it always shows it as the possible cause. If drivers are Microsoft it looks at *triage.ini* file located in *triage* folder under *Debugging Tools for Windows* installation folder where certain modules and functions are listed with appropriate actions for WinDbg, for example:

```
nt!KeBugCheck*=ignore
nt!ExAllocatePool=Pool_corruption
```

Let's add the following entry at the end of that INI file:

```
3rdPartyAVDrv!*=ignore
```

Now, if we load the dump in WinDbg, set the symbols and run the analysis, we get different results:

```
3: kd> .symfix
No downstream store given, using C:\Program Files\Debugging Tools for
Windows\sym

3: kd> !analyze -v
...
...
...
FOLLOWUP_NAME:  MachineOwner

MODULE_NAME: nt

DEBUG_FLR_IMAGE_TIMESTAMP:  3e8015c6

SYMBOL_NAME:  nt!MmGetSizeOfBigPoolAllocation+1cb

IMAGE_NAME:  memory_corruption

FAILURE_BUCKET_ID:  0xc2_47_nt!MmGetSizeOfBigPoolAllocation+1cb

BUCKET_ID:  0xc2_47_nt!MmGetSizeOfBigPoolAllocation+1cb

Followup: MachineOwner
---------
```

Because *nt!MmGetSizeOfBigPoolAllocation* is not listed in *triage.ini* WinDbg reports **nt** module and memory corruption. The latter cause is probably inferred from either BAD_POOL_CALLER bugcheck name or *Mm* function prefix.

Let's add more lines to tiage.ini:

```
3rdPartyAVDrv!*=ignore
nt!MmGetSizeOfBigPoolAllocation=ignore
nt!ExFreePoolWithTag=Dynamic memory corruption detected when freeing
memory
```

Now the analysis reports our custom follow-up message:

```
3: kd> !analyze -v
...
...
...
FOLLOWUP_IP:
nt!ExFreePoolWithTag+1d0
805689c2 e9c8f0ffff      jmp     nt!ExFreePoolWithTag+0x1d0 (80567a8f)

SYMBOL_STACK_INDEX:  2
```

```
FOLLOWUP_NAME:  Dynamic memory corruption detected when freeing memory

MODULE_NAME: nt

IMAGE_NAME:  ntkrnlmp.exe

DEBUG_FLR_IMAGE_TIMESTAMP:  3e8015c6

SYMBOL_NAME:  nt!ExFreePoolWithTag+1d0

FAILURE_BUCKET_ID:  0xc2_47_nt!ExFreePoolWithTag+1d0

BUCKET_ID:  0xc2_47_nt!ExFreePoolWithTag+1d0

Followup: Dynamic memory corruption detected when freeing memory
---------
```

Let's look at STACK_TEXT data:

```
STACK_TEXT:
b325db68 8054d2eb 000000c2 00000047 85083000 nt!KeBugCheckEx+0x19
b325db94 805689c2 85083000 00080000 85083000
nt!MmGetSizeOfBigPoolAllocation+0x1cb
b325dbe4 f77c8098 00000000 00000000 00000004 nt!ExFreePoolWithTag+0x1d0
WARNING: Stack unwind information not available. Following frames may be
wrong.
b325dc24 f77c8234 8599d4e0 8599d4e0 88cecf38 3rdPartyAVDrv+0x1098
b325dc3c 804f04f3 871d2cf0 00004808 8743b6a0 3rdPartyAVDrv+0x1234
b325dc4c 80585208 8599d550 872c8028 8599d4e0 nt!IofCallDriver+0x3f
b325dc60 80585fe6 871d2cf0 8599d4f0 872c8028
nt!IopSynchronousServiceTail+0x6f
b325dd00 80586028 00000468 00000614 00000000 nt!IopXxxControlFile+0x607
b325dd34 804dfd24 00000468 00000614 00000000 nt!NtDeviceIoControlFile+0x28
b325dd34 7ffe0304 00000468 00000614 00000000 nt!KiSystemService+0xd0
0087b6c0 00000000 00000000 00000000 00000000
SharedUserData!SystemCallStub+0x4
```

We see that WinDbg is not sure that it correctly identified *3rdPartyAVDrv* module. We can check this manually by subtracting **0x1098** from **f77c8098**. The latter address is the so-called return address saved when *nt!ExFreePoolWithTag* was called and can be located in the second column. We can see that it falls within the *3rdPartyAVDrv* address range, and, therefore, the stack looks correct:

```
3: kd> ? f77c8098-0x1098
Evaluate expression: -142839808 = f77c7000
```

```
3: kd> lmv m 3rdPartyAVDrv
f77c7000 f77cf000   3rdPartyAVDrv 3rdPartyAVDrv.sys
    Loaded symbol image file: 3rdPartyAVDrv.sys
    Symbol file: 3rdPartyAVDrv.sys
    Image path: 3rdPartyAVDrv.sys
    Browse all global symbols  functions  data
    Timestamp:        Wed Jul 28 07:15:21 2004 (410752C5)
    CheckSum:         00011518
    ImageSize:        00008000
    Translations:     0000.04b0 0000.04e0 0409.04b0 0409.04e0
```

The driver is dated Jul 2004, and therefore, we can try either disable it or contact the vendor for any updates. The "Timestamp" refers to the time when the driver was built at the vendor software factory and not the time when it was installed. It is a way to identify the version of the software if no more information except the time is present in the output of **lmv** command.

Also, note the PROCESS_NAME field in the analysis output. It is a process that was active at the time of the system failure. The application that the process belongs to might be from the same vendor as the suspicious driver, but usually, they are independent; for example, if there is a bug in a display driver, it might manifest when any application is running.

Sometimes stack trace (STACK_TEXT) starts with a warning as in this example:

```
STACK_TEXT:
WARNING: Stack unwind information not available. Following frames may be
wrong.
b4f528b0 b4f52904 e24079e0 000000ab 000003cb DisplayDriver+0x21bca6
b4f528b4 e24079e0 000000ab 000003cb 43f0027f 0xb4f52904
b4f52904 00000000 000003cb 0000027a 00000135 0xe24079e0
```

In such cases we can look at a crash point (FAULTING_IP) and notice the module there:

```
FAULTING_IP:
DisplayDriver+21bca6
bfbf0ca6 8b3e            mov     edi,dword ptr [esi]
```

```
0: kd> lmv m DisplayDriver
start    end        module name
bf9d5000 bff42500   DisplayDriver T (no symbols)
    Loaded symbol image file: DisplayDriver.dll
    Image path: DisplayDriver.dll
    Image name: DisplayDriver.dll
    Timestamp:        Fri Jun 29 09:13:08 2007 (4684BF14)
    CheckSum:         00570500
    ImageSize:        0056D500
    Translations:     0000.04b0 0000.04e0 0409.04b0 0409.04e0
```

Raw Stack Data Analysis

Unfortunately, stack traces reported by WinDbg, especially involving 3rd-party components, are usually incomplete and sometimes not even correct. They can also point to stable drivers when the system failure happened after slowly accumulated corruption caused by some intermediate driver or a combination of them.

Sometimes, there are other 3rd-party drivers involved in the system crash that are not visible in the output of **!analyze -v** command and only removing them, disabling, or upgrading software they are part of makes the system stable. To see them, we can look at the so-called raw stack data. Because the kernel mode thread stack size is small (12Kb or 0x3000 on x86 and 24Kb on x64), we can simply dump memory range between ESP-3000 and ESP+3000. We can use RSP register for x64 dumps, but the output is the same.

Let's look at our minidump again. The stack trace is small, incomplete, and points to *DisplayDriver*. It is because we don't have symbolic information (a PDB file) for *DisplayDriver.dll*. Could it be the case that *DisplayDriver.dll* was misused by another driver or operating system component? What are other components that might have been used before BSOD? Raw stack dump shows additional symbols like *DisplayDriver_mini*, *win32k*, and *dxg*:

```
0: kd> dps esp-3000 esp+3000
b4f4f8b4  ????????
b4f4f8b8  ????????
b4f4f8bc  ????????
b4f4f8c0  ????????
...
...
...
b4f51ffc  ????????
b4f52000  00001000
b4f52004  00006000
b4f52008  b4f5204c
b4f5200c  89025978
b4f52010  89139000
b4f52014  00000000
b4f52018  b4f527ec
b4f5201c  b4f52840
b4f52020  bfbf0ca6 DisplayDriver+0x21bca6
b4f52024  00000000
b4f52028  89025978
...
...
...
b4f52100  e24079e0
```

```
b4f52104  bfbf0ca6 DisplayDriver+0x21bca6
b4f52108  00000008
...
...
...
b4f52364  b4f52414
b4f52368  804dc0b2 nt!ExecuteHandler+0x24
b4f5236c  b4f527ec
b4f52370  b4f52d40
b4f52374  b4f524e8
b4f52378  b4f52400
b4f5237c  bf9d2132 dxg!_except_handler3
b4f52380  2a2a2a0a
...
...
...
b4f523e8  b4f52408
b4f523ec  8053738a nt!KeBugCheckEx+0x1b
b4f523f0  0000008e
b4f523f4  c0000005
b4f523f8  bfbf0ca6 DisplayDriver+0x21bca6
b4f523fc  b4f52840
b4f52400  00000000
b4f52404  00000000
b4f52408  b4f527d0
b4f5240c  80521fed nt!KiDispatchException+0x3b1
b4f52410  0000008e
b4f52414  c0000005
b4f52418  bfbf0ca6 DisplayDriver+0x21bca6
b4f5241c  b4f52840
b4f52420  00000000
b4f52424  03a3fb4c
b4f52428  03a3fb4c
b4f5242c  b4f52800
b4f52430  00000000
b4f52434  00000000
b4f52438  00000000
b4f5243c  b9deffc6 DisplayDriver_mini+0x4bfc6
b4f52440  897c621c
b4f52444  00000086
b4f52448  0000003c
b4f5244c  b9f3af5a DisplayDriver_mini+0x196f5a
b4f52450  897c6200
b4f52454  00000086
b4f52458  897c6200
b4f5245c  00000000
b4f52460  00000000
b4f52464  00000000
b4f52468  b9f38b4e DisplayDriver_mini+0x194b4e
b4f5246c  00000000
...
...
...
b4f5250c  00002800
```

```
b4f52510  b9f3ac10 DisplayDriver_mini+0x196c10
b4f52514  897c6200
b4f52518  00002504
b4f5251c  00000010
b4f52520  897c6200
b4f52524  b9f2d194 DisplayDriver_mini+0x189194
b4f52528  897c6200
b4f5252c  00002504
b4f52530  00000010
b4f52534  897c6200
b4f52538  898cca80
b4f5253c  00000080
b4f52540  89654008
b4f52544  b9f358e2 DisplayDriver_mini+0x1918e2
b4f52548  897c6200
...
...
...
b4f5256c  00000000
b4f52570  b9deff5c DisplayDriver_mini+0x4bf5c
b4f52574  00000000
...
...
...
b4f5259c  e24079e0
b4f525a0  bfbf0ca6 DisplayDriver+0x21bca6
b4f525a4  00000008
b4f525a8  00010246
b4f525ac  b4f528b4
b4f525b0  00000010
b4f525b4  0000003c
b4f525b8  b9f3af5a DisplayDriver_mini+0x196f5a
b4f525bc  897c6200
b4f525c0  00000086
b4f525c4  89b81008
b4f525c8  897c6200
b4f525cc  00000000
b4f525d0  00007c00
b4f525d4  b9deff5c DisplayDriver_mini+0x4bf5c
b4f525d8  b9deff5c DisplayDriver_mini+0x4bf5c
b4f525dc  8988d7d8
b4f525e0  b9deff66 DisplayDriver_mini+0x4bf66
b4f525e4  b9deff5c DisplayDriver_mini+0x4bf5c
b4f525e8  8961c288
b4f525ec  b9deff66 DisplayDriver_mini+0x4bf66
b4f525f0  8961c288
b4f525f4  00000000
b4f525f8  00000046
b4f525fc  00000000
b4f52600  89903000
b4f52604  b9e625a9 DisplayDriver_mini+0xbe5a9
b4f52608  8961c288
b4f5260c  00000046
b4f52610  00000000
```

```
b4f52614  b9deff5c DisplayDriver_mini+0x4bf5c
b4f52618  896ac008
...
...
...
b4f52630  898a8000
b4f52634  b9e9f220 DisplayDriver_mini+0xfb220
b4f52638  89941400
b4f5263c  b9e2ffec DisplayDriver_mini+0x8bfec
b4f52640  00000000
b4f52644  00000000
b4f52648  00000050
b4f5264c  b9e790d3 DisplayDriver_mini+0xd50d3
b4f52650  897c6200
...
...
...
b4f5266c  89bf6200
b4f52670  805502fa nt!ExFreePoolWithTag+0x664
b4f52674  00000000
b4f52678  88f322e0
b4f5267c  88c9d708
b4f52680  00000001
b4f52684  898cf918
b4f52688  ffdff538
b4f5268c  804dc766 nt!KiUnlockDispatcherDatabase+0x1c
b4f52690  b4f52901
b4f52694  b4f526ac
b4f52698  00000001
b4f5269c  804eaf06 nt!IopFreeIrp+0xed
b4f526a0  00000000
b4f526a4  00000000
b4f526a8  88c9d708
b4f526ac  b4f52700
b4f526b0  804f2b9f nt!IopCompleteRequest+0x319
b4f526b4  804f2bb5 nt!IopCompleteRequest+0x32f
b4f526b8  88c9d748
b4f526bc  89025978
b4f526c0  890259ac
b4f526c4  897752e8
b4f526c8  89025978
b4f526cc  b4f52910
b4f526d0  b4f527c8
b4f526d4  00000000
b4f526d8  b9e0d300 DisplayDriver_mini+0x69300
b4f526dc  88c9d708
b4f526e0  00000000
b4f526e4  00000086
b4f526e8  b4f526b8
b4f526ec  b9f3ad28 DisplayDriver_mini+0x196d28
b4f526f0  ffffffff
b4f526f4  804e2ed8 nt!_except_handler3
b4f526f8  804f2bb8 nt!GUID_DOCK_INTERFACE+0x424
b4f526fc  ffffffff
```

```
b4f52700  804f2bb5 nt!IopCompleteRequest+0x32f
b4f52704  804f2db5 nt!KiDeliverApc+0xb3
b4f52708  88c9d748
b4f5270c  b4f5274c
b4f52710  b4f52728
b4f52714  890259ac
b4f52718  804dce74 nt!KiDeliverApc+0x1e0
b4f5271c  806ffae4 hal!KeReleaseQueuedSpinLock+0x3c
...
...
...
b4f52738  88e775c8
b4f5273c  804f2a72 nt!IopCompleteRequest
...
...
...
b4f52754  806ffef2 hal!HalpApcInterrupt+0xc6
b4f52758  00000000
b4f5275c  00000000
b4f52760  b4f52768
b4f52764  00000000
b4f52768  b4f527f8
b4f5276c  806ffae4 hal!KeReleaseQueuedSpinLock+0x3c
b4f52770  badb0d00
b4f52774  00000000
b4f52778  00000000
b4f5277c  806ffae4 hal!KeReleaseQueuedSpinLock+0x3c
b4f52780  00000008
b4f52784  00000246
b4f52788  804e5d2c nt!KeInsertQueueApc+0x6d
b4f5278c  88c9d748
...
...
...
b4f527c0  b4f52c10
b4f527c4  804e2ed8 nt!_except_handler3
b4f527c8  804faca0 nt!KiFindFirstSetLeft+0x120
b4f527cc  ffffffff
b4f527d0  b4f52840
b4f527d4  804de403 nt!CommonDispatchException+0x4d
b4f527d8  b4f527ec
...
...
...
b4f527f4  00000000
b4f527f8  bfbf0ca6 DisplayDriver+0x21bca6
b4f527fc  00000002
...
...
...
b4f52828  b4f52840
b4f5282c  804e0944 nt!KiTrap0E+0xd0
b4f52830  00000000
b4f52834  03a3fb4c
```

```
b4f52838  00000000
b4f5283c  804de3b4 nt!Kei386EoiHelper+0x18a
b4f52840  e24079e0
b4f52844  bfbf0ca6 DisplayDriver+0x21bca6
b4f52848  badb0d00
...
...
...
b4f52884  00000000
b4f52888  bfdba6c7 DisplayDriver+0x3e56c7
b4f5288c  b4f52c10
...
...
...
b4f528a4  00000000
b4f528a8  bfbf0ca6 DisplayDriver+0x21bca6
b4f528ac  00000008
...
...
...
b4f528d8  000000f3
b4f528dc  bfb6269f DisplayDriver+0x18d69f
b4f528e0  9745d083
b4f528e4  00000001
b4f528e8  e9a18d4c
b4f528ec  ffffffff
b4f528f0  bfb268e7 DisplayDriver+0x1518e7
b4f528f4  000000ab
...
...
...
b4f52960  0000027a
b4f52964  bfb2696c DisplayDriver+0x15196c
b4f52968  00000000
...
...
...
b4f5298c  e2004308
b4f52990  bfab8ce4 DisplayDriver+0xe3ce4
b4f52994  000000ab
...
...
...
b4f52bd0  00000000
b4f52bd4  bf804779 win32k!GreReleaseFastMutex+0x14
b4f52bd8  b4f52be8
b4f52bdc  bf8a04e3 win32k!dhpdevRetrieveNode+0x32
b4f52be0  89b20128
b4f52be4  b4f52c50
b4f52be8  b4f52c20
b4f52bec  bf907d15 win32k!WatchdogDdBlt+0x38
b4f52bf0  b4f52c50
...
...
```

```
...
b4f52c10  b4f52d40
b4f52c14  bf9877ae win32k!_except_handler3
b4f52c18  bf995380 win32k!`string'+0x2b4
b4f52c1c  00000000
b4f52c20  b4f52d50
b4f52c24  bf9cdd78 dxg!DxDdBlt+0x374
b4f52c28  b4f52c50
b4f52c2c  b4f52d64
b4f52c30  038dfaf4
b4f52c34  bf907ca3 win32k!NtGdiDdBlt
b4f52c38  00000001
...
...
...
b4f52c90  000000b0
b4f52c94  bf805b42 win32k!AllocateObject+0xaa
b4f52c98  00000001
b4f52c9c  00000006
b4f52ca0  b4f52cb0
b4f52ca4  32040ddf
b4f52ca8  bf805734 win32k!HANDLELOCK::vLockHandle+0x75
b4f52cac  00000ff4
b4f52cb0  00000000
b4f52cb4  bc40ddf0
b4f52cb8  b4f52cd0
b4f52cbc  00000001
b4f52cc0  804da3ee nt!ExAcquireResourceExclusiveLite+0x67
b4f52cc4  00000008
...
...
...
b4f52ce8  80001005
b4f52cec  804dc605 nt!ExReleaseResourceLite+0x8d
b4f52cf0  00000000
...
...
...
b4f52d08  b4f52d18
b4f52d0c  bf8018bf win32k!GreReleaseSemaphore+0xa
b4f52d10  bf803d1e win32k!GreUnlockDisplay+0x24
b4f52d14  00000000
...
...
...
b4f52d40  ffffffff
b4f52d44  bf9d2132 dxg!_except_handler3
b4f52d48  bf9d2928 dxg!GUID_MiscellaneousCallbacks+0x42c
b4f52d4c  ffffffff
b4f52d50  b4f52d64
b4f52d54  804dd99f nt!KiFastCallEntry+0xfc
b4f52d58  02400002
...
...
```

```
...
b4f52ddc  00000023
b4f52de0  804ec781 nt!KiThreadStartup+0x16
b4f52de4  f7849b85 NDIS!ndisWorkerThread
b4f52de8  88c9d4d0
b4f52dec  00000000
b4f52df0  0020027f
b4f52df4  011c0000
b4f52df8  bfdb97b7 DisplayDriver+0x3e47b7
b4f52dfc  00000008
...
...
...
b4f52e70  00000000
b4f52e74  f7800000 InCDPass+0x1000
b4f52e78  00004026
...
...
...
b4f52ff8  00000000
b4f52ffc  00000000
b4f53000  ????????
b4f53004  ????????
```

Some are coincidental like *InCDPass* and *NDIS*. *DisplayDriver*, *DisplayDriver_mini*, *dxg*, and *win32k* should be related due to their functional purpose: Display, DirectX, GDI (Graphics Device Interface). Now we can check their module information:

```
0: kd> lmv m DisplayDriver
start    end        module name
bf9d5000 bff42500   DisplayDriver T (no symbols)
    Loaded symbol image file: DisplayDriver.dll
    Image path: DisplayDriver.dll
    Image name: DisplayDriver.dll
    Timestamp:        Fri Jun 29 09:13:08 2007 (4684BF14)
    CheckSum:         00570500
    ImageSize:        0056D500
    Translations:     0000.04b0 0000.04e0 0409.04b0 0409.04e0
```

```
0: kd> lmv m DisplayDriver_mini
start    end        module name
b9da4000 ba421f20   DisplayDriver_mini T (no symbols)
    Loaded symbol image file: DisplayDriver_mini.sys
    Image path: DisplayDriver_mini.sys
    Image name: DisplayDriver_mini.sys
    Timestamp:        Fri Jun 29 09:16:41 2007 (4684BFE9)
    CheckSum:         00680F20
    ImageSize:        0067DF20
    Translations:     0000.04b0 0000.04e0 0409.04b0 0409.04e0

0: kd> lmv m dxg
start    end        module name
bf9c3000 bf9d4580   dxg        (pdb symbols)
    Loaded symbol image file: dxg.sys
    Mapped memory image file: c:\websymbols\dxg.sys\41107B9311580\dxg.sys
    Image path: dxg.sys
    Image name: dxg.sys
    Timestamp:        Wed Aug 04 07:00:51 2004 (41107B93)
    CheckSum:         0001D181
    ImageSize:        00011580
    File version:     5.1.2600.2180
    Product version:  5.1.2600.2180
    File flags:       0 (Mask 3F)
    File OS:          40004 NT Win32
    File type:        3.7 Driver
    File date:        00000000.00000000
    Translations:     0409.04b0
    CompanyName:      Microsoft Corporation
    ProductName:      Microsoft® Windows® Operating System
    InternalName:     dxg.sys
    OriginalFilename: dxg.sys
    ProductVersion:   5.1.2600.2180
    FileVersion:      5.1.2600.2180 (xpsp_sp2_rtm.040803-2158)
    FileDescription:  DirectX Graphics Driver
    LegalCopyright:   © Microsoft Corporation. All rights reserved.

0: kd> lmv m win32k
start    end        module name
bf800000 bf9c2180   win32k   # (pdb symbols)
    Loaded symbol image file: win32k.sys
    Mapped memory image file:
c:\websymbols\win32k.sys\45F013F61c2180\win32k.sys
    Image path: win32k.sys
    Image name: win32k.sys
    Timestamp:        Thu Mar 08 13:47:34 2007 (45F013F6)
    CheckSum:         001C4886
    ImageSize:        001C2180
    File version:     5.1.2600.3099
    Product version:  5.1.2600.3099
    File flags:       0 (Mask 3F)
    File OS:          40004 NT Win32
    File type:        3.7 Driver
```

```
    File date:          00000000.00000000
    Translations:       0406.04b0
    CompanyName:        Microsoft Corporation
    ProductName:        Microsoft® Windows® Operativsystem
    InternalName:       win32k.sys
    OriginalFilename: win32k.sys
    ProductVersion:     5.1.2600.3099
    FileVersion:        5.1.2600.3099 (xpsp_sp2_gdr.070308-0222)
    FileDescription:    Win32-flerbrugerdriver
    LegalCopyright:     © Microsoft Corporation. Alle rettigheder
forbeholdes.
```

Symbols and Images

Suppose, we have a minidump with a stack trace that involves our product driver, and due to some reason, WinDbg doesn't pick symbols automatically and shows the following stack trace and crash address pointing to *driver.sys* module:

```
1: kd> kL
ChildEBP RetAddr
WARNING: Stack unwind information not available. Following frames may be
wrong.
ba0fd0e4 bfabd64b driver+0x2df2a
ba0fd1c8 bf8b495d driver+0x1f64b
ba0fd27c bf9166ae win32k!NtGdiBitBlt+0x52d
ba0fd2d8 bf9168d0 win32k!TileWallpaper+0xd4
ba0fd2f8 bf826c83 win32k!xxxDrawWallpaper+0x50
ba0fd324 bf8651df win32k!xxxDesktopPaintCallback+0x48
ba0fd388 bf8280f3 win32k!xxxEnumDisplayMonitors+0x13a
ba0fd3d4 bf8283ab win32k!xxxInternalPaintDesktop+0x66
ba0fd3f8 80833bdf win32k!NtUserPaintDesktop+0x41
ba0fd3f8 7c9485ec nt!KiFastCallEntry+0xfc
```

```
1: kd> r
eax=000007d0 ebx=000007d0 ecx=00000086 edx=bfb371a3 esi=bc492000
edi=bfb3775b
eip=bfacbf2a esp=ba0fd0b8 ebp=ba0fd0e4 iopl=0 nv up ei pl nz na po nc
cs=0008 ss=0010 ds=0023 es=0023 fs=0030 gs=0000 efl=00010202
driver+0x2df2a:
bfacbf2a f3a5 rep movs dword ptr es:[edi],dword ptr [esi]
es:0023:bfb3775b=e4405a64 ds:0023:bc492000=????????
```

Let's get the timestamp of this module too:

```
1: kd> lmv m driver
start    end        module name
bfa9e000 bfb42a00   driver    T (no symbols)
    Loaded symbol image file: driver.sys
    Image path: driver.sys
    Image name: driver.sys
    Timestamp:        Thu Mar 01 20:50:04 2007 (45E73C7C)
    CheckSum:         000A5062
    ImageSize:        000A4A00
    Translations:     0000.04b0 0000.04e0 0409.04b0 0409.04e0
```

We see that no symbols for driver.sys were found, and this is also indicated by the absence of function names and the presence of huge code offsets like **0x2df2a**. Perhaps we don't have a symbol server and store our symbol files somewhere. Or we got symbols from the developer of the recent fix that bugchecks, and we want to apply them. In any case, if we add a path to Symbol Search Path dialog (*File -> Symbol File Path …*) or use **.sympath** WinDbg command we can get a better stack trace and crash point:

```
1: kd> .reload
Loading Kernel Symbols
...
Loading User Symbols
Loading unloaded module list
...
Unable to load image driver.sys, Win32 error 0n2
*** WARNING: Unable to verify timestamp for driver.sys

1: kd> kL
ChildEBP RetAddr
ba0fd0c0 bfabc399 driver!ProcessBytes+0x18
ba0fd0e4 bfabd64b driver!ProcessObject+0xc9
ba0fd1c8 bf8b495d driver!CacheBitBlt+0x13d
ba0fd27c bf9166ae win32k!NtGdiBitBlt+0x52d
ba0fd2d8 bf9168d0 win32k!TileWallpaper+0xd4
ba0fd2f8 bf826c83 win32k!xxxDrawWallpaper+0x50
ba0fd324 bf8651df win32k!xxxDesktopPaintCallback+0x48
ba0fd388 bf8280f3 win32k!xxxEnumDisplayMonitors+0x13a
ba0fd3d4 bf8283ab win32k!xxxInternalPaintDesktop+0x66
ba0fd3f8 80833bdf win32k!NtUserPaintDesktop+0x41
ba0fd3f8 7c9485ec nt!KiFastCallEntry+0xfc

1: kd> r
eax=000007d0 ebx=000007d0 ecx=00000086 edx=bfb371a3 esi=bc492000
edi=bfb3775b
eip=bfacbf2a esp=ba0fd0b8 ebp=ba0fd0e4 iopl=0 nv up ei pl nz na po nc
cs=0008 ss=0010 ds=0023 es=0023 fs=0030 gs=0000 efl=00010202
driver!ProcessBytes+0x18:
bfacbf2a f3a5 rep movs dword ptr es:[edi],dword ptr [esi]
es:0023:bfb3775b=e4405a64 ds:0023:bc492000=????????
```

Because WinDbg reports that it was unable to verify timestamp for *driver.sys*, we might want to double-check the return address saved when *ProcessBytes* function was called. If symbols are correct, then disassembling the return address backward will most likely show *ProcessObject* function code and "call" instruction with *ProcessBytes* address. Unfortunately, minidumps don't have executable code regions except for the currently executing function:

```
1: kd> ub bfabc399
                   ^ Unable to find valid previous instruction for 'ub
bfabc399'

1: kd> uf driver!ProcessObject
No code found, aborting
```

Therefore, we need to point WinDbg to our *driver.sys* which contains executable code. It can be done by specifying a path in Executable Image Search Path dialog (*File -> Image File Path ...*) or using **.exepath** WinDbg command.

Now we get a complete stack trace, and we can double-check the return address:

```
1: kd> .reload
Loading Kernel Symbols
...
Loading User Symbols
Loading unloaded module list
...

1: kd> kL
ChildEBP RetAddr
ba0fd0c0 bfabc399 driver!ProcessBytes+0x18
ba0fd0e4 bfabd64b driver!ProcessObject+0xc9
ba0fd104 bfac5aac driver!CacheBitBlt+0x13d
ba0fd114 bfac6840 driver!ProcessCommand+0x150
ba0fd140 bfac1878 driver!CheckSurface+0x258
ba0fd178 bfaba0ee driver!CopyBitsEx+0xfa
ba0fd1c8 bf8b495d driver!DrvCopyBits+0xb6
ba0fd27c bf9166ae win32k!NtGdiBitBlt+0x52d
ba0fd2d8 bf9168d0 win32k!TileWallpaper+0xd4
ba0fd2f8 bf826c83 win32k!xxxDrawWallpaper+0x50
ba0fd324 bf8651df win32k!xxxDesktopPaintCallback+0x48
ba0fd388 bf8280f3 win32k!xxxEnumDisplayMonitors+0x13a
ba0fd3d4 bf8283ab win32k!xxxInternalPaintDesktop+0x66
ba0fd3f8 80833bdf win32k!NtUserPaintDesktop+0x41
ba0fd3f8 7c9485ec nt!KiFastCallEntry+0xfc

1: kd> ub bfabc399
driver!ProcessObject+0xb7:
bfabc387 57              push    edi
bfabc388 40              inc     eax
bfabc389 50              push    eax
bfabc38a e861fb0000      call    driver!convert (bfacbef0)
bfabc38f ff7508          push    dword ptr [ebp+8]
bfabc392 57              push    edi
bfabc393 50              push    eax
bfabc394 e879fb0000      call    driver!ProcessBytes (bfacbf12)
```

Interrupts and Exceptions Explained

Exceptions Ab Initio

Where do native exceptions come from? How do they propagate from hardware and eventually result in crash dumps? I was asking these questions when I started doing crash dump analysis in 2003, and I tried to find answers using IA-32 Intel® Architecture Software Developer's Manual, WinDbg, and complete memory dumps. Let's look at some findings.

X86 Interrupts

How do exceptions happen in the first place, and how does the execution flow reach *KiDispatchException* function? When some abnormal condition happens such as a breakpoint, division by zero, or memory protection violation, then the normal CPU execution flow (code stream) is interrupted. I use the terms "interrupt" and "exception" interchangeably here. The type of interrupt is specified by a number called interrupt vector number. CPU has to transfer execution to some procedure in memory to handle that interrupt. CPU has to find that procedure, theoretically either having one procedure for all interrupts and specifying an interrupt vector number as a parameter or having a table containing pointers to various procedures that correspond to different interrupt vectors. Intel x86 and x64 CPUs use the latter approach, which is depicted in the following diagram:

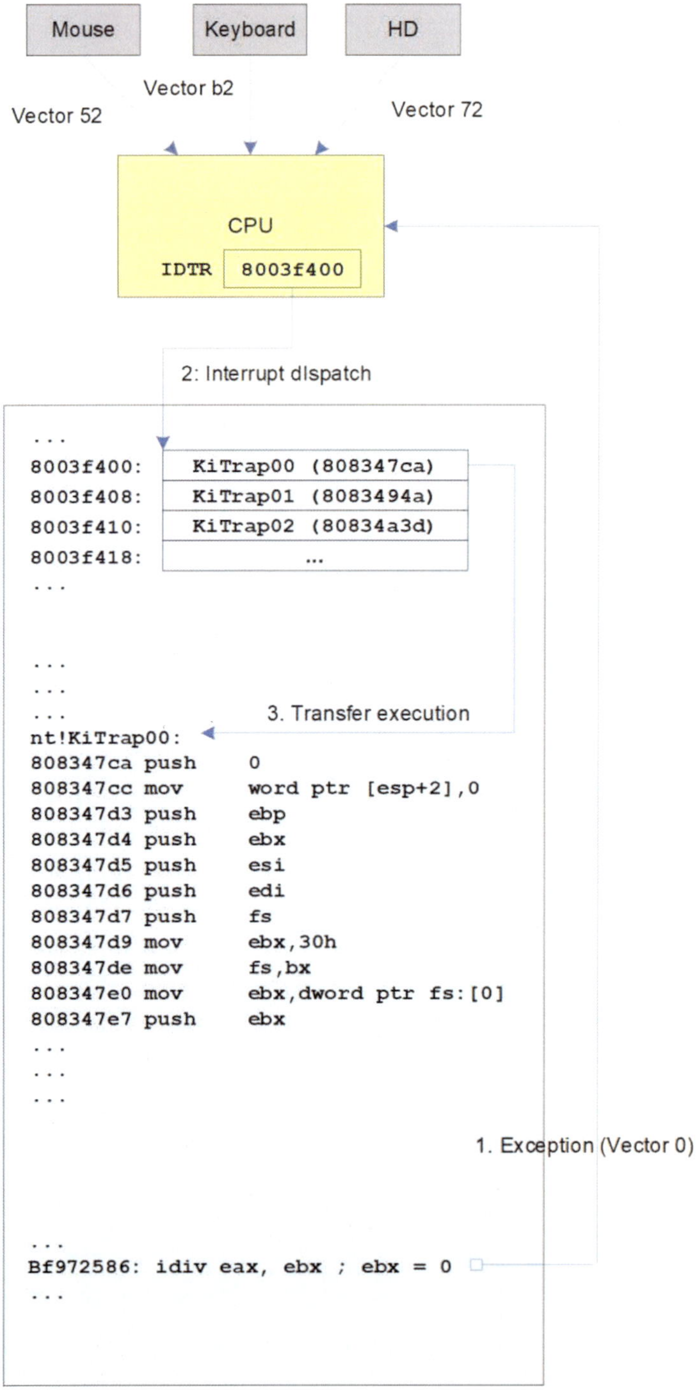
Mouse
Keyboard
HD
Vector b2
Vector 52
Vector 72
CPU
IDTR 8003f400
2: Interrupt dispatch
...
8003f400: KiTrap00 (808347ca)
8003f408: KiTrap01 (8083494a)
8003f410: KiTrap02 (80834a3d)
8003f418: ...
...
...
...
...
3. Transfer execution
nt!KiTrap00:
808347ca push 0
808347cc mov word ptr [esp+2],0
808347d3 push ebp
808347d4 push ebx
808347d5 push esi
808347d6 push edi
808347d7 push fs
808347d9 mov ebx,30h
808347de mov fs,bx
808347e0 mov ebx,dword ptr fs:[0]
808347e7 push ebx
...
...
...
1. Exception (Vector 0)
...
Bf972586: idiv eax, ebx ; ebx = 0
...

When an exception happens, for example, divide by zero, CPU gets the address of the procedure table from IDTR (Interrupt Descriptor Table Register). This IDT (Interrupt Descriptor Table) is a zero-based array of 8-byte descriptors (x86) or 16-byte descriptors (x64). CPU calculates the location of the necessary procedure to call and does some necessary steps like saving appropriate registers before the call.

The same happens when some external I/O device interrupts. For I/O devices, the term "interrupt" is more appropriate. On the picture above, I/O hardware interrupt vector numbers were taken from some crash dump. These are OS and user-defined numbers. The first 32 vectors are reserved by Intel. Before Windows switches CPU to protected mode during the boot process, it creates an IDT table in memory and sets IDTR to point to it by using SIDT instruction.

Let me now illustrate this by using a UML class diagram annotated by pseudo-code that shows what CPU does before calling the appropriate procedure. The pseudo-code on the diagram below is valid for interrupts and exceptions happening when the current CPU execution mode is kernel mode. For interrupts and exceptions generated when CPU executes code in user mode, the picture is a little more complicated because the processor has to switch the current user-mode stack to kernel mode stack.

The following diagram is for 32-bit x86 processor:

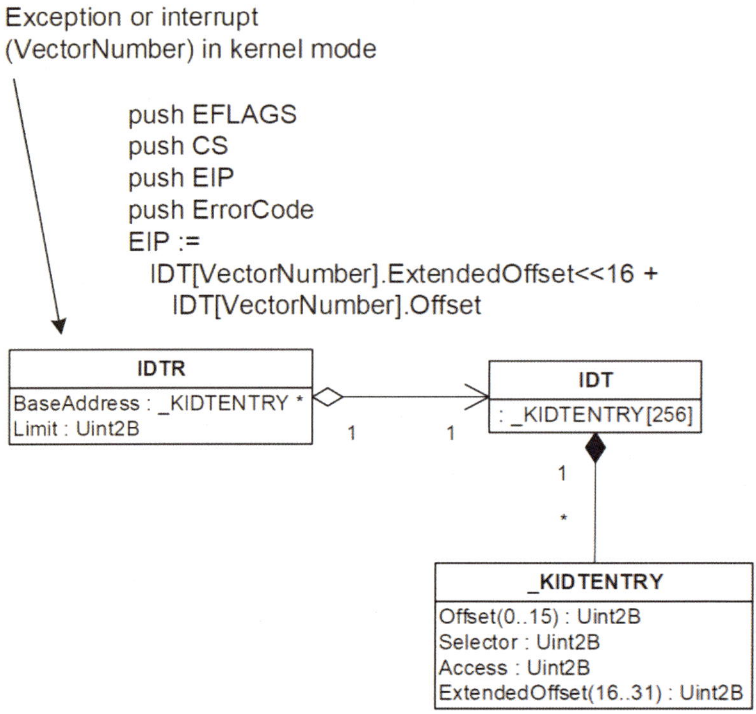

Let's see all this in some kernel memory dump. The address of IDT can be found by using **!pcr** *[processor number]* command. Every processor on a multiprocessor machine has its own IDT:

```
0: kd> !pcr 0
KPCR for Processor 0 at ffdff000:
    Major 1 Minor 1
 NtTib.ExceptionList: f2178b8c
     NtTib.StackBase: 00000000
    NtTib.StackLimit: 00000000
  NtTib.SubSystemTib: 80042000
       NtTib.Version: 0005c645
   NtTib.UserPointer: 00000001
       NtTib.SelfTib: 7ffdf000
             SelfPcr: ffdff000
                Prcb: ffdff120
                Irql: 0000001f
                 IRR: 00000000
                 IDR: ffffffff
       InterruptMode: 00000000
                 IDT: 8003f400
                 GDT: 8003f000
```

```
             TSS: 80042000
   CurrentThread: 88c1d3c0
      NextThread: 00000000
      IdleThread: 808a68c0
       DpcQueue:
```

Every entry in IDT has the type _KIDTENTRY, and we can get the first entry for divide by zero exceptions which has vector number 0:

```
0: kd> dt _KIDTENTRY 8003f400
   +0x000 Offset           : 0x47ca
   +0x002 Selector         : 8
   +0x004 Access           : 0x8e00
   +0x006 ExtendedOffset   : 0x8083
```

By gluing together *ExtendedOffset* and *Offset* fields, we get the address of the interrupt handling procedure (0x808347ca) which is *KiTrap00*:

```
0: kd> ln 0x808347ca
(808347ca)   nt!KiTrap00    |  (808348a5)   nt!Dr_kit1_a
Exact matches:
    nt!KiTrap00
```

We can also see the interrupt trace in a raw stack. For example, we have the following stack trace and registers in the output of **!analyze -v** command:

```
ErrCode = 00000000
eax=00001b00 ebx=00001b00 ecx=00000000 edx=00000000 esi=f2178cb4
edi=bc15a838
eip=bf972586 esp=f2178c1c ebp=f2178c90 iopl=0 nv up ei ng nz ac po cy
cs=0008 ss=0010 ds=0023 es=0023 fs=0030 gs=0000 efl=00010293
driver!foo+0xf9:
bf972586 f77d10 idiv eax,dword ptr [ebp+10h] ss:0010:f2178ca0=00000000
STACK_TEXT:
f2178b44 809989be nt!KeBugCheck+0x14
f2178b9c 8083484f nt!Ki386CheckDivideByZeroTrap+0x41
f2178b9c bf972586 nt!KiTrap00+0x88
f2178c90 bf94c23c driver!foo+0xf9
f2178d54 80833bdf driver!bar+0x11c
```

Dumping memory around ESP value (f2178c1c) shows the values processor pushes when divide by zero exception happens:

```
0: kd> dds f2178c1c-100 f2178c1c+100
...
...
...
f2178b80  00000000
f2178b84  f2178b50
f2178b88  00000000
f2178b8c  f2178d44
f2178b90  8083a8cc nt!_except_handler3
f2178b94  80870828 nt!`string'+0xa4
f2178b98  ffffffff
f2178b9c  f2178ba8
f2178ba0  8083484f nt!KiTrap00+0x88
f2178ba4  f2178ba8
f2178ba8  f2178c90
f2178bac  bf972586 driver!foo+0xf9
f2178bb0  badb0d00
f2178bb4  00000000
f2178bb8  0000006d
f2178bbc  bf842315
f2178bc0  f2178c6c
...
...
...
f2178be8  00000000
f2178bec  00001b00
f2178bf0  f2178c0c
f2178bf4  f2178d44
f2178bf8  f2170030
f2178bfc  bc15a838
f2178c00  f2178cb4
f2178c04  00001b00
f2178c08  f2178c90
f2178c0c  00000000 ; ErrorCode
f2178c10  bf972586 driver!foo+0xf9 ; EIP
f2178c14  00000008 ; CS
f2178c18  00010293 ; EFLAGS
f2178c1c  00000000 ; <- ESP before interrupt
f2178c20  0013c220
f2178c24  00000000
f2178c28  60000000
f2178c2c  00000001
f2178c30  00000000
f2178c34  00000000
...
...
...
```

ErrorCode is not the same as the interrupt vector number, although it is the same number here (0). I don't cover interrupt error codes here. If you are interested, please consult Intel Architecture Software Developer's Manual.

If we try to execute **!idt** extension command it will show us only user-defined hardware interrupt vectors:

```
0: kd> !idt
Dumping IDT:
37: 80a7d1ac hal!PicSpuriousService37
50: 80a7d284 hal!HalpApicRebootService
51: 89495044 serial!SerialCIsrSw (KINTERRUPT 89495008)
52: 89496044 i8042prt!I8042MouseInterruptService (KINTERRUPT 89496008)
53: 894ea044 USBPORT!USBPORT_InterruptService (KINTERRUPT 894ea008)
63: 894f2044 USBPORT!USBPORT_InterruptService (KINTERRUPT 894f2008)
72: 89f59044 atapi!IdePortInterrupt (KINTERRUPT 89f59008)
73: 89580044 NDIS!ndisMIsr (KINTERRUPT 89580008)
83: 899e7824 NDIS!ndisMIsr (KINTERRUPT 899e77e8)
92: 89f56044 atapi!IdePortInterrupt (KINTERRUPT 89f56008)
93: 89f1e044 SCSIPORT!ScsiPortInterrupt (KINTERRUPT 89f1e008)
a3: 894fa044 USBPORT!USBPORT_InterruptService (KINTERRUPT 894fa008)
a4: 894a3044 cpqcidrv+0x22AE (KINTERRUPT 894a3008)
b1: 89f697dc ACPI!ACPIInterruptServiceRoutine (KINTERRUPT 89f697a0)
b3: 89498824 i8042prt!I8042KeyboardInterruptService (KINTERRUPT 894987e8)
b4: 894a2044 cpqasm2+0x5B99 (KINTERRUPT 894a2008)
c1: 80a7d410 hal!HalpBroadcastCallService
d1: 80a7c754 hal!HalpClockInterrupt
e1: 80a7d830 hal!HalpIpiHandler
e3: 80a7d654 hal!HalpLocalApicErrorService
fd: 80a7e11c hal!HalpProfileInterrupt
```

X64 Interrupts

Now I describe changes in 64-bit Windows. The size of IDTR is 10 bytes, where 8 bytes hold the 64-bit address of IDT. The size of IDT entry is 16 bytes, and it holds the address of an interrupt procedure corresponding to an interrupt vector. However, interrupt procedure names are different in x64 Windows; they do not follow the same pattern as *KiTrapXX*.

The following UML class diagram describes the relationship and also shows what registers are saved. In native x64 mode, SS and RSP are saved regardless of kernel or user mode.

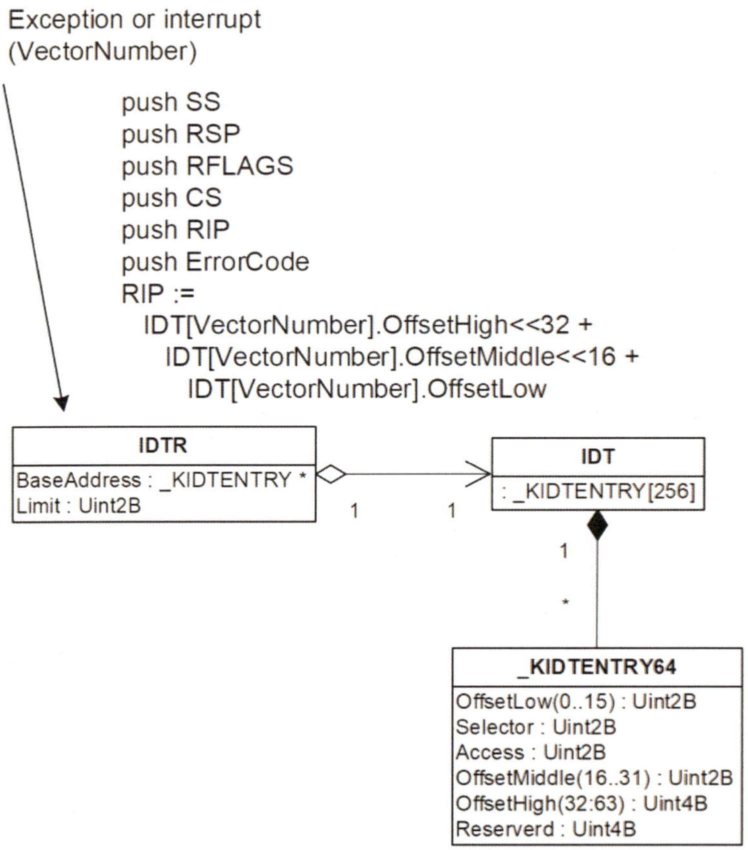

Let's dump all architecture-defined interrupt procedure names. It is a good exercise because we use WinDbg scripting. **!pcr** extension reports wrong IDT base, so we use **dt** command:

```
kd> !pcr 0
KPCR for Processor 0 at fffff80001176000:
    Major 1 Minor 1
 NtTib.ExceptionList: fffff80000124000
     NtTib.StackBase: fffff80000125070
    NtTib.StackLimit: 0000000000000000
  NtTib.SubSystemTib: fffff80001176000
       NtTib.Version: 0000000001176180
   NtTib.UserPointer: fffff800011767f0
       NtTib.SelfTib: 000000007ef95000
             SelfPcr: 0000000000000000
                Prcb: fffff80001176180
                Irql: 0000000000000000
                 IRR: 0000000000000000
                 IDR: 0000000000000000
       InterruptMode: 0000000000000000
                 IDT: 0000000000000000
                 GDT: 0000000000000000
                 TSS: 0000000000000000
       CurrentThread: fffffadfe669f890
          NextThread: 0000000000000000
          IdleThread: fffff8000117a300
           DpcQueue:

kd> dt _KPCR fffff80001176000
nt!_KPCR
   +0x000 NtTib            : _NT_TIB
   +0x000 GdtBase          : 0xfffff800`00124000 _KGDTENTRY64
   +0x008 TssBase          : 0xfffff800`00125070 _KTSS64
   +0x010 PerfGlobalGroupMask : (null)
   +0x018 Self             : 0xfffff800`01176000 _KPCR
   +0x020 CurrentPrcb      : 0xfffff800`01176180 _KPRCB
   +0x028 LockArray        : 0xfffff800`011767f0 _KSPIN_LOCK_QUEUE
   +0x030 Used_Self        : 0x00000000`7ef95000
   +0x038 IdtBase          : 0xfffff800`00124070 _KIDTENTRY64
   +0x040 Unused           : [2] 0
   +0x050 Irql             : 0 ''
   +0x051 SecondLevelCacheAssociativity : 0x10 ''
   +0x052 ObsoleteNumber   : 0 ''
   +0x053 Fill0            : 0 ''
   +0x054 Unused0          : [3] 0
   +0x060 MajorVersion     : 1
   +0x062 MinorVersion     : 1
   +0x064 StallScaleFactor : 0x892
   +0x068 Unused1          : [3] (null)
   +0x080 KernelReserved   : [15] 0
   +0x0bc SecondLevelCacheSize : 0x100000
   +0x0c0 HalReserved      : [16] 0x82c5c880
   +0x100 Unused2          : 0
   +0x108 KdVersionBlock   : 0xfffff800`01174ca0
   +0x110 Unused3          : (null)
   +0x118 PcrAlign1        : [24] 0
   +0x180 Prcb             : _KPRCB
```

Next, we dump the first entry of IDT array and glue together *OffsetHigh*, *OffsetMiddle,* and *OffsetLow* fields to form the interrupt procedure address corresponding to the interrupt vector 0, divide by zero exception:

```
kd> dt _KIDTENTRY64 0xfffff800`00124070
nt!_KIDTENTRY64
   +0x000 OffsetLow          : 0xf240
   +0x002 Selector           : 0x10
   +0x004 IstIndex           : 0y000
   +0x004 Reserved0          : 0y00000 (0)
   +0x004 Type               : 0y01110 (0xe)
   +0x004 Dpl                : 0y00
   +0x004 Present            : 0y1
   +0x006 OffsetMiddle       : 0x103
   +0x008 OffsetHigh         : 0xfffff800
   +0x00c Reserved1          : 0
   +0x000 Alignment          : 0x1038e00`0010f240

kd> u 0xfffff8000103f240
nt!KiDivideErrorFault:
fffff800`0103f240 4883ec08        sub     rsp,8
fffff800`0103f244 55              push    rbp
fffff800`0103f245 4881ec58010000  sub     rsp,158h
fffff800`0103f24c 488dac2480000000 lea     rbp,[rsp+80h]
fffff800`0103f254 c645ab01        mov     byte ptr [rbp-55h],1
fffff800`0103f258 488945b0        mov     qword ptr [rbp-50h],rax
fffff800`0103f25c 48894db8        mov     qword ptr [rbp-48h],rcx
fffff800`0103f260 488955c0        mov     qword ptr [rbp-40h],rdx

kd> ln 0xfffff8000103f240
(fffff800`0103f240)   nt!KiDivideErrorFault   |
(fffff800`0103f300)   nt!KiDebugTrapOrFault
Exact matches:
    nt!KiDivideErrorFault = <no type information>
```

We see that the name of the procedure is *KiDivideErrorFault* and not *KiTrap00*. We can dump the second IDT entry manually by adding 0x10 offset but in order to automate this I wrote the following WinDbg script to dump the first 20 vectors and get their interrupt procedure names:

```
r? $t0=(_KIDTENTRY64 *)0xfffff800`00124070; .for (r $t1=0; @$t1 <= 13; r?
$t0=(_KIDTENTRY64 *)@$t0+1) { .printf "Interrupt vector %d (0x%x):\n",
@$t1, @$t1; ln @@c++(@$t0->OffsetHigh*0x100000000 + @$t0-
>OffsetMiddle*0x10000 + @$t0->OffsetLow); r $t1=$t1+1 }
```

Here is the same script but formatted:

```
r? $t0=(_KIDTENTRY64 *)0xfffff800`00124070;
.for (r $t1=0; @$t1 <= 13; r? $t0=(_KIDTENTRY64 *)@$t0+1)
{
    .printf "Interrupt vector %d (0x%x):\n", @$t1, @$t1;
    ln @@c++(@$t0->OffsetHigh*0x100000000 +
        @$t0->OffsetMiddle*0x10000 + @$t0->OffsetLow);
    r $t1=$t1+1
}
```

The output on my Windows 2003 Server system is:

```
Interrupt vector 0 (0x0):
(fffff800`0103f240) nt!KiDivideErrorFault | (fffff800`0103f300)
nt!KiDebugTrapOrFault
Exact matches:
  nt!KiDivideErrorFault = <no type information>
Interrupt vector 1 (0x1):
(fffff800`0103f300) nt!KiDebugTrapOrFault | (fffff800`0103f440)
nt!KiNmiInterrupt
Exact matches:
  nt!KiDebugTrapOrFault = <no type information>
Interrupt vector 2 (0x2):
(fffff800`0103f440) nt!KiNmiInterrupt | (fffff800`0103f680)
nt!KxNmiInterrupt
Exact matches:
  nt!KiNmiInterrupt = <no type information>
Interrupt vector 3 (0x3):
(fffff800`0103f780) nt!KiBreakpointTrap | (fffff800`0103f840)
nt!KiOverflowTrap
Exact matches:
  nt!KiBreakpointTrap = <no type information>
Interrupt vector 4 (0x4):
(fffff800`0103f840) nt!KiOverflowTrap | (fffff800`0103f900)
nt!KiBoundFault
Exact matches:
  nt!KiOverflowTrap = <no type information>
Interrupt vector 5 (0x5):
(fffff800`0103f900) nt!KiBoundFault | (fffff800`0103f9c0)
nt!KiInvalidOpcodeFault
Exact matches:
  nt!KiBoundFault = <no type information>
Interrupt vector 6 (0x6):
(fffff800`0103f9c0) nt!KiInvalidOpcodeFault | (fffff800`0103fb80)
nt!KiNpxNotAvailableFault
Exact matches:
  nt!KiInvalidOpcodeFault = <no type information>
```

```
Interrupt vector 7 (0x7):
(fffff800`0103fb80) nt!KiNpxNotAvailableFault | (fffff800`0103fc40)
nt!KiDoubleFaultAbort
Exact matches:
  nt!KiNpxNotAvailableFault = <no type information>
Interrupt vector 8 (0x8):
(fffff800`0103fc40) nt!KiDoubleFaultAbort | (fffff800`0103fd00)
nt!KiNpxSegmentOverrunAbort
Exact matches:
  nt!KiDoubleFaultAbort = <no type information>
Interrupt vector 9 (0x9):
(fffff800`0103fd00) nt!KiNpxSegmentOverrunAbort | (fffff800`0103fdc0)
nt!KiInvalidTssFault
Exact matches:
  nt!KiNpxSegmentOverrunAbort = <no type information>
Interrupt vector 10 (0xa):
(fffff800`0103fdc0) nt!KiInvalidTssFault | (fffff800`0103fe80)
nt!KiSegmentNotPresentFault
Exact matches:
  nt!KiInvalidTssFault = <no type information>
Interrupt vector 11 (0xb):
(fffff800`0103fe80) nt!KiSegmentNotPresentFault | (fffff800`0103ff80)
nt!KiStackFault
Exact matches:
  nt!KiSegmentNotPresentFault = <no type information>
Interrupt vector 12 (0xc):
(fffff800`0103ff80) nt!KiStackFault | (fffff800`01040080)
nt!KiGeneralProtectionFault
Exact matches:
  nt!KiStackFault = <no type information>
Interrupt vector 13 (0xd):
(fffff800`01040080) nt!KiGeneralProtectionFault | (fffff800`01040180)
nt!KiPageFault
Exact matches:
  nt!KiGeneralProtectionFault = <no type information>
Interrupt vector 14 (0xe):
(fffff800`01040180) nt!KiPageFault | (fffff800`010404c0)
nt!KiFloatingErrorFault
Exact matches:
  nt!KiPageFault = <no type information>
Interrupt vector 15 (0xf):
(fffff800`01179090) nt!KxUnexpectedInterrupt0+0xf0 | (fffff800`0117a0c0)
nt!KiNode0
Interrupt vector 16 (0x10):
(fffff800`010404c0) nt!KiFloatingErrorFault | (fffff800`01040600)
nt!KiAlignmentFault
Exact matches:
  nt!KiFloatingErrorFault = <no type information>
Interrupt vector 17 (0x11):
(fffff800`01040600) nt!KiAlignmentFault | (fffff800`010406c0)
nt!KiMcheckAbort
Exact matches:
  nt!KiAlignmentFault = <no type information>
```

```
Interrupt vector 18 (0x12):
(fffff800`010406c0) nt!KiMcheckAbort | (fffff800`01040900)
nt!KxMcheckAbort
Exact matches:
  nt!KiMcheckAbort = <no type information>
Interrupt vector 19 (0x13):
(fffff800`01040a00) nt!KiXmmException | (fffff800`01040b80)
nt!KiRaiseAssertion
Exact matches:
  nt!KiXmmException = <no type information>
```

Let's look at some dump.

```
BugCheck 1E, {ffffffffc0000005, fffffade5ba2d643, 0, 28}
```

It is KMODE_EXCEPTION_NOT_HANDLED bugcheck, and it could have been invalid memory access. And indeed, the stack WinDbg shows after opening a dump and entering **!analyze -v** command is:

```
RSP
fffffade`4e88fe68 nt!KeBugCheckEx
fffffade`4e88fe70 nt!KiDispatchException+0x128
fffffade`4e8905f0 nt!KiPageFault+0x1e1
fffffade`4e890780 driver!foo+0x9b
```

We have the following exception context:

```
2: kd> r
Last set context:
rax=fffffade4e8907f4 rbx=fffffade6de0c2e0 rcx=fffffa8014412000
rdx=fffffade71e7e2ac rsi=0000000000000000 rdi=fffffadffff03000
rip=fffffade5ba2d643 rsp=fffffade4e890780 rbp=fffffade71e7ffff
r8=00000000000005b0 r9=fffffade4e890a88 r10=fffffadffd077898
r11=fffffade71e7e260 r12=0000000000000000 r13=0000000000000000
r14=0000000000000000 r15=0000000000000000
iopl=0 nv up ei pl zr na po nc
cs=0010 ss=0018 ds=0950 es=4e89 fs=fade gs=ffff efl=00010246
driver!foo+0x9b:
fffffade`5ba2d643 8b4e28 mov ecx,dword ptr [rsi+28h] ds:0950:0028=????????
```

KiPageFault function was called, and from the dumped IDT we see that it corresponds to the interrupt vector 14 (0xE) called on any memory reference that is not present in physical memory.

Now I'm going to dump the raw stack around fffffade`4e890780 address to see data the processor saved before calling *KiPageFault* function:

```
2: kd> dps fffffade`4e890780-50 fffffade`4e890780+50
fffffade`4e890730  fffffade`6de0c2e0
fffffade`4e890738  fffffadf`fff03000
fffffade`4e890740  00000000`00000000
fffffade`4e890748  fffffade`71e7ffff
fffffade`4e890750  00000000`00000000 ; ErrorCode
fffffade`4e890758  fffffade`5ba2d643 driver!foo+0x9b ; RIP
fffffade`4e890760  00000000`00000010 ; CS
fffffade`4e890768  00000000`00010246 ; RFLAGS
fffffade`4e890770  fffffade`4e890780 ; RSP
fffffade`4e890778  00000000`00000018 ; SS
fffffade`4e890780  00000000`00000000 ; RSP before interrupt
fffffade`4e890788  00000000`00000000
fffffade`4e890790  00000000`00000000
fffffade`4e890798  00000000`00000000
fffffade`4e8907a0  00000000`00000000
fffffade`4e8907a8  00000000`00000000
fffffade`4e8907b0  00000000`00000000
fffffade`4e8907b8  00000000`00000000
fffffade`4e8907c0  00000000`00000000
fffffade`4e8907c8  00000000`00000000
fffffade`4e8907d0  00000000`00000000
```

We see that the values are exactly the same as WinDbg shows in the saved context above. Actually, if we look at Page Fault Error Code bits in Intel Architecture Software Developer's Manual Volume 3A, you will see that for this case, all zeroes, we have:

- the page was not present in memory
- the fault was caused by the read access
- the processor was executing in kernel mode
- no reserved bits in page directory were set to 1 when 0s were expected
- it was not caused by instruction fetch.

Interrupt Frames and Stack Reconstruction

When an interrupt happens, and an x86 processor is in privileged, protected mode (ring 0) it pushes interrupt frame shown in the following pseudo-code:

```
push EFLAGS
push CS
push EIP
push ErrorCode
EIP := IDT[VectorNumber].ExtendedOffset<<16 +
   IDT[VectorNumber].Offset
```

This is an interrupt frame that is created by CPU and not a trap frame created by a software interrupt handler to save CPU state (_KTRAP_FRAME).

If an interrupt happens when an x86 processor is in user mode (ring 3), then the stack switch occurs before the processor saves user mode stack pointer SS:ESP and pushes the rest of the interrupt frame. Pushing both SS:RSP always happens on x64 processor regardless of the current execution mode, kernel or user. The following x86 pseudo-code shows how interrupt frame is pushed on the current stack (to be precise, on the kernel space stack if the interrupt happened in user mode):

```
push SS
push ESP
push EFLAGS
push CS
push EIP
push ErrorCode
EIP := IDT[VectorNumber].ExtendedOffset<<16 +
   IDT[VectorNumber].Offset
```

Usually, CS is 0x1b, and SS is 0x23 for x86 Windows flat memory model, so we can quickly identify this pattern on raw stack data.

Why should we care about an interrupt frame? This is because in complete memory dumps we can see exceptions that happened in user space and processed at the time the dump was saved.

Let's look at one example:

```
PROCESS 89a94800 SessionId: 1 Cid: 1050 Peb: 7ffd7000 ParentCid: 08a4
DirBase: 390f5000 ObjectTable: e36ee0b8 HandleCount: 168.
Image: processA.exe
VadRoot 8981d0a0 Vads 309 Clone 0 Private 222555. Modified 10838. Locked
0.
DeviceMap                             e37957e0
Token                                 e395b8f8
ElapsedTime                           07:44:38.505
UserTime                              00:54:52.906
KernelTime                            00:00:58.109
QuotaPoolUsage[PagedPool]             550152
QuotaPoolUsage[NonPagedPool]          14200
Working Set Sizes (now,min,max)       (213200, 50, 345) (852800KB, 200KB,
1380KB)
PeakWorkingSetSize                    227093
VirtualSize                           1032 Mb
PeakVirtualSize                       1032 Mb
PageFaultCount                        232357
MemoryPriority                        BACKGROUND
BasePriority                          8
CommitCharge                          233170
DebugPort                             899b6a40
```

We see that *processA* has a *DebugPort* and the presence of it usually indicates that some exception happened. Therefore, if we dump all processes by entering **!process 0 1** command we can search for any unhandled exceptions.

Indeed, if we switch to this process (we can also use **!process 89a94800 3f** command for dumps coming from XP and higher systems) we see *KiDispatchException* in one of the processA thread stack traces:

```
0: kd> .process 89a94800

0: kd> .reload

0: kd> !process 89a94800
...
...
...
THREAD 89a93020 Cid 1050.1054 Teb: 7ffdf000 Win32Thread: bc1da760 WAIT:
(Unknown) KernelMode Non-Alertable SuspendCount 1
    f44dc3a8 SynchronizationEvent
Not impersonating
DeviceMap               e37957e0
Owning Process          89a94800        Image:         processA.exe
Wait Start TickCount    4244146         Ticks: 1232980 (0:05:21:05.312)
Context Switch Count    1139234         LargeStack
```

```
UserTime                00:54:51.0531
KernelTime              00:00:53.0937
Win32 Start Address processA!WinMainCRTStartup (0x00c534c8)
Start Address kernel32!BaseProcessStartThunk (0x77e617f8)
Stack Init f44dcbd0 Current f44dc2ec Base f44dd000 Limit f44d7000 Call
f44dcbd8
Priority 12 BasePriority 8 PriorityDecrement 2
ChildEBP RetAddr
f44dc304 8083d5b1 nt!KiSwapContext+0x26
f44dc330 8083df9e nt!KiSwapThread+0x2e5
f44dc378 809c3cff nt!KeWaitForSingleObject+0x346
f44dc458 809c4f09 nt!DbgkpQueueMessage+0x178
f44dc47c 80977ad9 nt!DbgkpSendApiMessage+0x45
f44dc508 8081a94f nt!DbgkForwardException+0x90
f44dc8c4 808346b4 nt!KiDispatchException+0x1ea
f44dc92c 80834650 nt!CommonDispatchException+0x4a
f44dc9b8 80a801ae nt!Kei386EoiHelper+0x16e
0012f968 0046915d hal!HalpDispatchSoftwareInterrupt+0x5e
0012f998 0047cb72 processA!CalculateClientSizeFromPoint+0x5f
0012f9bc 0047cc1d processA!CalculateFromPoint+0x30
0012fa64 0047de83 processA!DrawUsingMemDC+0x1b9
0012fac0 0099fb43 processA!OnDraw+0x13
0012fb5c 7c17332d processA!OnPaint+0x56
0012fbe8 7c16e0b0 MFC71!CWnd::OnWndMsg+0x340
0012fc08 00c6253a MFC71!CWnd::WindowProc+0x22
0012fc24 0096cf9d processA!WindowProc+0x38
0012fcb8 7c16e1b8 MFC71!AfxCallWndProc+0x91
0012fcd8 7c16e1f6 MFC71!AfxWndProc+0x46
0012fd04 7739b6e3 MFC71!AfxWndProcBase+0x39
0012fd30 7739b874 USER32!InternalCallWinProc+0x28
0012fda8 7739c8b8 USER32!UserCallWinProcCheckWow+0x151
0012fe04 7739c9c6 USER32!DispatchClientMessage+0xd9
0012fe2c 7c828536 USER32!__fnDWORD+0x24
0012fe2c 80832dee ntdll!KiUserCallbackDispatcher+0x2e
f44dcbf0 8092d605 nt!KiCallUserMode+0x4
f44dcc48 bf8a26d3 nt!KeUserModeCallback+0x8f
f44dcccc bf89e985 win32k!SfnDWORD+0xb4
f44dcd0c bf89eb27 win32k!xxxDispatchMessage+0x223
f44dcd58 80833bdf win32k!NtUserDispatchMessage+0x4c
f44dcd58 7c8285ec nt!KiFastCallEntry+0xfc
0012fe2c 7c828536 ntdll!KiFastSystemCallRet
0012fe58 7739c57b ntdll!KiUserCallbackDispatcher+0x2e
0012fea8 773a16e5 USER32!NtUserDispatchMessage+0xc
0012feb8 7c169076 USER32!DispatchMessageA+0xf
0012fec8 7c16913e MFC71!AfxInternalPumpMessage+0x3e
0012fee4 0041cb0b MFC71!CWinThread::Run+0x54
0012ff08 7c172fc5 processA!CMain::Run+0x3b
0012ff18 00c5364d MFC71!AfxWinMain+0x68
0012ffc0 77e6f23b processA!WinMainCRTStartup+0x185
0012fff0 00000000 kernel32!BaseProcessStart+0x23
```

We might think that the exception happened in *CalculateClientSizeFromPoint* function. However, we see that there is no *nt!KiTrapXXX* call, and kernel space *hal!HalpDispatchSoftwareInterrupt* function has user space return address. This is suspicious. We need to look at raw stack data and find our interrupt frame. We look for *KiDispatchException*, then for *KiTrap* substring and, finally, for 0000001b. If 0000001b and 00000023 are separated by two double words then we have found out interrupt frame:

```
0: kd> .thread 89a93020
Implicit thread is now 89a93020

0: kd> dds esp esp+1000
...
...
...
f44dc2f8 f44dc330
f44dc2fc 89a93098
f44dc300 ffdff120
f44dc304 89a93020
f44dc308 8083d5b1 nt!KiSwapThread+0x2e5
f44dc30c 89a93020
f44dc310 89a930c8
f44dc314 00000000
...
...
...
f44dc4e8 f44dcc38
f44dc4ec 8083a8cc nt!_except_handler3
f44dc4f0 80870868 nt!`string'+0xa4
f44dc4f4 ffffffff
f44dc4f8 80998bfd nt!Ki386CheckDivideByZeroTrap+0x273
f44dc4fc 8083484f nt!KiTrap00+0x88    ; first KiTrap00
f44dc500 00000001
f44dc504 0000bb40
f44dc508 f44dc8c4
f44dc50c 8081a94f nt!KiDispatchException+0x1ea
f44dc510 f44dc8e0
f44dc514 00000001
f44dc518 00000000
f44dc51c 00469583 processA!LPtoDP+0x19
f44dc520 16b748f0
f44dc524 00469583 processA!LPtoDP+0x19
f44dc528 00000000
f44dc52c 00000000
...
...
...
f44dc8c0 ffffffff
f44dc8c4 f44dc934
f44dc8c8 808346b4 nt!CommonDispatchException+0x4a
f44dc8cc f44dc8e0
f44dc8d0 00000000
```

```
f44dc8d4 f44dc934
f44dc8d8 00000001
f44dc8dc 00000001
f44dc8e0 c0000094
f44dc8e4 00000000
f44dc8e8 00000000
f44dc8ec 00469583 processA!LPtoDP+0x19
f44dc8f0 00000000
f44dc8f4 808a3988 nt!KiAbiosPresent+0x4
f44dc8f8 ffffffff
f44dc8fc 0000a6f2
f44dc900 00469585 processA!LPtoDP+0x1b
f44dc904 00000004
f44dc908 00000000
f44dc90c f9000001
f44dc910 f44dc8dc
f44dc914 ffffffff
f44dc918 f44dcc38
f44dc91c 8083a8cc nt!_except_handler3
f44dc920 80870868 nt!`string'+0xa4
f44dc924 ffffffff
f44dc928 80998bfd nt!Ki386CheckDivideByZeroTrap+0x273
f44dc92c 8083484f nt!KiTrap00+0x88    ; second KiTrap00
f44dc930 80834650 nt!Kei386EoiHelper+0x16e
f44dc934 0012f968
f44dc938 00469583 processA!LPtoDP+0x19
f44dc93c badb0d00
f44dc940 00000000
f44dc944 ffffffff
f44dc948 00007fff
f44dc94c 00000000
f44dc950 fffff800
f44dc954 ffffffff
f44dc958 00007fff
f44dc95c 00000000
f44dc960 00000000
f44dc964 80a80000 hal!HalpInitIrqlAuditFlag+0x4e
f44dc968 00000023
f44dc96c 00000023
f44dc970 00000000
f44dc974 00000000
...
...
...
f44dc994 0012f968
f44dc998 00000000 ; ErrorCode
f44dc99c 00469583 processA!LPtoDP+0x19 ; EIP
f44dc9a0 0000001b ; CS
f44dc9a4 00010246 ; EFLAGS
f44dc9a8 0012f934 ; ESP
f44dc9ac 00000023 ; SS
f44dc9b0 8982e7e0
f44dc9b4 00000000
```

Why did we skip the first *KiTrap00*? Because *KiDispatchException* is called after *KiTrap00* so we should see it before *KiTrap00* in raw stack region. To see all these calls we can disassemble return addresses:

```
0: kd> .asm no_code_bytes
Assembly options: no_code_bytes

0: kd> ub nt!KiTrap00+0x88
nt!KiTrap00+0x74:
8083483b test byte ptr [ebp+6Ch],1
8083483f je   nt!KiTrap00+0x81 (80834848)
80834841 cmp  word ptr [ebp+6Ch],1Bh
80834846 jne  nt!KiTrap00+0x9e (80834865)
80834848 sti
80834849 push ebp
8083484a call nt!Ki386CheckDivideByZeroTrap (8099897d)
8083484f mov  ebx,dword ptr [ebp+68h]
```

nt!KiTrap00+0x88 address is not equal to *nt!KiTrap00+0x74* address so we have OMAP code optimization case here, and we have to disassemble raw addresses from the raw stack fragment repeated here:

```
...
...
...
f44dc8c8 808346b4 nt!CommonDispatchException+0x4a
...
...
...
f44dc924 ffffffff
f44dc928 80998bfd nt!Ki386CheckDivideByZeroTrap+0x273
f44dc92c 8083484f nt!KiTrap00+0x88
f44dc930 80834650 nt!Kei386EoiHelper+0x16e
f44dc934 0012f968
...
...
...

0: kd> u 8083484f
nt!KiTrap00+0x88:
8083484f mov  ebx,dword ptr [ebp+68h]
80834852 jmp  nt!Kei386EoiHelper+0x167 (80834649)
80834857 sti
80834858 mov  ebx,dword ptr [ebp+68h]
8083485b mov  eax,0C0000094h
80834860 jmp  nt!Kei386EoiHelper+0x167 (80834649)
80834865 mov  ebx,dword ptr fs:[124h]
8083486c mov  ebx,dword ptr [ebx+38h]
```

```
0: kd> u 80834649
nt!Kei386EoiHelper+0x167:
80834649 xor   ecx,ecx
8083464b call  nt!CommonDispatchException (8083466a)
80834650 xor   edx,edx ; nt!Kei386EoiHelper+0x16e
80834652 mov   ecx,1
80834657 call  nt!CommonDispatchException (8083466a)
8083465c xor   edx,edx
8083465e mov   ecx,2
80834663 call  nt!CommonDispatchException (8083466a)
```

```
0: kd> ub 808346b4
nt!CommonDispatchException+0x38:
808346a2 mov   eax,dword ptr [ebp+6Ch]
808346a5 and   eax,1
808346a8 push  1
808346aa push  eax
808346ab push  ebp
808346ac push  0
808346ae push  ecx
808346af call  nt!KiDispatchException (80852a53)
```

We see that *KiTrap00* function calls *CommonDispatchException* function which calls *KiDispatchException* function. If we look at our found interrupt frame we see that EIP of the exception was 00469583 and ESP was 0012f934:

```
...
...
...
f44dc998 00000000 ; ErrorCode
f44dc99c 00469583 processA!LPtoDP+0x19 ; EIP
f44dc9a0 0000001b ; CS
f44dc9a4 00010246 ; EFLAGS
f44dc9a8 0012f934 ; ESP
f44dc9ac 00000023 ; SS
...
...
...
```

Now we try to reconstruct stack trace by putting the values of ESP and EIP:

```
0: kd> k L=0012f934 0012f934 00469583 ; EBP ESP EIP format
ChildEBP RetAddr
0012f930 00469a16 processA!LPtoDP+0x19
0012f934 00000000 processA!GetColumnWidth+0x45
```

Stack trace doesn't look good to us because there is no *BaseProcessStart* or *BaseThreadStart* function, perhaps because we specified ESP value twice instead of EBP and ESP. Let's hope to find EBP value by dumping the memory around ESP:

```
0: kd> dds 0012f934-10 0012f934+100
0012f924 00000000
0012f928 0012f934 ; the same as ESP
0012f92c 0012f968 ; looks good to us
0012f930 00469572 processA!LPtoDP+0x8
0012f934 00469a16 processA!GetColumnWidth+0x45
0012f938 00005334
...
...
...
0012f964 00005334
0012f968 0012f998
0012f96c 0046915d processA!CalculateClientSizeFromPoint+0x5f
0012f970 00000000
0012f974 0012f9fc
0012f978 16b748f0
0012f97c 0012fa48
0012f980 00000000
0012f984 00000000
0012f988 000003a0
0012f98c 00000237
0012f990 00000014
0012f994 00000000
0012f998 0012f9bc
0012f99c 0047cb72 processA!CalculateFromPoint+0x30
0012f9a0 0012f9fc
0012f9a4 0012f9b4
0012f9a8 0012fa48
...
...
...
```

Finally, we get our stack trace:

```
0: kd> k L=0012f968 0012f934 00469583 100
ChildEBP RetAddr
0012f930 00469a16 processA!LPtoDP+0x19
0012f968 0046915d processA!GetColumnWidth+0x45
0012f998 0047cb72 processA!CalculateClientSizeFromPoint+0x5f
0012f9bc 0047cc1d processA!CalculateFromPoint+0x30
0012fa64 0047de83 processA!DrawUsingMemDC+0x1b9
0012fac0 0099fb43 processA!OnDraw+0x13
0012fb5c 7c17332d processA!OnPaint+0x56
0012fbe8 7c16e0b0 MFC71!CWnd::OnWndMsg+0x340
0012fc08 00c6253a MFC71!CWnd::WindowProc+0x22
0012fc24 0096cf9d processA!WindowProc+0x38
0012fcb8 7c16e1b8 MFC71!AfxCallWndProc+0x91
0012fcd8 7c16e1f6 MFC71!AfxWndProc+0x46
0012fd04 7739b6e3 MFC71!AfxWndProcBase+0x39
0012fd30 7739b874 USER32!InternalCallWinProc+0x28
0012fda8 7739c8b8 USER32!UserCallWinProcCheckWow+0x151
0012fe04 7739c9c6 USER32!DispatchClientMessage+0xd9
0012fe2c 7c828536 USER32!__fnDWORD+0x24
0012fe2c 80832dee ntdll!KiUserCallbackDispatcher+0x2e
f44dcbf0 8092d605 nt!KiCallUserMode+0x4
f44dcc48 bf8a26d3 nt!KeUserModeCallback+0x8f
f44dcccc bf89e985 win32k!SfnDWORD+0xb4
f44dcd0c bf89eb27 win32k!xxxDispatchMessage+0x223
f44dcd58 80833bdf win32k!NtUserDispatchMessage+0x4c
f44dcd58 7c8285ec nt!KiFastCallEntry+0xfc
0012fe2c 7c828536 ntdll!KiFastSystemCallRet
0012fe58 7739c57b ntdll!KiUserCallbackDispatcher+0x2e
0012fea8 773a16e5 USER32!NtUserDispatchMessage+0xc
0012feb8 7c169076 USER32!DispatchMessageA+0xf
0012fec8 7c16913e MFC71!AfxInternalPumpMessage+0x3e
0012fee4 0041cb0b MFC71!CWinThread::Run+0x54
0012ff08 7c172fc5 processA!CMain::Run+0x3b
0012ff18 00c5364d MFC71!AfxWinMain+0x68
0012ffc0 77e6f23b processA!WinMainCRTStartup+0x185
0012fff0 00000000 kernel32!BaseProcessStart+0x23
```

Trap Command on x86

Now I explain WinDbg **.trap** command and show how to simulate it manually.

Upon an interrupt, a processor saves the current instruction pointer and transfers execution to an interrupt handler, as explained in **x86 Interrupts** article (page 69). This interrupt handler has to save the full thread context before calling other functions to do complex interrupt processing. For example, if we disassemble *KiTrap0E* handler from x86 Windows 2003 crash dump, we see that it saves many registers, including segment registers:

```
3: kd> uf nt!KiTrap0E
...
...
...
nt!KiTrap0E:
e088bb2c mov     word ptr [esp+2],0
e088bb33 push    ebp
e088bb34 push    ebx
e088bb35 push    esi
e088bb36 push    edi
e088bb37 push    fs
e088bb39 mov     ebx,30h
e088bb3e mov     fs,bx
e088bb41 mov     ebx,dword ptr fs:[0]
e088bb48 push    ebx
e088bb49 sub     esp,4
e088bb4c push    eax
e088bb4d push    ecx
e088bb4e push    edx
e088bb4f push    ds
e088bb50 push    es
e088bb51 push    gs
e088bb53 mov     ax,23h
e088bb57 sub     esp,30h
e088bb5a mov     ds,ax
e088bb5d mov     es,ax
e088bb60 mov     ebp,esp
e088bb62 test    dword ptr [esp+70h],20000h
e088bb6a jne     nt!V86_kite_a (e088bb04)
...
...
...
```

The saved processor state information (context) forms the so-called Windows kernel trap frame:

```
3: kd> dt _KTRAP_FRAME
   +0x000 DbgEbp           : Uint4B
   +0x004 DbgEip           : Uint4B
   +0x008 DbgArgMark       : Uint4B
   +0x00c DbgArgPointer    : Uint4B
   +0x010 TempSegCs        : Uint4B
   +0x014 TempEsp          : Uint4B
   +0x018 Dr0              : Uint4B
   +0x01c Dr1              : Uint4B
   +0x020 Dr2              : Uint4B
   +0x024 Dr3              : Uint4B
   +0x028 Dr6              : Uint4B
   +0x02c Dr7              : Uint4B
   +0x030 SegGs            : Uint4B
   +0x034 SegEs            : Uint4B
   +0x038 SegDs            : Uint4B
   +0x03c Edx              : Uint4B
   +0x040 Ecx              : Uint4B
   +0x044 Eax              : Uint4B
   +0x048 PreviousPreviousMode : Uint4B
   +0x04c ExceptionList    : Ptr32 _EXCEPTION_REGISTRATION_RECORD
   +0x050 SegFs            : Uint4B
   +0x054 Edi              : Uint4B
   +0x058 Esi              : Uint4B
   +0x05c Ebx              : Uint4B
   +0x060 Ebp              : Uint4B
   +0x064 ErrCode          : Uint4B
   +0x068 Eip              : Uint4B
   +0x06c SegCs            : Uint4B
   +0x070 EFlags           : Uint4B
   +0x074 HardwareEsp      : Uint4B
   +0x078 HardwareSegSs    : Uint4B
   +0x07c V86Es            : Uint4B
   +0x080 V86Ds            : Uint4B
   +0x084 V86Fs            : Uint4B
   +0x088 V86Gs            : Uint4B
```

This Windows trap frame is not the same as an interrupt frame a processor saves in the current thread stack region when an interrupt occurs in kernel mode. The latter frame is very small and consists only of EIP, CS, EFLAGS, and *ErrorCode*. When an interrupt occurs in user mode, an x86 processor additionally saves the current stack pointer SS:ESP.

The **.trap** command finds the trap frame on the current thread stack and sets the current thread register context using the values from that saved structure. We can see that command in action for certain bugchecks when we use **!analyze –v** command:

```
3: kd> !analyze -v
KERNEL_MODE_EXCEPTION_NOT_HANDLED (8e)
...
...
...
Arguments:
Arg1: c0000005, The exception code that was not handled
Arg2: de65190c, The address that the exception occurred at
Arg3: f24f8a74, Trap Frame
Arg4: 00000000
...
...
...
TRAP_FRAME:  f24f8a74 -- (.trap ffffffffff24f8a74)
.trap ffffffffff24f8a74
ErrCode = 00000000
eax=dbc128c0 ebx=dbe4a010 ecx=f24f8ac4 edx=00000001 esi=46525356
edi=00000000
eip=de65190c esp=f24f8ae8 ebp=f24f8b18 iopl=0 nv up ei pl nz na pe nc
cs=0008 ss=0010 ds=0023 es=0023 fs=0030 gs=0000 efl=00010206
driver!foo+0x16:
de65190c 837e1c00         cmp     dword ptr [esi+1Ch],0
ds:0023:46525372=????????
...
...
...
```

If we look at the trap frame, we see the same register values that WinDbg reports above:

```
3: kd> dt _KTRAP_FRAME f24f8a74
   +0x000 DbgEbp           : 0xf24f8b18
   +0x004 DbgEip           : 0xde65190c
   +0x008 DbgArgMark       : 0xbadb0d00
   +0x00c DbgArgPointer    : 1
   +0x010 TempSegCs        : 0xb0501cd
   +0x014 TempEsp          : 0xdcc01cd0
   +0x018 Dr0              : 0xf24f8aa8
   +0x01c Dr1              : 0xde46c90a
   +0x020 Dr2              : 0
   +0x024 Dr3              : 0
   +0x028 Dr6              : 0xdbe4a000
   +0x02c Dr7              : 0
   +0x030 SegGs            : 0
   +0x034 SegEs            : 0x23
   +0x038 SegDs            : 0x23
   +0x03c Edx              : 1
   +0x040 Ecx              : 0xf24f8ac4
   +0x044 Eax              : 0xdbc128c0
   +0x048 PreviousPreviousMode : 0xdbe4a010
   +0x04c ExceptionList    : 0xffffffff _EXCEPTION_REGISTRATION_RECORD
   +0x050 SegFs            : 0x30
   +0x054 Edi              : 0
   +0x058 Esi              : 0x46525356
```

```
   +0x05c Ebx                  : 0xdbe4a010
   +0x060 Ebp                  : 0xf24f8b18
   +0x064 ErrCode              : 0
   +0x068 Eip                  : 0xde65190c ; driver!foo+0x16
   +0x06c SegCs                : 8
   +0x070 EFlags               : 0x10206
   +0x074 HardwareEsp          : 0xdbc171b0
   +0x078 HardwareSegSs        : 0xde667677
   +0x07c V86Es                : 0xdbc128c0
   +0x080 V86Ds                : 0xdbc171c4
   +0x084 V86Fs                : 0xf24f8bc4
   +0x088 V86Gs                : 0
```

It is good to know how to find a trap frame manually when the stack is corrupt, or WinDbg cannot find a trap frame automatically. In this case, we can take advantage of the fact that DS and ES segment registers have the same value in Windows flat memory model:

```
   +0x034 SegEs                : 0x23
   +0x038 SegDs                : 0x23
```

We need to find two consecutive 0x23 values in the stack region. There may be several such places, but, usually, the correct one comes between *KiTrapXX* address in the stack region and the initial processor trap frame shown below in bold. This is because *KiTrapXX* calls other functions to process an interrupt further, so its return address is saved in the stack.

```
3: kd> r
eax=f535713c ebx=de65190c ecx=00000000 edx=e088e1d2 esi=f5357120
edi=00000000
eip=e0827451 esp=f24f8628 ebp=f24f8640 iopl=0 nv up ei ng nz na pe nc
cs=0008 ss=0010 ds=0023 es=0023 fs=0030 gs=0000 efl=00000286
nt!KeBugCheckEx+0x1b:
e0827451 5d              pop     ebp

3: kd> dds f24f8628 f24f8628+1000
...
...
...
f24f8784  de4b2995 win32k!NtUserQueryWindow
f24f8788  00000000
f24f878c  fe76a324
f24f8790  f24f8d64
f24f8794  0006e43c
f24f8798  e087c041 nt!ExReleaseResourceAndLeaveCriticalRegion+0x5
f24f879c  83f3b801
f24f87a0  f24f8a58
f24f87a4  0000003b
f24f87a8  00000000
```

```
f24f87ac  00000030
f24f87b0  00000023
f24f87b4  00000023
f24f87b8  00000000
...
...
...
f24f8a58  00000111
f24f8a5c  f24f8a74
f24f8a60  e088bc08 nt!KiTrap0E+0xdc
f24f8a64  00000000
f24f8a68  46525372
f24f8a6c  00000000
f24f8a70  e0889686 nt!Kei386EoiHelper+0x186
f24f8a74  f24f8b18
f24f8a78  de65190c driver!foo+0x16
f24f8a7c  badb0d00
f24f8a80  00000001
f24f8a84  0b0501cd
f24f8a88  dcc01cd0
f24f8a8c  f24f8aa8
f24f8a90  de46c90a win32k!HANDLELOCK::vLockHandle+0x80
f24f8a94  00000000
f24f8a98  00000000
f24f8a9c  dbe4a000
f24f8aa0  00000000
f24f8aa4  00000000
f24f8aa8  00000023
f24f8aac  00000023
f24f8ab0  00000001
f24f8ab4  f24f8ac4
f24f8ab8  dbc128c0
f24f8abc  dbe4a010
f24f8ac0  ffffffff
f24f8ac4  00000030
f24f8ac8  00000000
f24f8acc  46525356
f24f8ad0  dbe4a010
f24f8ad4  f24f8b18
f24f8ad8  00000000
f24f8adc  de65190c driver!foo+0x16
f24f8ae0  00000008
f24f8ae4  00010206
f24f8ae8  dbc171b0
f24f8aec  de667677 driver!bar+0x173
f24f8af0  dbc128c0
f24f8af4  dbc171c4
f24f8af8  f24f8bc4
f24f8afc  00000000
...
...
...
```

Subtracting the offset 0x38 from the address of the 00000023 value (f24f8aac) and using **dt** command, we can check _KTRAP_FRAME structure and apply **.trap** command afterward:

```
3: kd> dt _KTRAP_FRAME f24f8aac-38
   +0x000 DbgEbp           : 0xf24f8b18
   +0x004 DbgEip           : 0xde65190c
   +0x008 DbgArgMark       : 0xbadb0d00
   +0x00c DbgArgPointer    : 1
   +0x010 TempSegCs        : 0xb0501cd
   +0x014 TempEsp          : 0xdcc01cd0
   +0x018 Dr0              : 0xf24f8aa8
   +0x01c Dr1              : 0xde46c90a
   +0x020 Dr2              : 0
   +0x024 Dr3              : 0
   +0x028 Dr6              : 0xdbe4a000
   +0x02c Dr7              : 0
   +0x030 SegGs            : 0
   +0x034 SegEs            : 0x23
   +0x038 SegDs            : 0x23
   +0x03c Edx              : 1
   +0x040 Ecx              : 0xf24f8ac4
   +0x044 Eax              : 0xdbc128c0
   +0x048 PreviousPreviousMode : 0xdbe4a010
   +0x04c ExceptionList    : 0xffffffff _EXCEPTION_REGISTRATION_RECORD
   +0x050 SegFs            : 0x30
   +0x054 Edi              : 0
   +0x058 Esi              : 0x46525356
   +0x05c Ebx              : 0xdbe4a010
   +0x060 Ebp              : 0xf24f8b18
   +0x064 ErrCode          : 0
   +0x068 Eip              : 0xde65190c
   +0x06c SegCs            : 8
   +0x070 EFlags           : 0x10206
   +0x074 HardwareEsp      : 0xdbc171b0
   +0x078 HardwareSegSs    : 0xde667677
   +0x07c V86Es            : 0xdbc128c0
   +0x080 V86Ds            : 0xdbc171c4
   +0x084 V86Fs            : 0xf24f8bc4
   +0x088 V86Gs            : 0

3: kd> ? f24f8aac-38
Evaluate expression: -229668236 = f24f8a74
```

```
3: kd> .trap f24f8a74
ErrCode = 00000000
eax=dbc128c0 ebx=dbe4a010 ecx=f24f8ac4 edx=00000001 esi=46525356
edi=00000000
eip=de65190c esp=f24f8ae8 ebp=f24f8b18 iopl=0 nv up ei pl nz na pe nc
cs=0008 ss=0010 ds=0023 es=0023 fs=0030 gs=0000 efl=00010206
driver!foo+0x16:
de65190c 837e1c00        cmp     dword ptr [esi+1Ch],0
ds:0023:46525372=????????
```

In complete memory dumps, we can see that _KTRAP_FRAME is saved too when system services are called:

```
3: kd> kL
ChildEBP RetAddr
f24f8ae8 de667677 driver!foo+0x16
f24f8b18 de667799 driver!bar+0x173
f24f8b90 de4a853e win32k!GreSaveScreenBits+0x69
f24f8bd8 de4922bd win32k!CreateSpb+0x167
f24f8c40 de490bb8 win32k!zzzChangeStates+0x448
f24f8c88 de4912de win32k!zzzBltValidBits+0xe2
f24f8ce0 de4926c6 win32k!xxxEndDeferWindowPosEx+0x13a
f24f8cfc de49aa8f win32k!xxxSetWindowPos+0xb1
f24f8d34 de4acf4d win32k!xxxShowWindow+0x201
f24f8d54 e0888c6c win32k!NtUserShowWindow+0x79
f24f8d54 7c94ed54 nt!KiFastCallEntry+0xfc (TrapFrame @ f24f8d64)
0006e48c 77e34f1d ntdll!KiFastSystemCallRet
0006e53c 77e2f12f USER32!NtUserShowWindow+0xc
0006e570 77e2b0fe USER32!InternalDialogBox+0xa9
0006e590 77e29005 USER32!DialogBoxIndirectParamAorW+0x37
0006e5b4 0103d569 USER32!DialogBoxParamW+0x3f
0006e5d8 0102d2f5 winlogon!Fusion_DialogBoxParam+0x24
```

We can get the current thread context before its transition to kernel mode:

```
3: kd> .trap f24f8d64
ErrCode = 00000000
eax=7ffff000 ebx=00000000 ecx=00000000 edx=7c94ed54 esi=00532e68
edi=0002002c
eip=7c94ed54 esp=0006e490 ebp=0006e53c iopl=0 nv up ei pl zr na pe nc
cs=001b ss=0023 ds=0023 es=0023 fs=003b gs=0000 efl=00000246
ntdll!KiFastSystemCallRet:
001b:7c94ed54 c3              ret
```

```
3: kd> kL
ChildEBP RetAddr
0006e48c 77e34f1d ntdll!KiFastSystemCallRet
0006e53c 77e2f12f USER32!NtUserShowWindow+0xc
0006e570 77e2b0fe USER32!InternalDialogBox+0xa9
0006e590 77e29005 USER32!DialogBoxIndirectParamAorW+0x37
0006e5b4 0103d569 USER32!DialogBoxParamW+0x3f
0006e5d8 0102d2f5 winlogon!Fusion_DialogBoxParam+0x24
```

Trap Command on x64

Now I show how to simulate **.trap** WinDbg command when we have x64 Windows kernel and complete memory dumps.

When we have a fault, an x64 processor saves some registers in the current thread stack, as explained in the **x64 Interrupts** article (page 76). Then an interrupt handler stores _KTRAP_FRAME in the stack region:

```
6: kd> uf nt!KiPageFault
nt!KiPageFault:
fffff800`0102d400 push    rbp
fffff800`0102d401 sub     rsp,158h
fffff800`0102d408 lea     rbp,[rsp+80h]
fffff800`0102d410 mov     byte ptr [rbp-55h],1
fffff800`0102d414 mov     qword ptr [rbp-50h],rax
fffff800`0102d418 mov     qword ptr [rbp-48h],rcx
fffff800`0102d41c mov     qword ptr [rbp-40h],rdx
fffff800`0102d420 mov     qword ptr [rbp-38h],r8
fffff800`0102d424 mov     qword ptr [rbp-30h],r9
fffff800`0102d428 mov     qword ptr [rbp-28h],r10
fffff800`0102d42c mov     qword ptr [rbp-20h],r11
...
...
...

6: kd> dt _KTRAP_FRAME
   +0x000 P1Home           : Uint8B
   +0x008 P2Home           : Uint8B
   +0x010 P3Home           : Uint8B
   +0x018 P4Home           : Uint8B
   +0x020 P5               : Uint8B
   +0x028 PreviousMode     : Char
   +0x029 PreviousIrql     : UChar
   +0x02a FaultIndicator   : UChar
   +0x02b ExceptionActive  : UChar
   +0x02c MxCsr            : Uint4B
   +0x030 Rax              : Uint8B
   +0x038 Rcx              : Uint8B
   +0x040 Rdx              : Uint8B
   +0x048 R8               : Uint8B
   +0x050 R9               : Uint8B
   +0x058 R10              : Uint8B
   +0x060 R11              : Uint8B
   +0x068 GsBase           : Uint8B
   +0x068 GsSwap           : Uint8B
   +0x070 Xmm0             : _M128A
   +0x080 Xmm1             : _M128A
   +0x090 Xmm2             : _M128A
   +0x0a0 Xmm3             : _M128A
```

```
+0x0b0 Xmm4                  : _M128A
+0x0c0 Xmm5                  : _M128A
+0x0d0 FaultAddress          : Uint8B
+0x0d0 ContextRecord         : Uint8B
+0x0d0 TimeStamp             : Uint8B
+0x0d8 Dr0                   : Uint8B
+0x0e0 Dr1                   : Uint8B
+0x0e8 Dr2                   : Uint8B
+0x0f0 Dr3                   : Uint8B
+0x0f8 Dr6                   : Uint8B
+0x100 Dr7                   : Uint8B
+0x108 DebugControl          : Uint8B
+0x110 LastBranchToRip       : Uint8B
+0x118 LastBranchFromRip : Uint8B
+0x120 LastExceptionToRip : Uint8B
+0x128 LastExceptionFromRip : Uint8B
+0x108 LastBranchControl : Uint8B
+0x110 LastBranchMSR         : Uint4B
+0x130 SegDs                 : Uint2B
+0x132 SegEs                 : Uint2B
+0x134 SegFs                 : Uint2B
+0x136 SegGs                 : Uint2B
+0x138 TrapFrame             : Uint8B
+0x140 Rbx                   : Uint8B
+0x148 Rdi                   : Uint8B
+0x150 Rsi                   : Uint8B
+0x158 Rbp                   : Uint8B
+0x160 ErrorCode             : Uint8B
+0x160 ExceptionFrame        : Uint8B
+0x168 Rip                   : Uint8B
+0x170 SegCs                 : Uint2B
+0x172 Fill1                 : [3] Uint2B
+0x178 EFlags                : Uint4B
+0x17c Fill2                 : Uint4B
+0x180 Rsp                   : Uint8B
+0x188 SegSs                 : Uint2B
+0x18a Fill3                 : [1] Uint2B
+0x18c CodePatchCycle        : Int4B
```

Unfortunately, the technique to use DS and ES pair to find the trap frame in x86 Windows crash dump doesn't work here because *KiPageFault* interrupt handler doesn't save them as can be found by inspecting its disassembly. Fortunately, the registers that an x64 processor pushes upon an interrupt are part of _KTRAP_FRAME shown in bold above. *Fill1*, *Fill2*, *Fill3*, and *CodePatchCycle* are just dummy values to fill 64-bit slots because CS and SS are 16-bit registers and in 64-bit RFLAGS only the first 32-bit EFLAGS part is currently used. Remember, a processor in 64-bit mode pushes 64-bit values even when values occupy only 16 or 32-bit. Therefore, we can try to find CS and SS in the stack region because they have the following constant values:

```
6: kd> r cs
cs=0010

6: kd> r ss
ss=0018

6: kd> k
Child-SP          RetAddr           Call Site
fffffadc`6e02b9e8 fffff800`013731b1 nt!KeBugCheckEx
...
...
...
fffffadc`6e02cd70 fffff800`010202d6 nt!PspSystemThreadStartup+0x3e
fffffadc`6e02cdd0 00000000`00000000 nt!KxStartSystemThread+0x16

6: kd> dqs fffffadc`6e02b9e8 fffffadc`6e02cd70
...
...
...
fffffadc`6e02c938 fffff800`0102d5e1 nt!KiPageFault+0x1e1
...
...
...
fffffadc`6e02ca70  fffff97f`f3937a8c
fffffadc`6e02ca78  fffff97f`ff57d28b driver+0x3028b
fffffadc`6e02ca80  00000000`00000000
fffffadc`6e02ca88  fffff97f`f3937030
fffffadc`6e02ca90  fffff97f`ff5c2990 driver+0x75990
fffffadc`6e02ca98  00000000`00000000
fffffadc`6e02caa0  00000000`00000000 ; ErrorCode
fffffadc`6e02caa8  fffff97f`ff591ed3 driver+0x44ed3 ; RIP
fffffadc`6e02cab0  00000000`00000010 ; CS
fffffadc`6e02cab8  00000000`00010282 ; RFLAGS
fffffadc`6e02cac0  fffffadc`6e02cad0 ; RSP
fffffadc`6e02cac8  00000000`00000018 ; SS
fffffadc`6e02cad0  fffff97f`f382b0e0
fffffadc`6e02cad8  fffffadc`6e02cbd0
fffffadc`6e02cae0  fffff97f`f3937a8c
fffffadc`6e02cae8  fffff97f`f3937030
fffffadc`6e02caf0  00000000`00000000
fffffadc`6e02caf8  00000000`00000001
...
...
...
```

Now we can calculate the trap frame address by subtracting *SegSs* offset in _KTRAP_FRAME structure (0x188) from fffffadc`6e02cac8 address:

```
6: kd> ? fffffadc`6e02cac8-188
Evaluate expression: -5650331285184 = fffffadc`6e02c940

6: kd> .trap fffffadc`6e02c940
NOTE: The trap frame does not contain all registers.
Some register values may be zeroed.
rax=fffffadcdac27298 rbx=0000000000000000 rcx=fffffadcdb45a4c0
rdx=0000000000000555 rsi=fffff97fff5c2990 rdi=fffff97ff3937030
rip=fffff97fff591ed3 rsp=fffffadc6e02cad0 rbp=0000000000000000
 r8=fffffadcdac27250  r9=fffff97ff3824030 r10=0000000000000020
r11=fffffadcdac27250 r12=0000000000000000 r13=0000000000000000
r14=0000000000000000 r15=0000000000000000
iopl=0 nv up ei ng nz na pe nc
driver+0x44ed3:
fffff97f`ff591ed3 0fb74514  movzx eax,word ptr [rbp+14h]
ss:0018:00000000`00000014=????

6: kd> k
Child-SP          RetAddr           Call Site
fffffadc`6e02cad0 fffff97f`ff5935f7 driver+0x44ed3
fffffadc`6e02cc40 fffff800`0124b972 driver+0x465f7
fffffadc`6e02cd70 fffff800`010202d6 nt!PspSystemThreadStartup+0x3e
fffffadc`6e02cdd0 00000000`00000000 nt!KxStartSystemThread+0x16
```

Our example shows how to find a trap frame manually in x64 kernel or complete memory dump. Usually, WinDbg finds trap frames automatically (call arguments are removed from verbose stack trace for clarity):

```
6: kd> kv
Child-SP          RetAddr           Call Site
fffffadc`6e02b9e8 fffff800`013731b1 nt!KeBugCheckEx
fffffadc`6e02b9f0 fffff800`010556ab nt!PspSystemThreadStartup+0x270
fffffadc`6e02ba40 fffff800`010549fd nt!_C_specific_handler+0x9b
fffffadc`6e02bad0 fffff800`01054f93 nt!RtlpExecuteHandlerForException+0xd
fffffadc`6e02bb00 fffff800`0100b901 nt!RtlDispatchException+0x2c0
fffffadc`6e02c1c0 fffff800`0102e76f nt!KiDispatchException+0xd9
fffffadc`6e02c7c0 fffff800`0102d5e1 nt!KiExceptionExit
fffffadc`6e02c940 fffff97f`ff591ed3 nt!KiPageFault+0x1e1 (TrapFrame @ 
fffffadc`6e02c940)
fffffadc`6e02cad0 fffff97f`ff5935f7 driver+0x44ed3
fffffadc`6e02cc40 fffff800`0124b972 driver+0x465f7
fffffadc`6e02cd70 fffff800`010202d6 nt!PspSystemThreadStartup+0x3e
fffffadc`6e02cdd0 00000000`00000000 nt!KxStartSystemThread+0x16
```

Exceptions in User Mode

Previous articles were dealing with exceptions in kernel mode. Now I'm going to investigate the flow of exception processing in user mode. In the **x86 Interrupts** article (page 69), I mentioned that interrupts and exceptions generated when CPU is in user mode require a processor to switch the current user mode stack to the kernel mode stack. This can be seen when we have a user debugger attached, and it gets an exception notification called a first chance exception. Because of the stack switch, we don't see any saved processor context in user mode thread stack when WinDbg breaks on a first-chance exception in TestDefaultDebugger64 (the module name is renamed to TDD64 for layout clarity):

```
0:000> r
rax=0000000000000000 rbx=0000000000000001 rcx=000000000012fd80
rdx=00000000000003e8 rsi=000000000012fd80 rdi=0000000140033fe0
rip=0000000140001690 rsp=000000000012f198 rbp=0000000000000111
 r8=0000000000000000  r9=0000000140001690 r10=0000000140001690
r11=000000000012f260 r12=0000000000000000 r13=00000000000003e8
r14=0000000000000110 r15=0000000000000001
iopl=0 nv up ei pl zr na po nc
cs=0033 ss=002b ds=002b es=002b fs=0053 gs=002b   efl=00010246
TDD64!CTestDefaultDebuggerDlg::OnBnClickedButton1:
00000001`40001690 c704250000000000000000 mov dword ptr [0],0
ds:00000000`00000000=????????

0:000> kL 100
Child-SP          RetAddr           Call Site
00000000`0012f198 00000001`40004ba0
TDD64!CTestDefaultDebuggerDlg::OnBnClickedButton1
00000000`0012f1a0 00000001`40004de0 TDD64!_AfxDispatchCmdMsg+0xc4
00000000`0012f1d0 00000001`4000564e TDD64!CCmdTarget::OnCmdMsg+0x180
00000000`0012f230 00000001`4000c6b4 TDD64!CDialog::OnCmdMsg+0x32
00000000`0012f270 00000001`4000d4d8 TDD64!CWnd::OnCommand+0xcc
00000000`0012f300 00000001`400082e0 TDD64!CWnd::OnWndMsg+0x60
00000000`0012f440 00000001`4000b77a TDD64!CWnd::WindowProc+0x38
00000000`0012f480 00000001`4000b881 TDD64!AfxCallWndProc+0xfe
00000000`0012f520 00000000`77c43abc TDD64!AfxWndProc+0x59
00000000`0012f560 00000000`77c4337a user32!UserCallWinProcCheckWow+0x1f9
00000000`0012f630 00000000`77c4341b user32!SendMessageWorker+0x68c
00000000`0012f6d0 000007ff`7f07c89f user32!SendMessageW+0x9d
00000000`0012f720 000007ff`7f07f2e1 comctl32!Button_ReleaseCapture+0x14f
00000000`0012f750 00000000`77c43abc comctl32!Button_WndProc+0xd51
00000000`0012f8b0 00000000`77c43f5c user32!UserCallWinProcCheckWow+0x1f9
00000000`0012f980 00000000`77c3966a user32!DispatchMessageWorker+0x3af
00000000`0012f9f0 00000001`40007148 user32!IsDialogMessageW+0x256
00000000`0012fac0 00000001`400087f8 TDD64!CWnd::IsDialogMessageW+0x38
00000000`0012faf0 00000001`4000560f TDD64!CWnd::PreTranslateInput+0x28
00000000`0012fb20 00000001`4000b2ca
TDD64!CDialog::PreTranslateMessage+0xc3
```

```
00000000`0012fb50 00000001`400034a7 TDD64!CWnd::WalkPreTranslateTree+0x3a
00000000`0012fb80 00000001`40003507
TDD64!AfxInternalPreTranslateMessage+0x67
00000000`0012fbb0 00000001`400036d2 TDD64!AfxPreTranslateMessage+0x23
00000000`0012fbe0 00000001`40003717 TDD64!AfxInternalPumpMessage+0x3a
00000000`0012fc10 00000001`4000a806 TDD64!AfxPumpMessage+0x1b
00000000`0012fc40 00000001`40005ff2 TDD64!CWnd::RunModalLoop+0xea
00000000`0012fca0 00000001`40001163 TDD64!CDialog::DoModal+0x1c6
00000000`0012fd50 00000001`4002ccb1
TDD64!CTestDefaultDebuggerApp::InitInstance+0xe3
00000000`0012fe80 00000001`40016150 TDD64!AfxWinMain+0x75
00000000`0012fec0 00000000`77d5964c TDD64!__tmainCRTStartup+0x260
00000000`0012ff80 00000000`00000000 kernel32!BaseProcessStart+0x29

0:000> dqs 000000000012f198-20 000000000012f198+20
00000000`0012f178  00000001`4000bc25 TDD64!CWnd::ReflectLastMsg+0x65
00000000`0012f180  00000000`00080334
00000000`0012f188  00000000`00000006
00000000`0012f190  00000000`0000000d
00000000`0012f198  00000001`40004ba0 TDD64!_AfxDispatchCmdMsg+0xc4
00000000`0012f1a0  ffffffff`fffffffe
00000000`0012f1a8  00000000`00000000
00000000`0012f1b0  00000000`00000000
00000000`0012f1b8  00000000`00000000
```

We see that there are no saved SS:RSP, RFLAGS, CS:RIP registers, which we see in a stack if an exception happens in kernel mode, as shown in the **x64 Interrupt** article (page 76). If we bugcheck our system using SystemDump tool to generate complete memory dump at that time, we can look later at the whole thread that experienced exception in user mode and its user mode and kernel mode stacks:

```
kd> !process fffffadfe7055c20 2
PROCESS fffffadfe7055c20
    SessionId: 0  Cid: 0c64    Peb: 7fffffd7000  ParentCid: 07b0
    DirBase: 27e3d000  ObjectTable: fffffa800073a550  HandleCount:  55.
    Image: TDD64.exe

        THREAD fffffadfe78f2bf0  Cid 0c64.0c68  Teb: 000007fffffde000
Win32Thread: fffff97ff4d71010 WAIT: (Unknown) KernelMode Non-Alertable
SuspendCount 1
            fffffadfdf7b6fc0  SynchronizationEvent

        THREAD fffffadfe734c3d0  Cid 0c64.0c88  Teb: 000007fffffdc000
Win32Thread: 0000000000000000 WAIT: (Unknown) KernelMode Non-Alertable
SuspendCount 1
FreezeCount 1
            fffffadfe734c670  Semaphore Limit 0x2
```

```
kd> .thread /r /p fffffadfe78f2bf0
Implicit thread is now fffffadf`e78f2bf0
Implicit process is now fffffadf`e7055c20
Loading User Symbols

kd> kL 100
Child-SP          RetAddr           Call Site
fffffadf`df7b6d30 fffff800`0103b063 nt!KiSwapContext+0x85
fffffadf`df7b6eb0 fffff800`0103c403 nt!KiSwapThread+0xc3
fffffadf`df7b6ef0 fffff800`013a9dc1 nt!KeWaitForSingleObject+0x528
fffffadf`df7b6f80 fffff800`01336dcf nt!DbgkpQueueMessage+0x281
fffffadf`df7b7130 fffff800`01011c69 nt!DbgkForwardException+0x1c5
fffffadf`df7b74f0 fffff800`0104146f nt!KiDispatchException+0x264
fffffadf`df7b7af0 fffff800`010402e1 nt!KiExceptionExit
fffffadf`df7b7c70 00000001`40001690 nt!KiPageFault+0x1e1
00000000`0012f198 00000001`40004ba0
TDD64!CTestDefaultDebuggerDlg::OnBnClickedButton1
00000000`0012f1a0 00000001`40004de0 TDD64!_AfxDispatchCmdMsg+0xc4
00000000`0012f1d0 00000001`4000564e TDD64!CCmdTarget::OnCmdMsg+0x180
00000000`0012f230 00000001`4000c6b4 TDD64!CDialog::OnCmdMsg+0x32
00000000`0012f270 00000001`4000d4d8 TDD64!CWnd::OnCommand+0xcc
00000000`0012f300 00000001`400082e0 TDD64!CWnd::OnWndMsg+0x60
00000000`0012f440 00000001`4000b77a TDD64!CWnd::WindowProc+0x38
00000000`0012f480 00000001`4000b881 TDD64!AfxCallWndProc+0xfe
00000000`0012f520 00000000`77c43abc TDD64!AfxWndProc+0x59
00000000`0012f560 00000000`77c4337a USER32!UserCallWinProcCheckWow+0x1f9
00000000`0012f630 00000000`77c4341b USER32!SendMessageWorker+0x68c
00000000`0012f6d0 000007ff`7f07c89f USER32!SendMessageW+0x9d
00000000`0012f720 000007ff`7f07f2e1 COMCTL32!Button_ReleaseCapture+0x14f
00000000`0012f750 00000000`77c43abc COMCTL32!Button_WndProc+0xd51
00000000`0012f8b0 00000000`77c43f5c USER32!UserCallWinProcCheckWow+0x1f9
00000000`0012f980 00000000`77c3966a USER32!DispatchMessageWorker+0x3af
00000000`0012f9f0 00000001`40007148 USER32!IsDialogMessageW+0x256
00000000`0012fac0 00000001`400087f8 TDD64!CWnd::IsDialogMessageW+0x38
00000000`0012faf0 00000001`4000560f TDD64!CWnd::PreTranslateInput+0x28
00000000`0012fb20 00000001`4000b2ca
TDD64!CDialog::PreTranslateMessage+0xc3
00000000`0012fb50 00000001`400034a7 TDD64!CWnd::WalkPreTranslateTree+0x3a
00000000`0012fb80 00000001`40003507
TDD64!AfxInternalPreTranslateMessage+0x67
00000000`0012fbb0 00000001`400036d2 TDD64!AfxPreTranslateMessage+0x23
00000000`0012fbe0 00000001`40003717 TDD64!AfxInternalPumpMessage+0x3a
00000000`0012fc10 00000001`4000a806 TDD64!AfxPumpMessage+0x1b
00000000`0012fc40 00000001`40005ff2 TDD64!CWnd::RunModalLoop+0xea
00000000`0012fca0 00000001`40001163 TDD64!CDialog::DoModal+0x1c6
00000000`0012fd50 00000000`00000000
TDD64!CTestDefaultDebuggerApp::InitInstance+0xe3
```

Dumping the kernel mode stack of our thread shows that the processor saved registers there:

```
kd> dqs fffffadf`df7b7c70  fffffadf`df7b7c70+200
fffffadf`df7b7c70  fffffadf`e78f2bf0
fffffadf`df7b7c78  00000000`00000000
fffffadf`df7b7c80  fffffadf`e78f2b01
fffffadf`df7b7c88  00000000`00000020
...
...
...
fffffadf`df7b7d90  00000000`00000000
fffffadf`df7b7d98  00000000`00000000
fffffadf`df7b7da0  00000000`00000000
fffffadf`df7b7da8  00000000`00000000
fffffadf`df7b7db0  00000000`001629b0
fffffadf`df7b7db8  00000000`00000001
fffffadf`df7b7dc0  00000000`00000001
fffffadf`df7b7dc8  00000000`00000111 ; RBP saved by KiPageFault
fffffadf`df7b7dd0  00000000`00000006 ; Page-Fault Error Code
fffffadf`df7b7dd8  00000001`40001690
TDD64!CTestDefaultDebuggerDlg::OnBnClickedButton1 ; RIP
fffffadf`df7b7de0  00000000`00000033 ; CS
fffffadf`df7b7de8  00000000`00010246 ; RFLAGS
fffffadf`df7b7df0  00000000`0012f198 ; RSP
fffffadf`df7b7df8  00000000`0000002b ; SS
fffffadf`df7b7e00  00000000`0000027f
fffffadf`df7b7e08  00000000`00000000
fffffadf`df7b7e10  00000000`00000000
fffffadf`df7b7e18  0000ffff`00001f80
fffffadf`df7b7e20  00000000`00000000
fffffadf`df7b7e20  00000000`00000000
fffffadf`df7b7e30  00000000`00000000
fffffadf`df7b7e38  00000000`00000000
...
...
...

kd> .asm no_code_bytes
Assembly options: no_code_bytes

kd> u KiPageFault
nt!KiPageFault:
fffff800`01040100 push    rbp
fffff800`01040101 sub     rsp,158h
fffff800`01040108 lea     rbp,[rsp+80h]
fffff800`01040110 mov     byte ptr [rbp-55h],1
fffff800`01040114 mov     qword ptr [rbp-50h],rax
fffff800`01040118 mov     qword ptr [rbp-48h],rcx
fffff800`0104011c mov     qword ptr [rbp-40h],rdx
fffff800`01040120 mov     qword ptr [rbp-38h],r8
```

Error code 6 is 110 in binary, and volume 3A of Intel manual tells us that "the fault was caused by a non-present page" (bit 0 is cleared), "the access causing the fault was a write" (bit 1 is set) and "the access causing the fault originated when the processor was executing in user mode" (bit 2 is set).

How to Distinguish Between 1st and 2nd Chances

Sometimes we look for **Early Crash Dump** pattern (page 466) but information about whether an exception was first-chance or second-chance is missing from a crash dump file name or in a crash dump itself, for example:

```
This dump file has an exception of interest stored in it.
The stored exception information can be accessed via .ecxr.
(1254.1124): Access violation - code c0000005 (first/second chance not
available)
TDD64!CTestDefaultDebuggerDlg::OnBnClickedButton1:
00000000`00401570 c70425000000000000000000 mov dword ptr [0],0
ds:00000000`00000000=????????
```

If we recall that first-chance exceptions don't leave any traces in user space thread stacks (see **Exceptions in User Mode**, page 104, for details) then we won't see any exception codes on thread raw stack:

```
0:000> !teb
TEB at 000007fffffde000
    ExceptionList:          0000000000000000
    StackBase:              0000000000130000
    StackLimit:             000000000012b000
    SubSystemTib:           0000000000000000
    FiberData:              0000000000001e00
    ArbitraryUserPointer:   0000000000000000
    Self:                   000007fffffde000
    EnvironmentPointer:     0000000000000000
    ClientId:               0000000000001254 . 0000000000001124
    RpcHandle:              0000000000000000
    Tls Storage:            000007fffffde058
    PEB Address:            000007fffffd5000
    LastErrorValue:         0
    LastStatusValue:        c0000034
    Count Owned Locks:      0
    HardErrorMode:          0

0:000> s -d 000000000012b000 0000000000130000 c0000005
```

However, we would definitely see it in a raw stack from a second-chance exception crash dump:

```
0:000> s -d 000000000012b000 0000000000130000 c0000005
00000000`0012f000  c0000005 00000000 00000000 00000000  .
```

From raw stack data, we can even tell when a crash dump was saved from a debugger handling a second-chance exception or saved by a postmortem debugger afterward. For example, on my Vista x64, I see the following difference:

Raw stack from a crash dump saved from WinDbg after receiving second-chance exception

```
00000000`0012e278  00000000`00000000
00000000`0012e280  00000000`00000000
00000000`0012e288  00000000`7790032c kernel32!IsDebugPortPresent+0x2c
00000000`0012e290  00000000`00000000
00000000`0012e298  00000000`00000000
00000000`0012e2a0  00000000`00000000
00000000`0012e2a8  00000000`7790032c kernel32!IsDebugPortPresent+0x2c
00000000`0012e2b0  00000001`00010000
00000000`0012e2b8  00000000`00000000
00000000`0012e2c0  00000000`00000000
00000000`0012e2c8  00000000`77b63c94 ntdll! ?? ::FNODOBFM::`string'+0xbd14
00000000`0012e2d0  00000000`00000000
00000000`0012e2d8  00000000`0012e420
00000000`0012e2e0  00000000`77b63cb0 ntdll! ?? ::FNODOBFM::`string'+0xbd30
00000000`0012e2e8  00000000`7793cf47
kernel32!UnhandledExceptionFilter+0xb7
00000000`0012e2f0  ffffffff`ffffffff
00000000`0012e2f8  00000000`00000000
00000000`0012e300  00000000`00000000
00000000`0012e308  00000000`00000000
00000000`0012e310  00000000`00318718
00000000`0012e318  00000000`7799eb89 user32!ImeWndProcWorker+0x331
00000000`0012e320  00000000`00000000
00000000`0012e328  00000000`00000000
00000000`0012e330  00000000`00000000
00000000`0012e338  00000000`004189b0 TDD64!_getptd_noexit+0x80
00000000`0012e340  00000000`01fb4b90
00000000`0012e348  00000000`0012e928
00000000`0012e350  00000000`00000000
00000000`0012e358  00000000`00418a50 TDD64!_getptd+0x80
00000000`0012e360  00000000`01fb4b90
00000000`0012e368  00000000`0041776d TDD64!_XcptFilter+0x1d
00000000`0012e370  00000000`0012e4f0
00000000`0012e378  00000000`77aa3cfa ntdll!RtlDecodePointer+0x2a
00000000`0012e380  00000000`00436fc4 TDD64!__rtc_tzz+0x1f8c
00000000`0012e388  00000000`00000001
00000000`0012e390  00000000`0012f000
```

```
00000000`0012e398  00000000`77a60000 ntdll!`string' <PERF> (ntdll+0x0)
00000000`0012e3a0  00000000`0004c6e1
00000000`0012e3a8  00000000`00000001
00000000`0012e3b0  00000000`0012ff90
00000000`0012e3b8  00000000`77afb1b5 ntdll!RtlUserThreadStart+0x95
00000000`0012e3c0  00000000`0012e420
```

Raw stack from a crash dump saved by CDB installed as a default postmortem debugger (WER)

```
0:000> dqs 00000000`0012e278 00000000`0012e3e8
00000000`0012e278  00000000`00000000
00000000`0012e280  00000000`00000000
00000000`0012e288  00000000`00000000
00000000`0012e290  ffffffff`ffffffff
00000000`0012e298  00000000`779257ef
kernel32!WerpReportExceptionInProcessContext+0x9f
00000000`0012e2a0  00000000`00000000
00000000`0012e2a8  00000000`0012ff90
00000000`0012e2b0  00000000`0012e420
00000000`0012e2b8  00000000`0041f4dc
TDD64!__CxxUnhandledExceptionFilter+0x5c
00000000`0012e2c0  00000000`00000000
00000000`0012e2c8  00000000`7a8b477b
00000000`0012e2d0  00000000`00000000
00000000`0012e2d8  fffff980`01000000
00000000`0012e2e0  00000000`00000001
00000000`0012e2e8  00000000`7793d07e
kernel32!UnhandledExceptionFilter+0x1ee
00000000`0012e2f0  00000000`77b63cb0 ntdll! ?? ::FNODOBFM::`string'+0xbd30
00000000`0012e2f8  000007fe`00000000
00000000`0012e300  00000000`00000000
00000000`0012e308  00000000`00000001
00000000`0012e310  00000000`00000000
00000000`0012e318  00000000`00000000
00000000`0012e320  000007ff`00000000
00000000`0012e328  00000000`00000000
00000000`0012e330  00000000`00000000
00000000`0012e338  00000000`004189b0 TDD64!_getptd_noexit+0x80
00000000`0012e340  00000000`023f4b90
00000000`0012e348  00000000`77ab8cf8
ntdll!RtlpFindNextActivationContextSection+0xaa
00000000`0012e350  00000000`00000000
00000000`0012e358  00000000`00418a50 TDD64!_getptd+0x80
00000000`0012e360  00000000`023f4b90
00000000`0012e368  00000000`0041776d TDD64!_XcptFilter+0x1d
00000000`0012e370  00000000`0012e4f0
00000000`0012e378  00000000`77aa3cfa ntdll!RtlDecodePointer+0x2a
00000000`0012e380  00000000`00436fc4 TDD64!__rtc_tzz+0x1f8c
00000000`0012e388  00000000`00000001
00000000`0012e390  00000000`0012f000
00000000`0012e398  00000000`77a60000 ntdll!`string' <PERF> (ntdll+0x0)
```

```
00000000`0012e3a0  00000000`0004c6e1
00000000`0012e3a8  00000000`00000001
00000000`0012e3b0  00000000`0012ff90
00000000`0012e3b8  00000000`77afb1b5 ntdll!RtlUserThreadStart+0x95
00000000`0012e3c0  00000000`0012e420
00000000`0012e3c8  00000000`7a8b477b
00000000`0012e3d0  00000000`00000000
```

Who Calls the Postmortem Debugger?

I was trying to understand who calls *dwwin.exe* (the part of Windows Error Reporting in Windows XP) when a crash happens. To find the answer, I launched TestDefaultDebugger application, and after pushing its crash button the following familiar WER dialog box appeared:

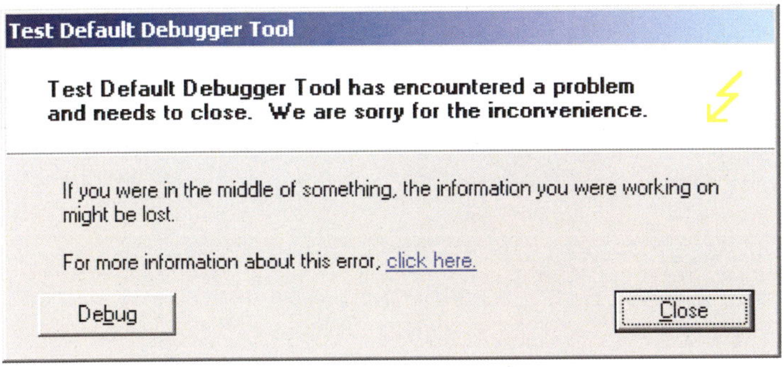

I repeated the same procedure while running ProcessHistory in the background, and from its log, I found that the parent process for *dwwin.exe* and the postmortem debugger (if we click on Debug button) was *TestDefaultDebugger.exe*. In my case, the default postmortem debugger was *drwtsn32.exe*. To dig further, I attached WinDbg to TestDefaultDebugger process when WER dialog box above was displayed and got the following stack trace:

```
0:000> k
ChildEBP RetAddr
0012d318 7c90e9ab ntdll!KiFastSystemCallRet
0012d31c 7c8094e2 ntdll!ZwWaitForMultipleObjects+0xc
0012d3b8 7c80a075 kernel32!WaitForMultipleObjectsEx+0x12c
0012d3d4 6945763c kernel32!WaitForMultipleObjects+0x18
0012dd68 694582b1 faultrep!StartDWException+0x5df
0012eddc 7c8633e9 faultrep!ReportFault+0x533
0012f47c 00411eaa kernel32!UnhandledExceptionFilter+0x587
0012f49c 0040e879 TestDefaultDebugger+0x11eaa
0012ffc0 7c816fd7 TestDefaultDebugger+0xe879
0012fff0 00000000 kernel32!BaseProcessStart+0x23
```

The combination of *StartDWException* and *WaitForMultipleObjects* suggests that *dwwin.exe* process is started there. Indeed, when I disassembled *StartDWException* function I saw *CreateProcess* call just before the "wait" call:

```
0:000> uf faultrep!StartDWException
...
...
...
69457585 8d8568f7ffff    lea     eax,[ebp-898h]
6945758b 50              push    eax
6945758c 8d8524f7ffff    lea     eax,[ebp-8DCh]
69457592 50              push    eax
69457593 8d85d4fbffff    lea     eax,[ebp-42Ch]
69457599 50              push    eax
6945759a 33c0            xor     eax,eax
6945759c 50              push    eax
6945759d 6820000004      push    4000020h
694575a2 6a01            push    1
694575a4 50              push    eax
694575a5 50              push    eax
694575a6 ffb5a4f7ffff    push    dword ptr [ebp-85Ch] ; second parameter
694575ac 50              push    eax ; first parameter
694575ad ff1558114569    call    dword ptr [faultrep!_imp__CreateProcessW
(69451158)]
...
...
...
```

The second parameter of *CreateProcess*, [ebp-85Ch], is the address of the process command line, and we know EBP value from the call stack above, 0012dd68, and we get the command line straight away:

```
0:000> dpu 0012dd68-85Ch l1
0012d50c  0012d3ec "C:\WINDOWS\system32\dwwin.exe -x -s 208"
```

If we dismiss WER dialog by clicking on the Debug button, then a postmortem debugger starts. It also starts without WER dialog displayed if we rename *faultrep.dll* beforehand. Therefore, the obvious place to look for a postmortem debugger launch is *UnhandledExceptionFilter* function. Indeed, we see it there:

```
0:000> uf kernel32!UnhandledExceptionFilter
...
...
...
7c8636a8 8d850cfaffff    lea     eax,[ebp-5F4h]
7c8636ae 50              push    eax
7c8636af 8d857cf9ffff    lea     eax,[ebp-684h]
7c8636b5 50              push    eax
7c8636b6 33c0            xor     eax,eax
```

```
7c8636b8 50              push    eax
7c8636b9 50              push    eax
7c8636ba 50              push    eax
7c8636bb 6a01            push    1
7c8636bd 50              push    eax
7c8636be 50              push    eax
7c8636bf 53              push    ebx  ; second parameter
7c8636c0 50              push    eax  ; first parameter
7c8636c1 e86cecf9ff      call    kernel32!CreateProcessW (7c802332)
...
...
...
```

Because this is the code that yet to be executed, we need to put a breakpoint at 7c8636c1 address, continue execution, and when the breakpoint is hit, dump the second parameter to *CreateProcess* that is the memory EBX points to:

```
0:000> bp 7c8636c1

0:000> g
Breakpoint 0 hit
eax=00000000 ebx=0012ed78 ecx=0012ec70 edx=7c90eb94 esi=0000003a
edi=00000000
eip=7c8636c1 esp=0012ed50 ebp=0012f47c iopl=0 nv up ei pl zr na pe nc
cs=001b  ss=0023  ds=0023  es=0023  fs=003b  gs=0000 efl=00000246
kernel32!UnhandledExceptionFilter+0x84b:
7c8636c1 e86cecf9ff      call    kernel32!CreateProcessW (7c802332)

0:000> du @ebx
0012ed78  "c:\drwatson\drwtsn32 -p 656 -e 1"
0012edb8  "72 -g"
```

We see that *UnhandledExceptionFilter* is about to launch my custom Dr. Watson postmortem debugger.

If we look further at *UnhandledExceptionFilter* disassembled code, we would see that after creating a postmortem debugger process and waiting for it to finish saving the process dump, the function calls *NtTerminateProcess*.

Therefore, all error reporting, calling a postmortem debugger, and final process termination are done in the same process that had the exception.

Starting from Windows XP, *UnhandledExceptionFilter* function locates and loads *faultrep.dll* which launches *dwwin.exe* to report an error:

```
kernel32!UnhandledExceptionFilter+0x4f7:
7c863359 8d85acfaffff    lea     eax,[ebp-554h]
7c86335f 50              push    eax
7c863360 8d8570faffff    lea     eax,[ebp-590h]
7c863366 50              push    eax
7c863367 56              push    esi
7c863368 56              push    esi
7c863369 e8fbacfaff      call    kernel32!LdrLoadDll (7c80e069)

0:000> dt _UNICODE_STRING 0012f47c-590
 "C:\WINDOWS\system32\faultrep.dll"
   +0x000 Length           : 0x40
   +0x002 MaximumLength    : 0x100
   +0x004 Buffer           :
0x0012f360  "C:\WINDOWS\system32\faultrep.dll"
```

We can also see that all processing is done using the same thread stack. So if something is wrong with that stack, then you have silent process termination, and no error is reported. In Vista, there are some improvements that I'm going to cover in the next article.

Inside Vista Error Reporting

Now we look inside the error reporting mechanism on Vista. After launching the TestDefaultDebugger application and pushing its crash button, we get the following Windows error reporting dialog:

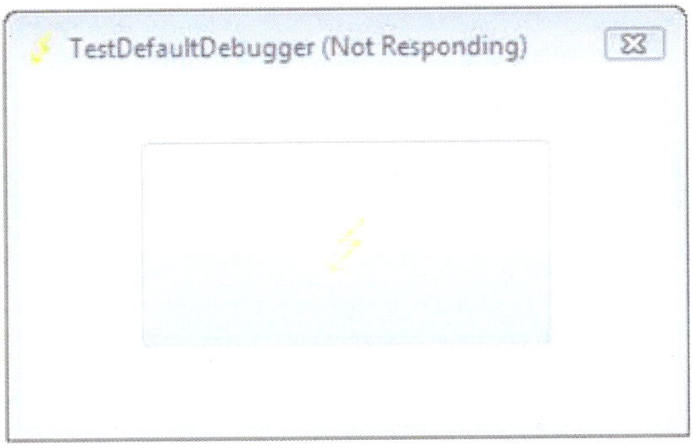

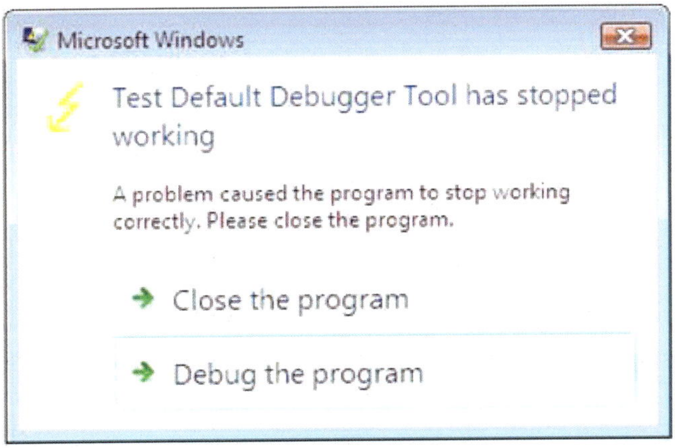

If we attach WinDbg to our TestDefaultDebugger process we would no longer see our default unhandled exception filter waiting for the error reporting process:

Windows XP

```
0:000> k
ChildEBP RetAddr
0012d318 7c90e9ab ntdll!KiFastSystemCallRet
0012d31c 7c8094e2 ntdll!ZwWaitForMultipleObjects+0xc
0012d3b8 7c80a075 kernel32!WaitForMultipleObjectsEx+0x12c
0012d3d4 6945763c kernel32!WaitForMultipleObjects+0x18
0012dd68 694582b1 faultrep!StartDWException+0x5df
0012eddc 7c8633e9 faultrep!ReportFault+0x533
0012f47c 00411eaa kernel32!UnhandledExceptionFilter+0x587
0012f8a4 00403263
TestDefaultDebugger!CTestDefaultDebuggerDlg::OnBnClickedButton1
0012f8b4 00403470 TestDefaultDebugger!_AfxDispatchCmdMsg+0x43
...
...
...
0012fff0 00000000 kernel32!BaseProcessStart+0x23
```

Windows Vista

```
0:001> ~*kL 100

0 Id: 120c.148c Suspend: 1 Teb: 7ffdf000 Unfrozen
ChildEBP RetAddr
0012f8a4 00403263
TestDefaultDebugger!CTestDefaultDebuggerDlg::OnBnClickedButton1
0012f8b4 00403470 TestDefaultDebugger!_AfxDispatchCmdMsg+0x43
0012f8e4 00402a27 TestDefaultDebugger!CCmdTarget::OnCmdMsg+0x118
0012f908 00408e69 TestDefaultDebugger!CDialog::OnCmdMsg+0x1b
0012f958 004098d9 TestDefaultDebugger!CWnd::OnCommand+0x90
0012f9f4 00406258 TestDefaultDebugger!CWnd::OnWndMsg+0x36
0012fa14 0040836d TestDefaultDebugger!CWnd::WindowProc+0x22
0012fa7c 004083f4 TestDefaultDebugger!AfxCallWndProc+0x9a
0012fa9c 77b71a10 TestDefaultDebugger!AfxWndProc+0x34
0012fac8 77b71ae8 USER32!InternalCallWinProc+0x23
0012fb40 77b7286a USER32!UserCallWinProcCheckWow+0x14b
0012fb80 77b72bba USER32!SendMessageWorker+0x4b7
0012fba0 7504e5cc USER32!SendMessageW+0x7c
0012fbc0 7504e583 COMCTL32!Button_NotifyParent+0x3d
0012fbdc 7504e680 COMCTL32!Button_ReleaseCapture+0x112
0012fc34 77b71a10 COMCTL32!Button_WndProc+0xa4b
0012fc60 77b71ae8 USER32!InternalCallWinProc+0x23
0012fcd8 77b72a47 USER32!UserCallWinProcCheckWow+0x14b
0012fd3c 77b72a98 USER32!DispatchMessageWorker+0x322
0012fd4c 77b6120c USER32!DispatchMessageW+0xf
0012fd70 0040568b USER32!IsDialogMessageW+0x586
0012fd80 004065d8 TestDefaultDebugger!CWnd::IsDialogMessageW+0x2e
0012fd88 00402a07 TestDefaultDebugger!CWnd::PreTranslateInput+0x29
0012fd98 00408041 TestDefaultDebugger!CDialog::PreTranslateMessage+0x96
0012fda8 00403ae3 TestDefaultDebugger!CWnd::WalkPreTranslateTree+0x1f
0012fdbc 00403c1e TestDefaultDebugger!AfxInternalPreTranslateMessage+0x3b
```

```
0012fdc4 00403b29 TestDefaultDebugger!CWinThread::PreTranslateMessage+0x9
0012fdcc 00403c68 TestDefaultDebugger!AfxPreTranslateMessage+0x15
0012fddc 00407920 TestDefaultDebugger!AfxInternalPumpMessage+0x2b
0012fe00 004030a1 TestDefaultDebugger!CWnd::RunModalLoop+0xca
0012fe4c 0040110d TestDefaultDebugger!CDialog::DoModal+0x12c
0012fef8 004206fb
TestDefaultDebugger!CTestDefaultDebuggerApp::InitInstance+0xdd
0012ff08 0040e852 TestDefaultDebugger!AfxWinMain+0x47
0012ffa0 77603833 TestDefaultDebugger!__tmainCRTStartup+0x176
0012ffac 779ea9bd kernel32!BaseThreadInitThunk+0xe
0012ffec 00000000 ntdll!_RtlUserThreadStart+0x23

# 1 Id: 120c.17e4 Suspend: 1 Teb: 7ffde000 Unfrozen
ChildEBP RetAddr
011cff70 77a3f0a9 ntdll!DbgBreakPoint
011cffa0 77603833 ntdll!DbgUiRemoteBreakin+0x3c
011cffac 779ea9bd kernel32!BaseThreadInitThunk+0xe
011cffec 00000000 ntdll!_RtlUserThreadStart+0x23
```

Let's look at the faulting thread's raw stack data:

```
0:001> ~0 s
eax=00000000 ebx=00000001 ecx=0012fe70 edx=00000000 esi=00425ae8
edi=0012fe70
eip=004014f0 esp=0012f8a8 ebp=0012f8b4 iopl=0 nv up ei ng nz ac pe cy
cs=001b ss=0023 ds=0023 es=0023 fs=003b gs=0000 efl=00010297
TestDefaultDebugger!CTestDefaultDebuggerDlg::OnBnClickedButton1:
004014f0 mov dword ptr ds:[0],0 ds:0023:00000000=????????

0:000> !teb
TEB at 7ffdf000
ExceptionList:          0012f9e8
StackBase:              00130000
StackLimit:             0012d000
SubSystemTib:           00000000
FiberData:              00001e00
ArbitraryUserPointer:   00000000
Self:                   7ffdf000
EnvironmentPointer:     00000000
ClientId:               0000120c . 0000148c
RpcHandle:              00000000
Tls Storage:            7ffdf02c
PEB Address:            7ffda000
LastErrorValue:         0
LastStatusValue:        c000008a
Count Owned Locks:      0
HardErrorMode:          0
```

```
0:000>dds 0012d000 00130000
...
...
...
0012f368 0012f3c0
0012f36c 7760fb01 kernel32!GetApplicationRecoveryCallback+0x33
0012f370 ffffffff
0012f374 0012f380
0012f378 00000001
0012f37c 00000000
0012f380 00000000
0012f384 00000000
0012f388 00000000
0012f38c 00000000
0012f390 00000000
0012f394 00000000
0012f398 00000000
0012f39c 00000000
0012f3a0 00000000
0012f3a4 00000000
0012f3a8 00000000
0012f3ac 00000000
0012f3b0 00000000
0012f3b4 00000000
0012f3b8 00000000
0012f3bc 00000000
0012f3c0 0012f410
0012f3c4 7767aa88 kernel32!WerpReportExceptionInProcessContext+0x82
0012f3c8 ffffffff
0012f3cc 0012f3ec
0012f3d0 00000000
0012f3d4 00000000
0012f3d8 7767aab7 kernel32!WerpReportExceptionInProcessContext+0xa7
0012f3dc 001257b9
0012f3e0 00000001
0012f3e4 00000000
0012f3e8 0012f4c8
0012f3ec 00000000
0012f3f0 00000000
0012f3f4 00000000
0012f3f8 0012f3dc
0012f3fc ffffffff
0012f400 0012f488
0012f404 775d5ac9 kernel32!_except_handler4
0012f408 77670969 kernel32!Internal_NotifyUILanguageChange+0x4a6
0012f40c fffffffe
0012f410 7767aab7 kernel32!WerpReportExceptionInProcessContext+0xa7
0012f414 77655b41 kernel32!UnhandledExceptionFilter+0x1b2
0012f418 77655cbd kernel32!UnhandledExceptionFilter+0x32e
0012f41c 00125731
0012f420 00000000
0012f424 0012f4c8
0012f428 00000000
0012f42c 00000000
```

```
0012f430 00000000
0012f434 00000000
0012f438 00000000
0012f43c 00000800
0012f440 00000000
0012f444 00000000
0012f448 00000000
0012f44c 00000000
0012f450 00000000
0012f454 00000005
0012f458 994ac7c4
0012f45c 00000011
0012f460 00000000
0012f464 0012f5c0
0012f468 775d5ac9 kernel32!_except_handler4
0012f46c 00000001
0012f470 00000000
0012f474 77655cbd kernel32!UnhandledExceptionFilter+0x32e
0012f478 00000000
0012f47c 00000000
0012f480 0012f41c
0012f484 00000024
0012f488 0012f4f4
0012f48c 775d5ac9 kernel32!_except_handler4
0012f490 7765ff59 kernel32!PEWriteResource<_IMAGE_NT_HEADERS>+0x50a
0012f494 fffffffe
0012f498 77655cbd kernel32!UnhandledExceptionFilter+0x32e
0012f49c 77a29f8e ntdll!_RtlUserThreadStart+0x6f
0012f4a0 00000000
0012f4a4 779b8dd4 ntdll!_EH4_CallFilterFunc+0x12
0012f4a8 00000000
0012f4ac 0012ffec
0012f4b0 779ff100 ntdll! ?? ::FNODOBFM::`string'+0xb6e
0012f4b4 0012f4dc
0012f4b8 779b40e4 ntdll!_except_handler4+0xcc
0012f4bc 00000000
0012f4c0 00000000
0012f4c4 00000000
0012f4c8 0012f5c0
0012f4cc 0012f5dc
0012f4d0 779ff118 ntdll! ?? ::FNODOBFM::`string'+0xb7e
0012f4d4 00000001
0012f4d8 0112f5c0
0012f4dc 0012f500
0012f4e0 77a11039 ntdll!ExecuteHandler2+0x26
0012f4e4 fffffffe
0012f4e8 0012ffdc
0012f4ec 0012f5dc
0012f4f0 0012f59c
0012f4f4 0012f9e8
0012f4f8 77a1104d ntdll!ExecuteHandler2+0x3a
0012f4fc 0012ffdc
0012f500 0012f5a8
0012f504 77a1100b ntdll!ExecuteHandler+0x24
```

```
0012f508 0012f5c0
0012f50c 0012ffdc
0012f510 0012fe70
0012f514 0012f59c
0012f518 779b8bf2 ntdll!_except_handler4
0012f51c 00000000
0012f520 0012f5c0
0012f524 0012f538
0012f528 779b94e3 ntdll!RtlCallVectoredContinueHandlers+0x15
0012f52c 0012f5c0
0012f530 0012f5dc
0012f534 77a754c0 ntdll!RtlpCallbackEntryList
0012f538 0012f5a8
0012f53c 779b94c1 ntdll!RtlDispatchException+0x11f
0012f540 0012f5c0
0012f544 0012f5dc
0012f548 00425ae8
TestDefaultDebugger!CTestDefaultDebuggerApp::`vftable'+0x154
0012f54c 00000000
0012f550 00000502
0012f554 00000000
0012f558 00a460e0
0012f55c 00000000
0012f560 00000000
0012f564 00000070
0012f568 ffffffff
0012f56c ffffffff
0012f570 77b60dba USER32!UserCallDlgProcCheckWow+0x5f
0012f574 77b60e63 USER32!UserCallDlgProcCheckWow+0x16e
0012f578 0000006c
0012f57c 00000000
0012f580 00000000
0012f584 00000000
0012f588 00000000
0012f58c 0000004e
0012f590 00000000
0012f594 0012f634
0012f598 77bb76cc USER32!_except_handler4
0012f59c 0012f634
0012f5a0 00130000
0012f5a4 00000000
0012f5a8 0012f8b4
0012f5ac 77a10060 ntdll!NtRaiseException+0xc
0012f5b0 77a10eb2 ntdll!KiUserExceptionDispatcher+0x2a
0012f5b4 0012f5c0
...
...
...
```

It shows the presence of *kernel32!UnhandledExceptionFilter* calls. Let's open *TestDefaultDebugger.exe* in WinDbg, put a breakpoint on *UnhandledExceptionFilter* function, and trace the execution. We have to change the return value of

IsDebugPortPresent to simulate the normal fault handling logic when no active debugger is attached:

```
0:000> bp kernel32!UnhandledExceptionFilter

0:000> g
(fb0.1190): Access violation - code c0000005 (first chance)
First chance exceptions are reported before any exception handling.
This exception may be expected and handled.
eax=00000000 ebx=00000001 ecx=0012fe70 edx=00000000 esi=00425ae8
edi=0012fe70
eip=004014f0 esp=0012f8a8 ebp=0012f8b4 iopl=0 nv up ei ng nz ac pe cy
cs=001b ss=0023 ds=0023 es=0023 fs=003b gs=0000 efl=00010297
TestDefaultDebugger!CTestDefaultDebuggerDlg::OnBnClickedButton1:
004014f0 mov dword ptr ds:[0],0 ds:0023:00000000=????????

0:000> g
Breakpoint 0 hit
eax=0042ae58 ebx=00000000 ecx=0042ae58 edx=0042ae58 esi=003b07d8
edi=c0000005
eip=77655984 esp=0012f478 ebp=0012f494 iopl=0 nv up ei pl zr na pe nc
cs=001b ss=0023 ds=0023 es=0023 fs=003b gs=0000 efl=00000246
kernel32!UnhandledExceptionFilter:
77655984 push 5Ch

0:000> g $$ skip first chance exception
Breakpoint 0 hit
eax=77655984 ebx=00000000 ecx=0012f404 edx=77a10f34 esi=0012f4c8
edi=00000000
eip=77655984 esp=0012f49c ebp=0012ffec iopl=0 nv up ei pl nz na pe nc
cs=001b ss=0023 ds=0023 es=0023 fs=003b gs=0000 efl=00000206
kernel32!UnhandledExceptionFilter:
77655984 push 5Ch

0:000> p
eax=77655984 ebx=00000000 ecx=0012f404 edx=77a10f34 esi=0012f4c8
edi=00000000
eip=77655986 esp=0012f498 ebp=0012ffec iopl=0 nv up ei pl nz na pe nc
cs=001b ss=0023 ds=0023 es=0023 fs=003b gs=0000 efl=00000206
kernel32!UnhandledExceptionFilter+0x2:
77655986 push offset kernel32!strcat_s+0x128d (77655cf0)
...
...
...
```

```
0:000> p
eax=00000000 ebx=0012f4c8 ecx=776558e5 edx=77a10f34 esi=00000000
edi=00000000
eip=77655a33 esp=0012f41c ebp=0012f498 iopl=0 nv up ei pl nz ac po cy
cs=001b ss=0023 ds=0023 es=0023 fs=003b gs=0000 efl=00000213
kernel32!UnhandledExceptionFilter+0xa5:
77655a33 call kernel32!IsDebugPortPresent (7765594c)

0:000> p
eax=00000001 ebx=0012f4c8 ecx=0012f3f4 edx=77a10f34 esi=00000000
edi=00000000
eip=77655a38 esp=0012f41c ebp=0012f498 iopl=0 nv up ei pl nz na po nc
cs=001b ss=0023 ds=0023 es=0023 fs=003b gs=0000 efl=00000202
kernel32!UnhandledExceptionFilter+0xaa:
77655a38 test eax,eax

0:000> r eax=0

0:000> p
eax=00000000 ebx=0012f4c8 ecx=0012f3f4 edx=77a10f34 esi=00000000
edi=00000000
eip=77655a3a esp=0012f41c ebp=0012f498 iopl=0 nv up ei pl zr na pe nc
cs=001b ss=0023 ds=0023 es=0023 fs=003b gs=0000 efl=00000246
kernel32!UnhandledExceptionFilter+0xac:
77655a3a jne kernel32!UnhandledExceptionFilter+0x22 (776559a6) [br=0]
```

Next, we continue to step over by using the **p** command until we see *WerpReportExceptionInProcessContext* function and step into it:

```
0:000> p
eax=c0000022 ebx=0012f4c8 ecx=0012f400 edx=77a10f34 esi=00000000
edi=00000001
eip=77655b3c esp=0012f418 ebp=0012f498 iopl=0 nv up ei pl nz na po nc
cs=001b ss=0023 ds=0023 es=0023 fs=003b gs=0000 efl=00000202
kernel32!UnhandledExceptionFilter+0x1ad:
77655b3c call kernel32!WerpReportExceptionInProcessContext (7767aa06)

0:000> t
eax=c0000022 ebx=0012f4c8 ecx=0012f400 edx=77a10f34 esi=00000000
edi=00000001
eip=7767aa06 esp=0012f414 ebp=0012f498 iopl=0 nv up ei pl nz na po nc
cs=001b ss=0023 ds=0023 es=0023 fs=003b gs=0000 efl=00000202
kernel32!WerpReportExceptionInProcessContext:
7767aa06 push 14h
```

At this point, if we look at the stack trace we would see:

```
0:000> kL 100
ChildEBP RetAddr
0012f410 77655b41 kernel32!WerpReportExceptionInProcessContext
0012f498 77a29f8e kernel32!UnhandledExceptionFilter+0x1b2
0012f4a0 779b8dd4 ntdll!_RtlUserThreadStart+0x6f
0012f4b4 779b40f0 ntdll!_EH4_CallFilterFunc+0x12
0012f4dc 77a11039 ntdll!_except_handler4+0x8e
0012f500 77a1100b ntdll!ExecuteHandler2+0x26
0012f5a8 77a10e97 ntdll!ExecuteHandler+0x24
0012f5a8 004014f0 ntdll!KiUserExceptionDispatcher+0xf
0012f8a4 00403263
TestDefaultDebugger!CTestDefaultDebuggerDlg::OnBnClickedButton1
0012f8b4 00403470 TestDefaultDebugger!_AfxDispatchCmdMsg+0x43
...
...
...
```

After that, we step over again and find that the code flow returns from all exception handlers until *KiUserExceptionDispatcher* function raises the exception again via *ZwRaiseException* call.

So it looks like the default unhandled exception filter in Vista only reports the exception and doesn't launch the error reporting process that displays the error box, *WerFault.exe*.

If we click on the Debug button on the error reporting dialog to launch the postmortem debugger (I have Visual Studio Just-In-Time Debugger configured in *AeDebug\Debugger* registry key) and look at its parent process by using Process Explorer, for example, we would see it is *WerFault.exe* which in turn has svchost.exe as its parent.

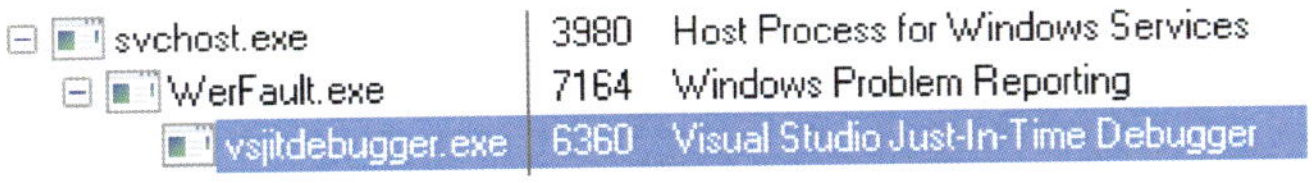

Now, we quit WinDbg and launch TestDefaultDebugger application again, push its big crash button, and, when the error reporting dialog appears, we attach another instance of WinDbg to *svchost.exe* process hosting Windows Error Reporting Service (*wersvc.dll*).

We see the following threads:

```
0:000> ~*k

. 0 Id: f8c.f90 Suspend: 1 Teb: 7ffdf000 Unfrozen
ChildEBP RetAddr
0008f5b4 77a10080 ntdll!KiFastSystemCallRet
0008f5b8 7760853f ntdll!ZwReadFile+0xc
0008f630 7709ffe2 kernel32!ReadFile+0x20e
0008f65c 7709fdfb ADVAPI32!ScGetPipeInput+0x2a
0008f6c4 7709bdd2 ADVAPI32!ScDispatcherLoop+0x6c
0008f93c 004a241d ADVAPI32!StartServiceCtrlDispatcherW+0xce
0008f944 004a2401 svchost!SvcHostMain+0x12
0008f948 004a2183 svchost!wmain+0x5
0008f98c 77603833 svchost!_initterm_e+0x163
0008f998 779ea9bd kernel32!BaseThreadInitThunk+0xe
0008f9d8 00000000 ntdll!_RtlUserThreadStart+0x23

1 Id: f8c.fa4 Suspend: 1 Teb: 7ffdd000 Unfrozen
ChildEBP RetAddr
0086f6d0 77a10690 ntdll!KiFastSystemCallRet
0086f6d4 779cb65b ntdll!ZwWaitForMultipleObjects+0xc
0086f870 77603833 ntdll!TppWaiterpThread+0x294
0086f87c 779ea9bd kernel32!BaseThreadInitThunk+0xe
0086f8bc 00000000 ntdll!_RtlUserThreadStart+0x23

2 Id: f8c.fa8 Suspend: 1 Teb: 7ffdc000 Unfrozen
ChildEBP RetAddr
0031f81c 77a0f2c0 ntdll!KiFastSystemCallRet
0031f820 71cb1545 ntdll!NtAlpcSendWaitReceivePort+0xc
0031fd3c 71cb63c4 wersvc!CWerService::LpcServerThread+0x9c
0031fd44 77603833 wersvc!CWerService::StaticLpcServerThread+0xd
0031fd50 779ea9bd kernel32!BaseThreadInitThunk+0xe
0031fd90 00000000 ntdll!_RtlUserThreadStart+0x23

3 Id: f8c.2cc Suspend: 1 Teb: 7ffde000 Unfrozen
ChildEBP RetAddr
00f8f768 77a106a0 ntdll!KiFastSystemCallRet
00f8f76c 776077d4 ntdll!NtWaitForSingleObject+0xc
00f8f7dc 77607742 kernel32!WaitForSingleObjectEx+0xbe
00f8f7f0 71cb6f4b kernel32!WaitForSingleObject+0x12
00f8f858 71cb6803 wersvc!CWerService::ReportCrashKernelMsg+0x256
00f8fb7c 71cb6770 wersvc!CWerService::DispatchPortRequestWorkItem+0x70a
00f8fb90 779c1fbb
wersvc!CWerService::StaticDispatchPortRequestWorkItem+0x17
00f8fbb4 77a1a2b8 ntdll!TppSimplepExecuteCallback+0x10c
00f8fcdc 77603833 ntdll!TppWorkerThread+0x522
00f8fce8 779ea9bd kernel32!BaseThreadInitThunk+0xe
00f8fd28 00000000 ntdll!_RtlUserThreadStart+0x23
```

```
4 Id: f8c.1b38 Suspend: 1 Teb: 7ffdb000 Unfrozen
ChildEBP RetAddr
00d3fe08 77a10850 ntdll!KiFastSystemCallRet
00d3fe0c 77a1a1b4 ntdll!NtWaitForWorkViaWorkerFactory+0xc
00d3ff34 77603833 ntdll!TppWorkerThread+0x1f6
00d3ff40 779ea9bd kernel32!BaseThreadInitThunk+0xe
00d3ff80 00000000 ntdll!_RtlUserThreadStart+0x23
```

First, it looks like some LPC notification mechanism is present here (*CWerService::LpcServerThread*). Next, if we look at *CWerService::ReportCrashKernelMsg* code, we see it calls *CWerService::ReportCrash*, which in turn loads *faultrep.dll:*

```
0:000> .asm no_code_bytes
Assembly options: no_code_bytes

0:000> uf wersvc!CWerService::ReportCrashKernelMsg
...
...
...
wersvc!CWerService::ReportCrashKernelMsg+0x226:
71cb6f13 lea   eax,[ebp-20h]
71cb6f16 push  eax
71cb6f17 push  dword ptr [ebp-34h]
71cb6f1a push  dword ptr [ebp-2Ch]
71cb6f1d call  dword ptr [wersvc!_imp__GetCurrentProcessId (71cb1120)]
71cb6f23 push  eax
71cb6f24 mov   ecx,dword ptr [ebp-38h]
71cb6f27 call  wersvc!CWerService::ReportCrash (71cb7008)
71cb6f2c mov   dword ptr [ebp-1Ch],eax
71cb6f2f cmp   eax,ebx
71cb6f31 jl    wersvc!CWerService::ReportCrashKernelMsg+0x279 (71cb6a10)
...
...
...

0:000> uf wersvc!CWerService::ReportCrash
...
...
...
wersvc!CWerService::ReportCrash+0x3d:
71cb7045 mov   dword ptr [ebp-4],edi
71cb7048 push  offset wersvc!`string' (71cb711c)
71cb704d call  dword ptr [wersvc!_imp__LoadLibraryW (71cb1144)]
71cb7053 mov   dword ptr [ebp-2Ch],eax
71cb7056 cmp   eax,edi
71cb7058 je    wersvc!CWerService::ReportCrash+0x52 (71cb9b47)
```

```
wersvc!CWerService::ReportCrash+0x88:
71cb705e push offset wersvc!`string' (71cb7100)
71cb7063 push eax
71cb7064 call dword ptr [wersvc!_imp__GetProcAddress (71cb1140)]
71cb706a mov  ebx,eax
71cb706c cmp  ebx,edi
71cb706e je   wersvc!CWerService::ReportCrash+0x9a (71cb9b7d)
...
...
...

0:000> du 71cb711c
71cb711c "faultrep.dll"

0:000> da 71cb7100
71cb7100 "WerpInitiateCrashReporting"
```

If we attach a new instance of WinDbg to *WerFault.exe* and inspect its threads, we see:

```
0:003> ~*k

0 Id: 1bfc.16c4 Suspend: 1 Teb: 7ffdf000 Unfrozen
ChildEBP RetAddr
0015de60 77a10690 ntdll!KiFastSystemCallRet
0015de64 77607e09 ntdll!ZwWaitForMultipleObjects+0xc
0015df00 77b6c4b7 kernel32!WaitForMultipleObjectsEx+0x11d
0015df54 77b68b83 USER32!RealMsgWaitForMultipleObjectsEx+0x13c
0015df70 6d46d90d USER32!MsgWaitForMultipleObjects+0x1f
0015dfc0 6d4acd77 wer!UtilMsgWaitForMultipleObjects+0x8a
0015dff4 6d4a7694 wer!CInitialConsentUI::Show+0x133
0015e040 6d4a9a69 wer!CEventUI::GetInitialDialogSelection+0xc6
0015e104 6d46df18 wer!CEventUI::Start+0x32
0015e39c 6d46b743 wer!CWatson::ReportProblem+0x438
0015e3ac 6d46b708 wer!WatsonReportSend+0x1e
0015e3c8 6d46b682 wer!CDWInstance::WatsonReportStub+0x17
0015e3ec 6d472a7f wer!CDWInstance::SubmitReport+0x21e
0015e410 730b6d0d wer!WerReportSubmit+0x5d
0015f33c 730b73c1 faultrep!CCrashWatson::GenerateCrashReport+0x5c4
0015f5d4 730b4de1 faultrep!CCrashWatson::ReportCrash+0x374
0015fad4 009bd895 faultrep!WerpInitiateCrashReporting+0x304
0015fb0c 009b60cd WerFault!UserCrashMain+0x14e
0015fb30 009b644a WerFault!wmain+0xbf
0015fb74 77603833 WerFault!_initterm_e+0x163
```

```
1 Id: 1bfc.894 Suspend: 1 Teb: 7ffde000 Unfrozen
ChildEBP RetAddr
024afbf8 77a10690 ntdll!KiFastSystemCallRet
024afbfc 77607e09 ntdll!ZwWaitForMultipleObjects+0xc
024afc98 77b6c4b7 kernel32!WaitForMultipleObjectsEx+0x11d
024afcec 74fa161a USER32!RealMsgWaitForMultipleObjectsEx+0x13c
024afd0c 74fa2cb6 DUser!CoreSC::Wait+0x59
024afd34 74fa2c55 DUser!CoreSC::WaitMessage+0x54
024afd44 77b615c0 DUser!MphWaitMessageEx+0x22
024afd60 77a10e6e USER32!__ClientWaitMessageExMPH+0x1e
024afd7c 77b6b5bc ntdll!KiUserCallbackDispatcher+0x2e
024afd80 77b61598 USER32!NtUserWaitMessage+0xc
024afdb4 77b61460 USER32!DialogBox2+0x202
024afddc 77b614a2 USER32!InternalDialogBox+0xd0
024afdfc 77b61505 USER32!DialogBoxIndirectParamAorW+0x37
024afe1c 75036c51 USER32!DialogBoxIndirectParamW+0x1b
024afe40 75036beb comctl32!SHFusionDialogBoxIndirectParam+0x2d
024afe74 6d4a65a4 comctl32!CTaskDialog::Show+0x100
024afebc 6d4acb72 wer!IsolationAwareTaskDialogIndirect+0x64
024aff4c 6d4acc39 wer!CInitialConsentUI::InitialDlgThreadRoutine+0x369
024aff54 77603833
wer!CInitialConsentUI::Static_InitialDlgThreadRoutine+0xd
024aff60 779ea9bd kernel32!BaseThreadInitThunk+0xe

2 Id: 1bfc.1a04 Suspend: 1 Teb: 7ffdc000 Unfrozen
ChildEBP RetAddr
012bf998 77a10690 ntdll!KiFastSystemCallRet
012bf99c 77607e09 ntdll!ZwWaitForMultipleObjects+0xc
012bfa38 77b6c4b7 kernel32!WaitForMultipleObjectsEx+0x11d
012bfa8c 74fa161a USER32!RealMsgWaitForMultipleObjectsEx+0x13c
012bfaac 74fa1642 DUser!CoreSC::Wait+0x59
012bfae0 74fac442 DUser!CoreSC::xwProcessNL+0xaa
012bfb00 74fac3a2 DUser!GetMessageExA+0x44
012bfb54 779262b6 DUser!ResourceManager::SharedThreadProc+0xb6
012bfb8c 779263de msvcrt!_endthreadex+0x44
012bfb94 77603833 msvcrt!_endthreadex+0xce
012bfba0 779ea9bd kernel32!BaseThreadInitThunk+0xe
012bfbe0 00000000 ntdll!_RtlUserThreadStart+0x23

# 3 Id: 1bfc.14a4 Suspend: 1 Teb: 7ffdb000 Unfrozen
ChildEBP RetAddr
02a1fc40 77a3f0a9 ntdll!DbgBreakPoint
02a1fc70 77603833 ntdll!DbgUiRemoteBreakin+0x3c
02a1fc7c 779ea9bd kernel32!BaseThreadInitThunk+0xe
02a1fcbc 00000000 ntdll!_RtlUserThreadStart+0x23
```

Next, we put a breakpoint on *CreateProcess*, push the Debug button in the error reporting dialog, and upon the breakpoint hit, inspect *CreateProcess* parameters:

```
0:003> .asm no_code_bytes
Assembly options: no_code_bytes
```

```
0:003> bp kernel32!CreateProcessW

0:003> g
Breakpoint 0 hit
eax=00000000 ebx=00000000 ecx=7ffdf000 edx=0015db30 esi=00000001
edi=00000000
eip=775c1d27 esp=0015dfe0 ebp=0015e408 iopl=0 nv up ei pl nz na po nc
cs=001b ss=0023 ds=0023 es=0023 fs=003b gs=0000 efl=00000202
kernel32!CreateProcessW:
775c1d27 mov edi,edi

0:000> ddu esp+8 l1
0015dfe8 008b0000 ""C:\WINDOWS\system32\vsjitdebugger.exe" -p 8064 -e 312"
```

ESP points to return address; ESP+4 points to the first *CreateProcess* parameter, and ESP+8 points to the second parameter. The thread stack now involves *faultrep.dll*:

```
0:000> k
ChildEBP RetAddr
0020dde0 730bb2b5 kernel32!CreateProcessW
0020e20c 730b6dae faultrep!WerpLaunchAeDebug+0x384
0020f140 730b73c1 faultrep!CCrashWatson::GenerateCrashReport+0x665
0020f3d8 730b4de1 faultrep!CCrashWatson::ReportCrash+0x374
0020f8d8 009bd895 faultrep!WerpInitiateCrashReporting+0x304
0020f910 009b60cd WerFault!UserCrashMain+0x14e
0020f934 009b644a WerFault!wmain+0xbf
0020f978 77603833 WerFault!_initterm_e+0x163
0020f984 779ea9bd kernel32!BaseThreadInitThunk+0xe
0020f9c4 00000000 ntdll!_RtlUserThreadStart+0x23
```

Therefore, it looks like calls to *faultrep.dll* module to report faults and launch the postmortem debugger were moved from *UnhandledExceptionFilter* to *WerFault.exe* in Vista.

Finally, let's go back to our *UnhandledExceptionFilter* function. If we disassemble it, we see that it can call *kernel32!WerpLaunchAeDebug* too:

```
0:000> .asm no_code_bytes
Assembly options: no_code_bytes

0:000> uf kernel32!UnhandledExceptionFilter
...
...
...
kernel32!UnhandledExceptionFilter+0x2d0:
77655c5f push dword ptr [ebp-28h]
77655c62 push dword ptr [ebp-1Ch]
77655c65 push dword ptr [ebx+4]
77655c68 push dword ptr [ebx]
```

```
77655c6a push 0FFFFFFFEh
77655c6c call kernel32!GetCurrentProcess (775e9145)
77655c71 push eax
77655c72 call kernel32!WerpLaunchAeDebug (7767baaf)
77655c77 test eax,eax
77655c79 jge  kernel32!UnhandledExceptionFilter+0x2f3 (77655c82)
...
...
...
kernel32!UnhandledExceptionFilter+0x303:
77655c92 mov  eax,dword ptr [ebx]
77655c94 push dword ptr [eax]
77655c96 push 0FFFFFFFFh
77655c98 call dword ptr [kernel32!_imp__NtTerminateProcess (775c14bc)]
```

If we look at *WerpLaunchAeDebug* code, we see that it calls *CreateProcess* too, and the code is the same as in *faultrep.dll*. This could mean that *faultrep.dll* imports that function from *kernel32.dll*. Therefore, some postmortem debugger launching code is still present in the default unhandled exception filter, perhaps for compatibility, or in case, WER doesn't work or disabled.

Another Look at Page Faults

I observed this bugcheck with reported "valid" address (in bold):

```
DRIVER_IRQL_NOT_LESS_OR_EQUAL (d1)
An attempt was made to access a pageable (or completely invalid) address
at an
interrupt request level (IRQL) that is too high.  This is usually
caused by drivers using improper addresses.
If kernel debugger is available get stack backtrace.
Arguments:
Arg1: e16623fc, memory referenced
Arg2: 00000002, IRQL
Arg3: 00000000, value 0 = read operation, 1 = write operation
Arg4: ae2b222e, address which referenced memory

TRAP_FRAME:  a54a4a40 -- (.trap 0xffffffffa54a4a40)
ErrCode = 00000000
eax=00000000 ebx=00000000 ecx=e16623f0 edx=00000000 esi=ae2ce428
edi=a54a4b4c
eip=ae2b222e esp=a54a4ab4 ebp=a54a4ac4 iopl=0 nv up ei pl nz ac po nc
cs=0008 ss=0010 ds=0023 es=0023 fs=0030 gs=0000 efl=00010212
driver!ProcessCommand+0x44:
ae2b222e 39590c cmp dword ptr [ecx+0Ch],ebx ds:0023:e16623fc=00000000

1: kd> dd e16623fc l4
e16623fc 00000000 00790000 004c4c44 00010204
```

The address belongs to a paged pool:

```
1: kd> !pool e16623fc
Pool page e16623fc region is Paged pool
 e1662000 size:  3a8 previous size:    0  (Allocated)  NtfF
 e16623a8 size:   10 previous size:  3a8  (Free)       ….
 e16623b8 size:   28 previous size:   10  (Allocated)  Ntfo
 e16623e0 size:    8 previous size:   28  (Free)       CMDa
*e16623e8 size:   20 previous size:    8  (Allocated) *DRV
```

So why do we have the bugcheck here if the memory wasn't paged out? This is because page faults occur not only when they are paged out to a disk but also when pages are marked as invalid in page tables. We can check whether an address belongs to an invalid page by using **!pte** command:

```
1: kd> !pte e16623fc
               VA e16623fc
PDE at 00000000C0603858    PTE at 00000000C070B310
contains 00000000F5434863  contains 00000000E817A8C2
pfn f5434 ---DA--KWEV                          not valid
                       Transition: e817a
                       Protect: 6 - ReadWriteExecute
```

Let's check our PTE (page table entry):

```
1: kd> .formats 00000000E817A8C2
Evaluate expression:
  Hex: e817a8c2
  Decimal: -401102654
  Octal: 35005724302
  Binary: 11101000 00010111 10101000 11000010
```

We see that the 0th (Valid) bit is cleared, and this means that PTE marks the page as invalid, and also, the 11th bit (Transition) is set, which marks that page as in standby or modified lists. When referenced and IRQL is less than 2, the page is made valid and added to a process working set. We see the address as "valid" in WinDbg because that page was not paged out and present in a crash dump. But it is marked as invalid and, therefore, triggers the page fault. Page fault handler sees that IRQL == 2 and generates a D1 bugcheck.

[This page is intentionally left blank]

Bugchecks Depicted

NMI_HARDWARE_FAILURE

WinDbg help states that NMI_HARDWARE_FAILURE (0x80) bugcheck indicates a hardware fault. This description can easily lead to the conclusion that a kernel or a complete crash dump we just got from our customer doesn't worth examining. But hardware malfunction is not always the case, especially if our customer mentions that their system was hanging, and they forced a manual dump. Here I would advise checking whether they have specialized hardware for debugging purposes, for example, a card or integrated iLO chip (Integrated Lights-Out) for remote server administration. Both can generate NMI (Non-Maskable Interrupt) on demand and therefore bugcheck the system. If this is the case, then it is worth examining their dump to see why the system was hanging.

IRQL_NOT_LESS_OR_EQUAL

During kernel debugging training I provided in the past, I came up with the idea of using UML sequence diagrams to depict various Windows kernel behavior, including bugchecks. I started with bugcheck A. To understand why this bugcheck is needed, I started explaining the difference between thread scheduling and IRQL, and I used the following diagram to illustrate it:

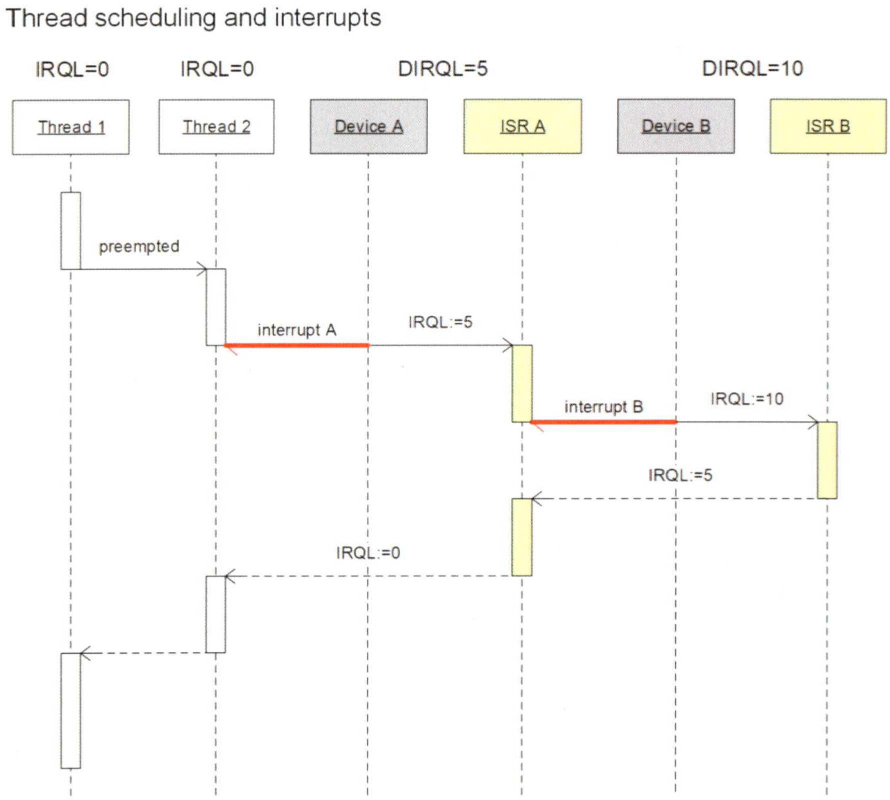

Then I explained interrupt masking:

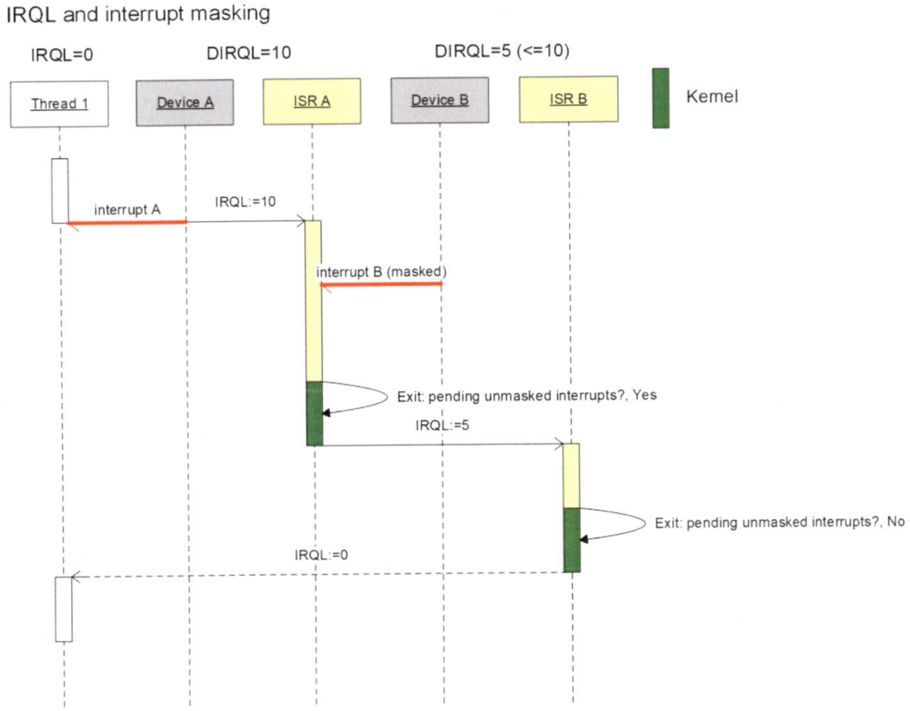

Next, I explained thread scheduling (thread dispatcher):

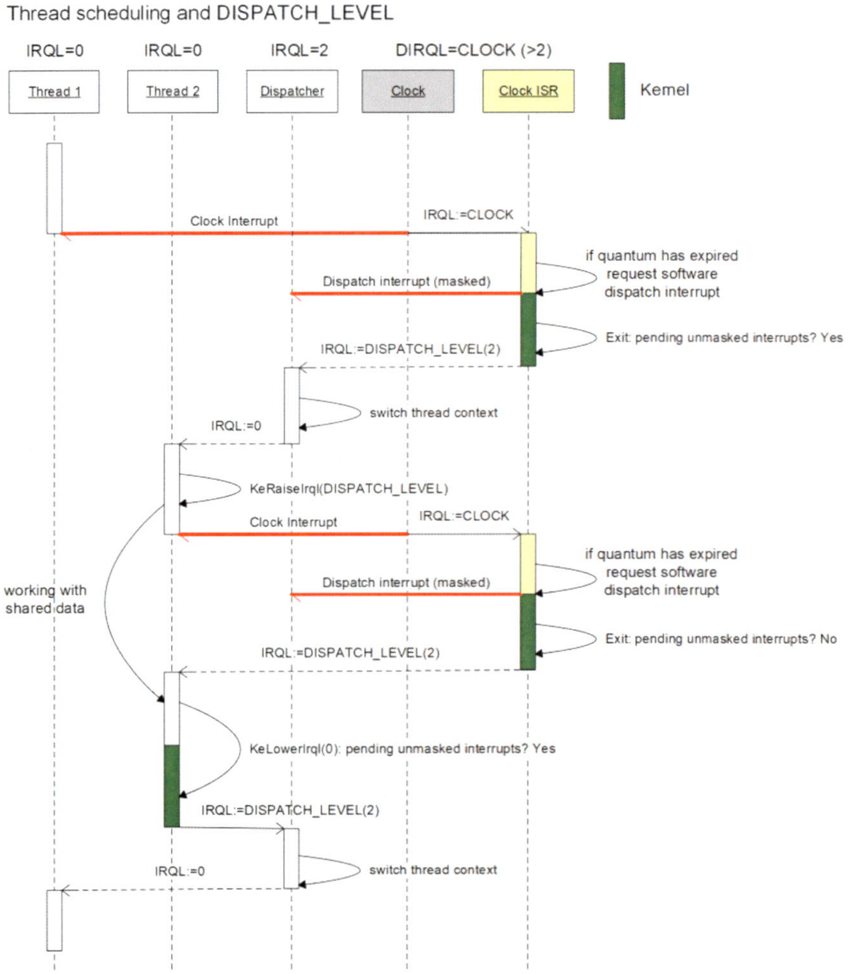

And finally, I presented the diagram showing why bugcheck A happens and what would have happened if it doesn't exist:

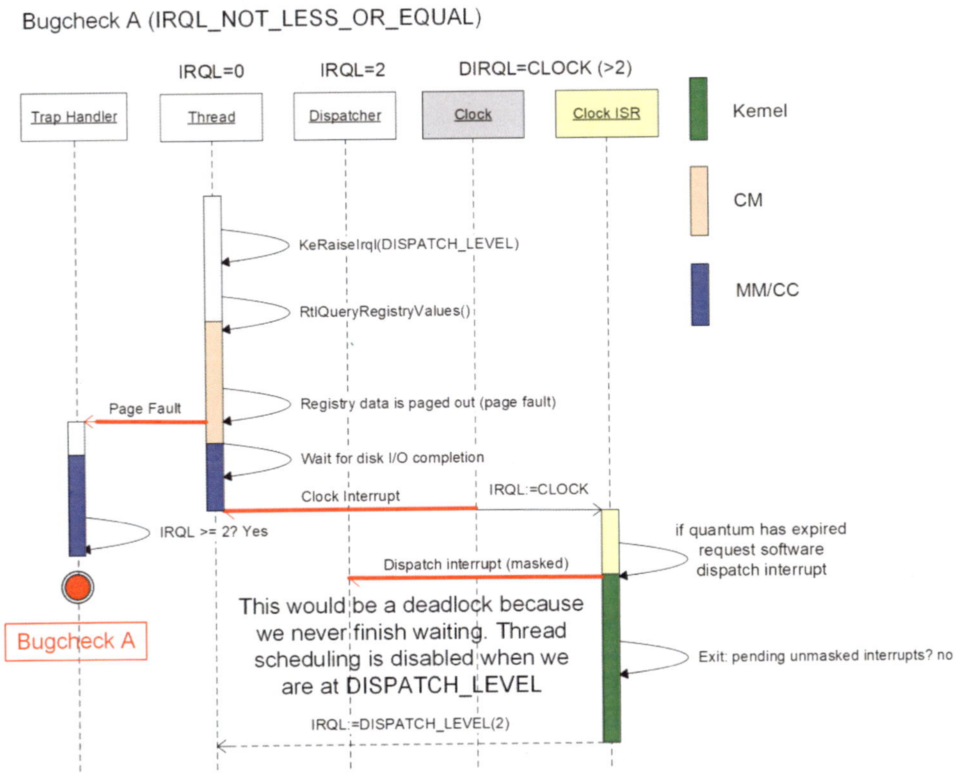

This bugcheck happens in the trap handler, and IRQL checking before the bugcheck happens in the memory manager, as you can see from the dump example below. There is no IRQL checking in the disassembled handler, so it must be in one of Mm functions:

```
BugCheck A, {3, 1c, 1, 8042d8f9}

0: kd> k
nt!KiTrap0E+0x210
driver!foo+0x209

0: kd> u nt!KiTrap0E nt!KiTrap0E+0x210
nt!KiTrap0E:
...
8046b05e call    nt!MmAccessFault (8044bfba)
...
8046b189 call    dword ptr [nt!_imp__KeGetCurrentIrql (8040063c)]
8046b18f lock    inc dword ptr [nt!KiHardwareTrigger (80470cc0)]
8046b196 mov     ecx,[ebp+0x64]
8046b199 and     ecx,0x2
8046b19c shr     ecx,1
8046b19e mov     esi,[ebp+0x68]
8046b1a1 push    esi
8046b1a2 push    ecx
8046b1a3 push    eax
8046b1a4 push    edi
8046b1a5 push    0xa
8046b1a7 call    nt!KeBugCheckEx (8042c1e2)
```

KERNEL_MODE_EXCEPTION_NOT_HANDLED

Here is the next depicted bugcheck: 0x8E. It is very common in kernel crash dumps, and it means that:

1. If an access violation exception happened, the reading or writing address was in user space.
2. Frame-based exception handling was allowed, a kernel debugger (if any) didn't handle the exception (first chance), then no exception handlers were willing to process the exception, and at last, the kernel debugger (if any) didn't handle the exception (second chance).
3. Frame-based exception handling wasn't allowed, and a kernel debugger (if any) didn't handle the exception.

The second option is depicted in the following UML sequence diagram:

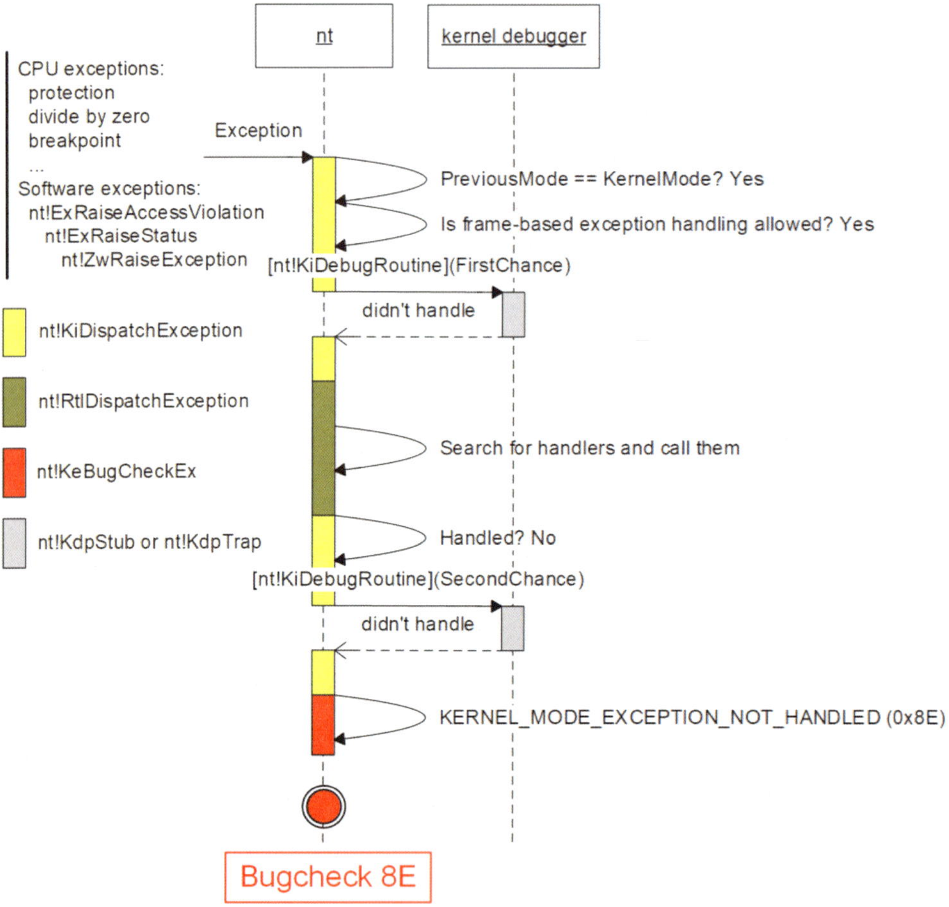

Note: If we have an access violation and reading or writing address is in kernel space, we get a different bugcheck as explained in **Invalid Pointer** pattern (page 267).

KMODE_EXCEPTION_NOT_HANDLED

This bugcheck (0x1E) is essentially the same as KERNEL_MODE_EXCEPTION_NOT_HANDLED (0x8E) bugcheck (page 141) although parameters are different:

```
KMODE_EXCEPTION_NOT_HANDLED (1e)
This is a very common bugcheck. Usually the exception address pinpoints
the driver/function that caused the problem. Always note this address as
well as the link date of the driver/image that contains this address.
Arguments:
Arg1: c0000005, The exception code that was not handled
Arg2: 8046ce72, The address that the exception occurred at
Arg3: 00000000, Parameter 0 of the exception
Arg4: 00000000, Parameter 1 of the exception

KERNEL_MODE_EXCEPTION_NOT_HANDLED (8e)
This is a very common bugcheck. Usually the exception address pinpoints
the driver/function that caused the problem. Always note this address as
well as the link date of the driver/image that contains this address. Some
common problems are exception code 0x80000003. This means a hard coded
breakpoint or assertion was hit, but this system was booted /NODEBUG. This
is not supposed to happen as developers should never have hardcoded
breakpoints in retail code, but … If this happens, make sure a debugger
gets connected, and the system is booted /DEBUG. This will let us see why
this breakpoint is happening.
Arguments:
Arg1: c0000005, The exception code that was not handled
Arg2: 808cbb8d, The address that the exception occurred at
Arg3: f5a84638, Trap Frame
Arg4: 00000000
```

Bugcheck 0x1E is called from the same routine *KiDispatchException* in x64 Windows Server 2003 and x86 Windows 2000 platforms, whereas 0x8E is called on x86 Windows Server 2003 and Vista platforms.

SYSTEM_THREAD_EXCEPTION_NOT_HANDLED

Another bugcheck that is similar to KMODE_EXCEPTION_NOT_HANDLED and KERNEL_MODE_EXCEPTION_NOT_HANDLED is SYSTEM_THREAD_EXCEPTION_NOT_HANDLED (0x7E).

This bugcheck happens when you have an exception in a system thread, and there is no exception handler to catch it, i.e., no *__try/__except* handler. System threads are created by calling *PsCreateSystemThread* function. Here is its description from DDK:

> *The PsCreateSystemThread routine creates a system thread that executes in kernel mode and returns a handle to the thread.*

By default, *PspUnhandledExceptionInSystemThread* function is set as a default exception handler, and its purpose is to call *KeBugCheckEx*.

The typical call stack in dumps with 7E bugcheck is:

```
1: kd> k
ChildEBP RetAddr
f70703cc 809a1eb2 nt!KeBugCheckEx+0x1b
f70703e8 80964a94 nt!PspUnhandledExceptionInSystemThread+0x1a
f7070ddc 80841a96 nt!PspSystemThreadStartup+0x56
00000000 00000000 nt!KiThreadStartup+0x16
```

To see how this bugcheck is generated from the processor trap, we need to look at the raw stack. Let's look at an example. **!analyze -v** command gives us the following output:

```
SYSTEM_THREAD_EXCEPTION_NOT_HANDLED (7e)
This is a very common bugcheck. Usually the exception address pinpoints
the driver/function that caused the problem. Always note this address as
well as the link date of the driver/image that contains this address.
Arguments:
Arg1: 80000003, The exception code that was not handled
Arg2: f69d9dd7, The address that the exception occurred at
Arg3: f70708c0, Exception Record Address
Arg4: f70705bc, Context Record Address
EXCEPTION_RECORD:  f70708c0 -- (.exr fffffffff70708c0)
ExceptionAddress: f69d9dd7 (driver+0x00014dd7)
   ExceptionCode: 80000003 (Break instruction exception)
  ExceptionFlags: 00000000
NumberParameters: 3
   Parameter[0]: 00000000
   Parameter[1]: 8a784020
```

```
   Parameter[2]: 00000044
CONTEXT:  f70705bc -- (.cxr ffffffff70705bc)
eax=00000001 ebx=00000032 ecx=8a37c000 edx=00000044 esi=8a37c000
edi=000000c7
eip=f69d9dd7 esp=f7070988 ebp=00004000 iopl=0 nv up ei pl zr na pe nc
cs=0008  ss=0010  ds=0023  es=0023  fs=0030  gs=0000 efl=00000246
driver+0x14dd7:
f69d9dd7 cc              int     3
STACK_TEXT:
WARNING: Stack unwind information not available. Following frames may be
wrong.
f7070998 f69dfbd1 80800000 00000000 8a37c000 driver+0x14dd7
00000000 00000000 00000000 00000000 00000000 driver+0x1abd1
```

We see that the thread encountered the breakpoint instruction, and we also see that the call stack that led to the breakpoint exception is incomplete. Here we must dump the raw stack data and try to reconstruct the stack manually. System threads are started with the execution of *KiThreadStartup* function. So let's dump the stack starting from ESP register and up to some value, find startup function there and try to walk EBP chain:

```
1: kd> dds esp esp+1000
...
...
...
f7070a04  f7070a40
f7070a08  f71172ec NDIS!ndisMCommonHaltMiniport+0x375
f7070a0c  8a37c000
f7070a10  8a60f5c0
f7070a14  8a610748
f7070a18  8a610748
f7070a1c  00000058
f7070a20  00000005
f7070a24  00000004
f7070a28  f7527000
f7070a2c  00000685
f7070a30  f710943a NDIS!ndisMDummyIndicatePacket
f7070a34  00000000
f7070a38  8a610778
f7070a3c  00010748
f7070a40  f7070b74
f7070a44  f7117640 NDIS!ndisMHaltMiniport+0x21
f7070a48  8a610990
...
... (intermediate frames are omitted to save space)
...
f7070d7c  e104a338
f7070d80  f7070dac
f7070d84  8083f72e nt!ExpWorkerThread+0xeb
f7070d88  894d0ed8
f7070d8c  00000000
f7070d90  8a784020
```

```
f7070d94  00000000
f7070d98  00000000
f7070d9c  00000000
f7070da0  00000001
f7070da4  00000000
f7070da8  808f0cb7 nt!PiWalkDeviceList
f7070dac  f7070ddc
f7070db0  8092ccff nt!PspSystemThreadStartup+0x2e
f7070db4  894d0ed8
f7070db8  00000000
f7070dbc  00000000
f7070dc0  00000000
f7070dc4  f7070db8
f7070dc8  f7070410
f7070dcc  ffffffff
f7070dd0  8083b9bc nt!_except_handler3
f7070dd4  808408f8 nt!ObWatchHandles+0x5f4
f7070dd8  00000000
f7070ddc  00000000
f7070de0  80841a96 nt!KiThreadStartup+0x16
f7070de4  8083f671 nt!ExpWorkerThread
```

The last EBP value we are able to get is f7070a04, and we can give it to the extended version of **k** command together with ESP and EIP values of the crash point:

```
1: kd> k L=f7070a04 f7070988 f69d9dd7
ChildEBP RetAddr
f7070998 f69dfbd1 driver+0x14dd7
f7070a40 f7117640 NDIS!ndisMCommonHaltMiniport+0x375
f7070a48 f711891a NDIS!ndisMHaltMiniport+0x21
f7070b74 f71196e5 NDIS!ndisPnPRemoveDevice+0x189
f7070ba4 8083f9d0 NDIS!ndisPnPDispatch+0x15d
f7070bb8 808f6a25 nt!IofCallDriver+0x45
f7070be4 808e20b5 nt!IopSynchronousCall+0xbe
f7070c38 8080beae nt!IopRemoveDevice+0x97
f7070c60 808e149b nt!IopRemoveLockedDeviceNode+0x160
f7070c78 808e18cc nt!IopDeleteLockedDeviceNode+0x50
f7070cac 808e1732 nt!IopDeleteLockedDeviceNodes+0x3f
f7070d40 808e19b6 nt!PiProcessQueryRemoveAndEject+0x7ad
f7070d5c 808e7879 nt!PiProcessTargetDeviceEvent+0x2a
f7070d80 8083f72e nt!PiWalkDeviceList+0x1d2
f7070dac 8092ccff nt!ExpWorkerThread+0xeb
f7070ddc 80841a96 nt!PspSystemThreadStartup+0x2e
00000000 00000000 nt!KiThreadStartup+0x16
```

This was the execution path before the exception. However, when **int 3** instruction was hit, then the processor generated the trap with the interrupt vector 3 (4th entry in interrupt descriptor table, zero-based) and the corresponding function in IDT, *KiTrap03*, was called. Therefore we need to find this function on the same raw stack and try to build the stack trace for our exception handling code path:

```
1: kd> dds esp esp+1000
f70703b4  0000007e
f70703b8  80000003
f70703bc  f69d9dd7 driver+0x14dd7
f70703c0  f70708c0
f70703c4  f70705bc
f70703c8  00000000
f70703cc  f70703e8
f70703d0  809a1eb2 nt!PspUnhandledExceptionInSystemThread+0x1a
f70703d4  0000007e
...
...
...
f7070418 f707043c
f707041c 8083b578 nt!ExecuteHandler2+0x26
f7070420 f70708c0
f7070424 f7070dcc
f7070428 f70705bc
f707042c f70704d8
f7070430 f7070894
f7070434 8083b58c nt!ExecuteHandler2+0x3a
f7070438 f7070dcc
f707043c f70704ec
f7070440 8083b54a nt!ExecuteHandler+0x24
f7070444 f70708c0
...
... (intermediate frames are omitted to save space)
...
f7070890  f7070410
f7070894  f7070dcc
f7070898  8083b9bc nt!_except_handler3
f707089c  80850c10 nt!`string'+0x10c
f70708a0  ffffffff
f70708a4  f7070914
f70708a8  808357a4 nt!CommonDispatchException+0x4a
f70708ac  f70708c0
f70708b0  00000000
f70708b4  f7070914
f70708b8  00000000
f70708bc  00000001
f70708c0  80000003
f70708c4  00000000
f70708c8  00000000
f70708cc  f69d9dd7 driver+0x14dd7
f70708d0  00000003
f70708d4  00000000
f70708d8  8a784020
f70708dc  00000044
f70708e0  ffffffff
f70708e4  00000001
f70708e8  f7737a7c
f70708ec  f7070934
f70708f0  8083f164 nt!KeWaitForSingleObject+0x346
f70708f4  000000c7
```

```
f70708f8  00000000
f70708fc  00000031
f7070900  00000000
f7070904  f707091c
f7070908  80840569 nt!KeSetTimerEx+0x179
f707090c  000000c7
f7070910  80835f39 nt!KiTrap03+0xb0
f7070914  00004000
```

The last EBP value we are able to get is f7070418, and the following stack trace emerges, albeit not accurate as it doesn't show that *KeBugCheckEx* was called from *PspUnhandledExceptionInSystemThread* as can be seen from disassembly. However, it does show that the main function that orchestrates our stack unwinding is *KiDispatchException*:

```
1: kd> k L=f7070418
ChildEBP RetAddr
f7070418 8083b578 nt!KeBugCheckEx+0x1b
f707043c 8083b54a nt!ExecuteHandler2+0x26
f70704ec 80810664 nt!ExecuteHandler+0x24
f70708a4 808357a4 nt!KiDispatchException+0x131
f707090c 80835f39 nt!CommonDispatchException+0x4a
f707090c f69d9dd8 nt!KiTrap03+0xb0
```

```
1: kd> uf nt!PspUnhandledExceptionInSystemThread
nt!PspUnhandledExceptionInSystemThread:
809a1e98 8bff            mov     edi,edi
809a1e9a 55              push    ebp
809a1e9b 8bec            mov     ebp,esp
809a1e9d 8b4d08          mov     ecx,dword ptr [ebp+8]
809a1ea0 ff7104          push    dword ptr [ecx+4]
809a1ea3 8b01            mov     eax,dword ptr [ecx]
809a1ea5 50              push    eax
809a1ea6 ff700c          push    dword ptr [eax+0Ch]
809a1ea9 ff30            push    dword ptr [eax]
809a1eab 6a7e            push    7Eh
809a1ead e8f197edff      call    nt!KeBugCheckEx (8087b6a3)
```

In the end, to illustrate this bugcheck, I created the following UML sequence diagram (trap processing that leads to *KiDispatchException* will be depicted in another post):

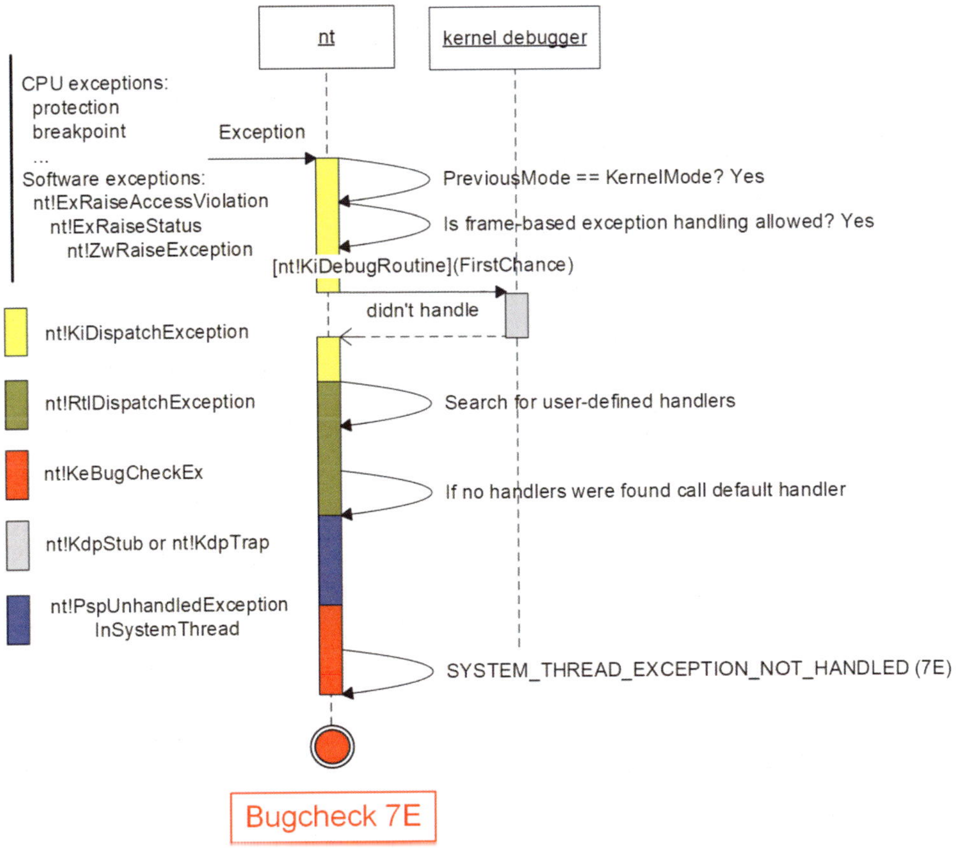
nt
kernel debugger
CPU exceptions:
protection
breakpoint
...
Software exceptions:
nt!ExRaiseAccessViolation
nt!ExRaiseStatus
nt!ZwRaiseException
Exception
PreviousMode == KernelMode? Yes
Is frame-based exception handling allowed? Yes
[nt!KiDebugRoutine](FirstChance)
didn't handle
nt!KiDispatchException
nt!RtlDispatchException
Search for user-defined handlers
nt!KeBugCheckEx
If no handlers were found call default handler
nt!KdpStub or nt!KdpTrap
nt!PspUnhandledException
InSystemThread
SYSTEM_THREAD_EXCEPTION_NOT_HANDLED (7E)
Bugcheck 7E

CAFF

userdump.sys generates it from userdump.exe request when process monitoring rules in Process Dumper from Microsoft userdump package are set to "Bugcheck after dumping":

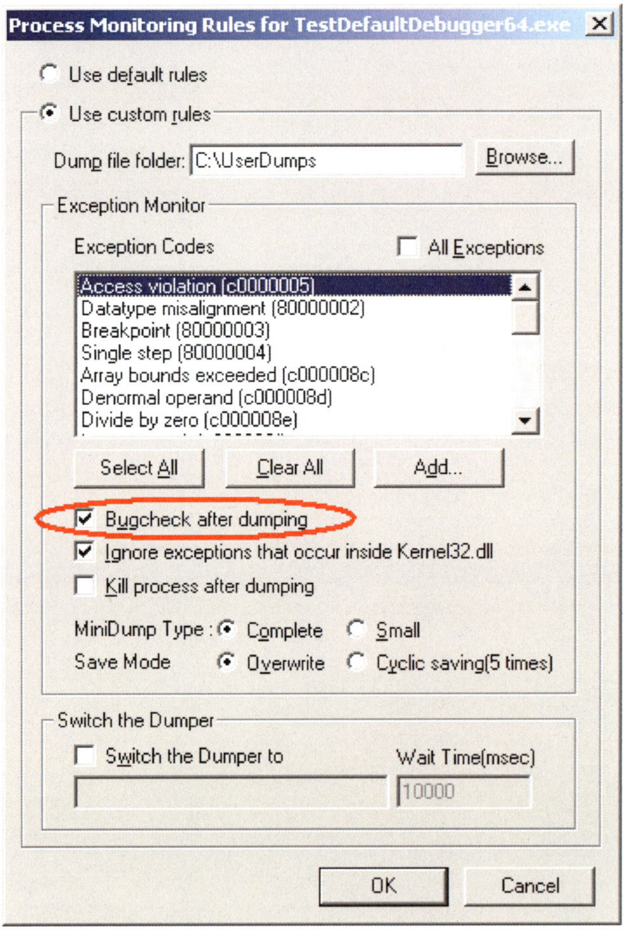


```
BUGCHECK_STR:  0xCAFF

PROCESS_NAME:  userdump.exe
```

```
kd> kL
Child-SP          RetAddr           Call Site
fffffadf`dfcf19b8 fffffadf`dfee38c4 nt!KeBugCheck
fffffadf`dfcf19c0 fffff800`012ce9cf userdump!UdIoctl+0x104
fffffadf`dfcf1a70 fffff800`012df026 nt!IopXxxControlFile+0xa5a
fffffadf`dfcf1b90 fffff800`010410fd nt!NtDeviceIoControlFile+0x56
fffffadf`dfcf1c00 00000000`77ef0a5a nt!KiSystemServiceCopyEnd+0x3
00000000`01eadd58 00000001`0000a755 ntdll!NtDeviceIoControlFile+0xa
00000000`01eadd60 00000000`77ef30a5
userdump_100000000!UdServiceWorkerAPC+0x1005
00000000`01eaf970 00000000`77ef0a2a ntdll!KiUserApcDispatcher+0x15
00000000`01eafe68 00000001`00007fe2 ntdll!NtWaitForSingleObject+0xa
00000000`01eafe70 00000001`00008a39
userdump_100000000!UdServiceWorker+0xb2
00000000`01eaff20 000007ff`7fee4db6
userdump_100000000!UdServiceStart+0x139
00000000`01eaff50 00000000`77d6b6da ADVAPI32!ScSvcctrlThreadW+0x25
00000000`01eaff80 00000000`00000000 kernel32!BaseThreadStart+0x3a
```

This might be useful if we want to see kernel data that happened to be at the exception time. In this case, we can avoid requesting a complete memory dump of physical memory and ask for kernel memory dump only together with a user dump.

Note: Do not set this option if you are unsure. It can have your production servers blu-escreen in the case of false positive dumps.

CF

Bugcheck CF name is the second longest one:

```
TERMINAL_SERVER_DRIVER_MADE_INCORRECT_MEMORY_REFERENCE (cf)
Arguments:
Arg1: a020b1d4, memory referenced
Arg2: 00000000, value 0 = read operation, 1 = write operation
Arg3: a020b1d4, If non-zero, the instruction address which referenced the
bad memory
 address.
Arg4: 00000000, Mm internal code.
 A driver has been incorrectly ported to Terminal Server. It is
referencing session space addresses from the system process
context.  Probably from queueing an item to a system worker thread. The
broken driver's name is displayed on the screen.
```

Although bugcheck explanation mentions only system process context, it can also happen in an arbitrary process context. Recall that kernel space address mapping is usually considered as persistent where virtual-to-physical mapping doesn't change between switching threads that belong to different processes. However, there is so-called session space in multi-user terminal services environments where different users can use different display drivers, for example:

- MS RDP users - RDPDD.DLL
- Citrix ICA users - VDTW30.DLL
- Vista users - TSDDD.DLL
- Console user - Some H/W related video drivers like ATI or NVIDIA

These drivers are not committed at the same time persistently since OS boot although their module addresses might remain fixed. Therefore, when a new user session is created the appropriate display driver corresponding to terminal services protocol is loaded and mapped to the so-called session space starting from A0000000 (x86) or FFFFF90000000000 (x64) after *win32k.sys* address range (on the first usage) and then committed to physical memory by proper PTE entries in process page tables. During thread switch, if the new process context belongs to a different session with a different display driver, the current display driver is decommitted by clearing its PTEs, and the new driver is committed by setting its proper PTE entries.

Therefore, in the system process context like worker threads, virtual addresses corresponding to display driver code, and data may be unknown. This can also happen in an arbitrary process context if we access the code that belongs to a display driver that doesn't correspond to the current session protocol. This can be illustrated with the following example where TSDD can be either RDP or ICA display driver.

In the list of loaded modules we can see that ATI and TSDD drivers are loaded:

```
0: kd> lm
start    end        module name
...
...
...
77d30000 77d9f000   RPCRT4     (deferred)
77e10000 77e6f000   USER32     (deferred)
77f40000 77f7c000   GDI32      (deferred)
77f80000 77ffc000   ntdll      (pdb symbols)
78000000 78045000   MSVCRT     (deferred)
7c2d0000 7c335000   ADVAPI32   (deferred)
7c340000 7c34f000   Secur32    (deferred)
7c570000 7c624000   KERNEL32   (deferred)
7cc30000 7cc70000   winsrv     (deferred)
80062000 80076f80   hal        (deferred)
80400000 805a2940   nt         (pdb symbols)
a0000000 a0190ce0   win32k     (pdb symbols)
a0191000 a01e8000   ati2drad   (deferred)
a01f0000 a0296000   tsdd       (no symbols)
b4a60000 b4a72320   naveng     (deferred)
b4a73000 b4b44c40   navex15    (deferred)

...
...
```

The bugcheck happens in *3rd-partyApp* process context running inside some terminal session:

```
PROCESS_NAME:  3rd-partyApp.exe

TRAP_FRAME:  b475f84c -- (.trap 0xffffffffb475f84c)
ErrCode = 00000000
eax=a020b1d4 ebx=00000000 ecx=04e0443b edx=ffffffff esi=a21b6778
edi=a201b018
eip=a020b1d4 esp=b475f8c0 ebp=b475f900 iopl=3 nv up ei pl zr na pe nc
cs=0008 ss=0010 ds=0023 es=0023 fs=0030 gs=0000 efl=00013246
TSDD+0x1b1d4:
a020b1d4 ??              ???
```

Examining display driver virtual address shows that it is unknown (PTE is NULL):

```
0: kd> !pte a020b1d4
A020B1D4  - PDE at C0300A00        PTE at C028082C
          contains 14AB6863      contains 00000000
        pfn 14ab6 -DA-KWV       not valid
```

ATI display driver address is unknown too:

```
0: kd> !pte a0191000
A0191000  - PDE at C0300A00        PTE at C0280644
          contains 3E301863      contains 00000000
        pfn 3e301 -DA-KWV       not valid
```

Let's switch to another terminal session:

```
PROCESS 87540a60  SessionId: 45  Cid: 3954    Peb: 7ffdf000  ParentCid:
0164
    DirBase: 2473d000  ObjectTable: 889b2c48  TableSize: 182.
    Image: csrss.exe

0: kd> .process /r /p 87540a60
Implicit process is now 87540a60
Loading User Symbols
................
```

Now TSDD display driver address is valid:

```
0: kd> !pte a020b1d4
A020B1D4   - PDE at C0300A00        PTE at C028082C
           contains 5D2C2863      contains 20985863
         pfn 5d2c2 -DA-KWV    pfn 20985 -DA-KWV
```

but ATI driver address is not. It is unknown, and this is expected because no real display hardware is used:

```
0: kd> !pte a0191000
A0191000   - PDE at C0300A00        PTE at C0280644
           contains 5D2C2863      contains 00000000
         pfn 5d2c2 -DA-KWV       not valid
```

Let's switch to session 0 where the display is "physical":

```
PROCESS 8898a5e0  SessionId: 0  Cid: 0180    Peb: 7ffdf000  ParentCid:
0164
    DirBase: 14c58000  ObjectTable: 8898b948  TableSize: 1322.
    Image: csrss.exe

0: kd> .process /r /p 8898a5e0
Implicit process is now 8898a5e0
Loading User Symbols
..............
```

TSDD driver address is unknown, and this is expected too because we no longer use terminal services protocol:

```
0: kd> !pte a020b1d4
A020B1D4   - PDE at C0300A00        PTE at C028082C
           contains 14AB6863      contains 00000000
         pfn 14ab6 -DA-KWV       not valid
```

However, ATI display driver addresses are not unknown (not NULL), and their two selected pages are either in transition or in a page file:

```
0: kd> !pte a0191000
A0191000  - PDE at C0300A00        PTE at C0280644
            contains 14AB6863      contains 156DD882
          pfn 14ab6 -DA-KWV       not valid
                                  Transition:  156dd
                                  Protect:  4

0: kd> !pte a0198000
A0198000  - PDE at C0300A00        PTE at C0280660
            contains 14AB6863      contains 000B9060
          pfn 14ab6 -DA-KWV       not valid
                                  PageFile    0
                                  Offset b9
                                  Protect:  3
```

Manual Stack Trace Reconstruction

This is a small case study to complement **Incorrect Stack Trace** pattern (page 288) and show how to reconstruct stack trace manually based on an example with complete source code.

For it, I created a small working multithreaded program:

```
#include "stdafx.h"
#include <stdio.h>
#include <process.h>

typedef void (*REQ_JUMP)();
typedef void (*REQ_RETURN)();

const char str[] = "\0\0\0\0\0\0\0";

bool loop = true;

void return_func()
{
  puts("Return Func");
  loop = false;
  _endthread();
}

void jump_func()
{
  puts("Jump Func");
}

void internal_func_2(void *param_jump,void *param_return)
{
  REQ_JUMP f_jmp = (REQ_JUMP)param_jump;
  REQ_RETURN f_ret = (REQ_RETURN)param_return;

  puts("Internal Func 2");
  // Uncomment memcpy to crash the program
  // Overwrite f_jmp and f_ret with NULL
  // memcpy(&f_ret, str, sizeof(str));
  __asm
  {
     push f_ret;
     mov  eax, f_jmp
     mov  ebp, 0 // use ebp as a general purpose register
     jmp  eax
  }
}
```

```
void internal_func_1(void *param)
{
  puts("Internal Func 1");
  internal_func_2(param, &return_func);
}

void thread_request(void *param)
{
  puts("Request");
  internal_func_1(param);
}

int _tmain(int argc, _TCHAR* argv[])
{
  _beginthread(thread_request, 0, (void *)jump_func);
  while (loop);
  return 0;
}
```

I had to disable optimizations in the Visual C++ compiler; otherwise, most of the code would have been eliminated because the program is very small and easy for code optimizer. If we run the program, it displays the following output:

```
Request
Internal Func 1
Internal Func 2
Jump Func
Return Func
```

internal_func_2 gets two parameters: the function address to jump and the function address to call upon the return. The latter sets the *loop* variable to *false* to break infinite main thread loop and calls *_endthread.* Why do we need this complexity in the small sample? Because I wanted to simulate FPO optimization in an inner function call and also gain control over a return address. This is why I set EBP to zero before jumping and pushed the custom return address, which I can change any time. If I used the *call* instruction, then the processor would have determined the return address as the next instruction address.

The code also copies two *internal_func_2* parameters into local variables *f_jmp* and *f_ret* because the commented *memcpy* call is crafted to overwrite them with zeroes and do not touch the saved EBP, return address, and function arguments. This is all to make the stack trace incorrect, but at the same time to make manual stack reconstruction as easy as possible in this example.

Let's suppose that the *memcpy* call is a bug that overwrites local variables. Then we obviously have a crash because EAX is zero and jump to a zero address will cause an access violation. EBP is also 0 because we assigned 0 to it explicitly. Let's pretend that we wanted to pass some constant via EBP, and it is zero.

What we have now:

EBP is 0
EIP is 0
Return address is 0

When we load a crash dump WinDbg is utterly confused because it has no clue on how to reconstruct the stack trace:

```
This dump file has an exception of interest stored in it.
The stored exception information can be accessed via .ecxr.
(bd0.ec8): Access violation - code c0000005 (first/second chance not
available)
eax=00000000 ebx=00595620 ecx=00000002 edx=00000000 esi=00000000
edi=00000000
eip=00000000 esp=0069ff54 ebp=00000000 iopl=0 nv up ei pl nz ac po nc
cs=0023 ss=002b ds=002b es=002b fs=0053 gs=002b efl=00010212
00000000 ??              ???

0:001> kv
ChildEBP RetAddr  Args to Child
WARNING: Frame IP not in any known module. Following frames may be wrong.
0069ff50 00000000 00000000 00000000 0069ff70 0x0
```

Fortunately, ESP is not zero, so we can look at the raw stack:

```
0:001> dds esp
0069ff54  00000000
0069ff58  00000000
0069ff5c  00000000
0069ff60  0069ff70
0069ff64  0040187f WrongIP!internal_func_1+0x1f
0069ff68  00401830 WrongIP!jump_func
0069ff6c  00401840 WrongIP!return_func
0069ff70  0069ff7c
0069ff74  0040189c WrongIP!thread_request+0xc
0069ff78  00401830 WrongIP!jump_func
0069ff7c  0069ffb4
0069ff80  78132848 msvcr80!_endthread+0x4b
0069ff84  00401830 WrongIP!jump_func
0069ff88  aa75565b
0069ff8c  00000000
0069ff90  00000000
```

```
0069ff94  00595620
0069ff98  c0000005
0069ff9c  0069ff88
0069ffa0  0069fb34
0069ffa4  0069ffdc
0069ffa8  78138cd9 msvcr80!_except_handler4
0069ffac  d207e277
0069ffb0  00000000
0069ffb4  0069ffec
0069ffb8  781328c8 msvcr80!_endthread+0xcb
0069ffbc  7d4dfe21 kernel32!BaseThreadStart+0x34
0069ffc0  00595620
0069ffc4  00000000
0069ffc8  00000000
0069ffcc  00595620
0069ffd0  c0000005
```

Here we can start searching for the following pairs:

```
EBP:          PreviousEBP
              Function return address
...
...
...
PreviousEBP:  PrePreviousEBP
              Function return address
...
...
...
```

For example:

```
0:001> dds esp
0069ff54 00000000
0069ff58 00000000
0069ff5c 00000000
0069ff60 0069ff70
0069ff64 0040187f WrongIP!internal_func_1+0x1f
0069ff68 00401830 WrongIP!jump_func
0069ff6c 00401840 WrongIP!return_func
0069ff70 0069ff7c
0069ff74 0040189c WrongIP!thread_request+0xc
0069ff78 00401830 WrongIP!jump_func
0069ff7c 0069ffb4
```

This is based on the fact that a function call saves its return address, and the standard function prolog saves the previous EBP value and sets ESP to point to it.

```
push ebp
mov ebp, esp
```

Therefore our stack looks like this:

```
0:001> dds esp
0069ff54 00000000
0069ff58 00000000
0069ff5c 00000000
0069ff60 0069ff70
0069ff64 0040187f WrongIP!internal_func_1+0x1f
0069ff68 00401830 WrongIP!jump_func
0069ff6c 00401840 WrongIP!return_func
0069ff70 0069ff7c
0069ff74 0040189c WrongIP!thread_request+0xc
0069ff78 00401830 WrongIP!jump_func
0069ff7c 0069ffb4
0069ff80 78132848 msvcr80!_endthread+0x4b
0069ff84 00401830 WrongIP!jump_func
0069ff88 aa75565b
0069ff8c 00000000
0069ff90 00000000
0069ff94 00595620
0069ff98 c0000005
0069ff9c 0069ff88
0069ffa0 0069fb34
0069ffa4 0069ffdc
0069ffa8 78138cd9 msvcr80!_except_handler4
0069ffac d207e277
0069ffb0 00000000
0069ffb4 0069ffec
0069ffb8 781328c8 msvcr80!_endthread+0xcb
0069ffbc 7d4dfe21 kernel32!BaseThreadStart+0x34
0069ffc0 00595620
0069ffc4 00000000
0069ffc8 00000000
0069ffcc 00595620
0069ffd0 c0000005
```

We also double check return addresses to see if they are valid code indeed. The best way is to disassemble them backward. This should show call instructions resulted in saved return addresses:

```
0:001> ub WrongIP!internal_func_1+0x1f
WrongIP!internal_func_1+0x1:
00401871 mov     ebp,esp
00401873 push    offset WrongIP!GS_ExceptionPointers+0x38 (00402124)
00401878 call    dword ptr [WrongIP!_imp__puts (004020ac)]
0040187e add     esp,4
00401881 push    offset WrongIP!return_func (00401850)
00401886 mov     eax,dword ptr [ebp+8]
00401889 push    eax
0040188a call    WrongIP!internal_func_2 (004017e0)
```

```
0:001> ub WrongIP!thread_request+0xc
WrongIP!internal_func_1+0x2d:
0040189d int     3
0040189e int     3
0040189f int     3
WrongIP!thread_request:
004018a0 push    ebp
004018a1 mov     ebp,esp
004018a3 mov     eax,dword ptr [ebp+8]
004018a6 push    eax
004018a7 call    WrongIP!internal_func_1 (00401870)

0:001> ub msvcr80!_endthread+0x4b
msvcr80!_endthread+0x2f:
7813282c pop     esi
7813282d push    0Ch
7813282f push    offset msvcr80!__rtc_tzz+0x64 (781b4b98)
78132834 call    msvcr80!_SEH_prolog4 (78138c80)
78132839 call    msvcr80!_getptd (78132e29)
7813283e and     dword ptr [ebp-4],0
78132842 push    dword ptr [eax+58h]
78132845 call    dword ptr [eax+54h]

0:001> ub msvcr80!_endthread+0xcb
msvcr80!_endthread+0xaf:
781328ac mov     edx,dword ptr [ecx+58h]
781328af mov     dword ptr [eax+58h],edx
781328b2 mov     edx,dword ptr [ecx+4]
781328b5 push    ecx
781328b6 mov     dword ptr [eax+4],edx
781328b9 call    msvcr80!_freefls (78132e41)
781328be call    msvcr80!_initp_misc_winxfltr (781493c1)
781328c3 call    msvcr80!_endthread+0x30 (7813282d)

0:001> ub BaseThreadStart+0x34
kernel32!BaseThreadStart+0x10:
7d4dfdfd mov     eax,dword ptr fs:[00000018h]
7d4dfe03 cmp     dword ptr [eax+10h],1E00h
7d4dfe0a jne     kernel32!BaseThreadStart+0x2e (7d4dfe1b)
7d4dfe0c cmp     byte ptr [kernel32!BaseRunningInServerProcess
(7d560008)],0
7d4dfe13 jne     kernel32!BaseThreadStart+0x2e (7d4dfe1b)
7d4dfe15 call    dword ptr [kernel32!_imp__CsrNewThread (7d4d0310)]
7d4dfe1b push    dword ptr [ebp+0Ch]
7d4dfe1e call    dword ptr [ebp+8]
```

Now we can use an extended version of **k** command and supply custom EBP, ESP and EIP values. We set EBP to the first found address of EBP:PreviousEBP pair, and set EIP to 0:

```
0:001> k L=0069ff60 0069ff60 0
ChildEBP RetAddr
WARNING: Frame IP not in any known module. Following frames may be wrong.
0069ff5c 0069ff70 0x0
0069ff60 0040188f 0x69ff70
0069ff70 004018ac WrongIP!internal_func_1+0x1f
0069ff7c 78132848 WrongIP!thread_request+0xc
0069ffb4 781328c8 msvcr80!_endthread+0x4b
0069ffb8 7d4dfe21 msvcr80!_endthread+0xcb
0069ffec 00000000 kernel32!BaseThreadStart+0x34
```

The stack trace looks good because it also shows *BaseThreadStart*. From the backward disassembly of the return address *WrongIP!internal_func_1+0x1f* we see that *internal_func_1* calls *internal_func_2* so we can disassemble the latter function:

```
0:001> uf internal_func_2
Flow analysis was incomplete, some code may be missing
WrongIP!internal_func_2:
   28 004017e0 push    ebp
   28 004017e1 mov     ebp,esp
   28 004017e3 sub     esp,8
   29 004017e6 mov     eax,dword ptr [ebp+8]
   29 004017e9 mov     dword ptr [ebp-4],eax
   30 004017ec mov     ecx,dword ptr [ebp+0Ch]
   30 004017ef mov     dword ptr [ebp-8],ecx
   32 004017f2 push    offset WrongIP!GS_ExceptionPointers+0x28 (00402114)
   32 004017f7 call    dword ptr [WrongIP!_imp__puts (004020ac)]
   32 004017fd add     esp,4
   33 00401800 push    8
   33 00401802 push    offset WrongIP!GS_ExceptionPointers+0x8 (004020f4)
   33 00401807 lea     edx,[ebp-8]
   33 0040180a push    edx
   33 0040180b call    WrongIP!memcpy (00401010)
   33 00401810 add     esp,0Ch
   35 00401813 push    dword ptr [ebp-8]
   36 00401816 mov     eax,dword ptr [ebp-4]
   37 00401819 mov     ebp,0
   38 0040181e jmp     eax
```

We see that it takes some value from [ebp-8], puts it into EAX, and then jumps to that address. The function uses standard prolog (in bold), and therefore EBP-4 is the local variable. From the code, we see that it comes from [EBP+8], which is the first function parameter:

```
EBP+C: second parameter
EBP+8: first parameter
EBP+4: return address
EBP:   previous EBP
EBP-4: local variable
EBP-8: local variable
```

If we examine the first parameter, we would see that it is the valid function address that we were supposed to call:

```
0:001> kv L=0069ff60 0069ff60 0
ChildEBP RetAddr  Args to Child
WARNING: Frame IP not in any known module. Following frames may be wrong.
0069ff5c 0069ff70 0040188f 00401830 00401850 0x0
0069ff60 0040188f 00401830 00401850 0069ff7c 0x69ff70
0069ff70 004018ac 00401830 0069ffb4 78132848 WrongIP!internal_func_1+0x1f
0069ff7c 78132848 00401830 6d5ba283 00000000 WrongIP!thread_request+0xc
0069ffb4 781328c8 7d4dfe21 00595620 00000000 msvcr80!_endthread+0x4b
0069ffb8 7d4dfe21 00595620 00000000 00000000 msvcr80!_endthread+0xcb
0069ffec 00000000 7813286e 00595620 00000000 kernel32!BaseThreadStart+0x34
```

```
0:001> u 00401830
WrongIP!jump_func:
00401830 push    ebp
00401831 mov     ebp,esp
00401833 push    offset WrongIP!GS_ExceptionPointers+0x1c (00402108)
00401838 call    dword ptr [WrongIP!_imp__puts (004020ac)]
0040183e add     esp,4
00401841 pop     ebp
00401842 ret
00401843 int     3
```

However, if we look at the code, we see that we call *memcpy* with EBP-8 address, and the number of bytes to copy is 8. In pseudo-code it looks like:

```
memcpy(ebp-8, 004020f4, 8);
```

```
   33 00401800 push     8
   33 00401802 push     offset WrongIP!GS_ExceptionPointers+0x8 (004020f4)
   33 00401807 lea      edx,[ebp-8]
   33 0040180a push     edx
   33 0040180b call     WrongIP!memcpy (00401010)
   33 00401810 add      esp,0Ch
```

If we examine 004020f4 address, we see that it contains 8 zeroes:

```
0:001> db 004020f4 l8
004020f4  00 00 00 00 00 00 00 00
```

Therefore, *memcpy* overwrites our local variables that contain a jump address with zeroes. This explains why we have jumped to 0 address and why EIP was zero.

Finally our reconstructed stack trace looks like this:

```
WrongIP!internal_func_2+offset ; here we jump
WrongIP!internal_func_1+0x1f
WrongIP!thread_request+0xc
msvcr80!_endthread+0x4b
msvcr80!_endthread+0xcb
kernel32!BaseThreadStart+0x34
```

This was based on the fact that ESP was valid. If we have zero or invalid ESP, we can look at the entire raw stack range from the thread environment block (TEB). Use **!teb** command to get thread stack range. In my example, this command doesn't work due to the lack of proper MS symbols, but it reports the TEB address, and we can dump it:

```
0:001> !teb
TEB at 7efda000
error InitTypeRead( TEB )...

0:001> dd 7efda000 l3
7efda000 0069ffa4 006a0000 0069e000
```

Usually, the second doubleword is the stack limit, and the third is the stack base address, so we can dump the range and start reconstructing stack trace for our example from the bottom of the stack (*BaseThreadStart*), or look after exception handling calls (shown in bold):

```
0:001> dds 0069e000 006a0000
0069e000  00000000
0069e004  00000000
...
...
...
0069fb24  7d535b43 kernel32!UnhandledExceptionFilter+0x851
...
...
...
0069fbb0  0069fc20
0069fbb4  7d6354c9 ntdll!RtlDispatchException+0x11f
0069fbb8  0069fc38
0069fbbc  0069fc88
0069fc1c  00000000
0069fc20  00000000
0069fc24  7d61dd26 ntdll!NtRaiseException+0x12
0069fc28  7d61ea51 ntdll!KiUserExceptionDispatcher+0x29
0069fc2c  0069fc38
```

```
...
...
...
0069ff38  00000000
0069ff3c  00000000
0069ff40  00000000
0069ff44  00000000
0069ff48  00000000
0069ff4c  00000000
0069ff50  00000000
0069ff54  00000000
0069ff58  00000000
0069ff5c  00000000
0069ff60  0069ff70
0069ff64  0040188f WrongIP!internal_func_1+0x1f
0069ff68  00401830 WrongIP!jump_func
0069ff6c  00401850 WrongIP!return_func
0069ff70  0069ff7c
0069ff74  004018ac WrongIP!thread_request+0xc
0069ff78  00401830 WrongIP!jump_func
0069ff7c  0069ffb4
0069ff80  78132848 msvcr80!_endthread+0x4b
0069ff84  00401830 WrongIP!jump_func
0069ff88  6d5ba283
0069ff8c  00000000
0069ff90  00000000
0069ff94  00595620
0069ff98  c0000005
0069ff9c  0069ff88
0069ffa0  0069fb34
0069ffa4  0069ffdc
0069ffa8  78138cd9 msvcr80!_except_handler4
0069ffac  152916af
0069ffb0  00000000
0069ffb4  0069ffec
0069ffb8  781328c8 msvcr80!_endthread+0xcb
0069ffbc  7d4dfe21 kernel32!BaseThreadStart+0x34
0069ffc0  00595620
0069ffc4  00000000
...
...
...
```

WinDbg Tips and Tricks

Looking for Strings in a Dump

There are wonderful WinDbg commands **dpu** (UNICODE strings) and **dpa** (ASCII strings) and other **d**** equivalents like **dpp**. For example, we can examine raw stack data and check if any pointers in the stack region are pointing to strings. For example:

```
0:143> !teb
TEB at 7ff2b000
...
    StackBase:              05e90000
    StackLimit:             05e89000
...
...
...
0:143> dpu 05e89000 05e90000
05e8f58c  00120010 ""
...
...
...
05e8f590  77e7723c "Debugger"
05e8f594  00000000
05e8f598  08dc0154
05e8f59c  01000040
05e8f5a0  05e8f5dc "G:\WINDOWS\system32\faultrep.dll"
05e8f5a4  0633adf0 ""
05e8f5a8  00000000
05e8f5ac  00000001
05e8f5b0  00000012
05e8f5b4  7c8723e0
05e8f5b8  ffffffff
05e8f5bc  00000004
05e8f5c0  69500000
05e8f5c4  00000000
05e8f5c8  00000aac
05e8f5cc  00000002
05e8f5d0  05e8f740
05e8f5d4  0633adfc "drwtsn32 -p %ld -e %ld -g"
05e8f5d8  00000000
...
...
...
```

Of course, we can apply these commands not only to stack but also to any memory range.

Tracing Win32 API While Debugging a Process

If we load an executable or attach WinDbg to an existing process then we can use **logexts** debugging extension to trace API calls (in the output below all API parameters and return values are omitted for visual clarity):

```
0:001> !logexts.loge

0:001> !logc e *
All categories enabled.

0:001> !logo e d
  Debugger            Enabled
  Text file           Disabled
  Verbose log         Enabled

0:001> g
Thrd 7c0 77555B59 BeginPaint( 0x001103AA) ...
Thrd 7c0 77555B65 GetClientRect( 0x001103AA) ...
Thrd 7c0 77555B96 DrawEdge( 0x01010072 ...) ...
Thrd 7c0 77555C8A DrawFrameControl( 0x01010072 ...) ...
Thrd 7c0 77555CE1 EndPaint( 0x001103AA ... ) ...
Thrd 7c0 004165F2 TlsGetValue( 0x00000006) ...
Thrd 7c0 4B8D54B5 CallNextHookEx( ... ) ...
Thrd 7c0 0040D7CC GetMessageW( ... ) ...
```

Then we can break in and put a breakpoint at a return address:

```
0:001> bp 0040D7CC

0:001> g
Thrd 7c0 0040D7CC GetMessageW( ... ) ...
Breakpoint 0 hit
ProcessHistory+0xd7cc:
0040d7cc 85c0             test    eax,eax

0:000> u 0040D7C0 0040D7CC
ProcessHistory+0xd7c0:
0040d7c0 50               push    eax
0040d7c1 50               push    eax
0040d7c2 8d7730           lea     esi,[edi+30h]
0040d7c5 56               push    esi
0040d7c6 ff15f8434300     call    dword ptr
[ProcessHistory+0x343f8 (004343f8)]

0:000> dd 004343f8
004343f8  3c001950 3c0018c4 3c00193c 3c0014dc
```

```
0:000> u 3c001950
3c001950 b889020000      mov     eax,289h
3c001955 e98e410014      jmp     logexts!LogHook
(50005ae8)
3c00195a b88a020000      mov     eax,28Ah
3c00195f e984410014      jmp     logexts!LogHook
(50005ae8)
3c001964 b88b020000      mov     eax,28Bh
3c001969 e97a410014      jmp     logexts!LogHook
(50005ae8)
3c00196e b88c020000      mov     eax,28Ch
3c001973 e970410014      jmp     logexts!LogHook
(50005ae8)
```

Here we can see that **logexts** patches import table.

We can trace different API categories:

```
0:001> !logexts.logc
Categories:
  1 AdvApi32                          Enabled
  2 AtomFunctions                     Enabled
  3 AVIFileExports                    Enabled
  4 Clipboard                         Enabled
  5 ComponentObjectModel              Enabled
  6 DebuggingAndErrorHandling         Enabled
  7 DeviceFunctions                   Enabled
  8 Direct3D                          Enabled
  9 DirectDraw                        Enabled
 10 DirectPlay                        Enabled
 11 DirectSound                       Enabled
 12 GDI                               Enabled
 13 HandleAndObjectFunctions          Enabled
 14 HookingFunctions                  Enabled
 15 IOFunctions                       Enabled
 16 MemoryManagementFunctions         Enabled
 17 Multimedia                        Enabled
 18 Printing                          Enabled
 19 ProcessesAndThreads               Enabled
 20 RegistryFunctions                 Enabled
 21 Shell                             Enabled
 22 StringManipulation                Enabled
 23 ThreadLocalStorage                Enabled
 24 User32                            Enabled
 25 User32StringExports               Enabled
 26 Version                           Enabled
 27 WinSock2                          Enabled
```

Exported NTDLL and Kernel Structures

During crash dump analysis or debugging session, we can forget the exact structure name when we want to use it in **dt** WinDbg command. In this case, wildcards can help us: **dt module!***, for example:

```
0:000> dt ntdll!*
          ntdll!LIST_ENTRY64
          ntdll!LIST_ENTRY32
          ntdll!_ULARGE_INTEGER
          ntdll!_LIST_ENTRY
          ntdll!_IMAGE_NT_HEADERS
          ntdll!_IMAGE_FILE_HEADER
          ntdll!_IMAGE_OPTIONAL_HEADER
          ntdll!_IMAGE_NT_HEADERS
          ntdll!_LARGE_INTEGER
          ntdll!_LUID
          ntdll!_KPRCB
          ntdll!_KTHREAD
          ntdll!_KPROCESSOR_STATE
          ntdll!_KSPIN_LOCK_QUEUE
          ntdll!_KNODE
          ntdll!_PP_LOOKASIDE_LIST
          ntdll!_KPRCB
          ntdll!_KDPC_DATA
          ntdll!_KEVENT
          ntdll!_KDPC
          ntdll!_SINGLE_LIST_ENTRY
          ntdll!_FX_SAVE_AREA
          ntdll!_PROCESSOR_POWER_STATE
          ntdll!_KPRCB
          ntdll!_KPCR
          ntdll!_NT_TIB
          ntdll!_EXCEPTION_REGISTRATION_RECORD
          ntdll!_KIDTENTRY
          ntdll!_KGDTENTRY
          ntdll!_KTSS
          ntdll!_KPCR
          ntdll!_KAPC
          ntdll!_SINGLE_LIST_ENTRY
          ntdll!_KDPC_IMPORTANCE
          ntdll!_KDPC
          ntdll!_DISPATCHER_HEADER
          ntdll!_KAPC_STATE
          ntdll!_KWAIT_BLOCK
          ntdll!_KGATE
          ntdll!_KQUEUE
          ntdll!_KTIMER
          ntdll!_KTRAP_FRAME
          ntdll!_KPROCESS
          ntdll!_KSEMAPHORE
          ntdll!_KTHREAD
          ntdll!_KSPIN_LOCK_QUEUE_NUMBER
          ntdll!_FAST_MUTEX
```

```
ntdll!_SLIST_HEADER
ntdll!_NPAGED_LOOKASIDE_LIST
ntdll!_GENERAL_LOOKASIDE
ntdll!_NPAGED_LOOKASIDE_LIST
ntdll!_PAGED_LOOKASIDE_LIST
ntdll!_PP_NPAGED_LOOKASIDE_NUMBER
ntdll!_POOL_TYPE
ntdll!_GENERAL_LOOKASIDE
ntdll!_EX_RUNDOWN_REF
ntdll!_EX_FAST_REF
ntdll!_EX_PUSH_LOCK
ntdll!_EX_PUSH_LOCK_WAIT_BLOCK
ntdll!_EX_PUSH_LOCK_CACHE_AWARE
ntdll!_ETHREAD
ntdll!_TERMINATION_PORT
ntdll!_CLIENT_ID
ntdll!_PS_IMPERSONATION_INFORMATION
ntdll!_DEVICE_OBJECT
ntdll!_EPROCESS
ntdll!_ETHREAD
ntdll!_HANDLE_TABLE
ntdll!_KGUARDED_MUTEX
ntdll!_MM_AVL_TABLE
ntdll!_EJOB
ntdll!_EPROCESS_QUOTA_BLOCK
ntdll!_PAGEFAULT_HISTORY
ntdll!_HARDWARE_PTE_X86
ntdll!_PEB
ntdll!_SE_AUDIT_PROCESS_CREATION_INFO
ntdll!_MMSUPPORT
ntdll!_EPROCESS
ntdll!_OBJECT_HEADER
ntdll!_OBJECT_TYPE
ntdll!_OBJECT_CREATE_INFORMATION
ntdll!_QUAD
ntdll!_OBJECT_HEADER
ntdll!_OBJECT_HEADER_QUOTA_INFO
ntdll!_OBJECT_HEADER_HANDLE_INFO
ntdll!_OBJECT_HANDLE_COUNT_DATABASE
ntdll!_OBJECT_HANDLE_COUNT_ENTRY
ntdll!_OBJECT_HEADER_HANDLE_INFO
ntdll!_OBJECT_HEADER_NAME_INFO
ntdll!_OBJECT_DIRECTORY
ntdll!_UNICODE_STRING
ntdll!_OBJECT_HEADER_NAME_INFO
ntdll!_OBJECT_HEADER_CREATOR_INFO
ntdll!_OBJECT_ATTRIBUTES
ntdll!_ERESOURCE
ntdll!_OBJECT_TYPE_INITIALIZER
ntdll!_OBJECT_TYPE
ntdll!_OBJECT_HANDLE_INFORMATION
ntdll!_PERFINFO_GROUPMASK
ntdll!_KGUARDED_MUTEX
ntdll!_DISPATCHER_HEADER
ntdll!_PF_SCENARIO_TYPE
ntdll!_HANDLE_TRACE_DEBUG_INFO
ntdll!_HANDLE_TABLE
```

```
ntdll!_KWAIT_BLOCK
ntdll!_MMSUPPORT_FLAGS
ntdll!_MMWSL
ntdll!_MMSUPPORT
ntdll!_EPROCESS_QUOTA_ENTRY
ntdll!_EPROCESS_QUOTA_BLOCK
ntdll!_UNICODE_STRING
ntdll!_NT_TIB
ntdll!_PS_JOB_TOKEN_FILTER
ntdll!_IO_COUNTERS
ntdll!_EJOB
ntdll!_PEB_LDR_DATA
ntdll!_RTL_USER_PROCESS_PARAMETERS
ntdll!_RTL_CRITICAL_SECTION
ntdll!_PEB_FREE_BLOCK
ntdll!_ACTIVATION_CONTEXT_DATA
ntdll!_ASSEMBLY_STORAGE_MAP
ntdll!_PEB
ntdll!_KGATE
ntdll!_IMAGE_FILE_HEADER
ntdll!_RTL_STACK_TRACE_ENTRY
ntdll!_PEB_FREE_BLOCK
ntdll!_KSPIN_LOCK_QUEUE
ntdll!_PP_LOOKASIDE_LIST
ntdll!_KEXECUTE_OPTIONS
ntdll!_KPROCESS
ntdll!_PEB_LDR_DATA
ntdll!_DPH_BLOCK_INFORMATION
ntdll!_SECURITY_IMPERSONATION_LEVEL
ntdll!_PS_IMPERSONATION_INFORMATION
ntdll!_EPROCESS_QUOTA_ENTRY
ntdll!_FNSAVE_FORMAT
ntdll!_FX_SAVE_AREA
ntdll!PROCESSOR_IDLE_TIMES
ntdll!PROCESSOR_PERF_STATE
ntdll!_PROCESSOR_POWER_STATE
ntdll!_IO_COUNTERS
ntdll!_KiIoAccessMap
ntdll!_KTSS
ntdll!_KIDTENTRY
ntdll!_MMSUPPORT_FLAGS
ntdll!_HEAP
ntdll!_HEAP_ENTRY
ntdll!_HEAP_TAG_ENTRY
ntdll!_HEAP_UCR_SEGMENT
ntdll!_HEAP_UNCOMMMTTED_RANGE
ntdll!_HEAP_SEGMENT
ntdll!_HEAP_PSEUDO_TAG_ENTRY
ntdll!_HEAP_LOCK
ntdll!_HEAP
ntdll!_TERMINATION_PORT
ntdll!LSA_FOREST_TRUST_RECORD_TYPE
ntdll!_HEAP_UNCOMMMTTED_RANGE
ntdll!_OBJECT_HANDLE_COUNT_DATABASE
ntdll!_FNSAVE_FORMAT
ntdll!PROCESSOR_PERF_STATE
ntdll!PROCESSOR_IDLE_TIMES
```

```
ntdll!_HANDLE_TRACE_DB_ENTRY
ntdll!_HANDLE_TRACE_DEBUG_INFO
ntdll!_PROCESS_WS_WATCH_INFORMATION
ntdll!_PAGEFAULT_HISTORY
ntdll!_SECURITY_QUALITY_OF_SERVICE
ntdll!_OBJECT_CREATE_INFORMATION
ntdll!_MMADDRESS_NODE
ntdll!_MM_AVL_TABLE
ntdll!_HARDWARE_PTE_X86
ntdll!_HEAP_ENTRY
ntdll!_GENERIC_MAPPING
ntdll!_OBJECT_DUMP_CONTROL
ntdll!_OB_OPEN_REASON
ntdll!_ACCESS_STATE
ntdll!_SECURITY_OPERATION_CODE
ntdll!_OBJECT_NAME_INFORMATION
ntdll!_OBJECT_TYPE_INITIALIZER
ntdll!_LARGE_INTEGER
ntdll!_RTL_TRACE_BLOCK
ntdll!_HEAP_UCR_SEGMENT
ntdll!_KEXECUTE_OPTIONS
ntdll!_OWNER_ENTRY
ntdll!_ERESOURCE
ntdll!_GENERIC_MAPPING
ntdll!_SID_AND_ATTRIBUTES
ntdll!_LUID_AND_ATTRIBUTES
ntdll!_PS_JOB_TOKEN_FILTER
ntdll!_MEMORY_CACHING_TYPE_ORIG
ntdll!_KiIoAccessMap
ntdll!_EXCEPTION_DISPOSITION
ntdll!_EXCEPTION_RECORD
ntdll!_CONTEXT
ntdll!_EXCEPTION_REGISTRATION_RECORD
ntdll!_DRIVER_OBJECT
ntdll!_IRP
ntdll!_IO_TIMER
ntdll!_VPB
ntdll!_WAIT_CONTEXT_BLOCK
ntdll!_KDEVICE_QUEUE
ntdll!_DEVOBJ_EXTENSION
ntdll!_DEVICE_OBJECT
ntdll!_PROCESS_WS_WATCH_INFORMATION
ntdll!_SECURITY_QUALITY_OF_SERVICE
ntdll!_FLOATING_SAVE_AREA
ntdll!_CONTEXT
ntdll!_IMAGE_DATA_DIRECTORY
ntdll!_IMAGE_OPTIONAL_HEADER
ntdll!_KUSER_SHARED_DATA
ntdll!_KSYSTEM_TIME
ntdll!_NT_PRODUCT_TYPE
ntdll!_ALTERNATIVE_ARCHITECTURE_TYPE
ntdll!_KUSER_SHARED_DATA
ntdll!_QUAD
ntdll!_KAPC_STATE
ntdll!_MODE
ntdll!_HEAP_PSEUDO_TAG_ENTRY
ntdll!_RTL_CRITICAL_SECTION_DEBUG
```

```
ntdll!_RTL_CRITICAL_SECTION
ntdll!_HEAP_SEGMENT
ntdll!_KTRAP_FRAME
ntdll!_KGDTENTRY
ntdll!_KDEVICE_QUEUE_ENTRY
ntdll!_IO_ALLOCATION_ACTION
ntdll!_WAIT_CONTEXT_BLOCK
ntdll!_KTIMER
ntdll!_MDL
ntdll!_IO_STATUS_BLOCK
ntdll!_IO_STACK_LOCATION
ntdll!_FILE_OBJECT
ntdll!_IRP
ntdll!_VPB
ntdll!_KOBJECTS
ntdll!_KSEMAPHORE
ntdll!_MMADDRESS_NODE
ntdll!_CURDIR
ntdll!_RTL_DRIVE_LETTER_CURDIR
ntdll!_RTL_USER_PROCESS_PARAMETERS
ntdll!_OWNER_ENTRY
ntdll!_SE_AUDIT_PROCESS_CREATION_INFO
ntdll!_OBJECT_HANDLE_COUNT_ENTRY
ntdll!_CLIENT_ID
ntdll!_RTL_TRACE_DATABASE
ntdll!_RTL_TRACE_SEGMENT
ntdll!_RTL_TRACE_DATABASE
ntdll!_HEAP_LOCK
ntdll!_HANDLE_TRACE_DB_ENTRY
ntdll!ReplacesCorHdrNumericDefines
ntdll!_MEMORY_TYPE
ntdll!_IO_TIMER
ntdll!_FXSAVE_FORMAT
ntdll!_OBJECT_DIRECTORY_ENTRY
ntdll!_DEVICE_MAP
ntdll!_OBJECT_DIRECTORY
ntdll!_STACK_TRACE_DATABASE
ntdll!_KDPC_DATA
ntdll!_STRING
ntdll!_RTL_DRIVE_LETTER_CURDIR
ntdll!_SID_AND_ATTRIBUTES
ntdll!_DPH_HEAP_ROOT
ntdll!_DPH_HEAP_BLOCK
ntdll!_RTL_AVL_TABLE
ntdll!_DPH_HEAP_ROOT
ntdll!_DEVICE_OBJECT_POWER_EXTENSION
ntdll!_DEVOBJ_EXTENSION
ntdll!_FLOATING_SAVE_AREA
ntdll!_KSYSTEM_TIME
ntdll!_KQUEUE
ntdll!_RTL_BALANCED_LINKS
ntdll!_RTL_GENERIC_COMPARE_RESULTS
ntdll!_RTL_AVL_TABLE
ntdll!_HEAP_TAG_ENTRY
ntdll!_RTL_CRITICAL_SECTION_DEBUG
ntdll!_MDL
ntdll!_DPH_HEAP_BLOCK
```

```
ntdll!_PS_QUOTA_TYPE
ntdll!_flags
ntdll!_KNODE
ntdll!_LDR_DATA_TABLE_ENTRY
ntdll!_ACTIVATION_CONTEXT
ntdll!_LDR_DATA_TABLE_ENTRY
ntdll!_TEB
ntdll!_ACTIVATION_CONTEXT_STACK
ntdll!_GDI_TEB_BATCH
ntdll!_TEB_ACTIVE_FRAME
ntdll!_TEB
ntdll!_KEVENT
ntdll!_IO_STATUS_BLOCK
ntdll!_RTL_TRACE_SEGMENT
ntdll!_SECURITY_SUBJECT_CONTEXT
ntdll!_INITIAL_PRIVILEGE_SET
ntdll!_PRIVILEGE_SET
ntdll!_ACCESS_STATE
ntdll!_KSPECIAL_REGISTERS
ntdll!_KPROCESSOR_STATE
ntdll!_STRING
ntdll!_flags
ntdll!_REG_NOTIFY_CLASS
ntdll!_OBJECT_DUMP_CONTROL
ntdll!_SECURITY_SUBJECT_CONTEXT
ntdll!_RTL_ACTIVATION_CONTEXT_STACK_FRAME
ntdll!_ACTIVATION_CONTEXT_STACK
ntdll!_MMSYSTEM_PTE_POOL_TYPE
ntdll!_KDEVICE_QUEUE
ntdll!_LUID_AND_ATTRIBUTES
ntdll!_EXCEPTION_RECORD
ntdll!_INITIAL_PRIVILEGE_SET
ntdll!_TEB_ACTIVE_FRAME_CONTEXT
ntdll!_TEB_ACTIVE_FRAME
ntdll!_OBJECT_NAME_INFORMATION
ntdll!_SECTION_OBJECT_POINTERS
ntdll!_IO_COMPLETION_CONTEXT
ntdll!_FILE_OBJECT
ntdll!_IO_COMPLETION_CONTEXT
ntdll!_DRIVER_EXTENSION
ntdll!_FAST_IO_DISPATCH
ntdll!_DRIVER_OBJECT
ntdll!_IO_CLIENT_EXTENSION
ntdll!_FS_FILTER_CALLBACKS
ntdll!_DRIVER_EXTENSION
ntdll!_TEB_ACTIVE_FRAME_CONTEXT
ntdll!_IMAGE_DATA_DIRECTORY
ntdll!_CURDIR
ntdll!_GDI_TEB_BATCH
ntdll!_RTL_BALANCED_LINKS
ntdll!_KDEVICE_QUEUE_ENTRY
ntdll!_SECTION_OBJECT_POINTERS
ntdll!_IO_CLIENT_EXTENSION
ntdll!_IO_SECURITY_CONTEXT
ntdll!_NAMED_PIPE_CREATE_PARAMETERS
ntdll!_MAILSLOT_CREATE_PARAMETERS
ntdll!_FILE_INFORMATION_CLASS
```

```
ntdll!_FSINFOCLASS
ntdll!_SCSI_REQUEST_BLOCK
ntdll!_FILE_GET_QUOTA_INFORMATION
ntdll!_DEVICE_RELATION_TYPE
ntdll!_GUID
ntdll!_INTERFACE
ntdll!_DEVICE_CAPABILITIES
ntdll!_IO_RESOURCE_REQUIREMENTS_LIST
ntdll!BUS_QUERY_ID_TYPE
ntdll!DEVICE_TEXT_TYPE
ntdll!_DEVICE_USAGE_NOTIFICATION_TYPE
ntdll!_SYSTEM_POWER_STATE
ntdll!_POWER_SEQUENCE
ntdll!_POWER_STATE_TYPE
ntdll!_POWER_STATE
ntdll!POWER_ACTION
ntdll!_CM_RESOURCE_LIST
ntdll!_IO_STACK_LOCATION
ntdll!_INTERFACE
ntdll!_DEVICE_POWER_STATE
ntdll!_POWER_STATE
ntdll!_FS_FILTER_CALLBACK_DATA
ntdll!_FS_FILTER_CALLBACKS
ntdll!_DEVICE_MAP
ntdll!_INTERFACE_TYPE
ntdll!_IO_RESOURCE_LIST
ntdll!_IO_RESOURCE_REQUIREMENTS_LIST
ntdll!_SID
ntdll!_FILE_GET_QUOTA_INFORMATION
ntdll!_FS_FILTER_PARAMETERS
ntdll!_FS_FILTER_CALLBACK_DATA
ntdll!_FILE_BASIC_INFORMATION
ntdll!_FILE_STANDARD_INFORMATION
ntdll!_FILE_NETWORK_OPEN_INFORMATION
ntdll!_COMPRESSED_DATA_INFO
ntdll!_FAST_IO_DISPATCH
ntdll!_FILE_BASIC_INFORMATION
ntdll!_PRIVILEGE_SET
ntdll!_DESCRIPTOR
ntdll!_KSPECIAL_REGISTERS
ntdll!_RTL_ACTIVATION_CONTEXT_STACK_FRAME
ntdll!_MAILSLOT_CREATE_PARAMETERS
ntdll!_NAMED_PIPE_CREATE_PARAMETERS
ntdll!_IO_RESOURCE_DESCRIPTOR
ntdll!_IO_RESOURCE_LIST
ntdll!_FILE_NETWORK_OPEN_INFORMATION
ntdll!_CM_FULL_RESOURCE_DESCRIPTOR
ntdll!_CM_RESOURCE_LIST
ntdll!_POWER_SEQUENCE
ntdll!_IO_RESOURCE_DESCRIPTOR
ntdll!_FS_FILTER_SECTION_SYNC_TYPE
ntdll!_FS_FILTER_PARAMETERS
ntdll!_COMPRESSED_DATA_INFO
ntdll!_FILE_STANDARD_INFORMATION
ntdll!_DESCRIPTOR
ntdll!_GUID
ntdll!_SID_IDENTIFIER_AUTHORITY
```

```
ntdll!_SID
ntdll!_SID_IDENTIFIER_AUTHORITY
ntdll!_CM_PARTIAL_RESOURCE_LIST
ntdll!_CM_FULL_RESOURCE_DESCRIPTOR
ntdll!_DEVICE_CAPABILITIES
ntdll!_CM_PARTIAL_RESOURCE_DESCRIPTOR
ntdll!_CM_PARTIAL_RESOURCE_LIST
ntdll!_CM_PARTIAL_RESOURCE_DESCRIPTOR
ntdll!__unnamed
```

Many structures are listed twice in the output. Actually, all of them appear twice, and there are many __unnamed (I edited the output to omit those). Visual Studio contains DIA SDK (Debug Interface Access SDK), and we can build DIA2Dump sample to dump PDB files. Unfortunately, this tool displays them twice too, without any hints:

```
UDT            : LIST_ENTRY32
Data           :   this+0x0, Member, Type: unsigned long, Flink
Data           :   this+0x4, Member, Type: unsigned long, Blink
UDT            : LIST_ENTRY32
Data           :   this+0x0, Member, Type: unsigned long, Flink
Data           :   this+0x4, Member, Type: unsigned long, Blink
```

__unnamed data type is for unions, for example:

```
0:000> dt -r _ULARGE_INTEGER
   +0x000 LowPart            : Uint4B
   +0x004 HighPart           : Uint4B
   +0x000 u                  : __unnamed
      +0x000 LowPart            : Uint4B
      +0x004 HighPart           : Uint4B
   +0x000 QuadPart           : Uint8B
```

To compare, here's the definition taken from *winnt.h*:

```
typedef union _ULARGE_INTEGER
{
   struct
   {
      DWORD LowPart;
      DWORD HighPart;
   };
   struct
   {
      DWORD LowPart;
      DWORD HighPart;
   } u;
   ULONGLONG QuadPart;
} ULARGE_INTEGER, *PULARGE_INTEGER;
```

Easy List Traversing

WinDbg **dt** command can be used for traversing linked lists. Many structures have LIST_ENTRY as their first member, and it is much easier to use **dt** command than **!list** command. For example:

```
0:000> dt _MYBIGSTRUCTURE
   +0x000 Links : _LIST_ENTRY
    ...
   +0x080 SomeName : [33] Uint2B

0:000> dd component!MyBigStructureListHead l1
01022cd0  0007fe58

0:000> .enable_unicode 1
```

The following command outputs the whole list of structures:

```
0:000> dt _MYBIGSTRUCTURE -l Links.Flink 0007fe58
```

And the following command outputs the list of *SomeName* members:

```
0:000> dt _MYBIGSTRUCTURE -l Links.Flink -y SomeName 0007fe58
Links.Flink at 0x7fe58
   +0x000 Links :   [ 0x8e090 - 0x1022cd0 ]
   +0x080 SomeName : [33]  "Foo"
Links.Flink at 0x8e090
   +0x000 Links :   [ 0x913f8 - 0x7fe58 ]
   +0x080 SomeName : [33]  "Bar"
```

If we don't remember exact member name we can specify the partial name and any member that matches would be shown:

```
0:000> dt _MYBIGSTRUCTURE -l Links.Flink -y S 0007fe58
```

However, if our structure doesn't have LIST_ENTRY as its first member, then we need to subtract its offset, for example:

```
kd> dd nt!PsActiveProcessHead l1
808af068  85fa48b0
```

```
kd> dt _EPROCESS
   +0x000 Pcb              : _KPROCESS
   +0x078 ProcessLock      : _EX_PUSH_LOCK
   +0x080 CreateTime       : _LARGE_INTEGER
   +0x088 ExitTime         : _LARGE_INTEGER
   +0x090 RundownProtect   : _EX_RUNDOWN_REF
   +0x094 UniqueProcessId  : Ptr32 Void
   +0x098 ActiveProcessLinks : _LIST_ENTRY

kd> dt _EPROCESS -l ActiveProcessLinks.Flink -y ImageFileName 85fa48b0-
0x98
ActiveProcessLinks.Flink at 0x85fa4818
   +0x098 ActiveProcessLinks :  [ 0x85d1ce20 - 0x808af068 ]
   +0x164 ImageFileName : [16]  "System"
ActiveProcessLinks.Flink at 0x85d1cd88
   +0x098 ActiveProcessLinks :  [ 0x85dba6b8 - 0x85fa48b0 ]
   +0x164 ImageFileName : [16]  "smss.exe"
ActiveProcessLinks.Flink at 0x85dba620
   +0x098 ActiveProcessLinks :  [ 0x858d20b8 - 0x85d1ce20 ]
   +0x164 ImageFileName : [16]  "csrss.exe"
ActiveProcessLinks.Flink at 0x858d2020
   +0x098 ActiveProcessLinks :  [ 0x858c20b8 - 0x85dba6b8 ]
   +0x164 ImageFileName : [16]  "winlogon.exe"
ActiveProcessLinks.Flink at 0x858c2020
   +0x098 ActiveProcessLinks :  [ 0x8589f0b8 - 0x858d20b8 ]
   +0x164 ImageFileName : [16]  "services.exe"
```

Here is another example, not involving LIST_ENTRY but rather a classic single list forward pointer:

```
0:000> !teb
TEB at 7FFDE000
    ExceptionList:      6fc54
    Stack Base:         70000
    Stack Limit:        6d000
    SubSystemTib:       0
    FiberData:          1e00
    ArbitraryUser:      0
    Self:               7ffde000
    EnvironmentPtr:     0
    ClientId:           22c.228
    Real ClientId:      22c.228
    RpcHandle:          0
    Tls Storage:        742b8
    PEB Address:        7ffdf000
    LastErrorValue:     997
    LastStatusValue:    103
    Count Owned Locks:0
    HardErrorsMode:     0
```

```
0:000> dt -r _TEB
   +0x000 NtTib : _NT_TIB
      +0x000 ExceptionList : Ptr32 _EXCEPTION_REGISTRATION_RECORD
         +0x000 Next : Ptr32 _EXCEPTION_REGISTRATION_RECORD
         +0x004 Handler : Ptr32
      +0x004 StackBase : Ptr32 Void
      +0x008 StackLimit : Ptr32 Void
      +0x00c SubSystemTib : Ptr32 Void
      +0x010 FiberData : Ptr32 Void
      +0x010 Version : Uint4B
      +0x014 ArbitraryUserPointer : Ptr32 Void
      +0x018 Self : Ptr32 _NT_TIB

0:000> dt _EXCEPTION_REGISTRATION_RECORD -l Next 7FFDE000
Next at 0x7ffde000
   +0x000 Next : 0x0006fc54 _EXCEPTION_REGISTRATION_RECORD
   +0x004 Handler : 0x00070000 +70000
Next at 0x6fc54
   +0x000 Next : 0x0006fcfc _EXCEPTION_REGISTRATION_RECORD
   +0x004 Handler : 0x7c5c1f44 KERNEL32!_except_handler3+0
Next at 0x6fcfc
   +0x000 Next : 0x0006ff5c _EXCEPTION_REGISTRATION_RECORD
   +0x004 Handler : 0x7c2e5649 ADVAPI32!_except_handler3+0
Next at 0x6ff5c
   +0x000 Next : 0x0006ffb0 _EXCEPTION_REGISTRATION_RECORD
   +0x004 Handler : 0x7c2e5649 ADVAPI32!_except_handler3+0
Next at 0x6ffb0
   +0x000 Next : 0x0006ffe0 _EXCEPTION_REGISTRATION_RECORD
   +0x004 Handler : 0x01015878 component!_except_handler3+0
Next at 0x6ffe0
   +0x000 Next : 0xffffffff _EXCEPTION_REGISTRATION_RECORD
   +0x004 Handler : 0x7c5c1f44 KERNEL32!_except_handler3+0
```

Suspending Threads

Suspending threads during live kernel debugging session can be useful for debugging or reproducing race condition issues. For example, when we have one thread that depends on another thread that finishes its work earlier. Sometimes, very rarely, the latter thread finishes after the moment the first thread would expect it. To model this race condition, we can simply patch the prolog code of the second thread worker function with **ret** instruction. This has the same effect as suspending the thread, so it cannot produce the required data.

Note: **~n** (suspend) and **~f** (freeze) are for user mode live debugging only.

Heap Stack Traces

If we have user mode stack trace DB enabled on Windows 2003 Server for some service or application and we get a crash dump and try to get saved stack traces using **!heap** extension command we might get these errors:

```
0:000> !heap -k -h 000a0000
    Heap entries for Segment00 in Heap 000a0000
        000a0c50: 00c50 . 00040 [01] - busy (40)
        000a0c90: 00040 . 01818 [07] - busy (1800), tail fill - unable to
read heap entry extra at 000a24a0
        000a24a8: 01818 . 00030 [07] - busy (18), tail fill - unable to
read heap entry extra at 000a24d0
        000a24d8: 00030 . 005a0 [07] - busy (588), tail fill - unable to
read heap entry extra at 000a2a70
```

The solution was to use old Windows 2000 extension *ntsdexts.dll*:

```
0:000> !.\w2kfre\ntsdexts.heap -k -h 000a0000
Stack trace (12) at 1021bfc:
   7c85fc22: ntdll!RtlAllocateHeapSlowly+0x00000041
   7c81d4df: ntdll!RtlAllocateHeap+0x00000E9F
   7c83467a: ntdll!LdrpAllocateUnicodeString+0x00000035
   7c8354f4: ntdll!LdrpCopyUnicodeString+0x00000031
   7c83517b: ntdll!LdrpResolveDllName+0x00000195
   7c834b2a: ntdll!LdrpMapDll+0x0000014F
   7c837474: ntdll!LdrpLoadImportModule+0x0000017C
   7c837368: ntdll!LdrpHandleOneNewFormatImportDescriptor+0x0000004D
   7c837317: ntdll!LdrpHandleNewFormatImportDescriptors+0x0000001D
   7c837441: ntdll!LdrpWalkImportDescriptor+0x00000195
   7c80f560: ntdll!LdrpInitializeProcess+0x00000E3E
   7c80ea0b: ntdll!_LdrpInitialize+0x000000D0
   7c82ec2d: ntdll!KiUserApcDispatcher+0x00000025
```

An example on how to enable user mode stack trace DB:

http://support.citrix.com/article/CTX106970

A note for the revised edition: this old extension is no longer included in the modern WinDbg distributions. We keep this article for historical reasons.

Hypertext Commands

Recent versions of WinDbg have a RichEdit command output window that allows syntax highlighting and can simulate hyperlinks.

A tooltip from Window2Dump shows its window class:

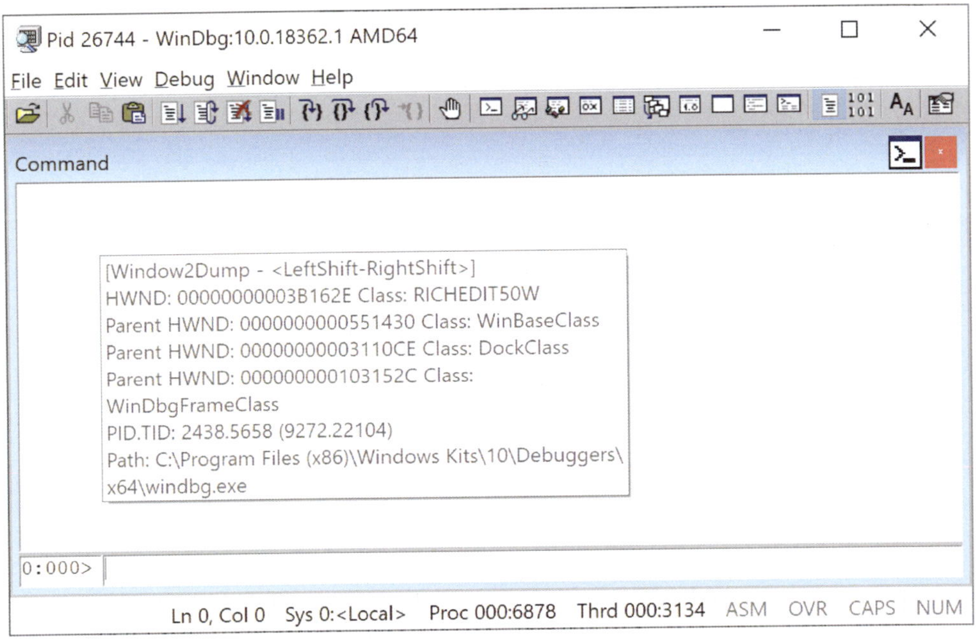

There is also Debugger Markup Language (DML) and new commands that take advantage of it. For documentation, please look at dml.doc located in your Debugging Tools for Windows folder.

Here is the output of some commands. The modern versions of WinDbg automatically enable this DML mode for commands, so the output of **k** and **kM**, **lm** and **lmD** are identical.

!dml_proc

```
0: kd> !dml_proc
Address            PID  Image file name
ffffa90b`1186c380 4    System
ffffa90b`118c0080 58   Registry
ffffa90b`14a66040 148  smss.exe
ffffa90b`1410d140 1a0  csrss.exe
ffffa90b`15513080 1ec  wininit.exe
ffffa90b`1410b080 1f4  csrss.exe
ffffa90b`1556f140 238  winlogon.exe
ffffa90b`15583080 278  services.exe
ffffa90b`14a1b080 28c  lsass.exe
ffffa90b`14a34240 2f4  svchost.exe
ffffa90b`15c41140 310  fontdrvhost.ex
ffffa90b`15c43140 318  fontdrvhost.ex
ffffa90b`15c45240 324  svchost.exe
ffffa90b`15c6c480 368  WUDFHost.exe
ffffa90b`15ccf2c0 3b4  svchost.exe
ffffa90b`15d16380 3f0  svchost.exe
ffffa90b`15d7a080 198  LogonUI.exe
ffffa90b`15d7c080 1a4  dwm.exe
ffffa90b`15dd8240 3d0  svchost.exe
ffffa90b`15e0c300 418  svchost.exe
[...]
```

Here we can click on a process link and get the list of threads:

```
0: kd> !dml_proc 0xffffa90b15513080
Address            PID  Image file name
ffffa90b`15513080 1ec  wininit.exe       Full details

Select user-mode state      Release user-mode state
Browse kernel module list   Browse user module list
Browse full module list

Thread s:
    Address            TID
    ffffa90b`14129080 1f0
    ffffa90b`14125040 214
    ffffa90b`15517140 248
    ffffa90b`14a32080 2a0
    ffffa90b`14929040 2f0
```

We can click either on "Full details" link or on an individual thread link to see its call stack. If we select "user-mode state" link we switch to process context automatically (useful for complete memory dumps):

```
0: kd> .process /p /r 0xffffa90b15513080
Implicit process is now 0xffffa90b15513080
Loading User Symbols
```

We can also navigate frames and local variables very easily:

```
0:007> !dml_proc
DbgId  PID    Image file name
0      6878   C:\WINDOWS\system32\notepad.exe

0:007> !dml_proc 0x0
DbgId  PID    Image file name
0      6878   C:\WINDOWS\system32\notepad.exe

Browse module list

Threads:
    DbgId  TID    Name (if available)
    0      3134   "<No name>"
    1      5a94   "<No name>"
    2      6238   "<No name>"
    3      59a0   "<No name>"
    4      640    "<No name>"
    5      5104   "<No name>"
    6      6e6c   "<No name>"
    7      599c   "<No name>"
```

If we click on a thread name (<No name> here) we get its context:

```
0:007> ~[0x0]s;kM
win32u!NtUserGetMessage+0x14:
00007ffb`8f701164 c3              ret
 # Child-SP          RetAddr           Call Site
00 000000b2`6b72f878 00007ffb`90cf3a4d win32u!NtUserGetMessage+0x14
01 000000b2`6b72f880 00007ff6`3cfaa3e3 USER32!GetMessageW+0x2d
02 000000b2`6b72f8e0 00007ff6`3cfc02c7 notepad!WinMain+0x293
03 000000b2`6b72f9b0 00007ffb`91417bd4 notepad!__mainCRTStartup+0x19f
04 000000b2`6b72fa70 00007ffb`9266ced1 KERNEL32!BaseThreadInitThunk+0x14
05 000000b2`6b72faa0 00000000`00000000 ntdll!RtlUserThreadStart+0x21
```

Clicking on a number sets the scope and shows local variables (if we have full PDB files):

```
0:000> dx
Debugger.Sessions[0].Processes[26744].Threads[12596].Stack.Frames[1].Switc
hTo();dv /t /v
Debugger.Sessions[0].Processes[26744].Threads[12596].Stack.Frames[1].Switc
hTo()

0:000> dx
Debugger.Sessions[0].Processes[26744].Threads[12596].Stack.Frames[3].Switc
hTo();dv /t /v
Debugger.Sessions[0].Processes[26744].Threads[12596].Stack.Frames[3].Switc
hTo()
```

Similar command is **kM**:

```
0:000> kM
 # Child-SP          RetAddr           Call Site
00 000000b2`6b72f878 00007ffb`90cf3a4d win32u!NtUserGetMessage+0x14
01 000000b2`6b72f880 00007ff6`3cfaa3e3 USER32!GetMessageW+0x2d
02 000000b2`6b72f8e0 00007ff6`3cfc02c7 notepad!WinMain+0x293
03 000000b2`6b72f9b0 00007ffb`91417bd4 notepad!__mainCRTStartup+0x19f
04 000000b2`6b72fa70 00007ffb`9266ced1 KERNEL32!BaseThreadInitThunk+0x14
05 000000b2`6b72faa0 00000000`00000000 ntdll!RtlUserThreadStart+0x21
```

Another useful command is **lmD** where we can easily inspect modules:

```
0:000> lmD
start             end                 module name
00007ff6`3cfa0000  00007ff6`3cfd2000       notepad            (pdb   symbols)
C:\ProgramData\dbg\sym\notepad.pdb\8633727A5D343C61309AA6D139FC9DD41\notep
ad.pdb
00007ffb`573f0000 00007ffb`574c7000   efswrt       (deferred)
00007ffb`6c730000 00007ffb`6c7ce000   TextInputFramework    (deferred)
00007ffb`75e70000 00007ffb`76116000   iertutil     (deferred)
00007ffb`766f0000 00007ffb`76802000   MrmCoreR     (deferred)
00007ffb`78610000 00007ffb`7862b000   MPR          (deferred)
00007ffb`7c4d0000 00007ffb`7c535000   oleacc       (deferred)
00007ffb`7c550000 00007ffb`7c7d5000   COMCTL32     (deferred)
00007ffb`89f00000 00007ffb`8a22a000   CoreUIComponents    (deferred)
00007ffb`8a630000 00007ffb`8a783000   wintypes     (deferred)
[...]

0:000> lmDvmnotepad
Browse full module list
start             end                 module name
00007ff6`3cfa0000  00007ff6`3cfd2000       notepad            (pdb   symbols)
C:\ProgramData\dbg\sym\notepad.pdb\8633727A5D343C61309AA6D139FC9DD41\notep
ad.pdb
    Loaded symbol image file: C:\WINDOWS\system32\notepad.exe
    Image path: C:\WINDOWS\system32\notepad.exe
    Image name: notepad.exe
    Browse all global symbols  functions  data
    Image was built with /Brepro flag.
    Timestamp:        6E3B99C1 (This is a reproducible build file hash, not
a timestamp)
    CheckSum:         0002C69F
    ImageSize:        00032000
    File version:     10.0.18362.693
    Product version:  10.0.18362.693
    File flags:       0 (Mask 3F)
    File OS:          40004 NT Win32
    File type:        1.0 App
    File date:        00000000.00000000
    Translations:     0409.04b0
[...]
```

Analyzing Hangs Faster

Google search shows that the additional parameter (**-hang**) to the venerable **!analyze -v** command is rarely used. Here is the command that we can use if we get a manually generated dump, and there is no exception in it reported by **!analyze -v**, and subsequent visual inspection of **~*kv** output doesn't show anything suspicious that is leading to hidden exception(s):

!analyze -hang -v

Then we should always double-check with **!locks** command because there could be multiple hang conditions in a crash dump.

The same parameter can be used for kernel memory dumps too. But double-checking ERESOURCE locks (**!locks**), kernel threads (**!stacks**), and DPC queues (**!dpcs**) manually is highly recommended.

Triple Dereference

WinDbg commands like **dpp** allow us to do double dereference in the following format:

```
pointer *pointer **pointer
```

For example:

```
0:000> dpp 004015a2
004015a2  00405068 7c80929c kernel32!GetTickCount
```

There are cases where we need triple dereference (or even quadruple dereference) done on a range of memory. Here we can utilize WinDbg scripts. The key is to use **$p** pseudo-register which shows the last value of **d*** commands (**dd**, **dps**, etc.):

```
.for (r $t0=00000000`004015a2, $t1=4; @$t1 >= 0; r $t1=$t1-1,
$t0=$t0+$ptrsize) { dps @$t0 l1; dps $p l1; dps $p l1; .printf "\n" }
```

where **$t0** and **$t1** are pseudo-registers holding the starting address of a memory block (we use 64-bit format) and the number of objects to be triple dereferenced and displayed. **$ptrsize** is a pointer size. The script is platform independent (can be used on both 32-bit and 64-bit targets). For example:

```
004015a2  00405068 component!_imp__GetTickCount
00405068  7c80929c kernel32!GetTickCount
7c80929c  fe0000ba

004015a6  458df033
458df033  ????????
458df033  ????????

004015aa  15ff50f0
15ff50f0  ????????
15ff50f0  ????????

004015ae  00405064 component!_imp__QueryPerformanceCounter
00405064  7c80a427 kernel32!QueryPerformanceCounter
7c80a427  8b55ff8b

004015b2  33f4458b
33f4458b  ????????
33f4458b  ????????
```

If we want quadruple dereferenced memory, we just need to add the additional **dps @$t0 l1;** to **.for** loop body. With this script even double dereference looks much better because it shows symbol information for the first dereference too whereas **dpp** command shows symbol name only for the second dereference.

Another less "elegant" variation without **$p** pseudo-register uses **poi** operator, but we need a **.catch** block to prevent the script termination on invalid memory access:

```
0:000> .for (r $t0=00000000`004015a2, $t1=4; @$t1 >= 0; r $t1=$t1-1,
$t0=$t0+$ptrsize) { .catch { dds $t0 l1; dds poi($t0) l1; dds
poi(poi($t0)) l1; }; .printf "\n" }

004015a2  00405068 component!_imp__GetTickCount
00405068  7c80929c kernel32!GetTickCount
7c80929c  fe0000ba

004015a6  458df033
458df033  ????????
Memory access error at ') '

004015aa  15ff50f0
15ff50f0  ????????
Memory access error at ') '

004015ae  00405064 component!_imp__QueryPerformanceCounter
00405064  7c80a427 kernel32!QueryPerformanceCounter
7c80a427  8b55ff8b

004015b2  33f4458b
33f4458b  ????????
Memory access error at ') '
```

We can also use **!list** extension but more formatting is necessary:

```
0:000> .for (r $t0=00000000`004015a2, $t1=4; @$t1 >= 0; r $t1=$t1-1,
$t0=$t0+$ptrsize) { .printf "%p:\n---------\n\n", $t0; !list -x "dds
@$extret l1" $t0; .printf "\n" }
004015a2:
---------
004015a2  00405068 component!_imp__GetTickCount
00405068  7c80929c kernel32!GetTickCount
7c80929c  fe0000ba
fe0000ba  ????????
Cannot read next element at fe0000ba
004015a6:
---------
004015a6  458df033
458df033  ????????
Cannot read next element at 458df033
004015aa:
---------
```

```
004015aa  15ff50f0
15ff50f0  ????????
Cannot read next element at 15ff50f0
004015ae:
---------
004015ae  00405064 component!_imp__QueryPerformanceCounter
00405064  7c80a427 kernel32!QueryPerformanceCounter
7c80a427  8b55ff8b
8b55ff8b  ????????
Cannot read next element at 8b55ff8b
004015b2:
---------
004015b2  33f4458b
33f4458b  ????????
Cannot read next element at 33f4458b
```

The advantage of **!list** is in unlimited number of pointer dereferences until invalid address is reached.

Finding a Needle in a Hay

There is a good WinDbg command to list unique threads in a process. Some processes have so many threads that it is difficult to find anomalies in the output of **~*kv** command, especially when most threads are similar, for example, waiting for LPC reply. In this case, we can use **!uniqstack** command to list only threads with unique call stacks and then list duplicate thread numbers.

```
0:046> !uniqstack
Processing 51 threads, please wait

.  0  Id: 1d50.1dc0 Suspend: 1 Teb: 7fffe000 Unfrozen
      Priority: 0  Priority class: 32
ChildEBP RetAddr
0012fbcc 7c821b84 ntdll!KiFastSystemCallRet
0012fbd0 77e4189f ntdll!NtReadFile+0xc
0012fc38 77f795ab kernel32!ReadFile+0x16c
0012fc64 77f7943c ADVAPI32!ScGetPipeInput+0x2a
0012fcd8 77f796c1 ADVAPI32!ScDispatcherLoop+0x51
0012ff3c 004018fb ADVAPI32!StartServiceCtrlDispatcherW+0xe3
...
...
...

. 26  Id: 1d50.44ec Suspend: 1 Teb: 7ffaf000 Unfrozen
      Priority: 1  Priority class: 32
ChildEBP RetAddr
0752fea0 7c822124 ntdll!KiFastSystemCallRet
0752fea4 77e6bad8 ntdll!NtWaitForSingleObject+0xc
0752ff14 77e6ba42 kernel32!WaitForSingleObjectEx+0xac
0752ff28 1b00999e kernel32!WaitForSingleObject+0x12
0752ff34 1b009966 msjet40!Semaphore::Wait+0xe
0752ff5c 1b00358c msjet40!Queue::GetMessageW+0xc9
0752ffb8 77e6608b msjet40!System::WorkerThread+0x41
0752ffec 00000000 kernel32!BaseThreadStart+0x34
...
...
...

Total threads: 51
Duplicate callstacks: 31 (windbg thread #s follow):
3, 4, 5, 7, 8, 9, 10, 11, 12, 13, 14, 15, 16, 17, 19, 21, 22, 23, 27, 28,
29, 33, 39, 40, 41, 42, 43, 44, 47, 49, 50
```

```
0:046> ~49kL
ChildEBP RetAddr
0c58fe18 7c821c54 ntdll!KiFastSystemCallRet
0c58fe1c 77c7538c ntdll!ZwReplyWaitReceivePortEx+0xc
0c58ff84 77c5778f RPCRT4!LRPC_ADDRESS::ReceiveLotsaCalls+0x198
0c58ff8c 77c5f7dd RPCRT4!RecvLotsaCallsWrapper+0xd
0c58ffac 77c5de88 RPCRT4!BaseCachedThreadRoutine+0x9d
0c58ffb8 77e6608b RPCRT4!ThreadStartRoutine+0x1b
0c58ffec 00000000 kernel32!BaseThreadStart+0x34

0:046> ~47kL
ChildEBP RetAddr
0b65fe18 7c821c54 ntdll!KiFastSystemCallRet
0b65fe1c 77c7538c ntdll!ZwReplyWaitReceivePortEx+0xc
0b65ff84 77c5778f RPCRT4!LRPC_ADDRESS::ReceiveLotsaCalls+0x198
0b65ff8c 77c5f7dd RPCRT4!RecvLotsaCallsWrapper+0xd
0b65ffac 77c5de88 RPCRT4!BaseCachedThreadRoutine+0x9d
0b65ffb8 77e6608b RPCRT4!ThreadStartRoutine+0x1b
0b65ffec 00000000 kernel32!BaseThreadStart+0x34
```

Guessing Stack Trace

Sometimes, instead of looking at raw stack data to identify all modules that might have been involved in a problem thread, we can use the following old Windows 2000 kdex2x86 WinDbg extension command that can even work with Windows 2003 or XP kernel memory dumps:

```
4: kd> !w2kfre\kdex2x86.stack -?
!stack - Do stack trace for specified thread
Usage : !stack [-?ha[0|1]] [address]
Arguments :
 -?,-h - display help information.
 -a - specifies display mode. This option is off, in default. If this
option is specified, output stack trace in detail.
 -0,-1 - specifies filter level for display. Default filter level is 0. In
level 0, display stackframes that are guessed return-adresses for reason
of its value and previous mnemonic. In level 1, display stackframes that
call other stackframe or is called by other stackframe, besides level 0.
 address - specifies thread address. When address is omitted, do stack
trace for the current thread.
```

For example:

```
Loading Dump File [MEMORY.DMP]
Kernel Summary Dump File: Only kernel address space is available
Windows Server 2003 Kernel Version 3790 (Service Pack 2) MP (8 procs) Free
x86 compatible
Product: Server, suite: Enterprise TerminalServer
Built by: 3790.srv03_sp2_gdr.070304 2240
Kernel base = 0x80800000 PsLoadedModuleList = 0x808a6ea8
Debug session time: Mon Jun 11 14:49:21.541 2007 (GMT+1)
System Uptime: 0 days 2:10:11.877

4: kd> k
ChildEBP RetAddr
b7a24e84 80949b48 nt!KeBugCheckEx+0x1b
b7a24ea0 80949ba4 nt!PspUnhandledExceptionInSystemThread+0x1a
b7a25ddc 8088e062 nt!PspSystemThreadStartup+0x56
00000000 00000000 nt!KiThreadStartup+0x16

4: kd> !w2kfre\kdex2x86.stack
T. Address  RetAddr  Called Procedure
*2 B7A24E68 80827C63 nt!KeBugCheck2(0000007E, C0000005, BFE5FEEA,...);
*2 B7A24E88 80949B48 nt!KeBugCheckEx(0000007E, C0000005, BFE5FEEA,...);
*2 B7A24EA4 80949BA4 nt!PspUnhandledExceptionInSystemThread(B7A24EC8,
80881801, B7A24ED0,...);
*0 B7A24EAC 80881801 dword ptr EAX(B7A24ED0, 00000000, B7A24ED0,...);
*1 B7A24ED4 8088ED4E dword ptr ECX(B7A25378, B7A25DCC, B7A25074,...);
*1 B7A24EF8 8088ED20 nt!ExecuteHandler2(B7A25378, B7A25DCC, B7A25074,...);
```

```
*1 B7A24F1C 80877C0C nt!RtlpExecuteHandlerForException(B7A25378, B7A25DCC,
B7A25074,...);
*0 B7A24F5C 808914F7 nt!RtlClearBits(893E3BF8, 0000014A, 00000001,...);
*1 B7A24FA8 8082D58F nt!RtlDispatchException(B7A25378, B7A25074,
00000008,...);
*1 B7A2501C 80A5C456 hal!HalpCheckForSoftwareInterrupt(89267D08, 00000000,
89267D00,...);
*1 B7A25030 80A5C456 hal!HalpCheckForSoftwareInterrupt(00000000, 89267D00,
B7A25060,...);
*1 B7A25040 80A5A56D hal!KfLowerIrql(8087C9C0, BC910000, 00000018,...);
*1 B7A25044 8087C9C0 hal!KeReleaseInStackQueuedSpinLock(BC910000,
00000018, BFEBC0A0,...);
*1 B7A25064 8087CA95 nt!ExReleaseResourceLite(B7A253CC, B7A25078,
B7A25378,...);
*0 B7A250F4 F346C646 termdd!IcaCallNextDriver(88F9E2A4, 00000002,
00000000,...);
*1 B7A25140 F764C20E termdd!_IcaCallSd(88F9E290, 00000002, B7A251EC,...);
*1 B7A25154 F3464959 termdd!IcaCallNextDriver(88F876B4, 00000002,
B7A251EC,...);
*1 B7A25174 F346632D component2+00000830(88F4F990, B7A251EC,
88F876B0,...);
*1 B7A25188 F764C1C7 dword ptr EAX(88F4F990, B7A251EC, 88DFB000,...);
*1 B7A251A4 F764C20E termdd!_IcaCallSd(88F876A0, 00000002, B7A251EC,...);
*1 B7A251B8 F36C9928 termdd!IcaCallNextDriver(88EAEC6C, F773F120,
F773F120,...);
*0 B7A251D0 80892853 nt!RtlpInterlockedPushEntrySList(00000000, 00000000,
808B4900,...);
*0 B7A251E8 8081C3DA nt!RtlpInterlockedPushEntrySList(89586178, 00000000,
00000000,...);
*0 B7A251FC 80821967 nt!ObDereferenceObjectDeferDelete(8082196C, 894E8648,
898B0020,...);
*0 B7A25200 8082196C nt!_SEH_epilog(894E8648, 898B0020, 80A5A530,...);
*0 B7A25248 8082196C nt!_SEH_epilog(8082DFC3, 894E8648, B7A25294,...);
*1 B7A2524C 8082DFC3 dword ptr [EBP-14](894E8648, B7A25294, B7A25288,...);
*1 B7A2529C 80A5C199 nt!KiDeliverApc(00000000, 00000000, 00000000,...);
*1 B7A252BC 80A5C3D9 hal!HalpDispatchSoftwareInterrupt(898B0001, 00000000,
00000000,...);
*1 B7A252D8 80A5C456 hal!HalpCheckForSoftwareInterrupt(00000001, 898B0000,
B7A25300,...);
*1 B7A252E8 8083129E hal!KfLowerIrql(898B0020, 894E8648, 89468504,...);
*1 B7A25304 8082AB7B nt!KiExitDispatcher(894E8648, 894E8608,
00000000,...);
*1 B7A25318 80864E45 nt!MiFindNodeOrParent(893F8E00, 00000000,
B7A2532C,...);
*1 B7A25334 8084D308 nt!MiLocateAddress(C0000000, C0600000, 0000BB40,...);
*1 B7A25360 8088A262 nt!KiDispatchException(B7A25378, 00000000,
B7A253CC,...);
*0 B7A253A0 F7648BFE termdd!_SEH_epilog(00000000, C0000005, 00000018,...);
*0 B7A253B8 8088C798 nt!MmAccessFault(00000000, 00000008, 00000000,...);
*1 B7A253C8 8088A216 nt!CommonDispatchException(B7A25488, BFE5FEEA,
BADB0D00,...);
*1 B7A25450 BFE7B854 component+0003D5D0(BC048FE0, 00000000, 00000003,...);
*1 B7A2548C BFE6C043 component+00021B70(04048FE0, BC912820, BFEBC0A0,...);
*1 B7A254A8 BFE6CCBD component+0002DFD0(BC912820, BC14A2B4, BC14A018,...);
```

```
*1 B7A254CC BFE6FCB6 component+0002EBE0(BFEBC0A0, BFEBC038, BFEBBF80,...);
*1 B7A255C8 80A5C456 hal!HalpCheckForSoftwareInterrupt(00000000, 8CE03500,
B7A255F8,...);
*1 B7A255D8 80A5A56D hal!KfLowerIrql(8087C9C0, 88F93F24, E1681348,...);
*1 B7A255DC 8087C9C0 hal!KeReleaseInStackQueuedSpinLock(88F93F24,
E1681348, 00000000,...);
*1 B7A255FC F7134586 nt!ExReleaseResourceLite(88F93EF8, B7A2561C,
F7134640,...);
*1 B7A25608 F7134640 Ntfs!NtfsReleaseFcb(88F93EF8, 88F93EF8,
00000000,...);
*1 B7A2561C F7133091 Ntfs!NtfsFreeSnapshotsForFcb(88F93EF8, 00000014,
88F93EF8,...);
*1 B7A25638 F7133177 Ntfs!NtfsCleanupIrpContext(88F93EF8, 00000001,
00000000,...);
*1 B7A25650 F7174936 Ntfs!NtfsCompleteRequest(88F93EF8, 00000000,
F7174943,...);
*0 B7A2565C F7174943 Ntfs!_SEH_epilog(00000000, B7A257A0, 88F103D8,...);
*1 B7A2568C 80A5C456 hal!HalpCheckForSoftwareInterrupt(00000000, 00000001,
00000001,...);
*1 B7A256D4 80A5C456 hal!HalpCheckForSoftwareInterrupt(00000001, 808B4300,
B7A256FC,...);
*1 B7A256E4 8083129E hal!KfLowerIrql(00000000, B7A25C90, 00000000,...);
*1 B7A25700 808281D6 nt!KiExitDispatcher(88F103D8, 00000000,
00000000,...);
*1 B7A25714 8081E1E9 nt!KeSetEvent(00A25C90, 00000001, 00000000,...);
*1 B7A2573C F7133177 Ntfs!NtfsCleanupIrpContext(B7A25750, B7A257A4,
00000000,...);
*1 B7A25780 80A5C456 hal!HalpCheckForSoftwareInterrupt(0000026C, 808B4900,
B7A25828,...);
*1 B7A25790 80A5A56D hal!KfLowerIrql(8085712D, 00000000, 00180000,...);
*1 B7A25794 8085712D hal!KeReleaseQueuedSpinLock(00000000, 00180000,
00181000,...);
*1 B7A2582C 8085755D nt!MiProcessValidPteList(B7A25844, 00000002,
C0000C08,...);
*1 B7A25890 80A5C456 hal!HalpCheckForSoftwareInterrupt(00000001, 808B4300,
F7747120,...);
*0 B7A258C4 F724DA0D fltmgr!FltDecodeParameters(88E3BD2C, B7A25924,
88E62020,...);
*0 B7A258E8 8082CD1F nt!KiEspFromTrapFrame(B7A25D64, 894CA9C8,
7FFDA000,...);
*0 B7A258F8 8082CF40 nt!__security_check_cookie(B7A25D64, 01A5C456,
892373F8,...);
*1 B7A25914 80A5C456 hal!HalpCheckForSoftwareInterrupt(8081C585, B7A25944,
B7A25948,...);
*1 B7A25918 8081C585 nt!RtlpGetStackLimits(B7A25944, B7A25948,
00000000,...);
*1 B7A25934 F713320E nt!IoGetStackLimits(000015ED, B7A25764,
B7A25A78,...);
*1 B7A25970 80A5C456 hal!HalpCheckForSoftwareInterrupt(8CE03598, 00000000,
8CE03500,...);
*0 B7A2598C 808347E4 nt!ProbeForWrite(0032FD14, 000002E4, 808348C6,...);
*0 B7A25998 808348C6 nt!_SEH_epilog(7FFDA000, 894CA9C8, 00000000,...);
*0 B7A259A8 F713435F Ntfs!ExFreeToNPagedLookasideList(F7150420, 88F93EF8,
B7A25ACC,...);
```

```
*0 B7A259D8 8082CBCF nt!KiEspFromTrapFrame(C0001978, 83F251EC,
00000000,...);
*0 B7A259F0 80865C32 nt!MiInsertPageInFreeList(C0001978, 00000000,
83F251EC,...);
*1 B7A25A30 80A5C456 hal!HalpCheckForSoftwareInterrupt(C0001980, C0600000,
808B4900,...);
*1 B7A25A44 80A5C456 hal!HalpCheckForSoftwareInterrupt(C0600008, 808B4900,
B7A25B2C,...);
*1 B7A25A54 80A5A56D hal!KfLowerIrql(808658FB, 0032FFFF, 890D4198,...);
*1 B7A25A58 808658FB hal!KeReleaseQueuedSpinLock(0032FFFF, 890D4198,
8CB0B7B0,...);
*1 B7A25A7C 80A5C456 hal!HalpCheckForSoftwareInterrupt(C0600018, 808B4900,
B7A25B44,...);
*1 B7A25A8C 80A5A56D hal!KfLowerIrql(808658FB, 88E62020, 89293DF0,...);
*1 B7A25A90 808658FB hal!KeReleaseQueuedSpinLock(88E62020, 89293DF0,
88F87718,...);
*0 B7A25AC4 80945FEA nt!ObReferenceObjectByHandle(00000000, 00000018,
0032FE64,...);
*0 B7A25AE0 80892853 nt!RtlpInterlockedPushEntrySList(8CB0B890, 890D4198,
8CB0B7B0,...);
*1 B7A25AF4 80A5C1AE nt!KiDispatchInterrupt(00000000, 00000000,
00000202,...);
*1 B7A25B08 80A5C3D9 hal!HalpDispatchSoftwareInterrupt(00000002, 00000000,
80A5C3F4,...);
*0 B7A25B20 8081C3DA nt!RtlpInterlockedPushEntrySList(89586178, 00000000,
00000000,...);
*0 B7A25B34 80821967 nt!ObDereferenceObjectDeferDelete(8082196C, 8C22B848,
898B0020,...);
*0 B7A25B38 8082196C nt!_SEH_epilog(8C22B848, 898B0020, 80A5A530,...);
*0 B7A25B4C 8081C3DA nt!RtlpInterlockedPushEntrySList(00000000, 00000000,
8C22B808,...);
*0 B7A25B80 8082196C nt!_SEH_epilog(8082DFC3, 8C22B848, B7A25BCC,...);
*1 B7A25B84 8082DFC3 dword ptr [EBP-14](8C22B848, B7A25BCC, B7A25BC0,...);
*1 B7A25BD4 80A5C199 nt!KiDeliverApc(00000000, 00000000, 00000000,...);
*1 B7A25BF4 80A5C3D9 hal!HalpDispatchSoftwareInterrupt(898B0001, 00000000,
00000000,...);
*1 B7A25C10 80A5C456 hal!HalpCheckForSoftwareInterrupt(00000001, 898B0000,
B7A25C38,...);
*1 B7A25C20 8083129E hal!KfLowerIrql(898B0020, 8C22B848, 00000010,...);
*1 B7A25C54 80A5C456 hal!HalpCheckForSoftwareInterrupt(F7757000, 00000002,
893F8BB0,...);
*1 B7A25C64 8088DBAC hal!KfLowerIrql(B7A25C88, BFE6BA78, 00000000,...);
*1 B7A25C78 80A5C1AE nt!KiDispatchInterrupt(B7A25CC0, B7A25D00,
00000002,...);
*1 B7A25C8C 80A5C3D9 hal!HalpDispatchSoftwareInterrupt(00000002, B7A25CC0,
B7A25CC0,...);
*1 B7A25CA8 80A5C57E nt!KiCheckForSListAddress(BC845018, B7A25CC0,
80A59902,...);
*1 B7A25CB4 80A59902 hal!HalEndSystemInterrupt(898B0000, 000000E1,
B7A25D40,...);
*1 B7A25CE0 80A5C456 hal!HalpCheckForSoftwareInterrupt(00000001, 894890F0,
894890D8,...);
*0 B7A25CF4 8087CDDC hal!KeReleaseInStackQueuedSpinLock(894890D8,
00000000, 89489100,...);
```

```
*1 B7A25D18 80A5A56D hal!KfLowerIrql(00000001, BC14A018, BC5F9003,...);
*1 B7A25D44 BFE708D4 component+000312D0(BFEBBF80, 00000000, 00000000,...);
```

Another thread stack example:

```
4: kd> ~1

1: kd> k
ChildEBP RetAddr
f37fe9b4 f57e8407 tcpip!_IPTransmit+0x172c
f37fea24 f57e861a tcpip!TCPSend+0x604
f37fea54 f57e6edd tcpip!TdiSend+0x242
f37fea90 f57e1d13 tcpip!TCPSendData+0xbf
f37feaac 8081df65 tcpip!TCPDispatchInternalDeviceControl+0x19a
f37feac0 f57305dc nt!IofCallDriver+0x45
8cde7030 8c297030 afd!AfdFastConnectionSend+0x238
WARNING: Frame IP not in any known module. Following frames may be wrong.
8cde7044 8cde70d8 0x8c297030
8cde7048 001a001a 0x8cde70d8
8cde70d8 00000000 0x1a001a

1: kd> !w2kfre\kdex2x86.stack
T. Address  RetAddr  Called Procedure
*1 F37FE8D4 80A5C456 hal!HalpCheckForSoftwareInterrupt(00000000, 00000000,
F37FE904,...);
*0 F37FE984 F57DE006 NDIS!NdisCopyBuffer(F37FE9AC, F37FE9B0,
00000000,...);
*2 F37FE9B8 F57E8407 tcpip!IPTransmitBeforeSym(F58224D8, 8C396348,
8C3962E0,...);
*0 F37FE9F0 F5815DB6 tcpip!NeedToOffloadConnection(88EBC720, 00000B55,
00000001,...);
*2 F37FEA28 F57E861A tcpip!TCPSend(8AF6F701, 7FEA6000, 001673CE,...);
*2 F37FEA58 F57E6EDD tcpip!TdiSend(00000000, 00000000, 00000B55,...);
*0 F37FEA88 F5722126 dword ptr [ESI+28](F58203C0, F37FEAAC, F57E1D13,...);
*2 F37FEA94 F57E1D13 tcpip!TCPSendData(88FEE99C, 00EE5FA0, 88EE5EB0,...);
*2 F37FEAB0 8081DF65
tcpip!TCPDispatchInternalDeviceControl+0000019A(8C2D7030, 88EE5EE8,
89242378,...);
*2 F37FEAC4 F57305DC nt!IofCallDriver(F37FEBB8, 00000002, F37FEB1C,...);
*2 F37FEB14 F5726191 afd!AfdFastConnectionSend(89315008, 00000000,
F5726191,...);
*1 F37FEB20 F5726191 afd!AfdFastConnectionSend(89315008, F37FEBA8,
00000B55,...);
*1 F37FEB68 80A5C456 hal!HalpCheckForSoftwareInterrupt(8908AE01, 808B4301,
F37FEB90,...);
*1 F37FEB78 8083129E hal!KfLowerIrql(88F24A58, 00000000, 8908AE01,...);
*1 F37FEB94 8082B96B nt!KiExitDispatcher(00000000, 8908AE30,
00000000,...);
*0 F37FEBF4 8082196C nt!_SEH_epilog(8082DFC3, 8908AE18, F37FEC40,...);
*0 F37FEBF8 8082DFC3 dword ptr [EBP-14](8908AE18, F37FEC40, F37FEC34,...);
*0 F37FEC2C 8098AA4A nt!ExpLookupHandleTableEntry(E18D5E38, 00000B55,
89315008,...);
```

```
*2 F37FEC60 808F5E2F afd!AfdFastIoDeviceControl+000003A3(89435340,
00000001, 00ECFDC4,...);
*1 F37FEC9C 80933491 nt!ExUnlockHandleTableEntry(E18D5E38, 00000001,
00000000,...);
*0 F37FECBC 8081C3DA nt!RtlpInterlockedPushEntrySList(0336E6D8, 0336E6EC,
00000000,...);
*1 F37FECD4 808ED600 nt!ObReferenceObjectByHandle(F37FED01, 89435340,
00000000,...);
*2 F37FED04 808EED08 nt!IopXxxControlFile(00000124, 00000000,
00000000,...);
*2 F37FED38 8088978C nt!NtDeviceIoControlFile+0000002A(00000124, 00000000,
00000000,...);
```

This command is called "heuristic stack walker" in OSR NT Insider article mentioned in the post about **Stack Overflow** pattern (page 314) in kernel space.

A note for the revised edition: this extension and its command are no longer available in modern WinDbg distributions.

Coping with Missing Symbolic Information

Sometimes there is no private PDB file available for a module in a crash dump although we know they exist for different versions of the same module. The typical example is when we have a public PDB file loaded automatically, and we need access to structure definitions, for example, _TEB or _PEB. In this case, we need to force WinDbg to load an additional PDB file just to be able to use these structure definitions. This can be achieved by loading an additional module at a different address and forcing it to use another private PDB file. At the same time, we want to keep the original module to reference the correct PDB file, albeit the public one. Let's look at one concrete example.

For example, we are trying to get stack limits for a thread by using **!teb** command but we get an error:

```
0:000> !teb
TEB at 7efdd000
*** Your debugger is not using the correct symbols
***
*** In order for this command to work properly, your symbol path
*** must point to .pdb files that have full type information.
***
*** Certain .pdb files (such as the public OS symbols) do not
*** contain the required information.  Contact the group that
*** provided you with these symbols if you need this command to
*** work.
***
*** Type referenced: ntdll!_TEB
***
error InitTypeRead( TEB )...
0:000> dt ntdll!*
```

lm command shows that the symbol file was loaded, and it was correct so perhaps it was the public symbol file or _TEB definition that was missing in it:

```
0:000> lm m ntdll
start    end        module name
7d600000 7d6f0000 ntdll (pdb symbols) c:\websymbols\wntdll.pdb\
40B574C84D5C42708465A7E4A1E4D7CC2\wntdll.pdb
```

The size of *wntdll.pdb* is 1,091Kb. The search for other *ntdll.pdb* files finds one with the bigger size 1,187Kb, and we can append it to our symbol search path:

```
0:000> .sympath+ C:\websymbols\ntdll.pdb\
DCE823FCF71A4BF5AA489994520EA18F2
Symbol search path is:
SRV*c:\websymbols*http://msdl.microsoft.com/download/symbols;
C:\websymbols\ntdll.pdb\DCE823FCF71A4BF5AA489994520EA18F2
```

Then we can look at our symbol cache folder for *ntdll.dll*, choose a path to a random one and load it at the address not occupied by other modules forcing to load symbol files and ignore a mismatch if any:

```
0:000> .reload /f /i
C:\websymbols\ntdll.dll\45D709FFf0000\ntdll.dll=7E000000
```

```
0:000> lm
start    end        module name
...
...
...
7d600000 7d6f0000   ntdll      (pdb
symbols)           c:\websymbols\wntdll.pdb\40B574C84D5C42708465A7E4A1E4D7C
C2\wntdll.pdb
7d800000 7d890000   GDI32      (deferred)
7d8d0000 7d920000   Secur32    (deferred)
7d930000 7da00000   USER32     (deferred)
7da20000 7db00000   RPCRT4     (deferred)
7e000000 7e000000   ntdll_7e000000   (pdb
symbols)           C:\websymbols\ntdll.pdb\DCE823FCF71A4BF5AA489994520EA18F
2\ntdll.pdb
```

The additional *ntdll.dll* is now loaded at 7e000000 address, and its module name is *ntdll_7e000000*. Because we know TEB address we can see the values of _TEB structure fields immediately (the output is shown in smaller font for better visual clarity):

```
0:000> dt -r1 ntdll_7e000000!_TEB 7efdd000
   +0x000 NtTib            : _NT_TIB
      +0x000 ExceptionList    : 0x0012fec0 _EXCEPTION_REGISTRATION_RECORD
      +0x004 StackBase        : 0x00130000
      +0x008 StackLimit       : 0x0011c000
      +0x00c SubSystemTib     : (null)
      +0x010 FiberData        : 0x00001e00
      +0x010 Version          : 0x1e00
      +0x014 ArbitraryUserPointer : (null)
      +0x018 Self             : 0x7efdd000 _NT_TIB
   +0x01c EnvironmentPointer : (null)
   +0x020 ClientId         : _CLIENT_ID
      +0x000 UniqueProcess    : 0x00000e0c
      +0x004 UniqueThread     : 0x000013dc
   +0x028 ActiveRpcHandle  : (null)
   +0x02c ThreadLocalStoragePointer : (null)
   +0x030 ProcessEnvironmentBlock : 0x7efde000 _PEB
      +0x000 InheritedAddressSpace : 0 ''
      +0x001 ReadImageFileExecOptions : 0x1 ''
```

```
+0x002 BeingDebugged    : 0x1 ''
+0x003 BitField         : 0 ''
+0x003 ImageUsesLargePages : 0y0
+0x003 SpareBits        : 0y0000000 (0)
+0x004 Mutant           : 0xffffffff
+0x008 ImageBaseAddress : 0x00400000
+0x00c Ldr              : 0x7d6a01e0 _PEB_LDR_DATA
+0x010 ProcessParameters : 0x00020000 _RTL_USER_PROCESS_PARAMETERS
+0x014 SubSystemData    : (null)
+0x018 ProcessHeap      : 0x00210000
+0x01c FastPebLock      : 0x7d6a00e0 _RTL_CRITICAL_SECTION
+0x020 AtlThunkSListPtr : (null)
+0x024 SparePtr2        : (null)
+0x028 EnvironmentUpdateCount : 1
+0x02c KernelCallbackTable : 0x7d9419f0
+0x030 SystemReserved   : [1] 0
+0x034 SpareUlong       : 0
+0x038 FreeList         : (null)
+0x03c TlsExpansionCounter : 0
+0x040 TlsBitmap        : 0x7d6a2058
+0x044 TlsBitmapBits    : [2] 0xf
+0x04c ReadOnlySharedMemoryBase : 0x7efe0000
+0x050 ReadOnlySharedMemoryHeap : 0x7efe0000
+0x054 ReadOnlyStaticServerData : 0x7efe0cd0  -> (null)
+0x058 AnsiCodePageData : 0x7efb0000
+0x05c OemCodePageData  : 0x7efc1000
+0x060 UnicodeCaseTableData : 0x7efd2000
+0x064 NumberOfProcessors : 8
+0x068 NtGlobalFlag     : 0x70
+0x070 CriticalSectionTimeout : _LARGE_INTEGER 0xffffe86d`079b8000
+0x078 HeapSegmentReserve : 0x100000
+0x07c HeapSegmentCommit : 0x2000
+0x080 HeapDeCommitTotalFreeThreshold : 0x10000
+0x084 HeapDeCommitFreeBlockThreshold : 0x1000
+0x088 NumberOfHeaps    : 5
+0x08c MaximumNumberOfHeaps : 0x10
+0x090 ProcessHeaps     : 0x7d6a06a0  -> 0x00210000
+0x094 GdiSharedHandleTable : (null)
+0x098 ProcessStarterHelper : (null)
+0x09c GdiDCAttributeList : 0
+0x0a0 LoaderLock       : 0x7d6a0180 _RTL_CRITICAL_SECTION
+0x0a4 OSMajorVersion   : 5
+0x0a8 OSMinorVersion   : 2
+0x0ac OSBuildNumber    : 0xece
+0x0ae OSCSDVersion     : 0x200
+0x0b0 OSPlatformId     : 2
+0x0b4 ImageSubsystem   : 2
+0x0b8 ImageSubsystemMajorVersion : 4
+0x0bc ImageSubsystemMinorVersion : 0
+0x0c0 ImageProcessAffinityMask : 0
+0x0c4 GdiHandleBuffer  : [34] 0
+0x14c PostProcessInitRoutine : (null)
+0x150 TlsExpansionBitmap : 0x7d6a2050
+0x154 TlsExpansionBitmapBits : [32] 1
+0x1d4 SessionId        : 1
+0x1d8 AppCompatFlags   : _ULARGE_INTEGER 0x0
+0x1e0 AppCompatFlagsUser : _ULARGE_INTEGER 0x0
+0x1e8 pShimData        : (null)
+0x1ec AppCompatInfo    : (null)
+0x1f0 CSDVersion       : _UNICODE_STRING "Service Pack 2"
+0x1f8 ActivationContextData : (null)
```

```
   +0x1fc ProcessAssemblyStorageMap : (null)
   +0x200 SystemDefaultActivationContextData : 0x00180000 _ACTIVATION_CONTEXT_DATA
   +0x204 SystemAssemblyStorageMap : (null)
   +0x208 MinimumStackCommit : 0
   +0x20c FlsCallback      : 0x002137b0  -> (null)
   +0x210 FlsListHead      : _LIST_ENTRY [ 0x2139c8 - 0x2139c8 ]
   +0x218 FlsBitmap        : 0x7d6a2040
   +0x21c FlsBitmapBits    : [4] 0x33
   +0x22c FlsHighIndex     : 5
+0x034 LastErrorValue   : 0
+0x038 CountOfOwnedCriticalSections : 0
+0x03c CsrClientThread  : (null)
+0x040 Win32ThreadInfo  : (null)
+0x044 User32Reserved   : [26] 0
+0x0ac UserReserved     : [5] 0
+0x0c0 WOW32Reserved    : 0x78b81910
+0x0c4 CurrentLocale    : 0x409
+0x0c8 FpSoftwareStatusRegister : 0
+0x0cc SystemReserved1  : [54] (null)
+0x1a4 ExceptionCode    : 0
+0x1a8 ActivationContextStackPointer : 0x00211ea0 _ACTIVATION_CONTEXT_STACK
   +0x000 ActiveFrame      : (null)
   +0x004 FrameListCache   : _LIST_ENTRY [ 0x211ea4 - 0x211ea4 ]
   +0x00c Flags            : 0
   +0x010 NextCookieSequenceNumber : 1
   +0x014 StackId          : 0x9444f8
+0x1ac SpareBytes1      : [40]  ""
+0x1d4 GdiTebBatch      : _GDI_TEB_BATCH
   +0x000 Offset           : 0
   +0x004 HDC              : 0
   +0x008 Buffer           : [310] 0
+0x6b4 RealClientId     : _CLIENT_ID
   +0x000 UniqueProcess    : 0x00000e0c
   +0x004 UniqueThread     : 0x000013dc
+0x6bc GdiCachedProcessHandle : (null)
+0x6c0 GdiClientPID     : 0
+0x6c4 GdiClientTID     : 0
+0x6c8 GdiThreadLocalInfo : (null)
+0x6cc Win32ClientInfo  : [62] 0
+0x7c4 glDispatchTable  : [233] (null)
+0xb68 glReserved1      : [29] 0
+0xbdc glReserved2      : (null)
+0xbe0 glSectionInfo    : (null)
+0xbe4 glSection        : (null)
+0xbe8 glTable          : (null)
+0xbec glCurrentRC      : (null)
+0xbf0 glContext        : (null)
+0xbf4 LastStatusValue  : 0xc0000135
+0xbf8 StaticUnicodeString : _UNICODE_STRING "mscoree.dll"
   +0x000 Length           : 0x16
   +0x002 MaximumLength    : 0x20a
   +0x004 Buffer           : 0x7efddc00  "mscoree.dll"
+0xc00 StaticUnicodeBuffer : [261] 0x6d
+0xe0c DeallocationStack : 0x00030000
+0xe10 TlsSlots         : [64] (null)
+0xf10 TlsLinks         : _LIST_ENTRY [ 0x0 - 0x0 ]
   +0x000 Flink            : (null)
   +0x004 Blink            : (null)
+0xf18 Vdm              : (null)
+0xf1c ReservedForNtRpc : (null)
+0xf20 DbgSsReserved    : [2] (null)
```

```
+0xf28 HardErrorMode    : 0
+0xf2c Instrumentation  : [14] (null)
+0xf64 SubProcessTag    : (null)
+0xf68 EtwTraceData     : (null)
+0xf6c WinSockData      : (null)
+0xf70 GdiBatchCount    : 0x7efdb000
+0xf74 InDbgPrint       : 0 ''
+0xf75 FreeStackOnTermination : 0 ''
+0xf76 HasFiberData     : 0 ''
+0xf77 IdealProcessor   : 0x3 ''
+0xf78 GuaranteedStackBytes : 0
+0xf7c ReservedForPerf  : (null)
+0xf80 ReservedForOle   : (null)
+0xf84 WaitingOnLoaderLock : 0
+0xf88 SparePointer1    : 0
+0xf8c SoftPatchPtr1    : 0
+0xf90 SoftPatchPtr2    : 0
+0xf94 TlsExpansionSlots : (null)
+0xf98 ImpersonationLocale : 0
+0xf9c IsImpersonating  : 0
+0xfa0 NlsCache         : (null)
+0xfa4 pShimData        : (null)
+0xfa8 HeapVirtualAffinity : 0
+0xfac CurrentTransactionHandle : (null)
+0xfb0 ActiveFrame      : (null)
+0xfb4 FlsData          : 0x002139c8
+0xfb8 SafeThunkCall    : 0 ''
+0xfb9 BooleanSpare     : [3]  ""
```

Because *StackBase* and *StackLimit* are the second and the third doublewords we could have just dumped the first 3 doublewords at TEB address:

```
0:000> dd 7efdd000 l3
7efdd000  0012fec0 00130000 0011c000
```

Resolving Symbol Messages

On one of my debugging workstations, I couldn't analyze kernel and complete memory dumps from Windows 2003 Server R02. I was always getting this message:

```
*** ERROR: Symbol file could not be found.  Defaulted to export symbols
for ntkrnlmp.exe -
```

An attempt to reload and overwrite PDB files using **.reload /o /f** command didn't resolve the issue, but the following WinDbg command helped in troubleshooting:

```
1: kd> !sym noisy
noisy mode - symbol prompts on
```

Reloading symbol files showed that the default symbol path contained corrupt *ntkrnlmp.pdb*:

```
1: kd> .reload
DBGHELP: C:\Program Files\Debugging Tools for
Windows\sym\ntkrnlmp.pdb\A91CA63E49A840F4A50509F90ADE10D52\ntkrnlmp.pdb -
E_PDB_CORRUPT
DBGHELP: ntkrnlmp.pdb - file not found
*** ERROR: Symbol file could not be found.  Defaulted to export symbols
for ntkrnlmp.exe -
DBGHELP: nt - export symbol
```

Deleting it and reloading symbols again showed problems with the file downloaded from MS symbol server too (seems it was left unpacked):

```
1: kd> .reload
SYMSRV:  c:\symdownstream\ntkrnlmp.pdb\A91CA63E49A840F4A50509F90ADE10D52\n
tkrnlmp.pd_
         The file or directory is corrupted and unreadable.
DBGHELP: ntkrnlmp.pdb - file not found
*** ERROR: Symbol file could not be found.  Defaulted to export symbols
for ntkrnlmp.exe -
DBGHELP: nt - export symbols
```

Removing the folder and reloading symbols finally resolved the problem:

```
1: kd> .reload
DBGHELP: nt - public symbols
         c:\symdownstream\ntkrnlmp.pdb\A91CA63E49A840F4A50509F90ADE10D52\n
tkrnlmp.pdb
```

Now it was time to switch noisy mode off:

```
1: kd> !sym quiet
quiet mode - symbol prompts on
```

The Search for Tags

Sometimes we get pool allocation failures, and the driver's tag is 'Ddk':

```
0: kd> !vm

*** Virtual Memory Usage ***
 Physical Memory:       851775 (   3407100 Kb)
 Page File: \??\C:\pagefile.sys
   Current:    4190208 Kb  Free Space:    4175708 Kb
   Minimum:    4190208 Kb  Maximum:       4190208 Kb
 Available Pages:       147274 (    589096 Kb)
 ResAvail Pages:        769287 (   3077148 Kb)
 Locked IO Pages:          118 (       472 Kb)
 Free System PTEs:      184910 (    739640 Kb)
 Free NP PTEs:             110 (       440 Kb)
 Free Special NP:            0 (         0 Kb)
 Modified Pages:           168 (       672 Kb)
 Modified PF Pages:        168 (       672 Kb)
 NonPagedPool Usage:     64445 (    257780 Kb)
 NonPagedPool Max:       64640 (    258560 Kb)
 ********** Excessive NonPaged Pool Usage *****
 PagedPool 0 Usage:      21912 (     87648 Kb)
 PagedPool 1 Usage:        691 (      2764 Kb)
 PagedPool 2 Usage:        706 (      2824 Kb)
 PagedPool 3 Usage:        704 (      2816 Kb)
 PagedPool 4 Usage:        708 (      2832 Kb)
 PagedPool Usage:        24721 (     98884 Kb)
 PagedPool Maximum:     134144 (    536576 Kb)

 ********** 429 pool allocations have failed **********

 Shared Commit:           5274 (     21096 Kb)
 Special Pool:               0 (         0 Kb)
 Shared Process:          3958 (     15832 Kb)
 PagedPool Commit:       24785 (     99140 Kb)
 Driver Commit:          19289 (     77156 Kb)
 Committed pages:       646282 (   2585128 Kb)
 Commit limit:         1860990 (   7443960 Kb)

0: kd> !poolused 3
   Sorting by  NonPaged Pool Consumed

  Pool Used:
            NonPaged
 Tag    Allocs    Frees     Diff     Used
 Ddk   9074558  3859522  5215036 225708304 Default for driver allocated
memory (user's of ntddk.h)
```

How do we find which driver had caused this memory leak? We can search for drivers using the following command:

```
C:\>findstr /S /m /l Ddk *.sys
```

or we can guess the driver by using the fact that long time ago *ExAllocatePool* was defined as *ExAllocatePoolWithTag*(, … 'Ddk '). Currently, all DDK samples use their separate driver tags and *ExAllocatePool* uses 'None':

```
0: kd> .asm no_code_bytes
Assembly options: no_code_bytes

0: kd> uf ExAllocatePool
nt!ExAllocatePool:
80894d1f mov     edi,edi
80894d21 push    ebp
80894d22 mov     ebp,esp
80894d24 push    656E6F4Eh
80894d29 push    dword ptr [ebp+0Ch]
80894d2c push    dword ptr [ebp+8]
80894d2f call    nt!ExAllocatePoolWithTag (8089b93f)
80894d34 pop     ebp
80894d35 ret     8

0: kd> .formats 656E6F4Eh
Evaluate expression:
  Hex:     656e6f4e
  Decimal: 1701736270
  Octal:   14533467516
  Binary:  01100101 01101110 01101111 01001110
  Chars:   enoN
  Time:    Tue Dec 05 00:31:10 2023
  Float:   low 7.03735e+022 high 0
  Double:  8.40769e-315
```

Note: We push 'None' but see 'enoN' in memory because of little-endian byte ordering.

Most of the recent drivers use their own tags, and it is common not to encounter 'None' at all:

```
kd> !poolused
   Sorting by  Tag

  Pool Used:
            NonPaged             Paged
 Tag     Allocs      Used    Allocs      Used
...
...
 None          0         0          1     8192 call to ExAllocatePool
...
...
```

Therefore, the driver must be old, and if we see most drivers dated 2006-2007 and some dated 1998-2001 the chances are that 2001 drivers were responsible for our memory leak:

```
b9840000 b9842980   newdriver     Sat Feb 10 00:33:41 2007 (45CD12E5)
b8cfa000 b8d39e00   olddriver     Tue Aug 21 12:18:35 2001 (3B82438B)
f79e5000 f79e6400   veryolddriver Wed Sep 23 13:09:52 1998 (3608E510)
```

However *veryolddriver.sys* doesn't use *ExAllocatePoolWithTag* so *olddriver.sys* is under suspicion:

```
0: kd> !dh f79e5000
...
...
     A00 [      33] address [size] of Export Directory
     C00 [      3C] address [size] of Import Directory
     E00 [     3A4] address [size] of Resource Directory
       0 [       0] address [size] of Exception Directory
       0 [       0] address [size] of Security Directory
    1200 [      34] address [size] of Base Relocation Directory
     440 [      54] address [size] of Debug Directory
       0 [       0] address [size] of Description Directory
       0 [       0] address [size] of Special Directory
       0 [       0] address [size] of Thread Storage Directory
       0 [       0] address [size] of Load Configuration Directory
       0 [       0] address [size] of Bound Import Directory
     400 [      34] address [size] of Import Address Table Directory
       0 [       0] address [size] of Delay Import Directory
       0 [       0] address [size] of COR20 Header Directory
       0 [       0] address [size] of Reserved Directory
...
...
```

```
0: kd> dds f79e5000+400
f79e5400  80a82264 hal!HalTranslateBusAddress
f79e5404  80a84358 hal!READ_PORT_BUFFER_UCHAR
f79e5408  00000000
f79e540c  80840bd9 nt!IofCompleteRequest
f79e5410  808e8f01 nt!IoCreateSymbolicLink
f79e5414  80838035 nt!RtlInitUnicodeString
f79e5418  808fbe85 nt!IoDeleteSymbolicLink
f79e541c  80816a6e nt!MmUnmapIoSpace
f79e5420  808ef1f1 nt!IoCreateDevice
f79e5424  80837e3a nt!READ_REGISTER_BUFFER_UCHAR
f79e5428  80815fc8 nt!IoDeleteDevice
f79e542c  80816814 nt!MmMapIoSpace
f79e5430  00000000
f79e5434  00000000
```

To confirm that *olddriver.sys* uses 'Ddk ' tag we can search its address space for code that calls *ExAllocatePoolWithTag*:

```
b8cfa000 b8d39e00 olddriver Tue Aug 21 12:18:35 2001 (3B82438B)
```

```
0: kd> !dh b8cfa000
...
...
...
       0 [       0] address [size] of Export Directory
   3D330 [      50] address [size] of Import Directory
   3DE00 [     380] address [size] of Resource Directory
       0 [       0] address [size] of Exception Directory
   3FE00 [      88] address [size] of Security Directory
   3E180 [    1BE8] address [size] of Base Relocation Directory
   3B640 [      1C] address [size] of Debug Directory
       0 [       0] address [size] of Description Directory
       0 [       0] address [size] of Special Directory
       0 [       0] address [size] of Thread Storage Directory
       0 [       0] address [size] of Load Configuration Directory
       0 [       0] address [size] of Bound Import Directory
   3B480 [     1B4] address [size] of Import Address Table Directory
       0 [       0] address [size] of Delay Import Directory
       0 [       0] address [size] of COR20 Header Directory
       0 [       0] address [size] of Reserved Directory
...
...
...
```

```
0: kd> dds b8cfa000+3B480 b8cfa000+3B480+1B4
b8d35480  80a83dba hal!KeQueryPerformanceCounter
b8d35484  80a7e3c0 hal!KfAcquireSpinLock
b8d35488  80a7e440 hal!KfReleaseSpinLock
b8d3548c  00000000
...
...
...
b8d35544  80812b1a nt!IoWriteErrorLogEntry
b8d35548  8081287b nt!IoAllocateErrorLogEntry
b8d3554c  8082f12f nt!swprintf
b8d35550  8089b93f nt!ExAllocatePoolWithTag
b8d35554  8087c465 nt!KeBugCheckEx
b8d35558  80815407 nt!wcsncat
b8d3555c  8083bc54 nt!ZwQueryValueKey
b8d35560  8083affb nt!ZwClose
b8d35564  80841a14 nt!_wcsicmp
b8d35568  80928d30 nt!ObReferenceObjectByHandle
...
...
...

0: kd> s-d b8cfa000 b8d39e00 b8d35550
b8d19f08  b8d35550 555425ff 25ffb8d3 b8d35480  PU…%TU…%.T..
b8d1a068  b8d35550 ff85f88b 75fc7d89 b85e5f0c  PU…….}.u._^.
b8d2c4e4  b8d35550 0375c085 89c35d5e 04c08330  PU….u.^]..0…

0: kd> u b8d19f08-2
olddriver!ExAllocatePoolWithTag:
b8d19f06 jmp     dword ptr [olddriver!_imp__ExAllocatePoolWithTag
(b8d35550)]

0: kd> u b8d2c4e4-2
olddriver!malloc+0x12
b8d2c4e2 call    dword ptr [olddriver!_imp__ExAllocatePoolWithTag
(b8d35550)]
b8d2c4e8 test    eax,eax
b8d2c4ea jne     olddriver!malloc+0x1f (b8d2c4ef)
b8d2c4ec pop     esi
b8d2c4ed pop     ebp
b8d2c4ee ret
b8d2c4ef mov     dword ptr [eax],esi
b8d2c4f1 add     eax,4
```

```
0: kd> ub b8d1a068-2
olddriver!TraceRoutine+0xc1
b8d1a051 mov     esp,ebp
b8d1a053 pop     ebp
b8d1a054 ret
b8d1a055 cmp     edi,8
b8d1a058 jbe     olddriver!TraceRoutine+0x157 (b8d1a0e7)
b8d1a05e push    206b6444h
b8d1a063 push    edx
b8d1a064 push    0

0: kd> .formats 206b6444
Evaluate expression:
  Hex:      206b6444
  Decimal:  543908932
  Octal:    04032662104
  Binary:   00100000 01101011 01100100 01000100
  Chars:     kdD
  Time:     Sat Mar 28 05:48:52 1987
  Float:    low 1.99384e-019 high 0
  Double:   2.68727e-315
```

Old Dumps, New Extensions

Sometimes we can use old Windows 2000 WinDbg extensions to extract information from Windows 2003 and XP crash dumps when their native extensions fail. We can also do the other way around to extract information from old Windows 2000 crash dumps using WinDbg extensions written for Windows XP and later. Here is an example. WinDbg **!stacks** command shows the following not helpful output from Windows 2000 complete memory dump:

```
2: kd> !stacks
Proc.Thread  Thread   Ticks   ThreadState Blocker
                                    [System]
   8.000004  89df8220 0000000 BLOCKED     nt!KiSwapThread+0x1b1
   8.00000c  89dc1860 0003734 BLOCKED     nt!KiSwapThread+0x1b1
   8.000010  89dc15e0 0003734 BLOCKED     nt!KiSwapThread+0x1b1
   8.000014  89dc1360 00003b4 BLOCKED     nt!KiSwapThread+0x1b1
   8.000018  89dc10e0 0003734 BLOCKED     nt!KiSwapThread+0x1b1
   8.00001c  89dc0020 0000381 BLOCKED     nt!KiSwapThread+0x1b1
   8.000020  89dc0da0 00066f6 BLOCKED     nt!KiSwapThread+0x1b1
   8.000024  89dc0b20 00025b4 BLOCKED     nt!KiSwapThread+0x1b1
   8.000028  89dc08a0 00025b4 BLOCKED     nt!KiSwapThread+0x1b1
   8.00002c  89dc0620 0003734 BLOCKED     nt!KiSwapThread+0x1b1
   8.000030  89dc03a0 0003734 BLOCKED     nt!KiSwapThread+0x1b1
   8.000034  89dbf020 00025b4 BLOCKED     nt!KiSwapThread+0x1b1
   8.000038  89dbfda0 00025b4 BLOCKED     nt!KiSwapThread+0x1b1
   8.00003c  89dbfb20 00007b4 BLOCKED     nt!KiSwapThread+0x1b1
   8.000040  89dbf8a0 00007b4 BLOCKED     nt!KiSwapThread+0x1b1
   8.000044  89dbf620 0000074 BLOCKED     nt!KiSwapThread+0x1b1
   8.000048  89dbf3a0 00007b4 BLOCKED     nt!KiSwapThread+0x1b1
...
...
...
```

This command belongs to several WinDbg extension DLLs (from old WinDbg help):

```
Windows NT 4.0         Unavailable
Windows 2000           Kdextx86.dll
Windows XP and later   Kdexts.dll
```

and we can try newer *kdexts.dll* with better results:

```
2: kd> !winxp\kdexts.stacks
Proc.Thread  .Thread  Ticks   ThreadState Blocker
                          [89df84a0 System]
   8.0000c8  89db77c0 0000000 Blocked    nt!MiRemoveUnusedSegments+0xf4
   8.0000f0  89c8a020 0019607 Blocked    cpqasm2+0x1ef0
   8.000108  89881900 0000085 Blocked    CPQCISSE+0x3ae8
   8.000110  8982cda0 000000a Blocked    cpqasm2+0x2a523
```

```
   8.00013c  8974a9a0 00007d7
Blocked     rdbss!RxSetMinirdrCancelRoutine+0x3d
   8.000148  89747b20 000010a Blocked    rdbss!RxIsOkToPurgeFcb+0x3f
   8.00014c  89758a80 0019493
Blocked     nt!NtNotifyChangeMultipleKeys+0x434
   8.0002dc  89620680 000000e Blocked    cpqasm2+0x5523
   8.0002e0  89620400 00000d2 Blocked    cpqasm2+0x584d
   8.0004ac  895ae9c0 000955b Blocked    srv!SrvOemStringTo8dot3+0xb7
   8.0004c0  8937b4e0 0018fea Blocked    srv!SrvOemStringTo8dot3+0xb7
   8.0004a0  895b09e0 0018fe9 Blocked    srv!SrvOemStringTo8dot3+0xb7
   8.0004cc  893784e0 0018fe8 Blocked    srv!SrvOemStringTo8dot3+0xb7
   8.0004d0  893774e0 000955b Blocked    srv!SrvOemStringTo8dot3+0xb7
   8.0004d4  893764e0 0018fe8 Blocked    srv!SrvOemStringTo8dot3+0xb7
   8.003d68  87abb580 00000b7
Blocked     rdbss!RxSearchForCollapsibleOpen+0x17c
   8.002b94  88e4f180 00000b9
Blocked     rdbss!RxSearchForCollapsibleOpen+0x17c

                              [89736940 smss.exe]

                              [896d3b20 csrss.exe]
 178.000180  896c8020 0000012 Blocked    ntdll!NtReplyWaitReceivePort+0xb
 178.00018c  896c5320 0000012 Blocked    ntdll!NtReplyWaitReceivePort+0xb
 178.001260  88fbcb20 0000060 Blocked    ntdll!NtReplyWaitReceivePort+0xb
 178.001268  88fbbda0 0000060 Blocked    ntdll!NtReplyWaitReceivePort+0xb

                              [896c8740 WINLOGON.EXE]
 174.00019c  896b7740 0000299 Blocked    ntdll!ZwDelayExecution+0xb
 174.0001a0  896b6020 00015dd Blocked    ntdll!NtRemoveIoCompletion+0xb
 174.000f08  8913eda0 00000b0
Blocked     ntdll!ZwWaitForMultipleObjects+0xb
 174.000f0c  8901b030 00000b0 Blocked    ntdll!ZwWaitForSingleObject+0xb
```

Object Names and Waiting Threads

Sometimes we have threads waiting for synchronization objects like events, and it is good to know their names or vice versa because it might give some clues to whether the particular thread and object are relevant to the problem. For example, we have a thread from **!process 0 3f** WinDbg command applied to a complete memory dump:

```
THREAD 86047968  Cid 01e8.04d4  Teb: 7ffaa000 Win32Thread: 00000000 WAIT:
(Unknown) UserMode Non-Alertable
    8604b750  NotificationEvent
    86013070  NotificationEvent
Not impersonating
DeviceMap                 e1007d00
Owning Process            86014ba0       Image:         winlogon.exe
Wait Start TickCount      997            Ticks: 788709 (0:03:25:23.578)
Context Switch Count      1
UserTime                  00:00:00.000
KernelTime                00:00:00.000
Win32 Start Address USERENV!NotificationThread (0x76929dd9)
Start Address kernel32!BaseThreadStartThunk (0x77e617ec)
Stack Init f5d48000 Current f5d47914 Base f5d48000 Limit f5d45000 Call 0
Priority 10 BasePriority 10 PriorityDecrement 0
Kernel stack not resident.
ChildEBP RetAddr
f5d4792c 8082ffb7 nt!KiSwapContext+0x25
f5d47944 808282b0 nt!KiSwapThread+0x83
f5d47978 80930d34 nt!KeWaitForMultipleObjects+0x320
f5d47bf4 80930e96 nt!ObpWaitForMultipleObjects+0x202
f5d47d48 80883908 nt!NtWaitForMultipleObjects+0xc8
f5d47d48 7c8285ec nt!KiFastCallEntry+0xf8
00f1fec0 7c827cfb ntdll!KiFastSystemCallRet
00f1fec4 77e6202c ntdll!NtWaitForMultipleObjects+0xc
00f1ff6c 77e62fbe kernel32!WaitForMultipleObjectsEx+0x11a
00f1ff88 76929e35 kernel32!WaitForMultipleObjects+0x18
00f1ffb8 77e64829 USERENV!NotificationThread+0x5f
00f1ffec 00000000 kernel32!BaseThreadStart+0x34
```

or we switched to *winlogon.exe* process, and we inspect this thread:

```
kd> .process 86014ba0
Implicit process is now 86014ba0

kd> .reload /user
Loading User Symbols

kd> .thread 86047968
Implicit thread is now 86047968
```

```
kd> kv
  *** Stack trace for last set context - .thread/.cxr resets it
ChildEBP RetAddr  Args to Child
f5d4792c 8082ffb7 86047968 ffdff120 00002700 nt!KiSwapContext+0x25
f5d47944 808282b0 86047968 00000002 00000000 nt!KiSwapThread+0x83
f5d47978 80930d34 00000002 f5d47aac 00000001
nt!KeWaitForMultipleObjects+0x320
f5d47bf4 80930e96 00000002 f5d47c1c 00000001
nt!ObpWaitForMultipleObjects+0x202
f5d47d48 80883908 00000002 00f1ff10 00000001
nt!NtWaitForMultipleObjects+0xc8
f5d47d48 7c8285ec 00000002 00f1ff10 00000001 nt!KiFastCallEntry+0xf8
00f1fec0 7c827cfb 77e6202c 00000002 00f1ff10 ntdll!KiFastSystemCallRet
00f1fec4 77e6202c 00000002 00f1ff10 00000001
ntdll!NtWaitForMultipleObjects+0xc
00f1ff6c 77e62fbe 00000002 769cd34c 00000000
kernel32!WaitForMultipleObjectsEx+0x11a
00f1ff88 76929e35 00000002 769cd34c 00000000
kernel32!WaitForMultipleObjects+0x18
00f1ffb8 77e64829 00000000 00000000 00000000
USERENV!NotificationThread+0x5f
00f1ffec 00000000 76929dd9 00000000 00000000 kernel32!BaseThreadStart+0x34

kd> dd f5d47aac l2
f5d47aac  8604b750 86013070
```

WinDbg **!object** command shows names for named synchronization objects:

```
kd> !object 8604b750
Object: 8604b750  Type: (86598990) Event
    ObjectHeader: 8604b738 (old version)
    HandleCount: 1  PointerCount: 2

kd> !object 86013070
Object: 86013070  Type: (86598990) Event
    ObjectHeader: 86013058 (old version)
    HandleCount: 10  PointerCount: 18
    Directory Object: e19b61c0  Name: userenv: Machine Group Policy has
been applied
```

We see that one object is named and related to group policies. The same technique can be applied in reverse. For example, we want to find which thread is waiting for 85efb848 event:

```
kd> !object \BaseNamedObjects
Object: e19b61c0  Type: (865cab50) Directory
    ObjectHeader: e19b61a8 (old version)
    HandleCount: 75  PointerCount: 259
    Directory Object: e10012c8  Name: BaseNamedObjects
```

```
    Hash Address  Type          Name
    ---- -------  ----          ----



...
...
...
         861697f0 Event         COM+ Tracker Push Event
         85f6fbb0 Event         WMI_ProcessIdleTasksComplete
         85efb848 Event         VMwareToolsServiceEvent
...
...
...
```

Looking at threads from **!process 0 3f** command we find that *VMwareService.exe* uses it:

```
THREAD 8633bd40  Cid 0664.0680  Teb: 7ffde000 Win32Thread: 00000000 WAIT:
(Unknown) UserMode Alertable
    85efb848  SynchronizationEvent
    8633bdb8  NotificationTimer
Not impersonating
DeviceMap                 e1007d00
Owning Process            862fa938       Image:         VMwareService.exe
Wait Start TickCount      789703         Ticks: 3 (0:00:00:00.046)
Context Switch Count      120485
UserTime                  00:00:00.093
KernelTime                00:00:00.062
Win32 Start Address ADVAPI32!ScSvcctrlThreadA (0x77f65e70)
Start Address kernel32!BaseThreadStartThunk (0x77e617ec)
Stack Init f5cc8000 Current f5cc7914 Base f5cc8000 Limit f5cc5000 Call 0
Priority 15 BasePriority 15 PriorityDecrement 0
ChildEBP RetAddr
f5cc792c 8082ffb7 nt!KiSwapContext+0x25
f5cc7944 808282b0 nt!KiSwapThread+0x83
f5cc7978 80930d34 nt!KeWaitForMultipleObjects+0x320
f5cc7bf4 80930e96 nt!ObpWaitForMultipleObjects+0x202
f5cc7d48 80883908 nt!NtWaitForMultipleObjects+0xc8
f5cc7d48 7c8285ec nt!KiFastCallEntry+0xf8
00a5fe4c 7c827cfb ntdll!KiFastSystemCallRet
00a5fe50 77e6202c ntdll!NtWaitForMultipleObjects+0xc
00a5fef8 0040158e kernel32!WaitForMultipleObjectsEx+0x11a
WARNING: Stack unwind information not available. Following frames may be
wrong.
00a5ff18 00402390 VMwareService+0x158e
00a5ff84 00402f5a VMwareService+0x2390
00a5ffa4 77f65e91 VMwareService+0x2f5a
00a5ffb8 77e64829 ADVAPI32!ScSvcctrlThreadW+0x21
00a5ffec 00000000 kernel32!BaseThreadStart+0x34
```

!object command is equivalent to WinObj tool (http://technet.microsoft.com/en-us/sysinternals/bb896657.aspx) and allows inspection of Windows Object Manager namespace that existed at the time of saving a memory dump. Here is the root directory from my x64 Vista workstation:

```
lkd> !object \
Object: fffff880000056c0  Type: (fffffa800183fde0) Directory
    ObjectHeader: fffff88000005690 (old version)
    HandleCount: 0  PointerCount: 50
    Directory Object: 00000000  Name: \

    Hash Address          Type          Name
    ---- -------          ----          ----
     01  fffff88000005510 Directory     ObjectTypes
     03  fffffa80047574e0 Event         NETLOGON_SERVICE_STARTED
     05  fffff8800156fb00 SymbolicLink  SystemRoot
     06  fffff880018bfeb0 Directory     Sessions
     07  fffffa800448eb90 ALPC Port     MmcssApiPort
     08  fffff8800000a060 Directory     ArcName
     09  fffff88000081e10 Directory     NLS
         fffffa80047523c0 ALPC Port     XactSrvLpcPort
     10  fffffa8004504e60 ALPC Port     ThemeApiPort
         fffff880018efce0 Directory     Windows
         fffff88000007bd0 Directory     GLOBAL??
         fffffa8004199de0 Event         LanmanServerAnnounceEvent
         fffffa80043027d0 Event         DSYSDBG.Debug.Trace.Memory.2a4
     11  fffff8800189feb0 Directory     RPC Control
     13  fffffa8003ed6490 Event         EFSInitEvent
     14  fffffa8002746bd0 Device        clfs
         fffff88000fb6b10 -
     15  fffffa8003dd5060 ALPC Port     SeRmCommandPort
         fffffa80040c7210 Event         CsrSbSyncEvent
     16  fffff880000052e0 SymbolicLink  DosDevices
         fffffa8004626c70 Device        Cdfs
     17  fffff8800471c210 Directory     KnownDlls32
         fffffa8004770490 ALPC Port     AELPort
         fffffa8004342680 Event         EFSSrvInitEvent
     18  fffff8800000a2b0 Key           \REGISTRY
         fffffa8004851900 ALPC Port     WindowsErrorReportingServicePort
     19  fffff88004732380 Directory     BaseNamedObjects
     21  fffff88000072d00 Directory     UMDFCommunicationPorts
         fffffa8004182120 ALPC Port     SmSsWinStationApiPort
         fffffa8003ddbe60 Event         UniqueInteractiveSessionIdEvent
     22  fffff88000875a00 Directory     KnownDlls
         fffffa8003ece330 Device        FatCdrom
         fffffa8003a16720 Device        Fat
     23  fffff88000005120 Directory     KernelObjects
         fffff88000081ab0 Directory     FileSystem
         fffffa8002a5f620 Device        Ntfs
     26  fffff88000007300 Directory     Callback
         fffffa80042e14c0 ALPC Port     SeLsaCommandPort
     28  fffff880000095f0 Directory     Security
     29  fffffa8004574e60 ALPC Port     UxSmsApiPort
     30  fffff88000013060 Directory     Device
```

```
        fffffa8004342700 Event            EFSSmbInitEvent
    32  fffffa8004342260 ALPC Port        LsaAuthenticationPort
    34  fffffa8003dd7e60 ALPC Port        SmApiPort
        fffff88004bf5080 Section          LsaPerformance
        fffffa8003f65160 Event            UniqueSessionIdEvent
    36  fffff88000081c60 Directory        Driver
        fffffa8004308c00 Event            SAM_SERVICE_STARTED
```

We can inspect any directory or object, for example:

```
lkd> !object \FileSystem
Object: fffff88000081ab0  Type: (fffffa800183fde0) Directory
    ObjectHeader: fffff88000081a80 (old version)
    HandleCount: 0  PointerCount: 31
    Directory Object: fffff880000056c0  Name: FileSystem

    Hash Address          Type            Name
    ---- -------          ----            ----
     02  Unable to read directory entry at fffff88004d46ca0
     03  fffffa80041a9bc0 Driver          mrxsmb20
     04  fffffa8004371450 Driver          luafv
     11  fffffa8003e3b530 Driver          rdbss
         fffffa8003c6e470 Device          CdfsRecognizer
     12  fffffa800261c300 Device          UdfsDiskRecognizer
         fffffa8003c6e680 Driver          Fs_Rec
     13  fffffa8002626e70 Driver          Msfs
     15  fffffa8003edc7e0 Driver          DfsC
     16  fffffa8004640e70 Driver          cdfs
     17  fffffa800410ed90 Driver          srvnet
     19  fffffa80046f9420 Driver          srv
         fffffa800468cc90 Driver          MRxDAV
         fffff88000072eb0 Directory       Filters
     21  fffffa80046be400 Driver          bowser
         fffffa8001c92c40 Driver          FltMgr
     22  fffffa800261cc40 Device          FatCdRomRecognizer
     23  fffffa8002756e70 Driver          Ntfs
     24  fffffa8003dc0530 Driver          Npfs
         fffffa80027abd20 Driver          Mup
         fffffa80018476a0 Driver          RAW
     27  fffffa8003f04270 Driver          fastfat
     28  fffffa8002745060 Driver          FileInfo
     31  fffffa800261ce50 Device          FatDiskRecognizer
     33  fffffa80046c4650 Driver          srv2
         fffffa8003eaf470 Driver          NetBIOS
         fffffa800261ca30 Device          ExFatRecognizer
     34  fffffa8003ce3610 Driver          SRTSP
     35  fffffa800261c060 Device          UdfsCdRomRecognizer
```

Memory Dumps from Virtual Images

Although I haven't found the way to distinguish the process dump taken from a physical machine versus virtualized machine there is a way to see it from kernel and complete memory dumps if VMware Tools are installed inside the guest Windows OS:

```
kd> !vm
...
...
...
        1098 VMwareUser.exe      350 (        1400 Kb)
...
        14e4 VMwareTray.exe      317 (        1268 Kb)
...
        0664 VMwareService.e     190 (         760 Kb)
...
...
...
```

In the case of a kernel minidump we can check for VMware drivers (as we can obviously do with kernel and complete memory dumps):

```
kd> lmt m vm*
start    end        module name
bf9e6000 bf9faa80   vmx_fb    Tue Oct 04 08:13:32 2005
f6e8b000 f6e8ed80   vmx_svga  Tue Oct 04 08:13:02 2005
f77e7000 f77ede80   vmxnet    Sat Apr 22 23:13:11 2006
f7997000 f7998200   vmmouse   Tue Aug 02 20:07:49 2005
f79c9000 f79ca5c0   vmmemctl  Thu Jul 26 21:50:03 2007
```

If VMware Tools are not installed we can check machine id:

```
kd> !sysinfo machineid
Machine ID Information [From Smbios 2.31, DMIVersion 0, Size=1642]
BiosVendor = Phoenix Technologies LTD
BiosVersion = 6.00
BiosReleaseDate = 04/17/2006
SystemManufacturer = VMware, Inc.
SystemProductName = VMware Virtual Platform
SystemVersion = None
BaseBoardManufacturer = Intel Corporation
BaseBoardProduct = 440BX Desktop Reference Platform
BaseBoardVersion = None
```

Filtering Processes

When I analyze memory dumps coming from Microsoft or Citrix terminal server environments, I frequently need to find a process hosting terminal service. In Windows 2000, it was the separate process *termsrv.exe*, and now it is *termsrv.dll,* which can be loaded into any of several instances of *svchost.exe*. The simplest way to narrow down that *svchost.exe* process if we have a complete memory dump is to use the module option of WinDbg **!process** command:

```
!process /m termsrv.dll 0

!process /m wsxica.dll 0

!process /m ctxrdpwsx.dll 0
```

Note: This option works only with W2K3, XP and later OS

Also, to list all processes with user space stacks having the same image name, we can use the following command:

```
!process 0 3f msiexec.exe
```

or

```
!process 0 3f svchost.exe
```

Note: This command works with W2K, too, as well as session option (**/s**).

WinDbg Scripts

First Encounters

Sometimes instead of writing a debugging extension, it is much faster to write a script. After spending some time, I wrote the final version of my first script (based on WinDbg help sample) which can enumerate processes in a complete memory dump and output their command line.

I saved the script below in a text file and used the following command to run it from WinDbg command prompt: $$><script.txt.

```
$$ WinDbg script to get process command line for all processes in complete
memory dump
r $t0 = nt!PsActiveProcessHead
.for (r $t1 = poi(@$t0); (@$t1 != 0) & (@$t1 != @$t0);
       r $t1 = poi(@$t1))
{
   r? $t2 = #CONTAINING_RECORD(@$t1,
      nt!_EPROCESS, ActiveProcessLinks);
   .process @$t2
   .if (@$peb != 0)
   {
      .catch
      {
         r $t3 = @@c++(@$peb->ProcessParameters)
         r? $t4 =
             @@c++(&((_RTL_USER_PROCESS_PARAMETERS *)
             @$t3)->CommandLine)
         .printf "_EPROCESS: %N Command Line: %msu\n",
          @$t2, @$t4
      }
   }
}
```

Yet another WinDbg Script

One day I got a Windows 2000 server crash dump with 30 IE processes running, and I wanted to find the only one waiting for a specific function. I knew there was one and I wrote the following script to list all processes and their stacks (of course, I already opened a log in WinDbg to save that huge amount of output):

```
$$
$$ List user processes and stacks
$$
r $t0 = nt!PsActiveProcessHead
.for (r $t1 = poi(@$t0); (@$t1 != 0) & (@$t1 != @$t0); r $t1 = poi(@$t1))
{
    r? $t2 = #CONTAINING_RECORD(@$t1, nt!_EPROCESS, ActiveProcessLinks);
    .process @$t2
    .reload
    !process @$t2
}
```

In memory dumps coming from XP/W2K3 and higher systems, you can get all of this plus PEB and module information for all processes by using **!process 0 3f** WinDbg command. The command with flags sets process context for every process and reloads user symbols accordingly.

Another alternative would be to use the following command instead of the script:

```
!for_each_process ".process /r /p @#Process; !process @#Process"
```

Deadlocks and Critical Sections

The following script uncovers deadlocks and critical section contention in user mode processes (including services) if we run it against complete memory dump:

```
$$
$$ List owned critical sections in user processes
$$
r $t0 = nt!PsActiveProcessHead
.for (r $t1 = poi(@$t0); (@$t1 != 0) & (@$t1 != @$t0); r $t1 = poi(@$t1))
{
    r? $t2 = #CONTAINING_RECORD(@$t1, nt!_EPROCESS, ActiveProcessLinks);
    .process @$t2
    .reload
    !ntsdexts.locks
}
```

To run it, we need to save in a file and use the following command in WinDbg: **$$>**<*script.txt.*

Another alternative would be to use the following command instead of the script:

```
!for_each_process ".process /r /p @#Process; !ntsdexts.locks"
```

Security Problem

Crash dumps may expose confidential information stored in memory (see **Crash Dumps and Security**, page 604). It seems a solution exists which allows doing some sort of crash dump analysis or at least to identify problem components without sending complete or kernel memory dumps.

This solution takes advantage of WinDbg's ability to execute scripts of arbitrary complexity. For example, the script that combines all frequent commands can be used for identification of potential problems in memory dumps:

- **!analyze -v**
- **!vm** 4
- **lmv**
- **!locks**
- **!poolused** 3
- **!poolused** 4
- **!exqueue** f
- **!irpfind**
- **!stacks**
- List of all processes' thread stacks, loaded modules and critical sections (for complete memory dump)

Other commands can be added if necessary.

How does all this work? A customer has to install Debugging Tools for Windows from Microsoft. This can be done on any workstation and not necessarily in a production environment. Then the customer has to run *WinDbg.exe* with some parameters including path(s) to symbols (**-y**, if necessary), a path to a memory dump (**-z**) and a path to the script (**-c**):

```
C:\Program Files (x86)\Windows Kits\10\Debuggers\x64>WinDbg.exe -z
MEMORY.DMP -c "$$><c:\WinDbgScripts\Dmp2Txt.txt;q" -Q -QS -QY -QSY
```

Once *WinDbg.exe* finishes processing the memory dump (it can run for couple of hours if we have many processes in our complete memory dump) we can copy the *.log* file created in *C:\Program Files (x86)\Windows Kits\10\Debuggers\x64* folder, archive it and send it to support for analysis. Kernel and process data and cached files are not exposed in the log! And because this is a text file, the customer can inspect it before sending it.

Here are the contents of *Dmp2Txt.txt* file:

```
$$
$$ Dmp2Txt: Dump all necessary information from complete full memory dump
into log
$$
.logopen /d
!analyze -v
!vm 4
lmv
!locks
!poolused 3
!poolused 4
!exqueue f
!irpfind
!stacks
r $t0 = nt!PsActiveProcessHead
.for (r $t1 = poi(@$t0); (@$t1 != 0) & (@$t1 != @$t0); r $t1 = poi(@$t1))
{
    r? $t2 = #CONTAINING_RECORD(@$t1, nt!_EPROCESS, ActiveProcessLinks);
    .process @$t2
    .reload
    !process @$t2
    !ntsdexts.locks
    lmv
}
.logclose
$$ Dmp2Txt: End of File
```

For the kernel dumps the script is simpler than the previous:

```
$$
$$ KeDmp2Txt: Dump all necessary information from kernel dump into log
$$
.logopen /d
!analyze -v
!vm 4
lmv
!locks
!poolused 3
!poolused 4
!exqueue f
!irpfind
!stacks
!process 0 7
.logclose
$$ KeDmp2Txt: End of File
```

Note: If the dump is *LiveKd.exe* generated, then due to inconsistency, scripts may run forever.

For XP/W2K3 and higher you can simplify the script at the cost of excluding process critical section locks:

```
$$
$$ Dmp2Txt: Dump all necessary information from complete full memory dump
into log
$$
.logopen /d
!analyze -v
!vm 4
lmv
!locks
!poolused 3
!poolused 4
!exqueue f
!irpfind
!stacks
!process 0 3f
.logclose
$$
$$ Dmp2Txt: End of File
$$
```

or use the following command instead of **.for** loop:

```
!for_each_process ".process /r /p @#Process; !process @#Process;
!ntsdexts.locks; lmv"
```

Hundreds of Crash Dumps

Suppose we have 100 - 200 user dumps from various user processes in the system, and we want to check their thread stacks, locks quickly, or to see something suspicious related to our product or its environment our customers are complaining about. It is much easier to collect such information into text files and browse them quickly than open every crash dump in WinDbg. We can use a shell script (VBScript) to automate loading dumps into WinDbg and use WinDbg scripts to run complex commands against loaded user dumps. For example, we can use the following shell script (in the past, we also needed to customize the symbol search path after **-y** parameter to point to our symbol folders):

```
'
' UDumps2Txt.vbs
'
Set fso = CreateObject("Scripting.FileSystemObject")
Set Folder = fso.GetFolder(".")
Set Files = Folder.Files
Set WshShell = CreateObject("WScript.Shell")
For Each File In Files
  Set oExec = WshShell.Exec("C:\Program Files (x86)\Windows
Kits\10\Debuggers\x64\WinDbg.exe -z " + File.Name + " -c
""$$><c:\scripts\UDmp2Txt.txt;q"" -Q -QS -QY -QSY")
  Do While oExec.Status = 0
     WScript.Sleep 1000
  Loop
Next
'
' UDumps2Txt.vbs: End of File
'
```

and the following WinDbg script:

```
$$
$$ UDmp2Txt: Dump information from user dump into log
$$
.logopen /d
!analyze -v
!locks
~*kv
lmv
.logclose
$$
$$ UDmp2Txt: End of File
$$
```

The following command launches multiple Dmp2Txt conversions:

```
C:\UserDumps>cscript /nologo c:\scripts\UDumps2Txt.vbs
```

We can also use CDB from Debugging Tools for Windows (console debugger) instead of WinDbg. I prefer to use WinDbg uniformly instead of using separately CDB for the user process dumps and KD for the kernel and complete memory dumps.

Now, when we have text files, we can search for patterns using regular expressions, or we can process text files further and feed them into our database – a part of the automated crash dump analysis system.

Parameterized Scripts

To pass arguments to WinDbg scripts, we can use the following WinDbg command:

$$>a< *Filename arg1 arg2 arg3 ... argn*

where *argn* specifies an argument that the debugger passes to the script. These parameters can be quoted strings or space-delimited strings. All arguments are optional (from WinDbg help)

We use *$arg1, ..., $argn* to reference parameters inside the script. This promises many possibilities to write cool scripts and use structured programming. Please refer to Roberto Alexis Farah's blog for many script examples: (https://docs.microsoft.com/en-gb/archive/blogs/debuggingtoolbox/)

Security Issues and Scripts

It is a well-known fact that crash dumps may contain sensitive and private information. Crash reports that contain binary process extracts may contain it too. There is a conflict here between the desire to get full memory contents for debugging purposes and possible security implications. The solution would be to have postmortem debuggers and user mode process dumpers to implement an option to save only the activity data like stack traces in a text form. Some problems on a system level can be corrected just by looking at thread stack traces, critical section list, full module information, and thread times. This can help to identify components that cause process crashes, hangs, or CPU spikes.

Users or system administrators can review text data before sending it outside their environment. This was already implemented as Dr. Watson logs. However, these logs don't usually have sufficient information required for crash dump analysis compared to information we can extract from a dump using WinDbg, for example. If we need to analyze the kernel and all process activities, we can use scripts to convert kernel and complete memory dumps to text files (page 224). Similar scripts can be applied to user dumps (page 226).

Generating good scripts in a production environment has one problem: the conversion tool or debugger needs to know about symbols. This can be easily done with Microsoft modules because of Microsoft public symbol server. Other companies may have an option to download public symbols.

Alternatively, one can write a WinDbg extension that loads a text file with stack traces, appropriate module images, finds the right PDB files, and presents stack traces with full symbolic information. This can also be a separate program that uses Visual Studio DIA (Debug Interface Access) SDK to access PDB files later after receiving a text file from a customer.

Raw Stack Dump of All Threads (Process Dump)

Sometimes we need to dump the whole thread stack data to find traces of hooks, printer drivers, or just string fragments. This is usually done by finding the appropriate TEB and dumping the data between *StackLimit* and *StackBase* addresses, for example:

```
0:000> ~
.  0  Id: 106c.4e4 Suspend: 1 Teb: 7ffde000 Unfrozen
   1  Id: 106c.4e0 Suspend: 1 Teb: 7ffdc000 Unfrozen
   2  Id: 106c.1158 Suspend: 1 Teb: 7ffdb000 Unfrozen
   3  Id: 106c.c3c Suspend: 1 Teb: 7ffd9000 Unfrozen
   4  Id: 106c.1174 Suspend: 1 Teb: 7ffd8000 Unfrozen
   5  Id: 106c.1168 Suspend: 1 Teb: 7ffd4000 Unfrozen
   6  Id: 106c.1568 Suspend: 1 Teb: 7ffaf000 Unfrozen
   7  Id: 106c.1574 Suspend: 1 Teb: 7ffad000 Unfrozen
   8  Id: 106c.964 Suspend: 1 Teb: 7ffac000 Unfrozen
   9  Id: 106c.1164 Suspend: 1 Teb: 7ffab000 Unfrozen
  10  Id: 106c.d84 Suspend: 1 Teb: 7ffaa000 Unfrozen
  11  Id: 106c.bf4 Suspend: 1 Teb: 7ffa9000 Unfrozen
  12  Id: 106c.eac Suspend: 1 Teb: 7ffa8000 Unfrozen
  13  Id: 106c.614 Suspend: 1 Teb: 7ffd5000 Unfrozen
  14  Id: 106c.cd8 Suspend: 1 Teb: 7ffa7000 Unfrozen
  15  Id: 106c.1248 Suspend: 1 Teb: 7ffa6000 Unfrozen
  16  Id: 106c.12d4 Suspend: 1 Teb: 7ffa4000 Unfrozen
  17  Id: 106c.390 Suspend: 1 Teb: 7ffa3000 Unfrozen
  18  Id: 106c.764 Suspend: 1 Teb: 7ffa1000 Unfrozen
  19  Id: 106c.f48 Suspend: 1 Teb: 7ff5f000 Unfrozen
  20  Id: 106c.14a8 Suspend: 1 Teb: 7ff53000 Unfrozen
  21  Id: 106c.464 Suspend: 1 Teb: 7ff4d000 Unfrozen
  22  Id: 106c.1250 Suspend: 1 Teb: 7ffa5000 Unfrozen
  23  Id: 106c.fac Suspend: 1 Teb: 7ff5c000 Unfrozen
  24  Id: 106c.1740 Suspend: 1 Teb: 7ffd7000 Unfrozen
  25  Id: 106c.ae4 Suspend: 1 Teb: 7ffd6000 Unfrozen
  26  Id: 106c.a4c Suspend: 1 Teb: 7ffdd000 Unfrozen
  27  Id: 106c.1710 Suspend: 1 Teb: 7ffda000 Unfrozen
  28  Id: 106c.1430 Suspend: 1 Teb: 7ffa2000 Unfrozen
  29  Id: 106c.1404 Suspend: 1 Teb: 7ff4e000 Unfrozen
  30  Id: 106c.9a8 Suspend: 1 Teb: 7ff4c000 Unfrozen
  31  Id: 106c.434 Suspend: 1 Teb: 7ff4b000 Unfrozen
  32  Id: 106c.c8c Suspend: 1 Teb: 7ff4a000 Unfrozen
  33  Id: 106c.4f0 Suspend: 1 Teb: 7ff49000 Unfrozen
  34  Id: 106c.be8 Suspend: 1 Teb: 7ffae000 Unfrozen
  35  Id: 106c.14e0 Suspend: 1 Teb: 7ff5d000 Unfrozen
  36  Id: 106c.fe0 Suspend: 1 Teb: 7ff5b000 Unfrozen
  37  Id: 106c.1470 Suspend: 1 Teb: 7ff57000 Unfrozen
  38  Id: 106c.16c4 Suspend: 1 Teb: 7ff5e000 Unfrozen
```

```
0:000> !teb 7ffad000
TEB at 7ffad000
    ExceptionList:         0181ff0c
    StackBase:             01820000
    StackLimit:            0181c000
    SubSystemTib:          00000000
    FiberData:             00001e00
    ArbitraryUserPointer: 00000000
    Self:                  7ffad000
    EnvironmentPointer:    00000000
    ClientId:              0000106c . 00001574
    RpcHandle:             00000000
    Tls Storage:           00000000
    PEB Address:           7ffdf000
    LastErrorValue:        0
    LastStatusValue:       c000000d
    Count Owned Locks:     0
    HardErrorMode:         0

0:000> dps 0181c000 01820000
0181c000  00000000
0181c004  00000000
0181c008  00000000
0181c00c  00000000
0181c010  00000000
0181c014  00000000
0181c018  00000000
0181c01c  00000000
0181c020  00000000
0181c024  00000000
...
...
...
0181ffb8  0181ffec
0181ffbc  77e6608b kernel32!BaseThreadStart+0x34
0181ffc0  00f31eb0
0181ffc4  00000000
0181ffc8  00000000
0181ffcc  00f31eb0
0181ffd0  8a38f7a8
0181ffd4  0181ffc4
0181ffd8  88a474b8
0181ffdc  ffffffff
0181ffe0  77e6b7d0 kernel32!_except_handler3
0181ffe4  77e66098 kernel32!`string'+0x98
0181ffe8  00000000
0181ffec  00000000
0181fff0  00000000
0181fff4  7923a709
0181fff8  00f31eb0
0181fffc  00000000
01820000  ????????
```

However, if our process has many threads, as in the example above, and we want to dump stack data from all of them, we need to automate this procedure. After several attempts, I created the following simple script which can be copy-pasted into the WinDbg command window or saved in a text file to be loaded and executed later via WinDbg **$$><** command. The script takes advantage of the following command:

~e (Thread-Specific Command)

The **~e** command executes one or more commands for a specific thread or all threads in the target process (from WinDbg help).

Here is the script:

```
~*e r? $t1 = ((ntdll!_NT_TIB *)@$teb)->StackLimit; r? $t2 =
((ntdll!_NT_TIB *)@$teb)->StackBase; !teb; dps @$t1 @$t2
```

Raw stack data from different stacks is separated by **!teb** output for clarity, for example:

```
0:000> .logopen rawdata.log

0:000> ~*e r? $t1 = ((ntdll!_NT_TIB *)@$teb)->StackLimit; r? $t2 =
((ntdll!_NT_TIB *)@$teb)->StackBase; !teb; dps @$t1 @$t2
TEB at 7ffde000
    ExceptionList:        0007fd38
    StackBase:            00080000
    StackLimit:           0007c000
    SubSystemTib:         00000000
    FiberData:            00001e00
    ArbitraryUserPointer: 00000000
    Self:                 7ffde000
    EnvironmentPointer:   00000000
    ClientId:             0000106c . 000004e4
    RpcHandle:            00000000
    Tls Storage:          00000000
    PEB Address:          7ffdf000
    LastErrorValue:       0
    LastStatusValue:      c0000034
    Count Owned Locks:    0
    HardErrorMode:        0
 0007c000  00000000
 0007c004  00000000
 0007c008  00000000
 0007c00c  00000000
 0007c010  00000000
 0007c014  00000000
 0007c018  00000000
 0007c01c  00000000
 0007c020  00000000
```

```
0007c024  00000000
...
...
...
...
...
...
...
0977ffb4  00000000
0977ffb8  0977ffec
0977ffbc  77e6608b kernel32!BaseThreadStart+0x34
0977ffc0  025c3728
0977ffc4  00000000
0977ffc8  00000000
0977ffcc  025c3728
0977ffd0  a50c4963
0977ffd4  0977ffc4
0977ffd8  000a5285
0977ffdc  ffffffff
0977ffe0  77e6b7d0 kernel32!_except_handler3
0977ffe4  77e66098 kernel32!`string'+0x98
0977ffe8  00000000
0977ffec  00000000
0977fff0  00000000
0977fff4  77bcb4bc msvcrt!_endthreadex+0x2f
0977fff8  025c3728
0977fffc  00000000
09780000  ????????
TEB at 7ffae000
    ExceptionList:        0071ff64
    StackBase:            00720000
    StackLimit:           0071c000
    SubSystemTib:         00000000
    FiberData:            00001e00
    ArbitraryUserPointer: 00000000
    Self:                 7ffae000
    EnvironmentPointer:   00000000
    ClientId:             0000106c . 00000be8
    RpcHandle:            00000000
    Tls Storage:          00000000
    PEB Address:          7ffdf000
    LastErrorValue:       0
    LastStatusValue:      c000000d
    Count Owned Locks:    0
    HardErrorMode:        0
0071c000  00000000
0071c004  00000000
0071c008  00000000
0071c00c  00000000
0071c010  00000000
0071c014  00000000
0071c018  00000000
0071c01c  00000000
0071c020  00000000
```

```
0071c024  00000000
0071c028  00000000
0071c02c  00000000
0071c030  00000000
0071c034  00000000
0071c038  00000000
0071c03c  00000000
0071c040  00000000
0071c044  00000000
0071c048  00000000
0071c04c  00000000
0071c050  00000000
0071c054  00000000
...
...
...
...
...
...
...

0:000> .logclose
```

Instead of (or in addition to) **dps** command used in the script, we can use **dpu** or **dpa** commands to dump all strings that are pointed to by stack data or create a more complex script that does triple dereference.

Raw Stack Dump of All Threads (Complete Dump)

We can use **!for_each_thread** WinDbg extension command to dump a stack trace and user space raw stack data for all threads except system threads because they don't have user space stack counterpart and their TEB address is NULL:

```
!for_each_thread ".thread /r /p @#Thread; .if (@$teb != 0) {!thread
@#Thread; r? $t1 = ((ntdll!_NT_TIB *)@$teb)->StackLimit; r? $t2 =
((ntdll!_NT_TIB *)@$teb)->StackBase; !teb; dps @$t1 @$t2}"
```

We need to create a log file here. If it is huge and we want to dump raw stack contents for a specific process only, we can filter the output of the script using **$proc** pseudo-register, the address of EPROCESS:

```
!for_each_thread ".thread /r /p @#Thread; .if (@$teb != 0 & @$proc ==
<EPROCESS>) {!thread @#Thread; r? $t1 = ((ntdll!_NT_TIB *)@$teb)-
>StackLimit; r? $t2 = ((ntdll!_NT_TIB *)@$teb)->StackBase; !teb; dps @$t1
@$t2}"
```

For example:

```
1: kd>!process 0 0
...
...
...
PROCESS 8596f9c8  SessionId: 0  Cid: 0fac    Peb: 7ffde000  ParentCid:
0f3c
    DirBase: 3fba6520  ObjectTable: d6654e28  HandleCount: 389.
    Image: explorer.exe
...
...
...

1: kd> !for_each_thread ".thread /r /p @#Thread; .if (@$teb != 0 & @$proc
== 8596f9c8) {!thread @#Thread; r? $t1 = ((ntdll!_NT_TIB *)@$teb)-
>StackLimit; r? $t2 = ((ntdll!_NT_TIB *)@$teb)->StackBase; !teb; dps @$t1
@$t2}"
Implicit thread is now 8659b208
Implicit process is now 8659b478
Loading User Symbols

Implicit thread is now 86599db0
Implicit process is now 8659b478
Loading User Symbols


...
...
```

```
...
Implicit thread is now 85b32db0
Implicit process is now 8596f9c8
Loading User Symbols

THREAD 85b32db0  Cid 0fac.0fb0  Teb: 7ffdd000 Win32Thread: bc0a6be8 WAIT:
(Unknown) UserMode Non-Alertable
    859bda20  SynchronizationEvent
Not impersonating
DeviceMap                 d743e440
Owning Process            8596f9c8       Image:         explorer.exe
Wait Start TickCount      376275         Ticks: 102 (0:00:00:01.593)
Context Switch Count      3509                 LargeStack
UserTime                  00:00:00.078
KernelTime                00:00:00.203
Win32 Start Address Explorer!ModuleEntry (0x010148a4)
Start Address kernel32!BaseProcessStartThunk (0x77e617f8)
Stack Init ba5fe000 Current ba5fdc50 Base ba5fe000 Limit ba5f9000 Call 0
Priority 10 BasePriority 8 PriorityDecrement 0
ChildEBP RetAddr  Args to Child
ba5fdc68 80833465 85b32db0 85b32e58 00000000 nt!KiSwapContext+0x26
ba5fdc94 80829a62 00000000 bc0a6be8 00000000 nt!KiSwapThread+0x2e5
ba5fdcdc bf89abe3 859bda20 0000000d 00000001
nt!KeWaitForSingleObject+0x346
ba5fdd38 bf89da53 000024ff 00000000 00000001 win32k!xxxSleepThread+0x1be
ba5fdd4c bf89e411 000024ff 00000000 0007fef8
win32k!xxxRealWaitMessageEx+0x12
ba5fdd5c 8088978c 0007ff08 7c8285ec badb0d00 win32k!NtUserWaitMessage+0x14
ba5fdd5c 7c8285ec 0007ff08 7c8285ec badb0d00 nt!KiFastCallEntry+0xfc
(TrapFrame @ ba5fdd64)
0007feec 7739bf53 7c92addc 77e619d1 000d9298 ntdll!KiFastSystemCallRet
0007ff08 7c8fadbd 00000000 0007ff5c 0100fff1 USER32!NtUserWaitMessage+0xc
0007ff14 0100fff1 000d9298 7ffde000 0007ffc0
SHELL32!SHDesktopMessageLoop+0x24
0007ff5c 0101490c 00000000 00000000 000207fa
Explorer!ExplorerWinMain+0x2c4
0007ffc0 77e6f23b 00000000 00000000 7ffde000 Explorer!ModuleEntry+0x6d
0007fff0 00000000 010148a4 00000000 78746341
kernel32!BaseProcessStart+0x23
```

```
Last set context:
TEB at 7ffdd000
    ExceptionList:          0007ffe0
    StackBase:              00080000
    StackLimit:             00072000
    SubSystemTib:           00000000
    FiberData:              00001e00
    ArbitraryUserPointer: 00000000
    Self:                   7ffdd000
    EnvironmentPointer:     00000000
    ClientId:               00000fac . 00000fb0
    RpcHandle:              00000000
    Tls Storage:            00000000
    PEB Address:            7ffde000
    LastErrorValue:         6
    LastStatusValue:        c0000008
    Count Owned Locks:      0
    HardErrorMode:          0
00072000  ????????
00072004  ????????
00072008  ????????
0007200c  ????????
00072010  ????????
00072014  ????????
00072018  ????????
0007201c  ????????
...
...
...
00079ff8  ????????
00079ffc  ????????
0007a000  00000000
0007a004  00000000
0007a008  00000000
0007a00c  00000000
0007a010  00000000
0007a014  00000000
0007a018  00000000
0007a01c  00000000
0007a020  00000000
0007a024  00000000
0007a028  00000000
0007a02c  00000000
...
...
...
0007ff04  0007ff14
0007ff08  0007ff14
0007ff0c  7c8fadbd SHELL32!SHDesktopMessageLoop+0x24
0007ff10  00000000
0007ff14  0007ff5c
0007ff18  0100fff1 Explorer!ExplorerWinMain+0x2c4
0007ff1c  000d9298
0007ff20  7ffde000
```

```
0007ff24  0007ffc0
0007ff28  00000000
0007ff2c  0007fd28
0007ff30  0007ff50
0007ff34  7ffde000
0007ff38  7c82758b ntdll!ZwQueryInformationProcess+0xc
0007ff3c  77e6c336 kernel32!GetErrorMode+0x18
0007ff40  ffffffff
0007ff44  0000000c
0007ff48  00000000
0007ff4c  00018fb8
0007ff50  000000ec
0007ff54  00000001
0007ff58  000d9298
0007ff5c  0007ffc0
0007ff60  0101490c Explorer!ModuleEntry+0x6d
0007ff64  00000000
0007ff68  00000000
0007ff6c  000207fa
0007ff70  00000001
0007ff74  00000000
0007ff78  00000000
0007ff7c  00000044
0007ff80  0002084c
0007ff84  0002082c
0007ff88  000207fc
0007ff8c  00000000
0007ff90  00000000
0007ff94  00000000
0007ff98  00000000
0007ff9c  f60e87fc
0007ffa0  00000002
0007ffa4  021a006a
0007ffa8  00000001
0007ffac  00000001
0007ffb0  00000000
0007ffb4  00000000
0007ffb8  00000000
0007ffbc  00000000
0007ffc0  0007fff0
0007ffc4  77e6f23b kernel32!BaseProcessStart+0x23
0007ffc8  00000000
0007ffcc  00000000
0007ffd0  7ffde000
0007ffd4  00000000
0007ffd8  0007ffc8
0007ffdc  b9a94ce4
0007ffe0  ffffffff
0007ffe4  77e61a60 kernel32!_except_handler3
0007ffe8  77e6f248 kernel32!`string'+0x88
0007ffec  00000000
0007fff0  00000000
0007fff4  00000000
0007fff8  010148a4 Explorer!ModuleEntry
```

```
0007fffc  00000000
00080000  78746341
...
...
...
```

Because complete memory dumps contain only physical memory contents, some pages of raw stack data can be in page files and, therefore, unavailable.

Case Study

Consider the following legacy C++/Win32 code fragment highlighted in WinDbg after opening a crash dump:

```
HANDLE hFile = CreateFile(str.GetBuffer(), GENERIC_READ,
FILE_SHARE_READ, NULL, OPEN_EXISTING, FILE_ATTRIBUTE_NORMAL, NULL);
if (hFile != INVALID_HANDLE_VALUE)
{
    DWORD dwSize = GetFileSize(hFile, NULL);
    DWORD dwRead = 0;
    CHAR *bufferA = new CHAR[dwSize+2];
    memset(bufferA, 0, dwSize+2);
    if (ReadFile(hFile, bufferA, dwSize, &dwRead, NULL))
    {
       DWORD i = 0, j = 0;
       for (; i < dwSize+2-7; ++i)
       {
          if (bufferA[i] == 0xD && bufferA[i+1] != 0xA)
```

At first glance, the code seems to be right: we open a file, get its size, and allocate a buffer to read. All loop indexes are within array bounds too. Let's look at disassembly and crash point:

```
0:000> uf component!CMyDlg::OnTimer
...
...
...
004021bc push    0
004021be push    esi
004021bf call    dword ptr [component!_imp__GetFileSize (0042e26c)]
004021c5 mov     edi,eax ; dwSize
004021c7 lea     ebx,[edi+2]  ; dwSize+2
004021ca push    ebx
004021cb mov     dword ptr [esp+34h],0
004021d3 call    component!operator new[] (00408e35)
004021d8 push    ebx
004021d9 mov     ebp,eax  ; bufferA
004021db push    0
004021dd push    ebp
004021de call    component!memset (00418500)
004021e3 add     esp,10h
004021e6 push    0
004021e8 lea     edx,[esp+34h]
004021ec push    edx
004021ed push    edi
004021ee push    ebp
004021ef push    esi
004021f0 call    dword ptr [component!_imp__ReadFile (0042e264)]
004021f6 test    eax,eax
```

```
004021f8 jne     component!CMyDlg::OnTimer+0x3b1 (00402331)
...
...
...
00402331 xor     esi,esi ; i
00402333 add     edi,0FFFFFFFBh ; +2-7 (edi contains dwSize)
00402336 cmp     edi,esi ; loop condition
00402338 mov     dword ptr [esp+24h],esi
0040233c jbe     component!CMyDlg::OnTimer+0x43e (004023be)
00402342 mov     al,byte ptr [esi+ebp] ; bufferA[i]
```

```
0:000> r
eax=00002b00 ebx=00000002 ecx=00431000 edx=00000000 esi=00002b28
edi=fffffffb
eip=00402342 esp=0012efd4 ebp=0095b4d8 iopl=0 nv up ei pl nz ac pe cy
cs=001b ss=0023 ds=0023 es=0023 fs=003b gs=0000 efl=00000217
component!CMyDlg::OnTimer+0x3c2:
00402342 8a042e mov al,byte ptr [esi+ebp] ds:0023:0095e000=??
```

If we look at **ebx** (dwSize+2) and **edi** registers (array upper bound, *dwSize+2-7*), we can easily see that *dwSize* was zero. Clearly, we had a buffer overrun because the upper array bound was calculated as 0+2-7 = FFFFFFFB (the loop index was an unsigned integer, DWORD). Were the index signed integer variable (int), we wouldn't have had any problem because the condition 0 < 0+2-7 is always false, and the loop body would have never been executed.

Based on that the following fix was proposed:

```
1: HANDLE hFile = CreateFile(str.GetBuffer(), GENERIC_READ,
FILE_SHARE_READ, NULL, OPEN_EXISTING, FILE_ATTRIBUTE_NORMAL, NULL);
2: if (hFile != INVALID_HANDLE_VALUE)
3: {
4:    DWORD dwSize = GetFileSize(hFile, NULL);
5:    DWORD dwRead = 0;
6:    CHAR *bufferA = new CHAR[dwSize+2];
7:    memset(bufferA, 0, dwSize+2);
8:    if (ReadFile(hFile, bufferA, dwSize, &dwRead, NULL))
9:    {
10:      DWORD i = 0, j = 0;
10:      int i = 0, j = 0;
11:      for (; i < dwSize+2-7; ++i)
11:      for (; i < (int)dwSize+2-7; ++i)
12:      {
```

GetFileSize can return INVALID_FILE_SIZE (0xFFFFFFFF), and operator *new* can fail theoretically (if the size is too big) so we can correct the code even further:

```
1: HANDLE hFile = CreateFile(str.GetBuffer(), GENERIC_READ,
FILE_SHARE_READ, NULL, OPEN_EXISTING, FILE_ATTRIBUTE_NORMAL, NULL);
2: if (hFile != INVALID_HANDLE_VALUE)
3: {
4:     DWORD dwSize = GetFileSize(hFile, NULL);
4a:    if (dwSize != INVALID_FILE_SIZE)
4b:    {
5:        DWORD dwRead = 0;
6:        CHAR *bufferA = new CHAR[dwSize+2];
6a:       if (bufferA)
6b:       {
7:           memset(bufferA, 0, dwSize+2);
8:           if (ReadFile(hFile, bufferA, dwSize, &dwRead, NULL))
9:           {
10:             int i = 0, j = 0;
11:             for (; i < (int)dwSize+2-7; ++i)
12:             {
```

Detecting Loops in Code

Sometimes, when we look at a stack trace and code disassembly, we see that a crash couldn't have happened if the code path was linear. In such cases, we need to see if there is any loop that changes some variables. This is greatly simplified if we have source code, but in cases where we don't have access to source code, it is still possible to detect loops. We just need to find a direct (JMP) or conditional jump instruction (Jxxx, for example, JE) after the crash point branching to the beginning of the loop before the crash point as shown in the following pseudo-code:

```
set the pointer value
...
label:
...
>>> crash when dereferencing the pointer
...
change the pointer value
...
jmp label
```

Let's look at one example I found very interesting because it also shows *__thiscall* calling convention for C++ code generated by Visual C++ compiler. Before we look at the dump, I quickly remind you about how C++ non-static class methods are called. Let's first look at a non-virtual method call.

```
class A
{
public:
        int foo() { return i; }
virtual int bar() { return i; }
private:
        int i;
};
```

Internally class members are accessed via implicit *this* pointer (passed via ECX):

```
int A::foo() { return this->i; }
```

Suppose we have an object instance of *class A*, and we call its *foo* method:

```
A obj;
obj.foo();
```

The compiler has to generate code that calls *foo* function, and the code inside the function has to know which object it is associated with. So internally, the compiler passes implicit parameter - a pointer to that object. In pseudo-code:

```
int foo_impl(A *this)
{
return this->i;
}

A obj;
foo_impl(&obj);
```

In x86 assembly language, it should be similar to this code:

```
lea ecx, obj
call foo_impl
```

If we have *obj* declared as a local variable the code is similar:

```
lea ecx, [ebp-N]
call foo_impl
```

If we have a pointer to *obj* then the compiler usually generates MOV instruction instead of LEA instruction:

```
A *pobj;
pobj->foo();

mov ecx, [ebp-N]
call foo_impl
```

If we have other function parameters, they are pushed on the stack from right to left. This is *__thiscall* calling convention. For a virtual function call, we have an indirect call through a virtual function table. The pointer to it is the first object layout member, and in the latter case where the pointer to *obj* is declared as the local variable we have the following x86 code:

```
A *pobj;
pobj->bar();

mov ecx, [ebp-N]
mov eax, [ecx]
call [eax]
```

Now let's look at the crash point and stack trace:

```
0:021> r
eax=020864ee ebx=00000000 ecx=0000005c edx=7518005c esi=020864dc
edi=00000000
eip=67dc5dda esp=075de820 ebp=075dea78 iopl=0 nv up ei pl nz na po nc
cs=001b ss=0023 ds=0023 es=0023 fs=003b gs=0000 efl=00010202
component!CDirectory::GetDirectory+0x8a:
67dc5dda 8b03 mov eax,dword ptr [ebx] ds:0023:00000000=????????

0:021> k
ChildEBP RetAddr
075dea78 004074f0 component!CDirectory::GetDirectory+0x8a
075deaac 0040e4fc component!CDirectory::FindFirstFileW+0xd0
075dffb8 77e64829 component!MonitorThread+0x13
075dffec 00000000 kernel32!BaseThreadStart+0x34
```

If we look at *GetDirectory* code we see:

```
0:021> .asm no_code_bytes
Assembly options: no_code_bytes

0:021> uf component!CDirectory::GetDirectory
component!CDirectory::GetDirectory:
67dc5d50 push    ebp
67dc5d51 mov     ebp,esp
67dc5d53 push    0FFFFFFFFh
67dc5d55 push    offset component!CreateErrorInfo+0x553 (67ded93b)
67dc5d5a mov     eax,dword ptr fs:[00000000h]
67dc5d60 push    eax
67dc5d61 mov     dword ptr fs:[0],esp
67dc5d68 sub     esp,240h
67dc5d6e mov     eax,dword ptr [component!__security_cookie (67e0113c)]
67dc5d73 mov     dword ptr [ebp-10h],eax
67dc5d76 mov     eax,dword ptr [ebp+8]
67dc5d79 test    eax,eax
67dc5d7b push    ebx
67dc5d7c mov     ebx,ecx
67dc5d7e mov     dword ptr [ebp-238h],ebx
67dc5d84 je      component!CDirectory::GetDirectory+0x2a1 (67dc5ff1)

component!CDirectory::GetDirectory+0x3a:
67dc5d8a cmp     word ptr [eax],0
67dc5d8e je      component!CDirectory::GetDirectory+0x2a1 (67dc5ff1)
```

```
component!CDirectory::GetDirectory+0x44:
67dc5d94 push    esi
67dc5d95 push    eax
67dc5d96 call    dword ptr [component!_imp__wcsdup (67df050c)]
67dc5d9c add     esp,4
67dc5d9f mov     dword ptr [ebp-244h],eax
67dc5da5 mov     dword ptr [ebp-240h],eax
67dc5dab push    5Ch
67dc5dad lea     ecx,[ebp-244h]
67dc5db3 mov     dword ptr [ebp-4],0
67dc5dba call    component!CStrToken::Next (67dc4f80)
67dc5dbf mov     esi,eax
67dc5dc1 test    esi,esi
67dc5dc3 je      component!CDirectory::GetDirectory+0x28c (67dc5fdc)

component!CDirectory::GetDirectory+0x79:
67dc5dc9 push    edi
67dc5dca lea     ebx,[ebx]

component!CDirectory::GetDirectory+0x80:
67dc5dd0 cmp     word ptr [esi],0
67dc5dd4 je      component!CDirectory::GetDirectory+0x28b (67dc5fdb)

component!CDirectory::GetDirectory+0x8a:
>>> 67dc5dda mov     eax,dword ptr [ebx]
67dc5ddc mov ecx,ebx
...
```

If we trace EBX backward, we see that it comes from ECX so ECX can be considered as an implicit *this* pointer according to *__thiscall* calling convention. Therefore it looks like the caller passed NULL *this* pointer via ECX.

Let's look at the caller. To see the code we can either disassemble *FindFirstFileW* or disassemble backward at the *GetDirectory* return address. We'll do the latter:

```
0:021> k
ChildEBP RetAddr
075dea78 004074f0 component!CDirectory::GetDirectory+0x8a
075deaac 0040e4fc component!CDirectory::FindFirstFileW+0xd0
075dffb8 77e64829 component!MonitorThread+0x13
075dffec 00000000 kernel32!BaseThreadStart+0x34
```

```
0:021> ub 004074f0
component!CDirectory::FindFirstFileW+0xbe:
004074de pop     ebp
004074df clc
004074e0 mov     ecx,dword ptr [esi+8E4h]
004074e6 mov     eax,dword ptr [ecx]
004074e8 push    0
004074ea push    0
004074ec push    edx
004074ed call    dword ptr [eax+10h]
```

We see that ECX is our *this* pointer. However, the virtual table pointer is taken from the memory it references:

```
004074e6 mov eax,dword ptr [ecx]
...
...
004074ed call dword ptr [eax+10h]
```

Were ECX a NULL, we would have had our crash at this point. However, we have our crash in the called function. So it couldn't be NULL. There is a contradiction here. The only plausible explanation is that in *GetDirectory* function, there is a loop that changes EBX (shown in bold in *GetDirectory* function code above). If we have a second look at the code we would see that EBX is saved in [ebp-238h] local variable before it is used:

```
0:021> uf component!CDirectory::GetDirectory
component!CDirectory::GetDirectory:
67dc5d50 push    ebp
67dc5d51 mov     ebp,esp
67dc5d53 push    0FFFFFFFFh
67dc5d55 push    offset component!CreateErrorInfo+0x553 (67ded93b)
67dc5d5a mov     eax,dword ptr fs:[00000000h]
67dc5d60 push    eax
67dc5d61 mov     dword ptr fs:[0],esp
67dc5d68 sub     esp,240h
67dc5d6e mov     eax,dword ptr [component!__security_cookie (67e0113c)]
67dc5d73 mov     dword ptr [ebp-10h],eax
67dc5d76 mov     eax,dword ptr [ebp+8]
67dc5d79 test    eax,eax
67dc5d7b push    ebx
67dc5d7c mov     ebx,ecx
67dc5d7e mov     dword ptr [ebp-238h],ebx
67dc5d84 je      component!CDirectory::GetDirectory+0x2a1 (67dc5ff1)
```

```
component!CDirectory::GetDirectory+0x3a:
67dc5d8a cmp     word ptr [eax],0
67dc5d8e je      component!CDirectory::GetDirectory+0x2a1 (67dc5ff1)

component!CDirectory::GetDirectory+0x44:
67dc5d94 push    esi
67dc5d95 push    eax
67dc5d96 call    dword ptr [component!_imp__wcsdup (67df050c)]
67dc5d9c add     esp,4
67dc5d9f mov     dword ptr [ebp-244h],eax
67dc5da5 mov     dword ptr [ebp-240h],eax
67dc5dab push    5Ch
67dc5dad lea     ecx,[ebp-244h]
67dc5db3 mov     dword ptr [ebp-4],0
67dc5dba call    component!CStrToken::Next (67dc4f80)
67dc5dbf mov     esi,eax
67dc5dc1 test    esi,esi
67dc5dc3 je      component!CDirectory::GetDirectory+0x28c (67dc5fdc)

component!CDirectory::GetDirectory+0x79:
67dc5dc9 push    edi
67dc5dca lea     ebx,[ebx]

component!CDirectory::GetDirectory+0x80:
67dc5dd0 cmp     word ptr [esi],0
67dc5dd4 je      component!CDirectory::GetDirectory+0x28b (67dc5fdb)

component!CDirectory::GetDirectory+0x8a:
>>> 67dc5dda mov     eax,dword ptr [ebx]
67dc5ddc mov ecx,ebx
...
```

If we look further past the crash point, we see that [ebp-238h] value is changed and then used again to change EBX:

```
component!CDirectory::GetDirectory+0x80:
67dc5dd0 cmp word ptr [esi],0
67dc5dd4 je component!CDirectory::GetDirectory+0x28b (67dc5fdb)
```

```
component!CDirectory::GetDirectory+0x8a:
>>> 67dc5dda mov eax,dword ptr [ebx]
67dc5ddc mov ecx,ebx
...
...
...
component!CDirectory::GetDirectory+0x11e:
67dc5e6e mov     eax,dword ptr [ebp-23Ch]
67dc5e74 mov     ecx,dword ptr [eax]
67dc5e76 mov     dword ptr [ebp-238h],ecx
67dc5e7c jmp     component!CDirectory::GetDirectory+0x20e (67dc5f5e)
...
...
...
component!CDirectory::GetDirectory+0x23e:
67dc5f8e cmp     esi,edi
67dc5f90 mov     ebx,dword ptr [ebp-238h]
67dc5f96 jne     component!CDirectory::GetDirectory+0x80 (67dc5dd0)
```

We see that after changing EBX, the code jumps to 67dc5dd0 address, and this address is just before our crash point. It looks like a loop. Therefore, there is no contradiction. ECX as **this** pointer was passed as a non-NULL and valid pointer. Before the loop started, its value was passed to EBX. In the loop body, EBX was changed, and after some loop iterations, the new value became NULL. It could be the case that there were no checks for NULL pointers in the loop code.

Crash Dump Analysis Checklist

Often the root cause of a problem is not evident from a memory dump. Here is the first version of the crash dump analysis checklist to help experienced engineers not to miss any important information. The checklist doesn't prescribe any specific steps, just lists all possible points to double-check when looking at a memory dump.

General:

- Symbol servers (*.symfix*)
- Internal database(s) search
- Google or Microsoft search for suspected components as this could be a known issue. Sometimes a simple search immediately points to the fix on a vendor's site
- The tool used to save a dump (to flag false positive, incomplete or inconsistent dumps)
- OS/SP version (*version*)
- Language
- Debug time
- System uptime
- Computer name (*dS srv!srvcomputername* or *!envvar COMPUTERNAME*)
- List of loaded and unloaded modules (*lmv* or *!dlls*)
- Hardware configuration (*!sysinfo*)
- *.kframes 1000*

Application or service:

- Default analysis (*!analyze -v* or *!analyze -v -hang* for hangs)
- Critical sections (*!cs -s -l -o*, *!locks*) for both crashes and hangs
- Component timestamps, duplication, and paths. DLL Hell? (*lmv* and *!dlls*)
- Do any newer components exist?
- Process threads (*~*kv* or *!uniqstack*) for multiple exceptions and blocking functions
- Process uptime
- Your components on the full raw stack of the problem thread
- Your components on the full raw stack of the main application thread
- Process size
- Number of threads
- Gflags value (*!gflag*)
- Time consumed by threads (*!runaway*)

- Environment (*!peb*)
- Import table (*!dh*)
- Hooked functions (*!chkimg*)
- Exception handlers (*!exchain*)
- Computer name (*!envvar COMPUTERNAME*)
- Process heap stats and validation (*!heap -s, !heap -s -v*)
- CLR threads? (*mscorwks* or *clr* modules on stack traces) Yes: use .NET checklist below
- Hidden (unhandled and handled) exceptions on thread raw stacks

System hang:

- Default analysis (*!analyze -v -hang*)
- ERESOURCE contention (*!locks*)
- Processes and virtual memory including session space (*!vm 4*)
- Important services are present and not hanging (for example, terminal or IMA services for Citrix environments)
- Pools (*!poolused*)
- Waiting threads (*!stacks*)
- Critical system queues (*!exqueue f*)
- I/O (*!irpfind*)
- The list of all thread stack traces (*!process 0 3f*)
- LPC/ALPC chain for suspected threads (*!lpc message* or *!alpc /m* after search for "*Waiting for reply to LPC*" or "*Waiting for reply to ALPC*" in *!process 0 3f* output)
- RPC threads (search for "*RPCRT4!OSF*" in *!process 0 3f* output)
- Mutants (search for "*Mutants - owning thread*" in *!process 0 3f* output)
- Critical sections for suspected processes (*!cs -l -o -s*)
- Sessions, session processes (*!session, !sprocess*)
- Processes (size, handle table size) (*!process 0 0*)
- Running threads (*!running*)
- Ready threads (*!ready*)
- DPC queues (*!dpcs*)
- The list of APCs (*!apc*)
- Internal queued spinlocks (*!qlocks*)
- Computer name (*dS srv!srvcomputername*)
- File cache, VACB (*!filecache*)
- File objects for blocked thread IRPs (*!irp -> !fileobj*)
- Network (*!ndiskd.miniports* and *!ndiskd.pktpools*)
- Disk (*!scsikd.classext -> !scsikd.classext class_device 2*)
- Modules rdbss, mrxdav, mup, mrxsmb in stack traces
- Functions Ntfs!Ntfs*, nt!Fs* and fltmgr!Flt* in stack traces

BSOD:

- Default analysis (*!analyze -v*)
- Pool address (*!pool*)
- Component timestamps (*lmv*)
- Processes and virtual memory (*!vm 4*)
- Current threads on other processors
- Raw stack
- Bugcheck description (including ln exception address for corrupt or truncated dumps)
- Bugcheck callback data (*!bugdump* for systems prior to Windows XP SP1)
- Bugcheck secondary callback data (*.enumtag*)
- Computer name (*dS srv!srvcomputername*)
- Hardware configuration (*!sysinfo*)

.NET application or service:

- CLR module and SOS extension versions (*lmv* and *.chain*)
- Managed exceptions (*~*e !pe*)
- Nested managed exceptions (*!pe -nested*)
- Managed threads (*!Threads -special*)
- Managed stack traces (*~*e !CLRStack*)
- Managed execution residue (*~*e !DumpStackObjects* and *!DumpRuntimeTypes*)
- Managed heap (*!VerifyHeap, !DumpHeap -stat* and *!eeheap -gc*)
- GC handles (*!GCHandles, !GCHandleLeaks*)
- Finalizer queue (*!FinalizeQueue*)
- Sync blocks (*!syncblk*)

Crash Dump Analysis Poster (HTML version)

There is an HTML version of Crash Dump Analysis Poster with hyperlinks. Command links launch WinDbg online help for a corresponding topic, for example, **!heap**. Its link is http://www.dumpanalysis.org/CDAPoster.html or simply go to WinDbg.org to locate it.

In one of my previous work environments, I kept this HTML file open locally on a second monitor and found it very easy to jump to an appropriate command help when I needed its parameter description.

PART 3: Crash Dump Analysis Patterns

Multiple Exceptions (User Mode)

After doing crash dump analysis for some time, I decided to organize my knowledge into a set of patterns (so to speak in a memory dump analysis pattern language and therefore try to facilitate its common vocabulary).

What is a pattern? It is a general solution we can apply in a specific context to a common recurrent problem.

The first pattern I'm going to introduce today is **Multiple Exceptions**. This pattern captures the known fact that there could be as many exceptions ("crashes") as many threads in a process. The following UML diagram depicts the relationship between Process, Thread, and Exception entities:

Every process in Windows has at least one execution thread, so there could be at least one exception per thread (like invalid memory reference) if things go wrong. There could be the second exception in that thread if exception handling code experiences another exception or the first exception was handled, and you have another one and so on.

So what is the **general solution** to that common problem when an application or service crashes, and we have a crash dump file **(common recurrent problem)** from a customer **(specific context)**? The general solution is to look at all threads and their stacks and do not rely on what tools say.

Here is a concrete example from one of the dumps. Internet Explorer crashed, and I opened it in WinDbg and ran **!analyze -v** command. This is what I got in my WinDbg output:

```
ExceptionAddress: 7c822583 (ntdll!DbgBreakPoint)
   ExceptionCode: 80000003 (Break instruction exception)
  ExceptionFlags: 00000000
NumberParameters: 3
   Parameter[0]: 00000000
   Parameter[1]: 8fb834b8
   Parameter[2]: 00000003
```

Break instruction, we might think, shows that the dump was taken manually from the running application, and there was no crash - the customer sent the wrong dump or misunderstood troubleshooting instructions. However, I looked at all threads, and noticed the following two stacks (threads 15 and 16):

```
0:016>~*kL
...
15  Id: 1734.8f4 Suspend: 1 Teb: 7ffab000 Unfrozen
ntdll!KiFastSystemCallRet
ntdll!NtRaiseHardError+0xc
kernel32!UnhandledExceptionFilter+0x54b
kernel32!BaseThreadStart+0x4a
kernel32!_except_handler3+0x61
ntdll!ExecuteHandler2+0x26
ntdll!ExecuteHandler+0x24
ntdll!KiUserExceptionDispatcher+0xe
componentA!xxx
componentB!xxx
mshtml!xxx
kernel32!BaseThreadStart+0x34

# 16  Id: 1734.11a4 Suspend: 1 Teb: 7ffaa000 Unfrozen
ntdll!DbgBreakPoint
ntdll!DbgUiRemoteBreakin+0x36
```

We see here that the real crash happened in *componentA.dll* and *componentB.dll* or *mshtml.dll* might have influenced that. Why did this happen? The customer might have dumped Internet Explorer manually while it was displaying an exception message box. *NtRaiseHardError* displays a message box containing an error message.

Perhaps something else happened. Many cases, where we see multiple thread exceptions in one process dump, happened because crashed threads displayed message boxes like Visual C++ debug message box and preventing that process from termination. In our dump under discussion, WinDbg automatic analysis command recognized only the last breakpoint exception (shown as # 16). In conclusion, we shouldn't rely on "automatic analysis" often.

Dynamic Memory Corruption (Process Heap)

The next pattern I would like to discuss is **Dynamic Memory Corruption** (and its user and kernel variants called **Heap Corruption** and **Pool Corruption**). It is so ubiquitous, and its manifestations are random and usually crashes happen far away from the original corruption point. In our user mode and space part of exception threads (don't forget about **Multiple Exceptions** pattern, page 255) you would see something like this:

```
ntdll!RtlpCoalesceFreeBlocks+0x10c
ntdll!RtlFreeHeap+0x142
MSVCRT!free+0xda
componentA!xxx
```

or this stack trace fragment:

```
ntdll!RtlpCoalesceFreeBlocks+0x10c
ntdll!RtlpExtendHeap+0x1c1
ntdll!RtlAllocateHeap+0x3b6
componentA!xxx
```

or any similar variants, and we need to know the exact component that corrupted the application heap (which usually is not the same as *componentA.dll* we see in the crashed thread stack).

For this **common recurrent problem**, we have a **general solution**: enable heap checking. This general solution has many variants applied in a **specific context**:

- parameter value checking for heap functions
- user space software heap checks before or after certain checkpoints (like "malloc"/"new" and/or "free"/"delete" calls): usually implemented by checking various fill patterns, etc.
- hardware/OS supported heap checks (like using guard and inaccessible pages to trap buffer overruns)

The latter variant is the mostly used according to my experience and mainly due to the fact that most heap corruptions originate from buffer overflows. And it is easier to rely on instant MMU support than on checking fill patterns. Here is the presentation describing how we can enable full page heap:

How to enable full page heap: Debugging TV episode 0x26
(http://www.debugging.tv/Frames/0x26/DebuggingTV_Frame_0x26.pdf
https://www.youtube.com/watch?v=F4cCxHkJVCQ)

The Windows kernel analog to user mode and space heap corruption is called a page and nonpaged pool corruption. If we consider Windows kernel pools as variants of heap, then exactly the same techniques are applicable there, for example, the so-called special pool enabled by Driver Verifier is implemented by inaccessible pages. Refer to the following Microsoft article for further details:

How to use the special pool feature to isolate pool damage
(http://support.microsoft.com/kb/188831)

False Positive Dump

Another frequent pattern is **False Positive Dump**. Here we get crash dump files pointing in the wrong direction or not useful for analysis. It usually happens when a wrong tool was selected, or the right one was not correctly configured for capturing crash dumps. Here is one example investigated in detail.

The customer experienced frequent spooler crashes on Windows Server 2003. The dump was sent for investigation to find an offending component. Usually, it is a printer driver. WinDbg revealed the following exception thread stack:

```
KERNEL32!RaiseException+0x56
KERNEL32!OutputDebugStringA+0x55
KERNEL32!OutputDebugStringW+0x39
PRINTER!ConvertTicket+0x3c90
PRINTER!DllGetClassObject+0x5d9b
PRINTER!DllGetClassObject+0x11bb
```

The immediate response is to point to *PRINTER.DLL*, but if we look at parameters to *KERNEL32!OutputDebugStringA* we would see that the string passed to it is a valid NULL-terminated string:

```
0:010> da 000d0040
000d0040  ".Lower DWORD of elapsed time = 3"
000d0060  "750000."
```

If we disassemble *OutputDebugStringA* up to *RaiseException* call we see:

```
0:010> u KERNEL32!OutputDebugStringA
KERNEL32!OutputDebugStringA+0x55
KERNEL32!OutputDebugStringA:
push    ebp
mov     ebp,esp
push    0FFFFFFFFh
push    offset KERNEL32!'string'+0x10
push    offset KERNEL32!_except_handler3
mov     eax,dword ptr fs:[00000000h]
push    eax
mov     dword ptr fs:[0],esp
push    ecx
push    ecx
sub     esp,228h
push    ebx
push    esi
push    edi
mov     dword ptr [ebp-18h],esp
```

```
and     dword ptr [ebp-4],0
mov     edx,dword ptr [ebp+8]
mov     edi,edx
or      ecx,0FFFFFFFFh
xor     eax,eax
repne scas byte ptr es:[edi]
not     ecx
mov     dword ptr [ebp-20h],ecx
mov     dword ptr [ebp-1Ch],edx
lea     eax,[ebp-20h]
push    eax
push    2
push    0
push    40010006h
call    KERNEL32!RaiseException
```

There are no jumps in the code before *KERNEL32!RaiseException* call, and this means that raising an exception is expected. Also, MSDN documentation says:

> *"If the application has no debugger, the system debugger displays the string. If the application has no debugger and the system debugger is not active, OutputDebugString does nothing."*

So *spoolsv.exe* might have been monitored by a debugger which caught that exception, and instead of dismissing, it dumped the spooler process.

If we look at **analyze -v** output we see the following:

```
Comment: 'Userdump generated complete user-mode minidump
with Exception Monitor function on WS002E0O-01-MFP'ERROR_CODE: (NTSTATUS)
0x40010006 -
Debugger printed exception on control C.
```

Now we see that the debugger was User Mode Process Dumper we can download from Microsoft web site:

How to use the Userdump.exe tool to create a dump file
(http://support.microsoft.com/kb/241215)

If we download it, install it and write a small console program in Visual C++ to reproduce this crash:

```
#include "stdafx.h"
#include
int _tmain(int argc, _TCHAR* argv[])
{
    OutputDebugString(_T("Sample string"));
    return 0;
}
```

and if we compile it in Release mode and configure Process Dumper applet in Control Panel to include *TestOutputDebugString.exe* with the following properties:

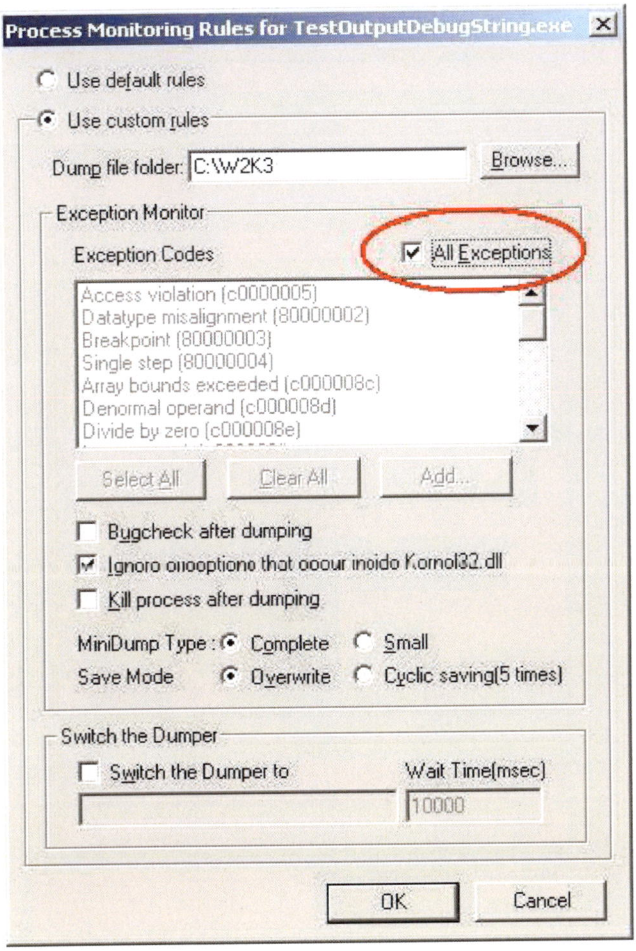

Then if we run our program, we see Process Dumper catching exceptions thrown by *KERNEL32!RaiseExceptionfunction* and saving the dump.

Even if we select to ignore exceptions that occur inside *kernel32.dll*, this tool still dumps our process. Now we can see that the customer most probably enabled 'All Exceptions' checkbox too. What the customer should have done is to use default rules shown in the picture below:

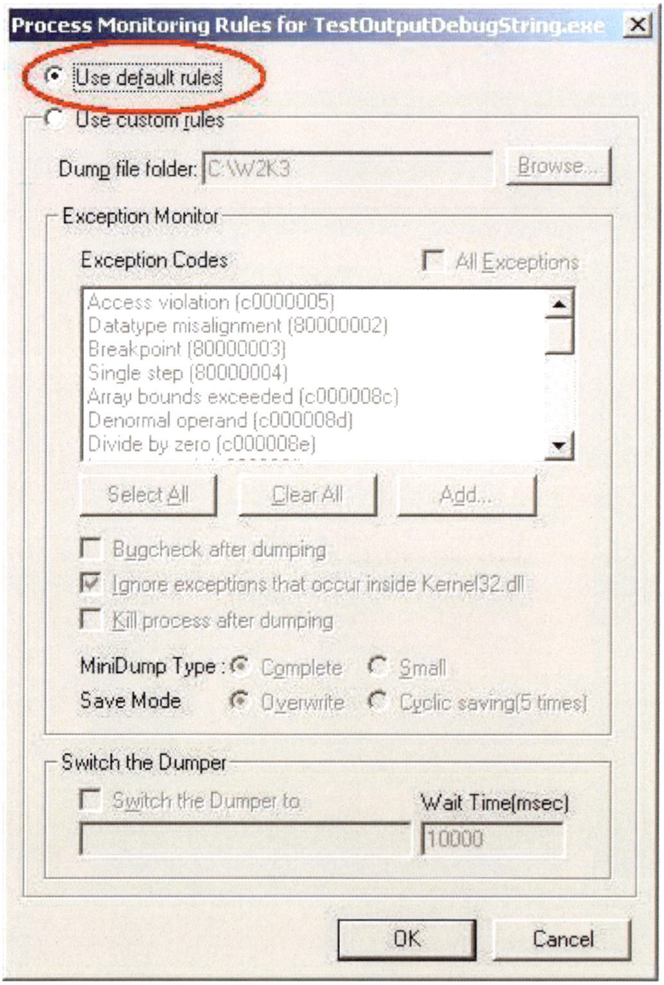

We can also select exception codes manually. In this case, no crash dump is generated even if we manually select all of them. Just to check that the latter configuration still catches access violations, we can add a line of code dereferencing a NULL pointer, and Process Dumper catches it and saves the dump.

The customer should have used NTSD as a default postmortem debugger. Then if a crash happened, we would have seen the real offending component or could have applied other patterns and requested additional dumps.

Lateral Damage (General)

After looking at one dump where all thread environment blocks were zeroed, the import table was corrupt, and recalling some similar cases encountered previously I came up with the next pattern: **Lateral Damage**.

When this problem happens, we don't have much choice, and our first temptation is to apply **Alien Component** anti-pattern (page 493) unless our module list is corrupt, and we have a manifestation of another widespread pattern **Corrupt Dump** (see volume 2).

An anti-pattern is not always a wrong solution if complemented by subsequent verification and backed by experience. If we get a damaged process and thread structures we can point to a suspicious component (supported by some evidence from raw stack analysis and educated guess), and then request additional crash dumps in hope to get less damaged process space or see that component again. At the very end, if removing a suspicious component stabilizes the customer environment, it proves that we were right.

Optimized Code (Function Parameter Reuse)

The next pattern is called **Optimized Code.** If we have such cases, we should not trust our crash dump analysis tools like WinDbg. Always suspect that compiler generated code might have been optimized if we see any suspicious or strange behavior of the tool. Let's consider this stack trace fragment:

```
Args to Child
77e44c24 000001ac 00000000 ntdll!KiFastSystemCallRet
000001ac 00000000 00000000 ntdll!NtFsControlFile+0xc
00000034 00000bb8 0013e3f4 kernel32!WaitNamedPipeW+0x2c3
0016fc60 00000000 67c14804 MyModule!PipeCreate+0x48
```

Third-party function *PipeCreate* from *MyModule* opens a named pipe, and its first parameter (0016fc60) points to a pipe name L"\\.\pipe\MyPipe". Inside the source code, it calls Win32 API function *WaitNamedPipeW* to wait for the pipe to be available for connection) and passes the same pipe name. But we see that the first parameter to *WaitNamedPipeW* is 00000034, which cannot be the pointer to a valid Unicode string. And the program should have been crashed if 00000034 were a pointer value.

Everything becomes clear if we look at *WaitNamedPipeW* disassembly:

```
0:000> uf kernel32!WaitNamedPipeW
mov     edi,edi
push    ebp
mov     ebp,esp
sub     esp,50h
push    dword ptr [ebp+8]   ; Use pipe name
lea     eax,[ebp-18h]
push    eax
call    dword ptr [kernel32!_imp__RtlCreateUnicodeString (77e411c8)]
...
...
...
...
call    dword ptr [kernel32!_imp__NtOpenFile (77e41014)]
cmp     dword ptr [ebp-4],edi
mov     esi,eax
jne     kernel32!WaitNamedPipeW+0x1d5 (77e93316)
cmp     esi,edi
jl      kernel32!WaitNamedPipeW+0x1ef (77e93331)
movzx   eax,word ptr [ebp-10h]
mov     ecx,dword ptr fs:[18h]
add     eax,0Eh
push    eax
push    dword ptr [kernel32!BaseDllTag (77ecd14c)]
mov     dword ptr [ebp+8],eax   ; reuse parameter slot
```

As we know, [ebp+8] is the first function parameter for non-FPO calls, and we see it is reused because after converting LPWSTR to UNICODE_STRING and calling *NtOpenFile* to get a handle we no longer need our parameter slot. The compiler can reuse it to store other information.

There is another compiler optimization we should be aware of, and it is called **OMAP** (page 294). It moves the code inside the code section and puts the most frequently accessed code fragments together. In that case, if we type in WinDbg, for example,

```
0:000> uf nt!someFunction
```

we get different disassembly code than if we type (assuming f4794100 is the address of the function we obtained from stack trace or disassembly)

```
0:000> uf f4794100
```

In conclusion, the advice is to be alert and conscious during crash dump analysis and inspect any inconsistencies closer.

Invalid Pointer (General)

Here I want to "introduce" **Invalid Pointer** pattern. It's just a number saved in a register or memory location. When we try to interpret it as a memory address itself and follow it (dereference) to fetch memory contents (value) it points to, OS with the help of hardware tells us that the address doesn't exist or inaccessible due to security restrictions.

In Windows, we have our process memory partitioned into two big regions: kernel space and process space. Space partition is a different concept than execution mode (kernel or user, ring 0 or ring 3), which is a processor state. Code executing in kernel mode (a driver or OS, for example) can access memory that belongs to user space.

Based on that, we can make a distinction between invalid pointers containing kernel space addresses (starting from 0x80000000 on x86, no /3Gb switch) and invalid pointers containing user space addresses (below 0x7FFFFFFF).

On Windows x64 user space addresses are below 0x0000070000000000 and kernel space addresses start from 0xFFFF080000000000.

When we dereference invalid kernel space address we get a bugcheck immediately:

UNEXPECTED_KERNEL_MODE_TRAP (7F)

PAGE_FAULT_IN_NONPAGED_AREA (50)

There is no way we can catch it in our code (by using SEH).

However, when we dereference user space address the course of action depends on whether our processor is in kernel mode (ring 0) or user mode (ring 3). In any mode, we can catch the exception (by using appropriate SEH handler) or leave this to the operating system or a debugger. If there was no component willing to process the exception when it happened in user mode we get our process crash and in kernel mode we get the following bugchecks:

SYSTEM_THREAD_EXCEPTION_NOT_HANDLED (7E)

KERNEL_MODE_EXCEPTION_NOT_HANDLED (8E)

I summarized all of this on the following UML class diagram:

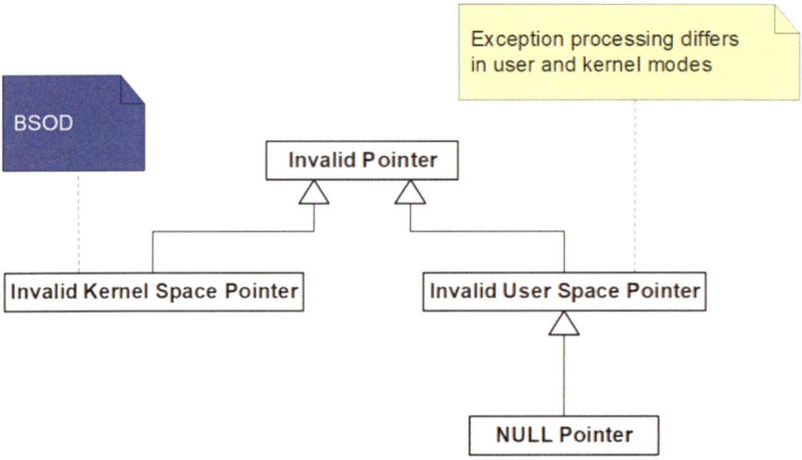

A NULL pointer is a special class of user space pointers. Usually, its value is in the range of 0x00000000 - 0x0000FFFF. We can see them used in instructions like

```
mov   esi, dword ptr [ecx+0x10]
```

where ECX value is 0x00000000, and we try to access the value located at 0x00000010 memory address.

When we get a crash dump, and we see an invalid pointer pattern, the next step is to interpret the pointer value, which should help in understanding possible steps that led to the crash.

Inconsistent Dump

Sometimes, we have to live with tools that produce inconsistent dumps. For example, LiveKd.exe from sysinternals.com was widely used by technical support to save complete memory dumps without a server reboot. In the past, before 2008, I wrote an article *Using LiveKD to Save a Complete Memory Dump for Session or System Hangs* (the link is no longer available). There was an important note there which is reproduced here:

> *LiveKd.exe-generated dumps are always inconsistent and cannot be a reliable source for certain types of dump analysis, for example, looking at resource contention. This is because it takes a considerable amount of time to save a dump on a live system, and the system is being changed during that process. The instantaneous traditional CrashOnCtrlScroll method or SystemDump tool always save a reliable and consistent dump because the system is frozen first (any process or kernel activity is disabled), then a dump is saved to a page file.*

If we look at such an inconsistent dump, we find that many useful kernel structures such as ERESOURCE lists (**!locks**) are broken, and even circularly referenced. Therefore, WinDbg commands display "strange" output.

Easy and painless (for customers) crash dump generation using such "Live" tools means that it is widely used, and we have to analyze memory dumps saved by these tools and sent from customers. This brings us to the next crash dump analysis pattern called **Inconsistent Dump**.

If we have such a memory dump, we should look at it to extract maximum useful information that helps in identifying the root cause or give us further directions. Not all information is inconsistent in such dumps. For example, drivers, processes, thread stacks, and IRP lists can give us some clues about activities. Even some information not visible in a consistent dump can surface in an inconsistent dump.

For example, I had a LiveKd memory dump from Windows Server 2003 where I looked at process stacks and found that for some processes in addition to their own threads there were additional terminated threads belonging to a completely different process (never seen in consistent memory dumps):

```
THREAD 8a665db0  Cid 16a8.16ac  Teb: 00000000 Win32Thread: 00000000 TERMINATED
Not impersonating
Owning Process            89d97d88       Image:          winlogon.exe
Wait Start TickCount      995838         Ticks: 2275 (0:00:00:35.546)
Context Switch Count      2287                 LargeStack
UserTime                  00:00:00.0468
KernelTime                00:00:00.0781
Start Address 0x0103d90f
Stack Init 0 Current f47fcc18 Base f47fd000 Limit f47f8000 Call 0
Priority 11 BasePriority 10 PriorityDecrement 0
```

Process 89d97d88 was not visible in the active process list (**!process 0 0** command). However, when I fed this memory address to **!process** command (or explore it as _EPROCESS structure, **dt** command) I got its contents:

```
0: kd> !process 89d97d88
PROCESS 89d97d88  SessionId: 2  Cid: 16a8    Peb: 7ffdf000  ParentCid: 0278
    DirBase: cc869000  ObjectTable: 00000000  HandleCount:   0.
    Image: winlogon.exe
    VadRoot 00000000 Vads 0 Clone 0 Private 0. Modified 1635. Locked 0.
    DeviceMap 00000000
    Token                             00000000
    ElapsedTime                       00:01:49.812
    UserTime                          00:00:00.531
    KernelTime                        00:00:01.171
    QuotaPoolUsage[PagedPool]         0
    QuotaPoolUsage[NonPagedPool]      0
    Working Set Sizes (now,min,max)  (4, 50, 345) (16KB, 200KB, 1380KB)
    PeakWorkingSetSize                3259
    VirtualSize                       63 Mb
    PeakVirtualSize                   63 Mb
    PageFaultCount                    8048
    MemoryPriority                    BACKGROUND
    BasePriority                      8
    CommitCharge                      0
```

What might have happened there: terminated process 89d97d88 was excluded from the active processes list, but its structure was left in memory, and due to inconsistency, thread lists were also broken, and, therefore, terminated threads surfaced when listing other processes and their threads.

I suspected here that *winlogon.exe* died in session 2 and left empty desktop window which the customer saw and complained about. The only left and visible process from session 2 was *csrss.exe*. The conclusion was to enable NTSD as a default postmortem debugger to catch *winlogon.exe* crash when it happens next time.

Note: Since the first edition of this book, LiveKd.exe was significantly extended with additional options to prevent **Inconsistent Dumps**.

Hidden Exception (User Space)

Another pattern that occurs frequently is called **Hidden Exception**. It manifests itself when we run **!analyze -v** command, and we don't see an exception, or we see only a breakpoint hit. In this case, manual analysis is required. Sometimes this happens because of another pattern: **Multiple Exceptions** (page 255). In other cases, an exception happens, and it is handled by an exception handler dismissing it, and a process continues its execution, slowly accumulating corruption inside its data leading to a new crash or hang. Sometimes we see a process hanging during its termination like the case shown below.

We have a process dump with only one thread:

```
0:000> kv
ChildEBP RetAddr
0096fcdc 7c822124 ntdll!KiFastSystemCallRet
0096fce0 77e6baa8 ntdll!NtWaitForSingleObject+0xc
0096fd50 77e6ba12 kernel32!WaitForSingleObjectEx+0xac
0096fd64 67f016ce kernel32!WaitForSingleObject+0x12
0096fd78 7c82257a component!DllInitialize+0xc2
0096fd98 7c8118b0 ntdll!LdrpCallInitRoutine+0x14
0096fe34 77e52fea ntdll!LdrShutdownProcess+0x130
0096ff20 77e5304d kernel32!_ExitProcess+0x43
0096ff34 77bcade4 kernel32!ExitProcess+0x14
0096ff40 77bcaefb msvcrt!__crtExitProcess+0x32
0096ff70 77bcaf6d msvcrt!_cinit+0xd2
0096ff84 77bcb555 msvcrt!_exit+0x11
0096ffb8 77e66063 msvcrt!_endthreadex+0xc8
0096ffec 00000000 kernel32!BaseThreadStart+0x34
```

We can look at its raw stack and try to find the following address:

KiUserExceptionDispatcher

This function calls *RtlDispatchException*:

```
0:000> !teb
TEB at 7ffdc000
    ExceptionList:          0096fd40
    StackBase:              00970000
    StackLimit:             0096a000
    SubSystemTib:           00000000
    FiberData:              00001e00
    ArbitraryUserPointer:   00000000
    Self:                   7ffdc000
    EnvironmentPointer:     00000000
    ClientId:               00000858 . 000008c0
```

```
    RpcHandle:               00000000
    Tls Storage:             00000000
    PEB Address:             7ffdd000
    LastErrorValue:          0
    LastStatusValue:         c0000135
    Count Owned Locks:       0
    HardErrorMode:           0

0:000>dds 0096a000 00970000
...
...
...
0096c770  7c8140cc ntdll!RtlDispatchException+0x91
0096c774  0096c808
0096c778  0096ffa8
0096c77c  0096c824
0096c780  0096c7e4
0096c784  77bc6c74 msvcrt!_except_handler3
0096c788  00000000
0096c78c  0096c808
0096c790  01030064
0096c794  00000000
0096c798  00000000
0096c79c  00000000
0096c7a0  00000000
0096c7a4  00000000
0096c7a8  00000000
0096c7ac  00000000
0096c7b0  00000000
0096c7b4  00000000
0096c7b8  00000000
0096c7bc  00000000
0096c7c0  00000000
0096c7c4  00000000
0096c7c8  00000000
0096c7cc  00000000
0096c7d0  00000000
0096c7d4  00000000
0096c7d8  00000000
0096c7dc  00000000
0096c7e0  00000000
0096c7e4  00000000
0096c7e8  00970000
0096c7ec  00000000
0096c7f0  0096caf0
0096c7f4  7c82ecc6 ntdll!KiUserExceptionDispatcher+0xe
0096c7f8  0096c000
0096c7fc  0096c824 ; a pointer to an exception context
0096c800  0096c808
0096c804  0096c824
0096c808  c0000005
0096c80c  00000000
0096c810  00000000
```

```
0096c814  77bd8df3 msvcrt!wcschr+0x15
0096c818  00000002
0096c81c  00000000
0096c820  01031000
0096c824  0001003f
0096c828  00000000
0096c82c  00000000
0096c830  00000000
0096c834  00000000
0096c838  00000000
0096c83c  00000000
```

A second parameter to both functions is a pointer to the so-called exception context (processor state when an exception occurred). We can use **.cxr** command to change thread execution context to what it was at exception time:

```
0:000> .cxr 0096c824
eax=01031000 ebx=0096eb70 ecx=01035000 edx=0000005b esi=01030064 edi=00000000
eip=77bd8df3 esp=0096caf0 ebp=0096caf0 iopl=0         nv up ei pl nz ac pe nc
cs=001b  ss=0023  ds=0023  es=0023  fs=003b  gs=0000             efl=00010216
msvcrt!wcschr+0x15:
77bd8df3 668b08          mov     cx,word ptr [eax]        ds:0023:01031000=????
```

After changing the context, we can see the thread stack before that exception:

```
0:000> kL
ChildEBP RetAddr
0096caf0 67b11808 msvcrt!wcschr+0x15
0096cb10 67b1194d component2!function1+0x50
0096cb24 67b11afb component2!function2+0x1a
0096eb5c 67b11e10 component2!function3+0x39
0096ed94 67b14426 component2!function4+0x155
0096fdc0 67b164b7 component2!function5+0x3b
0096fdcc 00402831 component2!function6+0x5b
0096feec 0096ff14 program!function+0x1d1
0096ffec 00000000 kernel32!BaseThreadStart+0x34
```

We see that the exception happened when *component2* was searching a Unicode string for a character (*wcschr*). Most likely the string was not zero-terminated:

```
0:000> r
Last set context:
eax=01031000 ebx=0096eb70 ecx=01035000 edx=0000005b esi=01030064 edi=00000000
eip=77bd8df3 esp=0096caf0 ebp=0096caf0 iopl=0         nv up ei pl nz ac pe nc
cs=001b  ss=0023  ds=0023  es=0023  fs=003b  gs=0000             efl=00010216
msvcrt!wcschr+0x15:
77bd8df3 668b08          mov     cx,word ptr [eax]        ds:0023:01031000=????

0:000> kv
ChildEBP RetAddr  Args to Child
0096caf0 67b11808 01030064 0000005b 00000000 msvcrt!wcschr+0x15
```

To summarize and show the common exception handling path in user space here is another thread stack taken from a different dump:

```
ntdll!KiFastSystemCallRet
ntdll!NtWaitForMultipleObjects+0xc
kernel32!UnhandledExceptionFilter+0x746
kernel32!_except_handler3+0x61
ntdll!ExecuteHandler2+0x26
ntdll!ExecuteHandler+0x24
ntdll!RtlDispatchException+0x91
ntdll!KiUserExceptionDispatcher+0xe
ntdll!RtlpCoalesceFreeBlocks+0x36e ; crash is here
ntdll!RtlFreeHeap+0x38e
msvcrt!free+0xc3
msvcrt!_freefls+0x124
msvcrt!_freeptd+0x27
msvcrt!__CRTDLL_INIT+0x1da
ntdll!LdrpCallInitRoutine+0x14
ntdll!LdrShutdownThread+0xd2
kernel32!ExitThread+0x2f
kernel32!BaseThreadStart+0x39
```

When *RtlpCoalesceFreeBlocks* (this function compacts a heap, and it is called from *RtlFreeHeap*) does an illegal memory access then this exception is first processed in kernel, and, because it happened in user space and mode, the execution is transferred to *RtlDispatchException* which searches for exception handlers, and in this case there is a default one installed: *UnhandledExceptionFilter*.

If we see this function on call stack we can also manually get an exception context and a thread stack leading to it like in this example below taken from some other crash dump:

```
  16  Id: 3354.37d8 Suspend: 1 Teb: 7ffdc000 Unfrozen
ChildEBP RetAddr  Args to Child
042be0d0 7c59c1f5 00000410 00000001 00000000 NTDLL!ZwWaitForSingleObject+0xb
042be80c 7c57b3a9 042be834 7c5c21b3 042be83c KERNEL32!UnhandledExceptionFilter+0x3a8
042bffec 00000000 77d37dd0 01effaf8 00000000 KERNEL32!BaseThreadStart+0x65

0:000> dt EXCEPTION_POINTERS 042be834
   +0x000 ExceptionRecord  : 0x042be900 _EXCEPTION_RECORD
   +0x004 ContextRecord    : 0x042be91c _CONTEXT

0:000> .cxr 042be91c
eax=00000000 ebx=002f0000 ecx=00000000 edx=002fe0e8 esi=002fdb50 edi=002fe0e8
eip=77fcc8e1 esp=042bebe8 ebp=042bebf4 iopl=0         nv up ei pl zr na pe nc
cs=001b  ss=0023  ds=0023  es=0023  fs=0038  gs=0000             efl=00010246
NTDLL!RtlpCoalesceFreeBlocks+0x2fb:
77fcc8e1 8901             mov     dword ptr [ecx],eax  ds:0023:00000000=????????
```

The most likely reason for this crash is an instance of **Dynamic Memory Corruption** pattern - heap corruption (page 257).

We can also search for exception codes like c0000005 using scripts to dump raw stack data (see pages 231 and 236). For example:

```
007cfa40 017d0000
007cfa44 007cfd90
007cfa48 7c82855e ntdll!KiUserExceptionDispatcher+0xe
007cfa4c 7c826d9b ntdll!NtContinue+0xc
007cfa50 7c82856c ntdll!KiUserExceptionDispatcher+0x1c
007cfa54 007cfa78
007cfa58 00000000
007cfa5c c0000005
007cfa60 00000000
007cfa64 00000000
007cfa68 0100e076 component!foo+0x1c4
007cfa6c 00000002
007cfa70 00000001
007cfa74 00000000
007cfa78 0001003f
007cfa7c 00000003
007cfa80 000000b0
007cfa84 00000001
007cfa88 00000000
007cfa8c 00000000
007cfa90 00000155
007cfa94 ffff027f
007cfa98 ffff0000
007cfa9c ffffffff
007cfaa0 00000000
007cfaa4 00000000
007cfaa8 00000000
007cfaac ffff0000
007cfab0 00000000
007cfab4 00000000
007cfab8 00000000

1. kd> .cxr 007cfa70
eax=01073bb0 ebx=7ffd9000 ecx=00000050 edx=01073bb0 esi=000003e5
edi=00000000
eip=0100e076 esp=007cfd44 ebp=007cfd90 iopl=0 nv up ei pl zr na pe nc
cs=001b ss=0023 ds=0023 es=0023 fs=003b gs=0000 efl=00000246
component!foo+0x1c4:
001b:0100e076 891a mov dword ptr [edx],ebx ds:0023:01073bb0=????????
```

The presence of unloaded fault handling modules can be the sign of hidden exceptions too:

```
Unloaded modules:
697b0000 697c7000 faultrep.dll
Timestamp: Fri Mar 25 02:11:44 2005 (42437360)
Checksum: 0001DC38
```

Deadlock (Critical Sections)

The next pattern is called **Deadlock**. If you don't know what "deadlock" is please read its explanation on page 31. Deadlocks not only happen with synchronization primitives like mutexes, events, or more complex objects (built upon primitives like critical sections or executive resources, ERESOURCE), but also from a high level or systems perspective in inter-process or inter-component communication, for example, when mutually waiting on messages: GUI window messages, LPC messages, and RPC calls.

How can we see deadlocks in memory dumps? Let's start with user dumps and critical sections.

First, I would recommend reading the following excellent MSDN article to understand various members of CRITICAL_SECTION structure:

Break Free of Code Deadlocks in Critical Sections Under Windows, MSDN Magazine, December 2003 (https://docs.microsoft.com/en-us/archive/msdn-magazine/2003/december/break-free-of-code-deadlocks-in-critical-sections-under-windows)

WinDbg **!locks** command examines process critical section list and displays all locked critical sections, lock count, and thread ID of current critical section owner. This is the output from a memory dump of hanging Windows print spooler process (*spoolsv.exe*):

```
0:000> !locks
CritSec NTDLL!LoaderLock+0 at 784B0348
LockCount          4
RecursionCount     1
OwningThread       624
EntryCount         6c3
ContentionCount    6c3
*** Locked

CritSec LOCALSPL!SpoolerSection+0 at 76AB8070
LockCount          3
RecursionCount     1
OwningThread       1c48
EntryCount         646
ContentionCount    646
*** Locked
```

If we look at threads #624 and #1c48, we see them mutually waiting for each other:

- TID#**624** owns CritSec **784B0348** and is waiting for CritSec **76AB8070**
- TID#**1c48** owns CritSec **76AB8070** and is waiting for CritSec **784B0348**

```
0:000>~*kv

. 12 Id: bc0.624 Suspend: 1 Teb: 7ffd3000 Unfrozen
0000024c 00000000 00000000 NTDLL!ZwWaitForSingleObject+0xb
76ab8000 76a815ef 76ab8070 NTDLL!RtlpWaitForCriticalSection+0x9e
76ab8070 76a844f8 00cd1f38 NTDLL!RtlEnterCriticalSection+0x46
00cd1f38 76a8a1d7 00000000 LOCALSPL!EnterSplSem+0xb
00000000 00000000 00cd1f38 LOCALSPL!FindSpoolerByNameIncRef+0x1f
00000000 777f19bc 00000001 LOCALSPL!LocalGetPrinterDriverDirectory+0xe
00000000 777f19bc 00000001 spoolss!GetPrinterDriverDirectoryW+0x59
00000000 777f19bc 00000001 spoolsv!YGetPrinterDriverDirectory+0x27
00000000 777f19bc 00000001 WINSPOOL!GetPrinterDriverDirectoryW+0x7b
50000000 00000001 00000000 BRHLUI04+0x14ea
50002ea0 50000000 00000001 BRHLUI04!DllGetClassObject+0x1705
00000000 00000000 000cb570 NTDLL!LdrpRunInitializeRoutines+0x1df
000cc8f8 0288ea30 0288ea38 NTDLL!LdrpLoadDll+0x2e6
000cc8f8 0288ea30 0288ea38 NTDLL!LdrLoadDll+0x17)
000c1258 00000000 00000008 KERNEL32!LoadLibraryExW+0x231
000c150c 0288efd8 00000000 UNIDRVUI!PLoadCommonInfo+0x17e
000c150c 0288efd8 00000007 UNIDRVUI!DwDeviceCapabilities+0x1a
00070000 00071378 00000045 UNIDRVUI!DrvDeviceCapabilities+0x19

. 13 Id: bc0.1c48 Suspend: 1 Teb: 7ffd2000 Unfrozen
0000010c 00000000 00000000 NTDLL!ZwWaitForSingleObject+0xb
784b0301 78468d38 784b0348 NTDLL!RtlpWaitForCriticalSection+0x9e
784b0348 74fb4344 00000000 NTDLL!RtlEnterCriticalSection+0x46
74fb0000 02c0f2a8 00000000 NTDLL!LdrpGetProcedureAddress+0x122
74fb0000 02c0f2a8 00000000 NTDLL!LdrGetProcedureAddress+0x17
74fb0000 74fb4344 02c0f449 KERNEL32!GetProcAddress+0x41
017924b0 00000000 00000001 ws2_32!CheckForHookersOrChainers+0x1f
00000101 02c0f344 017924b0 ws2_32!WSAStartup+0x10f
00cdf79c 02c0f4f4 76a8c9bc LOCALSPL!GetDNSMachineName+0x1e
00000000 76a8c9bc 780276a2 LOCALSPL!GetPrinterUrl+0x2c
0176f570 ffffffff 01000000 LOCALSPL!UpdateDsSpoolerKey+0x322
0176f570 76a8c9bc 01792b90 LOCALSPL!RecreateDsKey+0x50
00000000 00000002 01792b90 LOCALSPL!SplAddPrinter+0x521
01791faa 0176a684 76a5cd34 WIN32SPL!InternalAddPrinterConnection+0x1b4
01791faa 02c0fa00 02c0fabc WIN32SPL!AddPrinterConnectionW+0x15
00076f1c 02c0fabc 01006873 spoolss!AddPrinterConnectionW+0x49
00076f1c 00000001 77107fb0 spoolsv!YAddPrinterConnection+0x17
00076f1c 02020202 00000001 spoolsv!RpcAddPrinterConnection+0xb
01006868 02c0fac0 00000001 rpcrt4!Invoke+0x30
00000000 00000000 000d22c8 rpcrt4!NdrStubCall2+0x655
000d22c8 00076fe0 000d22c8 rpcrt4!NdrServerCall2+0x17
010045fc 000d22c8 02c0fe0c rpcrt4!DispatchToStubInC+0x32
0000002b 00000000 02c0fe0c
```

```
rpcrt4!RPC_INTERFACE::DispatchToStubWorker+0x100
000d22c8 00000000 02c0fe0c rpcrt4!RPC_INTERFACE::DispatchToStub+0x5e
000d3210 00076608 813b0013 rpcrt4!LRPC_SCALL::DealWithRequestMessage+0x1dd
000d21d0 02c0fe50 000d3210 rpcrt4!LRPC_ADDRESS::DealWithLRPCRequest+0x10c
770c9ad0 00076608 770cb6d8 rpcrt4!LRPC_ADDRESS::ReceiveLotsaCalls+0x229
00076608 770cb6d8 0288f9a8 rpcrt4!RecvLotsaCallsWrapper+0x9
00074a50 02c0ffec 77e7438b rpcrt4!BaseCachedThreadRoutine+0x11f
00076e68 770cb6d8 0288f9a8 rpcrt4!ThreadStartRoutine+0x18
770d1c54 00076e68 00000000 KERNEL32!BaseThreadStart+0x52
```

This analysis looks pretty simple and easy. What about kernel and complete memory dumps? Of course, we cannot see user space critical sections in kernel memory dumps, but we can see them in complete memory dumps after switching to the appropriate process context and using **!ntsdexts.locks**. This can be done via a simple script adapted from *debugger.chm* (see Deadlocks and Critical Sections section there).

Why is it so easy to see deadlocks when critical sections are involved? This is because their structures have a member that records their owner. So it is straightforward to map them to corresponding threads. The same is with kernel ERESOURCE synchronization objects. Other objects do not have an owner. For example, in the case of events, it is not so easy to find an owner just by looking at an event object. We need to examine thread call stacks, other structures or have access to source code.

There is also **!cs** WinDbg extension where **!cs -l** command lists all locked sections with stack traces and **!cs -t** shows critical section tree. For the latter, we need to enable Application Verifier using *gflags.exe* or set 0x100 in the registry for your image:

```
HKEY_LOCAL_MACHINE\SOFTWARE\Microsoft\Windows NT\CurrentVersion\Image File
Execution Options
GlobalFlag=0x00000100
```

Here is another deadlock example in hanging IE process (stack traces are shown in smaller font for visual clarity):

```
0:000> !locks

CritSec ntdll!LdrpLoaderLock+0 at 7c8877a0
WaiterWoken No
LockCount 3
RecursionCount 2
OwningThread d5a8
EntryCount 0
ContentionCount 5a
*** Locked
```

```
CritSec shell32!CMountPoint::_csDL+0 at 7cae42d0
WaiterWoken No
LockCount 1
RecursionCount 1
OwningThread b7b4
EntryCount 0
ContentionCount 7
*** Locked

Scanned 1024 critical sections
```

```
0:000> ~*kb 100

. 0 Id: c068.b7b4 Suspend: 1 Teb: 7ffdd000 Unfrozen
ChildEBP RetAddr Args to Child
0013bd0c 7c827d0b 7c83d236 000001d0 00000000 ntdll!KiFastSystemCallRet
0013bd10 7c83d236 000001d0 00000000 00000000 ntdll!NtWaitForSingleObject+0xc
0013bd4c 7c83d281 000001d0 00000004 00000001 ntdll!RtlpWaitOnCriticalSection+0x1a3
0013bd6c 7c82f20c 7c8877a0 00000000 0013be68 ntdll!RtlEnterCriticalSection+0xa8
0013bda0 7c82f336 00000000 00000000 0013bde8 ntdll!LdrLockLoaderLock+0x133
0013be1c 7c82f2a3 00000001 00000001 00000000 ntdll!LdrGetDllHandleEx+0x94
0013be38 77e65185 00000001 00000000 0013bea0 ntdll!LdrGetDllHandle+0x18
0013be84 77e6528f 0013bea0 00000000 7cae2f60 kernel32!GetModuleHandleForUnicodeString+0x20
0013c2fc 77e65155 00000001 00000002 7c8d8828 kernel32!BasepGetModuleHandleExW+0x17f
0013c314 7c91079e 7c8d8828 7c9107b8 0013c350 kernel32!GetModuleHandleW+0x29
0013c31c 7c9107b8 0013c350 7c91078d 00000001 shell32!IsProcessAnExplorer+0xb
0013c324 7c91078d 00000001 7c91373b 00000018 shell32!IsMainShellProcess2+0x46
0013c32c 7c91373b 00000018 00000000 7cae42d0 shell32!_Shell32LoadedInDesktop+0x7
0013c350 7c913776 00000018 00000000 7cae42d0 shell32!CMountPoint::_IsNetDriveLazyLoadNetDLLs+0x7b
0013c37c 7c9136dc 00000018 00000001 0013c634 shell32!CMountPoint::_GetMountPointDL+0x1c
0013c398 7c96dfd7 00000018 00000001 00000001 shell32!CMountPoint::GetMountPoint+0x46
0013c5e4 7c90f37d 0018e988 00000001 001a0ea8 shell32!CDrivesFolder::GetAttributesOf+0x7b
0013c624 779cc875 0018e9b0 00000001 04002000 shell32!CRegFolder::GetAttributesOf+0x122
0013c648 779cc917 0018e9b0 001e4dc8 04002000 shdocvw!SHGetAttributes+0x53
0013d728 779cd9c8 0013ddac 00193a50 80004005 shdocvw!CNscTree::_OnCDNotify+0x85
0013d754 779cd964 0013ddac 001a06c8 11281f2a shdocvw!CNscTree::_OnNotify+0x2e1
0013d768 779cd8ff 001a06c8 00010090 0000004e shdocvw!CNscTree::OnWinEvent+0x51
0013d798 75eba756 00193a50 00010090 0000004e shdocvw!CNSCBand::OnWinEvent+0x70
0013d7b8 75eba2a2 00193a50 00010090 0000004e browseui!_FwdWinEvent+0x1d
0013d7cc 75eba357 00010090 0000004e 00000064 browseui!CBandSite::_SendToToolband+0x44
0013d818 75ee2a72 0017de98 00010088 00000000 browseui!CBandSite::OnWinEvent+0x143
0013d864 75ee2b32 0017de98 00010088 0000004e browseui!CBrowserBandSite::OnWinEvent+0x14c
0013d890 75ee2a9a 0000004e 00000064 0013ddac browseui!CBaseBar::_CheckForwardWinEvent+0x88
0013d8ac 75ee29dc 0000004e 00000064 0013ddac browseui!CBaseBar::_OnNotify+0x1c
0013d8c8 75ee2965 00010088 0000004e 00000064 browseui!CBaseBar::v_WndProc+0xd4
0013d918 75ee28fa 00010088 0000004e 00000064 browseui!CDockingBar::v_WndProc+0x447
0013d948 75ee2880 00010088 0000004e 00000064 browseui!CBrowserBar::v_WndProc+0x99
0013d96c 7739b6e3 00010088 0000004e 00000064 browseui!CImpWndProc::s_WndProc+0x65
0013d998 7739b874 75ee2841 00010088 0000004e user32!InternalCallWinProc+0x28
0013da10 7739c2d3 00172e34 75ee2841 00010088 user32!UserCallWinProcCheckWow+0x151
0013da4c 7739c337 006172a0 00618f18 00000064 user32!SendMessageWorker+0x4bd
0013da6c 7743b07f 00010088 0000004e 00000064 user32!SendMessageW+0x7f
0013db04 7743b1ef 0013db1c fffffff4 0013ddac comctl32!CCSendNotify+0xc24
0013db40 774a5ab0 00010088 ffffffff fffffff4 comctl32!SendNotifyEx+0x57
0013dbac 774a652d 0001008a 0000004e 00000064 comctl32!CReBar::_WndProc+0x257
0013dbd0 7739b6e3 0001008a 0000004e 00000064 comctl32!CReBar::s_WndProc+0x2c
0013dbfc 7739b874 774a6501 0001008a 0000004e user32!InternalCallWinProc+0x28
0013dc74 7739c2d3 00172e34 774a6501 0001008a user32!UserCallWinProcCheckWow+0x151
0013dcb0 7739c337 00617350 0060a9c0 00000064 user32!SendMessageWorker+0x4bd
0013dcd0 7743b07f 0001008a 0000004e 00000064 user32!SendMessageW+0x7f
0013dd68 7743b10d 001c8900 fffffff4 0013ddac comctl32!CCSendNotify+0xc24
0013dd7c 7748a032 001c8900 00010001 0013ddac comctl32!CICustomDrawNotify+0x2c
0013e070 7748a8bb 001c8900 001d2aa8 01010060 comctl32!TV_DrawItem+0x356
0013e0f4 7748a9ac 00000154 01010060 00000000 comctl32!TV_DrawTree+0x136
0013e158 7745bdd0 001c8900 00000000 0013e21c comctl32!TV_Paint+0x65
0013e1a4 7739b6e3 00010090 0000000f 00000000 comctl32!TV_WndProc+0x6ea
0013e1d0 7739b874 7745b6e6 00010090 0000000f user32!InternalCallWinProc+0x28
0013e248 7739bfce 0015fce4 7745b6e6 00010090 user32!UserCallWinProcCheckWow+0x151
```

```
0013e278 7739bf74 7745b6e6 00010090 0000000f user32!CallWindowProcAorW+0x98
0013e298 77431848 7745b6e6 00010090 0000000f user32!CallWindowProcW+0x1b
0013e2b4 77431b9b 00010090 0000000f 00000000 comctl32!CallOriginalWndProc+0x1a
0013e310 77431d5d 001cf0f8 00010090 0000000f comctl32!CallNextSubclassProc+0x3c
0013e334 779cd761 00010090 0000000f 00000000 comctl32!DefSubclassProc+0x46
0013e350 77431b9b 00010090 0000000f 00000000 shdocvw!CNotifySubclassWndProc::_SubclassWndProc+0xa7
0013e3ac 77431d5d 001cf0f8 00010090 0000000f comctl32!CallNextSubclassProc+0x3c
0013e3d0 779cd86f 00010090 0000000f 00000000 comctl32!DefSubclassProc+0x46
0013e41c 779cd7e4 00010090 0000000f 00000000 shdocvw!CNscTree::_SubClassTreeWndProc+0x3ae
0013e43c 77431b9b 00010090 0000000f 00000000 shdocvw!CNscTree::s_SubClassTreeWndProc+0x34
0013e498 77431dc0 001cf0f8 00010090 0000000f comctl32!CallNextSubclassProc+0x3c
0013e4ec 7739b6e3 00010090 0000000f 00000000 comctl32!MasterSubclassProc+0x54
0013e518 7739b874 77431d6c 00010090 0000000f user32!InternalCallWinProc+0x28
0013e590 7739c8b8 0015fce4 77431d6c 00010090 user32!UserCallWinProcCheckWow+0x151
0013e5ec 7739c9c6 00617618 0000000f 00000000 user32!DispatchClientMessage+0xd9
0013e614 7c828536 0013e62c 00000018 0013e750 user32!__fnDWORD+0x24
0013e640 7739cbb2 7739cb75 00010090 0000005e ntdll!KiUserCallbackDispatcher+0x2e
0013e654 77459d14 00010090 00000200 001c8900 user32!NtUserCallHwndLock+0xc
0013e66c 7745bd2d 00000004 016b0055 00000000 comctl32!TV_OnMouseMove+0x62
0013e6bc 7739b6e3 00010090 00000200 00000000 comctl32!TV_WndProc+0x647
0013e6e8 7739b874 7745b6e6 00010090 00000200 user32!InternalCallWinProc+0x28
0013e760 7739bfce 0015fce4 7745b6e6 00010090 user32!UserCallWinProcCheckWow+0x151
0013e790 7739bf74 7745b6e6 00010090 00000200 user32!CallWindowProcAorW+0x98
0013e7b0 77431848 7745b6e6 00010090 00000200 user32!CallWindowProcW+0x1b
0013e7cc 77431b9b 00010090 00000200 00000000 comctl32!CallOriginalWndProc+0x1a
0013e828 77431d5d 001cf0f8 00010090 00000200 comctl32!CallNextSubclassProc+0x3c
0013e84c 779cd761 00010090 00000200 00000000 comctl32!DefSubclassProc+0x46
0013e868 77431b9b 00010090 00000200 00000000 shdocvw!CNotifySubclassWndProc::_SubclassWndProc+0xa7
0013e8c4 77431d5d 001cf0f8 00010090 00000200 comctl32!CallNextSubclassProc+0x3c
0013e8e8 779cd86f 00010090 00000200 00000000 comctl32!DefSubclassProc+0x46
0013e934 779cd7e4 00010090 00000200 00000000 shdocvw!CNscTree::_SubClassTreeWndProc+0x3ae
0013e954 77431b9b 00010090 00000200 00000000 shdocvw!CNscTree::s_SubClassTreeWndProc+0x34
0013e9b0 77431dc0 001cf0f8 00010090 00000200 comctl32!CallNextSubclassProc+0x3c
0013ea04 7739b6e3 00010090 00000200 00000000 comctl32!MasterSubclassProc+0x54
0013ea30 7739b874 77431d6c 00010090 00000200 user32!InternalCallWinProc+0x28
0013eaa8 7739ba92 0015fce4 77431d6c 00010090 user32!UserCallWinProcCheckWow+0x151
0013eb10 7739bad0 0013eb50 00000000 0013eb38 user32!DispatchMessageWorker+0x327
0013eb20 75ed1410 0013eb50 00000000 00176388 user32!DispatchMessageW+0xf
0013eb38 75ed14fc 0013eb50 0013ee50 00000000 browseui!TimedDispatchMessage+0x33
0013ed98 75ec1c83 0015f7e8 0013ee50 0015f7e8 browseui!BrowserThreadProc+0x336
0013ee24 75ec61ef 0015f7e8 0015f7e8 00000000 browseui!BrowserProtectedThreadProc+0x44
0013fea8 779ba3a6 0015f7e8 00000001 00000000 browseui!SHOpenFolderWindow+0x22c
0013fec8 0040243d 00152552 00020d02 ffffffff shdocvw!IEWinMain+0x129
0013ff1c 00402744 00400000 00000000 00152552 iexplore!WinMain+0x316
0013ffc0 77e6f23b 00000000 00000000 7ffde000 iexplore!WinMainCRTStartup+0x182
0013fff0 00000000 004025c2 00000000 78746341 kernel32!BaseProcessStart+0x23

1 Id: c068.d71c Suspend: 1 Teb: 7ffdc000 Unfrozen
ChildEBP RetAddr Args to Child
00d4fea0 7c827cfb 7c80e5bb 00000002 00d4fef0 ntdll!KiFastSystemCallRet
00d4fea4 7c80e5bb 00000002 00d4fef0 00000001 ntdll!NtWaitForMultipleObjects+0xc
00d4ff48 7c80e4a2 00000002 00d4ff70 00000000 ntdll!EtwpWaitForMultipleObjectsEx+0xf7
00d4ffb8 77e64829 00000000 00000000 00000000 ntdll!EtwpEventPump+0x27f
00d4ffec 00000000 7c80e1fa 00000000 00000000 kernel32!BaseThreadStart+0x34

2 Id: c068.cba4 Suspend: 1 Teb: 7ffdb000 Unfrozen
ChildEBP RetAddr Args to Child
012bfe18 7c82783b 77c885ac 000001c4 012bff74 ntdll!KiFastSystemCallRet
012bfe1c 77c885ac 000001c4 012bff74 00000000 ntdll!NtReplyWaitReceivePortEx+0xc
012bff84 77c88792 012bffac 77c8872d 00153cf0 rpcrt4!LRPC_ADDRESS::ReceiveLotsaCalls+0x198
012bff8c 77c8872d 00153cf0 00000000 00000000 rpcrt4!RecvLotsaCallsWrapper+0xd
012bffac 77c7b110 00167030 012bffec 77e64829 rpcrt4!BaseCachedThreadRoutine+0x9d
012bffb8 77e64829 00172088 00000000 00000000 rpcrt4!ThreadStartRoutine+0x1b
012bffec 00000000 77c7b0f5 00172088 00000000 kernel32!BaseThreadStart+0x34
```

```
3 Id: c068.8604 Suspend: 1 Teb: 7ffda000 Unfrozen
ChildEBP RetAddr Args to Child
013bfe28 7c827d0b 7c83d236 000001d0 00000000 ntdll!KiFastSystemCallRet
013bfe2c 7c83d236 000001d0 00000000 00000000 ntdll!NtWaitForSingleObject+0xc
013bfe68 7c83d281 000001d0 00000004 00000000 ntdll!RtlpWaitOnCriticalSection+0x1a3
013bfe88 7c839844 7c8877a0 00000000 77670000 ntdll!RtlEnterCriticalSection+0xa8
013bff90 77e52860 77670000 77670000 00171698 ntdll!LdrUnloadDll+0x35
013bffa4 776b171d 77670000 00000000 00000000 kernel32!FreeLibraryAndExitThread+0x38
013bffb8 77e64829 00171698 00000000 00000000 ole32!CRpcThreadCache::RpcWorkerThreadEntry+0x39
013bffec 00000000 776b16e4 00171698 00000000 kernel32!BaseThreadStart+0x34

4 Id: c068.d6dc Suspend: 1 Teb: 7ffd9000 Unfrozen
ChildEBP RetAddr Args to Child
016dfd24 7c827cfb 77e6202c 00000005 016dfd74 ntdll!KiFastSystemCallRet
016dfd28 77e6202c 00000005 016dfd74 00000001 ntdll!NtWaitForMultipleObjects+0xc
016dfdd0 7739bbd1 00000005 016dfdf8 00000000 kernel32!WaitForMultipleObjectsEx+0x11a
016dfe2c 7c919b2e 00000004 016dfe54 ffffffff user32!RealMsgWaitForMultipleObjectsEx+0x141
016dff50 7c8f7ada 77da3f12 00000000 00000000 shell32!CChangeNotify::_MessagePump+0x3b
016dff54 77da3f12 00000000 00000000 00000000 shell32!CChangeNotify::ThreadProc+0x1e
016dffb8 77e64829 00000000 00000000 00000000 shlwapi!WrapperThreadProc+0x94
016dffec 00000000 77da3ea5 0013dea8 00000000 kernel32!BaseThreadStart+0x34

5 Id: c068.caf4 Suspend: 1 Teb: 7ffd8000 Unfrozen
ChildEBP RetAddr Args to Child
01b1fdb4 7c827cfb 77e6202c 00000002 01b1fe04 ntdll!KiFastSystemCallRet
01b1fdb8 77e6202c 00000002 01b1fe04 00000001 ntdll!NtWaitForMultipleObjects+0xc
01b1fe60 7739bbd1 00000002 01b1fe88 00000000 kernel32!WaitForMultipleObjectsEx+0x11a
01b1febc 6c296601 00000001 01b1fef0 ffffffff user32!RealMsgWaitForMultipleObjectsEx+0x141
01b1fedc 6c29684b 000004ff ffffffff 00000001 duser!CoreSC::Wait+0x3a
01b1ff10 6c28f9e6 01b1ff50 00000000 00000000 duser!CoreSC::xwProcessNL+0xab
01b1ff30 6c28bce1 01b1ff50 00000000 00000000 duser!GetMessageExA+0x44
01b1ff84 77bcb530 00000000 00000000 00000000 duser!ResourceManager::SharedThreadProc+0xb6
01b1ffb8 77e64829 000385f0 00000000 00000000 msvcrt!_endthreadex+0xa3
01b1ffec 00000000 77bcb4bc 000385f0 00000000 kernel32!BaseThreadStart+0x34

6 Id: c068.d624 Suspend: 1 Teb: 7ffd7000 Unfrozen
ChildEBP RetAddr Args to Child
01c9ff9c 7c826f4b 7c83d424 00000001 01c9ffb0 ntdll!KiFastSystemCallRet
01c9ffa0 7c83d424 00000001 01c9ffb0 00000000 ntdll!NtDelayExecution+0xc
01c9ffb8 77e64829 00000000 00000000 00000000 ntdll!RtlpTimerThread+0x47
01c9ffec 00000000 7c83d3dd 00000000 00000000 kernel32!BaseThreadStart+0x34

7 Id: c068.b4e0 Suspend: 1 Teb: 7ffd6000 Unfrozen
ChildEBP RetAddr Args to Child
01d9fd58 7c827d0b 7c83d236 000001d0 00000000 ntdll!KiFastSystemCallRet
01d9fd5c 7c83d236 000001d0 00000000 00000000 ntdll!NtWaitForSingleObject+0xc
01d9fd98 7c83d281 000001d0 00000004 00000000 ntdll!RtlpWaitOnCriticalSection+0x1a3
01d9fdb8 7c839844 7c8877a0 75eb8b7c 75eb0000 ntdll!RtlEnterCriticalSection+0xa8
01d9fec0 77e6b1bb 75eb0000 75eb0000 001e2f98 ntdll!LdrUnloadDll+0x35
01d9fed4 77da4c1c 75eb0000 0020eec8 77da591b kernel32!FreeLibrary+0x41
01d9feec 7c83a827 0020eec8 7c889080 001e4ec0 shlwapi!ExecuteWorkItem+0x28
01d9ff44 7c83aa0b 77da591b 0020eec8 00000000 ntdll!RtlpWorkerCallout+0x71
01d9ff64 7c83aa82 00000000 0020eec8 001e4ec0 ntdll!RtlpExecuteWorkerRequest+0x4f
01d9ff78 7c839f60 7c83a9ca 00000000 0020eec8 ntdll!RtlpApcCallout+0x11
01d9ffb8 77e64829 00000000 00000000 00000000 ntdll!RtlpWorkerThread+0x61
01d9ffec 00000000 7c839efb 00000000 00000000 kernel32!BaseThreadStart+0x34
```

```
8 Id: c068.d5a8 Suspend: 1 Teb: 7ffd5000 Unfrozen
ChildEBP RetAddr Args to Child
01fbb41c 7c827d0b 7c83d236 00000468 00000000 ntdll!KiFastSystemCallRet
01fbb420 7c83d236 00000468 00000000 00000000 ntdll!NtWaitForSingleObject+0xc
01fbb45c 7c83d281 00000468 00000004 00000000 ntdll!RtlpWaitOnCriticalSection+0x1a3
01fbb47c 7c9136c9 7cae42d0 001c97b0 80070003 ntdll!RtlEnterCriticalSection+0xa8
01fbb494 7c913b75 0000000c 00000000 00000001 shell32!CMountPoint::GetMountPoint+0x33
01fbb4c8 7c91358d 01fbb4fc 0000000c 00000000 shell32!CDrivesFolder::_FillIDDrive+0x5c
01fbb52c 7c9109e7 0018e988 00000000 001c97b0 shell32!CDrivesFolder::ParseDisplayName+0x9f
01fbb594 7c9119ff 0018e9b0 00000000 001c97b0 shell32!CRegFolder::ParseDisplayName+0x93
01fbb5bc 7c910bb8 00000000 001a8e30 00000000 shell32!CDesktopFolder::_ChildParseDisplayName+0x22
01fbb60c 7c9109e7 0017cde0 00000000 001c97b0 shell32!CDesktopFolder::ParseDisplayName+0x7e
01fbb674 7c910a9b 0015f058 00000000 001c97b0 shell32!CRegFolder::ParseDisplayName+0x93
01fbb6ac 7c911ab4 00000000 00000000 00000000 shell32!SHParseDisplayName+0xa3
01fbb6d0 7c911a6e 01fbbe60 00000000 00000002 shell32!ILCreateFromPathEx+0x3d
01fbb6ec 7c911a4b 01fbbe60 01fbb700 00000000 shell32!SHILCreateFromPath+0x17
01fbb704 7c95e055 01fbbe60 00000104 01fbc0a0 shell32!ILCreateFromPathW+0x18
01fbbb84 7c9ef49d 01fbbe60 00000000 01fbbbac shell32!SHGetFileInfoW+0x117
01fbc06c 01b4d195 01fbc200 00000000 01fbc0a0 shell32!SHGetFileInfoA+0x6a
WARNING: Stack unwind information not available. Following frames may be wrong.
01fbc0a4 01b54a20 0000073c 02541f28 00000000 issftran!SSCopyFile+0x27ad
00000000 00000000 00000000 00000000 00000000 issftran!DllUnregisterServer+0x70ad

9 Id: c068.d750 Suspend: 1 Teb: 7ffd4000 Unfrozen
ChildEBP RetAddr Args to Child
0228ff7c 7c8277db 71b25914 000004b4 0228ffc0 ntdll!KiFastSystemCallRet
0228ff80 71b25914 000004b4 0228ffc0 0228ffb4 ntdll!ZwRemoveIoCompletion+0xc
0228ffb8 77e64829 71b259de 00000000 00000000 mswsock!SockAsyncThread+0x69
0228ffec 00000000 71b258ab 001fcd20 00000000 kernel32!BaseThreadStart+0x34
```

```
0:000> du 7c8d8828
7c8d8828 "EXPLORER.EXE"

0:000> da 01fbc200
01fbc200 "M:\WINDOWS"
```

Changed Environment

Sometimes the change of operating system version or installing an intrusive product reveals hidden bugs in software that was working correctly before that.

What happens after installing the new software? If we look at the process dump, we see many DLLs loaded at their specific virtual addresses. Here is the output from **lm** WinDbg command after attaching to iexplore.exe process running on Windows XP SP2 workstation:

```
0:000> lm
start    end        module name
00400000 00419000 iexplore
01c80000 01d08000 shdoclc
01d10000 01fd5000 xpsp2res
022b0000 022cd000 xpsp3res
02680000 02946000 msi
031f0000 031fd000 LvHook
03520000 03578000 PortableDeviceApi
037e0000 037f7000 odbcint
0ffd0000 0fff8000 rsaenh
20000000 20012000 browselc
30000000 302ee000 Flash9b
325c0000 325d2000 msohev
4d4f0000 4d548000 WINHTTP
5ad70000 5ada8000 UxTheme
5b860000 5b8b4000 NETAPI32
5d090000 5d12a000 comctl32_5d090000
5e310000 5e31c000 pngfilt
63000000 63014000 SynTPFcs
662b0000 66308000 hnetcfg
66880000 6688c000 ImgUtil
6bdd0000 6be06000 dxtrans
6be10000 6be6a000 dxtmsft
6d430000 6d43a000 ddrawex
71a50000 71a8f000 mswsock
71a90000 71a98000 wshtcpip
71aa0000 71aa8000 WS2HELP
71ab0000 71ac7000 WS2_32
71ad0000 71ad9000 wsock32
71b20000 71b32000 MPR
71bf0000 71c03000 SAMLIB
71c10000 71c1e000 ntlanman
71c80000 71c87000 NETRAP
71c90000 71cd0000 NETUI1
71cd0000 71ce7000 NETUI0
71d40000 71d5c000 actxprxy
722b0000 722b5000 sensapi
72d10000 72d18000 msacm32
72d20000 72d29000 wdmaud
```

```
73300000 73367000 vbscript
73760000 737a9000 DDRAW
73bc0000 73bc6000 DCIMAN32
73dd0000 73ece000 MFC42
74320000 7435d000 ODBC32
746c0000 746e7000 msls31
746f0000 7471a000 msimtf
74720000 7476b000 MSCTF
754d0000 75550000 CRYPTUI
75970000 75a67000 MSGINA
75c50000 75cbe000 jscript
75cf0000 75d81000 mlang
75e90000 75f40000 SXS
75f60000 75f67000 drprov
75f70000 75f79000 davclnt
75f80000 7607d000 BROWSEUI
76200000 76271000 mshtmled
76360000 76370000 WINSTA
76390000 763ad000 IMM32
763b0000 763f9000 comdlg32
76600000 7661d000 CSCDLL
767f0000 76817000 schannel
769c0000 76a73000 USERENV
76b20000 76b31000 ATL
76b40000 76b6d000 WINMM
76bf0000 76bfb000 PSAPI
76c30000 76c5e000 WINTRUST
76c90000 76cb8000 IMAGEHLP
76d60000 76d79000 iphlpapi
76e80000 76e8e000 rtutils
76e90000 76ea2000 rasman
76eb0000 76edf000 TAPI32
76ee0000 76f1c000 RASAPI32
76f20000 76f47000 DNSAPI
76f60000 76f8c000 WLDAP32
76fc0000 76fc6000 rasadhlp
76fd0000 7704f000 CLBCATQ
77050000 77115000 COMRes
77120000 771ac000 OLEAUT32
771b0000 77256000 WININET
773d0000 774d3000 comctl32
774e0000 7761d000 ole32
77920000 77a13000 SETUPAPI
77a20000 77a74000 cscui
77a80000 77b14000 CRYPT32
77b20000 77b32000 MSASN1
77b40000 77b62000 appHelp
77bd0000 77bd7000 midimap
77be0000 77bf5000 MSACM32_77be0000
77c00000 77c08000 VERSION
77c10000 77c68000 msvcrt
77c70000 77c93000 msv1_0
77d40000 77dd0000 USER32
77dd0000 77e6b000 ADVAPI32
```

```
77e70000 77f01000 RPCRT4
77f10000 77f57000 GDI32
77f60000 77fd6000 SHLWAPI
77fe0000 77ff1000 Secur32
7c800000 7c8f4000 kernel32
7c900000 7c9b0000 ntdll
7c9c0000 7d1d5000 SHELL32
7dc30000 7df20000 mshtml
7e1e0000 7e280000 urlmon
7e290000 7e3ff000 SHDOCVW
```

Installing or upgrading software can change the distribution of loaded DLLs and their addresses. This also happens when we install some monitoring software that usually injects their DLLs into every process. As a result, some DLLs may be relocated, or even the new ones appear loaded. And this may influence 3rd-party program behavior, therefore, exposing its hidden bugs being dormant when executing the process in the old environment. I call this pattern **Changed Environment**.

Let's look at a hypothetical example. Suppose our program has the following code fragment:

```
if (*p)
{
// do something useful
}
```

Suppose the pointer *p* is invalid, dangling, its value has been overwritten, and this happened because of some bug. If invalid, that pointer can point to a valid memory location nevertheless, and the value it points to most likely is non-zero. Therefore, the body of the "if" statement is executed. Suppose it always happens when we run the program, and every time we execute it, the value of the pointer happens to be the same.

Here is the picture illustrating the point:

The pointer value 0x40010024, due to some reason, always points to the value 0x00BADBAD. Although in the correct program, the pointer itself should have had a completely different value and pointed to 0x1, for example, we see that dereferencing its current invalid value doesn't crash the process.

After installing the new software, *NewComponent DLL* is loaded at the address range previously occupied by *ComponentC*:

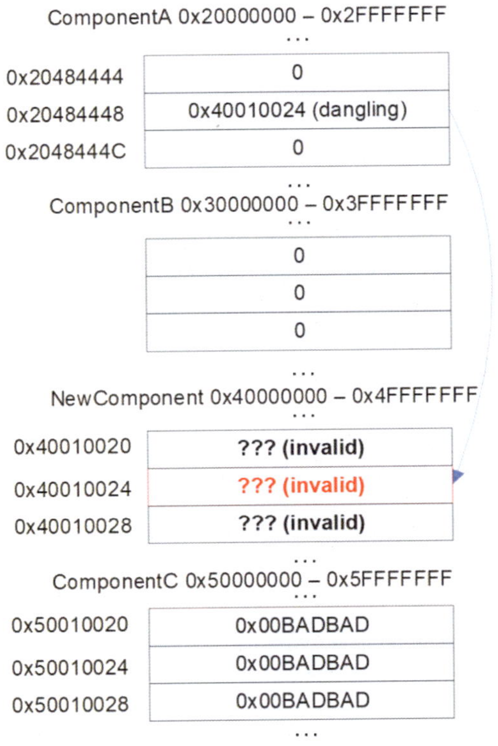

Now the address 0x40010024 happens to be completely invalid, and we have an access violation and the crash dump.

Incorrect Stack Trace

One of the mistakes beginners make is trusting WinDbg **!analyze** or **kv** commands displaying a stack trace. WinDbg is only a tool, sometimes information necessary to get the correct stack trace is missing, and, therefore, some critical thought is required to distinguish between correct and incorrect stack traces. I call this pattern **Incorrect Stack Trace**. Incorrect stack traces usually:

- Have WinDbg warning: "Following frames may be wrong."
- Don't have the correct bottom frame like *kernel32!BaseThreadStart* (in user mode).
- Have function calls that don't make any sense.
- Have strange-looking disassembled function code or code that doesn't make any sense from a compiler perspective.
- Have ChildEBP and RetAddr addresses that don't make any sense.

Consider the following stack trace:

```
0:011> k
ChildEBP RetAddr
WARNING: Frame IP not in any known module. Following frames may be wrong.
0184e434 7c830b10 0x184e5bf
0184e51c 7c81f832 ntdll!RtlGetFullPathName_Ustr+0x15b
0184e5f8 7c83b1dd ntdll!RtlpLowFragHeapAlloc+0xc6a
00099d30 00000000 ntdll!RtlpLowFragHeapFree+0xa7
```

Here we have almost all attributes of the wrong stack trace. At the first glance it looks like some heap corruption happened (runtime heap allocation and freeing functions are present) but if we give it second thought we see that the low fragmentation heap *Free* function shouldn't call the low fragmentation heap *Alloc* function and the latter shouldn't query the full path name. That doesn't make any sense.

What should we do here? Look at the raw stack region and try to build the correct stack trace ourselves. In our case, this is very easy. We need to traverse stack frames from *BaseThreadStart+0x34* until we don't find any function call or reach the top. When functions are called (no optimization, most compilers) EBP registers are linked together as explained on the following slide from my Practical Foundations of Debugging seminars:

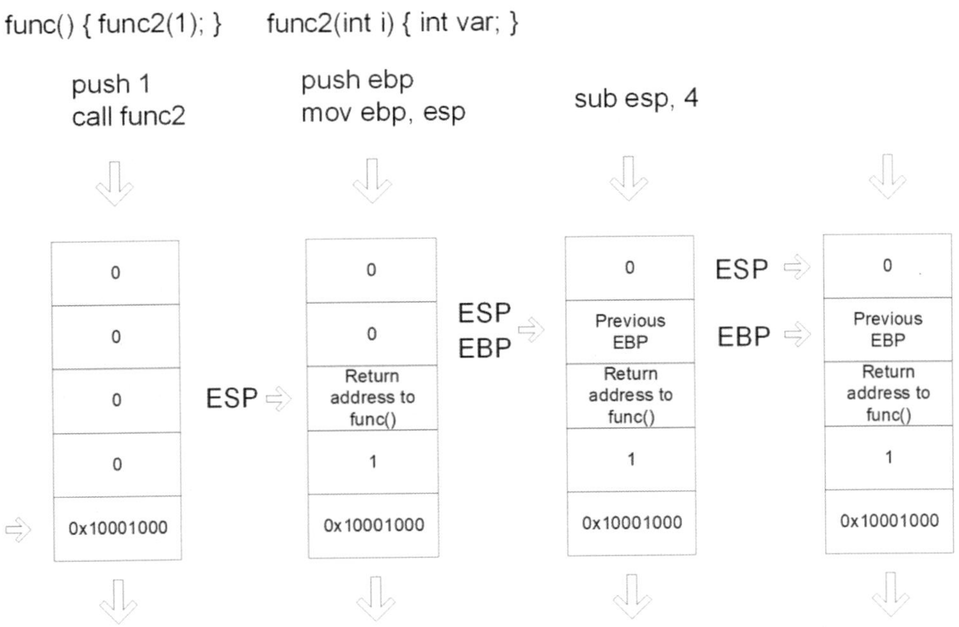


```
0:011> !teb
TEB at 7ffd8000
    ExceptionList:          0184ebdc
    StackBase:              01850000
    StackLimit:             01841000
    SubSystemTib:           00000000
    FiberData:              00001e00
    ArbitraryUserPointer:   00000000
    Self:                   7ffd8000
    EnvironmentPointer:     00000000
    ClientId:               0000061c . 00001b60
    RpcHandle:              00000000
    Tls Storage:            00000000
    PEB Address:            7ffdf000
    LastErrorValue:         0
    LastStatusValue:        c0000034
    Count Owned Locks:      0
    HardErrorMode:          0
```

```
0:011> dds 01841000 01850000
01841000  00000000
...
...
...
0184eef0  0184ef0c
0184eef4  7615dff2 localspl!SplDriverEvent+0x21
0184eef8  00bc3e08
0184eefc  00000003
0184ef00  00000001
0184ef04  00000000
0184ef08  0184efb0
0184ef0c  0184ef30
0184ef10  7615f9d0 localspl!PrinterDriverEvent+0x46
0184ef14  00bc3e08
0184ef18  00000003
0184ef1c  00000000
0184ef20  0184efb0
0184ef24  00b852a8
0184ef28  00c3ec58
0184ef2c  00bafcc0
0184ef30  0184f3f8
0184ef34  7614a9b4 localspl!SplAddPrinter+0x5f3
0184ef38  00c3ec58
0184ef3c  00000003
0184ef40  00000000
0184ef44  0184efb0
0184ef48  00c117f8
...
...
...
0184ff28  00000000
0184ff2c  00000000
0184ff30  0184ff84
0184ff34  77c75286 RPCRT4!LRPC_ADDRESS::ReceiveLotsaCalls+0x3a
0184ff38  0184ff4c
0184ff3c  77c75296 RPCRT4!LRPC_ADDRESS::ReceiveLotsaCalls+0x4a
0184ff40  7c82f2fc ntdll!RtlLeaveCriticalSection
0184ff44  000de378
0184ff48  00097df0
0184ff4c  4d2fa200
0184ff50  ffffffff
0184ff54  ca5b1700
0184ff58  ffffffff
0184ff5c  8082d821
0184ff60  0184fe38
0184ff64  00097df0
0184ff68  000000aa
0184ff6c  80020000
0184ff70  0184ff54
0184ff74  80020000
0184ff78  000b0c78
0184ff7c  00a50180
0184ff80  0184fe38
```

```
0184ff84  0184ff8c
0184ff88  77c5778f RPCRT4!RecvLotsaCallsWrapper+0xd
0184ff8c  0184ffac
0184ff90  77c5f7dd RPCRT4!BaseCachedThreadRoutine+0x9d
0184ff94  0009c410
0184ff98  00000000
0184ff9c  00000000
0184ffa0  00097df0
0184ffa4  00097df0
0184ffa8  00015f90
0184ffac  0184ffb8
0184ffb0  77c5de88 RPCRT4!ThreadStartRoutine+0x1b
0184ffb4  00088258
0184ffb8  0184ffec
0184ffbc  77e6608b kernel32!BaseThreadStart+0x34
0184ffc0  00097df0
0184ffc4  00000000
0184ffc8  00000000
0184ffcc  00097df0
0184ffd0  8ad84818
0184ffd4  0184ffc4
0184ffd8  8980a700
0184ffdc  ffffffff
0184ffe0  77e6b7d0 kernel32!_except_handler3
0184ffe4  77e66098 kernel32!`string'+0x98
0184ffe8  00000000
0184ffec  00000000
0184fff0  00000000
77c5de6d  RPCRT4!ThreadStartRoutine
0184fff8  00097df0
0184fffc  00000000
01850000  00000008
```

Next, we need to use custom **k** command and specify the base pointer. In our case, the last found stack address that links EBP pointers is 0184eef0:

```
0:011> k L=0184eef0
ChildEBP RetAddr
WARNING: Frame IP not in any known module. Following frames may be wrong.
0184eef0 7615dff2 0x184e5bf
0184ef0c 7615f9d0 localspl!SplDriverEvent+0x21
0184ef30 7614a9b4 localspl!PrinterDriverEvent+0x46
0184f3f8 761482de localspl!SplAddPrinter+0x5f3
0184f424 74067c8f localspl!LocalAddPrinterEx+0x2e
0184f874 74067b76 SPOOLSS!AddPrinterExW+0x151
0184f890 01007e29 SPOOLSS!AddPrinterW+0x17
0184f8ac 01006ec3 spoolsv!YAddPrinter+0x75
0184f8d0 77c70f3b spoolsv!RpcAddPrinter+0x37
0184f8f8 77ce23f7 RPCRT4!Invoke+0x30
0184fcf8 77ce26ed RPCRT4!NdrStubCall2+0x299
0184fd14 77c709be RPCRT4!NdrServerCall2+0x19
0184fd48 77c7093f RPCRT4!DispatchToStubInCNoAvrf+0x38
```

```
0184fd9c 77c70865 RPCRT4!RPC_INTERFACE::DispatchToStubWorker+0x117
0184fdc0 77c734b1 RPCRT4!RPC_INTERFACE::DispatchToStub+0xa3
0184fdfc 77c71bb3 RPCRT4!LRPC_SCALL::DealWithRequestMessage+0x42c
0184fe20 77c75458 RPCRT4!LRPC_ADDRESS::DealWithLRPCRequest+0x127
0184ff84 77c5778f RPCRT4!LRPC_ADDRESS::ReceiveLotsaCalls+0x430
0184ff8c 77c5f7dd RPCRT4!RecvLotsaCallsWrapper+0xd
```

Stack traces make more sense now, but we don't see BaseThreadStart+0x34. By default, WinDbg displays only a certain amount of function calls (stack frames) so we need to specify stack frame count, for example, 100:

```
0:011> k L=0184eef0 100
ChildEBP RetAddr
WARNING: Frame IP not in any known module. Following frames may be wrong.
0184eef0 7615dff2 0x184e5bf
0184ef0c 7615f9d0 localspl!SplDriverEvent+0x21
0184ef30 7614a9b4 localspl!PrinterDriverEvent+0x46
0184f3f8 761482de localspl!SplAddPrinter+0x5f3
0184f424 74067c8f localspl!LocalAddPrinterEx+0x2e
0184f874 74067b76 SPOOLSS!AddPrinterExW+0x151
0184f890 01007e29 SPOOLSS!AddPrinterW+0x17
0184f8ac 01006ec3 spoolsv!YAddPrinter+0x75
0184f8d0 77c70f3b spoolsv!RpcAddPrinter+0x37
0184f8f8 77ce23f7 RPCRT4!Invoke+0x30
0184fcf8 77ce26ed RPCRT4!NdrStubCall2+0x299
0184fd14 77c709be RPCRT4!NdrServerCall2+0x19
0184fd48 77c7093f RPCRT4!DispatchToStubInCNoAvrf+0x38
0184fd9c 77c70865 RPCRT4!RPC_INTERFACE::DispatchToStubWorker+0x117
0184fdc0 77c734b1 RPCRT4!RPC_INTERFACE::DispatchToStub+0xa3
0184fdfc 77c71bb3 RPCRT4!LRPC_SCALL::DealWithRequestMessage+0x42c
0184fe20 77c75458 RPCRT4!LRPC_ADDRESS::DealWithLRPCRequest+0x127
0184ff84 77c5778f RPCRT4!LRPC_ADDRESS::ReceiveLotsaCalls+0x430
0184ff8c 77c5f7dd RPCRT4!RecvLotsaCallsWrapper+0xd
0184ffac 77c5de88 RPCRT4!BaseCachedThreadRoutine+0x9d
0184ffb8 77e6608b RPCRT4!ThreadStartRoutine+0x1b
0184ffec 00000000 kernel32!BaseThreadStart+0x34
```

Now our stack trace looks much better. For another complete example, please see **Manual Stack Trace Reconstruction**, page 157.

Sometimes, incorrect stack trace is reported when symbols were not applied. Non-symbol gaps in stack traces can be the sign of this pattern too:

```
STACK_TEXT:
WARNING: Stack unwind information not available. Following frames may be
wrong.
00b2f42c 091607aa mydll!foo+0x8338
00b2f4cc 7c83ab9e mydll!foo+0x8fe3
00b2f4ec 7c832d06 ntdll!RtlFindNextActivationContextSection+0x46
00b2f538 001a5574 ntdll!RtlFindActivationContextSectionString+0xe1
00b2f554 7c8302b3 0x1a5574
00b2f560 7c82f9c1 ntdll!RtlpFreeToHeapLookaside+0x22
00b2f640 7c832b7f ntdll!RtlFreeHeap+0x20e
001dd000 00080040 ntdll!LdrUnlockLoaderLock+0xad
001dd00c 0052005c 0x80040
001dd010 00470045 0x52005c
0052005c 00000000 0x470045
```

OMAP Code Optimization

This pattern is a follow up to **Optimized Code** pattern (page 265). Now we discuss the following feature that often bewilders beginners. It is called OMAP code optimization. It is used to generate code that needs to be present in memory smaller. So instead of a flat address space for compiled function, we have pieces of it scattered here and there. This leads to an ambiguity when we try to disassemble OMAP code at its address because WinDbg doesn't know whether it should treat address range as a function offset (starting from the beginning of the function source code) or just a memory layout offset (starting from the address of that function). Let me illustrate this on *IoCreateDevice* function code.

Let's first evaluate a random address starting from the first address of the function (memory layout offset):

```
kd> ? nt!IoCreateDevice
Evaluate expression: -8796073668256 = fffff800`01275160

kd> ? nt!IoCreateDevice+0x144
Evaluate expression: -8796073667932 = fffff800`012752a4

kd> ? fffff800`012752a4-fffff800`01275160
Evaluate expression: 324 = 00000000`00000144
```

If we try to disassemble code at the same address, the expression is also evaluated as the memory layout offset:

```
kd> u nt!IoCreateDevice+0x144
nt!IoCreateDevice+0x1a3:
fffff800`012752a4 or      eax,10h
fffff800`012752a7 mov     dword ptr [rsp+0B0h],eax
fffff800`012752ae test    ebp,ebp
fffff800`012752b0 mov     ebx,ebp
fffff800`012752b2 jne     nt!IoCreateDevice+0x1b3
fffff800`012752b8 add     ebx,dword ptr [rsp+54h]
fffff800`012752bc mov     rdx,qword ptr [nt!IoDeviceObjectType]
fffff800`012752c3 lea     rcx,[rsp+88h]
```

We see the difference: we give +0x144 offset, but the code is shown from +0x1a3! This is because OMAP optimization moved the code from the function offset +0x1a3 to memory locations starting from +0x144. The following picture illustrates this:

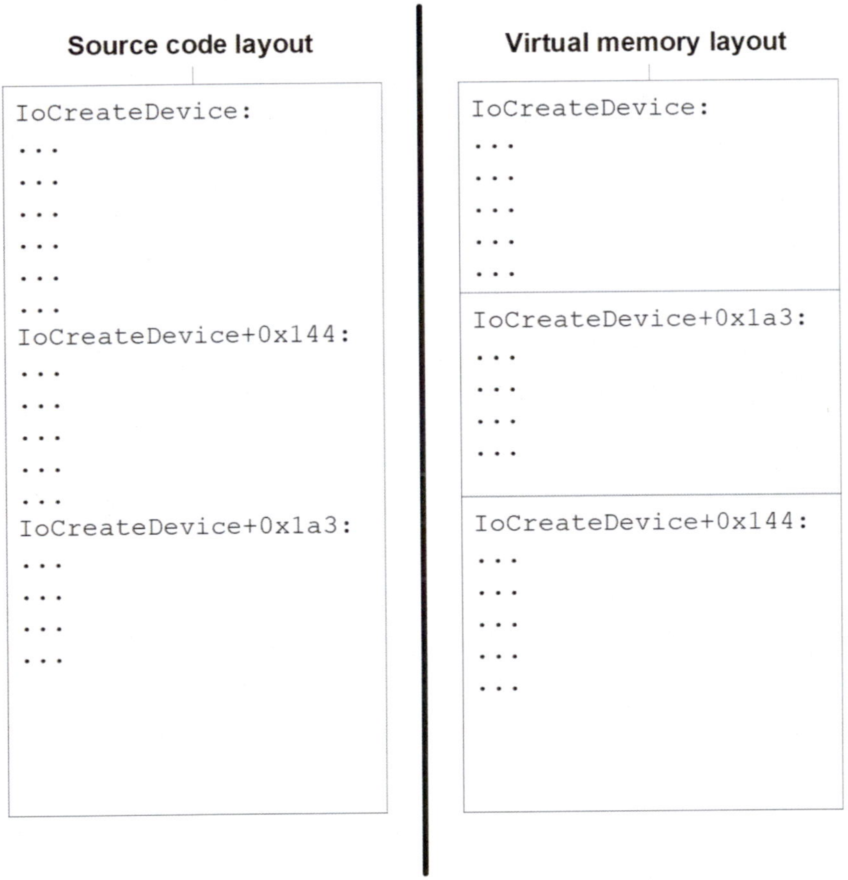

If we see this when disassembling a *function name+offset* address from a thread stack trace we can use a raw address instead:

```
kd> k
Child-SP          RetAddr           Call Site
fffffadf`e3a18d30 fffff800`012b331e component!function+0x72
fffffadf`e3a18d70 fffff800`01044196 nt!PspSystemThreadStartup+0x3e
fffffadf`e3a18dd0 00000000`00000000 nt!KxStartSystemThread+0x16
```

```
kd> u fffff800`012b331e
nt!PspSystemThreadStartup+0x3e:
fffff800`012b331e nop
fffff800`012b331f test    byte ptr [rbx+3FCh],40h
fffff800`012b3326 jne     nt!PspSystemThreadStartup+0x4c
fffff800`012b332c mov     rax,qword ptr gs:[188h]
fffff800`012b3335 cmp     rbx,rax
fffff800`012b3338 jne     nt!PspSystemThreadStartup+0x10c
fffff800`012b333e or      dword ptr [rbx+3FCh],1
fffff800`012b3345 xor     ecx,ecx
```

We also see OMAP in action when we try to disassemble the function body using **uf** command:

```
kd> uf nt!IoCreateDevice
nt!IoCreateDevice+0x34d:
fffff800`0123907d or      dword ptr [rdi+30h],8
fffff800`01239081 jmp     nt!IoCreateDevice+0x351
...
...
...
nt!IoCreateDevice+0x14c:
fffff800`0126f320 mov     r14w,200h
fffff800`0126f325 jmp     nt!IoCreateDevice+0x158
nt!IoCreateDevice+0x3cc:
fffff800`01270bd0 lea     rax,[rdi+50h]
fffff800`01270bd4 mov     qword ptr [rax+8],rax
fffff800`01270bd8 mov     qword ptr [rax],rax
fffff800`01270bdb jmp     nt!IoCreateDevice+0x3d7
nt!IoCreateDevice+0xa4:
fffff800`01273eb9 mov     r8d,1
fffff800`01273ebf lea     rdx,[nt!`string']
fffff800`01273ec6 lea     rcx,[rsp+0D8h]
fffff800`01273ece xadd    dword ptr [nt!IopUniqueDeviceObjectNumber],r8d
fffff800`01273ed6 inc     r8d
fffff800`01273ed9 call    nt!swprintf
fffff800`01273ede test    r13b,r13b
fffff800`01273ee1 jne     nt!IoCreateDevice+0xce
...
...
...
```

Another example of OMAP optimization when we try to disassemble backward:

```
ChildEBP RetAddr Args to Child
0006f87c 01034efb application!MultiUserLogonAttempt+0x5ba
0006fee4 01037120 application!LogonAttempt+0x406

1: kd> ub application!LogonAttempt+0x406
^ Unable to find valid previous instruction for 'ub
application!LogonAttempt+0x406'

1: kd> u application!LogonAttempt+0x406
application!LogonAttempt+0x20b:
010348d5 add dword ptr [edx+10h],ebp
```

We have to specify the return address for *MultiUserLogonAttempt* then:

```
1: kd> ub 01034efb
application!LogonAttempt+0x3e4:
01034ed9 mov  dword ptr [ebp-628h],ecx
01034edf mov  ecx,dword ptr [ebp-61Ch]
01034ee5 mov  dword ptr [eax+24h],ecx
01034ee8 push dword ptr [ebp-61Ch]
01034eee lea  eax,[ebp-638h]
01034ef4 push eax
01034ef5 push ebx
01034ef6 call application!MultiUserLogonAttempt (0102c822)

1: kd> u 01034efb
application!LogonAttempt+0x406:
01034efb mov  ecx,dword ptr [ebp-628h]
01034f01 mov  dword ptr [ebp-608h],eax
01034f07 mov  eax,dword ptr [ebx+8]
01034f0a mov  dword ptr [eax+24h],ecx
01034f0d cmp  dword ptr [application!g_SessionId (010742dc)],0
01034f14 je   application!LogonAttempt+0x47e (01034f73)
01034f16 lea  eax,[ebx+1078h]
01034f1c push eax
```

No Component Symbols

Another pattern that happens so often in crash dumps: **No Component Symbols**. In this case, we can guess what a component does by looking at its name, overall thread stack where it is called, and also, at its import table. Here is an example. We have component.sys driver visible on some thread stack in a kernel dump, but we don't know what that component can potentially do. Because we don't have symbols, we cannot see its imported functions:

```
kd> x component!*
kd>
```

We use **!dh** command to dump its image headers:

```
kd> lmv m component
start             end                 module name
fffffadf`e0eb5000 fffffadf`e0ebc000   component   (no symbols)
    Loaded symbol image file: component.sys
    Image path: \??\C:\Component\x64\component.sys
    Image name: component.sys
    Timestamp:        Sat Jul 01 19:06:16 2006 (44A6B998)
    CheckSum:         000074EF
    ImageSize:        00007000
    Translations:     0000.04b0 0000.04e0 0409.04b0 0409.04e0

kd> !dh fffffadf`e0eb5000
File Type: EXECUTABLE IMAGE
FILE HEADER VALUES
    8664 machine (X64)
       6 number of sections
44A6B998 time date stamp Sat Jul 01 19:06:16 2006
       0 file pointer to symbol table
       0 number of symbols
      F0 size of optional header
      22 characteristics
            Executable
            App can handle >2gb addresses
OPTIONAL HEADER VALUES
     20B magic #
    8.00 linker version
     C00 size of code
     A00 size of initialized data
       0 size of uninitialized data
    5100 address of entry point
    1000 base of code
         ----- new -----
0000000000010000 image base
    1000 section alignment
     200 file alignment
```

```
       1 subsystem (Native)
    5.02 operating system version
    5.02 image version
    5.02 subsystem version
    7000 size of image
     400 size of headers
    74EF checksum
0000000000040000 size of stack reserve
0000000000001000 size of stack commit
0000000000100000 size of heap reserve
0000000000001000 size of heap commit
       0 [       0] address [size] of Export Directory
    51B0 [      28] address [size] of Import Directory
    6000 [     3B8] address [size] of Resource Directory
    4000 [      6C] address [size] of Exception Directory
       0 [       0] address [size] of Security Directory
       0 [       0] address [size] of Base Relocation Directory
    2090 [      1C] address [size] of Debug Directory
       0 [       0] address [size] of Description Directory
       0 [       0] address [size] of Special Directory
       0 [       0] address [size] of Thread Storage Directory
       0 [       0] address [size] of Load Configuration Directory
       0 [       0] address [size] of Bound Import Directory
    2000 [      88] address [size] of Import Address Table Directory
       0 [       0] address [size] of Delay Import Directory
       0 [       0] address [size] of COR20 Header Directory
       0 [       0] address [size] of Reserved Directory
...
...
...
```

Then we display the contents of Import Address Table Directory using **dps** command:

```
kd> dps fffffadf`e0eb5000+2000 fffffadf`e0eb5000+2000+88
fffffadf`e0eb7000  fffff800`01044370 nt!IoCompleteRequest
fffffadf`e0eb7008  fffff800`01019700 nt!IoDeleteDevice
fffffadf`e0eb7010  fffff800`012551a0 nt!IoDeleteSymbolicLink
fffffadf`e0eb7018  fffff800`01056a90 nt!MiResolveTransitionFault+0x7c2
fffffadf`e0eb7020  fffff800`0103a380 nt!ObDereferenceObject
fffffadf`e0eb7028  fffff800`0103ace0 nt!KeWaitForSingleObject
fffffadf`e0eb7030  fffff800`0103c570 nt!KeSetTimer
fffffadf`e0eb7038  fffff800`0102d070 nt!IoBuildPartialMdl+0x3
fffffadf`e0eb7040  fffff800`012d4480 nt!PsTerminateSystemThread
fffffadf`e0eb7048  fffff800`01041690 nt!KeBugCheckEx
fffffadf`e0eb7050  fffff800`010381b0 nt!KeInitializeTimer
fffffadf`e0eb7058  fffff800`0103ceb0 nt!ZwClose
fffffadf`e0eb7060  fffff800`012b39f0 nt!ObReferenceObjectByHandle
fffffadf`e0eb7068  fffff800`012b7380 nt!PsCreateSystemThread
fffffadf`e0eb7070  fffff800`01251f90 nt!FsRtlpIsDfsEnabled+0x114
fffffadf`e0eb7078  fffff800`01275160 nt!IoCreateDevice
fffffadf`e0eb7080  00000000`00000000
fffffadf`e0eb7088  00000000`00000000
```

We see that this driver under certain circumstances can bugcheck the system using *KeBugCheckEx*, it creates system thread(s) (*PsCreateSystemThread*) and uses timer(s) (*KeInitializeTimer*, *KeSetTimer*).

If we see *name+offset* in the import table (I think this is an effect of OMAP code optimization) we can get the function by using **ln** command (list nearest symbols):

```
kd> ln fffff800`01056a90
(fffff800`01056760)   nt!MiResolveTransitionFault+0x7c2   |  (fffff800`010
56a92)   nt!RtlInitUnicodeString

kd> ln fffff800`01251f90
(fffff800`01251e90)   nt!FsRtlpIsDfsEnabled+0x114   |  (fffff800`01251f92)
   nt!IoCreateSymbolicLink
```

This technique is useful if we have a bugcheck that happens when a driver calls certain functions or must call particular functions in pairs, like bugcheck 0x20:

```
kd> !analyze -show 0x20
KERNEL_APC_PENDING_DURING_EXIT (20)
The key data item is the thread's APC disable count. If this is non-zero,
then this is the source of the problem. The APC disable count is
decremented each time a driver calls KeEnterCriticalRegion,
KeInitializeMutex, or FsRtlEnterFileSystem. The APC disable count is
incremented each time a driver calls KeLeaveCriticalRegion,
KeReleaseMutex, or FsRtlExitFileSystem. Since these calls should always be
in pairs, this value should be zero when a thread exits. A negative value
indicates that a driver has disabled APC calls without re-enabling them. A
positive value indicates that the reverse is true. If you ever see this
error, be very suspicious of all drivers installed on the machine —
especially unusual or non-standard drivers. Third party file system
redirectors are especially suspicious since they do not generally receive
the heavy duty testing that NTFS, FAT, RDR, etc receive. This current IRQL
should also be 0. If it is not, that a driver's cancelation routine can
cause this bugcheck by returning at an elevated IRQL. Always attempt to
note what you were doing/closing at the time of the crash, and note all of
the installed drivers at the time of the crash.  This symptom is usually a
severe bug in a third party driver.
```

Then we can see at least whether the suspicious driver could have potentially used those functions and if it imports one of them we can see whether it imports the corresponding counterpart function.

No Component Symbols pattern can be easily identified in stack traces by huge function offsets or no exported functions at all:

```
STACK_TEXT:
WARNING: Stack unwind information not available. Following frames may be
wrong.
00b2f42c 091607aa mydll!foo+0x8338
00b2f4cc 7c83ab9e mydll2+0x8fe3
```

Insufficient Memory (Committed Memory)

Insufficient Memory pattern can be seen in many complete and kernel memory dumps. This condition can cause a system to crash, become slow, hang, or refuse to provide the expected functionality, for example, refuse new terminal server connections. There are many types of memory resources, and we can classify them initially into the following categories:

- Committed memory
- Virtual memory
    - Kernel space
        - Paged pool
        - Non-paged pool
        - Session pool
        - PTE limits
        - Desktop heap
        - GDI limits
    - User space
        - Virtual regions
        - Process heap

What we outline here is committed memory exhaustion. Committed memory is an allocated memory backed up by some physical memory or by a reserved space in the page file(s). Reserving the space needs to be done in case OS wants to swap out that memory data to disk when it is not used, and there is no physical memory available for other processes. If that data is needed again, OS brings it back to physical memory. If there is no space in the page file(s), then physical memory is filled up. If committed memory is exhausted, most likely, the system hangs or results in a bugcheck soon, so checking memory statistics shall always be done when we get a kernel or a complete memory dump. Even access violation bugchecks could result from insufficient memory when some memory allocation operation failed, but a kernel mode component didn't check the return value for NULL. Here is an example:

```
BugCheck 8E, {c0000005, 809203af, aa647c0c, 0}

0: kd> !analyze -v
...
...
...
TRAP_FRAME: aa647c0c -- (.trap ffffffffaa647c0c)
...
```

```
...
...

0: kd> .trap ffffffffaa647c0c
ErrCode = 00000000
eax=00000000 ebx=bc1f3cfc ecx=89589250 edx=000018c1 esi=bc1f3ce0
edi=aa647d14
eip=809203af esp=aa647c80 ebp=aa647c80 iopl=0 nv up ei pl zr na pe nc
cs=0008 ss=0010 ds=0023 es=0023 fs=0030 gs=0000 efl=00010246
nt!SeTokenType+0x8:
809203af 8b8080000000 mov eax,dword ptr [eax+80h]
ds:0023:00000080=????????

0: kd> k
ChildEBP RetAddr
aa647c80 bf8173c5 nt!SeTokenType+0x8
aa647cdc bf81713b win32k!GreGetSpoolMessage+0xb0
aa647d4c 80834d3f win32k!NtGdiGetSpoolMessage+0x96
aa647d4c 7c82ed54 nt!KiFastCallEntry+0xfc
```

If we enter **!vm** command to display memory statistics we would see that all committed memory is filled up:

```
0: kd> !vm
*** Virtual Memory Usage ***
 Physical Memory:        999294 (   3997176 Kb)
 Page File: \??\C:\pagefile.sys
   Current:   4193280 Kb  Free Space:     533744 Kb
   Minimum:   4193280 Kb  Maximum:       4193280 Kb
 Available Pages:         18698 (     74792 Kb)
 ResAvail Pages:         865019 (   3460076 Kb)
 Locked IO Pages:           290 (      1160 Kb)
 Free System PTEs:       155265 (    621060 Kb)
 Free NP PTEs:            32766 (    131064 Kb)
 Free Special NP:             0 (         0 Kb)
 Modified Pages:            113 (       452 Kb)
 Modified PF Pages:          61 (       244 Kb)
 NonPagedPool Usage:      12380 (     49520 Kb)
 NonPagedPool Max:        64799 (    259196 Kb)
 PagedPool 0 Usage:       40291 (    161164 Kb)
 PagedPool 1 Usage:        2463 (      9852 Kb)
 PagedPool 2 Usage:        2455 (      9820 Kb)
 PagedPool 3 Usage:        2453 (      9812 Kb)
 PagedPool 4 Usage:        2488 (      9952 Kb)
 PagedPool Usage:         50150 (    200600 Kb)
 PagedPool Maximum:       67584 (    270336 Kb)

 ********** 18 pool allocations have failed **********

 Shared Commit:           87304 (    349216 Kb)
 Special Pool:                0 (         0 Kb)
```

```
Shared Process:          56241 (    224964 Kb)
PagedPool Commit:        50198 (    200792 Kb)
Driver Commit:            1892 (      7568 Kb)
Committed pages:       2006945 (   8027780 Kb)
Commit limit:          2008205 (   8032820 Kb)

********** 1216024 commit requests have failed  **********
```

There might have been a memory leak or too many terminal sessions with fat applications to fit in physical memory and the page file.

Spiking Thread

The next pattern is **Spiking Thread**. If we have a process dump with many threads, it is sometimes difficult to see which thread there was spiking CPU. This is why it is always good to have some screenshots or notes from QSlice or Process Explorer showing spiking thread ID and process ID. The latter ID is to make sure that the process dump was from the correct process. New process dumpers and tools from Microsoft (userdump.exe, for example) save thread time information so we can open the dump and see the time spent in kernel and user mode for any thread by entering **!runaway** command. However, if that command shows many threads with similar CPU consumption, it doesn't highlight the particular thread that was spiking at the time the crash dump was saved, so screenshots are still useful in some cases.

What to do if we don't have the spiking thread ID? We need to look at all threads and find those that are not waiting. Almost all threads are waiting most of the time. So the chances to dump the normal process and see some active threads are very low. If the thread is waiting the top function on its stack usually is (for XP/W2K3/Vista):

```
ntdll!KiFastSystemCallRet
```

and below it, we can see some blocking calls waiting for some synchronization object, *Sleep* API call, IO completion or for LPC reply:

```
0:085> ~*kv
...
...
...
64 Id: 1b0.120c Suspend: -1 Teb: 7ff69000 Unfrozen
ChildEBP RetAddr Args to Child
02defe18 7c90e399 ntdll!KiFastSystemCallRet
02defe1c 77e76703 ntdll!NtReplyWaitReceivePortEx+0xc
02deff80 77e76c22 rpcrt4!LRPC_ADDRESS::ReceiveLotsaCalls+0xf4
02deff88 77e76a3b rpcrt4!RecvLotsaCallsWrapper+0xd
02deffa8 77e76c0a rpcrt4!BaseCachedThreadRoutine+0x79
02deffb4 7c80b683 rpcrt4!ThreadStartRoutine+0x1a
02deffec 00000000 kernel32!BaseThreadStart+0x37

65 Id: 1b0.740 Suspend: -1 Teb: 7ff67000 Unfrozen
ChildEBP RetAddr Args to Child
02edff44 7c90d85c ntdll!KiFastSystemCallRet
02edff48 7c8023ed ntdll!NtDelayExecution+0xc
02edffa0 57cde2dd kernel32!SleepEx+0x61
02edffb4 7c80b683 component!foo+0x35
02edffec 00000000 kernel32!BaseThreadStart+0x37
```

```
66 Id: 1b0.131c Suspend: -1 Teb: 7ff66000 Unfrozen
ChildEBP RetAddr Args to Child
02f4ff38 7c90e9c0 ntdll!KiFastSystemCallRet
02f4ff3c 7c8025cb ntdll!ZwWaitForSingleObject+0xc
02f4ffa0 72001f65 kernel32!WaitForSingleObjectEx+0xa8
02f4ffb4 7c80b683 component!WorkerThread+0x15
02f4ffec 00000000 kernel32!BaseThreadStart+0x37

67 Id: 1b0.1320 Suspend: -1 Teb: 7ff65000 Unfrozen
ChildEBP RetAddr Args to Child
02f8fe1c 7c90e9ab ntdll!KiFastSystemCallRet
02f8fe20 7c8094e2 ntdll!ZwWaitForMultipleObjects+0xc
02f8febc 7e4195f9 kernel32!WaitForMultipleObjectsEx+0x12c
02f8ff18 7e4196a8 user32!RealMsgWaitForMultipleObjectsEx+0x13e
02f8ff34 720019f6 user32!MsgWaitForMultipleObjects+0x1f
02f8ffa0 72001a29 component!bar+0xd9
02f8ffb4 7c80b683 component!MonitorWorkerThread+0x11
02f8ffec 00000000 kernel32!BaseThreadStart+0x37

68 Id: 1b0.1340 Suspend: -1 Teb: 7ff63000 Unfrozen
ChildEBP RetAddr Args to Child
0301ff1c 7c90e31b ntdll!KiFastSystemCallRet
0301ff20 7c80a746 ntdll!ZwRemoveIoCompletion+0xc
0301ff4c 57d46e65 kernel32!GetQueuedCompletionStatus+0x29
0301ffb4 7c80b683 component!AsyncEventsThread+0x91
0301ffec 00000000 kernel32!BaseThreadStart+0x37
...
...
...

# 85 Id: 1b0.17b4 Suspend: -1 Teb: 7ffd4000 Unfrozen
ChildEBP RetAddr Args to Child
00daffc8 7c9507a8 ntdll!DbgBreakPoint
00dafff4 00000000 ntdll!DbgUiRemoteBreakin+0x2d
```

Therefore, if we have a different thread like this one below the chances that it was spiking are bigger:

```
58 Id: 1b0.9f4 Suspend: -1 Teb: 7ff75000 Unfrozen
ChildEBP RetAddr Args to Child
0280f64c 500af723 componentB!DoSomething+32
0280f85c 500b5391 componentB!CheckSomething+231
0280f884 500b7a3f componentB!ProcessWorkIteme+9f
0301ffec 00000000 kernel32!BaseThreadStart+0x37
```

There is no *KiFastSystemCallRet* on top, and if we look at the currently executing instruction, we see that it does some copy operation:

```
0:085> ~58r
eax=00000000 ebx=0280fdd4 ecx=0000005f edx=00000000 esi=03d30444
edi=0280f6dc
eip=500a4024 esp=0280f644 ebp=0280f64c iopl=0 nv up ei pl nz na po nc
cs=001b ss=0023 ds=0023 es=0023 fs=003b gs=0000 efl=00010202
componentB!DoSomething+32:
500a4024 f3a5 rep movs dword ptr es:[edi],dword ptr [esi]
es:0023:0280f6dc=00000409 ds:0023:03d30444=00000409
```

In a kernel or a complete memory dump we can see CPU spikes by checking *KernelTime* and *UserTime*:

```
0: kd> !thread 88b66768
THREAD 88b66768 Cid 01fc.1550 Teb: 7ffad000 Win32Thread: bc18f240 RUNNING
on processor 1
IRP List:
89716008: (0006,0094) Flags: 00000a00 Mdl: 00000000
Impersonation token: e423a030 (Level Impersonation)
DeviceMap e3712480
Owning Process 8a0a56a0 Image: SomeSvc.exe
Wait Start TickCount 1782229 Ticks: 0
Context Switch Count 877610 LargeStack
UserTime 00:00:01.0078
KernelTime 02:23:21.0718
```

By default, **!runaway** shows only user mode time. By specifying additional flags, it is possible to see both kernel and user time:

```
0:000> !runaway 3
User Mode Time
Thread Time
8:15a4 0 days 0:12:32.812
0:1c00 0 days 0:00:00.312
9:1b50 0 days 0:00:00.296
22:2698 0 days 0:00:00.046
17:22b8 0 days 0:00:00.031
14:2034 0 days 0:00:00.031
21:21b4 0 days 0:00:00.000
20:27b0 0 days 0:00:00.000
19:278c 0 days 0:00:00.000
18:2788 0 days 0:00:00.000
16:2194 0 days 0:00:00.000
15:2064 0 days 0:00:00.000
13:2014 0 days 0:00:00.000
12:1e38 0 days 0:00:00.000
11:1c54 0 days 0:00:00.000
10:1d40 0 days 0:00:00.000
7:1994 0 days 0:00:00.000
6:1740 0 days 0:00:00.000
5:1c18 0 days 0:00:00.000
4:c10 0 days 0:00:00.000
```

```
3:1774 0 days 0:00:00.000
2:1a08 0 days 0:00:00.000
1:fb8 0 days 0:00:00.000
Kernel Mode Time
Thread Time
9:1b50 0 days 1:21:54.125
8:15a4 0 days 0:02:48.390
0:1c00 0 days 0:00:00.328
14:2034 0 days 0:00:00.234
22:2698 0 days 0:00:00.156
17:22b8 0 days 0:00:00.015
21:21b4 0 days 0:00:00.000
20:27b0 0 days 0:00:00.000
19:278c 0 days 0:00:00.000
18:2788 0 days 0:00:00.000
16:2194 0 days 0:00:00.000
15:2064 0 days 0:00:00.000
13:2014 0 days 0:00:00.000
12:1e38 0 days 0:00:00.000
11:1c54 0 days 0:00:00.000
10:1d40 0 days 0:00:00.000
7:1994 0 days 0:00:00.000
6:1740 0 days 0:00:00.000
5:1c18 0 days 0:00:00.000
4:c10 0 days 0:00:00.000
3:1774 0 days 0:00:00.000
2:1a08 0 days 0:00:00.000
1:fb8 0 days 0:00:00.000
```

We see that the thread #**15a4** spikes mostly in user mode, but the thread #**1b50** spikes mostly in kernel mode!

In the kernel and complete memory dumps we can scan all threads with *Ticks: 0* or *Elapsed Ticks: 0* to check their kernel and user times:

```
PROCESS 8782cd60 SessionId: 52 Cid: 4a58 Peb: 7ffdf000 ParentCid: 1ea4
DirBase: 0a0260c0 ObjectTable: 88ab33a8 TableSize: 486.
Image: IEXPLORE.EXE
VadRoot 87f59ea8 Clone 0 Private 2077. Modified 123. Locked 0.
DeviceMap 880f6828
Token e8217cd0
ElapsedTime 0:03:09.0765
UserTime 0:00:00.0890
KernelTime 0:00:10.0171
QuotaPoolUsage[PagedPool] 100320
QuotaPoolUsage[NonPagedPool] 58100
Working Set Sizes (now,min,max) (4944, 50, 345) (19776KB, 200KB, 1380KB)
PeakWorkingSetSize 4974
VirtualSize 83 Mb
PeakVirtualSize 83 Mb
PageFaultCount 8544
MemoryPriority FOREGROUND
BasePriority 8
CommitCharge 2262
```

```
THREAD 87836580 Cid 4a58.57cc Teb: 7ffde000 Win32Thread: a224f1d8 WAIT:
(Executive) KernelMode Non-Alertable
89dee788 Semaphore Limit 0x7fffffff
87836668 NotificationTimer
Not impersonating
Owning Process 8782cd60
Wait Start TickCount 123758 Elapsed Ticks: 0
Context Switch Count 97636 LargeStack
UserTime 0:00:00.0593
KernelTime 0:00:08.0359
Start Address 0x7c57b70c
Win32 Start Address 0x00401ee6
Stack Init ac154770 Current ac154320 Base ac155000 Limit ac14d000 Call
ac15477c
Priority 11 BasePriority 8 PriorityDecrement 0 DecrementCount 0

ChildEBP RetAddr Args to Child
ac154338 8042d8d7 00000000 8047bd00 00000001 nt!KiSwapThread+0x1b1
ac154360 80415d61 89dee788 00000000 00000000
nt!KeWaitForSingleObject+0x1a3
ac15439c 8041547c 00000000 00000001 8051c501 nt!ExpWaitForResource+0x2d
ac1543b4 8046907a 8047bd00 00000001 805225e9
nt!ExAcquireResourceSharedLite+0xc6
ac1543c0 805225e9 00000000 00000001 8051c501 nt!CmpLockRegistry+0x18
ac154430 8051c718 e7c5fd08 ac15448c 00000001 nt!CmSetValueKey+0x31
ac1544b4 8046b2a9 00000798 00125c04 00000000 nt!NtSetValueKey+0x196
ac1544b4 77f88de7 00000798 00125c04 00000000 nt!KiSystemService+0xc9
00125bb0 00000000 00000000 00000000 00000000 +0x77f88de7
```

For complete and kernel dumps, we can also pay attention to the output of **!running** command and to the output of **!stacks** command (*Ticks* and *ThreadState* columns).

Module Variety

Sometimes when we look at the list of loaded modules in a process address space, we see an instance of the pattern that I call **Module Variety**. It means, literally, that there are so many different loaded modules that we start thinking that their coexistence created the problem. We can also call this pattern **Component Variety** or **DLL Variety**, but I prefer the former because WinDbg refers to loaded executables, DLLs, drivers, ActiveX controls as modules.

Modules can be roughly classified into 4 broad categories:

- Application modules - components that were developed specifically for this application, one of them is the main application module.
- 3rd-party modules - we can easily identify them if the company name is the same in the output of **lmv** WinDbg command.
- Common system modules - Windows DLLs supplied by OS and implementing native OS calls, Windows API, and also C/C++ runtime functions, for example, *ntdll.dll, kernel32.dll, user32.dll, gdi32.dll, advapi32.dll, msvcrt.dll.*
- Specific system modules - optional Windows DLLs supplied by Microsoft that are specific to the application functionality and implementation, like MFC DLLs, .NET runtime or *tapi32.dll.*

Although **lmv** is verbose for a quick check of component timestamps, we can use **lmt** WinDbg command. Here is an example of the great module variety from Windows Server 2003:

```
Loading Dump File [application.dmp]
...
...
...
Windows Server 2003 Version 3790 (Service Pack 1)
...
...
...

0:001> lmt
start    end        module name
00400000 030ba000   app_main  Mon Dec 04 21:22:42 2006
04120000 04193000   Dformd    Mon Jan 31 02:27:58 2000
041a0000 04382000   sqllib2   Mon May 29 22:50:11 2006
04490000 044d3000   udNet     Mon May 29 23:22:43 2006
04e30000 04f10000   abchook   Wed Aug 01 20:47:17 2006
05e10000 05e15000   token_manager  Fri Mar 12 11:54:17 1999
06030000 06044000   ODBCINT   Thu Mar 24 22:59:58 2005
```

```
06150000 0618d000   sgl5NET   Mon May 29 23:25:22 2006
06190000 0622f000   OPENGL32  Mon Nov 06 21:30:52 2006
06230000 06240000   pwrpc32   Thu Oct 22 16:22:40 1998
06240000 07411000   app_dll_1 Tue Aug 08 12:14:39 2006
07420000 07633000   app_dll_2 Mon Dec 04 22:11:59 2006
07640000 07652000   zlib      Fri Aug 30 08:12:24 2002
07660000 07f23000   app_dll_3 Wed Oct 19 11:43:34 2005
0dec0000 0dedc000   app_dll_4 Mon Dec 04 22:11:36 2006
10000000 110be000   des       Tue Jul 18 20:42:02 2006
129c0000 12f1b000   xpsp2res  Fri Mar 25 00:26:47 2005
1b000000 1b170000   msjet40   Tue Jul 06 19:16:05 2004
1b2c0000 1b2cd000   msjter40  Thu May 09 19:09:53 2002
1b2d0000 1b2ea000   msjint40  Thu May 09 19:09:53 2002
1b570000 1b5c5000   msjetoledb40  Thu Nov 13 23:40:06 2003
1b5d0000 1b665000   mswstr10  Thu May 09 19:09:56 2002
1e000000 1e0f0000   python23  Fri Jan 30 13:03:24 2004
4b070000 4b0c1000   MSCTF     Fri Mar 25 02:10:36 2005
4b610000 4b64d000   ODBC32    Fri Mar 25 02:09:33 2005
4b9e0000 4ba59000   OLEDB32   Fri Mar 25 02:09:56 2005
4c310000 4c31d000   OLEDB32R  Fri Mar 25 02:09:57 2005
4c3b0000 4c3de000   MSCTFIME  Fri Mar 25 02:10:37 2005
5f400000 5f4f2000   mfc42     Wed Oct 27 22:35:22 1999
62130000 6213d000   mfc42loc  Wed Mar 26 03:35:58 2003
62460000 6246e000   msadrh15  Fri Mar 25 02:10:29 2005
63050000 63059000   lpk       Fri Mar 25 02:09:21 2005
63270000 632c7000   hnetcfg   Fri Mar 25 02:09:11 2005
65340000 653d2000   OLEAUT32  Wed Sep 01 00:15:11 1999
68000000 6802f000   rsaenh    Fri Mar 25 00:30:55 2005
68a50000 68a70000   glu32     Fri Mar 25 02:09:03 2005
71990000 71998000   wshtcpip  Wed Mar 26 03:34:24 2003
719d0000 71a11000   mswsock   Fri Mar 25 02:12:06 2005
71a60000 71a6b000   wsock32   Wed Mar 26 03:34:24 2003
71a90000 71a91000   mpr       Wed Mar 26 03:34:24 2003
71aa0000 71aa8000   ws2help   Fri Mar 25 02:10:19 2005
71ab0000 71ac7000   ws2_32    Fri Mar 25 02:10:18 2005
71ad0000 71ae2000   tsappcmp  Fri Mar 25 02:09:56 2005
71af0000 71b48000   netapi32  Fri Aug 11 11:00:07 2006
72ec0000 72ee7000   winspool  Fri Mar 25 02:09:48 2005
73290000 73295000   riched32  Wed Mar 26 03:34:14 2003
73ee0000 73ee5000   icmp      Wed Mar 26 03:34:09 2003
74920000 7493a000   msdart    Fri Mar 25 02:10:48 2005
74b10000 74b80000   riched20  Fri Mar 25 02:09:36 2005
75220000 75281000   usp10     Fri Mar 25 02:09:51 2005
75810000 758d0000   userenv   Fri Mar 25 02:09:50 2005
75d00000 75d27000   apphelp   Fri Mar 25 02:09:21 2005
76120000 7613d000   imm32     Fri Mar 25 02:09:37 2005
76140000 76188000   comdlg32  Fri Mar 25 02:10:11 2005
76810000 76949000   comsvcs   Fri Aug 26 23:19:45 2005
76a60000 76a6b000   psapi     Fri Mar 25 02:09:57 2005
76c00000 76c1a000   iphlpapi  Fri May 19 04:21:07 2006
76de0000 76e0f000   dnsapi    Wed Jul 12 20:02:12 2006
76e20000 76e4e000   wldap32   Fri Mar 25 02:09:59 2005
76e60000 76e73000   secur32   Fri Mar 25 02:10:01 2005
76e80000 76e87000   winrnr    Fri Mar 25 02:09:45 2005
```

```
76e90000 76e98000    rasadhlp  Wed Jul 12 20:02:15 2006
76f20000 77087000    comres    Wed Mar 26 03:33:48 2003
77330000 773c7000    comctl32  Mon Aug 28 09:26:02 2006
77470000 775a4000    ole32     Thu Jul 21 04:25:12 2005
77640000 776c3000    clbcatq   Thu Jul 21 04:25:13 2005
77b30000 77b38000    version   Fri Mar 25 02:09:50 2005
77b40000 77b9a000    msvcrt    Fri Mar 25 02:11:59 2005
77ba0000 77be8000    gdi32     Tue Mar 07 03:55:05 2006
77bf0000 77c8f000    rpcrt4    Fri Mar 25 02:09:42 2005
77ca0000 77da3000    comctl32_77ca0000  Mon Aug 28 09:25:59 2006
77db0000 77dc1000    winsta    Fri Mar 25 02:09:51 2005
77de0000 77e71000    user32    Fri Mar 25 02:09:49 2005
77e80000 77ed2000    shlwapi   Wed Sep 20 01:33:12 2006
77ee0000 77ef1000    regapi    Fri Mar 25 02:09:51 2005
77f20000 77fcb000    advapi32  Fri Mar 25 02:09:06 2005
780a0000 780b2000    MSVCIRT   Wed Jun 17 19:45:46 1998
780c0000 78121000    MSVCP60   Wed Jun 17 19:52:10 1998
79040000 79085000    fusion    Fri Feb 18 20:57:41 2005
79170000 79198000    mscoree   Fri Feb 18 20:57:48 2005
791b0000 79417000    mscorwks  Fri Feb 18 20:59:56 2005
79510000 79523000    mscorsn   Fri Feb 18 20:30:38 2005
79780000 7998c000    mscorlib  Fri Feb 18 20:48:36 2005
79990000 79cce000    mscorlib_79990000  Thu Nov 02 04:53:27 2006
7c340000 7c396000    msvcr71   Fri Feb 21 12:42:20 2003
7c800000 7c93e000    kernel32  Tue Jul 25 13:37:16 2006
7c940000 7ca19000    ntdll     Fri Mar 25 02:09:53 2005
7ca20000 7d20a000    shell32   Thu Jul 13 13:58:56 2006
```

Note: We can use the **lmtD** command to take advantage of WinDbg hypertext commands. In that case, we can quickly click on a module name to view its detailed information.

We see that some components are very old, 1998-1999, and some are from 2006. We also see 3rd-party libraries: OpenGL, Visual Fortran RTL, Python language runtime. Common system modules include two versions of C/C++ runtime library, 6.0 and 7.0. Specific system modules include MFC and .NET, MSJET, ODBC, and OLE DB support. There is a sign of DLL Hell (https://en.wikipedia.org/wiki/DLL_Hell) here too. OLE Automation DLL in system32 folder seems to be very old and doesn't correspond to Windows 2003 SP1 which should have file version 5.2.3790.1830:

```
0:001> lmv m OLEAUT32
start    end         module name
65340000 653d2000    OLEAUT32    (deferred)
    Image path: C:\WINDOWS\system32\OLEAUT32.DLL
    Image name: OLEAUT32.DLL
    Timestamp:        Wed Sep 01 00:15:11 1999 (37CC61FF)
    CheckSum:         0009475A
    ImageSize:        00092000
    File version:     2.40.4277.1
    Product version:  2.40.4277.1
    File flags:       2 (Mask 3F) Pre-release
```

```
    File OS:            40004 NT Win32
    File type:          2.0 Dll
    File date:          00000000.00000000
    Translations:       0409.04e4
    CompanyName:        Microsoft Corporation
    ProductName:        Microsoft OLE 2.40  for Windows NT(TM) and
Windows 95(TM) Operating Systems
    InternalName:       OLEAUT32.DLL
    ProductVersion:     2.40.4277
    FileVersion:        2.40.4277
    FileDescription:    Microsoft OLE 2.40  for Windows NT(TM) and
Windows 95(TM) Operating Systems
    LegalCopyright:     Copyright © Microsoft Corp. 1993-1998.
    LegalTrademarks:    Microsoft® is a registered trademark
of Microsoft Corporation. Windows NT(TM) and Windows 95(TM) are
trademarks of Microsoft Corporation.
    Comments:           Microsoft OLE 2.40  for Windows NT(TM) and
Windows 95(TM) Operating Systems
```

Stack Overflow (Kernel Mode)

Now I show one example of **Stack Overflow** pattern in x86 Windows kernel. When it happens in kernel mode, we usually have bugcheck 7F with the first argument being EXCEPTION_DOUBLE_FAULT (8):

```
UNEXPECTED_KERNEL_MODE_TRAP (7f)
This means a trap occurred in kernel mode, and it's a trap of a kind that
the kernel isn't allowed to have/catch (bound trap) or that is always
instant death (double fault). The first number in the bugcheck params is
the number of the trap (8 = double fault, etc). Consult an Intel x86
family manual to learn more about what these traps are. Here is a
*portion* of those codes:
If kv shows a taskGate
  use .tss on the part before the colon, then kv.
Else if kv shows a trapframe
  use .trap on that value
Else
  .trap on the appropriate frame will show where the trap was taken (on
x86, this will be the ebp that goes with the procedure KiTrap)
Endif
kb will then show the corrected stack.
Arguments:
Arg1: 00000008, EXCEPTION_DOUBLE_FAULT
Arg2: f7747fe0
Arg3: 00000000
Arg4: 00000000
```

The kernel stack size for a thread is limited to 12Kb on x86 platforms (24kb on x64 platforms) and is guarded by an invalid page. Therefore, when we hit an invalid address on that page, the processor generates a page fault, tries to push registers, and gets a second page fault. This is what "double fault" means. In this scenario, the processor switches to another stack via TSS (task state segment) task switching mechanism because IDT entry for trap 8 contains not an interrupt handler address but the so-called TSS segment selector. This selector points to a memory segment that contains a new kernel stack pointer. The difference between a normal IDT entry and double fault entry can be seen by inspecting IDT:

```
5: kd> !pcr 5
KPCR for Processor 5 at f7747000:
    Major 1 Minor 1
 NtTib.ExceptionList: b044e0b8
     NtTib.StackBase: 00000000
    NtTib.StackLimit: 00000000
  NtTib.SubSystemTib: f7747fe0
       NtTib.Version: 00ae1064
   NtTib.UserPointer: 00000020
```

```
      NtTib.SelfTib: 7ffdf000
            SelfPcr: f7747000
               Prcb: f7747120
               Irql: 00000000
                IRR: 00000000
                IDR: ffffffff
      InterruptMode: 00000000
                IDT: f774d800
                GDT: f774d400
                TSS: f774a2e0
      CurrentThread: 8834c020
         NextThread: 00000000
         IdleThread: f774a090

5: kd> dt _KIDTENTRY f774d800
   +0x000 Offset            : 0x97e8
   +0x002 Selector          : 8
   +0x004 Access            : 0x8e00
   +0x006 ExtendedOffset    : 0x8088

5: kd> ln 0x808897e8
(808897e8)   nt!KiTrap00   |  (808898c0)   nt!Dr_kit1_a
Exact matches:
    nt!KiTrap00

5: kd> dt _KIDTENTRY f774d800+7*8
   +0x000 Offset            : 0xa880
   +0x002 Selector          : 8
   +0x004 Access            : 0x8e00
   +0x006 ExtendedOffset    : 0x8088

5: kd> ln 8088a880
(8088a880)   nt!KiTrap07   |  (8088ab72)   nt!KiTrap08
Exact matches:
    nt!KiTrap07

5: kd> dt _KIDTENTRY f774d800+8*8
   +0x000 Offset            : 0x1238
   +0x002 Selector          : 0x50
   +0x004 Access            : 0x8500
   +0x006 ExtendedOffset    : 0

5: kd> dt _KIDTENTRY f774d800+9*8
  +0x000 Offset : 0xac94
  +0x002 Selector : 8
  +0x004 Access : 0x8e00
  +0x006 ExtendedOffset : 0x8088
```

```
5: kd> ln 8088ac94
(8088ac94) nt!KiTrap09 | (8088ad10) nt!Dr_kita_a
Exact matches:
  nt!KiTrap09
```

If we switch to selector 50 explicitly, we see *nt!KiTrap08* function which does our bugcheck and saves a crash dump in *KeBugCheck2* function:

```
5: kd> .tss 50
eax=00000000 ebx=00000000 ecx=00000000 edx=00000000 esi=00000000
edi=00000000
eip=8088ab72 esp=f774d3c0 ebp=00000000 iopl=0 nv up di pl nz na po nc
cs=0008 ss=0010 ds=0023 es=0023 fs=0030 gs=0000 efl=00000000
nt!KiTrap08:
8088ab72 fa              cli

5: kd> .asm no_code_bytes
Assembly options: no_code_bytes

5: kd> uf nt!KiTrap08
nt!KiTrap08:
8088ab72 cli
8088ab73 mov     eax,dword ptr fs:[00000040h]
8088ab79 mov     ecx,dword ptr fs:[124h]
8088ab80 mov     edi,dword ptr [ecx+38h]
8088ab83 mov     ecx,dword ptr [edi+18h]
8088ab86 mov     dword ptr [eax+1Ch],ecx
8088ab89 mov     cx,word ptr [edi+30h]
8088ab8d mov     word ptr [eax+66h],cx
8088ab91 mov     ecx,dword ptr [edi+20h]
8088ab94 test    ecx,ecx
8088ab96 je      nt!KiTrap08+0x2a (8088ab9c)

nt!KiTrap08+0x26:
8088ab98 mov     cx,48h

nt!KiTrap08+0x2a:
8088ab9c mov     word ptr [eax+60h],cx
8088aba0 mov     ecx,dword ptr fs:[3Ch]
8088aba7 lea     eax,[ecx+50h]
8088abaa mov     byte ptr [eax+5],89h
8088abae pushfd
8088abaf and     dword ptr [esp],0FFFFBFFFh
8088abb6 popfd
8088abb7 mov     eax,dword ptr fs:[0000003Ch]
8088abbd mov     ch,byte ptr [eax+57h]
8088abc0 mov     cl,byte ptr [eax+54h]
8088abc3 shl     ecx,10h
8088abc6 mov     cx,word ptr [eax+52h]
8088abca mov     eax,dword ptr fs:[00000040h]
8088abd0 mov     dword ptr fs:[40h],ecx
```

```
nt!KiTrap08+0x65:
8088abd7 push    0
8088abd9 push    0
8088abdb push    0
8088abdd push    eax
8088abde push    8
8088abe0 push    7Fh
8088abe2 call    nt!KeBugCheck2 (80826a92)
8088abe7 jmp     nt!KiTrap08+0x65 (8088abd7)
```

We can inspect the TSS address shown in the **!pcr** command output above:

```
5: kd> dt _KTSS f774a2e0
   +0x000 Backlink         : 0x28
   +0x002 Reserved0        : 0
   +0x004 Esp0             : 0xf774d3c0
   +0x008 Ss0              : 0x10
   +0x00a Reserved1        : 0
   +0x00c NotUsed1         : [4] 0
   +0x01c CR3              : 0x646000
   +0x020 Eip              : 0x8088ab72
   +0x024 EFlags           : 0
   +0x028 Eax              : 0
   +0x02c Ecx              : 0
   +0x030 Edx              : 0
   +0x034 Ebx              : 0
   +0x038 Esp              : 0xf774d3c0
   +0x03c Ebp              : 0
   +0x040 Esi              : 0
   +0x044 Edi              : 0
   +0x048 Es               : 0x23
   +0x04a Reserved2        : 0
   +0x04c Cs               : 8
   +0x04e Reserved3        : 0
   +0x050 Ss               : 0x10
   +0x052 Reserved4        : 0
   +0x054 Ds               : 0x23
   +0x056 Reserved5        : 0
   +0x058 Fs               : 0x30
   +0x05a Reserved6        : 0
   +0x05c Gs               : 0
   +0x05e Reserved7        : 0
   +0x060 LDT              : 0
   +0x062 Reserved8        : 0
   +0x064 Flags            : 0
   +0x066 IoMapBase        : 0x20ac
   +0x068 IoMaps           : [1] _KiIoAccessMap
   +0x208c IntDirectionMap  : [32]  "???"
```

We see that EIP points to *nt!KiTrap08* and we see that *Backlink* value is 28 which is the previous TSS selector value that was before the double fault trap:

```
5: kd> .tss 28
eax=00000020 ebx=8bef5100 ecx=01404800 edx=8bee4aa8 esi=01404400
edi=00000000
eip=80882e4b esp=b044e000 ebp=b044e034 iopl=0 nv up ei ng nz na po nc
cs=0008 ss=0010 ds=0023 es=0023 fs=0030 gs=0000 efl=00010282
nt!_SEH_prolog+0x1b:
80882e4b push    esi

5: kd> k 100
ChildEBP RetAddr
b044e034 f7b840ac nt!_SEH_prolog+0x1b
b044e054 f7b846e6 Ntfs!NtfsMapStream+0x4b
b044e0c8 f7b84045 Ntfs!NtfsReadMftRecord+0x86
b044e100 f7b840f4 Ntfs!NtfsReadFileRecord+0x7a
b044e138 f7b7cdb5 Ntfs!NtfsLookupInFileRecord+0x37
b044e210 f7b6efef Ntfs!NtfsWriteFileSizes+0x76
b044e260 f7b6eead Ntfs!NtfsFlushAndPurgeScb+0xd4
b044e464 f7b7e302 Ntfs!NtfsCommonCleanup+0x1ca8
b044e5d4 8081dce5 Ntfs!NtfsFsdCleanup+0xcf
b044e5e8 f70fac53 nt!IofCallDriver+0x45
b044e610 8081dce5 fltMgr!FltpDispatch+0x6f
b044e624 f420576a nt!IofCallDriver+0x45
b044e634 f4202621 component2!DispatchEx+0xa4
b044e640 8081dce5 component2!Dispatch+0x53
b044e654 f4e998c7 nt!IofCallDriver+0x45
b044e67c f4e9997c component!PassThrough+0xbb
b044e688 8081dce5 component!Dispatch+0x78
b044e69c f41e72ff nt!IofCallDriver+0x45
WARNING: Stack unwind information not available. Following frames may be
wrong.
b044e6c0 f41e71ed driver+0xc2ff
00000000 00000000 driver+0xc1ed
```

This is what **!analyze -v** does for this crash dump:

```
STACK_COMMAND:  .tss 0x28 ; kb
```

In our case, NTFS tries to process an exception and SEH exception handler causes double fault when trying to save registers on the stack. Let's look at the stack trace and crash point. We see that ESP points to the beginning of the valid stack page, but the push decrements ESP before memory access, and the previous page is clearly invalid:

```
TSS:  00000028 -- (.tss 28)
eax=00000020 ebx=8bef5100 ecx=01404800 edx=8bee4aa8 esi=01404400
edi=00000000
eip=80882e4b esp=b044e000 ebp=b044e034 iopl=0  nv up ei ng nz na po nc
cs=0008 ss=0010 ds=0023 es=0023 fs=0030 gs=0000 efl=00010282
nt!_SEH_prolog+0x1b:
80882e4b 56              push    esi
```

```
5: kd> dd b044e000-4
b044dffc  ???????? 8bef5100 00000000 00000000
b044e00c  00000000 00000000 00000000 00000000
b044e01c  00000000 00000000 b044e0b8 80880c80
b044e02c  808b6426 80801300 b044e054 f7b840ac
b044e03c  8bece5e0 b044e064 00000400 00000001
b044e04c  b044e134 b044e164 b044e0c8 f7b846e6
b044e05c  b044e480 8bee4aa8 01404400 00000000
b044e06c  00000400 b044e134 b044e164 e143db08
```

```
5: kd> !pte b044e000-4
               VA b044dffc
PDE at 00000000C0602C10    PTE at 00000000C0582268
contains 000000010AA3C863  contains 0000000000000000
pfn 10aa3c —DA-KWEV
```

WinDbg was unable to get all stack frames, and we don't see large frame values ("Memory" column below):

```
5: kd> knf 100
  *** Stack trace for last set context - .thread/.cxr resets it
 #   Memory  ChildEBP RetAddr
00           b044e034 f7b840ac nt!_SEH_prolog+0x1b
01        20 b044e054 f7b846e6 Ntfs!NtfsMapStream+0x4b
02        74 b044e0c8 f7b84045 Ntfs!NtfsReadMftRecord+0x86
03        38 b044e100 f7b840f4 Ntfs!NtfsReadFileRecord+0x7a
04        38 b044e138 f7b7cdb5 Ntfs!NtfsLookupInFileRecord+0x37
05        d8 b044e210 f7b6efef Ntfs!NtfsWriteFileSizes+0x76
06        50 b044e260 f7b6eead Ntfs!NtfsFlushAndPurgeScb+0xd4
07       204 b044e464 f7b7e302 Ntfs!NtfsCommonCleanup+0x1ca8
08       170 b044e5d4 8081dce5 Ntfs!NtfsFsdCleanup+0xcf
09        14 b044e5e8 f70fac53 nt!IofCallDriver+0x45
0a        28 b044e610 8081dce5 fltMgr!FltpDispatch+0x6f
0b        14 b044e624 f420576a nt!IofCallDriver+0x45
0c        10 b044e634 f4202621 component2!DispatchEx+0xa4
0d         c b044e640 8081dce5 component2!Dispatch+0x53
0e        14 b044e654 f4e998c7 nt!IofCallDriver+0x45
0f        28 b044e67c f4e9997c component!PassThrough+0xbb
10         c b044e688 8081dce5 component!Dispatch+0x78
11        14 b044e69c f41e72ff nt!IofCallDriver+0x45
WARNING: Stack unwind information not available. Following frames may be
wrong.
12        24 b044e6c0 f41e71ed driver+0xc2ff
13           00000000 00000000 driver+0xc1ed
```

To see all components involved, we need to dump raw stack data (12Kb is 0x3000). There we can also see some software exceptions processed and get some partial stack traces for them. Some caution is required because stack traces might be incomplete and misleading due to overwritten stack data.

```
5: kd> dds b044e000 b044e000+3000
...
...
...
...
b044ebc4  b044ec74
b044ebc8  b044ec50
b044ebcc  f41f9458 driver+0x1e458
b044ebd0  b044f140
b044ebd4  b044ef44
b044ebd8  b044f138
b044ebdc  80877290 nt!RtlDispatchException+0x8c
b044ebe0  b044ef44
b044ebe4  b044f138
b044ebe8  b044ec74
b044ebec  b044ec50
b044ebf0  f41f9458 driver+0x1e458
b044ebf4  8a7668c0
b044ebf8  e16c2e80
b044ebfc  00000000
b044ec00  00000000
b044ec04  00000002
b044ec08  01000000
b044ec0c  00000000
b044ec10  00000000
...
...
...
b044ec60  00000000
b044ec64  b044ef94
b044ec68  8088e13f nt!RtlRaiseStatus+0x47
b044ec6c  b044ef44
b044ec70  b044ec74
b044ec74  00010007
...
...
...
b0450fe8  00000000
b0450fec  00000000
b0450ff0  00000000
b0450ff4  00000000
b0450ff8  00000000
b0450ffc  00000000
b0451000  ????????
```

```
5: kd> .exr b044ef44
ExceptionAddress: f41dde6d (driver+0x00002e6d)
   ExceptionCode: c0000043
  ExceptionFlags: 00000001
NumberParameters: 0

5: kd> .cxr b044ec74
eax=c0000043 ebx=00000000 ecx=89fe1bc0 edx=b044f084 esi=e16c2e80
edi=8a7668c0
eip=f41dde6d esp=b044efa0 ebp=b044f010 iopl=0 nv up ei pl zr na pe nc
cs=0008 ss=0010 ds=0023 es=0023 fs=0030 gs=0000 efl=00000246
driver+0x2e6d:
f41dde6d e92f010000      jmp     driver+0x2fa1 (f41ddfa1)

5: kd> knf
  *** Stack trace for last set context - .thread/.cxr resets it
 #   Memory  ChildEBP RetAddr
WARNING: Stack unwind information not available. Following frames may be
wrong.
00           b044f010 f41ddce6 driver+0x2e6d
01        b0 b044f0c0 f41dd930 driver+0x2ce6
02        38 b044f0f8 f41e88eb driver+0x2930
03        2c b044f124 f6598eba driver+0xd8eb
04        24 b044f148 f41dcd40 driver2!AllocData+0x84da
05        18 b044f160 8081dce5 driver+0x1d40
06        14 b044f174 f6596741 nt!IofCallDriver+0x45
07        28 b044f19c f659dd70 driver2!AllocData+0x5d61
08        1c b044f1b8 f65967b9 driver2!EventObjectCreate+0xa60
09        40 b044f1f8 8081dce5 driver2!AllocData+0x5dd9
0a        14 b044f20c 808f8255 nt!IofCallDriver+0x45
0b        e8 b044f2f4 80936af5 nt!IopParseDevice+0xa35
0c        80 b044f374 80932de6 nt!ObpLookupObjectName+0x5a9
0d        54 b044f3c8 808ea211 nt!ObOpenObjectByName+0xea
0e        7c b044f444 808eb4ab nt!IopCreateFile+0x447
0f        5c b044f4a0 808edf2a nt!IoCreateFile+0xa3
10        40 b044f4e0 80888c6c nt!NtCreateFile+0x30
11         0 b044f4e0 8082e105 nt!KiFastCallEntry+0xfc
12        a4 b044f584 f657f20d nt!ZwCreateFile+0x11
13        54 b044f5d8 f65570f6 driver3+0x2e20d
```

Therefore, the following components found on raw stack look suspicious:

driver.sys, driver2.sys and *driver3.sys*.

We should check their timestamps using **lmv** command and contact their vendors for any existing updates. The workaround would be to remove these products. The rest are Microsoft modules and drivers *component.sys* and *component2.sys*.

For the latter two, we don't have significant local variable usage in their functions.

OSR NT Insider article provides another example:
http://www.osronline.com/article.cfm?article=254

Deadlock (Executive Resources)

This is a follow up to the previous **Deadlock** pattern post (page 276). Now I'm going to show an example of ERESOURCE deadlock in the Windows kernel.

ERESOURCE (executive resource) is a Windows synchronization object that has ownership semantics.

An executive resource can be owned exclusively or can have shared ownership. This is similar to the following file sharing analogy: when a file is opened for writing others can't write or read it; if we have that file opened for reading, others can read it but can't write to it.

ERESOURCE structure is linked into a list and has threads as owners that allows us to quickly find deadlocks using **!locks** command in the kernel and complete memory dumps. Here is the definition of _ERESOURCE from x86 and x64 Windows:

```
0: kd> dt -r1 _ERESOURCE
   +0x000 SystemResourcesList : _LIST_ENTRY
      +0x000 Flink            : Ptr32 _LIST_ENTRY
      +0x004 Blink            : Ptr32 _LIST_ENTRY
   +0x008 OwnerTable       : Ptr32 _OWNER_ENTRY
      +0x000 OwnerThread      : Uint4B
      +0x004 OwnerCount       : Int4B
      +0x004 TableSize        : Uint4B
   +0x00c ActiveCount      : Int2B
   +0x00e Flag             : Uint2B
   +0x010 SharedWaiters    : Ptr32 _KSEMAPHORE
      +0x000 Header           : _DISPATCHER_HEADER
      +0x010 Limit            : Int4B
   +0x014 ExclusiveWaiters : Ptr32 _KEVENT
      +0x000 Header           : _DISPATCHER_HEADER
   +0x018 OwnerThreads     : [2] _OWNER_ENTRY
      +0x000 OwnerThread      : Uint4B
      +0x004 OwnerCount       : Int4B
      +0x004 TableSize        : Uint4B
   +0x028 ContentionCount  : Uint4B
   +0x02c NumberOfSharedWaiters : Uint2B
   +0x02e NumberOfExclusiveWaiters : Uint2B
   +0x030 Address          : Ptr32 Void
   +0x030 CreatorBackTraceIndex : Uint4B
   +0x034 SpinLock         : Uint4B
```

```
0: kd> dt -r1  _ERESOURCE
nt!_ERESOURCE
   +0x000 SystemResourcesList : _LIST_ENTRY
      +0x000 Flink            : Ptr64 _LIST_ENTRY
```

```
      +0x008 Blink              : Ptr64 _LIST_ENTRY
   +0x010 OwnerTable          : Ptr64 _OWNER_ENTRY
      +0x000 OwnerThread        : Uint8B
      +0x008 OwnerCount         : Int4B
      +0x008 TableSize          : Uint4B
   +0x018 ActiveCount         : Int2B
   +0x01a Flag                : Uint2B
   +0x020 SharedWaiters       : Ptr64 _KSEMAPHORE
      +0x000 Header             : _DISPATCHER_HEADER
      +0x018 Limit              : Int4B
   +0x028 ExclusiveWaiters    : Ptr64 _KEVENT
      +0x000 Header             : _DISPATCHER_HEADER
   +0x030 OwnerThreads        : [2] _OWNER_ENTRY
      +0x000 OwnerThread        : Uint8B
      +0x008 OwnerCount         : Int4B
      +0x008 TableSize          : Uint4B
   +0x050 ContentionCount     : Uint4B
   +0x054 NumberOfSharedWaiters : Uint2B
   +0x056 NumberOfExclusiveWaiters : Uint2B
   +0x058 Address             : Ptr64 Void
   +0x058 CreatorBackTraceIndex : Uint8B
   +0x060 SpinLock            : Uint8B
```

If we have a list of resources from **!locks** output, we can start following threads that own these resources. Owner threads are marked with a star character (*):

```
0: kd> !locks
**** DUMP OF ALL RESOURCE OBJECTS ****
KD: Scanning for held locks......

Resource @ 0x8815b928    Exclusively owned
    Contention Count = 6234751
    NumberOfExclusiveWaiters = 53
     Threads: 89ab8db0-01<*>
     Threads Waiting On Exclusive Access:
        8810fa08       880f5b40       88831020       87e33020
        880353f0       88115020       88131678       880f5db0
        89295420       88255378       880f8b40       8940d020
        880f58d0       893ee500       880edac8       880f8db0
        89172938       879b3020       88091510       88038020
        880407b8       88051020       89511db0       8921f020
        880e9db0       87c33020       88064cc0       88044730
        8803f020       87a2a020       89529380       8802d330
        89a53020       89231b28       880285b8       88106b90
        8803cbc8       88aa3020       88093400       8809aab0
        880ea540       87d46948       88036020       8806e198
        8802d020       88038b40       8826b020       88231020
        890a2020       8807f5d0
```

We see that 53 threads are waiting for _KTHREAD 89ab8db0 to release _ERESOURCE 8815b928. Searching for this thread address reveals the following:

```
Resource @ 0x88159560    Exclusively owned
    Contention Count = 166896
    NumberOfExclusiveWaiters = 1
     Threads: 8802a790-01<*>
     Threads Waiting On Exclusive Access:
              89ab8db0
```

We see that the thread 89ab8db0 is waiting for 8802a790 to release the resource 88159560. We continue searching for the thread 8802a790 waiting for another thread, but we skip occurrences when this thread is not waiting:

```
Resource @ 0x881f7b60    Exclusively owned
     Threads: 8802a790-01<*>

Resource @ 0x8824b418    Exclusively owned
    Contention Count = 34
     Threads: 8802a790-01<*>

Resource @ 0x8825e5a0    Exclusively owned
     Threads: 8802a790-01<*>

Resource @ 0x88172428    Exclusively owned
    Contention Count = 5
    NumberOfExclusiveWaiters = 1
     Threads: 8802a790-01<*>
     Threads Waiting On Exclusive Access:
              880f5020
```

Searching further we see that the thread **8802a790** is waiting for the thread **880f5020** to release the resource 89bd7bf0:

```
Resource @ 0x89bd7bf0    Exclusively owned
    Contention Count = 1
    NumberOfExclusiveWaiters = 1
     Threads: 880f5020-01<*>
     Threads Waiting On Exclusive Access:
              8802a790
```

If we look carefully we see that we have already seen the thread **880f5020** above, and I repeat the fragment:

```
Resource @ 0x88172428    Exclusively owned
    Contention Count = 5
    NumberOfExclusiveWaiters = 1
     Threads: 8802a790-01<*>
     Threads Waiting On Exclusive Access:
              880f5020
```

We see that the thread **880f5020** is waiting for the thread **8802a790**, and the thread **8802a790** is waiting for the thread **880f5020**.

Therefore, we have identified the classical deadlock. What we have to do now is to look at stack traces of these threads to see involved components.

Insufficient Memory (Handle Leak)

Sometimes handle leaks also result in insufficient memory, especially if handles point to structures allocated by OS. Here is the typical example of the handle leak resulted in freezing several servers. The complete memory dump shows exhausted non-paged pool:

```
0: kd> !vm

*** Virtual Memory Usage ***
 Physical Memory:      1048352 (   4193408 Kb)
 Page File: \??\C:\pagefile.sys
   Current:    4190208 Kb  Free Space:    3749732 Kb
   Minimum:    4190208 Kb  Maximum:       4190208 Kb
 Available Pages:       697734 (   2790936 Kb)
 ResAvail Pages:        958085 (   3832340 Kb)
 Locked IO Pages:           95 (       380 Kb)
 Free System PTEs:      199971 (    799884 Kb)
 Free NP PTEs:             105 (       420 Kb)
 Free Special NP:            0 (         0 Kb)
 Modified Pages:           195 (       780 Kb)
 Modified PF Pages:        195 (       780 Kb)
 NonPagedPool Usage:     65244 (    260976 Kb)
 NonPagedPool Max:       65503 (    262012 Kb)
 ********** Excessive NonPaged Pool Usage *****
 PagedPool 0 Usage:       6576 (     26304 Kb)
 PagedPool 1 Usage:        629 (      2516 Kb)
 PagedPool 2 Usage:        624 (      2496 Kb)
 PagedPool 3 Usage:        608 (      2432 Kb)
 PagedPool 4 Usage:        625 (      2500 Kb)
 PagedPool Usage:         9062 (     36240 Kb)
 PagedPool Maximum:      66560 (    266240 Kb)

********** 184 pool allocations have failed **********

 Shared Commit:           7711 (     30844 Kb)
 Special Pool:               0 (         0 Kb)
 Shared Process:         10625 (     42500 Kb)
 PagedPool Commit:        9102 (     36408 Kb)
 Driver Commit:           1759 (      7036 Kb)
 Committed pages:       425816 (   1703264 Kb)
 Commit limit:         2052560 (   8210240 Kb)
```

Looking at non-paged pool consumption reveals an excessive number of thread objects:

```
0: kd> !poolused 3
   Sorting by  NonPaged Pool Consumed


  Pool Used:
            NonPaged
 Tag    Allocs     Frees      Diff     Used
 Thre   772672    463590    309082 192867168   Thread objects , Binary: nt!ps
 MmCm       42         9        33 12153104   Calls made to
MmAllocateContiguousMemory , Binary: nt!mm
...
...
...
```

The next logical step would be to list processes and find their handle usage. Indeed, there is such a process:

```
0: kd> !process 0 0
...
...
...
PROCESS 88b75020  SessionId: 7  Cid: 172e4    Peb: 7ffdf000  ParentCid:
17238
    DirBase: c7fb6bc0  ObjectTable: e17f50a0  HandleCount: 143428.
    Image: iexplore.exe
...
...
...
```

Making the process current and listing its handles shows contiguously allocated handles to thread objects:

```
0: kd> .process 88b75020
Implicit process is now 88b75020

0: kd> .reload /user

0: kd> !handle
...
...
...
0d94: Object: 88a6b020  GrantedAccess: 001f03ff Entry: e35e1b28
Object: 88a6b020  Type: (8b780c68) Thread
    ObjectHeader: 88a6b008
        HandleCount: 1  PointerCount: 1
```

```
0d98: Object: 88a97320  GrantedAccess: 001f03ff Entry: e35e1b30
Object: 88a97320  Type: (8b780c68) Thread
    ObjectHeader: 88a97308
        HandleCount: 1  PointerCount: 1

0d9c: Object: 88b2b020  GrantedAccess: 001f03ff Entry: e35e1b38
Object: 88b2b020  Type: (8b780c68) Thread
    ObjectHeader: 88b2b008
        HandleCount: 1  PointerCount: 1

0da0: Object: 88b2a730  GrantedAccess: 001f03ff Entry: e35e1b40
Object: 88b2a730  Type: (8b780c68) Thread
    ObjectHeader: 88b2a718
        HandleCount: 1  PointerCount: 1

0da4: Object: 88b929a0  GrantedAccess: 001f03ff Entry: e35e1b48
Object: 88b929a0  Type: (8b780c68) Thread
    ObjectHeader: 88b92988
        HandleCount: 1  PointerCount: 1

0da8: Object: 88a57db0  GrantedAccess: 001f03ff Entry: e35e1b50
Object: 88a57db0  Type: (8b780c68) Thread
    ObjectHeader: 88a57d98
        HandleCount: 1  PointerCount: 1

0dac: Object: 88b92db0  GrantedAccess: 001f03ff Entry: e35e1b58
Object: 88b92db0  Type: (8b780c68) Thread
    ObjectHeader: 88b92d98
        HandleCount: 1  PointerCount: 1

0db0: Object: 88b4a730  GrantedAccess: 001f03ff Entry: e35e1b60
Object: 88b4a730  Type: (8b780c68) Thread
    ObjectHeader: 88b4a718
        HandleCount: 1  PointerCount: 1

0db4: Object: 88a7e730  GrantedAccess: 001f03ff Entry: e35e1b68
Object: 88a7e730  Type: (8b780c68) Thread
    ObjectHeader: 88a7e718
        HandleCount: 1  PointerCount: 1

0db8: Object: 88a349a0  GrantedAccess: 001f03ff Entry: e35e1b70
Object: 88a349a0  Type: (8b780c68) Thread
    ObjectHeader: 88a34988
        HandleCount: 1  PointerCount: 1

0dbc: Object: 88a554c0  GrantedAccess: 001f03ff Entry: e35e1b78
Object: 88a554c0  Type: (8b780c68) Thread
    ObjectHeader: 88a554a8
        HandleCount: 1  PointerCount: 1
...
```

Examination of these threads shows their stack traces and start addresses:

```
0: kd> !thread 88b4a730
THREAD 88b4a730  Cid 0004.1885c  Teb: 00000000 Win32Thread: 00000000
TERMINATED
Not impersonating
DeviceMap                 e1000930
Owning Process            8b7807a8       Image:         System
Wait Start TickCount      975361         Ticks: 980987 (0:04:15:27.921)
Context Switch Count      1
UserTime                  00:00:00.0000
KernelTime                00:00:00.0000
Start Address mydriver!StatusWaitThread (0xf5c5d128)
Stack Init 0 Current f3c4cc98 Base f3c4d000 Limit f3c4a000 Call 0
Priority 8 BasePriority 8 PriorityDecrement 0
ChildEBP RetAddr  Args to Child
f3c4ccac 8083129e ffdff5f0 8697ba00 a674c913 hal!KfLowerIrql+0x62
f3c4ccc8 00000000 808ae498 8697ba00 00000000 nt!KiExitDispatcher+0x130

0: kd> !thread 88a554c0
THREAD 88a554c0  Cid 0004.1888c  Teb: 00000000 Win32Thread: 00000000
TERMINATED
Not impersonating
DeviceMap                 e1000930
Owning Process            8b7807a8       Image:         System
Wait Start TickCount      975380         Ticks: 980968 (0:04:15:27.625)
Context Switch Count      1
UserTime                  00:00:00.0000
KernelTime                00:00:00.0000
Start Address mydriver!StatusWaitThread (0xf5c5d128)
Stack Init 0 Current f3c4cc98 Base f3c4d000 Limit f3c4a000 Call 0
Priority 8 BasePriority 8 PriorityDecrement 0
ChildEBP RetAddr  Args to Child
f3c4ccac 8083129e ffdff5f0 8697ba00 a674c913 hal!KfLowerIrql+0x62
f3c4ccc8 00000000 808ae498 8697ba00 00000000 nt!KiExitDispatcher+0x130
```

We can see that these threads have been terminated, and their start address belongs to *mydriver.sys*. Therefore, we can say that *mydriver* code has to be examined to find the source of our handle leak.

Managed Code Exception

.NET programs also crash either from defects in .NET runtime (Common Language Runtime, CLR) or from non-handled runtime exceptions in managed code executed by .NET virtual machine. The latter exceptions are re-thrown from .NET runtime to be handled by the operating system and intercepted by native debuggers. Therefore, our next crash dump analysis pattern is called **Managed Code Exception**.

When we get a crash dump from .NET application, it is the dump from a native process. **!analyze -v** output can usually tell us that the exception is actually CLR exception and give us other hints to look at managed code stack (CLR stack):

```
FAULTING_IP:
kernel32!RaiseException+53
77e4bee7 5e              pop     esi

EXCEPTION_RECORD:  ffffffff -- (.exr 0xffffffffffffffff)
ExceptionAddress: 77e4bee7 (kernel32!RaiseException+0x00000053)
   ExceptionCode: e0434f4d (CLR exception)
  ExceptionFlags: 00000001
NumberParameters: 1
   Parameter[0]: 80131604

DEFAULT_BUCKET_ID:  CLR_EXCEPTION

PROCESS_NAME:  mmc.exe

ERROR_CODE: (NTSTATUS) 0xe0434f4d - <Unable to get error code text>

MANAGED_STACK: !dumpstack -EE
No export dumpstack found

STACK_TEXT:
05faf3d8 79f97065 e0434f4d 00000001 00000001 kernel32!RaiseException+0x53
WARNING: Stack unwind information not available. Following frames may be
wrong.
05faf438 7a0945a4 023f31e0 00000000 00000000
mscorwks!DllCanUnloadNowInternal+0x37a9
05faf4fc 00f2f00a 02066be4 02085ee8 023d0df0
mscorwks!CorLaunchApplication+0x12005
05faf500 02066be4 02085ee8 023d0df0 023d0e2c 0xf2f00a
05faf504 02085ee8 023d0df0 023d0e2c 05e00dfa 0x2066be4
05faf508 023d0df0 023d0e2c 05e00dfa 023d0e10 0x2085ee8
05faf50c 023d0e2c 05e00dfa 023d0e10 05351d30 0x23d0df0
05faf510 05e00dfa 023d0e10 05351d30 023d0e10 0x23d0e2c
```

```
FOLLOWUP_IP:
mscorwks!DllCanUnloadNowInternal+37a9
79f97065 c745fcfeffffff  mov     dword ptr [ebp-4],0FFFFFFFEh

SYMBOL_NAME:  mscorwks!DllCanUnloadNowInternal+37a9

MODULE_NAME: mscorwks

IMAGE_NAME:  mscorwks.dll

PRIMARY_PROBLEM_CLASS:  CLR_EXCEPTION

BUGCHECK_STR:  APPLICATION_FAULT_CLR_EXCEPTION
```

Sometimes we can see *mscorwks.dll* on a raw stack region or see it loaded and can find it on other thread stacks than the current one.

When we get such hints, we might want to get managed code stack as well. First, we need to load the appropriate WinDbg SOS extension (Son of Strike) corresponding to .NET runtime version. This can be done by the following command:

```
0:015> .loadby sos mscorwks
```

We can check which SOS extension version was loaded by using **.chain** command:

```
0:015> .chain
Extension DLL search Path:
...
...
...
Extension DLL chain:
    C:\WINDOWS\Microsoft.NET\Framework\v2.0.50727\sos: image 2.0.50727.42,
API 1.0.0, built Fri Sep 23 08:27:26 2005
        [path: C:\WINDOWS\Microsoft.NET\Framework\v2.0.50727\sos.dll]
    dbghelp: image 6.6.0007.5, API 6.0.6, built Sat Jul 08 21:11:32 2006
        [path: C:\Program Files\Debugging Tools for Windows\dbghelp.dll]
    ext: image 6.6.0007.5, API 1.0.0, built Sat Jul 08 21:10:52 2006
        [path: C:\Program Files\Debugging Tools for
Windows\winext\ext.dll]
    exts: image 6.6.0007.5, API 1.0.0, built Sat Jul 08 21:10:48 2006
        [path: C:\Program Files\Debugging Tools for
Windows\WINXP\exts.dll]
    uext: image 6.6.0007.5, API 1.0.0, built Sat Jul 08 21:11:02 2006
        [path: C:\Program Files\Debugging Tools for
Windows\winext\uext.dll]
    ntsdexts: image 6.0.5457.0, API 1.0.0, built Sat Jul 08 21:29:38 2006
        [path: C:\Program Files\Debugging Tools for
Windows\WINXP\ntsdexts.dll]
```

Then we can use **!dumpstack** to dump the current stack or **!EEStack** command to dump all thread stacks. The native stack trace would be mixed with managed stack trace:

```
0:015> !dumpstack
OS Thread Id: 0x16e8 (15)
Current frame: kernel32!RaiseException+0x53
ChildEBP RetAddr Caller,Callee
05faf390 77e4bee7 kernel32!RaiseException+0x53, calling
ntdll!RtlRaiseException
05faf3a8 79e814da mscorwks!Binder::RawGetClass+0x23, calling
mscorwks!Module::LookupTypeDef
05faf3bc 79e87ff4 mscorwks!Binder::IsClass+0x21, calling
mscorwks!Binder::RawGetClass
05faf3c8 79f958b8 mscorwks!Binder::IsException+0x13, calling
mscorwks!Binder::IsClass
05faf3d8 79f97065 mscorwks!RaiseTheExceptionInternalOnly+0x226, calling
kernel32!RaiseException
05faf438 7a0945a4 mscorwks!JIT_Throw+0xd0, calling
mscorwks!RaiseTheExceptionInternalOnly
05faf4ac 7a0944ea mscorwks!JIT_Throw+0x1e, calling
mscorwks!LazyMachStateCaptureState
05faf4c8 793d424e (MethodDesc 0x7924ad68 +0x2e
System.Threading.WaitHandle.WaitOne(Int64, Boolean)), calling
mscorwks!WaitHandleNative::CorWaitOneNative
05faf4fc 00f2f00a (MethodDesc 0x4f97500 +0x9a
Ironring.Management.MMC.SnapinBase+MmcWindow.Invoke(System.Delegate,
System.Object[])), calling mscorwks!JIT_Throw
05faf510 05e00dfa (MethodDesc 0x4f98fd8 +0xca
MyNamespace.MyClass.MyMethod(Boolean)), calling 05fc7124
05faf55c 00f62fbc (MethodDesc 0x4f95f90 +0x16f4
MyNamespace.MyClass.MyMethod.Initialise(System.Object))
05faf740 793d912f (MethodDesc 0x7925fc70 +0x2f
System.Threading._ThreadPoolWaitCallback.WaitCallback_Context(System.Objec
t))
05faf748 793683dd (MethodDesc 0x7913f3d0 +0x81
System.Threading.ExecutionContext.Run(System.Threading.ExecutionContext,
System.Threading.ContextCallback, System.Object))
05faf75c 793d9218 (MethodDesc 0x7925fc80 +0x6c
System.Threading._ThreadPoolWaitCallback.PerformWaitCallback(System.Object
)), calling (MethodDesc 0x7913f3d0 +0
System.Threading.ExecutionContext.Run(System.Threading.ExecutionContext,
System.Threading.ContextCallback, System.Object))
05faf774 79e88f63 mscorwks!CallDescrWorker+0x33
05faf784 79e88ee4 mscorwks!CallDescrWorkerWithHandler+0xa3, calling
mscorwks!CallDescrWorker
05faf804 79f20212 mscorwks!DispatchCallBody+0x1e, calling
mscorwks!CallDescrWorkerWithHandler
05faf824 79f201bc mscorwks!DispatchCallDebuggerWrapper+0x3d, calling
mscorwks!DispatchCallBody
05faf888 79f2024b mscorwks!DispatchCallNoEH+0x51, calling
mscorwks!DispatchCallDebuggerWrapper
05faf8bc 7a07bdf0 mscorwks!Holder,2>::~Holder,2>+0xbb, calling
mscorwks!DispatchCallNoEH
```

```
05faf90c 77e61d1e kernel32!WaitForSingleObjectEx+0xac, calling
ntdll!ZwWaitForSingleObject
05faf91c 79ecb4a4 mscorwks!Thread::UserResumeThread+0xfb
05faf92c 79ecb442 mscorwks!Thread::DoADCallBack+0x355, calling
mscorwks!Thread::UserResumeThread+0xae
05faf950 79e74afe mscorwks!Thread::EnterRuntimeNoThrow+0x9b, calling
mscorwks!_EH_epilog3
05faf988 79e77fe8 mscorwks!PEImage::LoadImage+0x1e1, calling
mscorwks!_SEH_epilog4
05faf9c0 79ecb364 mscorwks!Thread::DoADCallBack+0x541, calling
mscorwks!Thread::DoADCallBack+0x2a5
05faf9fc 7a0e1b7e mscorwks!Thread::DoADCallBack+0x575, calling
mscorwks!Thread::DoADCallBack+0x4d4
05fafa24 7a0e1bab mscorwks!ManagedThreadBase::ThreadPool+0x13, calling
mscorwks!Thread::DoADCallBack+0x550
05fafa38 7a07cae8 mscorwks!QueueUserWorkItemCallback+0x9d, calling
mscorwks!ManagedThreadBase::ThreadPool
05fafa54 7a07ca48 mscorwks!QueueUserWorkItemCallback, calling
mscorwks!UnwindAndContinueRethrowHelperAfterCatch
05fafa90 7a110f08 mscorwks!ThreadpoolMgr::ExecuteWorkRequest+0x40
05fafaa8 7a112328 mscorwks!ThreadpoolMgr::WorkerThreadStart+0x1f2, calling
mscorwks!ThreadpoolMgr::ExecuteWorkRequest
05fafad0 79e7839d mscorwks!EEHeapFreeInProcessHeap+0x21, calling
mscorwks!EEHeapFree
05fafae0 79e782dc mscorwks!operator delete[]+0x30, calling
mscorwks!EEHeapFreeInProcessHeap
05fafb14 79ecb00b mscorwks!Thread::intermediateThreadProc+0x49
05fafb48 77e65512 kernel32!FlsSetValue+0xc7, calling kernel32!_SEH_epilog
05fafb6c 75da14d0 sxs!_calloc_crt+0x19, calling sxs!calloc
05fafb80 77e65512 kernel32!FlsSetValue+0xc7, calling kernel32!_SEH_epilog
05fafb88 75da1401 sxs!_CRT_INIT+0x17e, calling sxs!_initptd
05fafb8c 75da1408 sxs!_CRT_INIT+0x185, calling kernel32!GetCurrentThreadId
05fafb9c 30403805 MMCFormsShim!DllMain+0x15, calling
MMCFormsShim!PrxDllMain
05fafbb0 30418b69 MMCFormsShim!__DllMainCRTStartup+0x7a, calling
MMCFormsShim!DllMain
05fafbdc 75de0e4c sxs!_SxsDllMain+0x87, calling sxs!DllStartup_CrtInit
05fafbf0 30418bf9 MMCFormsShim!__DllMainCRTStartup+0x10a, calling
MMCFormsShim!__SEH_epilog4
05fafbf4 30418c22 MMCFormsShim!_DllMainCRTStartup+0x1d, calling
MMCFormsShim!__DllMainCRTStartup
05fafbfc 7c81a352 ntdll!LdrpCallInitRoutine+0x14
05fafc24 7c82ee8b ntdll!LdrpInitializeThread+0x1a5, calling
ntdll!RtlLeaveCriticalSection
05fafc2c 7c82edec ntdll!LdrpInitializeThread+0x18f, calling
ntdll!_SEH_epilog
05fafc7c 7c82ed71 ntdll!LdrpInitializeThread+0xd8, calling
ntdll!RtlActivateActivationContextUnsafeFast
05fafc80 7c82ed35 ntdll!LdrpInitializeThread+0x12c, calling
ntdll!RtlDeactivateActivationContextUnsafeFast
05fafcb4 7c82edec ntdll!LdrpInitializeThread+0x18f, calling
ntdll!_SEH_epilog
05fafcb8 7c827c3b ntdll!NtTestAlert+0xc
05fafcbc 7c82ecb1 ntdll!_LdrpInitialize+0x1de, calling ntdll!_SEH_epilog
```

```
05fafd10 7c82ecb1 ntdll!_LdrpInitialize+0x1de, calling ntdll!_SEH_epilog
05fafd14 7c826d9b ntdll!NtContinue+0xc
05fafd18 7c8284da ntdll!KiUserApcDispatcher+0x3a, calling ntdll!NtContinue
05faffa4 79ecaff9 mscorwks!Thread::intermediateThreadProc+0x37, calling
mscorwks!_alloca_probe_16
05faffb8 77e64829 kernel32!BaseThreadStart+0x34
```

Symbolic .NET language names are usually reconstructed from .NET assembly metadata.

We can examine a CLR exception and get a managed stack trace by using **!PrintException** and **!CLRStack** commands, for example:

```
0:014> !PrintException
Exception object: 02320314
Exception type: System.Reflection.TargetInvocationException
Message: Exception has been thrown by the target of an invocation.
InnerException: System.Runtime.InteropServices.COMException, use
!PrintException 023201a8 to see more
StackTrace (generated):
    SP       IP       Function
    075AF4FC 016BFD9A
Ironring.Management.MMC.SnapinBase+MmcWindow.Invoke(System.Delegate,
System.Object[])
    ...
    ...
    ...
    075AF740 793D87AF
System.Threading._ThreadPoolWaitCallback.WaitCallback_Context(System.Objec
t)
    075AF748 793608FD
System.Threading.ExecutionContext.Run(System.Threading.ExecutionContext,
System.Threading.ContextCallback, System.Object)
    075AF760 793D8898
System.Threading._ThreadPoolWaitCallback.PerformWaitCallback(System.Object
)

StackTraceString: <none>
HResult: 80131604

0:014> !PrintException 023201a8
Exception object: 023201a8
Exception type: System.Runtime.InteropServices.COMException
Message: Error HRESULT E_FAIL has been returned from a call to a COM
component.
InnerException: <none>
StackTrace (generated):
    SP       IP       Function
    00000000 00000001
Ironring.Management.MMC.IMMCFormsShim.HostUserControl3(System.Object,
System.Object, System.String, System.String, Int32, Int32)
    0007F724 073875B9
```

```
Ironring.Management.MMC.FormNode.SetShimControl(System.Object)
    0007F738 053D9DDE
Ironring.Management.MMC.FormNode.set_ControlType(System.Type)
    ...
    ...
    ...

StackTraceString: <none>
HResult: 80004005

0:014> !CLRStack
OS Thread Id: 0x11ec (14)
ESP       EIP
075af4fc 016bfd9a
Ironring.Management.MMC.SnapinBase+MmcWindow.Invoke(System.Delegate,
System.Object[])
...
...
...
075af740 793d87af
System.Threading._ThreadPoolWaitCallback.WaitCallback_Context(System.Objec
t)
075af748 793608fd
System.Threading.ExecutionContext.Run(System.Threading.ExecutionContext,
System.Threading.ContextCallback, System.Object)
075af760 793d8898
System.Threading._ThreadPoolWaitCallback.PerformWaitCallback(System.Object
)
075af8f0 79e7be1b [GCFrame: 075af8f0]
```

!help command gives the list of other available SOS extension commands:

```
0:014> !help

Object Inspection

DumpObj (do)
DumpArray (da)
DumpStackObjects (dso)
DumpHeap
DumpVC
GCRoot
ObjSize
FinalizeQueue
PrintException (pe)
TraverseHeap

Examining code and stacks

Threads
CLRStack
IP2MD
U
DumpStack
EEStack
GCInfo
EHInfo
COMState
BPMD

Examining CLR data structures

DumpDomain
EEHeap
Name2EE
SyncBlk
DumpMT
DumpClass
DumpMD
Token2EE
EEVersion
DumpModule
ThreadPool
DumpAssembly
DumpMethodSig
DumpRuntimeTypes
DumpSig
RCWCleanupList
DumpIL
```

```
Diagnostic Utilities


VerifyHeap
DumpLog
FindAppDomain
SaveModule
GCHandles
GCHandleLeaks
VMMap
VMStat
ProcInfo
StopOnException (soe)
MinidumpMode


Other


FAQ
```

In the case where .NET CLR runtime is version 1.x we might get messages pointing to some .NET DLL, and this could be the indication that some threads have managed code:

```
*** WARNING: Unable to verify checksum for mscorlib.dll
*** ERROR: Module load completed but symbols could not be loaded for
mscorlib.dll
```

In some cases we cannot load the appropriate SOS extension automatically:

```
0:000> .loadby sos mscorwks
Unable to find module "mscorwks"
```

Then we can try SOS version 1.0

```
0:000> !clr10\sos.EEStack
Loaded Son of Strike data table version 5 from
"C:\WINDOWS\Microsoft.NET\Framework\v1.1.4322\mscorsvr.dll"
```

The following message means that the server version of CLR is used:

```
0:000> .loadby sos mscorwks
Unable to find module "mscorwks"

0:000> .loadby sos mscorsvr

0:000> !help
SOS : Help
```

For some crash dumps we get the following message saying that *sos.dll* cannot be found:

```
0:000> .loadby sos mscorwks
The call to LoadLibrary(C:\WIN_NO_SP\Microsoft.NET
\Framework\v2.0.50727\sos) failed, Win32 error 0n126
"The specified module could not be found."
Please check your debugger configuration and/or network access
```

Here we need to check where *Microsoft.NET\Framework\v2.0.50727\sos.dll* is installed on our crash dump analysis host and use **.load** command:

```
0:000> .load C:\WINDOWS\Microsoft.NET\Framework\v2.0.50727\sos.dll
```

The version of WinDbg since 6.8.4.0 and **!analyze -v** command show both native and managed stack traces from .NET 64-bit application memory dump, so there is no need to load SOS manually there.

Truncated Dump

Sometimes the page file size is less than the amount of physical memory. If this is the case, and we have configured "Complete memory dump" in Startup and Recovery settings in Control Panel, we get truncated memory dumps. Therefore, we can call our next pattern **Truncated Dump**. WinDbg prints a warning when we open such a dump file:

```
************************************************************
WARNING: Dump file has been truncated.  Data may be missing.
************************************************************
```

We can double check this with **!vm** command:

```
kd> !vm

*** Virtual Memory Usage ***
        Physical Memory:       511859 (   2047436 Kb)
        Paging File Name paged out
          Current:   1536000 Kb  Free Space:    1522732 Kb
          Minimum:   1536000 Kb  Maximum:       1536000 Kb
```

We see that the page file size is 1.5Gb, but the amount of physical memory is 2Gb. When BSOD happens, the physical memory contents are saved to the page file, and the dump file size is no more than 1.5Gb, effectively truncating the data needed for crash dump analysis.

Sometimes we can still access some data in truncated dumps, but we need to pay attention to what WinDbg says. For example, in the truncated dump shown above the stack and driver code are not available:

```
kd> kv
ChildEBP RetAddr  Args to Child
WARNING: Stack unwind information not available. Following frames may be
wrong.
f408b004 00000000 00000000 00000000 00000000 driver+0x19237

kd> r
Last set context:
eax=89d55230 ebx=89d21130 ecx=89d21130 edx=89c8cc20 esi=89e24ac0
edi=89c8cc20
eip=f7242237 esp=f408afec ebp=f408b004 iopl=0 nv up ei ng nz ac po nc
cs=0008 ss=0010 ds=0023 es=0023 fs=0030 gs=0000 efl=00010292
driver+0x19237:
f7242237 ??              ???
```

```
kd> dds esp
f408afec  ????????
f408aff0  ????????
f408aff4  ????????
f408aff8  ????????
f408affc  ????????
f408b000  ????????
f408b004  ????????
f408b008  ????????
f408b00c  ????????
f408b010  ????????
f408b014  ????????
f408b018  ????????
f408b01c  ????????
f408b020  ????????
f408b024  ????????
f408b028  ????????
f408b02c  ????????
f408b030  ????????
f408b034  ????????
f408b038  ????????
f408b03c  ????????
f408b040  ????????
f408b044  ????????
f408b048  ????????
f408b04c  ????????
f408b050  ????????
f408b054  ????????
f408b058  ????????
f408b05c  ????????
f408b060  ????????
f408b064  ????????
f408b068  ????????

kd> lmv m driver
start    end        module name
f7229000 f725f000   driver     T (no symbols)
    Loaded symbol image file: driver.sys
    Image path: driver.sys
    Image name: driver.sys
    Timestamp:        unavailable (FFFFFFFE)
    CheckSum:         missing
    ImageSize:        00036000

kd> dd f7229000
f7229000  ???????? ???????? ???????? ????????
f7229010  ???????? ???????? ???????? ????????
f7229020  ???????? ???????? ???????? ????????
f7229030  ???????? ???????? ???????? ????????
f7229040  ???????? ???????? ???????? ????????
f7229050  ???????? ???????? ???????? ????????
f7229060  ???????? ???????? ???????? ????????
f7229070  ???????? ???????? ???????? ????????
```

If, due to some reasons, we cannot increase the size of our page file, we just should configure “Kernel memory dump” in Startup and Recovery. For most all bugchecks, kernel memory dump is sufficient except manual crash dumps when we need to inspect user process space.

Waiting Thread Time (Kernel Dumps)

Almost all threads in any system are waiting for resources or waiting in ready-to-run queues to be scheduled. At any moment, the number of running threads is equal to the number of processors. The rest, hundreds and thousands of threads, are waiting. Looking at their waiting times in the kernel and complete memory dumps provides some interesting observations that worth their own pattern name: **Waiting Thread Time**.

When a thread starts waiting that time is recorded in the **WaitTime** field of _KTHREAD structure:

```
1: kd> dt _KTHREAD 8728a020
   +0x000 Header            : _DISPATCHER_HEADER
   +0x010 MutantListHead    : _LIST_ENTRY [ 0x8728a030 - 0x8728a030 ]
   +0x018 InitialStack      : 0xa3a1f000
   +0x01c StackLimit        : 0xa3a1a000
   +0x020 KernelStack       : 0xa3a1ec08
   +0x024 ThreadLock        : 0
   +0x028 ApcState          : _KAPC_STATE
   +0x028 ApcStateFill      : [23]  "H???"
   +0x03f ApcQueueable      : 0x1 ''
   +0x040 NextProcessor     : 0x3 ''
   +0x041 DeferredProcessor : 0x3 ''
   +0x042 AdjustReason      : 0 ''
   +0x043 AdjustIncrement   : 1 ''
   +0x044 ApcQueueLock      : 0
   +0x048 ContextSwitches   : 0x6b7
   +0x04c State             : 0x5 ''
   +0x04d NpxState          : 0xa ''
   +0x04e WaitIrql          : 0 ''
   +0x04f WaitMode          : 1 ''
   +0x050 WaitStatus        : 0
   +0x054 WaitBlockList     : 0x8728a0c8 _KWAIT_BLOCK
   +0x054 GateObject        : 0x8728a0c8 _KGATE
   +0x058 Alertable         : 0 ''
   +0x059 WaitNext          : 0 ''
   +0x05a WaitReason        : 0x11 ''
   +0x05b Priority          : 12 ''
   +0x05c EnableStackSwap   : 0x1 ''
   +0x05d SwapBusy          : 0 ''
   +0x05e Alerted           : [2]  ""
   +0x060 WaitListEntry     : _LIST_ENTRY [ 0x88091e10 - 0x88029ce0 ]
   +0x060 SwapListEntry     : _SINGLE_LIST_ENTRY
   +0x068 Queue             : (null)
   +0x06c WaitTime          : 0x82de9b
   +0x070 KernelApcDisable  : 0
...
```

This value is also displayed in the decimal format as *Wait Start TickCount* when we list threads or use **!thread** command:

```
0: kd> ? 0x82de9b
Evaluate expression: 8576667 = 0082de9b
```

```
1: kd> !thread 8728a020
THREAD 8728a020  Cid 4c9c.59a4  Teb: 7ffdf000 Win32Thread: bc012008 WAIT:
(Unknown) UserMode Non-Alertable
    8728a20c  Semaphore Limit 0x1
Waiting for reply to LPC MessageId 017db413:
Current LPC port e5fcff68
Impersonation token:  e2b07028 (Level Impersonation)
DeviceMap                 e1da6518
Owning Process            89d20740       Image:         winlogon.exe
Wait Start TickCount      8576667        Ticks: 7256 (0:00:01:53.375)
Context Switch Count      1719                 LargeStack
UserTime                  00:00:00.0359
KernelTime                00:00:00.0375
```

Tick is a system unit of time, and *KeTimeIncrement* double-word value contains its equivalent as the number of 100-nanosecond units:

```
0: kd> dd KeTimeIncrement l1
808a6304  0002625a
```

```
0: kd> ? 0002625a
Evaluate expression: 156250 = 0002625a
```

```
0: kd> ?? 156250.0/10000000.0
double 0.015625
```

Therefore on that system, one tick is 0.015625 of a second.

The current tick count is available via *KeTickCount* variable:

```
0: kd> dd KeTickCount l1
8089c180  0082faf3
```

If we subtract the recorded start wait time from the current tick count we get the number of ticks passed since the thread began waiting:

```
0: kd> ? 0082faf3-82de9b
Evaluate expression: 7256 = 00001c58
```

Using our previously calculated constant of the number of seconds per tick (0.015625) we get the number of seconds passed:

```
0: kd> ?? 7256.0 * 0.015625
double 113.37499999999999
```

113.375 seconds is 1 minute 53 seconds and 375 milliseconds:

```
0: kd> ?? 113.375-60.0
double 53.374999999999986
```

We can see that this value corresponds to the *Ticks* value that WinDbg shows for the thread:

```
Wait Start TickCount 8576667 Ticks: 7256 (0:00:01:53.375)
```

Why do we need to concern ourselves with these ticks? If we know that some activity was frozen for 15 minutes, we can filter out threads from our search space because threads with a significantly smaller number of ticks were running at some time and not waiting for 15 minutes.

Threads with a low number of ticks were running recently:

```
THREAD 86ced020  Cid 0004.3908  Teb: 00000000 Win32Thread: 00000000 WAIT:
(Unknown) KernelMode Non-Alertable
    b99cb7d0  QueueObject
    86ced098  NotificationTimer
Not impersonating
DeviceMap                 e10038e0
Owning Process            8ad842a8       Image:         System
Wait Start TickCount      8583871        Ticks: 52 (0:00:00:00.812)
Context Switch Count      208
UserTime                  00:00:00.0000
KernelTime                00:00:00.0000
Start Address rdbss!RxWorkerThreadDispatcher (0xb99cdc2e)
Stack Init ad21d000 Current ad21ccd8 Base ad21d000 Limit ad21a000 Call 0
Priority 8 BasePriority 8 PriorityDecrement
ChildEBP RetAddr
ad21ccf0 808330c6 nt!KiSwapContext+0x26
ad21cd1c 8082af7f nt!KiSwapThread+0x284
ad21cd64 b99c00e9 nt!KeRemoveQueue+0x417
ad21cd9c b99cdc48 rdbss!RxpWorkerThreadDispatcher+0x4b
ad21cdac 80948e74 rdbss!RxWorkerThreadDispatcher+0x1a
ad21cddc 8088d632 nt!PspSystemThreadStartup+0x2e
00000000 00000000 nt!KiThreadStartup+0x16
```

Another application would be to find all threads from different processes whose wait time roughly corresponds to 15 minutes, and, therefore, they might be related to the same frozen activity. For example, these RPC threads below from different processes are most likely related because one is the RPC client thread, the other is the RPC server thread waiting for some object and their common Ticks value is the same: 15131.

```
THREAD 89cc9750  Cid 0f1c.0f60  Teb: 7ffd6000 Win32Thread: 00000000 WAIT:
(Unknown) UserMode Non-Alertable
    89cc993c  Semaphore Limit 0x1
Waiting for reply to LPC MessageId 0000a7e7:
Current LPC port e18fcae8
Not impersonating
DeviceMap                 e10018a8
Owning Process            88d3b938       Image:         svchost.exe
Wait Start TickCount      29614          Ticks: 15131 (0:00:03:56.421)
Context Switch Count      45
UserTime                  00:00:00.0000
KernelTime                00:00:00.0000
Win32 Start Address 0x0000a7e6
LPC Server thread working on message Id a7e6
Start Address kernel32!BaseThreadStartThunk (0x7c82b5bb)
Stack Init f29a6000 Current f29a5c08 Base f29a6000 Limit f29a3000 Call 0
Priority 11 BasePriority 10 PriorityDecrement 0
Kernel stack not resident.
ChildEBP RetAddr
f29a5c20 80832f7a nt!KiSwapContext+0x26
f29a5c4c 8082927a nt!KiSwapThread+0x284
f29a5c94 8091df86 nt!KeWaitForSingleObject+0x346
f29a5d50 80888c6c nt!NtRequestWaitReplyPort+0x776
f29a5d50 7c94ed54 nt!KiFastCallEntry+0xfc
0090f6b8 7c941c94 ntdll!KiFastSystemCallRet
0090f6bc 77c42700 ntdll!NtRequestWaitReplyPort+0xc
0090f708 77c413ba RPCRT4!LRPC_CCALL::SendReceive+0x230
0090f714 77c42c7f RPCRT4!I_RpcSendReceive+0x24
0090f728 77cb5d63 RPCRT4!NdrSendReceive+0x2b
0090f9cc 67b610ca RPCRT4!NdrClientCall+0x334
0090f9dc 67b61c07 component!NotifyOfEvent+0x14
...
...
...
0090ffec 00000000 kernel32!BaseThreadStart+0x34
```

```
THREAD 89b49590  Cid 098c.01dc  Teb: 7ff92000 Win32Thread: 00000000 WAIT:
(Unknown) UserMode Non-Alertable
    88c4e020  Thread
    89b49608  NotificationTimer
Not impersonating
DeviceMap                 e10018a8
Owning Process            89d399c0       Image:         MyService.exe
Wait Start TickCount      29614          Ticks: 15131 (0:00:03:56.421)
Context Switch Count      310
UserTime                  00:00:00.0015
KernelTime                00:00:00.0000
Win32 Start Address 0x0000a7e7
LPC Server thread working on message Id a7e7
Start Address kernel32!BaseThreadStartThunk (0x7c82b5bb)
Stack Init f2862000 Current f2861c60 Base f2862000 Limit f285f000 Call 0
Priority 11 BasePriority 10 PriorityDecrement 0
Kernel stack not resident.
ChildEBP RetAddr
f2861c78 80832f7a nt!KiSwapContext+0x26
f2861ca4 8082927a nt!KiSwapThread+0x284
f2861cec 80937e4c nt!KeWaitForSingleObject+0x346
f2861d50 80888c6c nt!NtWaitForSingleObject+0x9a
f2861d50 7c94ed54 nt!KiFastCallEntry+0xfc
0a6cf590 7c942124 ntdll!KiFastSystemCallRet
0a6cf594 7c82baa8 ntdll!NtWaitForSingleObject+0xc
0a6cf604 7c82ba12 kernel32!WaitForSingleObjectEx+0xac
0a6cf618 3f691c11 kernel32!WaitForSingleObject+0x12
0a6cf658 09734436 component2!WaitForResponse+0x75
...
...
...
0a6cf8b4 77cb23f7 RPCRT4!Invoke+0x30
0a6cfcb4 77cb260d RPCRT4!NdrStubCall2+0x299
0a6cfcd0 77c409be RPCRT4!NdrServerCall2+0x19
0a6cfd04 77c4093f RPCRT4!DispatchToStubInCNoAvrf+0x38
0a6cfd58 77c40865 RPCRT4!RPC_INTERFACE::DispatchToStubWorker+0x117
0a6cfd7c 77c357eb RPCRT4!RPC_INTERFACE::DispatchToStub+0xa3
0a6cfdbc 77c41e26 RPCRT4!RPC_INTERFACE::DispatchToStubWithObject+0xc0
0a6cfdfc 77c41bb3 RPCRT4!LRPC_SCALL::DealWithRequestMessage+0x42c
0a6cfe20 77c45458 RPCRT4!LRPC_ADDRESS::DealWithLRPCRequest+0x127
0a6cff84 77c2778f RPCRT4!LRPC_ADDRESS::ReceiveLotsaCalls+0x430
0a6cff8c 77c2f7dd RPCRT4!RecvLotsaCallsWrapper+0xd
0a6cffac 77c2de88 RPCRT4!BaseCachedThreadRoutine+0x9d
0a6cffb8 7c826063 RPCRT4!ThreadStartRoutine+0x1b
0a6cffec 00000000 kernel32!BaseThreadStart+0x34
```

To convert ticks to the time interval, we can use **!whattime** command:

```
3: kd> !whattime 0n7256
7256 Ticks in Standard Time: 01:53.375s
```

Also **!stacks** command shows *Ticks* data for threads.

Deadlock (Mixed Objects, User Space)

This pattern is another variant of **Deadlock** pattern (page 276) when we have mixed synchronization objects, for example, events and critical sections. An event may be used to signal the availability of some work item for processing it, the fact that the queue is not empty, and a critical section may be used to protect some shared data.

The typical deadlock scenario here is when one thread resets an event by calling *WaitForSingleObject* and tries to acquire a critical section. In the meantime the second thread has already acquired that critical section and now is waiting for the event to be set:

```
Thread A       | Thread B
..             | ..
reset Event    | ..
..             | acquire CS
wait for CS    | ..
               | wait for Event
```

The classical fix to this bug is to acquire the critical section and wait for the event in the same order in both threads.

In our example crash dump we can easily identify the second thread that acquired the critical section and is waiting for the event 0x480 (stack traces are shown in smaller font for visual clarity):

```
0:000> !locks

CritSec ntdll!LdrpLoaderLock+0 at 7c889d94
WaiterWoken        No
LockCount          9
RecursionCount     1
OwningThread       2038
EntryCount         0
ContentionCount    164
*** Locked
```

```
  13  Id: 590.2038 Suspend: 1 Teb: 7ffaa000 Unfrozen
ChildEBP RetAddr  Args to Child
0483fd5c 7c822124 77e6bad8 00000480 00000000 ntdll!KiFastSystemCallRet
0483fd60 77e6bad8 00000480 00000000 00000000 ntdll!NtWaitForSingleObject+0xc
0483fdd0 77e6ba42 00000480 ffffffff 00000000 kernel32!WaitForSingleObjectEx+0xac
0483fde4 776cfb30 00000480 ffffffff 777904f8 kernel32!WaitForSingleObject+0x12
0483fe00 776adfaa 00000480 00000000 00000080 ole32!CDllHost::ClientCleanupFinish+0x2a
0483fe2c 776adf1a 00000000 0483fe7c 77790828 ole32!DllHostProcessUninitialize+0x80
0483fe4c 776b063f 00000000 00000000 0c9ecee0 ole32!ApartmentUninitialize+0xf8
0483fe64 776b06e3 0483fe7c 00000000 00000001 ole32!wCoUninitialize+0x48
```

```
0483fe80 776e43f5 00000001 77670000 776afef0 ole32!CoUninitialize+0x65
0483fe8c 776afef0 0483feb4 776b5cb8 77670000 ole32!DoThreadSpecificCleanup+0x63
0483fe94 776b5cb8 77670000 00000003 00000000 ole32!ThreadNotification+0x37
0483feb4 776b5c1b 77670000 00000003 00000000 ole32!DllMain+0x176
0483fed4 7c82257a 77670000 00000003 00000000 ole32!_DllMainCRTStartup+0x52
0483fef4 7c83c195 776b5bd3 77670000 00000003 ntdll!LdrpCallInitRoutine+0x14
0483ffa8 77e661d6 00000000 00000000 0483ffec ntdll!LdrShutdownThread+0xd2
0483ffb8 77e66090 00000000 00000000 00000000 kernel32!ExitThread+0x2f
0483ffec 00000000 77c5de6d 0ab24f68 00000000 kernel32!BaseThreadStart+0x39
```

```
0:000> !handle 480 ff
Handle 00000480
  Type          Event
  Attributes    0
  GrantedAccess 0x1f0003:
         Delete,ReadControl,WriteDac,WriteOwner,Synch
         QueryState,ModifyState
  HandleCount   2
  PointerCount  4
  Name          <none>
  No object specific information available
```

It is difficult to find the first thread, the one which has reset the event and is waiting for the critical section. In our dump we have 9 such threads from **!locks** command output:

```
LockCount          9
```

An event as a synchronization primitive doesn't have an owner. Despite this, we can try to find 0x480 and *WaitForSingleObject* address nearby on some other thread raw stack if that information wasn't overwritten. Let's do a virtual memory search:

```
0:000> s -d 0 L4000000 00000480
000726ec 00000480 00000022 000004a4 00000056
008512a0 00000480 00000480 00000000 00000000
008512a4 00000480 00000000 00000000 01014220
0085ab68 00000480 00000480 00000092 00000000
0085ab6c 00000480 00000092 00000000 01014234
00eb12a0 00000480 00000480 00000000 00000000
00eb12a4 00000480 00000000 00000000 0101e614
00ebeb68 00000480 00000480 00000323 00000000
00ebeb6c 00000480 00000323 00000000 0101e644
03ffb4fc 00000480 d772c13b ce753966 00fa840f
040212a0 00000480 00000480 00000000 00000000
040212a4 00000480 00000000 00000000 01063afc
0402ab68 00000480 00000480 00000fb6 00000000
0402ab6c 00000480 00000fb6 00000000 01063b5c
041312a0 00000480 00000480 00000000 00000000
041312a4 00000480 00000000 00000000 01065b28
0413eb68 00000480 00000480 00001007 00000000
0413eb6c 00000480 00001007 00000000 01065b7c
```

```
043412a0 00000480 00000480 00000000 00000000
043412a4 00000480 00000000 00000000 01066b44
0434ab68 00000480 00000480 00001033 00000000
0434ab6c 00000480 00001033 00000000 01066b9c
0483fd68 00000480 00000000 00000000 00000000
0483fdd8 00000480 ffffffff 00000000 0483fe00
0483fdec 00000480 ffffffff 777904f8 77790738
0483fe08 00000480 00000000 00000080 776b0070
0483fe20 00000480 00000000 00000000 0483fe4c
05296f58 00000480 ffffffff ffffffff ffffffff
05297eb0 00000480 00000494 000004a4 000004c0
0557cf9c 00000480 00000000 00000000 00000000
05580adc 00000480 00000000 00000000 00000000
0558715c 00000480 00000000 00000000 00000000
0558d3cc 00000480 00000000 00000000 00000000
0559363c 00000480 00000000 00000000 00000000
0559ee0c 00000480 00000000 00000000 00000000
055a507c 00000480 00000000 00000000 00000000
056768ec 00000480 00000000 00000000 00000000
0568ef14 00000480 00000000 00000000 00000000
0581ff88 00000480 07ca7ee0 0581ff98 776cf2a3
05ed1260 00000480 00000480 00000000 00000000
05ed1264 00000480 00000000 00000000 01276efc
05ed8b68 00000480 00000480 00005c18 00000000
05ed8b6c 00000480 00005c18 00000000 01276f74
08f112a0 00000480 00000480 00000000 00000000
08f112a4 00000480 00000000 00000000 00000000
08f1ab68 00000480 00000480 00007732 00000000
08f1ab6c 00000480 00007732 00000000 01352db0
```

In blue color, I highlighted the thread #13 raw stack occurrences, and in red color, I highlighted memory locations that belong to another thread raw stack region. In fact, these are the only memory locations from search results that make any sense from the code perspective. The only meaningful stack traces can be found in memory locations highlighted in bold above.

This can be seen if we feed search results to WinDbg **dds** command:

```
0:000> .foreach (place { s-[1]d 0 L4000000 00000480 }) { dds place -30;
.printf "\n" }
000726bc  00000390
000726c0  00000022
000726c4  000003b4
000726c8  00000056
000726cc  00000004
000726d0  6dc3f6fd
000726d4  0000040c
000726d8  0000001e
000726dc  0000042c
000726e0  00000052
000726e4  00000004
```

```
000726e8  eacb0f6d
000726ec  00000480
000726f0  00000022
000726f4  000004a4
000726f8  00000056
000726fc  00000004
00072700  62b796d2
00072704  000004fc
00072708  0000001e
0007270c  0000051c
00072710  00000052
00072714  00000004
00072718  2a615cff
0007271c  00000570
00072720  00000024
00072724  00000598
00072728  00000058
0007272c  00000004
00072730  51913e59
00072734  000005f0
00072738  00000016
...
...
...
0568eee4  05680008 xpsp2res+0x1b0008
0568eee8  01200000
0568eeec  00001010
0568eef0  00200001
0568eef4  00000468
0568eef8  00000121
0568eefc  00000000
0568ef00  00000028
0568ef04  00000030
0568ef08  00000060
0568ef0c  00040001
0568ef10  00000000
0568ef14  00000480
0568ef18  00000000
0568ef1c  00000000
0568ef20  00000000
0568ef24  00000000
0568ef28  00000000
0568ef2c  00800000
0568ef30  00008000
0568ef34  00808000
0568ef38  00000080
0568ef3c  00800080
0568ef40  00008080
0568ef44  00808080
0568ef48  00c0c0c0
0568ef4c  00ff0000
0568ef50  0000ff00
0568ef54  00ffff00
0568ef58  000000ff
```

```
0568ef5c  00ff00ff
0568ef60  0000ffff

0581ff58  0581ff70
0581ff5c  776b063f ole32!wCoUninitialize+0x48
0581ff60  00000001
0581ff64  00007530
0581ff68  77790438 ole32!gATHost
0581ff6c  00000000
0581ff70  0581ff90
0581ff74  776cf370 ole32!CDllHost::WorkerThread+0xdd
0581ff78  0581ff8c
0581ff7c  00000001
0581ff80  77e6ba50 kernel32!WaitForSingleObjectEx
0581ff84  0657cfe8
0581ff88  00000480
0581ff8c  07ca7ee0
0581ff90  0581ff98
0581ff94  776cf2a3 ole32!DLLHostThreadEntry+0xd
0581ff98  0581ffb8
0581ff9c  776b2307 ole32!CRpcThread::WorkerLoop+0x1e
0581ffa0  77790438 ole32!gATHost
0581ffa4  00000000
0581ffa8  0657cfe8
0581ffac  77670000 ole32!_imp__InstallApplication <PERF> (ole32+0x0)
0581ffb0  776b2374 ole32!CRpcThreadCache::RpcWorkerThreadEntry+0x20
0581ffb4  00000000
0581ffb8  0581ffec
0581ffbc  77e6608b kernel32!BaseThreadStart+0x34
0581ffc0  0657cfe8
0581ffc4  00000000
0581ffc8  00000000
0581ffcc  0657cfe8
0581ffd0  3cfb5963
0581ffd4  0581ffc4

05ed1230  0101f070
05ed1234  05ed1274
05ed1238  05ed1174
05ed123c  05ed0000
05ed1240  05ed1280
05ed1244  00000000
05ed1248  00000000
05ed124c  00000000
05ed1250  05ed8b80
05ed1254  05ed8000
05ed1258  00002000
05ed125c  00001000
05ed1260  00000480
05ed1264  00000480
05ed1268  00000000
05ed126c  00000000
05ed1270  01276efc
```

```
05ed1274  05ed12b4
05ed1278  05ed1234
05ed127c  05ed0000
05ed1280  05ed2d00
05ed1284  05ed1240
05ed1288  05ed1400
05ed128c  00000000
05ed1290  05edade0
05ed1294  05eda000
05ed1298  00002000
05ed129c  00001000
05ed12a0  00000220
05ed12a4  00000220
05ed12a8  00000000
05ed12ac  00000000
...
...
...
08f1ab3c  00000000
08f1ab40  00000000
08f1ab44  00000000
08f1ab48  00000000
08f1ab4c  00000000
08f1ab50  00000000
08f1ab54  00000000
08f1ab58  00000000
08f1ab5c  00000000
08f1ab60  abcdbbbb
08f1ab64  08f11000
08f1ab68  00000480
08f1ab6c  00000480
08f1ab70  00007732
08f1ab74  00000000
08f1ab78  01352db0
08f1ab7c  dcbabbbb
08f1ab80  ffffffff
08f1ab84  c0c00ac1
08f1ab88  00000000
08f1ab8c  c0c0c0c0
08f1ab90  c0c0c0c0
08f1ab94  c0c0c0c0
08f1ab98  c0c0c0c0
08f1ab9c  c0c0c0c0
08f1aba0  c0c0c0c0
08f1aba4  ffffffff
08f1aba8  c0c00ac1
08f1abac  00000000
08f1abb0  c0c0c0c0
08f1abb4  c0c0c0c0
08f1abb8  c0c0c0c0
```

We see that the address 0581ff88 is the most meaningful and it also has *WaitForSingleObjectEx* nearby. This address belongs to the raw stack of the following thread #16:

```
  16  Id: 590.1a00 Suspend: 1 Teb: 7ffa9000 Unfrozen
ChildEBP RetAddr
0581fc98 7c822124 ntdll!KiFastSystemCallRet
0581fc9c 7c83970f ntdll!NtWaitForSingleObject+0xc
0581fcd8 7c839620 ntdll!RtlpWaitOnCriticalSection+0x19c
0581fcf8 7c83a023 ntdll!RtlEnterCriticalSection+0xa8
0581fe00 77e67bcd ntdll!LdrUnloadDll+0x35
0581fe14 776b46fb kernel32!FreeLibrary+0x41
0581fe20 776b470f
ole32!CClassCache::CDllPathEntry::CFinishObject::Finish+0x2f
0581fe34 776b44a0 ole32!CClassCache::CFinishComposite::Finish+0x1d
0581ff0c 776b0bfd ole32!CClassCache::CleanUpDllsForApartment+0x1d0
0581ff38 776b0b1f ole32!FinishShutdown+0xd7
0581ff58 776b063f ole32!ApartmentUninitialize+0x94
0581ff70 776cf370 ole32!wCoUninitialize+0x48
0581ff90 776cf2a3 ole32!CDllHost::WorkerThread+0xdd
0581ff98 776b2307 ole32!DLLHostThreadEntry+0xd
0581ffac 776b2374 ole32!CRpcThread::WorkerLoop+0x1e
0581ffb8 77e6608b ole32!CRpcThreadCache::RpcWorkerThreadEntry+0x20
0581ffec 00000000 kernel32!BaseThreadStart+0x34
```

And if we disassemble *ole32!CRpcThread::WorkerLoop* function which is found below *WaitForSingleObjectEx* function on both stack trace and raw stack data from search results we would see that the former function calls the latter function indeed:

```
0:000> uf ole32!CRpcThread::WorkerLoop
ole32!CRpcThread::WorkerLoop:
776b22e9 mov     edi,edi
776b22eb push    esi
776b22ec mov     esi,ecx
776b22ee cmp     dword ptr [esi+4],0
776b22f2 jne     ole32!CRpcThread::WorkerLoop+0x67 (776b234d)

ole32!CRpcThread::WorkerLoop+0xb:
776b22f4 push    ebx
776b22f5 push    edi
776b22f6 mov     edi,dword ptr [ole32!_imp__WaitForSingleObjectEx
(77671304)]
776b22fc mov     ebx,7530h

ole32!CRpcThread::WorkerLoop+0x18:
776b2301 push    dword ptr [esi+0Ch]
776b2304 call    dword ptr [esi+8]
776b2307 call    dword ptr [ole32!_imp__GetCurrentThread (7767130c)]
776b230d push    eax
```

```
776b230e call     dword ptr
[ole32!_imp__RtlCheckForOrphanedCriticalSections (77671564)]
776b2314 xor      eax,eax
776b2316 cmp      dword ptr [esi],eax
776b2318 mov      dword ptr [esi+8],eax
776b231b mov      dword ptr [esi+0Ch],eax
776b231e je       ole32!CRpcThread::WorkerLoop+0x65 (776b234b)

ole32!CRpcThread::WorkerLoop+0x37:
776b2320 push     esi
776b2321 mov      ecx,offset ole32!gRpcThreadCache (7778fc28)
776b2326 call     ole32!CRpcThreadCache::AddToFreeList (776de78d)

ole32!CRpcThread::WorkerLoop+0x55:
776b232b push     0
776b232d push     ebx
776b232e push     dword ptr [esi]
776b2330 call     edi
776b2332 test     eax,eax
776b2334 je       ole32!CRpcThread::WorkerLoop+0x60 (776cf3be)

ole32!CRpcThread::WorkerLoop+0x44:
776b233a push     esi
776b233b mov      ecx,offset ole32!gRpcThreadCache (7778fc28)
776b2340 call     ole32!CRpcThreadCache::RemoveFromFreeList (776e42de)
776b2345 cmp      dword ptr [esi+4],0
776b2349 je       ole32!CRpcThread::WorkerLoop+0x55 (776b232b)

ole32!CRpcThread::WorkerLoop+0x65:
776b234b pop      edi
776b234c pop      ebx

ole32!CRpcThread::WorkerLoop+0x67:
776b234d pop      esi
776b234e ret

ole32!CRpcThread::WorkerLoop+0x60:
776cf3be cmp      dword ptr [esi+4],eax
776cf3c1 je       ole32!CRpcThread::WorkerLoop+0x18 (776b2301)

ole32!CRpcThread::WorkerLoop+0x69:
776cf3c7 jmp      ole32!CRpcThread::WorkerLoop+0x65 (776b234b)
```

Therefore, we have possibly identified thread #16 that resets the event by calling *WaitForSingleObjectEx* and tries to acquire the critical section. We also know the second thread #13 that has already acquired that critical section and is now waiting for the event to be signaled.

Memory Leak (Process Heap)

Memory Leak is another pattern that may be finally manifested as **Insufficient Memory** pattern (page 302) in a crash dump. Here I'll cover process heap memory leaks. They are usually identified when the process virtual memory size grows over time. It starts with 80Mb, and instead of fluctuating normally below 100Mb, it suddenly starts growing to 150Mb after some time and then to 300Mb the next day and then grows to 600Mb and so on.

Usually, a process heap is under suspicion here. To confirm this, we need to sample 2-3 consecutive user memory dumps at process sizes 100Mb, 200Mb, and 300Mb, for example. This can be done by using Microsoft *userdump.exe* command line tool. Then we can see whether there is any heap growth by using **!heap -s** WinDbg command:

1st dump

```
0:000> !heap -s
  Heap      Flags     Reserv  Commit  Virt
                       (k)     (k)     (k)
---------------------------------------
00140000 00000002    2048    1048    1112
00240000 00008000      64      12      12
00310000 00001002    7232    4308    4600
00420000 00001002    1024     520     520
00340000 00001002     256      40      40
00720000 00001002      64      32      32
00760000 00001002      64      48      48
01020000 00001002     256      24      24
02060000 00001002      64      16      16
02070000 00001003     256     120     120
020b0000 00001003     256       4       4
020f0000 00001003     256       4       4
02130000 00001003     256       4       4
02170000 00001003     256       4       4
021f0000 00001002    1088      76      76
021e0000 00001002      64      16      16
02330000 00001002    1088     428     428
02340000 00011002     256      12      12
02380000 00001002      64      12      12
024c0000 00001003      64       8       8
028d0000 00001002    7232    3756    6188
02ce0000 00001003      64       8       8
07710000 00001002      64      20      20
07b20000 00001002      64      16      16
07f30000 00001002      64      16      16
09050000 00001002     256      12      12
09c80000 00001002  130304  102340  102684
```

```
007d0000 00001003      256      192      192
00810000 00001003      256        4        4
0bdd0000 00001003      256        4        4
0be10000 00001003      256        4        4
0be50000 00001003      256        4        4
0be90000 00001003      256       56       56
0bed0000 00001003      256        4        4
0bf10000 00001003      256        4        4
0bf50000 00001003      256        4        4
0bf90000 00001003      256        4        4
00860000 00001002       64       20       20
00870000 00001002       64       20       20
0d760000 00001002      256       12       12
0dc60000 00001002     1088      220      220
0c3a0000 00001002       64       12       12
0c3d0000 00001002     1088      160      364
08420000 00001002       64       64       64
```

2nd dump

```
0:000> !heap -s
  Heap     Flags   Reserv  Commit  Virt
                    (k)     (k)    (k)
-----------------------------------------
00140000 00000002     8192     4600     4600
00240000 00008000       64       12       12
00310000 00001002     7232     4516     4600
00420000 00001002     1024      520      520
00340000 00001002      256       44       44
00720000 00001002       64       32       32
00760000 00001002       64       48       48
01020000 00001002      256       24       24
02060000 00001002       64       16       16
02070000 00001003      256      124      124
020b0000 00001003      256        4        4
020f0000 00001003      256        4        4
02130000 00001003      256        4        4
02170000 00001003      256        4        4
021f0000 00001002     1088       76       76
021e0000 00001002       64       16       16
02330000 00001002     1088      428      428
02340000 00011002      256       12       12
02380000 00001002       64       12       12
024c0000 00001003       64        8        8
028d0000 00001002     7232     3796     6768
02ce0000 00001003       64        8        8
07710000 00001002       64       20       20
07b20000 00001002       64       16       16
07f30000 00001002       64       16       16
09050000 00001002      256       12       12
09c80000 00001002   261376   221152   221928
007d0000 00001003      256      192      192
00810000 00001003      256        4        4
```

```
0bdd0000 00001003      256        4        4
0be10000 00001003      256        4        4
0be50000 00001003      256        4        4
0be90000 00001003      256       60       60
0bed0000 00001003      256        4        4
0bf10000 00001003      256        4        4
0bf50000 00001003      256        4        4
0bf90000 00001003      256        4        4
00860000 00001002       64       20       20
00870000 00001002       64       20       20
0d760000 00001002      256       12       12
0dc60000 00001002     1088      228      228
0c3a0000 00001002       64       12       12
0c3d0000 00001002     1088      168      224
08450000 00001002       64       64       64
```

We see that the only significant heap growth is at 09c80000 address, from 130Mb to 260Mb. However, this doesn't say which code uses it. To find the code, we need to enable the so-called user mode stack trace database. Please refer to the following Citrix article:

http://support.citrix.com/article/CTX106970

The example in the article is for Citrix IMA service, but we can replace *ImaSrv.exe* with any other executable name.

Suppose that after enabling user mode stack trace database and restarting the program or service we see the growth, and we get memory dumps with the following suspicious heap highlighted in bold:

```
0:000> !gflag
Current NtGlobalFlag contents: 0x00001000
ust - Create user mode stack trace database

0:000> !heap -s
NtGlobalFlag enables following debugging aids for new heaps:
  stack back traces
LFH Key: 0x2687ed29
  Heap     Flags   Reserv  Commit  Virt
                    (k)     (k)     (k)
-----------------------------------------
00140000 58000062     4096      488      676
00240000 58008060       64       12       12
00360000 58001062     3136     1152     1216
003b0000 58001062       64       32       32
01690000 58001062      256       32       32
016d0000 58001062     1024      520      520
003e0000 58001062       64       48       48
```

```
02310000 58001062      256      24       24
02b30000 58001062       64      16       16
02b40000 58001063      256      64       64
02b80000 58001063      256       4        4
02bc0000 58001063      256       4        4
02c00000 58001063      256       4        4
02c40000 58001063      256       4        4
02c80000 58001063      256       4        4
02cc0000 58001063      256       4        4
02d30000 58001063       64       4        4
03140000 58001062     7232    4160     4896
03550000 58001063       64       4        4
07f70000 58001062       64      12       12
08380000 58001062       64      12       12
08790000 58001062       64      12       12
091d0000 58011062      256      12       12
09210000 58001062       64      16       16
09220000 58001062       64      12       12
092a0000 58001062       64      12       12
09740000 58001062      256      12       12
0b1a0000 58001062       64      12       12
0b670000 58001062    64768   39508    39700
0b7b0000 58001062       64      12       12
0c650000 58001062     1088     192      192
```

Every heap is subdivided into several segments and to see which segments have grown the most we can use **!heap -m <heap address>** command:

```
0:000> !heap -m 0b670000
Index   Address  Name      Debugging options enabled
29:   0b670000
    Segment at 0b670000 to 0b6b0000 (00040000 bytes committed)
    Segment at 0c760000 to 0c860000 (00100000 bytes committed)
    Segment at 0c980000 to 0cb80000 (001fe000 bytes committed)
    Segment at 0cb80000 to 0cf80000 (003cc000 bytes committed)
    Segment at 0dc30000 to 0e430000 (00800000 bytes committed)
    Segment at 12330000 to 13330000 (01000000 bytes committed)
    Segment at 13330000 to 15330000 (0078b000 bytes committed)
...
...
...
```

If we use **!heap -a <heap address>** command, then in addition to the list of heap segments, individual heap allocation entries are dumped as well. This could be a considerable output, and we should create the log file in advance by using **.logopen <file name>** command.

The output can be like this (taken from another dump):

```
0:000> !heap -a 000a0000
...
...
...
    Segment00 at 000a0000:
        Flags:           00000000
        Base:            000a0000
        First Entry:     000a0580
        Last Entry:      000b0000
        Total Pages:     00000010
        Total UnCommit:  00000002
        Largest UnCommit:00000000
        UnCommitted Ranges: (1)

    Heap entries for Segment00 in Heap 000a0000
        000a0000: 00000 . 00580 [101] - busy (57f)
        000a0580: 00580 . 00240 [101] - busy (23f)
        000a07c0: 00240 . 00248 [101] - busy (22c)
        000a0a08: 00248 . 00218 [101] - busy (200)
        000a0c20: 00218 . 00ce0 [100]
        000a1900: 00ce0 . 00f88 [101] - busy (f6a)
        000a2888: 00f88 . 04418 [101] - busy (4400)
        000a6ca0: 04418 . 05958 [101] - busy (5940)
        000ac5f8: 05958 . 00928 [101] - busy (90c)
        000acf20: 00928 . 010c0 [100]
        000adfe0: 010c0 . 00020 [111] - busy (1d)
        000ae000:      00002000      - uncommitted bytes.
```

Then we can inspect individual entries to see stack traces that allocated them by using **!heap -p -a <heap entry address>** command:

```
0:000> !heap -p -a 000a6ca0
    address 000a6ca0 found in
    _HEAP @ a0000
      HEAP_ENTRY Size Prev Flags    UserPtr UserSize - state
        000a6ca0 0b2b 0000  [00]   000a6cb8    05940 - (busy)
        Trace: 2156ac
        7704dab4 ntdll!RtlAllocateHeap+0x0000021d
        75c59b12 USP10!UspAllocCache+0x0000002b
        75c62381 USP10!AllocSizeCache+0x00000048
        75c61c74
USP10!FindOrCreateSizeCacheWithoutRealizationID+0x00000124
        75c61bc0 USP10!FindOrCreateSizeCacheUsingRealizationID+0x00000070
        75c59a97 USP10!UpdateCache+0x0000002b
        75c59a61 USP10!ScriptCheckCache+0x0000005c
        75c59d04 USP10!ScriptStringAnalyse+0x0000012a
        7711140f LPK!LpkStringAnalyse+0x00000114
        7711159e LPK!LpkCharsetDraw+0x00000302
        77111488 LPK!LpkDrawTextEx+0x00000044
```

```
76a4beb3 USER32!DT_DrawStr+0x0000013a
76a4be45 USER32!DT_DrawJustifiedLine+0x0000005f
76a49d68 USER32!AddEllipsisAndDrawLine+0x00000186
76a4bc31 USER32!DrawTextExWorker+0x000001b1
76a4bedc USER32!DrawTextExW+0x0000001e
746051d8 uxtheme!CTextDraw::GetTextExtent+0x000000be
7460515a uxtheme!GetThemeTextExtent+0x00000065
74611ed4 uxtheme!CThemeMenuBar::MeasureItem+0x00000124
746119c1 uxtheme!CThemeMenu::OnMeasureItem+0x0000003f
74611978 uxtheme!CThemeWnd::_PreDefWindowProc+0x00000117
74601ea5 uxtheme!_ThemeDefWindowProc+0x00000090
74601f61 uxtheme!ThemeDefWindowProcW+0x00000018
76a4a09e USER32!DefWindowProcW+0x00000068
931406 notepad!NPWndProc+0x00000084
76a51a10 USER32!InternalCallWinProc+0x00000023
76a51ae8 USER32!UserCallWinProcCheckWow+0x0000014b
76a51c03 USER32!DispatchClientMessage+0x000000da
76a3bc24 USER32!__fnINOUTLPUAHMEASUREMENUITEM+0x00000027
77040e6e ntdll!KiUserCallbackDispatcher+0x0000002e
76a51d87 USER32!RealDefWindowProcW+0x00000047
74601f2f uxtheme!_ThemeDefWindowProc+0x000001b8
```

If we want to dump all heap entries with their corresponding stack traces, we can use **!heap -k -h <heap address>** command.

A historical note: sometimes, in the past, all these commands didn't work. In such cases, we used old Windows 2000 extension (page 182).

Some prefer to use *umdh.exe* and get text file logs, but the advantage of embedding heap allocation stack traces in a crash dump is that we are not concerned with sending and configuring symbol files at a customer site.

When analyzing heap various pageheap options **!heap -p** are useful such as (taken from WinDbg help):

> ***-t[c|s] [Traces]***
> *"Causes the debugger to display the collected traces of the heavy heap users. Traces specifies the number of traces to display; the default is four. If there are more traces than the specified number, the earliest traces are displayed. If -t or -tc is used, the traces are sorted by count usage. If -ts is used, the traces are sorted by size."*

In the past we also used Microsoft Debug Diagnostics tool:
https://docs.microsoft.com/en-us/archive/blogs/debugdiag/welcome-back-to-the-debug-diagnostics-blog

Missing Thread

Sometimes it is possible that a process crash dump doesn't have all usual threads inside. For example, we expect at least 4 threads, including the main process thread, but in the dump, we see only 3. If we know that some access violations were reported in the event log before (not necessarily for the same PID), we may suspect that one of the threads had been terminated due to some reason. I call this pattern **Missing Thread**.

To simulate this problem, I created a small multithreaded program in Visual C++:

```
#include "stdafx.h"
#include <process.h>

void thread_request(void *param)
{
    while (true);
}

int _tmain(int argc, _TCHAR* argv[])
{
    _beginthread(thread_request, 0, NULL);

    try
    {
        if (argc == 2)
        {
            *(int *)NULL = 0;
        }
    }
    catch (...)
    {
        _endthread();
    }

    while (true);

    return 0;
}
```

If there is a command-line argument, then the main thread simulates access violation and finishes in the exception handler. To use SEH exceptions with C++ *try/catch* blocks you have to enable **/EHa** option in C++ Code Generation properties:

Enable String Pooling	No
Enable Minimal Rebuild	No
Enable C++ Exceptions	**Yes With SEH Exceptions (/EHa)**
Smaller Type Check	No
Basic Runtime Checks	Default
Runtime Library	**Multi-threaded (/MT)**
Struct Member Alignment	Default
Buffer Security Check	Yes
Enable Function-Level Linking	No
Enable Enhanced Instruction Set	Not Set
Floating Point Model	Precise (/fp:precise)
Enable Floating Point Exceptions	No

If we run the program without command line parameter and take a manual dump from it, we see two threads:

```
0:000> ~*kL

.  0  Id: 1208.fdc Suspend: 1 Teb: 7efdd000 Unfrozen
ChildEBP RetAddr
0012ff70 00401403 MissingThread!wmain+0x58
0012ffc0 7d4e7d2a MissingThread!__tmainCRTStartup+0x15e
0012fff0 00000000 kernel32!BaseProcessStart+0x28

   1  Id: 1208.102c Suspend: 1 Teb: 7efda000 Unfrozen
ChildEBP RetAddr
005dff7c 004010ef MissingThread!thread_request
005dffb4 00401188 MissingThread!_callthreadstart+0x1b
005dffb0 7d4dfe21 MissingThread!_threadstart+0x73
005dffec 00000000 kernel32!BaseThreadStart+0x34

0:000> ~
.  0  Id: 1208.fdc Suspend: 1 Teb: 7efdd000 Unfrozen
   1  Id: 1208.102c Suspend: 1 Teb: 7efda000 Unfrozen

0:000> dd 7efdd000 l4
7efdd000  0012ff64 00130000 0012e000 00000000
```

I also dumped TEB of the main thread. However, if we run the program with any command line parameter and look at its manual dump we would see only one thread with the main thread missing:

```
0:000> ~*kL

.  0  Id: 1004.12e8 Suspend: 1 Teb: 7efda000 Unfrozen
ChildEBP RetAddr
005dff7c 004010ef MissingThread!thread_request
005dffb4 00401188 MissingThread!_callthreadstart+0x1b
005dffb8 7d4dfe21 MissingThread!_threadstart+0x73
005dffec 00000000 kernel32!BaseThreadStart+0x34

0:000> ~
.  0  Id: 1004.12e8 Suspend: 1 Teb: 7efda000 Unfrozen
```

If we try to dump TEB address and stack data from the missing main thread we would see that the memory was already decommitted:

```
0:000> dd 7efdd000 l4
7efdd000  ???????? ???????? ???????? ????????

0:000> dds 0012e000  00130000
0012e000  ????????
0012e004  ????????
0012e008  ????????
0012e00c  ????????
0012e010  ????????
0012e014  ????????
0012e018  ????????
0012e01c  ????????
0012e020  ????????
0012e024  ????????
```

The same effect can be achieved in the similar program that exits the thread in the custom unhandled exception filter:

```
#include "stdafx.h"
#include <process.h>
#include <windows.h>

LONG WINAPI CustomUnhandledExceptionFilter(struct _EXCEPTION_POINTERS*
ExceptionInfo)
{
    ExitThread(-1);
}

void thread_request(void *param)
{
    while (true);
}
```

```
int _tmain(int argc, _TCHAR* argv[])
{
    _beginthread(thread_request, 0, NULL);
    SetUnhandledExceptionFilter(CustomUnhandledExceptionFilter);

    *(int *)NULL = 0;

    while (true);

    return 0;
}
```

The solution to catch an exception that results in a thread termination would be to run the program under WinDbg or any other debugger:

```
CommandLine: C:\MissingThread\MissingThread.exe 1
Symbol search path is:
SRV*c:\websymbols*http://msdl.microsoft.com/download/symbols
Executable search path is:
ModLoad: 00400000 0040f000   MissingThread.exe
ModLoad: 7d4c0000 7d5f0000   NOT_AN_IMAGE
ModLoad: 7d600000 7d6f0000   C:\W2K3\SysWOW64\ntdll32.dll
ModLoad: 7d4c0000 7d5f0000   C:\W2K3\syswow64\kernel32.dll
(df0.12f0): Break instruction exception - code 80000003 (first chance)
eax=7d600000 ebx=7efde000 ecx=00000005 edx=00000020 esi=7d6a01f4
edi=00221f38
eip=7d61002d esp=0012fb4c ebp=0012fcac iopl=0 nv up ei pl nz na po nc
cs=0023 ss=002b ds=002b es=002b fs=0053 gs=002b efl=00000202
ntdll32!DbgBreakPoint:
7d61002d cc              int     3

0:000> g
ModLoad: 71c20000 71c32000   C:\W2K3\SysWOW64\tsappcmp.dll
ModLoad: 77ba0000 77bfa000   C:\W2K3\syswow64\msvcrt.dll
ModLoad: 00410000 004ab000   C:\W2K3\syswow64\ADVAPI32.dll
ModLoad: 7da20000 7db00000   C:\W2K3\syswow64\RPCRT4.dll
ModLoad: 7d8d0000 7d920000   C:\W2K3\syswow64\Secur32.dll
(df0.12f0): Access violation - code c0000005 (first chance)
First chance exceptions are reported before any exception handling.
This exception may be expected and handled.
eax=000007a0 ebx=7d4d8df9 ecx=78b842d9 edx=00000000 esi=00000002
edi=00000ece
eip=00401057 esp=0012ff50 ebp=0012ff70 iopl=0 nv up ei pl zr na pe nc
cs=0023 ss=002b ds=002b es=002b fs=0053 gs=002b efl=00010246
MissingThread!wmain+0x47:
00401057 c705000000000000000000 mov dword ptr
ds:[0],0  ds:002b:00000000=????????
```

```
0:000> kL
ChildEBP RetAddr
0012ff70 00401403 MissingThread!wmain+0x47
0012ffc0 7d4e7d2a MissingThread!__tmainCRTStartup+0x15e
0012fff0 00000000 kernel32!BaseProcessStart+0x28
```

If live debugging is not possible, and we are interested in crash dumps saved upon a first chance exception before it is processed by an exception handler, then we can also use MS userdump tool after we install it and enable *All Exceptions* in the *Process Monitoring Rules* dialog box. Another tool that can be used is *ADPlus* in crash mode from Debugging Tools for Windows.

Unknown Component

Sometimes we suspect that a problem was caused by some module, but WinDbg **lmv** command doesn't show the company name and other verbose information for it, and Google search has no results for the file name. I call this pattern **Unknown Component**.

In such cases, additional information can be obtained by dumping the module resource section or the whole module address range and looking for ASCII and UNICODE strings. For example (byte values in **db** output are omitted for clarity):

```
2: kd> lmv m driver
start    end        module name
f5022000 f503e400   driver   (deferred)
    Image path: \SystemRoot\System32\drivers\driver.sys
    Image name: driver.sys
    Timestamp:        Tue Jun 12 11:33:16 2007 (466E766C)
    CheckSum:         00021A2C
    ImageSize:        0001C400
    Translations:     0000.04b0 0000.04e0 0409.04b0 0409.04e0

2: kd> db f5022000 f503e400
f5022000  MZ..............
f5022010  ........@.......
f5022020  ................
f5022030  ................
f5022040  ........!..L.!Th
f5022050  is program canno
f5022060  t be run in DOS
f5022070  mode....$.......
f5022080  .g,._.B._.B._.B.
f5022090  _.C.=.B..%Q.X.B.
f50220a0  _.B.].B.Y%H.|.B.
f50220b0  ..D.^.B.Rich_.B.
f50220c0  ........PE..L...
f50220d0  lvnF............
...
...
...
f503ce30  ................
f503ce40  ................
f503ce50  ................
f503ce60  ............0...
f503ce70  ................
f503ce80  ....H...........
f503ce90  ..........4...V.
f503cea0  S._.V.E.R.S.I.O.
f503ceb0  N._.I.N.F.O.....
f503cec0  ................
f503ced0  ........?.......
```

```
f503cee0  ................
f503cef0  ....P.....S.t.r.
f503cf00  i.n.g.F.i.l.e.I.
f503cf10  n.f.o...,.....0.
f503cf20  4.0.9.0.4.b.0...
f503cf30  4.....C.o.m.p.a.
f503cf40  n.y.N.a.m.e.....
f503cf50  M.y.C.o.m.p. .A.
f503cf60  G...p.$...F.i.l.
f503cf70  e.D.e.s.c.r.i.p.
f503cf80  t.i.o.n.....M.y.
f503cf90  .B.i.g. .P.r.o.
f503cfa0  d.u.c.t. .H.o.o.
f503cfb0  k...............
f503cfc0  ................
f503cfd0  ....4.....F.i.l.
f503cfe0  e.V.e.r.s.i.o.n.
f503cff0  ....5...1...0...
f503d000  ????????????????
f503d010  ????????????????
f503d020  ????????????????
f503d030  ????????????????
...
...
...
```

We see that *CompanyName* is "MyComp AG", *FileDescription* is "My Big Product Hook", and *FileVersion* is "5.0.1".

In our example, the same information can be retrieved by dumping the image file header and then finding and dumping the resource section:

```
2: kd> lmv m driver
start    end         module name
f5022000 f503e400   driver   (deferred)
    Image path: \SystemRoot\System32\drivers\driver.sys
    Image name: driver.sys
    Timestamp:        Tue Jun 12 11:33:16 2007 (466E766C)
    CheckSum:         00021A2C
    ImageSize:        0001C400
    Translations:     0000.04b0 0000.04e0 0409.04b0 0409.04e0
```

```
2: kd> !dh f5022000 -f

File Type: EXECUTABLE IMAGE
FILE HEADER VALUES
     14C machine (i386)
       6 number of sections
466E766C time date stamp Tue Jun 12 11:33:16 2007

       0 file pointer to symbol table
       0 number of symbols
      E0 size of optional header
     10E characteristics
            Executable
            Line numbers stripped
            Symbols stripped
            32 bit word machine

OPTIONAL HEADER VALUES
     10B magic #
    6.00 linker version
   190A0 size of code
    30A0 size of initialized data
       0 size of uninitialized data
   1A340 address of entry point
     2C0 base of code
         ----- new -----
00010000 image base
      20 section alignment
      20 file alignment
       1 subsystem (Native)
    4.00 operating system version
    0.00 image version
    4.00 subsystem version
   1C400 size of image
     2C0 size of headers
   21A2C checksum
00100000 size of stack reserve
00001000 size of stack commit
00100000 size of heap reserve
00001000 size of heap commit
       0 [       0] address [size] of Export Directory
   1A580 [      50] address [size] of Import Directory
   1AE40 [     348] address [size] of Resource Directory
       0 [       0] address [size] of Exception Directory
       0 [       0] address [size] of Security Directory
   1B1A0 [    1084] address [size] of Base Relocation Directory
     420 [      1C] address [size] of Debug Directory
       0 [       0] address [size] of Description Directory
       0 [       0] address [size] of Special Directory
       0 [       0] address [size] of Thread Storage Directory
       0 [       0] address [size] of Load Configuration Directory
       0 [       0] address [size] of Bound Import Directory
     2C0 [     15C] address [size] of Import Address Table Directory
```

```
       0 [       0] address [size] of Delay Import Directory
       0 [       0] address [size] of COR20 Header Directory
       0 [       0] address [size] of Reserved Directory

2: kd> db f5022000+1AE40 f5022000+1AE40+348
f503ce40  ................
f503ce50  ................
f503ce60  ............0...
f503ce70  ................
f503ce80  ....H...........
f503ce90  ..........4...V.
f503cea0  S._.V.E.R.S.I.O.
f503ceb0  N._.I.N.F.O.....
f503cec0  ................
f503ced0  ........?.......
f503cee0  ................
f503cef0  ....P.....S.t.r.
f503cf00  i.n.g.F.i.l.e.I.
f503cf10  n.f.o...,.....0.
f503cf20  4.0.9.0.4.b.0...
f503cf30  4.....C.o.m.p.a.
f503cf40  n.y.N.a.m.e.....
f503cf50  M.y.C.o.m.p. .A.
f503cf60  G...p.$...F.i.l.
f503cf70  e.D.e.s.c.r.i.p.
f503cf80  t.i.o.n.....M.y.
f503cf90  .B.i.g. .P.r.o.
f503cfa0  d.u.c.t. .H.o.o.
f503cfb0  k...............
f503cfc0  ................
f503cfd0  ....4.....F.i.l.
f503cfe0  e.V.e.r.s.i.o.n.
f503cff0  ....5...1...0...
f503d000  ????????????????
f503d010  ????????????????
...
...
...
```

Memory Leak (.NET Heap)

Sometimes the process size steadily grows, but there is no difference in the process heap size. In such cases, we need to check whether the process uses Microsoft .NET runtime (CLR). If one of the loaded modules is *mscorwks.dll* or *mscorsvr.dll* then it is most likely. Then we should check CLR heap statistics.

In .NET world, dynamically allocated objects are garbage collected (GC), and therefore, simple allocate-and-forget memory leaks are not possible. To simulate that I created the following C# program:

```
using System;

namespace CLRHeapLeak
{
    class Leak
    {
        private byte[] m_data;


        public Leak()
        {
            m_data = new byte[1024];
        }
    }

    class Program
    {
        static void Main(string[] args)
        {
            Leak leak = new Leak();

            while (true)
            {
                leak = new Leak();
                System.Threading.Thread.Sleep(100);
            }
        }
    }
}
```

If we run it, the process size never grows. The GC thread collects and frees unreferenced Leak classes. This can be seen from inspecting memory dumps that were taken with *userdump.exe* after the start, 2, 6, and 12 minutes. The GC heap never grows higher than 1Mb and the number of *CLRHeapLeak.Leak* and *System.Byte[]* objects always fluctuates between 100 and 500. For example, on 12th minute, we have the following statistics:

```
0:000> .loadby sos mscorwks

0:000> !eeheap -gc
Number of GC Heaps: 1
generation 0 starts at 0x0147160c
generation 1 starts at 0x0147100c
generation 2 starts at 0x01471000
ephemeral segment allocation context: (0x014dc53c, 0x014dd618)
 segment    begin allocated     size
004aedb8 790d7ae4  790f7064 0x0001f580(128384)
01470000 01471000  014dd618 0x0006c618(443928)
Large object heap starts at 0x02471000
 segment    begin allocated     size
02470000 02471000  02473250 0x00002250(8784)
Total Size   0x8dde8(581096)
------------------------------
GC Heap Size   0x8dde8(581096)

0:000> !dumpheap -stat
total 2901 objects
Statistics:
Count    TotalSize Class Name
    1           12 System.Security.Permissions.SecurityPermission
    1           24 System.OperatingSystem
    1           24 System.Version
    1           24 System.Reflection.Assembly
    1           28 System.SharedStatics
    1           36 System.Int64[]
    1           40 System.AppDomainSetup
    3           60 System.RuntimeType
    5           60 System.Object
    2           72 System.Security.PermissionSet
    1           72 System.ExecutionEngineException
    1           72 System.StackOverflowException
    1           72 System.OutOfMemoryException
    1          100 System.AppDomain
    7          100      Free
    2          144 System.Threading.ThreadAbortException
    4          328 System.Char[]
  418         5016 CLRHeapLeak.Leak
    5         8816 System.Object[]
 2026       128632 System.String
  418       433048 System.Byte[]
Total 2901 objects
```

However, we can make Leak objects always referenced by introducing the following changes into the program:

```
using System;

namespace CLRHeapLeak
{
    class Leak
    {
        private byte[] m_data;
        private Leak m_prevLeak;

        public Leak()
        {
            m_data = new byte[1024];
        }

        public Leak(Leak prevLeak)
        {
            m_prevLeak = prevLeak;
            m_data = new byte[1024];
        }
    }

    class Program
    {
        static void Main(string[] args)
        {
            Leak leak = new Leak();

            while (true)
            {
                leak = new Leak(leak);
                System.Threading.Thread.Sleep(100);
            }
        }
    }
}
```

Then, if we run the program, we would see in Task Manager that it grows over time. Taking consecutive memory dumps after the start, 10 and 16 minutes, shows that Win32 heap segments always have the same size:

```
0:000> !heap 0 0
Index   Address  Name      Debugging options enabled
  1:   00530000
    Segment at 00530000 to 00630000 (0003d000 bytes committed)
  2:   00010000
    Segment at 00010000 to 00020000 (00003000 bytes committed)
```

```
  3:    00520000
    Segment at 00520000 to 00530000 (00003000 bytes committed)
  4:    00b10000
    Segment at 00b10000 to 00b50000 (00001000 bytes committed)
  5:    001a0000
    Segment at 001a0000 to 001b0000 (00003000 bytes committed)
  6:    00170000
    Segment at 00170000 to 00180000 (00008000 bytes committed)
  7:    013b0000
    Segment at 013b0000 to 013c0000 (00003000 bytes committed)
```

But GC heap and the number of *Leak* and *System.Byte[]* objects in it were growing significantly:

```
Process Uptime: 0 days 0:00:04.000

0:000> !eeheap -gc
Number of GC Heaps: 1
generation 0 starts at 0x013c1018
generation 1 starts at 0x013c100c
generation 2 starts at 0x013c1000
ephemeral segment allocation context: (0x013cd804, 0x013cdff4)
 segment    begin allocated     size
0055ee08 790d7ae4  790f7064 0x0001f580(128384)
013c0000 013c1000  013cdff4 0x0000cff4(53236)
Large object heap starts at 0x023c1000
 segment    begin allocated     size
023c0000 023c1000  023c3250 0x00002250(8784)
Total Size   0x2e7c4(190404)
------------------------------
GC Heap Size   0x2e7c4(190404)

0:000> !dumpheap -stat
total 2176 objects
Statistics:
Count     TotalSize Class Name
...
...
...
   46           736 CLRHeapLeak.Leak
    5          8816 System.Object[]
   46         47656 System.Byte[]
 2035        129604 System.String
Total 2176 objects

Process Uptime: 0 days 0:09:56.000

0:000> !eeheap -gc
Number of GC Heaps: 1
generation 0 starts at 0x018cddbc
generation 1 starts at 0x01541ec4
```

```
generation 2 starts at 0x013c1000
ephemeral segment allocation context: (0x0192d668, 0x0192ddc8)
 segment    begin allocated     size
0055ee08 790d7ae4  790f7064 0x0001f580(128384)
013c0000 013c1000  0192ddc8 0x0056cdc8(5688776)
Large object heap starts at 0x023c1000
 segment    begin allocated     size
023c0000 023c1000  023c3240 0x00002240(8768)
Total Size  0x58e588(5825928)
------------------------------
GC Heap Size  0x58e588(5825928)

0:000> !dumpheap -stat
total 12887 objects
Statistics:
Count     TotalSize Class Name
...
...
...
    5          8816 System.Object[]
 5403         86448 CLRHeapLeak.Leak
 2026        128632 System.String
 5403       5597508 System.Byte[]
Total 12887 objects

Process Uptime: 0 days 0:16:33.000

0:000> !eeheap -gc
Number of GC Heaps: 1
generation 0 starts at 0x01c59cb4
generation 1 starts at 0x0194fd20
generation 2 starts at 0x013c1000
ephemeral segment allocation context: (0x01cd3050, 0x01cd3cc0)
 segment    begin allocated     size
0055ee08 790d7ae4  790f7064 0x0001f580(128384)
013c0000 013c1000  01cd3cc0 0x00912cc0(9514176)
Large object heap starts at 0x023c1000
 segment    begin allocated     size
023c0000 023c1000  023c3240 0x00002240(8768)
Total Size  0x934480(9651328)
------------------------------
GC Heap Size  0x934480(9651328)

0:000> !dumpheap -stat
total 20164 objects
Statistics:
Count     TotalSize Class Name
    5          8816 System.Object[]
 2026        128632 System.String
 9038        144608 CLRHeapLeak.Leak
 9038       9363368 System.Byte[]
Total 20164 objects
```

This is not the traditional memory leak because we have the reference chain. However, uncontrolled memory growth can be considered as a memory leak too, caused by poor application design, bad input validation or error handling.

There are situations when customers think there is a memory leak, but it is not. One of them is unusually big size of a process when running it on a multi-processor server. If *dllhost.exe* hosting typical .NET assembly DLL occupies less than 100Mb on a local workstation starts consuming more than 300Mb on a 4-processor server than it can be the case that the server version of CLR uses per processor GC heaps:

```
0:000> .loadby sos mscorsvr

0:000> !EEHeap -gc
generation 0 starts at 0x05c80154
generation 1 starts at 0x05c7720c
generation 2 starts at 0x102d0030
generation 0 starts at 0x179a0444
generation 1 starts at 0x1799b7a4
generation 2 starts at 0x142d0030
generation 0 starts at 0x0999ac88
generation 1 starts at 0x09990cc4
generation 2 starts at 0x182d0030
generation 0 starts at 0x242eccb0
generation 1 starts at 0x242d0030
generation 2 starts at 0x1c2d0030
...
...
...
GC Heap Size  0x109702ec(278332140)
```

Or, if this is CLR 1.x the old extension will tell us the same too:

```
0:000> !.\clr10\sos.eeheap -gc
Loaded Son of Strike data table version 5 from
"C:\WINDOWS\Microsoft.NET\Framework\v1.1.4322\mscorsvr.dll"
Number of GC Heaps: 4
------------------------------
Heap 0 (0x000f9af0)
generation 0 starts at 0x05c80154
generation 1 starts at 0x05c7720c
generation 2 starts at 0x102d0030
...
...
...
Heap Size  0x515ed60(85,323,104)
------------------------------
Heap 1 (0x000fa070)
generation 0 starts at 0x179a0444
generation 1 starts at 0x1799b7a4
```

```
generation 2 starts at 0x142d0030
...
...
...
Heap Size  0x37c7bf0(58,489,840)
------------------------------
Heap 2 (0x000fab80)
generation 0 starts at 0x0999ac88
generation 1 starts at 0x09990cc4
generation 2 starts at 0x182d0030
...
...
...
Heap Size  0x485de34(75,882,036)
------------------------------
Heap 3 (0x000fb448)
generation 0 starts at 0x242eccb0
generation 1 starts at 0x242d0030
generation 2 starts at 0x1c2d0030
...
...
...
Heap Size  0x41ea570(69,117,296)
------------------------------
Reserved segments:
------------------------------
GC Heap Size  0x1136ecf4(288,812,276)
```

The more processors we have, the more heaps are contributing to the overall VM size. Although the process occupies almost 400Mb if it doesn't steadily grow over time beyond that value, then it is normal.

Double Free (Process Heap)

Double-free bugs lead to **Dynamic Memory Corruption** pattern (page 257). The reason why **Double Free** deserves its own pattern name is the fact that either debug runtime libraries or even OS itself detect such bugs and save crash dumps immediately.

For some heap implementations, double free doesn't lead to an immediate heap corruption and subsequent crash. For example, if we allocate 3 blocks in a row and then free the middle one twice there will be no crash as the second free call is able to detect that the block was already freed and does nothing. The following program loops forever and never crashes:

```
#include "stdafx.h"
#include <windows.h>

int _tmain(int argc, _TCHAR* argv[])
{
  while (true)
  {
    puts("Allocate: p1");
    void *p1 = malloc(100);
    puts("Allocate: p2");
    void *p2 = malloc(100);
    puts("Allocate: p3");
    void *p3 = malloc(100);

    puts("Free: p2");
    free(p2);
    puts("Double-Free: p2");
    free(p2);
    puts("Free: p1");
    free(p1);
    puts("Free: p3");
    free(p3);

    Sleep(100);
  }

  return 0;
}
```

The output of the program:

```
...
...
...
Allocate: p1
Allocate: p2
Allocate: p3
Free: p2
Double-Free: p2
Free: p1
Free: p3
Allocate: p1
Allocate: p2
Allocate: p3
Free: p2
Double-Free: p2
Free: p1
Free: p3
Allocate: p1
Allocate: p2
Allocate: p3
Free: p2
Double-Free: p2
...
...
...
```

However, if *free* call triggered heap coalescence (adjacent free blocks form the bigger free block) then we have a heap corruption crash on the next double-free call because the coalescence triggered by the previous *free* call erased free block information:

```
#include "stdafx.h"
#include <windows.h>

int _tmain(int argc, _TCHAR* argv[])
{
  while (true)
  {
    puts("Allocate: p1");
    void *p1 = malloc(100);
    puts("Allocate: p2");
    void *p2 = malloc(100);
    puts("Allocate: p3");
    void *p3 = malloc(100);

    puts("Free: p3");
    free(p3);
    puts("Free: p1");
    free(p1);
    puts("Free: p2");
```

```
    free(p2);
    puts("Double-Free: p2");
    free(p2);

    Sleep(100);
  }

  return 0;
}
```

The output of the program:

```
Allocate: p1
Allocate: p2
Allocate: p3
Free: p3
Free: p1
Free: p2
Double-Free: p2
Crash!
```

If we open a crash dump we would see the following stack trace:

```
0:000> r
eax=00922130 ebx=00920000 ecx=10101010 edx=10101010 esi=00922128
edi=00921fc8
eip=76ee1ad5 esp=0012fd6c ebp=0012fd94 iopl=0 nv up ei pl zr na pe nc
cs=001b ss=0023 ds=0023 es=0023 fs=003b gs=0000 efl=00010246
ntdll!RtlpCoalesceFreeBlocks+0x6ef:
76ee1ad5 8b4904          mov     ecx,dword ptr [ecx+4]
ds:0023:10101014=????????

0:000> kL
ChildEBP RetAddr
0012fd94 76ee1d37 ntdll!RtlpCoalesceFreeBlocks+0x6ef
0012fe8c 76ee1c21 ntdll!RtlpFreeHeap+0x1e2
0012fea8 758d7a7e ntdll!RtlFreeHeap+0x14e
0012febc 6cff4c39 kernel32!HeapFree+0x14
0012ff08 0040107b msvcr80!free+0xcd
0012ff5c 004011f1 DoubleFree!wmain+0x7b
0012ffa0 758d3833 DoubleFree!__tmainCRTStartup+0x10f
0012ffac 76eba9bd kernel32!BaseThreadInitThunk+0xe
0012ffec 00000000 ntdll!_RtlUserThreadStart+0x23
```

This is illustrated by the following picture where *free* calls result in heap coalescence, and the subsequent *free* call (double-free) corrupts the heap:

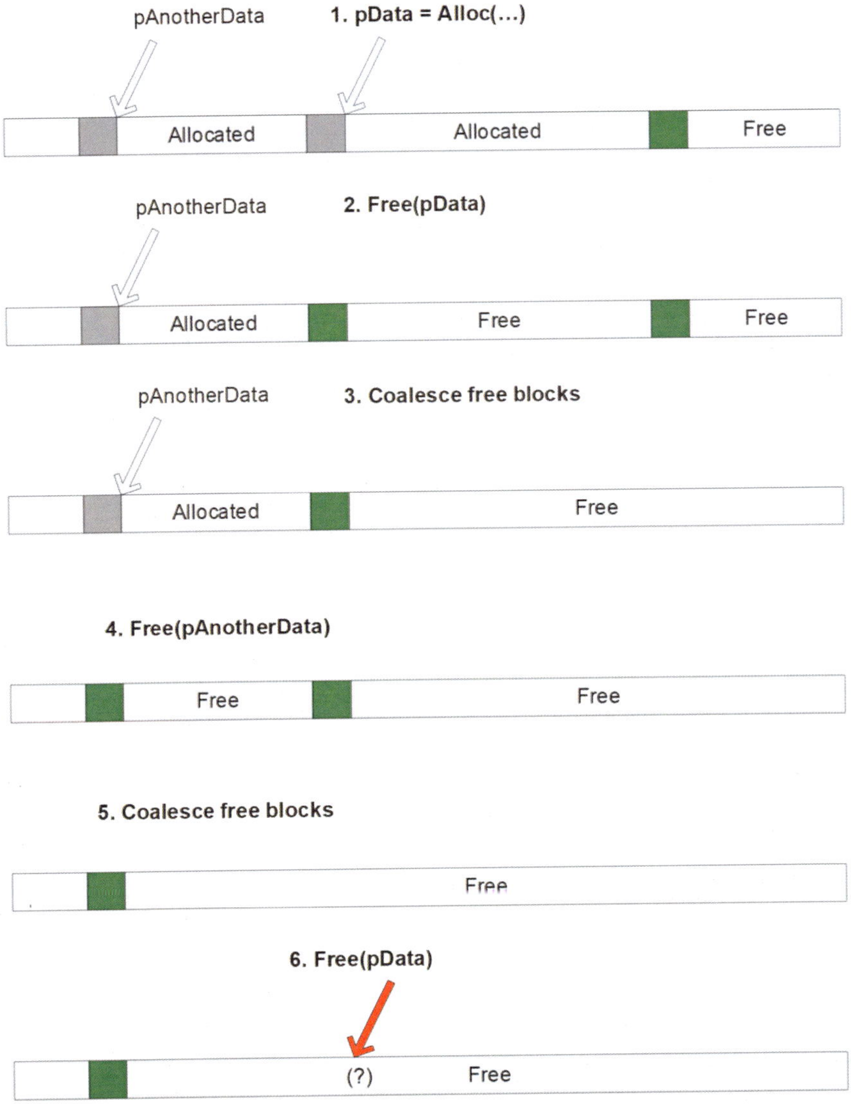

The problem here is that heap coalescence can be triggered sometime after the double *free*, so we need some solution to diagnose double-free bugs earlier, ideally at the first double-free call. For example, the following program crashes during the normal *free* operation long after the first double-free happened:

```
#include "stdafx.h"
#include <windows.h>

int _tmain(int argc, _TCHAR* argv[])
{
  while (true)
  {
    puts("Allocate: p1");
    void *p1 = malloc(100);
    puts("Allocate: p2");
    void *p2 = malloc(100);
    puts("Allocate: p3");
    void *p3 = malloc(100);

    puts("Free: p1");
    free(p1);
    puts("Free: p2");
    free(p2);
    puts("Double-Free: p2");
    free(p2);
    puts("Double-Free: p3");
    free(p3);

    Sleep(100);
  }

  return 0;
}
```

The output of the program:

```
Allocate: p1
Allocate: p2
Allocate: p3
Free: p1
Free: p2
Double-Free: p2
Free: p3
Allocate: p1
Allocate: p2
Allocate: p3
Free: p1
Free: p2
Double-Free: p2
Free: p3
Allocate: p1
Allocate: p2
Allocate: p3
Free: p1
Free: p2
Double-Free: p2
```

```
Free: p3
Allocate: p1
Allocate: p2
Allocate: p3
Free: p1
Free: p2
Double-Free: p2
Free: p3
Crash!
```

If we enable full page heap using *gflags.exe* from Debugging Tools for Windows the program crashes immediately on the double *free* call:

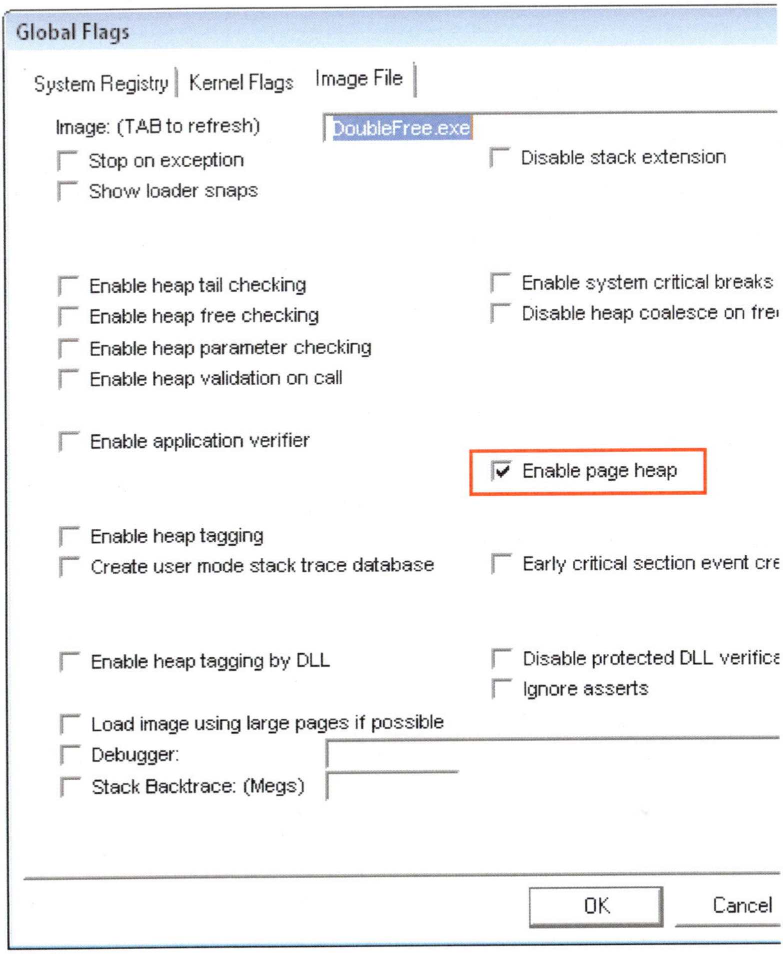

```
Allocate: p1
Allocate: p2
Allocate: p3
Free: p1
Free: p2
Double-Free: p2
Crash!
```

The crash dump shows the following stack trace:

```
0:000> kL
ChildEBP RetAddr
0012f810 71aa4ced ntdll!DbgBreakPoint+0x1
0012f834 71aa9fc2 verifier!VerifierStopMessage+0x1fd
0012f890 71aaa4da verifier!AVrfpDphReportCorruptedBlock+0x102
0012f8a4 71ab2c98 verifier!AVrfpDphCheckNormalHeapBlock+0x18a
0012f8b8 71ab2a0e verifier!_EH4_CallFilterFunc+0x12
0012f8e0 76ee1039 verifier!_except_handler4+0x8e
0012f904 76ee100b ntdll!ExecuteHandler2+0x26
0012f9ac 76ee0e97 ntdll!ExecuteHandler+0x24
0012f9ac 71aaa3ad ntdll!KiUserExceptionDispatcher+0xf
0012fcf0 71aaa920 verifier!AVrfpDphCheckNormalHeapBlock+0x5d
0012fd0c 71aa879b verifier!AVrfpDphNormalHeapFree+0x20
0012fd60 76f31c8f verifier!AVrfDebugPageHeapFree+0x1cb
0012fda8 76efd9fa ntdll!RtlDebugFreeHeap+0x2f
0012fe9c 76ee1c21 ntdll!RtlpFreeHeap+0x5f
0012feb8 758d7a7e ntdll!RtlFreeHeap+0x14e
0012fecc 6cff4c39 kernel32!HeapFree+0x14
0012ff18 0040105f msvcr80!free+0xcd
0012ff5c 004011f1 DoubleFree!wmain+0x5f
0012ffa0 758d3833 DoubleFree!__tmainCRTStartup+0x10f
0012ffac 76eba9bd kernel32!BaseThreadInitThunk+0xe

0:000> !gflag
Current NtGlobalFlag contents: 0x02000000
    hpa - Place heap allocations at ends of pages
```

If we enable heap free checking instead of page heap we get our crash on the first double *free* call immediately too:

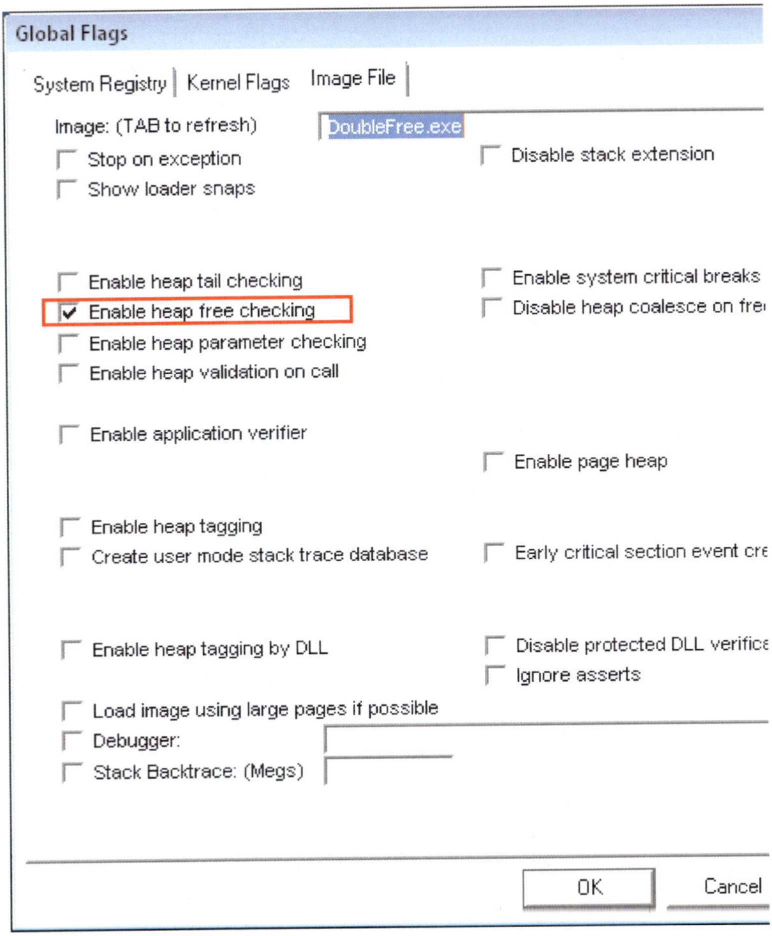


```
Allocate: p1
Allocate: p2
Allocate: p3
Free: p1
Free: p2
Double-Free: p2
Crash!
```

The crash dump shows the following stack trace:

```
0:000> r
eax=feeefeee ebx=001b2040 ecx=001b0000 edx=001b2040 esi=d4476047
edi=001b2038
eip=76ee2086 esp=0012fe68 ebp=0012fe9c iopl=0 nv up ei ng nz na pe nc
cs=001b ss=0023 ds=0023 es=0023 fs=003b gs=0000 efl=00010286
ntdll!RtlpLowFragHeapFree+0x31:
76ee2086 8b4604          mov     eax,dword ptr [esi+4]
ds:0023:d447604b=????????
```

```
0:000> kL
ChildEBP RetAddr
0012fe9c 76ee18c3 ntdll!RtlpLowFragHeapFree+0x31
0012feb0 758d7a7e ntdll!RtlFreeHeap+0x101
0012fec4 6cff4c39 kernel32!HeapFree+0x14
0012ff10 0040106d msvcr80!free+0xcd
0012ff5c 004011f1 DoubleFree!wmain+0x6d
0012ffa0 758d3833 DoubleFree!__tmainCRTStartup+0x10f
0012ffac 76eba9bd kernel32!BaseThreadInitThunk+0xe
0012ffec 00000000 ntdll!_RtlUserThreadStart+0x23

0:000> !gflag
Current NtGlobalFlag contents: 0x00000020
    hfc - Enable heap free checking
```

Double Free (Kernel Pool)

In contrast to **Double Free** pattern (page 378) in a user mode process heap double free in a kernel mode pool results in an immediate bugcheck in order to identify the driver causing the problem (BAD_POOL_CALLER bugcheck with Arg1 == 7):

```
2: kd> !analyze -v
...
...
...
BAD_POOL_CALLER (c2)
The current thread is making a bad pool request. Typically this is at a
bad IRQL level or double freeing the same allocation, etc.
Arguments:
Arg1: 00000007, Attempt to free pool which was already freed
Arg2: 0000121a, (reserved)
Arg3: 02140001, Memory contents of the pool block
Arg4: 89ba74f0, Address of the block of pool being deallocated
```

If we look at the block being deallocated we would see that it was marked as "Free" block:

```
2: kd> !pool 89ba74f0
Pool page 89ba74f0 region is Nonpaged pool
 89ba7000 size:  270 previous size:    0  (Allocated)  Thre (Protected)
 89ba7270 size:    8 previous size:  270  (Free)       ....
 89ba7278 size:   18 previous size:    8  (Allocated)  ReEv
 89ba7290 size:   80 previous size:   18  (Allocated)  Mdl
 89ba7310 size:   80 previous size:   80  (Allocated)  Mdl
 89ba7390 size:   30 previous size:   80  (Allocated)  Vad
 89ba73c0 size:   98 previous size:   30  (Allocated)  File (Protected)
 89ba7458 size:    8 previous size:   98  (Free)       Wait
 89ba7460 size:   28 previous size:    8  (Allocated)  FSfm
 89ba74a0 size:   40 previous size:   18  (Allocated)  Ntfr
 89ba74e0 size:    8 previous size:   40  (Free)       File
*89ba74e8 size:   a0 previous size:    8  (Free )     *ABCD
  Owning component : Unknown (update pooltag.txt)
 89ba7588 size:   38 previous size:   a0  (Allocated)  Sema (Protected)
 89ba75c0 size:   38 previous size:   38  (Allocated)  Sema (Protected)
 89ba75f8 size:   10 previous size:   38  (Free)       Nbtl
 89ba7608 size:   98 previous size:   10  (Allocated)  File (Protected)
 89ba76a0 size:   28 previous size:   98  (Allocated)  Ntfn
 89ba76c8 size:   40 previous size:   28  (Allocated)  Ntfr
 89ba7708 size:   28 previous size:   40  (Allocated)  NtFs
 89ba7730 size:   40 previous size:   28  (Allocated)  Ntfr
 89ba7770 size:   40 previous size:   40  (Allocated)  Ntfr
 89ba7a10 size:  270 previous size:  260  (Allocated)  Thre (Protected)
 89ba7c80 size:   20 previous size:  270  (Allocated)  VadS...
```

The pool tag is a 4-byte character sequence used to associate drivers with pool blocks and is useful to identify a driver allocated or freed a block. In our case, the pool tag is ABCD, and it is associated with the driver who previously freed the block. All known pool tags corresponding to kernel components can be found in pooltag.txt located in triage subfolder where WinDbg. Is installed. However, our ABCD tag is not listed there. We can try to find the driver corresponding to ABCD tag using **findstr** CMD command:

```
C:\Windows\System32\drivers>findstr /m /l ABCD *.sys
```

The results of the search help us to identify the driver that freed the block first. The driver which double freed the same block can be found on the call stack, and it may be the same driver or a different driver:

```
2: kd> k
ChildEBP RetAddr
f78be910 8089c8f4 nt!KeBugCheckEx+0x1b
f78be978 8089c622 nt!ExFreePoolWithTag+0x477
f78be988 f503968b nt!ExFreePool+0xf
WARNING: Stack unwind information not available. Following frames may be
wrong.
f78be990 f5024a6e driver+0x1768b
f78be9a0 f50249e7 driver+0x2a6e
f78be9a4 84b430e0 driver+0x29e7
```

Because we don't have symbol files for *driver.sys*, WinDbg warns us that it was unable to identify the correct stack trace and *driver.sys* might not have called *ExFreePool* or *ExFreePoolWithTag* function. To verify that *driver.sys* called *ExFreePool* function, we disassemble backward the return address of it:

```
2: kd> ub f503968b
driver+0x1767b:
f503967b 90              nop
f503967c 90              nop
f503967d 90              nop
f503967e 90              nop
f503967f 90              nop
f5039680 8b442404        mov     eax,dword ptr [esp+4]
f5039684 50              push    eax
f5039685 ff15202302f5    call    dword ptr [driver+0x320 (f5022320)]
```

Finally, we can get some info from the driver:

```
2: kd> lmv m driver
start    end        module name
f5022000 f503e400   driver   (no symbols)
    Loaded symbol image file: driver.sys
    Image path: \SystemRoot\System32\drivers\driver.sys
    Image name: driver.sys
    Timestamp:  Tue Aug 12 11:32:16 2007
```

If the name of a company that developed the driver is absent, we can try techniques outlined in **Unknown Component** pattern (page 367).

If we have symbols it is very easy to identify the code as can be seen from this 64-bit crash dump:

```
BAD_POOL_CALLER (c2)
The current thread is making a bad pool request. Typically this is at a
bad IRQL level or double freeing the same allocation, etc.
Arguments:
Arg1: 0000000000000007, Attempt to free pool which was already freed
Arg2: 000000000000121a, (reserved)
Arg3: 0000000000000080, Memory contents of the pool block
Arg4: fffffade6d54e270, Address of the block of pool being deallocated
```

```
0: kd> kL
fffffade`45517b08 fffff800`011ad905 nt!KeBugCheckEx
fffffade`45517b10 fffffade`5f5991ac nt!ExFreePoolWithTag+0x401
fffffade`45517bd0 fffffade`5f59a0b0 driver64!ProcessDataItem+0x198
fffffade`45517c70 fffffade`5f5885a6 driver64!OnDataArrival+0x2b4
fffffade`45517cd0 fffff800`01299cae driver64!ReaderThread+0x15a
fffffade`45517d70 fffff800`0102bbe6 nt!PspSystemThreadStartup+0x3e
fffffade`45517dd0 00000000`00000000 nt!KiStartSystemThread+0x16
```

Coincidental Symbolic Information

Raw stack dumps can be useful for finding any suspicious modules that might have caused the problem. For example, it is common for some programs to install hooks to monitor GUI changes, intercept window messages to provide value-added services on top of the existing applications. These hooks are implemented as DLLs. Another use would be to examine raw stack data for printer drivers that caused problems before. The fact that these modules had been loaded doesn't mean that they were used. If we find references to their code, it means that they might have been used.

However, when looking at raw stack dump with symbol information, we should be aware of **Coincidental Symbolic Information** pattern. Here is the first example. Loading the crash dump and displaying the problem thread stack shows the following reference:

```
...
...
...
00b1ed00  0063006f
00b1ed04  006d0075
00b1ed08  006e0065
00b1ed0c  00200074
00b1ed10  006f004c
00b1ed14  00640061
00b1ed18  00720065
00b1ed1c  005b0020
00b1ed20  00500055
00b1ed24  003a0044
00b1ed28  00430050 Application!Array::operator=+0x2f035
00b1ed2c  0035004c
00b1ed30  005d0063
00b1ed34  00630000
00b1ed38  0000005d
...
...
...
```

Applying symbols gives us more meaningful name:

```
...
...
...
00b1ed00  0063006f
00b1ed04  006d0075
00b1ed08  006e0065
00b1ed0c  00200074
00b1ed10  006f004c
00b1ed14  00640061
```

```
00b1ed18  00720065
00b1ed1c  005b0020
00b1ed20  00500055
00b1ed24  003a0044
00b1ed28  00430050 Application!Print::DocumentLoad+0x5f
00b1ed2c  0035004c
00b1ed30  005d0063
00b1ed34  00630000
...
...
...
```

However, this is the pure coincidence. The data pattern 00NN00NN clearly belongs to a Unicode string:

```
0:020> du 00b1ed00
00b1ed00  "ocument Loader [UPD:PCL5c]"
```

It just happens that 00430050 value can be interpreted as an address that falls within *Application* module address range and its code section:

```
0:020> lm
start    end         module name
00400000 0044d000   Application
```

In the second example, the crash dump is from some 3rd-party application called *AppSql* for which we don't have PDB files. Also, we know that *myhook.dll* is installed as a system-wide hook, and it had some problems in the past. It is loaded into any address space but is not necessarily used. We want to see if there are traces of it on the problem thread stack. Dumping stack contents shows us the only one reference:

```
...
...
...
00118cb0  37302f38
00118cb4  00000000
00118cb8  10008e00 myhook!notify_me+0x22c
00118cbc  01400000
00118cc0  00118abc
00118cc4  06a129f0
00118cc8  00118d04
00118ccc  02bc57d0
00118cd0  04ba5d74
00118cd4  00118d30
00118cd8  0000001c
00118cdc  00000010
00118ce0  075922bc
00118ce4  04a732e0
00118ce8  075922bc
```

```
00118cec  04a732e0
00118cf0  0066a831 AppSql+0x26a831
00118cf4  04a732d0
00118cf8  02c43190
00118cfc  00000001
00118d00  0000001c
00118d04  00118d14
00118d08  0049e180 AppSql+0x9e180
00118d0c  02c43190
00118d10  0000001c
00118d14  00118d34
...
...
...

0:020> lm
start    end        module name
00400000 00ba8000   AppSql
...
...
...
10000000 100e0000   myhook
```

The address 10008e00 looks very "round," and it might be the set of bit flags and also, if we disassemble the code at this address backward, we don't see the usual *call* instruction that saved that address on the stack:

```
0:000> ub 10008e00
myhook!notify_me+0x211
10008de5 81c180000000    add     ecx,80h
10008deb 899578ffffff    mov     dword ptr [ebp-88h],edx
10008df1 89458c          mov     dword ptr [ebp-74h],eax
10008df4 894d98          mov     dword ptr [ebp-68h],ecx
10008df7 6a01            push    1
10008df9 8d45ec          lea     eax,[ebp-14h]
10008dfc 50              push    eax
10008dfd ff75e0          push    dword ptr [ebp-20h]
```

In contrast, the other two addresses are return addresses saved on the stack:

```
0:000> ub 0066a831
AppSql+0x26a81e:
0066a81e 8bfb            mov     edi,ebx
0066a820 f3a5            rep movs dword ptr es:[edi],dword ptr [esi]
0066a822 8bca            mov     ecx,edx
0066a824 83e103          and     ecx,3
0066a827 f3a4            rep movs byte ptr es:[edi],byte ptr [esi]
0066a829 8b00            mov     eax,dword ptr [eax]
0066a82b 50              push    eax
0066a82c e8affeffff      call    AppSql+0x26a6e0 (0066a6e0)
```

```
0:000> ub 0049e180
AppSql+0x9e16f:
0049e16f cc              int     3
0049e170 55              push    ebp
0049e171 8bec            mov     ebp,esp
0049e173 8b4510          mov     eax,dword ptr [ebp+10h]
0049e176 8b4d0c          mov     ecx,dword ptr [ebp+0Ch]
0049e179 50              push    eax
0049e17a 51              push    ecx
0049e17b e840c61c00      call    AppSql+0x26a7c0 (0066a7c0)
```

Therefore, the appearance of *myhook!notify_me+0x22c* symbolic address could be a coincidence unless it was a pointer to a function. However, if it were a function pointer address then it wouldn't have pointed to the middle of the function call sequence that pushes arguments:

```
0:000> ub 10008e00
myhook!notify_me+0x211
10008de5 81c180000000    add     ecx,80h
10008deb 899578ffffff    mov     dword ptr [ebp-88h],edx
10008df1 89458c          mov     dword ptr [ebp-74h],eax
10008df4 894d98          mov     dword ptr [ebp-68h],ecx
10008df7 6a01            push    1
10008df9 8d45ec          lea     eax,[ebp-14h]
10008dfc 50              push    eax
10008dfd ff75e0          push    dword ptr [ebp-20h]
0:000> u 10008e00
myhook!notify_me+0x22c
10008e00 e82ff1ffff      call    myhook!copy_data (10007f34)
10008e05 8b8578ffffff    mov     eax,dword ptr [ebp-88h]
10008e0b 3945ac          cmp     dword ptr [ebp-54h],eax
10008e0e 731f            jae     myhook!notify_me+0x25b (10008e2f)
10008e10 8b4598          mov     eax,dword ptr [ebp-68h]
10008e13 0fbf00          movsx   eax,word ptr [eax]
10008e16 8945a8          mov     dword ptr [ebp-58h],eax
10008e19 8b45e0          mov     eax,dword ptr [ebp-20h]
```

Also, because we have the source code and private symbols, we know that if it were a function pointer, then it would have been *myhook!notify*_me address and not *notify_me+0x22c* address.

All this evidence supports the hypothesis that *myhook* occurrence in the problem stack region is just the coincidence and should be ignored.

To add, the most coincidental symbolic information I have found so far in one crash dump is an accidental correspondence between exported *_DebuggerHookData* and the location of the postmortem debugger NTSD:

```
002dd434 003a0043
002dd438 0057005c
002dd43c 004e0049 LegacyApp!_DebuggerHookData+0xc4a5
002dd440 004f0044 LegacyApp!_DebuggerHookData+0x1c4a0
002dd444 00530057
002dd448 0073005c
002dd44c 00730079
002dd450 00650074
002dd454 0033006d
002dd458 005c0032
002dd45c 0074006e
002dd460 00640073
002dd464 0065002e
002dd468 00650078

0:000> du 002dd434
002dd434 "C:\WINDOWS\system32\ntsd.exe"
```

Stack Trace

The most important pattern that is used for problem identification and resolution is **Stack Trace**. Consider the following fragment of **!analyze -v** output from *w3wp.exe* crash dump:

```
STACK_TEXT:
WARNING: Frame IP not in any known module. Following frames may be wrong.
1824f90c 5a39f97e 01057b48 01057bd0 5a3215b4 0x0
1824fa50 5a32cf7c 01057b48 00000000 79e651c0
w3core!ISAPI_REQUEST::SendResponseHeaders+0x5d
1824fa78 5a3218ad 01057bd0 79e651c0 79e64d9c
w3isapi!SSFSendResponseHeader+0xe0
1824fae8 79e76127 01057bd0 00000003 79e651c0
w3isapi!ServerSupportFunction+0x351
1824fb0c 79e763a3 80000411 00000000 00000000
aspnet_isapi!HttpCompletion::ReportHttpError+0x3a
1824fd50 79e761c3 34df6cf8 79e8e42f 79e8e442
aspnet_isapi!HttpCompletion::ProcessRequestInManagedCode+0x1d1
1824fd5c 79e8e442 34df6cf8 00000000 00000000
aspnet_isapi!HttpCompletion::ProcessCompletion+0x24
1824fd70 791d6211 34df6cf8 18e60110 793ee0d8
aspnet_isapi!CorThreadPoolWorkitemCallback+0x13
1824fd84 791d616a 18e60110 00000000 791d60fa
mscorsvr!ThreadpoolMgr::ExecuteWorkRequest+0x19
1824fda4 791fe95c 00000000 8083d5c7 00000000
mscorsvr!ThreadpoolMgr::WorkerThreadStart+0x129
1824ffb8 77e64829 17bb9c18 00000000 00000000
mscorsvr!ThreadpoolMgr::intermediateThreadProc+0x44
1824ffec 00000000 791fe91b 17bb9c18 00000000 kernel32!BaseThreadStart+0x34
```

Ignoring the first 5 numeric columns gives us the following trace:

```
0x0
w3core!ISAPI_REQUEST::SendResponseHeaders+0x5d
w3isapi!SSFSendResponseHeader+0xe0
w3isapi!ServerSupportFunction+0x351
aspnet_isapi!HttpCompletion::ReportHttpError+0x3a
aspnet_isapi!HttpCompletion::ProcessRequestInManagedCode+0x1d1
aspnet_isapi!HttpCompletion::ProcessCompletion+0x24
aspnet_isapi!CorThreadPoolWorkitemCallback+0x13
mscorsvr!ThreadpoolMgr::ExecuteWorkRequest+0x19
mscorsvr!ThreadpoolMgr::WorkerThreadStart+0x129
mscorsvr!ThreadpoolMgr::intermediateThreadProc+0x44
kernel32!BaseThreadStart+0x34
```

In general, we have something like this:

```
moduleA!functionX+offsetN
moduleB!functionY+offsetM
...
...
...
```

Sometimes function names are not available, or offsets are huge like 0x2380. If this is the case, then we probably don't have symbol files for *moduleA* and *moduleB*:

```
moduleA+offsetN
moduleB+offsetM
...
...
...
```

Usually, there is some kind of a database of previous issues we can use to match *moduleA!functionX+offsetN* against. If there is no such match we can try *functionX+offsetN*, *moduleA!functionX* or just *functionX*. If there is no such match again, we can try the next signature, *moduleB!functionY+offsetM*, and *moduleB!functionY*. Usually, the further in the trace, the less useful the signature is for problem resolution. For example, *mscorsvr!ThreadpoolMgr::WorkerThreadStart+0x129* probably matches many issues because this signature is common for many ASP.NET applications.

If there is no match in internal databases, we can try Google. For our example, Google search for *SendResponseHeaders+0x5d* gives the following search results:

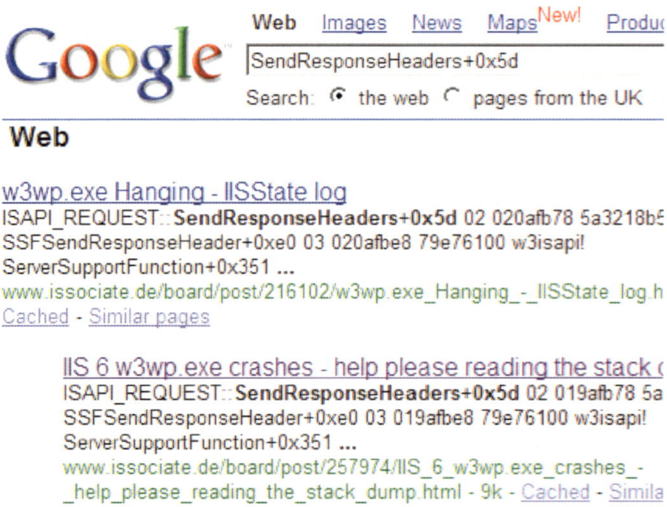

Browsing search results reveals the following discussion:

http://groups.google.com/group/microsoft.public.inetserver.iis/browse_frm/thread/34bc2be635b26531?tvc=1

which can be found directly by searching Google groups:

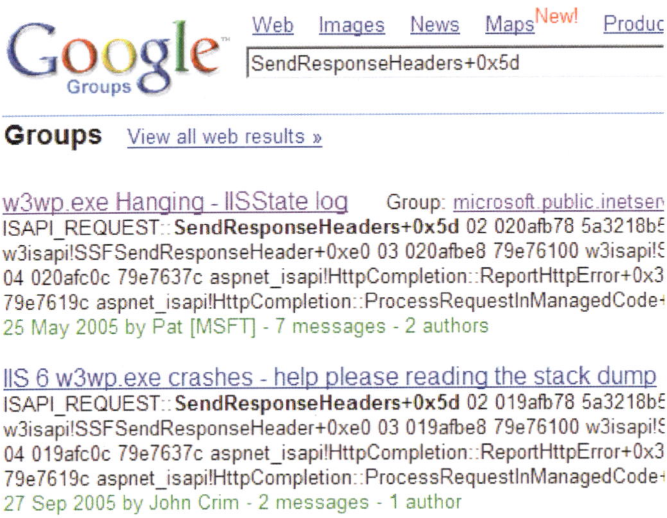

Another example is from BSOD complete memory dump. Analysis command has the following output:

```
MODE_EXCEPTION_NOT_HANDLED (1e)
This is a very common bugcheck. Usually the exception address pinpoints
the driver/function that caused the problem. Always note this address as
well as the link date of the driver/image that contains this address.
Arguments:
Arg1: c0000005, The exception code that was not handled
Arg2: bff90ca3, The address that the exception occurred at
Arg3: 00000000, Parameter 0 of the exception
Arg4: 00000000, Parameter 1 of the exception
```

```
TRAP_FRAME: bdf80834 -- (.trap ffffffffbdf80834)
ErrCode = 00000000
eax=00000000 ebx=bdf80c34 ecx=89031870 edx=88096928 esi=88096928
edi=8905e7f0
eip=bff90ca3 esp=bdf808a8 ebp=bdf80a44 iopl=0 nv up ei ng nz na po nc
cs=0008 ss=0010 ds=0023 es=0023 fs=0030 gs=0000 efl=00010282
tsmlvsa+0xfca3:
bff90ca3 8b08 mov ecx,dword ptr [eax] ds:0023:00000000=????????
Resetting default scope

STACK_TEXT:
bdf807c4 80467a15 bdf807e0 00000000 bdf80834 nt!KiDispatchException+0x30e
bdf8082c 804679c6 00000000 bdf80860 804d9f69
nt!CommonDispatchException+0x4d
bdf80838 804d9f69 00000000 00000005 e56c6946
nt!KiUnexpectedInterruptTail+0x207
00000000 00000000 00000000 00000000 00000000 nt!ObpAllocateObject+0xe1
```

Because the crash point *tsmlvsa+0xfca3* is not in the stack trace we use **.trap** command:

```
1: kd> .trap ffffffffbdf80834
ErrCode = 00000000
eax=00000000 ebx=bdf80c34 ecx=89031870 edx=88096928 esi=88096928
edi=8905e7f0
eip=bff90ca3 esp=bdf808a8 ebp=bdf80a44 iopl=0 nv up ei ng nz na po nc
cs=0008 ss=0010 ds=0023 es=0023 fs=0030 gs=0000 efl=00010282
tsmlvsa+0xfca3:
bff90ca3 8b08 mov ecx,dword ptr [eax] ds:0023:00000000=????????

1: kd> k
*** Stack trace for last set context - .thread/.cxr resets it
ChildEBP RetAddr
WARNING: Stack unwind information not available. Following frames may be
wrong.
00000000 bdf80afc tsmlvsa+0xfca3
89080c00 00000040 nt!ObpLookupObjectName+0x504
00000000 00000001 nt!ObOpenObjectByName+0xc5
c0100080 0012b8d8 nt!IopCreateFile+0x407
c0100080 0012b8d8 nt!IoCreateFile+0x36
c0100080 0012b8d8 nt!NtCreateFile+0x2e
c0100080 0012b8d8 nt!KiSystemService+0xc9
c0100080 0012b8d8 ntdll!NtCreateFile+0xb
c0000000 00000000 KERNEL32!CreateFileW+0x343
```

```
1: kd> lmv m tsmlvsa
bff81000 bff987c0 tsmlvsa (no symbols)
Loaded symbol image file: tsmlvsa.sys
Image path: tsmlvsa.sys
Image name: tsmlvsa.sys
Timestamp: Thu Mar 18 06:18:51 2004 (40593F4B)
CheckSum: 0002D102
ImageSize: 000177C0
Translations: 0000.04b0 0000.04e0 0409.04b0 0409.04e0
```

Google search for *tsmlvsa+0xfca3* fails, but if we search just for *tsmlvsa*, we get some links towards problem resolution.

Virtualized Process (WOW64)

Sometimes we get a process dump from x64 Windows, and when we load it into WinDbg, we get the output telling us that an exception or a breakpoint comes from *wow64.dll*. For example:

```
Loading Dump File [X:\ppid2088.dmp]
User Mini Dump File with Full Memory: Only application data is available

Comment: 'Userdump generated complete user-mode minidump with Exception
Monitor function on SERVER01'
Symbol search path is:
srv*c:\mss*http://msdl.microsoft.com/download/symbols
Executable search path is:
Windows Server 2003 Version 3790 (Service Pack 2) MP (4 procs) Free x64
Product: Server, suite: TerminalServer
Debug session time: Tue Sep  4 13:36:14.000 2007 (GMT+2)
System Uptime: 6 days 3:32:26.081
Process Uptime: 0 days 0:01:54.000
WARNING: tsappcmp overlaps ws2_32
WARNING: msvcp60 overlaps oleacc
WARNING: tapi32 overlaps rasapi32
WARNING: rtutils overlaps rasman
WARNING: dnsapi overlaps rasapi32
WARNING: wldap32 overlaps dnsapi
WARNING: ntshrui overlaps userenv
WARNING: wtsapi32 overlaps dnsapi
WARNING: winsta overlaps setupapi
WARNING: activeds overlaps rtutils
WARNING: activeds overlaps rasman
WARNING: adsldpc overlaps activeds
WARNING: drprov overlaps apphelp
WARNING: netui1 overlaps netui0
WARNING: davclnt overlaps apphelp
...
This dump file has an exception of interest stored in it.
The stored exception information can be accessed via .ecxr.
(2088.2fe4): Unknown exception - code 000006d9 (first/second chance not
available)
wow64!Wow64NotifyDebugger+0x9:
00000000`6b006369 b001            mov     al,1
```

The analysis shows that the run-time exception was raised, but the stack trace shows only WOW64 CPU simulation code in all process threads:

```
0:000> !analyze -v
*******************************************************************************
*                                                                             *
*                        Exception Analysis                                   *
*                                                                             *
*******************************************************************************

FAULTING_IP:
kernel32!RaiseException+53
00000000`7d4e2366 5e              pop     rsi

EXCEPTION_RECORD:  ffffffffffffffff -- (.exr 0xffffffffffffffff)
ExceptionAddress: 000000007d4e2366
(kernel32!RaiseException+0x0000000000000053)
   ExceptionCode: 000006d9
  ExceptionFlags: 00000001
NumberParameters: 0

DEFAULT_BUCKET_ID:  STACK_CORRUPTION

PROCESS_NAME:  App.exe

ERROR_CODE: (NTSTATUS) 0x6d9 - There are no more endpoints available from
the endpoint mapper.

NTGLOBALFLAG:  0

APPLICATION_VERIFIER_FLAGS:  0

LAST_CONTROL_TRANSFER:  from 000000006b0064f2 to 000000006b006369

FOLLOWUP_IP:
wow64!Wow64NotifyDebugger+9
00000000`6b006369 b001            mov     al,1

SYMBOL_STACK_INDEX:  0

SYMBOL_NAME:  wow64!Wow64NotifyDebugger+9

FOLLOWUP_NAME:  MachineOwner

MODULE_NAME: wow64

IMAGE_NAME:  wow64.dll

DEBUG_FLR_IMAGE_TIMESTAMP:  45d6943d

FAULTING_THREAD:  0000000000002fe4
```

```
PRIMARY_PROBLEM_CLASS:  STACK_CORRUPTION

BUGCHECK_STR:  APPLICATION_FAULT_STACK_CORRUPTION

STACK_COMMAND:  ~0s; .ecxr ; dt ntdll!LdrpLastDllInitializer BaseDllName ;
dt ntdll!LdrpFailureData ; kb

FAILURE_BUCKET_ID:  X64_APPLICATION_FAULT_STACK_CORRUPTION_wow64!Wow64Noti
fyDebugger+9

BUCKET_ID:  X64_APPLICATION_FAULT_STACK_CORRUPTION_wow64!Wow64NotifyDebugg
er+9

Followup: MachineOwner
---------

0:000> ~*k

.  0  Id: 2088.2fe4 Suspend: 1 Teb: 00000000`7efdb000 Unfrozen
Child-SP          RetAddr           Call Site
00000000`0016e190 00000000`6b0064f2 wow64!Wow64NotifyDebugger+0x9
00000000`0016e1c0 00000000`6b006866 wow64!Wow64KiRaiseException+0x172
00000000`0016e530 00000000`78b83c7d wow64!Wow64SystemServiceEx+0xd6
00000000`0016edf0 00000000`6b006a5a wow64cpu!ServiceNoTurbo+0x28
00000000`0016ee80 00000000`6b005e0d wow64!RunCpuSimulation+0xa
00000000`0016eeb0 00000000`77ed8030 wow64!Wow64LdrpInitialize+0x2ed
00000000`0016f3f0 00000000`77ed582f ntdll!LdrpInitializeProcess+0x1538
00000000`0016f6f0 00000000`77ef30a5 ntdll!LdrpInitialize+0x18f
00000000`0016f7d0 00000000`7d4d1510 ntdll!KiUserApcDispatcher+0x15
00000000`0016fcc8 00000000`00000000 kernel32!BaseProcessStartThunk
00000000`0016fcd0 00000000`00000000 0x0
00000000`0016fcd8 00000000`00000000 0x0
00000000`0016fce0 00000000`00000000 0x0
00000000`0016fce8 00000000`00000000 0x0
00000000`0016fcf0 00000000`00000000 0x0
00000000`0016fcf8 00000000`00000000 0x0
00000000`0016fd00 00010007`00000000 0x0
00000000`0016fd08 00000000`00000000 0x10007`00000000
00000000`0016fd10 00000000`00000000 0x0
00000000`0016fd18 00000000`00000000 0x0

   1  Id: 2088.280c Suspend: 1 Teb: 00000000`7efd8000 Unfrozen
Child-SP          RetAddr           Call Site
00000000`0200f0d8 00000000`6b006a5a wow64cpu!WaitForMultipleObjects32+0x3a
00000000`0200f180 00000000`6b005e0d wow64!RunCpuSimulation+0xa
00000000`0200f1b0 00000000`77f109f0 wow64!Wow64LdrpInitialize+0x2ed
00000000`0200f6f0 00000000`77ef30a5 ntdll!LdrpInitialize+0x2aa
00000000`0200f7d0 00000000`7d4d1504 ntdll!KiUserApcDispatcher+0x15
00000000`0200fcc8 00000000`00000000 kernel32!BaseThreadStartThunk
00000000`0200fcd0 00000000`00000000 0x0
00000000`0200fcd8 00000000`00000000 0x0
```

```
00000000`0200fce0 00000000`00000000 0x0
00000000`0200fce8 00000000`00000000 0x0
00000000`0200fcf0 00000000`00000000 0x0
00000000`0200fcf8 00000000`00000000 0x0
00000000`0200fd00 0001002f`00000000 0x0
00000000`0200fd08 00000000`00000000 0x1002f`00000000
00000000`0200fd10 00000000`00000000 0x0
00000000`0200fd18 00000000`00000000 0x0
00000000`0200fd20 00000000`00000000 0x0
00000000`0200fd28 00000000`00000000 0x0
00000000`0200fd30 00000000`00000000 0x0
00000000`0200fd38 00000000`00000000 0x0

   2  Id: 2088.1160 Suspend: 1 Teb: 00000000`7efd5000 Unfrozen
Child-SP          RetAddr           Call Site
00000000`0272e7c8 00000000`6b29c464 wow64win!ZwUserGetMessage+0xa
00000000`0272e7d0 00000000`6b006866 wow64win!whNtUserGetMessage+0x34
00000000`0272e830 00000000`78b83c7d wow64!Wow64SystemServiceEx+0xd6
00000000`0272f0f0 00000000`6b006a5a wow64cpu!ServiceNoTurbo+0x28
00000000`0272f180 00000000`6b005e0d wow64!RunCpuSimulation+0xa
00000000`0272f1b0 00000000`77f109f0 wow64!Wow64LdrpInitialize+0x2ed
00000000`0272f6f0 00000000`77ef30a5 ntdll!LdrpInitialize+0x2aa
00000000`0272f7d0 00000000`7d4d1504 ntdll!KiUserApcDispatcher+0x15
00000000`0272fcc8 00000000`00000000 kernel32!BaseThreadStartThunk
00000000`0272fcd0 00000000`00000000 0x0
00000000`0272fcd8 00000000`00000000 0x0
00000000`0272fce0 00000000`00000000 0x0
00000000`0272fce8 00000000`00000000 0x0
00000000`0272fcf0 00000000`00000000 0x0
00000000`0272fcf8 00000000`00000000 0x0
00000000`0272fd00 00010003`00000000 0x0
00000000`0272fd08 00000000`00000000 0x10003`00000000
00000000`0272fd10 00000000`00000000 0x0
00000000`0272fd18 00000000`00000000 0x0
00000000`0272fd20 00000000`00000000 0x0

   3  Id: 2088.2d04 Suspend: 1 Teb: 00000000`7efad000 Unfrozen
Child-SP          RetAddr           Call Site
00000000`0289f108 00000000`78b84191 wow64cpu!CpupSyscallStub+0x9
00000000`0289f110 00000000`6b006a5a
wow64cpu!Thunk2ArgNSpNSpReloadState+0x21
00000000`0289f180 00000000`6b005e0d wow64!RunCpuSimulation+0xa
00000000`0289f1b0 00000000`77f109f0 wow64!Wow64LdrpInitialize+0x2ed
00000000`0289f6f0 00000000`77ef30a5 ntdll!LdrpInitialize+0x2aa
00000000`0289f7d0 00000000`7d4d1504 ntdll!KiUserApcDispatcher+0x15
00000000`0289fcc8 00000000`00000000 kernel32!BaseThreadStartThunk
00000000`0289fcd0 00000000`00000000 0x0
00000000`0289fcd8 00000000`00000000 0x0
00000000`0289fce0 00000000`00000000 0x0
00000000`0289fce8 00000000`00000000 0x0
00000000`0289fcf0 00000000`00000000 0x0
00000000`0289fcf8 00000000`00000000 0x0
00000000`0289fd00 0001002f`00000000 0x0
```

```
00000000`0289fd08 00000000`00000000 0x1002f`00000000
00000000`0289fd10 00000000`00000000 0x0
00000000`0289fd18 00000000`00000000 0x0
00000000`0289fd20 00000000`00000000 0x0
00000000`0289fd28 00000000`00000000 0x0
00000000`0289fd30 00000000`00000000 0x0

   4  Id: 2088.15c4 Suspend: 1 Teb: 00000000`7efa4000 Unfrozen
Child-SP          RetAddr           Call Site
00000000`02def0a8 00000000`6b006a5a wow64cpu!RemoveIoCompletionFault+0x41
00000000`02def180 00000000`6b005e0d wow64!RunCpuSimulation+0xa
00000000`02def1b0 00000000`77f109f0 wow64!Wow64LdrpInitialize+0x2ed
00000000`02def6f0 00000000`77ef30a5 ntdll!LdrpInitialize+0x2aa
00000000`02def7d0 00000000`7d4d1504 ntdll!KiUserApcDispatcher+0x15
00000000`02defcc8 00000000`00000000 kernel32!BaseThreadStartThunk
00000000`02defcd0 00000000`00000000 0x0
00000000`02defcd8 00000000`00000000 0x0
00000000`02defce0 00000000`00000000 0x0
00000000`02defce8 00000000`00000000 0x0
00000000`02defcf0 00000000`00000000 0x0
00000000`02defcf8 00000000`00000000 0x0
00000000`02defd00 0001002f`00000000 0x0
00000000`02defd08 00000000`00000000 0x1002f`00000000
00000000`02defd10 00000000`00000000 0x0
00000000`02defd18 00000000`00000000 0x0
00000000`02defd20 00000000`00000000 0x0
00000000`02defd28 00000000`00000000 0x0
00000000`02defd30 00000000`00000000 0x0
00000000`02defd38 00000000`00000000 0x0
```

This is a clear indication that the process was, in fact, 32-bit, but the dump is 64-bit. This situation is depicted in the article **Dumps, Debuggers, and Virtualization** (page 516), and we need a debugger plug-in to understand virtualized CPU architecture.

This crash dump pattern can be called **Virtualized Process**. In our case, we need to load *wow64exts.dll* WinDbg extension and set the target processor mode to x86 by using **.effmach** command

```
0:000> .load wow64exts

0:000> .effmach x86
Effective machine: x86 compatible (x86)
```

Then analysis gives us more meaningful results:

```
0:000:x86> !analyze -v
*******************************************************
*                                                     *
*                Exception Analysis                   *
*                                                     *
*******************************************************


FAULTING_IP:
kernel32!RaiseException+53
00000000`7d4e2366 5e              pop     esi

EXCEPTION_RECORD:  ffffffffffffffff -- (.exr 0xffffffffffffffff)
ExceptionAddress: 000000007d4e2366
(kernel32!RaiseException+0x0000000000000053)
   ExceptionCode: 000006d9
  ExceptionFlags: 00000001
NumberParameters: 0

BUGCHECK_STR:  6d9

DEFAULT_BUCKET_ID:  APPLICATION_FAULT

PROCESS_NAME:  App.exe

ERROR_CODE: (NTSTATUS) 0x6d9 - There are no more endpoints available from
the endpoint mapper.

NTGLOBALFLAG:  0

APPLICATION_VERIFIER_FLAGS:  0

LAST_CONTROL_TRANSFER:  from 000000007da4a631 to 000000007d4e2366

STACK_TEXT:
0012d98c 7da4a631 kernel32!RaiseException+0x53
0012d9a4 7da4a5f7 rpcrt4!RpcpRaiseException+0x24
0012d9b4 7dac0140 rpcrt4!NdrGetBuffer+0x46
0012dda0 5f2a2fba rpcrt4!NdrClientCall2+0x197
0012ddbc 5f29c6a6 hnetcfg!FwOpenDynamicFwPort+0x1d
0012de68 7db4291f hnetcfg!IcfOpenDynamicFwPort+0x6a
0012df00 71c043db mswsock!WSPBind+0x2e3
WARNING: Frame IP not in any known module. Following frames may be wrong.
0012df24 76ed91c8 ws2_32+0x43db
0012df6c 76ed9128 rasapi32+0x491c8
0012df98 76ed997c rasapi32+0x49128
0012dfc0 76ed8ac2 rasapi32+0x4997c
0012dfd4 76ed89cd rasapi32+0x48ac2
0012dff0 76ed82e5 rasapi32+0x489cd
```

```
0012e010 76ed827f rasapi32+0x482e5
0012e044 76ed8bf0 rasapi32+0x4827f
0012e0c8 76ed844d rasapi32+0x48bf0
0012e170 76ed74b5 rasapi32+0x4844d
0012e200 76ed544f rasapi32+0x474b5
0012e22c 76ed944d rasapi32+0x4544f
0012e24c 76ed93a4 rasapi32+0x4944d
0012e298 76ed505f rasapi32+0x493a4
0012e2bc 7db442bf rasapi32+0x4505f
0012e2ec 7db4418b mswsock!SaBlob_Query+0x2d
0012e330 7db4407c mswsock!Rnr_DoDnsLookup+0xf0
0012e5c8 71c06dc0 mswsock!Dns_NSPLookupServiceNext+0x24b
0012e5e0 71c06da0 ws2_32+0x6dc0
0012e5fc 71c06d6a ws2_32+0x6da0
0012e628 71c06d08 ws2_32+0x6d6a
0012e648 71c08282 ws2_32+0x6d08
0012ef00 71c07f68 ws2_32+0x8282
0012ef34 71c08433 ws2_32+0x7f68
0012efa0 71c03236 ws2_32+0x8433
0012f094 71c03340 ws2_32+0x3236
0012f0bc 7dab22fb ws2_32+0x3340
0012f11c 7dab3a0e rpcrt4!IP_ADDRESS_RESOLVER::NextAddress+0x13e
0012f238 7dab3c11 rpcrt4!TCPOrHTTP_Open+0xdb
0012f270 7da44c85 rpcrt4!TCP_Open+0x55
0012f2b8 7da44b53 rpcrt4!OSF_CCONNECTION::TransOpen+0x5e
0012f31c 7da447d7 rpcrt4!OSF_CCONNECTION::OpenConnectionAndBind+0xbe
0012f360 7da44720 rpcrt4!OSF_CCALL::BindToServer+0xfa
0012f378 7da3a9df rpcrt4!OSF_BINDING_HANDLE::InitCCallWithAssociation+0x63
0012f3f4 7da3a8dd rpcrt4!OSF_BINDING_HANDLE::AllocateCCall+0x49d
0012f428 7da37a1c rpcrt4!OSF_BINDING_HANDLE::NegotiateTransferSyntax+0x2e
0012f440 7da3642c rpcrt4!I_RpcGetBufferWithObject+0x5b
0012f450 7da37bff rpcrt4!I_RpcGetBuffer+0xf
0012f460 7dac0140 rpcrt4!NdrGetBuffer+0x2e
0012f84c 766f41f1 rpcrt4!NdrClientCall2+0x197
0012f864 766f40b8 ntdsapi!_IDL_DRSBind+0x1c
0012f930 7d8ecaa2 ntdsapi!DsBindWithSpnExW+0x223
0012f9b0 7d8ed028 secur32!SecpTranslateName+0x1f3
0012f9d0 00434aa0 secur32!TranslateNameW+0x2d
0012fab4 00419a7f App+0x34aa0
0012fb0c 0041a61b App+0x19a7f
0012fbc0 0045a293 App+0x1a61b
0012fbc8 0043682f App+0x5a293
0012fbcc 004188f3 App+0x3682f
0043682f 00000000 App+0x188f3

STACK_COMMAND:  kb

FOLLOWUP_IP:
hnetcfg!FwOpenDynamicFwPort+1d
00000000`5f2a2fba 83c40c          add     esp,0Ch

SYMBOL_STACK_INDEX:  4
```

```
SYMBOL_NAME:  hnetcfg!FwOpenDynamicFwPort+1d

FOLLOWUP_NAME:  MachineOwner

MODULE_NAME: hnetcfg

IMAGE_NAME:  hnetcfg.dll

DEBUG_FLR_IMAGE_TIMESTAMP:  45d6cc2a

FAULTING_THREAD:  0000000000002fe4

FAILURE_BUCKET_ID:  X64_6d9_hnetcfg!FwOpenDynamicFwPort+1d

BUCKET_ID:  X64_6d9_hnetcfg!FwOpenDynamicFwPort+1d

Followup: MachineOwner
---------

0:000:x86> ~*k

.  0  Id: 2088.2fe4 Suspend: 1 Teb: 00000000`7efdb000 Unfrozen
ChildEBP         RetAddr
0012d98c 7da4a631 kernel32!RaiseException+0x53
0012d9a4 7da4a5f7 rpcrt4!RpcpRaiseException+0x24
0012d9b4 7dac0140 rpcrt4!NdrGetBuffer+0x46
0012dda0 5f2a2fba rpcrt4!NdrClientCall2+0x197
0012ddbc 5f29c6a6 hnetcfg!FwOpenDynamicFwPort+0x1d
0012de68 7db4291f hnetcfg!IcfOpenDynamicFwPort+0x6a
0012df00 71c043db mswsock!WSPBind+0x2e3
WARNING: Frame IP not in any known module. Following frames may be wrong.
0012df24 76ed91c8 ws2_32+0x43db
0012df6c 76ed9128 rasapi32+0x491c8
0012df98 76ed997c rasapi32+0x49128
0012dfc0 76ed8ac2 rasapi32+0x4997c
0012dfd4 76ed89cd rasapi32+0x48ac2
0012dff0 76ed82e5 rasapi32+0x489cd
0012e010 76ed827f rasapi32+0x482e5
0012e044 76ed8bf0 rasapi32+0x4827f
0012e0c8 76ed844d rasapi32+0x48bf0
0012e170 76ed74b5 rasapi32+0x4844d
0012e200 76ed544f rasapi32+0x474b5
0012e22c 76ed944d rasapi32+0x4544f
0012e24c 76ed93a4 rasapi32+0x4944d
```

```
   1  Id: 2088.280c Suspend: 1 Teb: 00000000`7efd8000 Unfrozen
ChildEBP          RetAddr
01fcfea4 7d63f501 ntdll_7d600000!NtWaitForMultipleObjects+0x15
01fcff48 7d63f988 ntdll_7d600000!EtwpWaitForMultipleObjectsEx+0xf7
01fcffb8 7d4dfe21 ntdll_7d600000!EtwpEventPump+0x27f
01fcffec 00000000 kernel32!BaseThreadStart+0x34

   2  Id: 2088.1160 Suspend: 1 Teb: 00000000`7efd5000 Unfrozen
ChildEBP          RetAddr
026eff50 0042f13b user32!NtUserGetMessage+0x15
WARNING: Stack unwind information not available. Following frames may be
wrong.
026effb8 7d4dfe21 App+0x2f13b
026effec 00000000 kernel32!BaseThreadStart+0x34

   3  Id: 2088.2d04 Suspend: 1 Teb: 00000000`7efad000 Unfrozen
ChildEBP          RetAddr
0285ffa0 7d634d69 ntdll_7d600000!ZwDelayExecution+0x15
0285ffb8 7d4dfe21 ntdll_7d600000!RtlpTimerThread+0x47
0285ffec 00000000 kernel32!BaseThreadStart+0x34

   4  Id: 2088.15c4 Suspend: 1 Teb: 00000000`7efa4000 Unfrozen
ChildEBP          RetAddr
02daff80 7db4b6c6 ntdll_7d600000!NtRemoveIoCompletion+0x15
02daffb8 7d4dfe21 mswsock!SockAsyncThread+0x69
02daffec 00000000 kernel32!BaseThreadStart+0x34
```

Stack Trace Collection (Unmanaged Space)

Sometimes a problem can be identified not from a single **Stack Trace** pattern but a **Stack Trace Collection**.

These include **Coupled Processes** (page 419), **Procedure Call Chains** (page 482), and **Blocked Threads** (see Volume 2). Here I only discuss various methods to list stack traces.

- Process dumps, including various process minidumps:

  ~*kv command lists all process threads.

  !findstack *module[!symbol]* **2** command filters all stack traces to show ones containing *module* or *module!symbol.*

  !uniqstack command.

- Kernel minidumps:

  have only one problem thread. **kv** command or its variant is sufficed.

- Kernel and complete memory dumps:

  !process 0 3f command lists all processes and their threads including user space process thread stacks for complete memory dumps. This command is valid for Windows XP and later. For older systems, we can use WinDbg scripts.

  !stacks 2 *[module[!symbol]]* command shows kernel mode stack traces, and we can filter the output based on *module* or *module!symbol.* Filtering is valid only for crash dumps from Windows XP and later systems.

  *~[ProcessorN]***s;.reload /user;kv** command sequence shows the stack trace for the running thread on the specified processor.

The processor change command is illustrated in this example:

```
0: kd> ~2s


2: kd> k
ChildEBP RetAddr
eb42bd58 00000000 nt!KiIdleLoop+0x14


2: kd> ~1s;.reload /user;k
Loading User Symbols
...
ChildEBP RetAddr
be4f8c30 eb091f43 i8042prt!I8xProcessCrashDump+0x53
be4f8c8c 8046bfe2 i8042prt!I8042KeyboardInterruptService+0x15d
be4f8c8c 8049470f nt!KiInterruptDispatch+0x32
be4f8d54 80468389 nt!NtSetEvent+0x71
be4f8d54 77f8290a nt!KiSystemService+0xc9
081cfefc 77f88266 ntdll!ZwSetEvent+0xb
081cff0c 77f881b1 ntdll!RtlpUnWaitCriticalSection+0x1b
081cff14 1b00c7d1 ntdll!RtlLeaveCriticalSection+0x1d
081cff4c 1b0034da msjet40!Database::ReadPages+0x81
081cffb4 7c57b3bc msjet40!System::WorkerThread+0x115
081cffec 00000000 KERNEL32!BaseThreadStart+0x52
```

Example of **!findstack** command (process dump):

```
0:000> !findstack kernel32!RaiseException 2
Thread 000, 1 frame(s) match
* 00 0013b3f8 72e8d3ef kernel32!RaiseException+0x53
  01 0013b418 72e9a26b msxml3!Exception::raiseException+0x5f
  02 0013b424 72e8ff00 msxml3!Exception::_throwError+0x22
  03 0013b46c 72e6abaa msxml3!COMSafeControlRoot::getBaseURL+0x3d
  04 0013b4bc 72e6a888 msxml3!Document::loadXML+0x82
  05 0013b510 64b73a9b msxml3!DOMDocumentWrapper::loadXML+0x5a
  06 0013b538 64b74eb6 iepeers!CPersistUserData::initXMLCache+0xa6
  07 0013b560 77d0516e iepeers!CPersistUserData::load+0xfc
  08 0013b57c 77d14abf oleaut32!DispCallFunc+0x16a
...
...
...
  66 0013fec8 0040243d shdocvw!IEWinMain+0x129
  67 0013ff1c 00402744 iexplore!WinMain+0x316
  68 0013ffc0 77e6f23b iexplore!WinMainCRTStartup+0x182
  69 0013fff0 00000000 kernel32!BaseProcessStart+0x23
```

Example of **!stacks** command (kernel dump):

```
2: kd> !stacks 2 nt!PspExitThread
Proc.Thread  .Thread  Ticks   ThreadState Blocker
                            [8a390818 System]

                            [8a1bbbf8 smss.exe]

                            [8a16cbf8 csrss.exe]

                            [89c14bf0 winlogon.exe]

                            [89dda630 services.exe]

                            [89c23af0 lsass.exe]

                            [8a227470 svchost.exe]

                            [89f03bb8 svchost.exe]

                            [89de3820 svchost.exe]

                            [89d09b60 svchost.exe]

                            [89c03530 ccEvtMgr.exe]

                            [89b8f4f0 ccSetMgr.exe]

                            [89dfe8c0 SPBBCSvc.exe]

                            [89c9db18 svchost.exe]

                            [89dfa268 spoolsv.exe]

                            [89dfa6b8 msdtc.exe]

                            [89df38f0 CpSvc.exe]

                            [89d97d88 DefWatch.exe]

                            [89e04020 IBMSPSVC.EXE]

                            [89b54710 IBMSPREM.EXE]

                            [89d9e4b0 IBMSPREM.EXE]
```

```
[89c2c4e8 svchost.exe]

[89d307c0 SavRoam.exe]

[89bfcd88 Rtvscan.exe]

[89b53b60 uphclean.exe]

[89c24020 AgentSVC.exe]

[89d75b60 sAginst.exe]

[89cf0d88 CdfSvc.exe]

[89d87020 cdmsvc.exe]

[89dafd88 ctxxmlss.exe]

[89d8dd88 encsvc.exe]

[89d06d88 ImaSrv.exe]

[89d37b60 mfcom.exe]

[89c8bb18 SmaService.exe]

[89d2ba80 svchost.exe]

[89ce8630 XTE.exe]

[89b64b60 XTE.exe]

[89b7c680 ctxcpusched.exe]

[88d94a88 ctxcpuusync.exe]

[89ba5418 unsecapp.exe]

[89d846e0 wmiprvse.exe]

[89cda9d8 ctxwmisvc.exe]

[88d6cb78 logon.scr]

[88ba0a70 csrss.exe]
```

```
                                [88961968 winlogon.exe]

                                [8865f740 rdpclip.exe]

                                [8858db20 wfshell.exe]

                                [88754020 explorer.exe]

                                [88846d88 BacsTray.exe]

                                [886b6180 ccApp.exe]

                                [884bc020 fppdis3a.exe]

                                [885cb350 ctfmon.exe]

                                [888bb918 cscript.exe]

                                [8880b3c8 cscript.exe]

                                [88ad2950 csrss.exe]
b68.00215c 88930020 0000000 RUNNING nt!KeBugCheckEx+0x1b
                                    nt!MiCheckSessionPoolAllocations+0xe3
                                    nt!MiDereferenceSessionFinal+0x183
                                    nt!MmCleanProcessAddressSpace+0x6b
                                    nt!PspExitThread+0x5f1
                                    nt!PspTerminateThreadByPointer+0x4b
                                    nt!PspSystemThreadStartup+0x3c
                                    nt!KiThreadStartup+0x16

                                [88629310 winlogon.exe]

                                [88a4d9b0 csrss.exe]

                                [88d9f8b0 winlogon.exe]

                                [88cd5840 wfshell.exe]

                                [8a252440 OUTLOOK.EXE]

                                [8a194bf8 WINWORD.EXE]

                                [88aabd20 ctfmon.exe]

                                [889ef440 EXCEL.EXE]

                                [88bec838 HogiaGUI2.exe]
```

```
                                        [88692020 csrss.exe]

                                        [884dd508 winlogon.exe]

                                        [88be1d88 wfshell.exe]

                                        [886a7d88 OUTLOOK.EXE]

                                        [889baa70 WINWORD.EXE]

                                        [8861e3d0 ctfmon.exe]

                                        [887bbb68 EXCEL.EXE]

                                        [884e4020 csrss.exe]

                                        [8889d218 winlogon.exe]

                                        [887c8020 wfshell.exe]

Threads Processed: 1101
```

What if we have a list of processes from a complete memory dump by using **!process 0 0** command and we want to interrogate the specific process? In this case, we need to switch to that process and reload user space symbol files (**.process /r /p** *address*).

There is also a separate command to reload user space symbol files any time (**.reload /user)**.

After switching, we can list threads (**!process** *address*), dump or search process virtual memory. For example:

```
1: kd> !process 0 0
**** NT ACTIVE PROCESS DUMP ****
PROCESS 890a3320  SessionId: 0  Cid: 0008    Peb: 00000000  ParentCid:
0000
    DirBase: 00030000  ObjectTable: 890a3e08  TableSize: 405.
    Image: System

PROCESS 889dfd60  SessionId: 0  Cid: 0144    Peb: 7ffdf000  ParentCid:
0008
    DirBase: 0b9e7000  ObjectTable: 889fdb48  TableSize: 212.
    Image: SMSS.EXE

PROCESS 890af020  SessionId: 0  Cid: 0160    Peb: 7ffdf000  ParentCid:
0144
```

```
    DirBase: 0ce36000  ObjectTable: 8898e308  TableSize: 747.
    Image: CSRSS.EXE

PROCESS 8893d020  SessionId: 0  Cid: 0178    Peb: 7ffdf000  ParentCid:
0144
    DirBase: 0d33b000  ObjectTable: 890ab4c8  TableSize: 364.
    Image: WINLOGON.EXE

PROCESS 88936020  SessionId: 0  Cid: 0194    Peb: 7ffdf000  ParentCid:
0178
    DirBase: 0d7d5000  ObjectTable: 88980528  TableSize: 872.
    Image: SERVICES.EXE

PROCESS 8897f020  SessionId: 0  Cid: 01a0    Peb: 7ffdf000  ParentCid:
0178
    DirBase: 0d89d000  ObjectTable: 889367c8  TableSize: 623.
    Image: LSASS.EXE

1: kd> .process /r /p 8893d020
Implicit process is now 8893d020
Loading User Symbols
...

1: kd> !process 8893d020
PROCESS 8893d020  SessionId: 0  Cid: 0178    Peb: 7ffdf000  ParentCid:
0144
    DirBase: 0d33b000  ObjectTable: 890ab4c8  TableSize: 364.
    Image: WINLOGON.EXE
    VadRoot 8893a508 Clone 0 Private 1320. Modified 45178. Locked 0.
    DeviceMap 89072448
    Token                             e392f8d0
    ElapsedTime                        9:54:06.0882
    UserTime                          0:00:00.0071
    KernelTime                        0:00:00.0382
    QuotaPoolUsage[PagedPool]         34828
    QuotaPoolUsage[NonPagedPool]      43440
    Working Set Sizes (now,min,max)  (737, 50, 345) (2948KB, 200KB,
1380KB)
    PeakWorkingSetSize                2764
    VirtualSize                       46 Mb
    PeakVirtualSize                   52 Mb
    PageFaultCount                    117462
    MemoryPriority                    FOREGROUND
    BasePriority                      13
    CommitCharge                      1861
```

```
        THREAD 8893dda0  Cid 178.15c  Teb: 7ffde000  Win32Thread: a2034908
WAIT: (WrUserRequest) UserMode Non-Alertable
            8893bee0  SynchronizationEvent
        Not impersonating
        Owning Process 8893d020
        Wait Start TickCount    29932455      Elapsed Ticks: 7
        Context Switch Count    28087                   LargeStack
        UserTime                  0:00:00.0023
        KernelTime                0:00:00.0084
        Start Address winlogon!WinMainCRTStartup (0x0101cbb0)
        Stack Init eb1b0000 Current eb1afcc8 Base eb1b0000 Limit eb1ac000
Call 0
        Priority 15 BasePriority 15 PriorityDecrement 0 DecrementCount 0

        ChildEBP RetAddr
        eb1afce0 8042d893 nt!KiSwapThread+0x1b1
        eb1afd08 a00019c2 nt!KeWaitForSingleObject+0x1a3
        eb1afd44 a0013993 win32k!xxxSleepThread+0x18a
        eb1afd54 a001399f win32k!xxxWaitMessage+0xe
        eb1afd5c 80468389 win32k!NtUserWaitMessage+0xb
        eb1afd5c 77e58b53 nt!KiSystemService+0xc9
        0006fdd0 77e33630 USER32!NtUserWaitMessage+0xb
        0006fe04 77e44327 USER32!DialogBox2+0x216
        0006fe28 77e38d37 USER32!InternalDialogBox+0xd1
        0006fe48 77e39eba USER32!DialogBoxIndirectParamAorW+0x34
        0006fe6c 01011749 USER32!DialogBoxParamW+0x3d
        0006fea8 01018bd3 winlogon!TimeoutDialogBoxParam+0x27
        0006fee0 76b93701 winlogon!WlxDialogBoxParam+0x7b
        0006ff08 010164c6 3rdPartyGINA!WlxDisplaySASNotice+0x43
        0006ff20 01014960 winlogon!MainLoop+0x96
        0006ff58 0101cd06 winlogon!WinMain+0x37a
        0006fff4 00000000 winlogon!WinMainCRTStartup+0x156
```

```
THREAD 88980020  Cid 178.188  Teb: 7ffdc000  Win32Thread: 00000000 WAIT:
(DelayExecution) UserMode Alertable
            88980108  NotificationTimer
        Not impersonating
        Owning Process 8893d020
        Wait Start TickCount    29930810      Elapsed Ticks: 1652
        Context Switch Count    15638
        UserTime                  0:00:00.0000
        KernelTime                0:00:00.0000
        Start Address KERNEL32!BaseThreadStartThunk (0x7c57b740)
        Win32 Start Address ntdll!RtlpTimerThread (0x77faa02d)
        Stack Init bf6f7000 Current bf6f6cc4 Base bf6f7000 Limit bf6f4000
Call 0
        Priority 13 BasePriority 13 PriorityDecrement 0 DecrementCount 0

        ChildEBP RetAddr
        bf6f6cdc 8042d340 nt!KiSwapThread+0x1b1
        bf6f6d04 8052aac9 nt!KeDelayExecutionThread+0x182
        bf6f6d54 80468389 nt!NtDelayExecution+0x7f
        bf6f6d54 77f82831 nt!KiSystemService+0xc9
        00bfff9c 77f842c4 ntdll!NtDelayExecution+0xb
        00bfffb4 7c57b3bc ntdll!RtlpTimerThread+0x42
        00bfffec 00000000 KERNEL32!BaseThreadStart+0x52

1: kd> dds 0006fee0
0006fee0  0006ff08
0006fee4  76b93701 3rdPartyGINA!WlxDisplaySASNotice+0x43
0006fee8  000755e8
0006feec  76b90000 3rdParty
0006fef0  00000578
0006fef4  00000000
0006fef8  76b9370b 3rdParty!WlxDisplaySASNotice+0x4d
0006fefc  0008d0e0
0006ff00  00000008
0006ff04  00000080
0006ff08  0006ff20
0006ff0c  010164c6 winlogon!MainLoop+0x96
0006ff10  0008d0e0
0006ff14  5ffa0000
0006ff18  000755e8
0006ff1c  00000000
0006ff20  0006ff58
0006ff24  01014960 winlogon!WinMain+0x37a
0006ff28  000755e8
0006ff2c  00000005
0006ff30  00072c9c
0006ff34  00000001
0006ff38  000001bc
0006ff3c  00000005
0006ff40  00000001
0006ff44  0000000d
0006ff48  00000000
0006ff4c  00000000
```

```
0006ff50  00000000
0006ff54  0000ffe4
0006ff58  0006fff4
0006ff5c  0101cd06 winlogon!WinMainCRTStartup+0x156
```

We can also filter stacks that belong to processes having the same module name, for example, ***svchost.exe*** (see Filtering Processes, page 220).

Sometimes the collection of all stack traces from all threads in the system can disprove or decrease the plausibility of the hypothesis that some module is involved. In one case, the customer claimed that the specific driver was involved in the server freeze. However, there was no such module found in all thread stacks.

Coupled Processes (Strong)

Sometimes we have a problem that some functionality is not available, or it is unresponsive when we request it. Then we can suppose that the process, which implements that functionality, has crashed or hangs. If we know the relationship between processes, we can request several user dumps at once or a complete memory dump to analyze the dependency between processes by looking at their stack traces. This is an example of the system level crash dump analysis pattern that I call **Coupled Processes.**

Process relationship can be implemented via different interprocess communication mechanisms (IPC), for example, Remote Procedure Call (RPC) via LPC (Local Procedure Call) which can be easily identified in stack traces.

My favorite example here is when some application tries to print and hangs. Printing API is exported from *WINSPOOL.DLL* and it forwards via RPC most requests to Windows Print Spooler service. Therefore, it is logical to take two dumps, one from that application, and one from *spoolsv.exe*. Similar example is from Citrix Presentation Server environments related to printer autocreation when there are dependencies between Citrix Printing Service *CpSvc.exe* and *spoolsv.exe*. Therefore if new user connections hang and restarting both printing services resolves the issue then we might need to analyze memory dumps from both services together to confirm this Procedure Call Chain and find the problem 3rd-party printing component or driver.

Back to my favorite example. In the hang application we have the following thread:

```
  18  Id: 2130.6320 Suspend: 1 Teb: 7ffa8000 Unfrozen
ChildEBP RetAddr
01eae170 7c821c94 ntdll!KiFastSystemCallRet
01eae174 77c72700 ntdll!NtRequestWaitReplyPort+0xc
01eae1c8 77c713ba rpcrt4!LRPC_CCALL::SendReceive+0x230
01eae1d4 77c72c7f rpcrt4!I_RpcSendReceive+0x24
01eae1e8 77ce219b rpcrt4!NdrSendReceive+0x2b
01eae5d0 7307c9ef rpcrt4!NdrClientCall2+0x22e
01eae5e8 73082d8d winspool!RpcAddPrinter+0x1c
01eaea70 0040d81a winspool!AddPrinterW+0x102
01eaef58 0040ee7c App!AddNewPrinter+0x816
...
...
...
```

Notice *winspool* and *rpcrt4* modules. The application is calling spooler service using RPC to add a new printer and waiting for a reply back. Looking at spooler service dump shows several threads displaying message boxes and waiting for user input:

```
  20  Id: 790.5950 Suspend: 1 Teb: 7ffa2000 Unfrozen
ChildEBP RetAddr  Args to Child
03deea70 7739d02f 77392bf3 00000000 00000000 ntdll!KiFastSystemCallRet
03deeaa8 7738f122 03dd0058 00000000 00000001 user32!NtUserWaitMessage+0xc
03deead0 773a1722 77380000 00123690 00000000 user32!InternalDialogBox+0xd0
03deed90 773a1004 03deeeec 03dae378 03dae160
user32!SoftModalMessageBox+0x94b
03deeee0 773b1a28 03deeeec 00000028 00000000 user32!MessageBoxWorker+0x2ba
03deef38 773b19c4 00000000 03defb9c 03def39c
user32!MessageBoxTimeoutW+0x7a
03deef58 773b19a0 00000000 03defb9c 03def39c user32!MessageBoxExW+0x1b
03deef74 021f265b 00000000 03defb9c 03def39c user32!MessageBoxW+0x45
WARNING: Stack unwind information not available. Following frames may be
wrong.
03deef88 00000000 03dae160 03deffec 03dae16a
PrinterDriver!UninstallerInstall+0x2cb
```

Dumping the 3rd parameter of *MessageBoxW* using WinDbg **du** command shows the message:

> *"Installation of the software for your printer is now complete. Restart your computer to make the new settings active."*

Another example is when one process starts another and then waiting for it to finish:

```
0 Id: 2a34.24d0 Suspend: 1 Teb: 7ffde000 Unfrozen
ChildEBP RetAddr
0007ec8c 7c822124 ntdll!KiFastSystemCallRet
0007ec90 77e6bad8 ntdll!NtWaitForSingleObject+0xc
0007ed00 77e6ba42 kernel32!WaitForSingleObjectEx+0xac
0007ed14 01002f4c kernel32!WaitForSingleObject+0x12
0007f79c 01003137 userinit!ExecApplication+0x2d3
0007f7dc 0100366b userinit!ExecProcesses+0x1bb
0007fe68 010041fd userinit!StartTheShell+0x132
0007ff1c 010056f1 userinit!WinMain+0x263
0007ffc0 77e523e5 userinit!WinMainCRTStartup+0x186
```

High Contention (Executive Resources)

Some Windows synchronization objects like executive resources and critical sections have a struct member called *ContentionCount*. This is the number of times a resource was accessed or, in other words, it is the accumulated number of threads waiting for an object: when a thread tries to acquire an object and is put into a wait state, the count is incremented. Hence the name of this pattern: **High Contention**.

Here is an example. In a kernel memory dump, we have just one exclusively owned lock, and it seems that no other threads were blocked by it at the time the dump was saved. However, the high contention count reveals CPU spike:

```
3: kd> !locks
**** DUMP OF ALL RESOURCE OBJECTS ****
KD: Scanning for held locks...

Resource @ 0x8abc11f0    Exclusively owned
    Contention Count = 19648535
     Threads: 896395f8-01<*>
KD: Scanning for held locks…

Resource @ 0x896fab88    Shared 1 owning threads
     Threads: 88c78608-01<*>
KD: Scanning for held locks...
15464 total locks, 2 locks currently held

3: kd> !thread 896395f8
THREAD 896395f8  Cid 04c0.0138  Teb: 7ffde000 Win32Thread: bc922d20
RUNNING on processor 1
Not impersonating
DeviceMap                 e3d4c008
Owning Process            8a035020       Image:         MyApp.exe
Wait Start TickCount      36969283       Ticks: 0
Context Switch Count      1926423                   LargeStack
UserTime                  00:00:53.843
KernelTime                00:13:10.703
Win32 Start Address 0x00401478
Start Address 0x77e617f8
Stack Init ba14b000 Current ba14abf8 Base ba14b000 Limit ba146000 Call 0
Priority 11 BasePriority 6 PriorityDecrement 5
ChildEBP RetAddr
ba14ac94 bf8c6505 001544c8 bf995948 000c000a nt!_wcsicmp+0x3a
ba14ace0 bf8c6682 00000000 00000000 00000000 win32k!_FindWindowEx+0xfb
ba14ad48 8088978c 00000000 00000000 0012f8d4
win32k!NtUserFindWindowEx+0xef
ba14ad48 7c8285ec 00000000 00000000 0012f8d4 nt!KiFastCallEntry+0xfc
```

```
3: kd> !process 8a035020
PROCESS 8a035020  SessionId: 9  Cid: 04c0    Peb: 7ffdf000  ParentCid:
10e8
    DirBase: cffaf7a0  ObjectTable: e4ba30a0  HandleCount:  73.
    Image: MyApp.exe
    VadRoot 88bc1bf8 Vads 82 Clone 0 Private 264. Modified 0. Locked 0.
    DeviceMap e3d4c008
    Token                             e5272028
    ElapsedTime                       00:14:19.360
    UserTime                          00:00:53.843
    KernelTime                        00:13:10.703
    QuotaPoolUsage[PagedPool]         40660
    QuotaPoolUsage[NonPagedPool]      3280
    Working Set Sizes (now,min,max)  (1139, 50, 345) (4556KB, 200KB,
1380KB)
    PeakWorkingSetSize                1141
    VirtualSize                       25 Mb
    PeakVirtualSize                   27 Mb
    PageFaultCount                    1186
    MemoryPriority                    BACKGROUND
    BasePriority                      6
    CommitCharge                      315
```

Accidental Lock

When a system is unresponsive or sluggish, we usually check _ERESOURCE locks in kernel or complete memory dumps to see **Deadlock** (page 323) or **High Resource Contention** (page 421) patterns. However, there is some chance that reported locks are purely accidental and appear in a crash dump because they just happened at that time. We need to look at *Contention Count*, *Ticks,* and *KernelTime* in both blocking and blocked threads to recognize an **Accidental Lock**. Also, the current version of WinDbg doesn't distinguish between prolonged and accidental locks when we use **!analyze -v -hang** command and merely reports some lock chain it finds among equal alternatives.

Here is an example. The system was reported hung, and kernel memory dump was saved. WinDbg analysis command reports one thread blocking 3 other threads and the driver on top of the blocking thread stack is *AVDriver.sys*. The algorithm WinDbg uses to point to specific image name is described in **Minidump Analysis** section (page 43) and in our case it chooses *AVDriver*:

```
BLOCKED_THREAD:  8089d8c0

BLOCKING_THREAD:  8aab4700

LOCK_ADDRESS:  8859a570 -- (!locks 8859a570)

Resource @ 0x8859a570    Exclusively owned
    Contention Count = 3
    NumberOfExclusiveWaiters = 3
     Threads: 8aab4700-01<*>
    Threads Waiting On Exclusive Access:
              885d0020       88a7c020       8aafc7d8

1 total locks, 1 locks currently held

BUGCHECK_STR:  LOCK_HELD

FAULTING_THREAD:  8aab4700
```

```
STACK_TEXT:
f592f698 80832f7a nt!KiSwapContext+0x26
f592f6c4 80828705 nt!KiSwapThread+0x284
f592f70c f720a394 nt!KeDelayExecutionThread+0x2ab
WARNING: Stack unwind information not available. Following frames may be
wrong.
f592f734 f720ae35 AVDriver+0x1394
f592f750 f720b208 AVDriver+0x1e35
f592f794 f721945a AVDriver+0x2208
f592f7cc 8081dcdf AVDriver+0x1045a
f592f7e0 f5b9f76a nt!IofCallDriver+0x45
f592f7f0 f5b9c621 Driver!FS_Dispatch+0xa4
f592f7fc 8081dcdf Driver!Kernel_dispatch+0x53
f592f810 f5eb2856 nt!IofCallDriver+0x45
f592f874 8081dcdf AVFilter!QueryFullName+0x5c10
f592f888 f5e9eae3 nt!IofCallDriver+0x45
f592f8b8 f5e9eca4 DrvFilter!PassThrough+0x115
f592f8d4 8081dcdf DrvFilter!Create+0xda
f592f8e8 808f8275 nt!IofCallDriver+0x45
f592f9d0 808f86bc nt!IopParseDevice+0xa35
f592fa08 80936689 nt!IopParseFile+0x46
f592fa88 80932e04 nt!ObpLookupObjectName+0x11f
f592fadc 808ea231 nt!ObOpenObjectByName+0xea
f592fb58 808eb4cb nt!IopCreateFile+0x447
f592fbb4 f57c8efd nt!IoCreateFile+0xa3
f592fc24 f57c9f29 srv!SrvIoCreateFile+0x36d
f592fcf0 f57ca5e4 srv!SrvNtCreateFile+0x5cc
f592fd78 f57adbc6 srv!SrvSmbNtCreateAndX+0x15c
f592fd84 f57c3451 srv!SrvProcessSmb+0xb7
f592fdac 80948bd0 srv!WorkerThread+0x138
f592fddc 8088d4e2 nt!PspSystemThreadStartup+0x2e
00000000 00000000 nt!KiThreadStartup+0x16

STACK_COMMAND:  .thread 0xffffffff8aab4700 ; kb

FOLLOWUP_IP:
AVDriver+1394
f720a394 eb85            jmp     AVDriver+0x131b (f720a31b)

MODULE_NAME: AVDriver

IMAGE_NAME:  AVDriver.sys
```

Motivated by this “discovery”, we want to see all locks:

```
0: kd> !locks
**** DUMP OF ALL RESOURCE OBJECTS ****
KD: Scanning for held locks...

Resource @ 0x895a62d8    Shared 1 owning threads
     Threads: 89570520-01<*>
```

```
Resource @ 0x897ceba8    Shared 1 owning threads
     Threads: 89584020-01<*>

Resource @ 0x8958e020    Shared 1 owning threads
     Threads: 89555020-01<*>

Resource @ 0x89590608    Shared 1 owning threads
     Threads: 89666020-01<*>

Resource @ 0x89efc398    Shared 1 owning threads
     Threads: 89e277c0-01<*>

Resource @ 0x88d70820    Shared 1 owning threads
     Threads: 88e43948-01<*>

Resource @ 0x89f2fb00    Shared 1 owning threads
     Threads: 89674688-01<*>

Resource @ 0x89c80370    Shared 1 owning threads
     Threads: 888496b8-01<*>

Resource @ 0x89bfdf08    Shared 1 owning threads
     Threads: 88b62910-01<*>

Resource @ 0x888b5488    Shared 1 owning threads
     Threads: 88536730-01<*>

Resource @ 0x89f2e348    Shared 1 owning threads
     Threads: 89295930-01<*>

Resource @ 0x891a0838    Shared 1 owning threads
     Threads: 88949020-01<*>

Resource @ 0x8825bf08    Shared 1 owning threads
     Threads: 882b9a08-01<*>

Resource @ 0x881a6510    Shared 1 owning threads
     Threads: 88a88338-01<*>

Resource @ 0x885c5890    Shared 1 owning threads
     Threads: 881ab020-01<*>

Resource @ 0x886633a8    Shared 1 owning threads
     Threads: 89b5f8b0-01<*>

Resource @ 0x88216390    Shared 1 owning threads
     Threads: 88820020-01<*>
```

```
Resource @ 0x88524490    Shared 1 owning threads
     Threads: 88073020-01<*>


Resource @ 0x88f6a020    Shared 1 owning threads
     Threads: 88e547b0-01<*>


Resource @ 0x88cf2020    Shared 1 owning threads
     Threads: 89af32d8-01<*>


Resource @ 0x889cea80    Shared 1 owning threads
     Threads: 88d18b40-01<*>


Resource @ 0x88486298    Shared 1 owning threads
     Threads: 88af7db0-01<*>


Resource @ 0x88b22270    Exclusively owned
    Contention Count = 4
    NumberOfExclusiveWaiters = 4
     Threads: 8aad07d8-01<*>
     Threads Waiting On Exclusive Access:
              8ad78020       887abdb0       88eb39a8       8aa1f668

Resource @ 0x88748c20    Exclusively owned
    Contention Count = 2
    NumberOfExclusiveWaiters = 2
     Threads: 8873c8d8-01<*>
     Threads Waiting On Exclusive Access:
              88477478       88db6020

Resource @ 0x8859a570    Exclusively owned
    Contention Count = 3
    NumberOfExclusiveWaiters = 3
     Threads: 8aab4700-01<*>
     Threads Waiting On Exclusive Access:
              885d0020       88a7c020       8aafc7d8

KD: Scanning for held locks...
18911 total locks, 25 locks currently held
```

We can ignore shared locks and then concentrate on the last 3 exclusively owned resources. It looks suspicious that *Contention Count* has the same number as the number of threads waiting for exclusive access (*NumberOfExclusiveWaiters*). This means that these resources had never been used before. If we dump locks, verbosely we would see that blocked threads had been waiting no more than 2 seconds, for example, for resource 0x8859a570:

```
0: kd> !thread 885d0020; !thread 88a7c020; !thread 8aafc7d8
THREAD 885d0020  Cid 0004.1c34  Teb: 00000000 Win32Thread: 00000000 WAIT:
(Unknown) KernelMode Non-Alertable
    89908d50  SynchronizationEvent
    885d0098  NotificationTimer
Not impersonating
DeviceMap                 e10022c8
Owning Process            8ad80648 Image:         System
Wait Start TickCount      7689055  Ticks: 127 (0:00:00:01.984)
Context Switch Count      248
UserTime                  00:00:00.000
KernelTime                00:00:00.000
Start Address srv!WorkerThread (0xf57c3394)
Stack Init b4136000 Current b4135b74 Base b4136000 Limit b4133000 Call 0
Priority 9 BasePriority 9 PriorityDecrement 0
ChildEBP RetAddr
b4135b8c 80832f7a nt!KiSwapContext+0x26
b4135bb8 8082925c nt!KiSwapThread+0x284
b4135c00 8087c1ad nt!KeWaitForSingleObject+0x346
b4135c3c 8087c3a1 nt!ExpWaitForResource+0xd5
b4135c5c f57c9e95 nt!ExAcquireResourceExclusiveLite+0x8d
b4135cf0 f57ca5e4 srv!SrvNtCreateFile+0x510
b4135d78 f57adbc6 srv!SrvSmbNtCreateAndX+0x15c
b4135d84 f57c3451 srv!SrvProcessSmb+0xb7
b4135dac 80948bd0 srv!WorkerThread+0x138
b4135ddc 8088d4e2 nt!PspSystemThreadStartup+0x2e
00000000 00000000 nt!KiThreadStartup+0x16

THREAD 88a7c020  Cid 0004.3448  Teb: 00000000 Win32Thread: 00000000 WAIT:
(Unknown) KernelMode Non-Alertable
    89908d50  SynchronizationEvent
    88a7c098  NotificationTimer
Not impersonating
DeviceMap                 e10022c8
Owning Process            8ad80648  Image:         System
Wait Start TickCount      7689112   Ticks: 70 (0:00:00:01.093)
Context Switch Count      210
UserTime                  00:00:00.000
KernelTime                00:00:00.000
Start Address srv!WorkerThread (0xf57c3394)
Stack Init b55dd000 Current b55dcb74 Base b55dd000 Limit b55da000 Call 0
Priority 9 BasePriority 9 PriorityDecrement 0
ChildEBP RetAddr
b55dcb8c 80832f7a nt!KiSwapContext+0x26
b55dcbb8 8082925c nt!KiSwapThread+0x284
b55dcc00 8087c1ad nt!KeWaitForSingleObject+0x346
b55dcc3c 8087c3a1 nt!ExpWaitForResource+0xd5
b55dcc5c f57c9e95 nt!ExAcquireResourceExclusiveLite+0x8d
b55dccf0 f57ca5e4 srv!SrvNtCreateFile+0x510
b55dcd78 f57adbc6 srv!SrvSmbNtCreateAndX+0x15c
b55dcd84 f57c3451 srv!SrvProcessSmb+0xb7
b55dcdac 80948bd0 srv!WorkerThread+0x138
```

```
b55dcddc 8088d4e2 nt!PspSystemThreadStartup+0x2e
00000000 00000000 nt!KiThreadStartup+0x16

THREAD 8aafc7d8  Cid 0004.058c  Teb: 00000000 Win32Thread: 00000000 WAIT:
(Unknown) KernelMode Non-Alertable
    89908d50  SynchronizationEvent
    8aafc850  NotificationTimer
Not impersonating
DeviceMap                 e10022c8
Owning Process            8ad80648  Image:          System
Wait Start TickCount      7689171   Ticks: 11 (0:00:00:00.171)
Context Switch Count      310
UserTime                  00:00:00.000
KernelTime                00:00:00.000
Start Address srv!WorkerThread (0xf57c3394)
Stack Init f592c000 Current f592bb18 Base f592c000 Limit f5929000 Call 0
Priority 9 BasePriority 9 PriorityDecrement 0
ChildEBP RetAddr
f592bb30 80832f7a nt!KiSwapContext+0x26
f592bb5c 8082925c nt!KiSwapThread+0x284
f592bba4 8087c1ad nt!KeWaitForSingleObject+0x346
f592bbe0 8087c3a1 nt!ExpWaitForResource+0xd5
f592bc00 f57c8267 nt!ExAcquireResourceExclusiveLite+0x8d
f592bc18 f57ff0ed srv!UnlinkRfcbFromLfcb+0x33
f592bc34 f57ff2ea srv!SrvCompleteRfcbClose+0x1df
f592bc54 f57b5e8f srv!CloseRfcbInternal+0xb6
f592bc78 f57ce8a9 srv!SrvCloseRfcbsOnSessionOrPid+0x74
f592bc94 f57e2b22 srv!SrvCloseSession+0xb0
f592bcb8 f57aeb12 srv!SrvCloseSessionsOnConnection+0xa9
f592bcd4 f57c79ed srv!SrvCloseConnection+0x143
f592bd04 f5808c50 srv!SrvCloseConnectionsFromClient+0x17f
f592bdac 80948bd0 srv!WorkerThread+0x138
f592bddc 8088d4e2 nt!PspSystemThreadStartup+0x2e
00000000 00000000 nt!KiThreadStartup+0x16
```

Blocking threads themselves are not blocked and active: the number of ticks passed since their last wait or preemption is 0. This could be a sign of a CPU spike pattern. However, their accumulated *KernelTime* is less than a second:

```
0: kd> !thread 8aad07d8
THREAD 8aad07d8  Cid 0004.0580  Teb: 00000000 Win32Thread: 00000000 WAIT:
(Unknown) KernelMode Non-Alertable
    8aad0850  NotificationTimer
IRP List:
    8927ade0: (0006,0220) Flags: 00000884  Mdl: 00000000
Impersonation token:  eafdc030 (Level Impersonation)
DeviceMap                 e5d69340
Owning Process            8ad80648      Image:          System
Wait Start TickCount      7689182       Ticks: 0
Context Switch Count      915582
UserTime                  00:00:00.000
KernelTime                00:00:00.125
```

```
Start Address srv!WorkerThread (0xf57c3394)
Stack Init f59d8000 Current f59d7680 Base f59d8000 Limit f59d5000 Call 0
Priority 9 BasePriority 9 PriorityDecrement 0

0: kd> !thread 8873c8d8
THREAD 8873c8d8  Cid 0004.2898  Teb: 00000000 Win32Thread: 00000000 WAIT:
(Unknown) KernelMode Non-Alertable
    8873c950  NotificationTimer
IRP List:
    882a8de0: (0006,0220) Flags: 00000884  Mdl: 00000000
Impersonation token:  eafdc030 (Level Impersonation)
DeviceMap                 e5d69340
Owning Process            8ad80648       Image:         System
Wait Start TickCount      7689182        Ticks: 0
Context Switch Count      917832
UserTime                  00:00:00.000
KernelTime                00:00:00.031
Start Address srv!WorkerThread (0xf57c3394)
Stack Init ac320000 Current ac31f680 Base ac320000 Limit ac31d000 Call 0
Priority 9 BasePriority 9 PriorityDecrement 0

0: kd> !thread 8aab4700
THREAD 8aab4700  Cid 0004.0588  Teb: 00000000 Win32Thread: 00000000 WAIT:
(Unknown) KernelMode Non-Alertable
    8aab4778  NotificationTimer
IRP List:
    88453008: (0006,0220) Flags: 00000884  Mdl: 00000000
Impersonation token:  e9a82728 (Level Impersonation)
DeviceMap                 eb45f108
Owning Process            8ad80648       Image:         System
Wait Start TickCount      7689182        Ticks: 0
Context Switch Count      1028220
UserTime                  00:00:00.000
KernelTime                00:00:00.765
Start Address srv!WorkerThread (0xf57c3394)
Stack Init f5930000 Current f592f680 Base f5930000 Limit f592d000 Call 0
Priority 9 BasePriority 9 PriorityDecrement 0
```

Based on this observation, we could say that locks were accidental, and indeed, when the problem happened again, the new dump didn't show them.

Passive Thread (User Space)

When trying to understand why the particular application or service hangs we look at **Stack Trace Collection** pattern (page 409) and hope to find some suspicious threads that are waiting for a response. These blocked threads are active**.** Other threads may appear waiting, but they are merely waiting for some notification or data that may or may not come during their lifetime and, therefore, are normal. In other words, they are passive and hence the name of the pattern **Passive Thread**. Typical examples from user space include:

- The main service thread and dispatch threads (when idle).
- A thread is waiting for file or registry notifications.
- A generic RPC/LPC/COM thread is waiting for messages.
- Worker threads are waiting for data to appear in a queue.
- Window message loops (when idle).
- Socket and network protocol threads (when idle).
- A thread with function names on its stack trace suggesting that it is a notification or listener thread.

Of course, sometimes these passive threads can be the reason for an application or service hang, but from my experience, most of the time they are not unless there are other threads which they block. Let's now look at example stack traces.

Note: Generic threads spawned to service various requests and waiting for data to arrive can be filtered using **!uniqstack** WinDbg command. Conceptually these threads are part of the so-called thread pool software design pattern.

LPC/RPC/COM threads waiting for requests:

```
  70  Id: 8f8.1100 Suspend: 1 Teb: 7ff80000 Unfrozen
ChildEBP RetAddr
0d82fe18 7c82783b ntdll!KiFastSystemCallRet
0d82fe1c 77c885ac ntdll!NtReplyWaitReceivePortEx+0xc
0d82ff84 77c88792 rpcrt4!LRPC_ADDRESS::ReceiveLotsaCalls+0x198
0d82ff8c 77c8872d rpcrt4!RecvLotsaCallsWrapper+0xd
0d82ffac 77c7b110 rpcrt4!BaseCachedThreadRoutine+0x9d
0d82ffb8 77e64829 rpcrt4!ThreadStartRoutine+0x1b
0d82ffec 00000000 kernel32!BaseThreadStart+0x34
```

```
  71  Id: 8f8.1e44 Suspend: 1 Teb: 7ffde000 Unfrozen
ChildEBP RetAddr
0c01fe18 7c82783b ntdll!KiFastSystemCallRet
0c01fe1c 77c885ac ntdll!NtReplyWaitReceivePortEx+0xc
0c01ff84 77c88792 rpcrt4!LRPC_ADDRESS::ReceiveLotsaCalls+0x198
0c01ff8c 77c8872d rpcrt4!RecvLotsaCallsWrapper+0xd
0c01ffac 77c7b110 rpcrt4!BaseCachedThreadRoutine+0x9d
0c01ffb8 77e64829 rpcrt4!ThreadStartRoutine+0x1b
0c01ffec 00000000 kernel32!BaseThreadStart+0x34

  72  Id: 8f8.1804 Suspend: 1 Teb: 7ff90000 Unfrozen
ChildEBP RetAddr
0e22fe18 7c82783b ntdll!KiFastSystemCallRet
0e22fe1c 77c885ac ntdll!NtReplyWaitReceivePortEx+0xc
0e22ff84 77c88792 rpcrt4!LRPC_ADDRESS::ReceiveLotsaCalls+0x198
0e22ff8c 77c8872d rpcrt4!RecvLotsaCallsWrapper+0xd
0e22ffac 77c7b110 rpcrt4!BaseCachedThreadRoutine+0x9d
0e22ffb8 77e64829 rpcrt4!ThreadStartRoutine+0x1b
0e22ffec 00000000 kernel32!BaseThreadStart+0x34

  73  Id: 8f8.1860 Suspend: 1 Teb: 7ff79000 Unfrozen
ChildEBP RetAddr
0da2fe18 7c82783b ntdll!KiFastSystemCallRet
0da2fe1c 77c885ac ntdll!NtReplyWaitReceivePortEx+0xc
0da2ff84 77c88792 rpcrt4!LRPC_ADDRESS::ReceiveLotsaCalls+0x198
0da2ff8c 77c8872d rpcrt4!RecvLotsaCallsWrapper+0xd
0da2ffac 77c7b110 rpcrt4!BaseCachedThreadRoutine+0x9d
0da2ffb8 77e64829 rpcrt4!ThreadStartRoutine+0x1b
0da2ffec 00000000 kernel32!BaseThreadStart+0x34

  74  Id: 8f8.f24 Suspend: 1 Teb: 7ff7e000 Unfrozen
ChildEBP RetAddr
0d20feac 7c8277db ntdll!KiFastSystemCallRet
0d20feb0 77e5bea2 ntdll!ZwRemoveIoCompletion+0xc
0d20fedc 77c7b900 kernel32!GetQueuedCompletionStatus+0x29
0d20ff18 77c7b703 rpcrt4!COMMON_ProcessCalls+0xa1
0d20ff84 77c7b9b5 rpcrt4!LOADABLE_TRANSPORT::ProcessIOEvents+0x117
0d20ff8c 77c8872d rpcrt4!ProcessIOEventsWrapper+0xd
0d20ffac 77c7b110 rpcrt4!BaseCachedThreadRoutine+0x9d
0d20ffb8 77e64829 rpcrt4!ThreadStartRoutine+0x1b
0d20ffec 00000000 kernel32!BaseThreadStart+0x34
```

```
  75  Id: 8f8.11f8 Suspend: 1 Teb: 7ffa1000 Unfrozen
ChildEBP RetAddr
08e0feac 7c8277db ntdll!KiFastSystemCallRet
08e0feb0 77e5bea2 ntdll!ZwRemoveIoCompletion+0xc
08e0fedc 77c7b900 kernel32!GetQueuedCompletionStatus+0x29
08e0ff18 77c7b703 rpcrt4!COMMON_ProcessCalls+0xa1
08e0ff84 77c7b9b5 rpcrt4!LOADABLE_TRANSPORT::ProcessIOEvents+0x117
08e0ff8c 77c8872d rpcrt4!ProcessIOEventsWrapper+0xd
08e0ffac 77c7b110 rpcrt4!BaseCachedThreadRoutine+0x9d
08e0ffb8 77e64829 rpcrt4!ThreadStartRoutine+0x1b
08e0ffec 00000000 kernel32!BaseThreadStart+0x34

   2  Id: ecc.c94 Suspend: 1 Teb: 7efac000 Unfrozen
ChildEBP RetAddr
0382f760 76e31330 ntdll!NtDelayExecution+0x15
0382f7c8 76e30dac kernel32!SleepEx+0x62
0382f7d8 75ec40f4 kernel32!Sleep+0xf
0382f7e4 75eafc0d ole32!CROIDTable::WorkerThreadLoop+0x14
0382f800 75eafc73 ole32!CRpcThread::WorkerLoop+0x26
0382f80c 76ea19f1 ole32!CRpcThreadCache::RpcWorkerThreadEntry+0x20
0382f818 7797d109 kernel32!BaseThreadInitThunk+0xe
0382f858 00000000 ntdll!_RtlUserThreadStart+0x23
```

Worker threads waiting for data items to process:

```
  43  Id: 8f8.17c0 Suspend: 1 Teb: 7ff8c000 Unfrozen
ChildEBP RetAddr
0c64ff20 7c8277db ntdll!KiFastSystemCallRet
0c64ff24 77e5bea2 ntdll!ZwRemoveIoCompletion+0xc
0c64ff50 67823549 kernel32!GetQueuedCompletionStatus+0x29
0c64ff84 77bcb530 component!WorkItemThread+0x1a9
0c64ffb8 77e64829 msvcrt!_endthreadex+0xa3
0c64ffec 00000000 kernel32!BaseThreadStart+0x34

  44  Id: 8f8.7b4 Suspend: 1 Teb: 7ff8b000 Unfrozen
ChildEBP RetAddr
0c77ff20 7c8277db ntdll!KiFastSystemCallRet
0c77ff24 77e5bea2 ntdll!ZwRemoveIoCompletion+0xc
0c77ff50 67823549 kernel32!GetQueuedCompletionStatus+0x29
0c77ff84 77bcb530 component!WorkItemThread+0x1a9
0c77ffb8 77e64829 msvcrt!_endthreadex+0xa3
0c77ffec 00000000 kernel32!BaseThreadStart+0x34

  45  Id: 8f8.1708 Suspend: 1 Teb: 7ff8a000 Unfrozen
ChildEBP RetAddr
0c87ff20 7c8277db ntdll!KiFastSystemCallRet
0c87ff24 77e5bea2 ntdll!ZwRemoveIoCompletion+0xc
0c87ff50 67823549 kernel32!GetQueuedCompletionStatus+0x29
0c87ff84 77bcb530 component!WorkItemThread+0x1a9
0c87ffb8 77e64829 msvcrt!_endthreadex+0xa3
0c87ffec 00000000 kernel32!BaseThreadStart+0x34
```

```
   5 Id: 11fc.16f4 Suspend: 1 Teb: 7ffd9000 Unfrozen
ChildEBP RetAddr
0109bf10 7c822124 ntdll!KiFastSystemCallRet
0109bf14 77e6baa8 ntdll!NtWaitForSingleObject+0xc
0109bf84 77e6ba12 kernel32!WaitForSingleObjectEx+0xac
0109bf98 66886519 kernel32!WaitForSingleObject+0x12
0109ff84 77bcb530 component!WorkerThread+0xe8
0109ffb8 77e66063 msvcrt!_endthreadex+0xa3
0109ffec 00000000 kernel32!BaseThreadStart+0x34
```

A thread waiting for registry change notification:

```
   1  Id: 13c4.350 Suspend: 1 Teb: 000007ff`fffde000 Unfrozen
Child-SP          RetAddr           Call Site
00000000`0012fdd8 000007fe`fd62c361 ntdll!ZwNotifyChangeKey+0xa
00000000`0012fde0 00000001`40001181 ADVAPI32!RegNotifyChangeKeyValue+0x115
00000000`0012ff30 00000000`76d9cdcd sample12!WaitForRegChange+0xe
00000000`0012ff60 00000000`76eec6e1 kernel32!BaseThreadInitThunk+0xd
00000000`0012ff90 00000000`00000000 ntdll!RtlUserThreadStart+0x1d
```

Idle main service thread and service dispatch threads:

```
.  0  Id: 65c.660 Suspend: 1 Teb: 000007ff`fffdc000 Unfrozen
Child-SP          RetAddr           Call Site
00000000`0011f2c8 00000000`76d926da ntdll!NtReadFile+0xa
00000000`0011f2d0 000007fe`fd6665aa kernel32!ReadFile+0x8a
00000000`0011f360 000007fe`fd6662e3 ADVAPI32!ScGetPipeInput+0x4a
00000000`0011f440 000007fe`fd6650f3 ADVAPI32!ScDispatcherLoop+0x9a
00000000`0011f540 00000000`ff0423a3
ADVAPI32!StartServiceCtrlDispatcherW+0x176
00000000`0011f7c0 00000000`ff042066 spoolsv!main+0x23
00000000`0011f850 00000000`76eec6e1 kernel32!BaseThreadInitThunk+0xd
00000000`0011f880 00000000`00000000 ntdll!RtlUserThreadStart+0x1d

   1  Id: 65c.664 Suspend: 1 Teb: 000007ff`fffda000 Unfrozen
Child-SP          RetAddr           Call Site
00000000`0009f9c8 00000000`76d9d820 ntdll!NtWaitForSingleObject+0xa
00000000`0009f9d0 00000000`ff04307f kernel32!WaitForSingleObjectEx+0x9c
00000000`0009fa90 000007fe`fd664bf5 spoolsv!SPOOLER_main+0x80
00000000`0009fac0 00000000`76d9cdcd ADVAPI32!ScSvcctrlThreadW+0x25
00000000`0009faf0 00000000`76eec6e1 kernel32!BaseThreadInitThunk+0xd
00000000`0009fb20 00000000`00000000 ntdll!RtlUserThreadStart+0x1d
```

Idle window message loops:

```
  10  Id: 65c.514 Suspend: 1 Teb: 000007ff`fffa2000 Unfrozen
Child-SP          RetAddr           Call Site
00000000`02c5fc18 00000000`76cae6ea USER32!ZwUserGetMessage+0xa
00000000`02c5fc20 000007fe`f88523f0 USER32!GetMessageW+0x34
00000000`02c5fc50 00000000`76d9cdcd
usbmon!CPNPNotifications::WindowMessageThread+0x1a0
00000000`02c5fd20 00000000`76eec6e1 kernel32!BaseThreadInitThunk+0xd
00000000`02c5fd50 00000000`00000000 ntdll!RtlUserThreadStart+0x1d

  11  Id: 65c.9bc Suspend: 1 Teb: 000007ff`fffa0000 Unfrozen
Child-SP          RetAddr           Call Site
00000000`037cf798 00000000`76cae6ea USER32!ZwUserGetMessage+0xa
00000000`037cf7a0 000007fe`f7ea0d3a USER32!GetMessageW+0x34
00000000`037cf7d0 00000000`76d9cdcd
WSDMon!Ncd::TPower::WindowMessageThread+0xe6
00000000`037cf870 00000000`76eec6e1 kernel32!BaseThreadInitThunk+0xd
00000000`037cf8a0 00000000`00000000 ntdll!RtlUserThreadStart+0x1d

  13  Id: ecc.b34 Suspend: 1 Teb: 7ef85000 Unfrozen
ChildEBP RetAddr
0621fc18 75b86458 USER32!NtUserGetMessage+0x15
0621fc3c 74aa1404 USER32!GetMessageA+0xa2
0621fc74 76ea19f1 WINMM!mciwindow+0x102
0621fc80 7797d109 kernel32!BaseThreadInitThunk+0xe
0621fcc0 00000000 ntdll!_RtlUserThreadStart+0x23
```

Idle socket and network protocol threads:

```
   5  Id: ecc.920 Suspend: 1 Teb: 7efa3000 Unfrozen
ChildEBP RetAddr
0412f534 751b3b28 ntdll!ZwWaitForSingleObject+0x15
0412f574 751b2690 mswsock!SockWaitForSingleObject+0x19f
0412f660 771d3781 mswsock!WSPSelect+0x38c
0412f6dc 760f60fd ws2_32!select+0x456
0412fa34 760f2a78 WININET!ICAsyncThread::SelectThread+0x242
0412fa3c 76ea19f1 WININET!ICAsyncThread::SelectThreadWrapper+0xd
0412fa48 7797d109 kernel32!BaseThreadInitThunk+0xe
0412fa88 00000000 ntdll!_RtlUserThreadStart+0x23

   6  Id: ecc.b1c Suspend: 1 Teb: 7ef9d000 Unfrozen
ChildEBP RetAddr
047afa6c 751b1b25 ntdll!NtRemoveIoCompletion+0x15
047afaa4 76ea19f1 mswsock!SockAsyncThread+0x69
047afab0 7797d109 kernel32!BaseThreadInitThunk+0xe
047afaf0 00000000 ntdll!_RtlUserThreadStart+0x23
```

```
   7 Id: 820.f90 Suspend: 1 Teb: 7ffd9000 Unfrozen
ChildEBP RetAddr
018dff84 7c93e9ab ntdll!KiFastSystemCallRet
018dff88 60620e6c ntdll!ZwWaitForMultipleObjects+0xc
018dffb4 7c80b683 NETAPI32!NetbiosWaiter+0x73
018dffec 00000000 kernel32!BaseThreadStart+0x37
```

Function names showing passive nature of threads:

```
   8  Id: 65c.b40 Suspend: 1 Teb: 000007ff`fffa6000 Unfrozen
Child-SP          RetAddr           Call Site
00000000`0259fdc8 00000000`76d9d820 ntdll!NtWaitForSingleObject+0xa
00000000`0259fdd0 000007fe`f8258084 kernel32!WaitForSingleObjectEx+0x9c
00000000`0259fe90 000007fe`fee994e7 wsnmp32!thrNotify+0x9c
00000000`0259fef0 000007fe`fee9967d msvcrt!endthreadex+0x47
00000000`0259ff20 00000000`76d9cdcd msvcrt!endthreadex+0x100
00000000`0259ff50 00000000`76eec6e1 kernel32!BaseThreadInitThunk+0xd
00000000`0259ff80 00000000`00000000 ntdll!RtlUserThreadStart+0x1d

  12  Id: 65c.908 Suspend: 1 Teb: 000007ff`fff9e000 Unfrozen
Child-SP          RetAddr           Call Site
00000000`0368fd48 00000000`76d9d820 ntdll!NtWaitForSingleObject+0xa
00000000`0368fd50 000007fe`fa49afd0 kernel32!WaitForSingleObjectEx+0x9c
00000000`0368fe10 00000000`76d9cdcd
FunDisc!CNotificationQueue::ThreadProc+0x2ec
00000000`0368fe70 00000000`76eec6e1 kernel32!BaseThreadInitThunk+0xd
00000000`0368fea0 00000000`00000000 ntdll!RtlUserThreadStart+0x1d

  13  Id: 65c.904 Suspend: 1 Teb: 000007ff`fff9c000 Unfrozen
Child-SP          RetAddr           Call Site
00000000`034af9f8 00000000`76d9ed73 ntdll!NtWaitForMultipleObjects+0xa
00000000`034afa00 00000000`76cae96d
kernel32!WaitForMultipleObjectsEx+0x10b
00000000`034afb10 00000000`76cae85e
USER32!RealMsgWaitForMultipleObjectsEx+0x129
00000000`034afbb0 00000000`76ca3680
USER32!MsgWaitForMultipleObjectsEx+0x46
00000000`034afbf0 000007fe`fa49b60a USER32!MsgWaitForMultipleObjects+0x20
00000000`034afc30 00000000`76d9cdcd FunDisc!ListenerThread+0x1a6
00000000`034afd20 00000000`76eec6e1 kernel32!BaseThreadInitThunk+0xd
00000000`034afd50 00000000`00000000 ntdll!RtlUserThreadStart+0x1d
```

```
  64  Id: 8f8.1050 Suspend: 1 Teb: 7ff74000 Unfrozen
ChildEBP RetAddr
0ef5fa48 7c82787b ntdll!KiFastSystemCallRet
0ef5fa4c 77c80a6e ntdll!NtRequestWaitReplyPort+0xc
0ef5fa98 77c7fcf0 rpcrt4!LRPC_CCALL::SendReceive+0x230
0ef5faa4 77c80673 rpcrt4!I_RpcSendReceive+0x24
0ef5fab8 77ce315a rpcrt4!NdrSendReceive+0x2b
0ef5fea0 771f4fbd rpcrt4!NdrClientCall2+0x22e
0ef5feb8 771f4f60 winsta!RpcWinStationWaitSystemEvent+0x1c
0ef5ff00 76f01422 winsta!WinStationWaitSystemEvent+0x51
0ef5ff24 0c922ace wtsapi32!WTSWaitSystemEvent+0x97
0ef5ff48 67823331 component!MonitorEvents+0xaf
0ef5ffb8 77e64829 msvcrt!_endthreadex+0xa3
0ef5ffec 00000000 kernel32!BaseThreadStart+0x34

  11 Id: 140c.e8c Suspend: 1 Teb: 7ffaf000 Unfrozen
ChildEBP RetAddr
01e3fec0 7c822114 ntdll!KiFastSystemCallRet
01e3fec4 77e6711b ntdll!NtWaitForMultipleObjects+0xc
01e3ff6c 77e61075 kernel32!WaitForMultipleObjectsEx+0x11a
01e3ff88 76928415 kernel32!WaitForMultipleObjects+0x18
01e3ffb8 77e66063 userenv!!NotificationThread+0x5f
01e3ffec 00000000 kernel32!BaseThreadStart+0x34
```

When in doubt, it is always a good idea to examine threads in non-hanging processes to see their normal idle stack traces. See Appendix: Reference Stack Traces.

Main Thread

When we look at a thread, and it is not in the **Passive Thread** pattern list (page 430), and it looks more like **Blocked Thread** (see Volume 2), we may ask whether it is **Main Thread**. Every process has at least one thread of execution called main or primary thread. Most GUI applications have window message processing loop inside their main process thread. When a memory dump is saved, it is most likely that this thread is blocked waiting for the windows or user-defined messages to arrive and can be considered as **Passive Thread**. If we see it blocked on something else waiting for some time, we may consider the application is hanging.

Here is an example of the normal *iexplore.exe* thread stack taken from a kernel dump:

```
PROCESS 88de4140  SessionId: 3  Cid: 15a8    Peb: 7ffdf000  ParentCid:
0e28
    DirBase: 0a43df40  ObjectTable: 88efe008  TableSize: 852.
    Image: IEXPLORE.EXE
    VadRoot 88dbbca8 Clone 0 Private 6604. Modified 951. Locked 0.
    DeviceMap 88de6408
    Token                             e3f5ccf0
    ElapsedTime                        0:10:52.0281
    UserTime                          0:00:06.0250
    KernelTime                        0:00:10.0421
    QuotaPoolUsage[PagedPool]         126784
    QuotaPoolUsage[NonPagedPool]      197704
    Working Set Sizes (now,min,max)  (8347, 50, 345) (33388KB, 200KB,
1380KB)
    PeakWorkingSetSize                10000
    VirtualSize                       280 Mb
    PeakVirtualSize                   291 Mb
    PageFaultCount                    15627
    MemoryPriority                    FOREGROUND
    BasePriority                      8
    CommitCharge                      7440

THREAD 88ee2b00  Cid 15a8.1654  Teb: 7ffde000  Win32Thread: a2242018 WAIT:
(WrUserRequest) UserMode Non-Alertable
    88f82ee0  SynchronizationEvent
Not impersonating
Owning Process 88de4140
Wait Start TickCount    104916        Elapsed Ticks: 0
Context Switch Count    100208                   LargeStack
UserTime                  0:00:04.0484
KernelTime                0:00:09.0859
Start Address KERNEL32!BaseProcessStartThunk (0x7c57b70c)
Stack Init be597000 Current be596cc8 Base be597000 Limit be58f000 Call 0
Priority 12 BasePriority 8 PriorityDecrement 0 DecrementCount 0
```

```
ChildEBP RetAddr
be596ce0 8042d8d7 nt!KiSwapThread+0x1b1
be596d08 a00019c2 nt!KeWaitForSingleObject+0x1a3
be596d44 a00138c5 win32k!xxxSleepThread+0x18a
be596d54 a00138d1 win32k!xxxWaitMessage+0xe
be596d5c 8046b2a9 win32k!NtUserWaitMessage+0xb
be596d5c 77e3c7cd nt!KiSystemService+0xc9
```

In the same kernel dump, there is another *iexplore.exe* process with the following main thread stack which had been blocked for 31 seconds:

```
PROCESS 8811ca00  SessionId: 21  Cid: 4d18    Peb: 7ffdf000  ParentCid:
34c8
    DirBase: 0a086ee0  ObjectTable: 87d07528  TableSize: 677.
    Image: IEXPLORE.EXE
    VadRoot 87a92ae8 Clone 0 Private 4600. Modified 227. Locked 0.
    DeviceMap 88b174e8
    Token                             e49508d0
    ElapsedTime                        0:08:03.0062
    UserTime                          0:00:01.0531
    KernelTime                        0:00:10.0375
    QuotaPoolUsage[PagedPool]         120792
    QuotaPoolUsage[NonPagedPool]      198376
    Working Set Sizes (now,min,max)  (7726, 50, 345) (30904KB, 200KB,
1380KB)
    PeakWorkingSetSize                7735
    VirtualSize                       272 Mb
    PeakVirtualSize                   275 Mb
    PageFaultCount                    11688
    MemoryPriority                    BACKGROUND
    BasePriority                      8
    CommitCharge                      6498

THREAD 87ce6da0  Cid 4d18.4c68  Teb: 7ffde000  Win32Thread: a22157b8 WAIT:
(Executive) KernelMode Non-Alertable
    b5bd6370  NotificationEvent
IRP List:
    885d4808: (0006,00dc) Flags: 00000014  Mdl: 00000000
Not impersonating
Owning Process 8811ca00
Wait Start TickCount     102908         Elapsed Ticks: 2008
Context Switch Count     130138                      LargeStack
UserTime                   0:00:01.0125
KernelTime                 0:00:08.0843
Start Address KERNEL32!BaseProcessStartThunk (0x7c57b70c)
Stack Init b5bd7000 Current b5bd62f4 Base b5bd7000 Limit b5bcf000 Call 0
Priority 8 BasePriority 8 PriorityDecrement 0 DecrementCount 0
```

```
ChildEBP RetAddr
b5bd630c 8042d8d7 nt!KiSwapThread+0x1b1
b5bd6334 bf09342d nt!KeWaitForSingleObject+0x1a3
b5bd6380 bf08896f mrxsmb!SmbCeAssociateExchangeWithMid+0x24b
b5bd63b0 bf0aa0ef mrxsmb!SmbCeTranceive+0xff
b5bd6490 bf0a92df mrxsmb!SmbTransactExchangeStart+0x559
b5bd64a8 bf0a9987 mrxsmb!SmbCeInitiateExchange+0x2ac
b5bd64c4 bf0a96e2 mrxsmb!SmbCeSubmitTransactionRequest+0x124
b5bd6524 bf0ac7c3 mrxsmb!_SmbCeTransact+0x86
b5bd6608 bf104ea0 mrxsmb!MRxSmbQueryFileInformation+0x553
b5bd66b4 bf103aff rdbss!__RxInitializeTopLevelIrpContext+0x52
b5bd6784 bf10da73 rdbss!WPP_SF_ZL+0x4b
b5bd67b4 bf0a8b29 rdbss!RxCleanupPipeQueues+0x117
b5bd67d4 8041ef05 mrxsmb!MRxSmbFsdDispatch+0x118
b5bd67e8 eb833839 nt!IopfCallDriver+0x35
b5bd6890 804a8109 nt!IopQueryXxxInformation+0x164
b5bd68b0 804c7d63 nt!IoQueryFileInformation+0x19
b5bd6a4c 80456562 nt!IopParseDevice+0xe8f
b5bd6ac4 804de0c0 nt!ObpLookupObjectName+0x504
b5bd6bd4 804a929b nt!ObOpenObjectByName+0xc8
b5bd6d54 8046b2a9 nt!NtQueryFullAttributesFile+0xe7
b5bd6d54 77f88887 nt!KiSystemService+0xc9

0: kd> !whattime 0n2008
2008 Ticks in Standard Time: 31.375s
```

Main Thread need not be a GUI thread. Most input console applications have *ReadConsole* calls in normal main process thread stack:

```
0:000> kL
ChildEBP RetAddr
0012fc6c 77d20190 ntdll!KiFastSystemCallRet
0012fc70 77d27fdf ntdll!NtRequestWaitReplyPort+0xc
0012fc90 765d705c ntdll!CsrClientCallServer+0xc2
0012fd8c 76634674 kernel32!ReadConsoleInternal+0x1cd
0012fe14 765eaf6a kernel32!ReadConsoleA+0x40
0012fe7c 6ec35196 kernel32!ReadFile+0x84
0012fec0 6ec35616 MSVCR80!_read_nolock+0x201
0012ff04 6ec45928 MSVCR80!_read+0xc0
0012ff1c 6ec49e47 MSVCR80!_filbuf+0x78
0012ff54 0040100d MSVCR80!getc+0x113
0012ff5c 0040117c ConsoleTest!wmain+0xd
0012ffa0 765d3833 ConsoleTest!__tmainCRTStartup+0x10f
0012ffac 77cfa9bd kernel32!BaseThreadInitThunk+0xe
0012ffec 00000000 ntdll!_RtlUserThreadStart+0x23
```

```
0:000> kL
ChildEBP RetAddr
001cf594 77d20190 ntdll!KiFastSystemCallRet
001cf598 77d27fdf ntdll!NtRequestWaitReplyPort+0xc
001cf5b8 765d705c ntdll!CsrClientCallServer+0xc2
001cf6b4 765d6efe kernel32!ReadConsoleInternal+0x1cd
001cf740 49ecd538 kernel32!ReadConsoleW+0x47
001cf7a8 49ecd645 cmd!ReadBufFromConsole+0xb5
001cf7d4 49ec2247 cmd!FillBuf+0x175
001cf7d8 49ec2165 cmd!GetByte+0x11
001cf7f4 49ec20d8 cmd!Lex+0x75
001cf80c 49ec207f cmd!GeToken+0x27
001cf81c 49ec200a cmd!ParseStatement+0x36
001cf830 49ec6038 cmd!Parser+0x46
001cf878 49ecc703 cmd!main+0x1de
001cf8bc 765d3833 cmd!_initterm_e+0x163
001cf8c8 77cfa9bd kernel32!BaseThreadInitThunk+0xe
001cf908 00000000 ntdll!_RtlUserThreadStart+0x23
```

Insufficient Memory (Kernel Pool)

Although handle leaks may result in insufficient pool memory, many drivers allocate their own private memory and specify a 4-letter ASCII tag. For example, here is a non-paged pool from my x64 Vista workstation (shown in a small font for visual clarity):

```
lkd> !poolused 3
   Sorting by  NonPaged Pool Consumed


  Pool Used:
            NonPaged
 Tag    Allocs     Frees      Diff     Used
 EtwB      304       134       170  6550080  Etw Buffer , Binary: nt!etw
 File 32630649 32618671    11978  3752928  File objects
 Pool       16        11         5  3363472  Pool tables, etc.
 Ntfr   204791    187152     17639  2258704  ERESOURCE , Binary: ntfs.sys
 FMsl   199039    187685     11354  2179968  STREAM_LIST_CTRL structure , Binary: fltmgr.sys
 MmCa   250092    240351      9741  2134368  Mm control areas for mapped files , Binary: nt!mm
 ViMm   135503    134021      1482  1783824  Video memory manager , Binary: dxgkrnl.sys
 Cont       53        12        41  1567664  Contiguous physical memory allocations for device
drivers
 Thre    72558     71527      1031  1234064  Thread objects , Binary: nt!ps
 VoSm      872       851        21  1220544  Bitmap allocations , Binary: volsnap.sys
 NtFs  8122505   8110933     11572  1190960  StrucSup.c , Binary: ntfs.sys
 AmlH        1         0         1  1048576  ACPI AMLI Pooltags
 SaSc    20281     14820      5461  1048512  UNKNOWN pooltag 'SaSc', please update pooltag.txt
 RaRS     1000         0      1000   960000  UNKNOWN pooltag 'RaRS', please update pooltag.txt
...
...
...
```

If the pool tag is unknown, the following Microsoft article explains how to locate the corresponding driver:

https://support.microsoft.com/en-us/help/298102/how-to-find-pool-tags-that-are-used-by-third-party-drivers

We can also use memory search in WinDbg to locate kernel space addresses and see what modules they correspond to.

WinDbg shows the number of failed pool allocations and also shows a message when pool usage is nearly its maximum. Below I put some examples with possible troubleshooting hints.

Session pool

```
3: kd> !vm

*** Virtual Memory Usage ***
        Physical Memory:      1572637 (    6290548 Kb)
```

```
        Page File: \??\C:\pagefile.sys
          Current:   3145728 Kb  Free Space:   3001132 Kb
          Minimum:   3145728 Kb  Maximum:      3145728 Kb
        Available Pages:      1317401 (    5269604 Kb)
        ResAvail Pages:       1478498 (    5913992 Kb)
        Locked IO Pages:          114 (        456 Kb)
        Free System PTEs:      194059 (     776236 Kb)
        Free NP PTEs:           32766 (     131064 Kb)
        Free Special NP:            0 (          0 Kb)
        Modified Pages:           443 (       1772 Kb)
        Modified PF Pages:        442 (       1768 Kb)
        NonPagedPool Usage:     13183 (      52732 Kb)
        NonPagedPool Max:       65215 (     260860 Kb)
        PagedPool 0 Usage:      11328 (      45312 Kb)
        PagedPool 1 Usage:       1473 (       5892 Kb)
        PagedPool 2 Usage:       1486 (       5944 Kb)
        PagedPool 3 Usage:       1458 (       5832 Kb)
        PagedPool 4 Usage:       1505 (       6020 Kb)
        PagedPool Usage:        17250 (      69000 Kb)
        PagedPool Maximum:      65536 (     262144 Kb)

        ********** 3441 pool allocations have failed **********

        Shared Commit:           8137 (      32548 Kb)
        Special Pool:               0 (          0 Kb)
        Shared Process:          8954 (      35816 Kb)
        PagedPool Commit:       17312 (      69248 Kb)
        Driver Commit:           2095 (       8380 Kb)
        Committed pages:       212476 (     849904 Kb)
        Commit limit:         2312654 (    9250616 Kb)
```

Paged and non-paged pool usage is far from maximum, therefore, we check session pool:

```
3: kd> !vm 4

        Terminal Server Memory Usage By Session:


        Session Paged Pool Maximum is 32768K
        Session View Space Maximum is 20480K


        Session ID 0 @ f79a1000:
        Paged Pool Usage:        9824K
        Commit Usage:           10148K


        Session ID 2 @ f7989000:
        Paged Pool Usage:        1212K
```

```
    Commit Usage:            2180K




    Session ID 9 @ f79b5000:
    Paged Pool Usage:        32552K

    *** 7837 Pool Allocation Failures ***

    Commit Usage:            33652K
```

Paged pool

We might have a direct warning:

```
1: kd> !vm

*** Virtual Memory Usage ***
 Physical Memory:    511881    ( 2047524 Kb)
 Page File: \??\S:\pagefile.sys
    Current:    2098176Kb Free Space:    1837740Kb
    Minimum:    2098176Kb Maximum:       2098176Kb
 Page File: \??\R:\pagefile.sys
    Current:    1048576Kb Free Space:     792360Kb
    Minimum:    1048576Kb Maximum:       1048576Kb
 Available Pages:    201353    (  805412 Kb)
 ResAvail Pages:     426839    ( 1707356 Kb)
 Modified Pages:      45405    (  181620 Kb)
 NonPagedPool Usage: 10042     (   40168 Kb)
 NonPagedPool Max:   68537     (  274148 Kb)
 PagedPool 0 Usage:  26820     (  107280 Kb)
 PagedPool 1 Usage:   1491     (    5964 Kb)
 PagedPool 2 Usage:   1521     (    6084 Kb)
 PagedPool 3 Usage:   1502     (    6008 Kb)
 PagedPool 4 Usage:   1516     (    6064 Kb)
 ********** Excessive Paged Pool Usage *****
 PagedPool Usage:     32850    (  131400 Kb)
 PagedPool Maximum:   40960    (  163840 Kb)
 Shared Commit:       14479    (   57916 Kb)
 Special Pool:            0    (       0 Kb)
 Free System PTEs:  135832     (  543328 Kb)
 Shared Process:      15186    (   60744 Kb)
 PagedPool Commit:    32850    (  131400 Kb)
 Driver Commit:        1322    (    5288 Kb)
 Committed pages:    426786    ( 1707144 Kb)
 Commit limit:      1259456    ( 5037824 Kb)
```

If there is no warning we can check the size manually and, if the paged pool usage is close to its maximum, but for the non-paged pool it is not, then most likely failed allocations were from the paged pool:

```
0: kd> !vm

*** Virtual Memory Usage ***
       Physical Memory:     4193696 (  16774784 Kb)
       Page File: \??\C:\pagefile.sys
         Current:   4193280 Kb  Free Space:   3313120 Kb
         Minimum:   4193280 Kb  Maximum:      4193280 Kb
       Available Pages:     3210617 (  12842468 Kb)
       ResAvail Pages:      4031978 (  16127912 Kb)
       Locked IO Pages:         120 (       480 Kb)
       Free System PTEs:      99633 (    398532 Kb)
       Free NP PTEs:          26875 (    107500 Kb)
       Free Special NP:           0 (         0 Kb)
       Modified Pages:          611 (      2444 Kb)
       Modified PF Pages:       590 (      2360 Kb)
       NonPagedPool 0 Used:    8271 (   33084 Kb)
       NonPagedPool 1 Used:   13828 (   55312 Kb)
       NonPagedPool Usage:    37846 (    151384 Kb)
       NonPagedPool Max:      65215 (    260860 Kb)
       PagedPool 0 Usage:     82308 (    329232 Kb)
       PagedPool 1 Usage:     12700 (     50800 Kb)
       PagedPool 2 Usage:     25702 (    102808 Kb)
       PagedPool Usage:      120710 (    482840 Kb)
       PagedPool Maximum:    134144 (    536576 Kb)

      ********** 818 pool allocations have failed **********

       Shared Commit:         80168 (    320672 Kb)
       Special Pool:              0 (         0 Kb)
       Shared Process:        55654 (    222616 Kb)
       PagedPool Commit:     120772 (    483088 Kb)
       Driver Commit:          1890 (      7560 Kb)
       Committed pages:     1344388 (   5377552 Kb)
       Commit limit:        5177766 (  20711064 Kb)
```

!poolused 4 WinDbg command sorts paged pool consumption by pool tag:

```
0: kd> !poolused 4
   Sorting by  Paged Pool Consumed


  Pool Used:
            NonPaged                   Paged
 Tag     Allocs       Used      Allocs       Used
 MmSt         0          0       85622 140642616      Mm section object
```

```
prototype ptes , Binary: nt!mm
 Ntff         5     1040     63715 51991440       FCB_DATA , Binary:
ntfs.sys
```

Non-paged pool

```
0: kd> !vm

 *** Virtual Memory Usage ***
        Physical Memory:       851775 (   3407100 Kb)
        Page File: \??\C:\pagefile.sys
          Current:   4190208 Kb  Free Space:   4175708 Kb
          Minimum:   4190208 Kb  Maximum:      4190208 Kb
        Available Pages:       147274 (    589096 Kb)
        ResAvail Pages:        769287 (   3077148 Kb)
        Locked IO Pages:          118 (       472 Kb)
        Free System PTEs:      184910 (    739640 Kb)
        Free NP PTEs:             110 (       440 Kb)
        Free Special NP:            0 (         0 Kb)
        Modified Pages:           168 (       672 Kb)
        Modified PF Pages:        168 (       672 Kb)
        NonPagedPool Usage:     64445 (    257780 Kb)
        NonPagedPool Max:       64640 (    258560 Kb)
        ********** Excessive NonPaged Pool Usage *****
        PagedPool 0 Usage:      21912 (     87648 Kb)
        PagedPool 1 Usage:        691 (      2764 Kb)
        PagedPool 2 Usage:        706 (      2824 Kb)
        PagedPool 3 Usage:        704 (      2816 Kb)
        PagedPool 4 Usage:        708 (      2832 Kb)
        PagedPool Usage:        24721 (     98884 Kb)
        PagedPool Maximum:     134144 (    536576 Kb)

        ********** 429 pool allocations have failed **********

        Shared Commit:           5274 (     21096 Kb)
        Special Pool:               0 (         0 Kb)
        Shared Process:          3958 (     15832 Kb)
        PagedPool Commit:       24785 (     99140 Kb)
        Driver Commit:          19289 (     77156 Kb)
        Committed pages:       646282 (   2585128 Kb)
        Commit limit:         1860990 (   7443960 Kb)
```

!poolused 3 WinDbg command sorts non-paged pool consumption by pool tag:

```
0: kd> !poolused 3
   Sorting by  NonPaged Pool Consumed

  Pool Used:
            NonPaged
 Tag    Allocs     Frees     Diff
```

```
 Ddk    9074558  3859522  5215036  Default for driver allocated memory
(user's of ntddk.h)
 MmCm     43787    42677     1110  Calls made to MmAllocateContiguousMemory
, Binary: nt!mm
 LSwi         1        0        1  initial work context
 TCPt   3281838  3281808       30  TCP/IP network protocol , Binary: TCP
```

Regarding *Ddk* tag, please see **The Search for Tags** case study (page 206).

The following Microsoft article KB293857 explains how we can use **xpool** command from old *kdex2x86.dll* extension which even works for Windows 2003 dumps (shown in a small font for visual clarity):

```
0: kd> !w2kfre\kdex2x86.xpool -map
unable to get NT!MmSizeOfNonPagedMustSucceed location
unable to get NT!MmSubsectionTopPage location
unable to get NT!MmKseg2Frame location
unable to get NT!MmNonPagedMustSucceed location


Status Map of Pool Area Pages
==============================
  'O': one page in use                                ('P': paged out)
  '<': start page of contiguous pages in use          ('{': paged out)
  '>': last page of contiguous pages in use           ('}': paged out)
  '=': intermediate page of contiguous pages in use   ('-': paged out)
  '.': one page not used


Non-Paged Pool Area Summary
----------------------------
Maximum Number of Pages   = 64640 pages
Number of Pages In Use    = 36721 pages (56.8%)


          +00000  +08000   +10000  +18000   +20000  +28000   +30000  +38000
82780000: ..OO.OO.OO..O.OO .O..OO.OO.OO..O. OO.O..OO.O..OO.. ..OO.O..OO.OO.OO
827c0000: .O..OO....OO..O. OO.OO.OO....OO.. O....O..OO....OO .O..OO.O..OO..O.
82800000: ..O............. ................ ................ ................
82840000: ................ ................ ................ ................
82880000: ......O.....O... ..O.O.....O..... O.....O.....O... ..O.....O.......
828c0000: ..O.........O... ......OOO.....O. ....O.....O..... O.....O.........
82900000: .O.........OO... O....O........O. ......OO........ OO.O..O.........
82940000: ...............O ..O.OO........OO ................ ...O.....O......
82980000: O.........O..O.. ....O.........O. ........O.....O. ..O.........O...
829c0000: ........O....... ..O...........O. .O..O...O..O.... ..O.........O...
82a00000: ......O..O...... O.........O..... ....O.........O. ................
82a40000: ............O... O..O.O......OO.. ......O.....O... ..O.....O...O.OO
...
...
...
893c0000: ................ ................ ................ ................
89400000: ..........=..=.. ....=.....=..... =..=......=..=.. ....=..=......=.
89440000: ..=............. ............=... =..=.....=..=... =...=.=.....==..
89480000: ....==......=.=. .........=...... ====.=.=........ ................
894c0000: ................ ................ ..........=.=... ...==...........
89500000: ..=............. ..=............. ..=............. ..=.............
89540000: ..=............. ..=............. ..=............. ..=...=.....=..=
89580000: ......=..=...... =..=......=.==== ==..==.=....=... .=....=....=.==.
895c0000: =.....==........ ..=............. =..=......=...=. ................
89600000: ........=...=..= .....=.......=.= ==....=......... .........=....=.
89640000: ..=...===...=... ==......=..=..=. ..=..=......=... ......=.=.....=.
...
...
...
```

Here is another example:

```
0: kd> !vm

*** Virtual Memory Usage ***
 Physical Memory:    786299    ( 3145196 Kb)
 Page File: \??\C:\pagefile.sys
    Current:   4193280Kb Free Space:   3407908Kb
    Minimum:   4193280Kb Maximum:      4193280Kb
 Available Pages:    200189    (  800756 Kb)
 ResAvail Pages:     657130    ( 2628520 Kb)
 Modified Pages:        762    (    3048 Kb)
 NonPagedPool Usage: 22948     (   91792 Kb)
 NonPagedPool Max:   70145     (  280580 Kb)
 PagedPool 0 Usage:  19666     (   78664 Kb)
 PagedPool 1 Usage:   3358     (   13432 Kb)
 PagedPool 2 Usage:   3306     (   13224 Kb)
 PagedPool 3 Usage:   3312     (   13248 Kb)
 PagedPool 4 Usage:   3309     (   13236 Kb)
 ********** Excessive Paged Pool Usage *****
 PagedPool Usage:     32951    (  131804 Kb)
 PagedPool Maximum:   40960    (  163840 Kb)
 Shared Commit:        9664    (   38656 Kb)
 Special Pool:            0    (       0 Kb)
 Free System PTEs:  103335     (  413340 Kb)
 Shared Process:      45024    (  180096 Kb)
 PagedPool Commit:    32951    (  131804 Kb)
 Driver Commit:        1398    (    5592 Kb)
 Committed pages:    864175    ( 3456700 Kb)
 Commit limit:      1793827    ( 7175308 Kb)

 0: kd> !poolused 4
    Sorting by Paged Pool Consumed

  Pool Used:
             NonPaged              Paged
 Tag    Allocs     Used     Allocs     Used
 CM         85     5440     11045  47915424
 MyAV        0        0       186  14391520
 MmSt        0        0     11795  13235744
 Obtb      709    90752      2712  11108352
 Ntff        5     1120      9886   8541504
...
...
...
```

MyAV tag seems to be the prefix for *MyAVDrv* module, and this is hardly a coincidence. Looking at the list of drivers, we see that *MyAVDrv.sys* was loaded and unloaded several times. Could it be that it didn't free its non-paged pool allocations?

```
0: kd> lmv m MyAVDrv.sys
start    end        module name

Unloaded modules:
a5069000 a5084000   MyAVDrv.sys
    Timestamp: unavailable (00000000)
    Checksum:  00000000
a5069000 a5084000   MyAVDrv.sys
    Timestamp: unavailable (00000000)
    Checksum:  00000000
a5069000 a5084000   MyAVDrv.sys
    Timestamp: unavailable (00000000)
    Checksum:  00000000
b93e1000 b93fc000   MyAVDrv.sys
    Timestamp: unavailable (00000000)
    Checksum:  00000000
b9ae5000 b9b00000   MyAVDrv.sys
    Timestamp: unavailable (00000000)
    Checksum:  00000000
be775000 be790000   MyAVDrv.sys
    Timestamp: unavailable (00000000)
    Checksum:  00000000
```

Also, we see that *CM* tag has the most allocations and **!locks** command shows hundreds of threads waiting for registry, one example of **High Contention** pattern (page 421):

```
0: kd> !locks

Resource @ nt!CmpRegistryLock (0x80478b00)    Shared 10 owning threads
    Contention Count = 9149810
    NumberOfSharedWaiters = 718
    NumberOfExclusiveWaiters = 21
```

Therefore, we see at least two problems in this memory dump: excessive paged pool usage and high thread contention around registry resource slowing down if not halting the system.

Busy System

If there are no CPU-bound threads in a system, then most of the time, processors are looping in the so-called idle thread where they are halted waiting for an interrupt to occur. When an interrupt occurs, they process a DPC list and then do thread scheduling if necessary, as evident from the stack trace and its functions disassembly below. If we have a memory dump, one of the running threads would be the one called *KeBugCheck(Ex)* function.

```
3: kd> !running

System Processors f (affinity mask)
  Idle Processors d

     Prcb      Current   Next
  1  f7737120  8a3da020            ................

3: kd> !thread 8a3da020 1f
THREAD 8a3da020  Cid 0ebc.0dec  Teb: 7ffdf000 Win32Thread: bc002328
RUNNING on processor 1
Not impersonating
DeviceMap                 e3e3e080
Owning Process            8a0aea88       Image:         SystemDump.exe
Wait Start TickCount      17154          Ticks: 0
Context Switch Count      568                 LargeStack
UserTime                  00:00:00.046
KernelTime                00:00:00.375
Win32 Start Address 0x0040fe92
Start Address 0x77e6b5c7
Stack Init f4266000 Current f4265c08 Base f4266000 Limit f4261000 Call 0
Priority 11 BasePriority 10 PriorityDecrement 0
ChildEBP RetAddr
f4265bec f79c9743 nt!KeBugCheckEx+0x1b
WARNING: Stack unwind information not available. Following frames may be
wrong.
f4265c38 8081dce5 SystemDump+0x743
f4265c4c 808f4797 nt!IofCallDriver+0x45
f4265c60 808f5515 nt!IopSynchronousServiceTail+0x10b
f4265d00 808ee0e4 nt!IopXxxControlFile+0x5db
f4265d34 80888c6c nt!NtDeviceIoControlFile+0x2a
f4265d34 7c82ed54 nt!KiFastCallEntry+0xfc

3: kd> !ready
Processor 0: No threads in READY state
Processor 1: No threads in READY state
Processor 2: No threads in READY state
Processor 3: No threads in READY state
```

```
3: kd> ~2s

2: kd> !thread -1 1f
THREAD f7742090  Cid 0000.0000  Teb: 00000000 Win32Thread: 00000000
RUNNING on processor 2
Not impersonating
Owning Process            8089db40       Image:         Idle
Wait Start TickCount      0              Ticks: 17154 (0:00:04:28.031)
Context Switch Count      193155
UserTime                  00:00:00.000
KernelTime                00:03:23.328
Stack Init f78b7000 Current f78b6d4c Base f78b7000 Limit f78b4000 Call 0
Priority 0 BasePriority 0 PriorityDecrement 0
ChildEBP RetAddr
f78b6d50 8088d262 intelppm!AcpiC1Idle+0x12
f78b6d54 00000000 nt!KiIdleLoop+0xa

2: kd> .asm no_code_bytes
Assembly options: no_code_bytes

2: kd> uf intelppm!AcpiC1Idle
intelppm!AcpiC1Idle:
f6e73c90 push    ecx
f6e73c91 push    0
f6e73c93 call    intelppm!KeQueryPerformanceCounter (f6e740c6)
f6e73c98 mov     ecx,dword ptr [esp]
f6e73c9b mov     dword ptr [ecx],eax
f6e73c9d mov     dword ptr [ecx+4],edx
f6e73ca0 sti
f6e73ca1 hlt
f6e73ca2 push    0
f6e73ca4 call    intelppm!KeQueryPerformanceCounter (f6e740c6)
f6e73ca9 pop     ecx
f6e73caa mov     dword ptr [ecx+8],eax
f6e73cad mov     dword ptr [ecx+0Ch],edx
f6e73cb0 xor     eax,eax
f6e73cb2 ret

2: kd> uf nt!KiIdleLoop
nt!KiIdleLoop:
8088d258 jmp     nt!KiIdleLoop+0xa (8088d262)

nt!KiIdleLoop+0x2:
8088d25a lea     ecx,[ebx+0EC0h]
8088d260 call    dword ptr [ecx]

nt!KiIdleLoop+0xa:
8088d262 pause ; http://www.asmpedia.org/index.php?title=PAUSE
8088d264 sti
8088d265 nop
8088d266 nop
```

```
8088d267 cli
8088d268 mov     eax,dword ptr [ebx+0A4Ch]
8088d26e or      eax,dword ptr [ebx+0A88h]
8088d274 or      eax,dword ptr [ebx+0C10h]
8088d27a je      nt!KiIdleLoop+0x37 (8088d28f)

nt!KiIdleLoop+0x24:
8088d27c mov     cl,2
8088d27e call    dword ptr [nt!_imp_HalClearSoftwareInterrupt (808010a8)]
8088d284 lea     ecx,[ebx+120h]
8088d28a call    nt!KiRetireDpcList (80831be8)

nt!KiIdleLoop+0x37:
8088d28f cmp     dword ptr [ebx+128h],0
8088d296 je      nt!KiIdleLoop+0xca (8088d322)

nt!KiIdleLoop+0x44:
8088d29c mov     ecx,1Bh
8088d2a1 call    dword ptr [nt!_imp_KfRaiseIrql (80801100)]
8088d2a7 sti
8088d2a8 mov     edi,dword ptr [ebx+124h]
8088d2ae mov     byte ptr [edi+5Dh],1
8088d2b2 lock bts dword ptr [ebx+0A7Ch],0
8088d2bb jae     nt!KiIdleLoop+0x70 (8088d2c8)

nt!KiIdleLoop+0x65:
8088d2bd lea     ecx,[ebx+0A7Ch]
8088d2c3 call    nt!KefAcquireSpinLockAtDpcLevel (80887fd0)

nt!KiIdleLoop+0x70:
8088d2c8 mov     esi,dword ptr [ebx+128h]
8088d2ce cmp     esi,edi
8088d2d0 je      nt!KiIdleLoop+0xb3 (8088d30b)

nt!KiIdleLoop+0x7a:
8088d2d2 and     dword ptr [ebx+128h],0
8088d2d9 mov     dword ptr [ebx+124h],esi
8088d2df mov     byte ptr [esi+4Ch],2
8088d2e3 and     byte ptr [ebx+0AA3h],0
8088d2ea and     dword ptr [ebx+0A7Ch],0

nt!KiIdleLoop+0x99:
8088d2f1 mov     ecx,1
8088d2f6 call    nt!SwapContext (8088d040)
8088d2fb mov     ecx,2
8088d300 call    dword ptr [nt!_imp_KfLowerIrql (80801104)]
8088d306 jmp     nt!KiIdleLoop+0xa (8088d262)

nt!KiIdleLoop+0xb3:
8088d30b and     dword ptr [ebx+128h],0
8088d312 and     dword ptr [ebx+0A7Ch],0
```

```
8088d319 and     byte ptr [edi+5Dh],0
8088d31d jmp     nt!KiIdleLoop+0xa (8088d262)

nt!KiIdleLoop+0xca:
8088d322 cmp     byte ptr [ebx+0AA3h],0
8088d329 je      nt!KiIdleLoop+0x2 (8088d25a)

nt!KiIdleLoop+0xd7:
8088d32f sti
8088d330 lea     ecx,[ebx+120h]
8088d336 call    nt!KiIdleSchedule (808343e6)
8088d33b test    eax,eax
8088d33d mov     esi,eax
8088d33f mov     edi,dword ptr [ebx+12Ch]
8088d345 jne     nt!KiIdleLoop+0x99 (8088d2f1)

nt!KiIdleLoop+0xef:
8088d347 jmp     nt!KiIdleLoop+0xa (8088d262)
```

In some memory dumps taken when systems or sessions were hanging or very slow for some time we might see **Busy System** pattern where all processors execute non-idle threads, and there are threads in ready queues waiting to be scheduled:

```
3: kd> !running

System Processors f (affinity mask)
  Idle Processors 0

     Prcb      Current   Next
  0  ffdff120  88cef850             ................
  1  f7727120  8940b7a0             ................
  2  f772f120  8776f020             ................
  3  f7737120  87b25360             ................

3: kd> !ready
Processor 0: Ready Threads at priority 8
    THREAD 88161668  Cid 3d58.43a0  Teb: 7ffdf000 Win32Thread: bc1eba48
READY
    THREAD 882d0020  Cid 1004.0520  Teb: 7ffdf000 Win32Thread: bc230838
READY
    THREAD 88716b40  Cid 2034.241c  Teb: 7ffdd000 Win32Thread: bc11b388
READY
    THREAD 88bf7978  Cid 2444.2564  Teb: 7ffde000 Win32Thread: bc1ccc18
READY
    THREAD 876f7a28  Cid 2308.4bfc  Teb: 7ffdd000 Win32Thread: bc1f7b98
READY
Processor 0: Ready Threads at priority 0
    THREAD 8a3925a8  Cid 0004.0008  Teb: 00000000 Win32Thread: 00000000
READY
Processor 1: Ready Threads at priority 9
```

```
    THREAD 87e69db0  Cid 067c.3930  Teb: 7ffdb000 Win32Thread: bc180990
READY
Processor 1: Ready Threads at priority 8
    THREAD 88398c70  Cid 27cc.15b4  Teb: 7ffde000 Win32Thread: bc159ea8
READY
Processor 2: Ready Threads at priority 8
    THREAD 8873cdb0  Cid 4c24.4384  Teb: 7ffdd000 Win32Thread: bc1c9838
READY
    THREAD 89f331e0  Cid 453c.4c68  Teb: 7ffdf000 Win32Thread: bc21dbd0
READY
    THREAD 889a03f0  Cid 339c.2fcc  Teb: 7ffdf000 Win32Thread: bc1cdbe8
READY
    THREAD 87aacdb0  Cid 3b80.4ed0  Teb: 7ffde000 Win32Thread: bc1c5d10
READY
Processor 3: No threads in READY state
```

Here is another example from a busy 8-processor system where only one CPU was idle at the time of the bugcheck:

```
5: kd> !ready
Processor 0: No threads in READY state
Processor 1: No threads in READY state
Processor 2: No threads in READY state
Processor 3: No threads in READY state
Processor 4: No threads in READY state
Processor 5: No threads in READY state
Processor 6: No threads in READY state
Processor 7: No threads in READY state

5: kd> !running

System Processors ff (affinity mask)
  Idle Processors 1

     Prcb      Current   Next
  1  f7727120  8713a5a0            ................
  2  f772f120  86214750            ................
  3  f7737120  86f87020            ................
  4  f773f120  86ffe700            ................
  5  f7747120  86803a90            ................
  6  f774f120  86043db0            ................
  7  f7757120  86bcbdb0            ................

5: kd> !thread 8713a5a0 1f
THREAD 8713a5a0  Cid 4ef4.4f04  Teb: 7ffdd000 Win32Thread: bc423920
RUNNING on processor 1
Not impersonating
DeviceMap                 e44e9a40
Owning Process            864d1d88       Image:         SomeExe.exe
Wait Start TickCount      1415535        Ticks: 0
Context Switch Count      7621092                 LargeStack
```

```
UserTime                  00:06:59.218
KernelTime                00:19:26.359
Win32 Start Address BROWSEUI!BrowserProtectedThreadProc (0x75ec1c3f)
Start Address kernel32!BaseThreadStartThunk (0x77e617ec)
Stack Init b68b8a70 Current b68b8c28 Base b68b9000 Limit b68b1000 Call
b68b8a7c
Priority 13 BasePriority 13 PriorityDecrement 0
ChildEBP RetAddr
00c1f4fc 773dc4e4 USER32!DispatchHookA+0x35
00c1f528 7739c9c6 USER32!fnHkINLPCWPRETSTRUCTA+0x60
00c1f550 7c828536 USER32!__fnDWORD+0x24
00c1f550 808308f4 ntdll!KiUserCallbackDispatcher+0x2e
b68b8a94 8091d6d1 nt!KiCallUserMode+0x4
b68b8aec bf8a26d3 nt!KeUserModeCallback+0x8f
b68b8b70 bf89dd4d win32k!SfnDWORD+0xb4
b68b8be8 bf89d79d win32k!xxxHkCallHook+0x22c
b68b8c90 bf89da19 win32k!xxxCallHook2+0x245
b68b8cac bf8a137a win32k!xxxCallHook+0x26
b68b8cec bf85af67 win32k!xxxSendMessageTimeout+0x1e3
b68b8d10 bf8c182c win32k!xxxWrapSendMessage+0x1b
b68b8d40 8088978c win32k!NtUserMessageCall+0x9d
b68b8d40 7c8285ec nt!KiFastCallEntry+0xfc
00c1f550 7c828536 ntdll!KiFastSystemCallRet
00c1f57c 7739d1ec ntdll!KiUserCallbackDispatcher+0x2e
00c1f5b8 7738cee9 USER32!NtUserMessageCall+0xc
00c1f5d8 01438f73 USER32!SendMessageA+0x7f

5: kd> !thread 86214750
THREAD 86214750  Cid 0b94.1238  Teb: 7ffdb000 Win32Thread: bc2f5ea8
RUNNING on processor 2
Not impersonating
DeviceMap                 e3482310
Owning Process            85790020       Image:         SomeExe.exe
Wait Start TickCount      1415535        Ticks: 0
Context Switch Count      1745682                LargeStack
UserTime                  00:01:20.031
KernelTime                00:04:03.484
Win32 Start Address 0x75ec1c3f
Start Address kernel32!BaseThreadStartThunk (0x77e617ec)
Stack Init b4861000 Current b4860558 Base b4861000 Limit b4856000 Call 0
Priority 13 BasePriority 13 PriorityDecrement 0
ChildEBP RetAddr
b4860bd8 bf8da699 nt!PsGetThreadProcess
b4860bf4 bf89d6e6 win32k!IsRestricted+0x2f
b4860c90 bf89da19 win32k!xxxCallHook2+0x12d
b4860cac bf8a137a win32k!xxxCallHook+0x26
b4860cec bf85af67 win32k!xxxSendMessageTimeout+0x1e3
b4860d10 bf8c182c win32k!xxxWrapSendMessage+0x1b
b4860d40 8088978c win32k!NtUserMessageCall+0x9d
b4860d40 7c8285ec nt!KiFastCallEntry+0xfc
00c1f5fc 00000000 ntdll!KiFastSystemCallRet
```

```
5: kd> !thread 86f87020 1f
THREAD 86f87020  Cid 0238.0ae8  Teb: 7ffa5000 Win32Thread: 00000000
RUNNING on processor 3
IRP List:
    86869200: (0006,0094) Flags: 00000900  Mdl: 00000000
    85b2a7f0: (0006,0094) Flags: 00000900  Mdl: 00000000
    86f80a20: (0006,0094) Flags: 00000800  Mdl: 00000000
    85e6af68: (0006,0094) Flags: 00000900  Mdl: 00000000
    892a6c78: (0006,0094) Flags: 00000900  Mdl: 00000000
    85d06070: (0006,0094) Flags: 00000900  Mdl: 00000000
    85da35e0: (0006,0094) Flags: 00000900  Mdl: 00000000
    87216340: (0006,0094) Flags: 00000900  Mdl: 00000000
Not impersonating
DeviceMap                 e1003940
Owning Process            8850e020       Image:         lsass.exe
Wait Start TickCount      1415535        Ticks: 0
Context Switch Count      39608
UserTime                  00:00:01.625
KernelTime                00:00:05.437
Win32 Start Address RPCRT4!ThreadStartRoutine (0x77c7b0f5)
Start Address kernel32!BaseThreadStartThunk (0x77e617ec)
Stack Init f4925000 Current f4924c38 Base f4925000 Limit f4922000 Call 0
Priority 10 BasePriority 9 PriorityDecrement 0
ChildEBP RetAddr
f4924640 80972e8e nt!SePrivilegeCheck+0x24
f4924678 80944aa0 nt!SeSinglePrivilegeCheck+0x3a
f4924770 8088978c nt!NtOpenProcess+0x13a
f4924770 8082eff5 nt!KiFastCallEntry+0xfc
f49247f8 f6037bee nt!ZwOpenProcess+0x11
WARNING: Stack unwind information not available. Following frames may be
wrong.
f4924830 f6002996 SomeDrv+0x48bee

5: kd> !thread 86ffe700 1f
THREAD 86ffe700  Cid 1ba4.1ba8  Teb: 7ffdf000 Win32Thread: bc23cea8
RUNNING on processor 4
Not impersonating
DeviceMap                 e44e9a40
Owning Process            87005708       Image:         WINWORD.EXE
Wait Start TickCount      1415535        Ticks: 0
Context Switch Count      1547251                   LargeStack
UserTime                  00:01:00.750
KernelTime                00:00:45.265
Win32 Start Address WINWORD (0x300019b0)
Start Address kernel32!BaseProcessStartThunk (0x77e617f8)
Stack Init f3465000 Current f3464c48 Base f3465000 Limit f345e000 Call 0
Priority 8 BasePriority 8 PriorityDecrement 0
ChildEBP RetAddr
f3464d64 7c8285eb nt!KiFastCallEntry+0x91
f3464d68 badb0d00 ntdll!KiFastSystemCall+0x3
```

```
5: kd> !thread 86803a90 1f
THREAD 86803a90  Cid 3c20.29f8  Teb: 7ffdf000 Win32Thread: bc295480
RUNNING on processor 5
Not impersonating
DeviceMap                 e518c6b8
Owning Process            857d5500       Image:         SystemDump.exe
Wait Start TickCount      1415535        Ticks: 0
Context Switch Count      310                 LargeStack
UserTime                  00:00:00.015
KernelTime                00:00:00.046
*** ERROR: Module load completed but symbols could not be loaded for
SystemDump.exe
Win32 Start Address SystemDump_400000 (0x0040fe92)
Start Address kernel32!BaseProcessStartThunk (0x77e617f8)
Stack Init b38a4000 Current b38a3c08 Base b38a4000 Limit b389f000 Call 0
Priority 11 BasePriority 8 PriorityDecrement 2
ChildEBP RetAddr  Args to Child
b38a3bf0 f79e3743 000000e2 cccccccc 866962b0 nt!KeBugCheckEx+0x1b
WARNING: Stack unwind information not available. Following frames may be
wrong.
b38a3c3c 8081df65 SystemDump+0x743
b38a3c50 808f5437 nt!IofCallDriver+0x45
b38a3c64 808f61bf nt!IopSynchronousServiceTail+0x10b
b38a3d00 808eed08 nt!IopXxxControlFile+0x5e5
b38a3d34 8088978c nt!NtDeviceIoControlFile+0x2a
b38a3d34 7c8285ec nt!KiFastCallEntry+0xfc
0012efc4 7c826fcb ntdll!KiFastSystemCallRet
0012efc8 77e416f5 ntdll!NtDeviceIoControlFile+0xc
0012f02c 00402208 kernel32!DeviceIoControl+0x137
0012f884 00404f8e SystemDump_400000+0x2208

5: kd> !thread 86043db0 1f
THREAD 86043db0  Cid 0610.55dc  Teb: 7ffa1000 Win32Thread: 00000000
RUNNING on processor 6
IRP List:
    86dc99a0: (0006,0094) Flags: 00000a00  Mdl: 00000000
Impersonation token:  e7b30030 (Level Impersonation)
DeviceMap                 e4e470a8
Owning Process            891374a8       Image:         SomeSvc.exe
Wait Start TickCount      1415215        Ticks: 320 (0:00:00:05.000)
Context Switch Count      11728
UserTime                  00:00:02.546
KernelTime                00:02:57.765
Win32 Start Address 0x0082b983
LPC Server thread working on message Id 82b983
Start Address kernel32!BaseThreadStartThunk (0x77e617ec)
Stack Init b49c1000 Current b49c0a7c Base b49c1000 Limit b49be000 Call 0
Priority 8 BasePriority 8 PriorityDecrement 0
ChildEBP RetAddr
b49c0b80 8087c9c0 hal!KeReleaseQueuedSpinLock+0x2d
b49c0ba0 8087ca95 nt!ExReleaseResourceLite+0xac
b49c0ba4 f6faa5ae nt!ExReleaseResourceAndLeaveCriticalRegion+0x5
b49c0bb8 f6faad05 termdd!_IcaCallStack+0x60
```

```
b49c0bdc f6fa6bda termdd!IcaCallDriver+0x71
b49c0c34 f6fa86dc termdd!IcaWriteChannel+0xd8
b49c0c50 f6fa8cc6 termdd!IcaWrite+0x40
b49c0c68 8081df65 termdd!IcaDispatch+0xd0
b49c0c7c 808f5437 nt!IofCallDriver+0x45
b49c0c90 808f3157 nt!IopSynchronousServiceTail+0x10b
b49c0d38 8088978c nt!NtWriteFile+0x663
b49c0d38 7c8285ec nt!KiFastCallEntry+0xfc
0254d814 7c827d3b ntdll!KiFastSystemCallRet
0254d818 77e5b012 ntdll!NtWriteFile+0xc
0254d878 004389f2 kernel32!WriteFile+0xa9

5: kd> !thread 86bcbdb0 1f
THREAD 86bcbdb0  Cid 34ac.1b04  Teb: 7ffdd000 Win32Thread: bc3d9a48
RUNNING on processor 7
IRP List:
    8581d900: (0006,01fc) Flags: 00000884  Mdl: 00000000
Not impersonating
DeviceMap                 e153fc48
Owning Process            872fb708       Image:         SomeExe.exe
Wait Start TickCount      1415535        Ticks: 0
Context Switch Count      7655285                 LargeStack
UserTime                  00:10:09.343
KernelTime                00:30:21.296
Win32 Start Address 0x75ec1c3f
Start Address 0x77e617ec
Stack Init b86cb000 Current b86ca58c Base b86cb000 Limit b86c2000 Call 0
Priority 13 BasePriority 13 PriorityDecrement 0
ChildEBP RetAddr
b86ca974 f724ffc2 fltmgr!FltpPerformPostCallbacks+0x260
b86ca988 f72504f1 fltmgr!FltpProcessIoCompletion+0x10
b86ca998 f7250b83 fltmgr!FltpPassThroughCompletion+0x89
b86ca9c8 f725e5de
fltmgr!FltpLegacyProcessingAfterPreCallbacksCompleted+0x269
b86caa04 8081df65 fltmgr!FltpCreate+0x26a
b86caa18 f75fa8c7 nt!IofCallDriver+0x45
b86caa40 f75faa5a SomeFlt!PassThrough+0xbb
b86caa5c 8081df65 SomeFlt!Create+0xda
b86caa70 808f8f71 nt!IofCallDriver+0x45
b86cab58 80937942 nt!IopParseDevice+0xa35
b86cabd8 80933a76 nt!ObpLookupObjectName+0x5b0
b86cac2c 808eae25 nt!ObOpenObjectByName+0xea
b86caca8 808ec0bf nt!IopCreateFile+0x447
b86cad04 808efc4f nt!IoCreateFile+0xa3
b86cad44 8088978c nt!NtOpenFile+0x27
b86cad44 7c8285ec nt!KiFastCallEntry+0xfc
```

Running threads have a good chance to be **Spiking Threads** (page 305).

Historical Information

Although crash dumps are static, they contain **Historical Information** about past system dynamics that might give clues to a problem and help with troubleshooting and debugging.

For example, IRP flow between user processes and drivers is readily available in any kernel or complete memory dump. WinDbg **!irpfind** command shows the list of currently present I/O request packets. **!irp** command gives individual packet details.

Driver Verifier improvements since Vista and Windows Server 2008 allow embedding stack traces associated with IRP allocation, completion, and cancelation. For information, please look at the following document:

https://docs.microsoft.com/en-us/windows-hardware/drivers/devtest/driver-verifier--what-s-new

Other information that can be included in process, kernel, and complete memory dumps may reveal some history of function calls beyond the current snapshot of thread stacks:

- Heap allocation stack traces that are usually used for debugging memory leaks.
- Handle traces that are used to debug handle leaks (**!htrace** command).
- Raw stack data interpreted symbolically. Some examples include dumping stack data from all process threads and dumping kernel mode stack data.
- LPC messages (**!lpc thread**).
- **Waiting Thread Time** pattern (page 343).

Distribution Anomaly (IRP)

In the kernel or complete memory dumps coming from hanging or slow workstations and servers **!irpfind** WinDbg command may show object **Distribution Anomaly** pattern when specific drivers have an excessive count of active IRPs not observed under normal circumstances. I created two IRP distribution graphs from two problem kernel dumps by preprocessing command output using Visual Studio keyboard macros to eliminate completed IRPs and then using Excel. In one case, it was a significant number of I/O request packets from 3rd-party antivirus filter driver:

\Driver\3rdPartyAvFilter

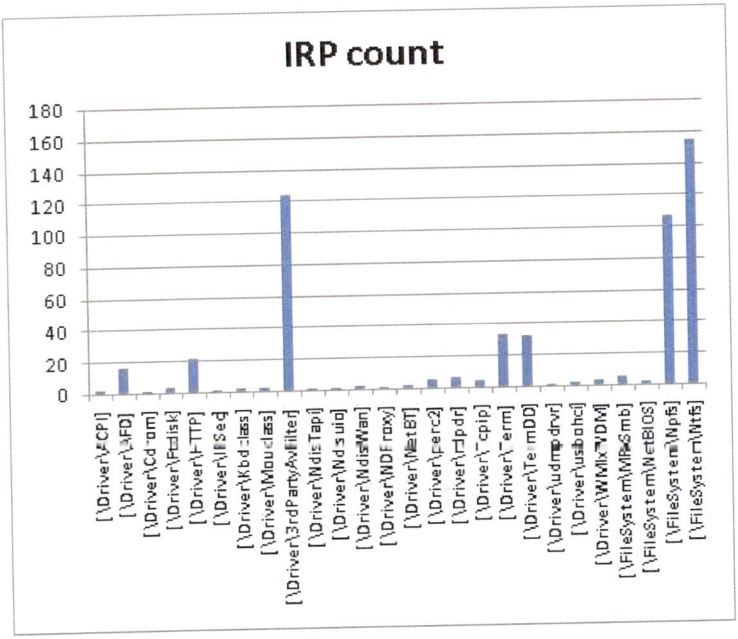

In the second case, it was the massive number of active IRPs targeted to kernel socket ancillary function driver:

\Driver\AFD

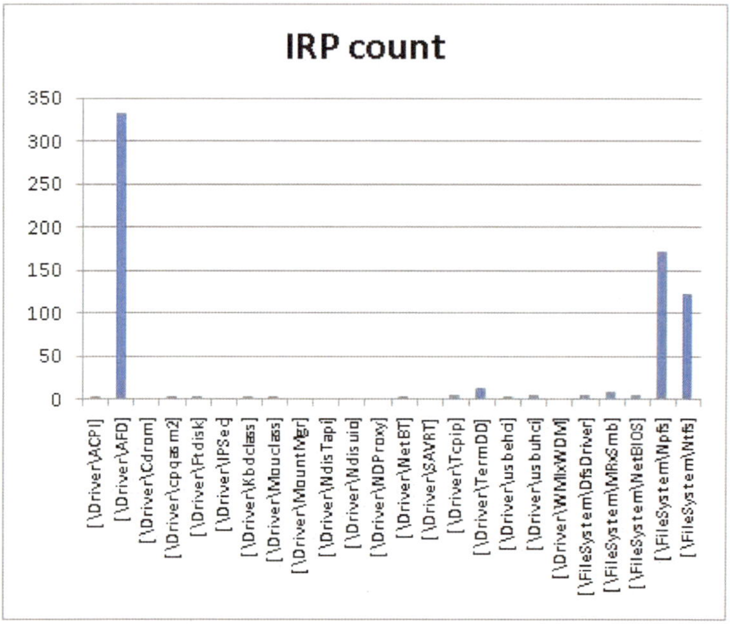

Two other peaks on both graphs are related to NTPS and NTFS, pipes and file system, and usually normal. Here is IRP distribution graph from my Vista workstation captured while I was writing this post:

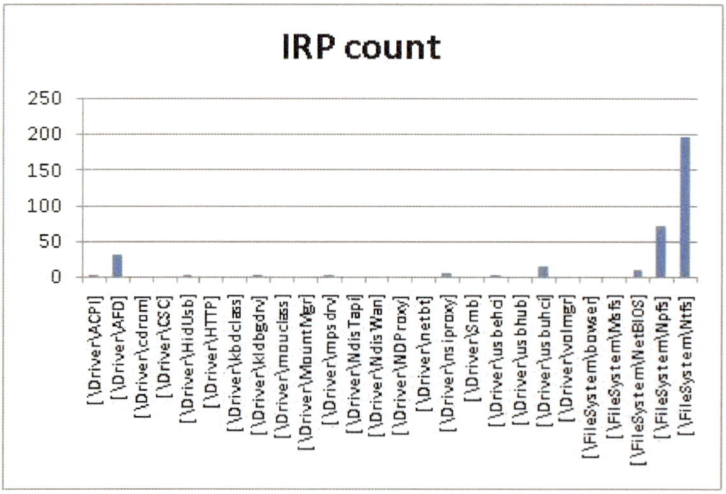

Local Buffer Overflow (User Space)

Local Buffer Overflow pattern is observed on x86 platforms when a local variable and a function return address or a saved frame pointer EBP are overwritten with some data. As a result, the instruction pointer EIP becomes **Wild Pointer** (see Volume 2), and we have a process crash in user mode or a bugcheck in kernel mode. Sometimes this pattern is diagnosed by looking at mismatched EBP and ESP values. In the case of ASCII or UNICODE buffer overflow, EIP register may contain 4-char or 2-wchar_t value, and ESP or EBP or both registers may point at some string fragment like in the example below:

```
0:000> r
eax=000fa101 ebx=0000c026 ecx=01010001 edx=bd43a010 esi=000003e0
edi=00000000
eip=0048004a esp=0012f158 ebp=00510044 iopl=0   nv up ei pl nz na po nc
cs=001b ss=0023 ds=0023 es=0023 fs=0038 gs=0000 efl=00000202
0048004a 0000 add     byte ptr [eax],al  ds:0023:000fa101=??

0:000> kL
ChildEBP RetAddr
WARNING: Frame IP not in any known module. Following frames may be wrong.
0012f154 00420047 0x48004a
0012f158 00440077 0x420047
0012f15c 00420043 0x440077
0012f160 00510076 0x420043
0012f164 00420049 0x510076
0012f168 00540041 0x420049
0012f16c 00540041 0x540041

...
...
```

Passive System Thread (Kernel Space)

Previously we discussed **Passive Thread** pattern (page 430) in user space. Here I continue with kernel space and passive system threads that don't run in any user process context. These threads belong to the so-called System process, don't have any user space stack and their full stack traces can be seen from the output of **!process** command (if not completely paged out) or from [System] portion of **!stacks 2** command:

```
1: kd> !process 0 3f System
```

Some system threads from that list belong to core OS functionality and are not passive (function offsets can vary for different OS versions and service packs):

```
nt!KiSwapContext+0x84
nt!KiSwapThread+0x125
nt!KeWaitForSingleObject+0x5f5
nt!MmZeroPageThread+0x180
nt!Phase1Initialization+0xe
nt!PspSystemThreadStartup+0x5b
nt!KiStartSystemThread+0x16

nt!KiSwapContext+0x84
nt!KiSwapThread+0x125
nt!KeWaitForSingleObject+0x5f5
nt!MiModifiedPageWriter+0x59
nt!PspSystemThreadStartup+0x5b
nt!KiStartSystemThread+0x16

nt!KiSwapContext+0x84
nt!KiSwapThread+0x125
nt!KeWaitForMultipleObjects+0x703
nt!MiMappedPageWriter+0xad
nt!PspSystemThreadStartup+0x5b
nt!KiStartSystemThread+0x16

nt!KiSwapContext+0x84
nt!KiSwapThread+0x125
nt!KeWaitForMultipleObjects+0x703
nt!KeBalanceSetManager+0x101
nt!PspSystemThreadStartup+0x5b
nt!KiStartSystemThread+0x16

nt!KiSwapContext+0x84
nt!KiSwapThread+0x125
nt!KeWaitForSingleObject+0x5f5
nt!KeSwapProcessOrStack+0x44
nt!PspSystemThreadStartup+0x5b
nt!KiStartSystemThread+0x16
```

```
nt!KiSwapContext+0x84
nt!KiSwapThread+0x125
nt!KeWaitForSingleObject+0x5f5
nt!EtwpLogger+0xdd
nt!PspSystemThreadStartup+0x5b
nt!KiStartSystemThread+0x16

nt!KiSwapContext+0x84
nt!KiSwapThread+0x125
nt!KeWaitForSingleObject+0x5f5
nt!KiExecuteDpc+0x198
nt!PspSystemThreadStartup+0x5b
nt!KiStartSystemThread+0x16

nt!KiSwapContext+0x84
nt!KiSwapThread+0x125
nt!KeWaitForMultipleObjects+0x703
nt!CcQueueLazyWriteScanThread+0x73
nt!PspSystemThreadStartup+0x5b
nt!KiStartSystemThread+0x16

nt!KiSwapContext+0x84
nt!KiSwapThread+0x125
nt!KeWaitForMultipleObjects+0x703
nt!ExpWorkerThreadBalanceManager+0x85
nt!PspSystemThreadStartup+0x5b
nt!KiStartSystemThread+0x16
```

Other threads belong to various worker queues (they can also be seen from **!exqueue ff** command output), and they wait for data items to arrive (passive threads):

```
nt!KiSwapContext+0x84
nt!KiSwapThread+0x125
nt!KeRemoveQueueEx+0x848
nt!ExpWorkerThread+0x104
nt!PspSystemThreadStartup+0x5b
nt!KiStartSystemThread+0x16
```

or

```
nt!KiSwapContext+0x26
nt!KiSwapThread+0x2e5
nt!KeRemoveQueue+0x417
nt!ExpWorkerThread+0xc8
nt!PspSystemThreadStartup+0x2e
nt!KiThreadStartup+0x16
```

Non-*Exp* system threads (no *nt!ExpWorkerThread* in their stack traces) having "Worker", "Logging" or "Logger" substrings in their function names are passive threads, and they wait for data too, for example:

```
nt!KiSwapContext+0x84
nt!KiSwapThread+0x125
nt!KeWaitForMultipleObjects+0x703
nt!PfTLoggingWorker+0x81
nt!PspSystemThreadStartup+0x5b
nt!KiStartSystemThread+0x16

nt!KiSwapContext+0x84
nt!KiSwapThread+0x125
nt!KeWaitForSingleObject+0x5f5
nt!EtwpLogger+0xdd
nt!PspSystemThreadStartup+0x5b
nt!KiStartSystemThread+0x16

nt!KiSwapContext+0x84
nt!KiSwapThread+0x125
nt!KeRemoveQueueEx+0x848
nt!KeRemoveQueue+0x21
rdpdr!RxpWorkerThreadDispatcher+0x6f
nt!PspSystemThreadStartup+0x5b
nt!KiStartSystemThread+0x16

nt!KiSwapContext+0x84
nt!KiSwapThread+0x125
nt!KeWaitForSingleObject+0x5f5
HTTP!UlpThreadPoolWorker+0x26c
nt!PspSystemThreadStartup+0x5b
nt!KiStartSystemThread+0x16

nt!KiSwapContext+0x84
nt!KiSwapThread+0x125
nt!KeRemoveQueueEx+0x848
nt!KeRemoveQueue+0x21
srv2!SrvProcWorkerThread+0x74
nt!PspSystemThreadStartup+0x5b
nt!KiStartSystemThread+0x16

nt!KiSwapContext+0x84
nt!KiSwapThread+0x125
nt!KeRemoveQueueEx+0x848
nt!KeRemoveQueue+0x21
srv!WorkerThread+0x90
nt!PspSystemThreadStartup+0x5b
nt!KiStartSystemThread+0x16
```

Any deviations in a memory dump can raise suspicion like in the stack below for *driver.sys*:

```
nt!KiSwapContext+0x26
nt!KiSwapThread+0x284
nt!KeWaitForSingleObject+0x346
nt!ExpWaitForResource+0xd5
nt!ExAcquireResourceExclusiveLite+0x8d
nt!ExEnterCriticalRegionAndAcquireResourceExclusive+0x19
driver!ProcessItem+0x2f
driver!DelayedWorker+0x27
nt!ExpWorkerThread+0x104
nt!PspSystemThreadStartup+0x5b
nt!KiStartSystemThread+0x16
```

Early Crash Dump

Some bugs are fixed using a brute-force approach via putting an exception handler to catch access violations and other exceptions. A long time ago, I saw one such "incredible fix" when the image processing application was crashing after approximately Nth heap free runtime call. To ignore crashes, an SEH handler was put in place, but the application started to crash in different places. Therefore, the additional fix was to skip free calls when approaching N and resume afterward. The application started to crash less frequently.

Here getting **Early Crash Dump** when a first-chance exception happens can help in component identification before corruption starts spreading across data. Recall that when an access violation happens in a process thread in user mode the system generates the first-chance exception which can be caught by an attached debugger and if there is no such debugger the system tries to find an exception handler and if that exception handler catches and dismisses the exception the thread resumes its normal execution path. If there are no such handlers found the system generates the so-called second-chance exception with the same exception context to notify the attached debugger and if it is not attached a default thread exception handler usually saves a postmortem user dump.

We can get first-chance exception memory dumps with:

- Debug Diagnostics (old tool)
- ADPlus in crash mode from Debugging Tools for Windows
- Exception Monitor from User Mode Process Dumper package (old tool)
- Procdump from Windows Sysinternals

Here is an example configuration rule for crashes in Debug Diagnostic tool for TestDefaultDebugger process (*Unconfigured First Chance Exceptions* option is set to *Full Userdump*):

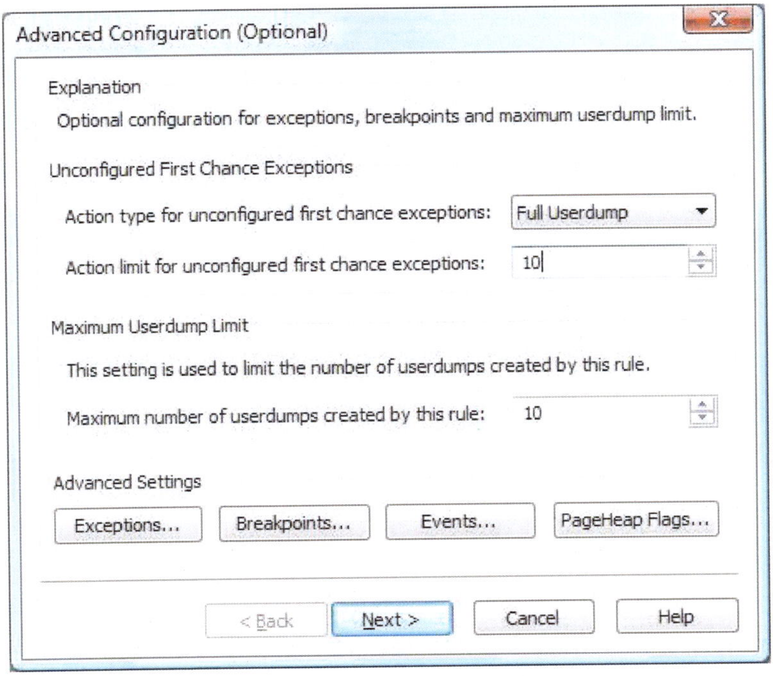

When we push the big crash button in TestDefaultDebugger dialog box, two crash dumps are saved, with the first and second-chance exceptions pointing to the same code:

```
Loading Dump File [C:\Program Files (x86)\DebugDiag\Logs\Crash rule for
all instances of TestDefaultDebugger.exe\TestDefaultDebugger__PID__4316__
Date__11_21_2007__Time_04_28_27PM__2__First chance exception
0XC0000005.dmp]
User Mini Dump File with Full Memory: Only application data is available

Comment: 'Dump created by DbgHost. First chance exception 0XC0000005'
Symbol search path is:
srv*c:\mss*http://msdl.microsoft.com/download/symbols
Executable search path is:
Windows Vista Version 6000 MP (2 procs) Free x86 compatible
Product: WinNt, suite: SingleUserTS
Debug session time: Wed Nov 21 16:28:27.000 2007 (GMT+0)
System Uptime: 0 days 23:45:34.711
Process Uptime: 0 days 0:01:09.000
```

```
This dump file has an exception of interest stored in it.
The stored exception information can be accessed via .ecxr.
(10dc.590): Access violation - code c0000005 (first/second chance not
available)
eax=00000000 ebx=00000001 ecx=0017fe70 edx=00000000 esi=00425ae8
edi=0017fe70
eip=004014f0 esp=0017f898 ebp=0017f8a4 iopl=0 nv up ei ng nz ac pe cy
cs=0023 ss=002b ds=002b es=002b fs=0053 gs=002b efl=00010297
TestDefaultDebugger!CTestDefaultDebuggerDlg::OnBnClickedButton1:
004014f0 c7050000000000000000 mov dword ptr
ds:[0],0 ds:002b:00000000=????????

Loading Dump File [C:\Program Files (x86)\DebugDiag\Logs\Crash rule for
all instances of TestDefaultDebugger.exe\TestDefaultDebugger__PID__4316__
Date__11_21_2007__Time_04_28_34PM__693__
Second_Chance_Exception_C0000005.dmp]
User Mini Dump File with Full Memory: Only application data is available

Comment: 'Dump created by DbgHost. Second_Chance_Exception_C0000005'
Symbol search path is:
srv*c:\mss*http://msdl.microsoft.com/download/symbols
Executable search path is:
Windows Vista Version 6000 MP (2 procs) Free x86 compatible
Product: WinNt, suite: SingleUserTS
Debug session time: Wed Nov 21 16:28:34.000 2007 (GMT+0)
System Uptime: 0 days 23:45:39.313
Process Uptime: 0 days 0:01:16.000

This dump file has an exception of interest stored in it.
The stored exception information can be accessed via .ecxr.
(10dc.590): Access violation - code c0000005 (first/second chance not
available)
eax=00000000 ebx=00000001 ecx=0017fe70 edx=00000000 esi=00425ae8
edi=0017fe70
eip=004014f0 esp=0017f898 ebp=0017f8a4 iopl=0 nv up ei ng nz ac pe cy
cs=0023 ss=002b ds=002b es=002b fs=0053 gs=002b efl=00010297
TestDefaultDebugger!CTestDefaultDebuggerDlg::OnBnClickedButton1:
004014f0 c7050000000000000000 mov dword ptr
ds:[0],0 ds:002b:00000000=????????
```

Hooked Functions (User Space)

Hooking functions using the trampoline method is so common on Windows that sometimes we need to check **Hooked Functions** in specific modules and determine which module hooked them for troubleshooting or memory forensic analysis needs. If original unhooked modules are available (via symbol server, for example) this can be done by using **!chkimg** WinDbg extension command:

```
0:002> !chkimg -lo 50 -d !kernel32 -v
Searching for module with expression: !kernel32
Will apply relocation fixups to file used for comparison
Will ignore NOP/LOCK errors
Will ignore patched instructions
Image specific ignores will be applied
Comparison image path:
c:\symdownstream\kernel32.dll\44C60F39102000\kernel32.dll
No range specified

Scanning section:    .text
Size: 564445
Range to scan: 77e41000-77ecacdd
    77e44004-77e44008  5 bytes - kernel32!GetDateFormatA
  [ 8b ff 55 8b ec:e9 f7 bf 08 c0 ]
    77e4412e-77e44132  5 bytes - kernel32!GetTimeFormatA (+0x12a)
  [ 8b ff 55 8b ec:e9 cd be 06 c0 ]
    77e4e857-77e4e85b  5 bytes - kernel32!FileTimeToLocalFileTime
(+0xa729)
  [ 8b ff 55 8b ec:e9 a4 17 00 c0 ]
    77e56b5f-77e56b63  5 bytes - kernel32!GetTimeZoneInformation (+0x8308)
  [ 8b ff 55 8b ec:e9 9c 94 00 c0 ]
    77e579a9-77e579ad  5 bytes - kernel32!GetTimeFormatW (+0xe4a)
  [ 8b ff 55 8b ec:e9 52 86 06 c0 ]
    77e57fc8-77e57fcc  5 bytes - kernel32!GetDateFormatW (+0x61f)
  [ 8b ff 55 8b ec:e9 33 80 08 c0 ]
    77e6f32b-77e6f32f  5 bytes - kernel32!GetLocalTime (+0x17363)
  [ 8b ff 55 8b ec:e9 d0 0c 00 c0 ]
    77e6f891-77e6f895  5 bytes - kernel32!LocalFileTimeToFileTime (+0x566)
  [ 8b ff 55 8b ec:e9 6a 07 01 c0 ]
    77e83499-77e8349d  5 bytes - kernel32!SetLocalTime (+0x13c08)
  [ 8b ff 55 8b ec:e9 62 cb 00 c0 ]
    77e88c32-77e88c36  5 bytes - kernel32!SetTimeZoneInformation (+0x5799)
  [ 8b ff 55 8b ec:e9 c9 73 01 c0 ]
Total bytes compared: 564445(100%)
Number of errors: 50
50 errors : !kernel32 (77e44004-77e88c36)
```

```
0:002> u 77e44004
kernel32!GetDateFormatA:
77e44004 e9f7bf08c0      jmp     37ed0000
77e44009 81ec18020000    sub     esp,218h
77e4400f a148d1ec77      mov     eax,dword ptr [kernel32!__security_cookie
(77ecd148)]
77e44014 53              push    ebx
77e44015 8b5d14          mov     ebx,dword ptr [ebp+14h]
77e44018 56              push    esi
77e44019 8b7518          mov     esi,dword ptr [ebp+18h]
77e4401c 57              push    edi

0:002> u 37ed0000
*** ERROR: Symbol file could not be found.  Defaulted to export symbols
for MyDateTimeHooks.dll -
37ed0000 e99b262f2d      jmp     MyDateTimeHooks+0x26a0 (651c26a0)
37ed0005 8bff            mov     edi,edi
37ed0007 55              push    ebp
37ed0008 8bec            mov     ebp,esp
37ed000a e9fa3ff73f      jmp     kernel32!GetDateFormatA+0x5 (77e44009)
37ed000f 0000            add     byte ptr [eax],al
37ed0011 0000            add     byte ptr [eax],al
37ed0013 0000            add     byte ptr [eax],al
```

Custom Exception Handler (User Space)

As discussed in **Early Crash Dump** pattern (page 466), saving crash dumps on first-chance exceptions helps to diagnose components that might have caused corruption and later crashes, hangs, or CPU spikes by ignoring abnormal exceptions like access violation. In such cases, we need to know whether an application installs its own **Custom Exception Handler** or several of them. If it uses only default handlers provided by runtime or windows subsystem, then most likely, a first-chance access violation exception results in a last-chance exception and a postmortem dump. To check a chain of exception handlers, we can use WinDbg **!exchain** extension command. For example:

```
0:000> !exchain
0017f9d8: TestDefaultDebugger!AfxWinMain+3f5 (00420aa9)
0017fa60: TestDefaultDebugger!AfxWinMain+34c (00420a00)
0017fb20: user32!_except_handler4+0 (770780eb)
0017fcc0: user32!_except_handler4+0 (770780eb)
0017fd24: user32!_except_handler4+0 (770780eb)
0017fe40: TestDefaultDebugger!AfxWinMain+16e (00420822)
0017feec: TestDefaultDebugger!AfxWinMain+797 (00420e4b)
0017ff90: TestDefaultDebugger!_except_handler4+0 (00410e00)
0017ffdc: ntdll!_except_handler4+0 (77961c78)
```

We see that TestDefaultDebugger doesn't have its own exception handlers except ones provided by MFC and C/C++ runtime libraries, which were linked statically. Here is another example. It was reported that a 3rd-party application was hanging and spiking CPU (**Spiking Thread** pattern, page 305), so a user dump was saved using command line userdump.exe:

```
0:000> vertarget
Windows Server 2003 Version 3790 (Service Pack 2) MP (4 procs) Free x86
compatible
Product: Server, suite: TerminalServer
kernel32.dll version: 5.2.3790.4062 (srv03_sp2_gdr.070417-0203)
Debug session time: Thu Nov 22 12:45:59.000 2007 (GMT+0)
System Uptime: 0 days 10:43:07.667
Process Uptime: 0 days 4:51:32.000
Kernel time: 0 days 0:08:04.000
User time: 0 days 0:23:09.000

0:000> !runaway 3
User Mode Time
Thread Time
0:1c1c      0 days 0:08:04.218
1:2e04      0 days 0:00:00.015
Kernel Mode Time
Thread Time
```

```
0:1c1c       0 days 0:23:09.156
1:2e04       0 days 0:00:00.031

0:000> kL
ChildEBP RetAddr
0012fb80 7739bf53 ntdll!KiFastSystemCallRet
0012fbb4 05ca73b0 user32!NtUserWaitMessage+0xc
WARNING: Stack unwind information not available. Following frames may be
wrong.
0012fd20 05c8be3f 3rdPartyDLL+0x573b0
0012fd50 05c9e9ea 3rdPartyDLL+0x3be3f
0012fd68 7739b6e3 3rdPartyDLL+0x4e9ea
0012fd94 7739b874 user32!InternalCallWinProc+0x28
0012fe0c 7739c8b8 user32!UserCallWinProcCheckWow+0x151
0012fe68 7739c9c6 user32!DispatchClientMessage+0xd9
0012fe90 7c828536 user32!__fnDWORD+0x24
0012febc 7739d1ec ntdll!KiUserCallbackDispatcher+0x2e
0012fef8 7738cee9 user32!NtUserMessageCall+0xc
0012ff18 0050aea9 user32!SendMessageA+0x7f
0012ff70 00452ae4 3rdPartyApp+0x10aea9
0012ffac 00511941 3rdPartyApp+0x52ae4
0012ffc0 77e6f23b 3rdPartyApp+0x111941
0012fff0 00000000 kernel32!BaseProcessStart+0x23
```

Exception chain listed custom exception handlers:

```
0:000> !exchain
0012fb8c: 3rdPartyDLL+57acb (05ca7acb)
0012fd28: 3rdPartyDLL+3be57 (05c8be57)
0012fd34: 3rdPartyDLL+3be68 (05c8be68)
0012fdfc: user32!_except_handler3+0 (773aaf18)
  CRT scope  0, func:   user32!UserCallWinProcCheckWow+156 (773ba9ad)
0012fe58: user32!_except_handler3+0 (773aaf18)
0012fea0: ntdll!KiUserCallbackExceptionHandler+0 (7c8284e8)
0012ff3c: 3rdPartyApp+53310 (00453310)
0012ff48: 3rdPartyApp+5334b (0045334b)
0012ff9c: 3rdPartyApp+52d06 (00452d06)
0012ffb4: 3rdPartyApp+38d4 (004038d4)
0012ffe0: kernel32!_except_handler3+0 (77e61a60)
  CRT scope  0, filter: kernel32!BaseProcessStart+29 (77e76a10)
                func:   kernel32!BaseProcessStart+3a (77e81469)
```

The customer then enabled MS Exception Monitor and selected only Access violation exception code (c0000005) to avoid **False Positive Dumps** (page 259). During application execution various 1st-chance exception crash dumps were saved pointing to numerous access violations including function calls into unloaded modules, for example:

```
0:000> kL 100
ChildEBP RetAddr
WARNING: Frame IP not in any known module. Following frames may be wrong.
0012f910 7739b6e3 <Unloaded_Another3rdParty.dll>+0x4ce58
0012f93c 7739b874 user32!InternalCallWinProc+0x28
0012f9b4 7739c8b8 user32!UserCallWinProcCheckWow+0x151
0012fa10 7739c9c6 user32!DispatchClientMessage+0xd9
0012fa38 7c828536 user32!__fnDWORD+0x24
0012fa64 7739d1ec ntdll!KiUserCallbackDispatcher+0x2e
0012faa0 7738cee9 user32!NtUserMessageCall+0xc
0012fac0 0a0f2e01 user32!SendMessageA+0x7f
0012fae4 0a0f2ac7 3rdPartyDLL+0x52e01
0012fb60 7c81a352 3rdPartyDLL+0x52ac7
0012fb80 7c839dee ntdll!LdrpCallInitRoutine+0x14
0012fc94 77e6b1bb ntdll!LdrUnloadDll+0x41a
0012fca8 0050c9c1 kernel32!FreeLibrary+0x41
0012fdf4 004374af 3rdPartyApp+0x10c9c1
0012fe24 0044a076 3rdPartyApp+0x374af
0012fe3c 7739b6e3 3rdPartyApp+0x4a076
0012fe68 7739b874 user32!InternalCallWinProc+0x28
0012fee0 7739ba92 user32!UserCallWinProcCheckWow+0x151
0012ff48 773a16e5 user32!DispatchMessageWorker+0x327
0012ff58 00452aa0 user32!DispatchMessageA+0xf
0012ffac 00511941 3rdPartyApp+0x52aa0
0012ffc0 77e6f23b 3rdPartyApp+0x111941
0012fff0 00000000 kernel32!BaseProcessStart+0x23
```

Deadlock (LPC)

Let's look at a good example of **Deadlock** pattern involving LPC. In the stack trace below *svchost.exe* thread (we call it thread A) receives an LPC call and dispatches it to *componentA* module which makes another LPC call (MessageId 000135b8) and then waiting for a reply:

```
THREAD 89143020  Cid 09b4.10dc  Teb: 7ff91000 Win32Thread: 00000000 WAIT:
(Unknown) UserMode Non-Alertable
    8914320c  Semaphore Limit 0x1
Waiting for reply to LPC MessageId 000135b8:
Current LPC port d64a5328
Not impersonating
DeviceMap                 d64028f0
Owning Process            891b8b80       Image:         svchost.exe
Wait Start TickCount      237408         Ticks: 1890 (0:00:00:29.531)
Context Switch Count      866
UserTime                  00:00:00.031
KernelTime                00:00:00.015
Win32 Start Address 0x000135b2
LPC Server thread working on message Id 135b2
Start Address kernel32!BaseThreadStartThunk (0x7c82b5f3)
Stack Init b91f9000 Current b91f8c08 Base b91f9000 Limit b91f6000 Call 0
Priority 9 BasePriority 8 PriorityDecrement 0
ChildEBP RetAddr
b91f8c20 8083e6a2 nt!KiSwapContext+0x26
b91f8c4c 8083f164 nt!KiSwapThread+0x284
b91f8c94 8093983f nt!KeWaitForSingleObject+0x346
b91f8d50 80834d3f nt!NtRequestWaitReplyPort+0x776
b91f8d50 7c94ed54 nt!KiFastCallEntry+0xfc
02bae928 7c941c94 ntdll!KiFastSystemCallRet
02bae92c 77c42700 ntdll!NtRequestWaitReplyPort+0xc
02bae984 77c413ba RPCRT4!LRPC_CCALL::SendReceive+0x230
02bae990 77c42c7f RPCRT4!I_RpcSendReceive+0x24
02bae9a4 77cb5d63 RPCRT4!NdrSendReceive+0x2b
02baec48 674825b6 RPCRT4!NdrClientCall+0x334
02baec5c 67486776 componentA!bar+0x16
...
...
...
02baf8d4 77c40f3b componentA!foo+0x157
02baf8f8 77cb23f7 RPCRT4!Invoke+0x30
02bafcf8 77cb26ed RPCRT4!NdrStubCall2+0x299
02bafd14 77c409be RPCRT4!NdrServerCall2+0x19
02bafd48 77c4093f RPCRT4!DispatchToStubInCNoAvrf+0x38
02bafd9c 77c40865 RPCRT4!RPC_INTERFACE::DispatchToStubWorker+0x117
02bafdc0 77c434b1 RPCRT4!RPC_INTERFACE::DispatchToStub+0xa3
02bafdfc 77c41bb3 RPCRT4!LRPC_SCALL::DealWithRequestMessage+0x42c
02bafe20 77c45458 RPCRT4!LRPC_ADDRESS::DealWithLRPCRequest+0x127
02baff84 77c2778f RPCRT4!LRPC_ADDRESS::ReceiveLotsaCalls+0x430
02baff8c 77c2f7dd RPCRT4!RecvLotsaCallsWrapper+0xd
```

```
02baffac 77c2de88 RPCRT4!BaseCachedThreadRoutine+0x9d
02baffb8 7c82608b RPCRT4!ThreadStartRoutine+0x1b
02baffec 00000000 kernel32!BaseThreadStart+0x34
```

We search for that LPC message to find the server thread:

```
1: kd> !lpc message 000135b8
Searching message 135b8 in threads ...
    Server thread 89115db0 is working on message 135b8
Client thread 89143020 waiting a reply from 135b8
...
...
...
```

It belongs to *Process.exe*, and we call it thread B (some output below is shown in smaller font for visual clarity):

```
1: kd> !thread 89115db0 0x16
THREAD 89115db0  Cid 098c.0384  Teb: 7ff79000 Win32Thread: 00000000 WAIT: (Unknown) UserMode Non-
Alertable
    8a114628  SynchronizationEvent
Not impersonating
DeviceMap                 d64028f0
Owning Process            8a2c9d88       Image:         Process.exe
Wait Start TickCount      237408         Ticks: 1890 (0:00:00:29.531)
Context Switch Count      1590
UserTime                  00:00:03.265
KernelTime                00:00:01.671
Win32 Start Address 0x000135b8
LPC Server thread working on message Id 135b8
Start Address kernel32!BaseThreadStartThunk (0x7c82b5f3)
Stack Init b952d000 Current b952cc60 Base b952d000 Limit b952a000 Call 0
Priority 9 BasePriority 8 PriorityDecrement 0
ChildEBP RetAddr  Args to Child
b952cc78 8083e6a2 89115e28 89115db0 89115e58 nt!KiSwapContext+0x26
b952cca4 8083f164 00000000 00000000 00000000 nt!KiSwapThread+0x284
b952ccec 8092db70 8a114628 00000006 ffffff01 nt!KeWaitForSingleObject+0x346
b952cd50 80834d3f 00000a7c 00000000 00000000 nt!NtWaitForSingleObject+0x9a
b952cd50 7c94ed54 00000a7c 00000000 00000000 nt!KiFastCallEntry+0xfc
22aceb48 7c942124 7c95970f 00000a7c 00000000 ntdll!KiFastSystemCallRet
22aceb4c 7c95970f 00000a7c 00000000 00000000 ntdll!NtWaitForSingleObject+0xc
22aceb88 7c959620 00000000 00000004 00002000 ntdll!RtlpWaitOnCriticalSection+0x19c
22aceba8 1b005744 06d30940 1b05ea80 06d30940 ntdll!RtlEnterCriticalSection+0xa8
22acebb0 1b05ea80 06d30940 feffffff 0cd410c0 componentB!bar+0xb
...
...
...
22acf8b0 77c40f3b 00080002 000800e2 00000001 componentB!foo+0xeb
22acf8e0 77cb23f7 0de110dc 22acfac8 00000007 RPCRT4!Invoke+0x30
22acfce0 77cb26ed 00000000 00000000 19f38f94 RPCRT4!NdrStubCall2+0x299
22acfcfc 77c409be 19f38f94 17316ef0 19f38f94 RPCRT4!NdrServerCall2+0x19
22acfd30 77c75e41 0de1dc58 19f38f94 22acfdec RPCRT4!DispatchToStubInCNoAvrf+0x38
22acfd48 77c4093f 0de1dc58 19f38f94 22acfdec RPCRT4!DispatchToStubInCAvrf+0x14
22acfd9c 77c40865 00000041 00000000 0de2b398 RPCRT4!RPC_INTERFACE::DispatchToStubWorker+0x117
22acfdc0 77c434b1 19f38f94 00000000 0de2b398 RPCRT4!RPC_INTERFACE::DispatchToStub+0xa3
22acfdfc 77c41bb3 1beeaec8 16b96f50 1baeef00 RPCRT4!LRPC_SCALL::DealWithRequestMessage+0x42c
22acfe20 77c45458 16b96f88 22acfe38 1beeaec8 RPCRT4!LRPC_ADDRESS::DealWithLRPCRequest+0x127
```

0x16 flags for **!thread** extension command are used to temporarily set the process context to the owning process and show the first three function call parameters. We see that the thread B is waiting for the critical section 06d30940, and we use user space **!locks** extension command to find who owns it after switching process context:

```
1: kd> .process /r /p 8a2c9d88
Implicit process is now 8a2c9d88
Loading User Symbols

1: kd> !ntsdexts.locks

CritSec +6d30940 at 06d30940
WaiterWoken        No
LockCount          1
RecursionCount     1
OwningThread       d6c
EntryCount         0
ContentionCount    1
*** Locked
```

Now we try to find a thread with TID d6c (thread C):

```
1: kd> !thread -t d6c
Looking for thread Cid = d6c ...
THREAD 890d8bb8  Cid 098c.0d6c  Teb: 7ff71000 Win32Thread: bc23cc20 WAIT: (Unknown) UserMode Non-Alertable
    890d8da4  Semaphore Limit 0x1
Waiting for reply to LPC MessageId 000135ea:
Current LPC port d649a678
Not impersonating
DeviceMap                 d64028f0
Owning Process            8a2c9d88       Image:         Process.exe
Wait Start TickCount      237641         Ticks: 1657 (0:00:00:25.890)
Context Switch Count      2102                 LargeStack
UserTime                  00:00:00.734
KernelTime                00:00:00.234
Win32 Start Address msvcrt!_endthreadex (0x77b9b4bc)
Start Address kernel32!BaseThreadStartThunk (0x7c82b5f3)
Stack Init ba91d000 Current ba91cc08 Base ba91d000 Limit ba919000 Call 0
Priority 13 BasePriority 8 PriorityDecrement 0
ChildEBP RetAddr  Args to Child
ba91cc20 8083e6a2 890d8c30 890d8bb8 890d8c60 nt!KiSwapContext+0x26
ba91cc4c 8083f164 890d8da4 890d8d78 890d8bb8 nt!KiSwapThread+0x284
ba91cc94 8093983f 890d8da4 00000011 8a2c9d01 nt!KeWaitForSingleObject+0x346
ba91cd50 80834d3f 000008bc 19c94f00 19c94f00 nt!NtRequestWaitReplyPort+0x776
ba91cd50 7c94ed54 000008bc 19c94f00 19c94f00 nt!KiFastCallEntry+0xfc
2709ebf4 7c941c94 77c42700 000008bc 19c94f00 ntdll!KiFastSystemCallRet
2709ebf8 77c42700 000008bc 19c94f00 19c94f00 ntdll!NtRequestWaitReplyPort+0xc
2709ec44 77c413ba 2709ec80 2709ec64 77c42c7f RPCRT4!LRPC_CCALL::SendReceive+0x230
2709ec50 77c42c7f 2709ec80 779b2770 2709f06c RPCRT4!I_RpcSendReceive+0x24
2709ec64 77cb219b 2709ecac 1957cfe4 1957ab38 RPCRT4!NdrSendReceive+0x2b
2709f04c 779b43a3 779b2770 779b1398 2709f06c RPCRT4!NdrClientCall2+0x22e
...
...
...
2709ff84 77b9b530 26658fb0 00000000 00000000 ComponentC!foo+0x18d
2709ffb8 7c82608b 26d9af70 00000000 00000000 msvcrt!_endthreadex+0xa3
2709ffec 00000000 77b9b4bc 26d9af70 00000000 kernel32!BaseThreadStart+0x34
```

We see that thread C makes another LPC call (MessageId 000135e) and is waiting for a reply. Let's find the server thread processing the message (thread D):

```
1: kd> !lpc message 000135ea
Searching message 135ea in threads ...
Client thread 890d8bb8 waiting a reply from 135ea
    Server thread 89010020 is working on message 135ea
...
...
...
```

```
1: kd> !thread 89010020 16
THREAD 89010020  Cid 09b4.1530  Teb: 7ff93000 Win32Thread: 00000000 WAIT: (Unknown) UserMode Non-
Alertable
    8903ba28  Mutant - owning thread 89143020
Not impersonating
DeviceMap                 d64028f0
Owning Process            891b8b80       Image:         svchost.exe
Wait Start TickCount      237641         Ticks: 1657 (0:00:00:25.890)
Context Switch Count      8
UserTime                  00:00:00.000
KernelTime                00:00:00.000
Win32 Start Address 0x000135ea
LPC Server thread working on message Id 135ea
Start Address kernel32!BaseThreadStartThunk (0x7c82b5f3)
Stack Init b9455000 Current b9454c60 Base b9455000 Limit b9452000 Call 0
Priority 9 BasePriority 8 PriorityDecrement 0
ChildEBP RetAddr  Args to Child
b9454c78 8083e6a2 89010098 89010020 890100c8 nt!KiSwapContext+0x26
b9454ca4 8083f164 00000000 00000000 00000000 nt!KiSwapThread+0x284
b9454cec 8092db70 8903ba28 00000006 00000001 nt!KeWaitForSingleObject+0x346
b9454d50 80834d3f 00000514 00000000 00000000 nt!NtWaitForSingleObject+0x9a
b9454d50 7c94ed54 00000514 00000000 00000000 nt!KiFastCallEntry+0xfc
02b5f720 7c942124 75fdbe44 00000514 00000000 ntdll!KiFastSystemCallRet
02b5f724 75fdbe44 00000514 00000000 00000000 ntdll!NtWaitForSingleObject+0xc
02b5f744 75fdc57f 000e6014 000da62c 02b5fca0 ComponentD!bar+0x42
…

…
02b5f8c8 77c40f3b 000d0a48 02b5fc90 00000001 ComponentD!foo+0x49
02b5f8f8 77cb23f7 75fdf8f2 02b5fae0 00000007 RPCRT4!Invoke+0x30
02b5fcf8 77cb26ed 00000000 00000000 000d4f24 RPCRT4!NdrStubCall2+0x299
02b5fd14 77c409be 000d4f24 000b5d70 000d4f24 RPCRT4!NdrServerCall2+0x19
02b5fd48 77c4093f 75fff834 000d4f24 02b5fdec RPCRT4!DispatchToStubInCNoAvrf+0x38
02b5fd9c 77c40865 00000005 00000000 7600589c RPCRT4!RPC_INTERFACE::DispatchToStubWorker+0x117
02b5fdc0 77c434b1 000d4f24 00000000 7600589c RPCRT4!RPC_INTERFACE::DispatchToStub+0xa3
02b5fdfc 77c41bb3 000d3550 000a78d0 001054b8 RPCRT4!LRPC_SCALL::DealWithRequestMessage+0x42c
02b5fe20 77c45458 000a7908 02b5fe38 000d3550 RPCRT4!LRPC_ADDRESS::DealWithLRPCRequest+0x127
02b5ff84 77c2778f 02b5ffac 77c2f7dd 000a78d0 RPCRT4!LRPC_ADDRESS::ReceiveLotsaCalls+0x430
02b5ff8c 77c2f7dd 000a78d0 00000000 00000000 RPCRT4!RecvLotsaCallsWrapper+0xd
02b5ffac 77c2de88 0008ae00 02b5ffec 7c82608b RPCRT4!BaseCachedThreadRoutine+0x9d
02b5ffb8 7c82608b 000d5c20 00000000 00000000 RPCRT4!ThreadStartRoutine+0x1b
02b5ffec 00000000 77c2de6d 000d5c20 00000000 kernel32!BaseThreadStart+0x34
```

We see that thread D is waiting for the mutant object owned by thread A (89143020). Therefore we have a deadlock spanning two process boundaries via RPC/LPC calls with the following dependency graph:

```
A (svchost.exe) LPC-> B (Process.exe) CritSec-> C (Process.exe) LPC-> D
(svchost.exe) Obj-> A (svchost.exe)
```

Special Stack Trace

Sometimes we encounter thread stacks related to debugger events like Exit a Process, Load or Unload a Module. These thread stacks are not usually encountered in healthy process dumps and, statistically speaking, when a process terminates or unloads a library, the chances to save a memory dump manually using process dumpers like *userdump.exe* or Task Manager in Vista are very low unless an interactive debugger was attached, or breakpoints were set in advance. Therefore, the presence of such threads in a captured crash dump usually indicates some problem or at least focuses attention on the procedure used to save a dump. Such a pattern merits its own name: **Special Stack Trace**.

For example, one process dump had the following stack trace showing process termination initiated from .NET runtime:

```
STACK_TEXT:
0012fc2c 7c827c1b ntdll!KiFastSystemCallRet
0012fc30 77e668c3 ntdll!NtTerminateProcess+0xc
0012fd24 77e66905 KERNEL32!_ExitProcess+0x63
0012fd38 01256d9b KERNEL32!ExitProcess+0x14
0012ff60 01256dc7 mscorwks!SafeExitProcess+0x11a
0012ff6c 011c5fa4 mscorwks!DisableRuntime+0xd0
0012ffb0 79181b5f mscorwks!_CorExeMain+0x8c
0012ffc0 77e6f23b mscoree!_CorExeMain+0x2c
0012fff0 00000000 KERNEL32!BaseProcessStart+0x23
```

The original problem was an error message box, and the application disappeared when a user dismissed the message. How was the dump saved? Someone advised to attach NTSD to that process, hit ‘g’ key, and then save the memory dump when the process breaks into the debugger again. So the problem was already gone by that time. The better way would have been to create the manual user dump of that process when it was displaying the error message.

Manual Dump (Kernel)

Some memory dumps are generated on purpose to troubleshoot process and system hangs. They are usually called **Manual Dumps,** manual crash dumps, or manual memory dumps. Kernel, complete, and kernel mini dumps can be generated using the famous keyboard method described in the following Microsoft article which has been updated for USB keyboards:

http://support.microsoft.com/kb/244139

The crash dump will show E2 bugcheck:

```
MANUALLY_INITIATED_CRASH (e2)
The user manually initiated this crash dump.
Arguments:
Arg1: 00000000
Arg2: 00000000
Arg3: 00000000
Arg4: 00000000
```

Various tools reuse E2 bug check code and its arguments. There are many other 3rd-party tools used to bugcheck Windows OS, such as NotMyFault from Sysinternals. The old one is *crash.exe* that loads *crashdrv.sys* and uses the following bugcheck:

```
Unknown bugcheck code (69696969)
Unknown bugcheck description
Arguments:
Arg1: 00000000
Arg2: 00000000
Arg3: 00000000
Arg4: 00000000
```

In a memory dump, we would see its characteristic stack trace pointing to *crashdrv* module:

```
STACK_TEXT:
b5b3ebe0 f615888d nt!KeBugCheck+0xf
WARNING: Stack unwind information not available. Following frames may be
wrong.
b5b3ebec f61584e3 crashdrv+0x88d
b5b3ec00 8041eec9 crashdrv+0x4e3
b5b3ec14 804b328a nt!IopfCallDriver+0x35
b5b3ec28 804b40de nt!IopSynchronousServiceTail+0x60
b5b3ed00 804abd0a nt!IopXxxControlFile+0x5d6
b5b3ed34 80468379 nt!NtDeviceIoControlFile+0x28
b5b3ed34 77f82ca0 nt!KiSystemService+0xc9
```

```
0006fed4 7c5794f4 ntdll!NtDeviceIoControlFile+0xb
0006ff38 01001a74 KERNEL32!DeviceIoControl+0xf8
0006ff70 01001981 crash+0x1a74
0006ff80 01001f93 crash+0x1981
0006ffc0 7c5989a5 crash+0x1f93
0006fff0 00000000 KERNEL32!BaseProcessStart+0x3d
```

Sometimes various hardware buttons are used to trigger NMI and generate a crash dump when a keyboard is not available. The bugcheck is:

```
NMI_HARDWARE_FAILURE (80)
This is typically due to a hardware malfunction. The hardware supplier
should be called.
Arguments:
Arg1: 004f4454
Arg2: 00000000
Arg3: 00000000
Arg4: 00000000
```

Critical process termination such as session 0 *csrss.exe* was also used to force a memory dump for older systems before Windows 10:

```
CRITICAL_OBJECT_TERMINATION (f4)
A process or thread crucial to system operation has unexpectedly exited or
been terminated.
Several processes and threads are necessary for the operation of the
system; when they are terminated (for any reason), the system can no
longer function.
Arguments:
Arg1: 00000003, Process
Arg2: 8a090d88, Terminating object
Arg3: 8a090eec, Process image file name
Arg4: 80967b74, Explanatory message (ascii)
```

Wait Chain (General)

Wait Chain pattern is simply a sequence of causal relations between events: a thread A is waiting for an event E to happen that threads B, C or D are supposed to signal at some time in the future, but they are all waiting for an event F to happen that a thread G is about to signal as soon as it finishes processing some critical task:

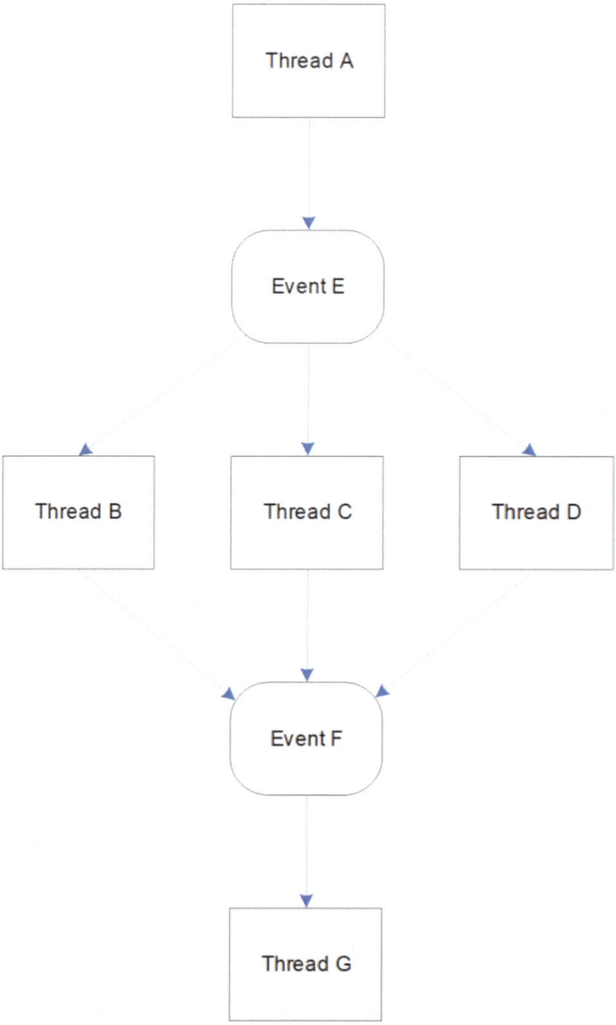

This subsumes various deadlock patterns too which are causal loops where a thread A is waiting for an event AB that a thread B signals as soon as the thread A signals an event BA the thread B is waiting for:

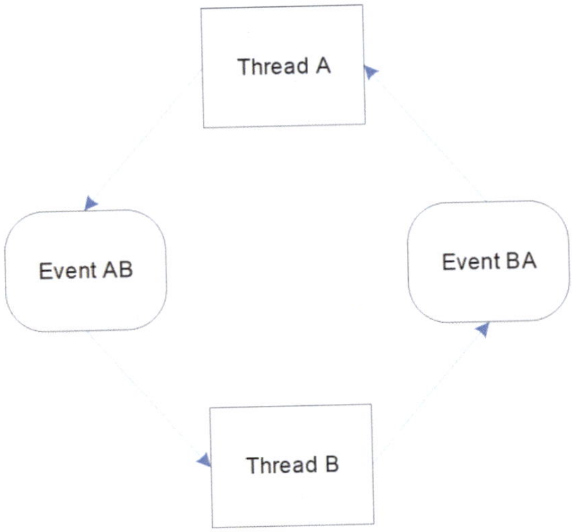

In this context, "Event" means not only a Win32 event object or kernel _KEVENT but also any type of a synchronization object, a critical section, LPC/RPC reply, or data arrival through some IPC channel.

As the first example of **Wait Chain** pattern, I show a process being terminated and waiting for another thread to finish or, in other words, considering thread termination as an event itself, the main process thread is waiting for the second thread object to be signaled. The second thread tries to cancel the previous I/O request directed to some device. However, that IRP is not cancellable, and the process hangs. This can be depicted in the following diagram:

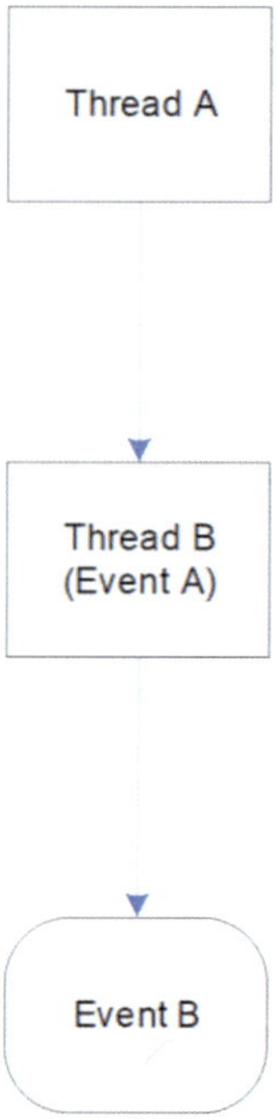

where Thread A is our main thread waiting for Event A, which is the thread B itself waiting for I/O cancelation (Event B). Their stack traces are:

```
THREAD 8a3178d0  Cid 04bc.01cc  Teb: 7ffdf000 Win32Thread: bc1b6e70 WAIT:
(Unknown) KernelMode Non-Alertable
    8af2c920  Thread
Not impersonating
DeviceMap                 e1032530
Owning Process            89ff8d88       Image:         processA.exe
Wait Start TickCount      80444          Ticks: 873 (0:00:00:13.640)
Context Switch Count      122                 LargeStack
UserTime                  00:00:00.015
KernelTime                00:00:00.156
Win32 Start Address 0x010148a4
Start Address 0x77e617f8
Stack Init f3f29000 Current f3f28be8 Base f3f29000 Limit f3f25000 Call 0
Priority 15 BasePriority 13 PriorityDecrement 0
ChildEBP RetAddr
f3f28c00 80833465 nt!KiSwapContext+0x26
f3f28c2c 80829a62 nt!KiSwapThread+0x2e5
f3f28c74 8094c0ea nt!KeWaitForSingleObject+0x346 ; stack trace
with arguments shows the first parameter as 8af2c920
f3f28d0c 8094c63f nt!PspExitThread+0x1f0
f3f28d24 8094c839 nt!PspTerminateThreadByPointer+0x4b
f3f28d54 8088978c nt!NtTerminateProcess+0x125
f3f28d54 7c8285ec nt!KiFastCallEntry+0xfc
```

```
THREAD 8af2c920  Cid 04bc.079c  Teb: 7ffd7000 Win32Thread: 00000000 WAIT:
(Unknown) KernelMode Non-Alertable
    8af2c998  NotificationTimer
IRP List:
    8ad26260: (0006,0220) Flags: 00000000  Mdl: 00000000
Not impersonating
DeviceMap                 e1032530
Owning Process            89ff8d88       Image:         processA.exe
Wait Start TickCount      81312          Ticks: 5 (0:00:00:00.078)
Context Switch Count      169                 LargeStack
UserTime                  00:00:00.000
KernelTime                00:00:00.000
Win32 Start Address 0x77da3ea5
Start Address 0x77e617ec
Stack Init f3e09000 Current f3e08bac Base f3e09000 Limit f3e05000 Call 0
Priority 13 BasePriority 13 PriorityDecrement 0
ChildEBP RetAddr
f3e08bc4 80833465 nt!KiSwapContext+0x26
f3e08bf0 80828f0b nt!KiSwapThread+0x2e5
f3e08c38 808ea7a4 nt!KeDelayExecutionThread+0x2ab
f3e08c68 8094c360 nt!IoCancelThreadIo+0x62
f3e08cf0 8094c569 nt!PspExitThread+0x466
f3e08cfc 8082e0b6 nt!PsExitSpecialApc+0x1d
f3e08d4c 80889837 nt!KiDeliverApc+0x1ae
f3e08d4c 7c8285ec nt!KiServiceExit+0x56
```

By inspecting IRP we can see a device it was directed to, see that it has the cancel bit but doesn't have a cancel routine:

```
0: kd> !irp 8ad26260  1
Irp is active with 5 stacks 4 is current (= 0x8ad2633c)
 No Mdl: No System Buffer: Thread 8af2c920:  Irp stack trace.
Flags = 00000000
ThreadListEntry.Flink = 8af2cb28
ThreadListEntry.Blink = 8af2cb28
IoStatus.Status = 00000000
IoStatus.Information = 00000000
RequestorMode = 00000001
Cancel = 01
CancelIrql = 0
ApcEnvironment = 00
UserIosb = 77ecb700
UserEvent = 00000000
Overlay.AsynchronousParameters.UserApcRoutine = 00000000
Overlay.AsynchronousParameters.UserApcContext = 00000000
Overlay.AllocationSize = 00000000 - 00000000
CancelRoutine = 00000000
UserBuffer = 77ecb720
&Tail.Overlay.DeviceQueueEntry = 8ad262a0
Tail.Overlay.Thread = 8af2c920
Tail.Overlay.AuxiliaryBuffer = 00000000
Tail.Overlay.ListEntry.Flink = 00000000
```

```
Tail.Overlay.ListEntry.Blink = 00000000
Tail.Overlay.CurrentStackLocation = 8ad2633c
Tail.Overlay.OriginalFileObject = 89ff8920
Tail.Apc = 00000000
Tail.CompletionKey = 00000000
     cmd  flg cl Device   File     Completion-Context
 [  0, 0]   0  0 00000000 00000000 00000000-00000000

   Args: 00000000 00000000 00000000 00000000
 [  0, 0]   0  0 00000000 00000000 00000000-00000000

   Args: 00000000 00000000 00000000 00000000
 [  0, 0]   0  0 00000000 00000000 00000000-00000000

   Args: 00000000 00000000 00000000 00000000
>[  c, 2]   0  1 8ab20388 89ff8920 00000000-00000000    pending
        \Device\DeviceA
   Args: 00000020 00000017 00000000 00000000
 [  c, 2]   0  0 8affa4b8 89ff8920 00000000-00000000
        \Device\DeviceB
   Args: 00000020 00000017 00000000 00000000
```

Manual Dump (Process)

Now we discuss **Manual Dump** pattern as seen in the process memory dumps. It is not possible to reliably identify manual dumps here because a debugger or another process dumper might have been attached to a process noninvasively and not leaving traces of intervention so we can only rely on the following information:

Comment field

```
Loading Dump File [C:\kktools\userdump8.1\x64\notepad.dmp]
User Mini Dump File with Full Memory: Only application data is available

Comment: 'Userdump generated complete user-mode minidump with Standalone
function on COMPUTER-NAME'
```

Absence of exceptions

```
Loading Dump File [C:\UserDumps\notepad.dmp]
User Mini Dump File with Full Memory: Only application data is available

Symbol search path is:
srv*c:\mss*http://msdl.microsoft.com/download/symbols
Executable search path is:
Windows Vista Version 6000 MP (2 procs) Free x64
Product: WinNt, suite: SingleUserTS
Debug session time: Mon Dec 17 16:31:31.000 2007 (GMT+0)
System Uptime: 0 days 0:45:11.148
Process Uptime: 0 days 0:00:36.000
....................
user32!ZwUserGetMessage+0xa:
00000000`76c8e6aa c3              ret
0:000> ~*kL

.  0  Id: 1b8.ed4 Suspend: 1 Teb: 000007ff`fffdc000 Unfrozen
Child-SP          RetAddr           Call Site
00000000`0029f618 00000000`76c8e6ea user32!ZwUserGetMessage+0xa
00000000`0029f620 00000000`ff2b6eca user32!GetMessageW+0x34
00000000`0029f650 00000000`ff2bcf8b notepad!WinMain+0x176
00000000`0029f6d0 00000000`76d7cdcd notepad!IsTextUTF8+0x24f
00000000`0029f790 00000000`76ecc6e1 kernel32!BaseThreadInitThunk+0xd
00000000`0029f7c0 00000000`00000000 ntdll!RtlUserThreadStart+0x1d
```

Wake debugger exception

```
Loading Dump File [C:\UserDumps\notepad2.dmp]
User Mini Dump File with Full Memory: Only application data is available

Symbol search path is:
srv*c:\mss*http://msdl.microsoft.com/download/symbols
Executable search path is:
Windows Vista Version 6000 MP (2 procs) Free x64
Product: WinNt, suite: SingleUserTS
Debug session time: Mon Dec 17 16:35:37.000 2007 (GMT+0)
System Uptime: 0 days 0:49:13.806
Process Uptime: 0 days 0:02:54.000
....................
This dump file has an exception of interest stored in it.
The stored exception information can be accessed via .ecxr.
(314.1b4): Wake debugger - code 80000007 (first/second chance not
available)"
user32!ZwUserGetMessage+0xa:
00000000`76c8e6aa c3              ret
```

Break instruction exception

```
Loading Dump File [C:\UserDumps\notepad3.dmp]
User Mini Dump File with Full Memory: Only application data is available

Symbol search path is:
srv*c:\mss*http://msdl.microsoft.com/download/symbols
Executable search path is:
Windows Vista Version 6000 MP (2 procs) Free x64
Product: WinNt, suite: SingleUserTS
Debug session time: Mon Dec 17 16:45:15.000 2007 (GMT+0)
System Uptime: 0 days 0:58:52.699
Process Uptime: 0 days 0:14:20.000
....................
This dump file has an exception of interest stored in it.
The stored exception information can be accessed via .ecxr.
ntdll!DbgBreakPoint:
00000000`76ecfdf0 cc              int     3

0:001> ~*kL

   0  Id: 1b8.ed4 Suspend: 1 Teb: 000007ff`fffdc000 Unfrozen
Child-SP          RetAddr           Call Site
00000000`0029f618 00000000`76c8e6ea user32!ZwUserGetMessage+0xa
00000000`0029f620 00000000`ff2b6eca user32!GetMessageW+0x34
00000000`0029f650 00000000`ff2bcf8b notepad!WinMain+0x176
00000000`0029f6d0 00000000`76d7cdcd notepad!IsTextUTF8+0x24f
00000000`0029f790 00000000`76ecc6e1 kernel32!BaseThreadInitThunk+0xd
00000000`0029f7c0 00000000`00000000 ntdll!RtlUserThreadStart+0x1d
```

```
# 1 Id: 1b8.ec4 Suspend: 1 Teb: 000007ff`fffda000 Unfrozen
Child-SP          RetAddr           Call Site
00000000`030df798 00000000`76f633e8 ntdll!DbgBreakPoint
00000000`030df7a0 00000000`76d7cdcd ntdll!DbgUiRemoteBreakin+0x38
00000000`030df7d0 00000000`76ecc6e1 kernel32!BaseThreadInitThunk+0xd
00000000`030df800 00000000`00000000 ntdll!RtlUserThreadStart+0x1d
```

The latter might also be some assertion statement in the code leading to a process crash like in the following instance of **Dynamic Memory Corruption** pattern (heap corruption, page 257):

```
FAULTING_IP:
ntdll!DbgBreakPoint+0
77f813b1 cc int 3

EXCEPTION_RECORD: ffffffff -- (.exr ffffffffffffffff)
ExceptionAddress: 77f813b1 (ntdll!DbgBreakPoint)
ExceptionCode: 80000003 (Break instruction exception)
ExceptionFlags: 00000000
NumberParameters: 3
Parameter[0]: 00000000
Parameter[1]: 09aef2ac
Parameter[2]: 09aeeee8

STACK_TEXT:
09aef0bc 77fb76aa ntdll!DbgBreakPoint
09aef0c4 77fa65c2 ntdll!RtlpBreakPointHeap+0x26
09aef2bc 77fb5367 ntdll!RtlAllocateHeapSlowly+0x212
09aef340 77fa64f6 ntdll!RtlDebugAllocateHeap+0xcb
09aef540 77fcc9e3 ntdll!RtlAllocateHeapSlowly+0x5a
09aef720 786f3f11 ntdll!RtlAllocateHeap+0x954
09aef730 786fd10e rpcrt4!operator new+0x12
09aef748 786fc042 rpcrt4!OSF_CCONNECTION::OSF_CCONNECTION+0x174
09aef79c 786fbe0d rpcrt4!OSF_CASSOCIATION::AllocateCCall+0xfa
09aef808 786fbd53 rpcrt4!OSF_BINDING_HANDLE::AllocateCCall+0x1cd
09aef83c 786f1f2f rpcrt4!OSF_BINDING_HANDLE::GetBuffer+0x28
09aef854 786f1ee4 rpcrt4!I_RpcGetBufferWithObject+0x6e
09aef860 786f1ea4 rpcrt4!I_RpcGetBuffer+0xb
09aef86c 78754762 rpcrt4!NdrGetBuffer+0x2b
09aefab8 796d78b5 rpcrt4!NdrClientCall2+0x3f9
09aefac8 796d7821 advapi32!LsarOpenPolicy2+0x14
09aefb1c 796d8b04 advapi32!LsaOpenPolicy+0xaf
09aefb84 796d8aa9 advapi32!LookupAccountSidInternal+0x63
09aefbac 0aaf5d8b advapi32!LookupAccountSidW+0x1f
WARNING: Stack unwind information not available. Following frames may be
wrong.
09aeff40 0aad1665 ComponentDLL+0x35d8b
09aeff5c 3f69264c ComponentDLL+0x11665
09aeff7c 780085bc ComponentDLL+0x264c
09aeffb4 77e5438b msvcrt!_endthreadex+0xc1
09aeffec 00000000 kernel32!BaseThreadStart+0x52
```

Wait Chain (Critical Sections)

Here is another example of **Wait Chain** pattern (page 482), where objects are critical sections.

WinDbg can detect them if we use **!analyze -v -hang** command, but it detects only one and not necessarily the longest or the widest chain in cases with multiple wait chains:

```
DERIVED_WAIT_CHAIN:

Dl Eid Cid     WaitType
-- --- ------- --------------------------
   2   8d8.90c Critical Section       -->
   4   8d8.914 Critical Section       -->
   66  8d8.f9c Unknown
```

Looking at threads, we see this chain, and we also see that the final thread is blocked waiting for a socket (shown in smaller font for visual clarity).

```
0:167> ~~[90c]kvL
ChildEBP RetAddr  Args to Child
00bbfd9c 7c942124 7c95970f 00000ea0 00000000 ntdll!KiFastSystemCallRet
00bbfda0 7c95970f 00000ea0 00000000 00000000 ntdll!NtWaitForSingleObject+0xc
00bbfddc 7c959620 00000000 00000004 00000000 ntdll!RtlpWaitOnCriticalSection+0x19c
00bbfdfc 6748d2f9 06018b50 00000000 00000000 ntdll!RtlEnterCriticalSection+0xa8
...
...
...
00bbffb8 7c82608b 00315218 00000000 00000000 msvcrt!_endthreadex+0xa3
00bbffec 00000000 77b9b4bc 00315218 00000000 kernel32!BaseThreadStart+0x34

0:167> ~~[914]kvL 100
ChildEBP RetAddr  Args to Child
00dbf1cc 7c942124 7c95970f 000004b0 00000000 ntdll!KiFastSystemCallRet
00dbf1d0 7c95970f 000004b0 00000000 00000000 ntdll!NtWaitForSingleObject+0xc
00dbf20c 7c959620 00000000 00000004 0031abcc ntdll!RtlpWaitOnCriticalSection+0x19c
00dbf22c 6748d244 0031abd8 003174e0 00dbf254 ntdll!RtlEnterCriticalSection+0xa8
...
...
...
00dbffb8 7c82608b 00315218 00000000 00000000 msvcrt!_endthreadex+0xa3
00dbffec 00000000 77b9b4bc 00315218 00000000 kernel32!BaseThreadStart+0x34

0:167> ~~[f9c]kvL 100
ChildEBP RetAddr  Args to Child
0fe2a09c 7c942124 71933a09 00000b50 00000001 ntdll!KiFastSystemCallRet
0fe2a0a0 71933a09 00000b50 00000001 0fe2a0c8 ntdll!NtWaitForSingleObject+0xc
0fe2a0dc 7194576e 00000b50 00000234 00000000 mswsock!SockWaitForSingleObject+0x19d
0fe2a154 71a12679 00000234 0fe2a1b4 00000001 mswsock!WSPRecv+0x203
0fe2a190 62985408 00000234 0fe2a1b4 00000001 WS2_32!WSARecv+0x77
0fe2a1d0 6298326b 00000234 0274ebc6 00000810 component!wait+0x338
...
...
...
0fe2ffb8 7c82608b 060cfc70 00000000 00000000 msvcrt!_endthreadex+0xa3
0fe2ffec 00000000 77b9b4bc 060cfc70 00000000 kernel32!BaseThreadStart+0x34
```

If we look at all held critical sections, we see another thread that blocked more than 125 other threads:

```
0:167> !locks

CritSec +31abd8 at 0031abd8
WaiterWoken        No
LockCount          6
RecursionCount     1
OwningThread       f9c
EntryCount         0
ContentionCount    17
*** Locked

CritSec +51e4bd8 at 051e4bd8
WaiterWoken        No
LockCount          125
RecursionCount     1
OwningThread       830
EntryCount         0
ContentionCount    7d
*** Locked

CritSec +5f40620 at 05f40620
WaiterWoken        No
LockCount          0
RecursionCount     1
OwningThread       920
EntryCount         0
ContentionCount    0
*** Locked

CritSec +60b6320 at 060b6320
WaiterWoken        No
LockCount          1
RecursionCount     1
OwningThread       8a8
EntryCount         0
ContentionCount    1
*** Locked

CritSec +6017c60 at 06017c60
WaiterWoken        No
LockCount          0
RecursionCount     1
OwningThread       914
EntryCount         0
ContentionCount    0
*** Locked
```

```
CritSec +6018b50 at 06018b50
WaiterWoken         No
LockCount           3
RecursionCount      1
OwningThread        914
EntryCount          0
ContentionCount     3
*** Locked

CritSec +6014658 at 06014658
WaiterWoken         No
LockCount           2
RecursionCount      1
OwningThread        928
EntryCount          0
ContentionCount     2
*** Locked
```

```
0:167> ~~[830]kvL 100
ChildEBP RetAddr  Args to Child
0ff2f300 7c942124 7c95970f 000004b0 00000000 ntdll!KiFastSystemCallRet
0ff2f304 7c95970f 000004b0 00000000 00000000 ntdll!NtWaitForSingleObject+0xc
0ff2f340 7c959620 00000000 00000004 0031abcc ntdll!RtlpWaitOnCriticalSection+0x19c
0ff2f360 6748d244 0031abd8 003174e0 0ff2f388 ntdll!RtlEnterCriticalSection+0xa8
...
...
...
0ff2ffb8 7c82608b 060cf9a0 00000000 00000000 msvcrt!_endthreadex+0xa3
0ff2ffec 00000000 77b9b4bc 060cf9a0 00000000 kernel32!BaseThreadStart+0x34
```

Searching for any thread waiting for critical section 051e4bd8 gives us:

```
   8  Id: 8d8.924 Suspend: 1 Teb: 7ffd5000 Unfrozen
ChildEBP RetAddr  Args to Child
011ef8e0 7c942124 7c95970f 00000770 00000000 ntdll!KiFastSystemCallRet
011ef8e4 7c95970f 00000770 00000000 00000000 ntdll!NtWaitForSingleObject+0xc
011ef920 7c959620 00000000 00000004 00000000 ntdll!RtlpWaitOnCriticalSection+0x19c
011ef940 677b209d 051e4bd8 011efa0c 057bd36c ntdll!RtlEnterCriticalSection+0xa8
...
...
...
011effb8 7c82608b 00315510 00000000 00000000 msvcrt!_endthreadex+0xa3
011effec 00000000 77b9b4bc 00315510 00000000 kernel32!BaseThreadStart+0x34
```

And we can construct yet another wait chain:

```
   8   8d8.924 Critical Section        -->
   67  8d8.830 Critical Section        -->
   66  8d8.f9c Unknown
```

PART 4: Crash Dump Analysis AntiPatterns

Alien Component

In any domain of activity where patterns exist, we can find anti-patterns too. They are the wrong or inadequate solutions to recurrent problems in specific contexts. One of them I would like to introduce briefly is called **Alien Component**. In essence, when every technique fails, or we run out of WinDbg commands, we look at an innocent component we have never seen before or don't have symbols for, be it a driver or hook. Of course, this component cannot be the component developed by the company we work for.

Zippocricy

Let's define **Zippocricy** – the common sin in software support environments worldwide: someone gets something from a customer in an archived form and without checking the contents forwards it further to another person in the support chain. By the time the evidence gets unzipped somewhere, checked, and found corrupt or irrelevant, the customer suffers not hours but days. It happens not only with crash dumps but with any type of problem evidence.

Word of Mouth

Many engineers say, "I didn't know about this debugging command, let's use it!" after a training session or reading other people's analysis of crash dumps. A year later, we hear the same phrase from them about another debugging command. In the meantime, they continue to use the same set of commands they know about until they hear the old new one.

This is a manifestation of **Word of Mouth** anti-pattern.

General solution: Know your tools. Study them proactively.

Example solution: periodically read and re-read WinDbg help.

Wrong Dump

A customer reports *application.exe* crashes, and we ask for a dump file. We get a dump, open it, and see that the dump is not from our application.exe. We ask for a print spooler crash dump, and we get *mplayer.exe* crash dump. I originally thought about calling it **Wrong Dump** pattern and placing it into the pattern category. Still, after writing about **Zippocricy** (page 494), I see it as an anti-pattern. It is not rocket science to check a process name in a dump file before sending it for analysis:

- Load the user process dump in WinDbg
- Type command **.symfix; .reload; !analyze -v** and wait

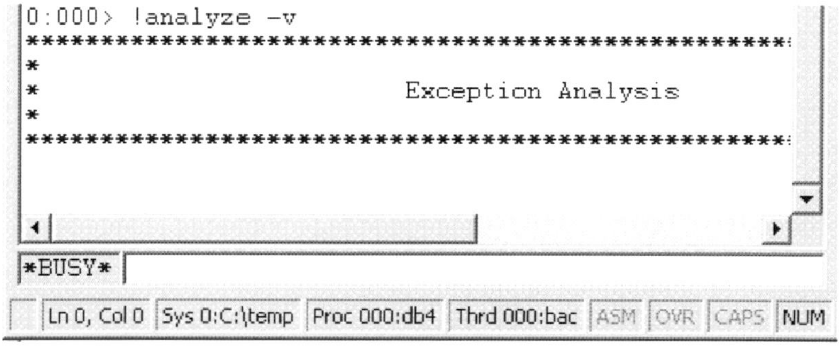

until WinDbg is not busy analyzing

- Find **PROCESS_NAME:** in the output. We get something like:

PROCESS_NAME: spoolsv.exe

We can also use *dumpchk.exe* from Debugging Tools for Windows.

Another example is when we ask for a complete memory dump, but we get a kernel dump or various mini-dumps. Fortunately, Citrix DumpCheck Explorer extension can warn users before they submit a dump file.

Fooled by Description

From my observation, an engineer with a software development background opens a crash dump after glancing at a problem description provided by a customer or even without reading it first. Only if the problem is not immediately obvious from the memory dump file, the engineer reads the problem description thoroughly. On the contrary, an engineer with a technical support or system administration background thoroughly reads the problem description first. In the latter case, the description may influence the direction of analysis.

Here is an example. The description says: slow application start, and we have a memory dump from a process. An engineer with a technical support background most likely looks for hang patterns inside the dump. An engineer with experience writing unmanaged applications in C and C++ opens the memory dump and checks an exception stored in it. If it is a breakpoint, the suspicion might arise that the memory dump was taken manually because of the hanging process. Based on the analysis, the engineer might even correct the problem description or add questions that clarify the discrepancy between what is seen in the dump and what users perceive.

Need the Crash Dump

This is might be the first thought when an engineer gets a stack trace fragment without symbolic information. It is usually based on the following presupposition:

We need an actual dump file to suggest further troubleshooting steps.

This is not true unless it is the first time we have the problem and a get stack trace for it. Consider the following fragment from one bugcheck kernel dump when no symbols were applied because the customer didn't have them:

```
b90529f8 8085eced nt!KeBugCheckEx+0x1b
b9052a70 8088c798 nt!MmAccessFault+0xb25
b9052a70 bfabd940 nt!_KiTrap0E+0xdc
WARNING: Stack unwind information not available. Following frames may be
wrong.
b9052b14 bfabe452 MyDriver+0x27940
```

We can convert *module+offset* information into *module!function+offset2* using MAP files or using DIA SDK (Debug Interface Access SDK) to query PDB files if we know module timestamp. This may be seen as a tedious exercise, but we don't need to do it if we keep raw stack trace signatures in some database when doing crash dump analysis. If we use our symbol servers, we want to remove references to them and reload symbols. Then redo previous stack trace commands.

In this case, similar previous bugcheck crash dumps were analyzed months ago, and engineers saved stacks trace prior to applying symbols. This helped to point to the solution without requesting the crash dump corresponding to that stack trace.

Be Language

This is about excessive use of "is" and was inspired by Alfred Korzybski's notion of how "is" affects our understanding of the world. In the context of technical support, the use of certain verbs sometimes leads to wrong troubleshooting and debugging paths. For example, the following phrase:

It is our pool tag. It is effected by driver A, driver B, and driver C.

Surely the driver A, driver B, and driver C were not developed by the same company that introduced the problem pool tag (smells **Alien Component** here, page 493). Unless supported by solid evidence the better phrase shall be:

It is our pool tag. It might have been effected by driver A, driver B or driver C.

I'm not advocating to completely eradicate "be" verbs but to be conscious of their use.

Fooled by Abbreviation

This anti-pattern happens when someone is so presupposed or engaged in identifying **Alien Components** (page 493) due to limited time and complexity of issues. For example, "Ctx" abbreviation in function names most likely means "Context" in general. Still, it can also be a function and data structure prefix used by a company with a similar sounding name. Opposite cases happen too when general is presupposed instead of particular, for example, "Mms" prefix is read as "Memory Management Subsystem" but belongs to a multimedia system vendor.

PART 5: A Bit of Science

Memory Dump - A Mathematical Definition

This post was inspired by reading the "Life Itself" book written by Robert Rosen, where computers are depicted as direct sums of states. As shown in that book, in the case of machines, their synthetic models (direct sums) are equivalent to analytic models (a direct product of observables). Taking every single bit as an observable having its values in Z_2 set {0, 1} we can make a definition of *an ideal memory dump* as a direct product or a direct sum of bits saved instantaneously at the given time:

$$\prod_i s_i = \sum_i s_i$$

Of course, we can also consider 8-bit bytes as observables having their values from the Z_{256} set.

In our case, we can simply rewrite the direct sum or product as the list of bits, bytes, words, or doublewords:

$(\ldots, s_{i-1}, s_i, s_{i+1}, \ldots, s_{j-1}, s_j, s_{j+1}, \ldots)$

According to Rosen, we include hardware states (registers, for example) and partition the memory into the input, output states for a particular computation and other states.

Saving a memory dump takes a certain amount of time. Suppose that it takes 3 discrete time events (ticks). During the first tick, we save memory up to $(\ldots, s_{i-1}, s_i)$, and that memory has some relationship to the s_j state. During the second tick, the s_j state changes its value, and during the 3rd tick, we copy the rest of the memory $(s_{i+1}, \ldots, s_{j-1}, \mathbf{s_j}, s_{j+1}, \ldots)$. Now we see that the final memory dump is inconsistent:

$(\ldots, s_{i-1}, s_i, s_{i+1}, \ldots, s_{j-1}, \mathbf{s_j}, s_{j+1}, \ldots)$

This is explained earlier in plain words in **Inconsistent Dump** pattern (page 269). Therefore, we may consider *a real memory dump* as a direct sum of disjoint memory areas M_t that were taken during some time interval (t_0, ..., t_n)

$$M = \sum_t M_t \text{ where } M_t = \sum_k S_{tk} \text{ or simply } M = \sum_t \sum_k S_{tk}$$

Threads as Braided Strings in Abstract Space

In the past, I was trying to find a way to depict running and blocked threads graphically perhaps as strings in some abstract n-dimensional space (manifold), preferably 3-dimensional manifold. If you have never encountered manifolds here is their informal definition:

> *A 3-dimensional manifold is a 3-dimensional space that looks like a 3-dimensional Euclidean space locally (in small regions), so we can explore the manifold space as we do in our 3-dimensional spatial world.*

Example: the surface of a sphere where small regions look like 2-dimensional rectangles (compare Earth surface and a football field on it)

My earlier attempts were not satisfactory, and only recently I found that it might be useful to represent threads as n-string braids.

Braids are strings that raise monotonically without reversing their direction. It sounds like an arrow of time during the computation. Braid theory is related to knot theory and might be an excellent metaphor to explore. To picture thread strings, we need to find abstract coordinates for our space. One of the axes is the time axis, and the other is the program counter axis (for example, the value of EIP register).

Here is a thread running through code sequentially without jumps or loops, acquiring and releasing a spinlock on its way:

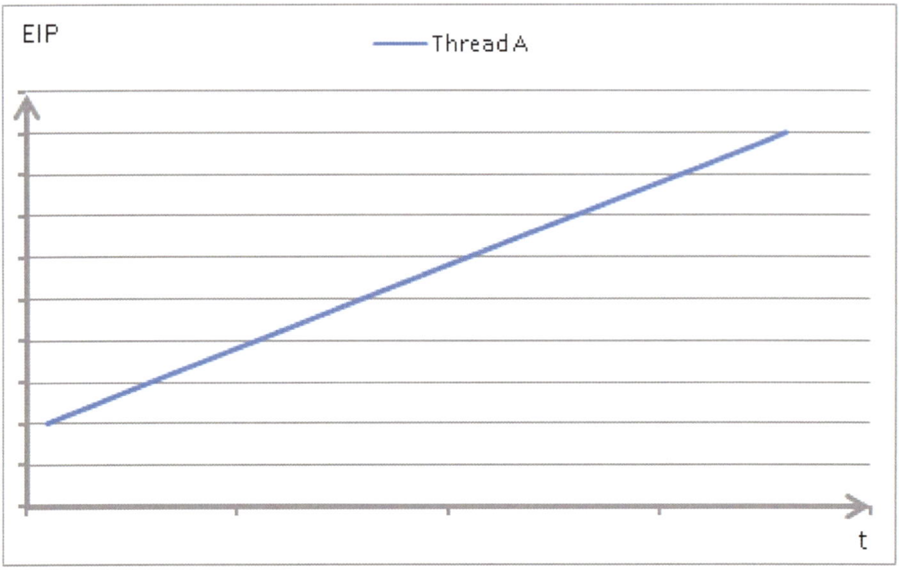

Here is another thread looping while trying to acquire a spinlock and finally taking ownership of it and then running the same code sequentially:

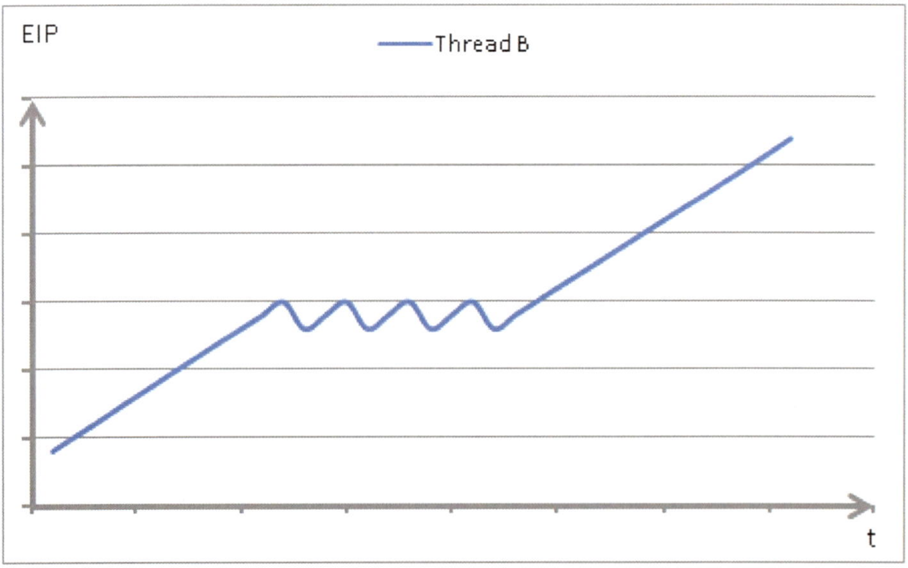

Suppose that both threads contend for the same spinlock, and there is a third thread doing the same. Let's overlay them on one single diagram:

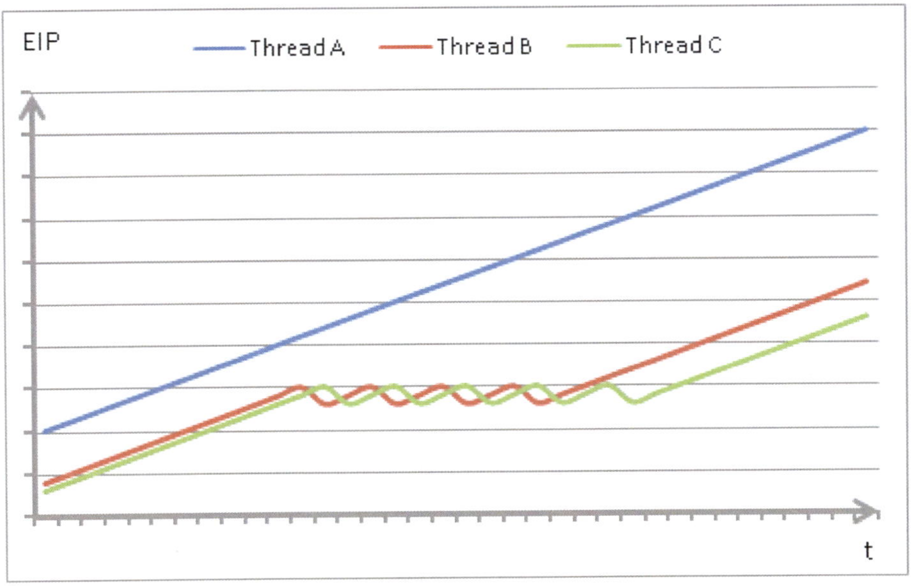

To have a perspective, we can add the third dimension: thread number or ID (TID):

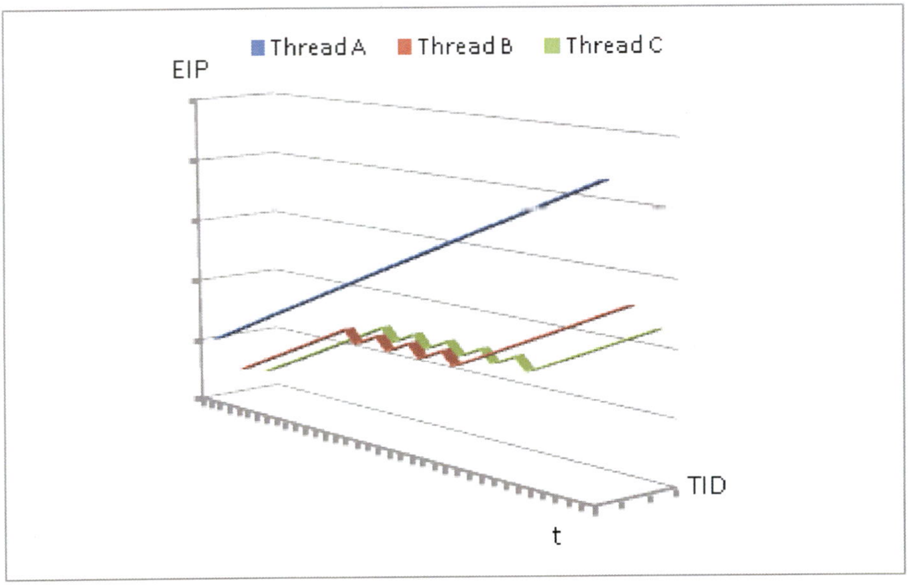

Instead of the TID axis, we can use the data address axis (the data address accessed by the current instruction) or have it as the fourth dimension. If we want to differentiate between read and write addresses, we can add the fifth axis.

What is Memory Dump Analysis?

From a computer system, we get a memory dump composed of fixed-size observable values called bit or byte values. Then we impose some structure on it in order to extract various derived objects like threads and processes, build some organization, and understand what had happened. This activity is called modeling and memory, crash, or core dump analysis is all about modeling a dynamical computer system based on its memory slice. Then we can make predictions and test them via controlled experiments called troubleshooting advice. Tools like WinDbg or GDB can be considered as abstract computers whose job is to model another computer when we feed memory dumps to them.

Memorillion and Quadrimemorillion

These are the names of the number of possible unique complete memory dumps when address space is 32 bit and 64-bit correspondingly:

$\mathbf{256^{2^{\wedge}32}}$ and $\mathbf{256^{2^{\wedge}64}}$

The first of them can be approximated by $\mathbf{10^{10^{\wedge}10}}$

The idea to name these numbers came to me after I learned about the so-called "immense number" proposed by Walter Elsasser. This number is so big that its digits cannot be listed because there are not enough particles in the observable Universe to write them.

Certainly, one memorillion is more than one googol $\mathbf{10^{100}}$, but it requires only approx. $\mathbf{10^{10}}$ particles in an ideal case to list its digits and, therefore, not an immense number. It is, however, far less than one googolplex $\mathbf{10^{10^{\wedge}100}}$.

Consider a complete memory dump with bytes written in hexadecimal notation:

```
0x50414745554d500f000000ce0e00000090...
```

This number has more than 8 billion digits. And it is one possible number out of memorillion of them. So one memorillion in hexadecimal notation is just

```
0xFFFFFFFFFFFFFFFFFFFF... + 1
```

where we have $\mathbf{2*2^{32}}$ 'F' symbols written sequentially. One quadrimemorillion has $\mathbf{2*2^{64}}$ 'F' symbols.

Four Causes of Crash Dumps

The appearance of crash dumps on a computer was caused by something. Was it a bug, a fault, a defect, or something else?

Aristotle suggested 4 types of causation 2 millennia ago, and they are:

- ***Material cause*** – the presence of some substance, usually material one (hardware), but can be machine code (software). The distinction between hardware and software is often blurred today because of virtualization.
- ***Formal cause*** - some form or arrangement (an algorithm)
- ***Efficient cause*** - an agent (data flow or event caused an algorithm to be executed)
- ***Final cause*** - the desire of someone (or something, operating system, for example).

We skip material causes because hardware and software are always involved. Obviously, final causality should be among of the crash dump causes because they were either anticipated or made deliberately. Let’s look at 3 examples with their possible causes:

<u>Buffer Overflow</u>

- *Formal cause* - a defect in the code which might have arisen from an incomplete or wrong model
- *Efficient cause* - data is too big to fit in a buffer
- *Final cause* - operating system and runtime library support decided to save a crash dump

<u>Bugcheck (NMI)</u>

- *Formal cause* - NMI handler
- *Efficient cause* - a button on a hardware panel or *KeBugCheckEx*
- *Final cause* - “I need a memory dump” desire. Also, crash dump saving functions were written before by kernel developers in anticipation of future crash dumps.

<u>Bugcheck (A)</u>

- *Formal cause* - a defect in the code again or a particular disposition of threads
- *Efficient cause* - Driver Verifier triggered paging out data

- *Final cause* - deliberate OS bugcheck (here we can also say that it was anticipated by OS designers)

Concrete causes depend on the organizational level we use, for example, software/hardware systems/components or modeling acts by humans.

Complexity and Memory Dumps

Asking the right questions at the appropriate hierarchical organization level is a known solution to complexity. In the case of memory dumps, it is sometimes useful to forget about bits, bytes, words, doublewords, qwords, memory addresses, pointers, runtime structures, API, and ask educated questions at the component level. The simplest of it is the question about component timestamp, in WinDbg parlance, using variants of **lm** command, for example:

```
0:008> lmt m ModuleA
start    end        module name
76290000 762ad000   ModuleA  Sat Feb 17 13:59:59 2007 (45D70A5F)

0:008> lmt m ModuleB
start    end        module name
66c50000 66c65000   ModuleB  Fri Feb 02 22:30:03 2007 (45C3BB6B)
```

The next step is obvious: test with the newer version. Another good question is about consistency to exclude cases caused by α-particle hits. This latter possibility was mentioned in Andreas Zeller's insightful book. It can be considered as the efficient cause of some crash dumps, according to Aristotelian causation categories (page 508).

What is a Software Defect?

Software can be considered as models of real or imagined systems which may be models themselves. Any modeling act involves a mapping between a system and a model that preserves causal, ordering, and inclusion relationships and a mapping from the model to the system that translates emerging relationships and causal structures back to that system. The latter I call modeling expectations, and any observed deviations in structure and behavior between the model and the system I call software defects which can be functional failures, error messages, crashes or hangs (bold line on diagrams below):

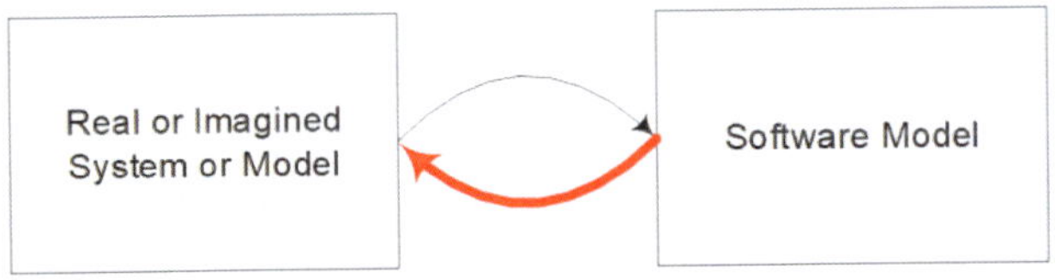

Consider ATM software as a venerable example. It models an imagined world of ATM transactions that we call ATM software requirements. The latter specifies ACID (atomic, consistent, isolated, and durable) transaction rules. If they are broken by the written software, we have the defect:

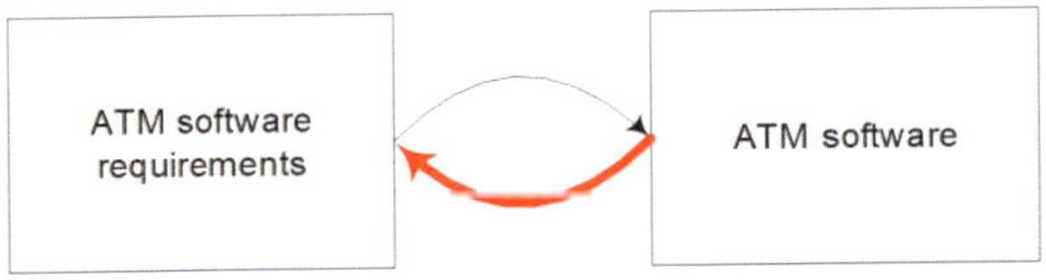

What are the software requirements? They are models of real or imagined systems or can be models of past causal and relationship experiences. If requirements are wrong, they do not translate back, and we still consider software as having a defect:

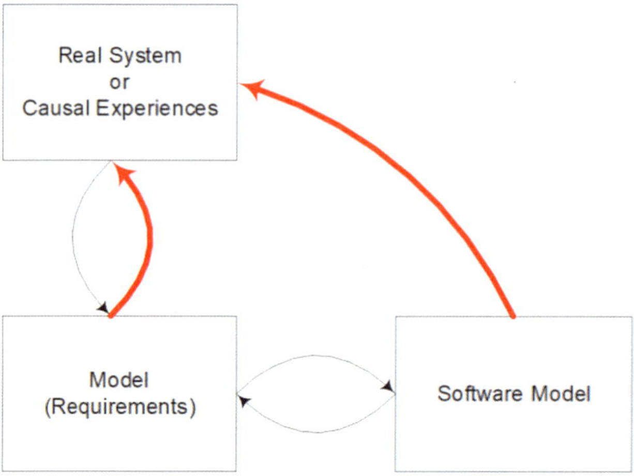

Translating this to ATM example we have:

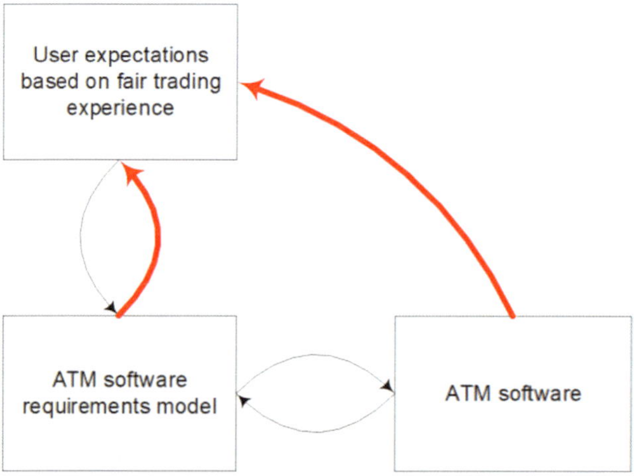

Another example where the perceived absence of failures can be considered as a defect is the program designed to model memory leaks that might not be leaking due to a defect in its source code.

PART 6: Fun with Crash Dumps

Dump Analysis and Voice Recognition

"Being so tired of typing endlessly ***!analyze -v*** *one day an idea came to me about using Voice Recognition.*

Taking advantage of spending 7 years in that field starting from 1992 and being the architect and designer/developer of the first pioneer speech recognition systems on Windows platforms (if you remember Covox and Voice Blaster - I was an employee there) VoiceMouse, JustVoice, SpeakingMouse, and recently my own project OpenTask I seriously consider using this for Dump Analysis.

More of this later..."

This was my first blog post ever, and now you are reading this book!

Sending SMS Messages via Dumps

SystemDump tool (page 646) allows crashing a computer and embedding a message in a memory dump. Dump files are becoming a universal medium of discourse between customers and support personnel.

WinDbg as a Big Calculator

I noticed one engineer frequently switching between WinDbg and Calc. Now we can forget about using *calc.exe* during debugging sessions and save valuable time. In other words, we no longer need to multiprocess. We can use **?** and **.formats** commands:

```
0:000> ? 2 + 2
Evaluate expression: 4 = 00000004
0:000> .formats 4
Evaluate expression:
  Hex:     00000004
  Decimal: 4
  Octal:   00000000004
  Binary:  00000000 00000000 00000000 00000100
  Chars:   ....
  Time:    Thu Jan 01 00:00:04 1970
  Float:   low 5.60519e-045 high 0
  Double:  1.97626e-323
```

Now we can do our finance calculations in WinDbg too.

The WinDbg Way!

Dumps, Debuggers, and Virtualization

Everyone now *(before 2008)* speaks about virtualization and its benefit. New horizons spring here and there. I would like to add my 2 cents from memory dump analysis and debugging perspective. There will be the more complex debugging environment as my recent experience with WOW64 tells me:

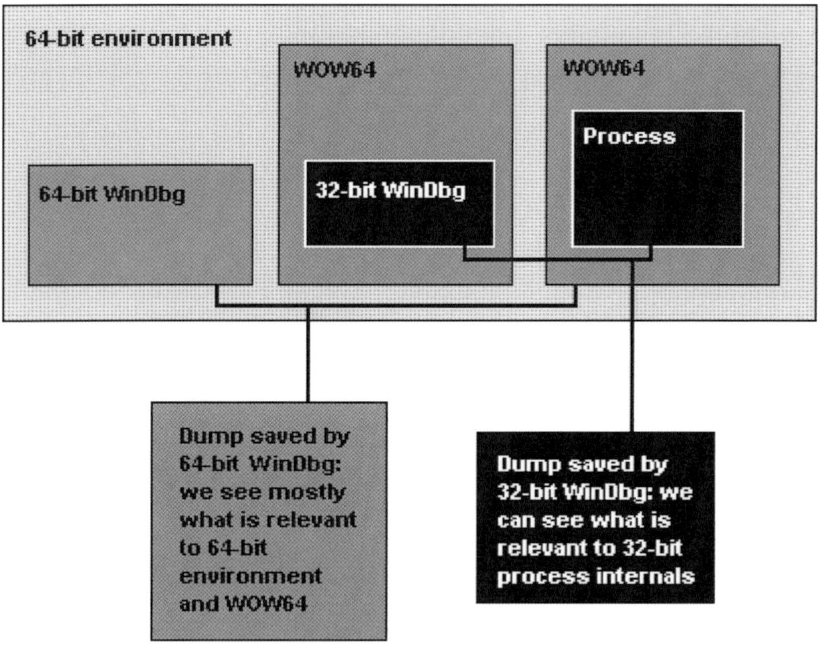

If we generalize this to a virtualization environment, we come up with the following picture:

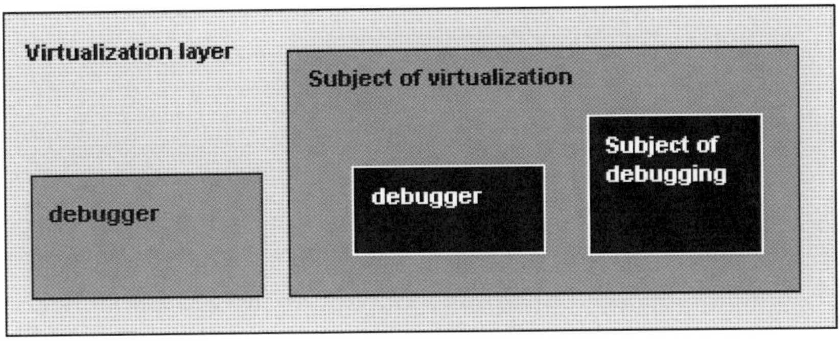

If we think more we come up with the following example of the general DDV architecture:

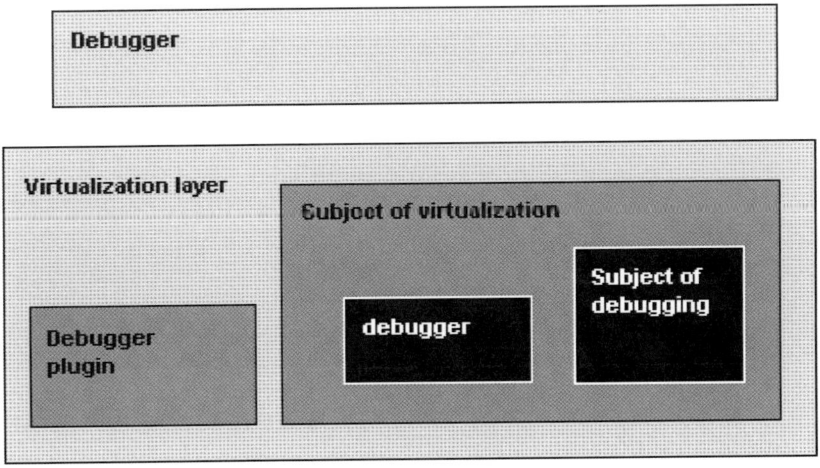

So we need:

- A "Debugger" to debug the "Virtualization layer."
- A "Debugger plugin" to help the "Debugger" to understand the "Subject of virtualization."
- Various virtualized "debuggers" debugging their virtualized subjects.

Musical Dumps

After listening to "An Anthology of Noise and Electronic Music" and remembering that long time ago I was asked to convert stock charts into sound waves an idea came to me to convert memory dump files into WAV files by appending an appropriate header in front of them. So depending on imposed sampling frequency (Hz), the quantization level (bits), and mono/stereo settings, we can enjoy listening to memory dumps.

Debugging the Debugger

Is it possible to debug a debugger when it debugs a debuggee? Good question. I never asked it to myself until one today and tried. And it works! First, I tried to attach WinDbg.exe to an instance of WinDbg.exe executing **!analyze -v** command and got these stacks:

```
0:002> ~*kL 100
0 Id: 1ff0.104c Suspend: 1 Teb: 7ffdf000 Unfrozen
ChildEBP RetAddr
0006df38 7739d02f ntdll!KiFastSystemCallRet
0006ff7c 01055e36 USER32!NtUserWaitMessage+0xc
0006ffc0 77e523e5 windbg!_initterm_e+0x170
0006fff0 00000000 kernel32!BaseProcessStart+0x23

1 Id: 1ff0.1af8 Suspend: 1 Teb: 7ffde000 Unfrozen
ChildEBP RetAddr
00ac3448 030a5677 dbghelp!CAllPubNameTrav::next+0x1b
00ac345c 0301e16e
dbghelp!CDiaEnumTraversalCSymRow::Next+0x48
00ac44fc 0301e452 dbghelp!diaGetGlobals+0x8fe
00ac4524 0304967a dbghelp!diaGetSymbols+0x42
00ac453c 03045ca3 dbghelp!diaEnumSymbols+0x1a
00ac4554 03031e5a dbghelp!modEnumSymbols+0x43
00ac459c 030338a5 dbghelp!ModLoop+0x10a
00ac6570 030391d8 dbghelp!EnumSymbols+0x155
00ac65a0 0220947b dbghelp!SymEnumSymbolsW+0x48
00ac7600 0220a53d dbgeng!FindTypeInfoInMod+0x18b
00aca5cc 0220caa2 dbgeng!TypeInfoFound+0xced
00acb62c 0220c95f dbgeng!SymbolTypeDumpNew+0xa2
00acb654 0220d36b dbgeng!FastSymbolTypeDump+0xef
00acb700 0213c753 dbgeng!SymbolTypeDump+0xbb
00acc25c 0147d632 dbgeng!ExtIoctl+0x1073
00acc2f4 0150e10e ext!GetFieldData+0xe2
00accc14 014f9f00 ext!UaThread::_Extract_UIThread+0x34e
00accc24 014fa1f9 ext!UaThread::CallExtractors+0x20
00accc34 01511126 ext!UaThread::ExtractAttributes+0x99
00accd78 015212e2
ext!UserAnalyze::ExtractAttributes+0x376
00acd02c 01521467 ext!UeFillAnalysis+0x462
00acd10c 01521650 ext!UeAnalyze+0x147
00acd208 0147c90c ext!AnalyzeUserException+0x1a0
00acd23c 02141299 ext!analyze+0x28c
00acd2c8 021414d9 dbgeng!ExtensionInfo::CallA+0x2e9
00acd458 021415a2 dbgeng!ExtensionInfo::Call+0x129
00acd474 0213feb1 dbgeng!ExtensionInfo::CallAny+0x72
00acd8ec 02181698 dbgeng!ParseBangCmd+0x661
00acd9dc 02182b29 dbgeng!ProcessCommands+0x508
00acda20 020c9049 dbgeng!ProcessCommandsAndCatch+0x49
00acdeb8 020c92aa dbgeng!Execute+0x2b9
```

```
00acdee8 010283bf dbgeng!DebugClient::ExecuteWide+0x6a
00acdf88 0102883b windbg!ProcessCommand+0xff
00acffa4 0102aabc windbg!ProcessEngineCommands+0x8b
00acffb8 77e6608b windbg!EngineLoop+0x3dc
00acffec 00000000 kernel32!BaseThreadStart+0x34

# 2 Id: 1ff0.116c Suspend: 1 Teb: 7ffdd000 Unfrozen
ChildEBP RetAddr
00fdffc8 7c845ea0 ntdll!DbgBreakPoint
00fdfff4 00000000 ntdll!DbgUiRemoteBreakin+0x36
```

Next, I thought, wait a moment, we are debugging the crash dump analysis session. Can we debug a debugger debugging a running process? So I attached *WinDbg.exe* to an instance of *WinDbg.exe* attached to an instance of *notepad.exe* and got these stacks:

```
0:002> ~*kL
0 Id: 11f0.164c Suspend: 1 Teb: 7ffde000 Unfrozen
ChildEBP RetAddr
0006df38 7739d02f ntdll!KiFastSystemCallRet
0006ff7c 01055e36 USER32!NtUserWaitMessage+0xc
0006ffc0 77e523e5 windbg!_initterm_e+0x170
0006fff0 00000000 kernel32!BaseProcessStart+0x23

1 Id: 11f0.1bb0 Suspend: 1 Teb: 7ffdd000 Unfrozen
ChildEBP RetAddr
00adff0c 7c822124 ntdll!KiFastSystemCallRet
00adff10 77e6bad8 ntdll!NtWaitForSingleObject+0xc
00adff80 020bf8aa kernel32!WaitForSingleObjectEx+0xac
00adffa0 0102aa42
dbgeng!DebugClient::DispatchCallbacks+0x4a
00adffb8 77e6608b windbg!EngineLoop+0x362
00adffec 00000000 kernel32!BaseThreadStart+0x34

# 2 Id: 11f0.100c Suspend: 1 Teb: 7ffdc000 Unfrozen
ChildEBP RetAddr
00beffc8 7c845ea0 ntdll!DbgBreakPoint
00befff4 00000000 ntdll!DbgUiRemoteBreakin+0x36
```

Given that many functions from *dbghelp.dll* and *dbgeng.dll* are described in WinDbg help, we can quickly reverse engineer *WinDbg.exe* and its extensions to understand their mechanics from a high-level perspective.

Musical Dumps: Dump2Wave

Dump2Wave command line tool is available for free download at:

http://www.dumpanalysis.org/downloads/Dump2Wave.zip

Simply run it from the command prompt and specify full paths to a dump file and output WAV file. The dump file will be converted by default into 44.1KHz 16bit stereo WAV file (CD quality). We can also specify our own conversion parameters like samples per second (22050, 11025), bits per sample (8 or 16) and the number of channels (1 - mono, 2 - stereo):

```
c:\Tools>Dump2Wave.exe

Dump2Wave version 1.3
Written by Dmitry Vostokov, 2006 - 2015

Usage: Dump2Wave dumpfile wavefile [192000|176400|96000|88200|44100|22050|11025|8000 24|16|8 2|1]
```

For example, I converted *notepad.dmp* to *notepad.wav*:

```
c:\Tools>Dump2Wave.exe c:\MemoryDumps\notepad.dmp c:\MemoryDumps\notepad.wav 22050 16 2

Dump2Wave version 1.3
Written by Dmitry Vostokov, 2006 - 2015
```

In 2006, I had a dump that was saved after *sndrec32.exe* played "*Windows XP Logon Sound.wav*" file from *Windows**Media* folder, and that wave file was originally sampled as 22050Hz 16bits stereo. By listening to *sndrec32.dmp*, I was able to hear a fragment from that logon sound because it was stored in a buffer inside the *sndrec32.exe* process.

Note: Due to limitations of the WAVE file format, Dump2Wave can't convert dump files greater than 4Gb.

Dump Tomography

There is an idea to interpret a process or a system dump as a picture (similar to interpreting it as a giant wave file: Dump2Wave:

http://www.dumpanalysis.org/forum/viewtopic.php?t=41

I would like to extend this idea and present it as **Dump Tomography** - a combination of images taken from a dump when looking at it from different perspectives, for example, memory, resources and subsystem hierarchy.

Dump Analysis becomes both Medicine and Art. We can finally hear how corruption sounds and how it looks like.

The Smallest Program

Can the smallest program that crashes be smaller than the smallest program that doesn't? It depends on a platform and a compiler/linker set. I chose x64 and MASM64 for my experiments. The smallest working program I came up first was this:

```
; ml64 /Zi TheSmallestProgram64.asm /link
;   /entry:main /SUBSYSTEM:CONSOLE

_text SEGMENT
main PROC
ret
main ENDP
_text ENDS

END
```

It compiles and links to an executable with only one-byte instruction in its *main* function:

```
0:000> u main
TheSmallestProgram64!main:
00000000`00401010 c3              ret
00000000`00401011 cc              int     3
00000000`00401012 cc              int     3
00000000`00401013 cc              int     3
00000000`00401014 cc              int     3
00000000`00401015 cc              int     3
00000000`00401016 cc              int     3
00000000`00401017 cc              int     3
```

Then I thought about removing *ret* instruction and supposed that if we compile and link and try to execute the program with 0 bytes, we get straight to *int 3* instruction, and in my case (I had NTSD set as a default postmortem debugger) a dump would be saved. So I did that, but I found that, unfortunately, compiler inserts *ret* instruction if the procedure body is empty. So I cheated them by putting *nop* instruction (which is also one byte) and got my dump!

```
; ml64 /Zi TheSmallestProgramWithBug64.asm /link
;    /entry:main /SUBSYSTEM:CONSOLE
_text SEGMENT
main PROC
nop
main ENDP
_text ENDS

END
```

```
Loading Dump File [new_2006-10-25_12-40-06-500_076C.dmp]
...

0:000> kL
TheSmallestProgramWithBug64!main+0x1
kernel32!BaseProcessStart+0x29

0:000> u main
TheSmallestProgramWithBug64!main:
00000000`00401010 90              nop
00000000`00401011 cc              int     3
00000000`00401012 cc              int     3
00000000`00401013 cc              int     3
00000000`00401014 cc              int     3
00000000`00401015 cc              int     3
00000000`00401016 cc              int     3
00000000`00401017 cc              int     3
```

So here is one answer to my question: The smallest working program and the smallest crashing program have the same size unless we use some binary editors.

Then I tried MS Visual C++ (this time a 32-bit project) and came up with the following C or C++ program without any prolog and epilog code:

```
__declspec(naked) void Main ()
{
}
```

I changed entry point from standard *main* function to my own capitalized *Main* function and here were my compiler/link options:

```
Compiler:

/Od /GL /D "WIN32" /D "NDEBUG" /D "_CONSOLE"
/D "_UNICODE" /D "UNICODE" /D "_AFXDLL"
/FD /MD /GS- /Fo"Release\"
/Fd"Releasevc80.pdb" /W3 /nologo /c
/Wp64 /Zi /TP /errorReport:prompt


Linker:

/OUT:"SmallestProgram.exe" /INCREMENTAL:NO
/NOLOGO /MANIFEST:NO /NODEFAULTLIB /DEBUG
/PDB:"SmallestProgram.pdb" /SUBSYSTEM:CONSOLE
/OPT:REF /OPT:ICF /LTCG /ENTRY:"Main"
/ERRORREPORT:PROMPT
```

The program crashed immediately because the body was empty:

```
Loading Dump File [new_2006-10-25_15-18-03-109_13B0.dmp]

0:000> u Main
SmallestProgram!Main:
00401000 cc              int     3
00401001 0000            add     byte ptr [eax],al
00401003 0000            add     byte ptr [eax],al
00401005 0000            add     byte ptr [eax],al
00401007 0000            add     byte ptr [eax],al
00401009 0000            add     byte ptr [eax],al
0040100b 0000            add     byte ptr [eax],al
0040100d 0000            add     byte ptr [eax],al

0:000> kL
ChildEBP RetAddr
002cfff0 00000000 SmallestProgram!Main

0:000> dds esp
002cffc4  7d4e992a kernel32!BaseProcessStart+0x28
002cffc8  00000000
002cffcc  00000000
002cffd0  7efdf000
002cffd4  80000003
002cffd8  002cffc8
002cffdc  002cfbbc
002cffe0  ffffffff
002cffe4  7d4d8998 kernel32!_except_handler3
002cffe8  7d4e9938 kernel32!`string'+0x28
002cffec  00000000
002cfff0  00000000
002cfff4  00000000
002cfff8  00401000 SmallestProgram!Main
002cfffc  00000000
```

So here is another answer to my question: The smallest crashing program can be less than the smallest working program and is actually 0 bytes.

Voices from Process Space

Following the release of **Dump2Wave** tool (page 521), some members of community had been asking me to provide some interesting sound fragments from dump files. I was also particularly interested in catching voices from the past: embedded fragments of the human voice. So I recorded my "Hello" message, played it by Media Player, and then saved a process dump. Then I converted the dump to CD-quality wave file and saved interesting sound fragments from it (to conserve space - the original wave file was 76Mb).

To listen to these fragments you can download wave files from the following location:

DumpSounds.zip (8Mb, http://www.dumpanalysis.org/Dump2Wave/DumpSounds.zip)

Here is the description of what I heard in these wave files:

- *dump1.wav*

  - violin
  - aliens
  - train sound
  - Hello

- *dump2.wav*

  - electric guitar
  - signals from cosmos

- *dump3.wav*

  - Morse code alphabet

- *dump4.wav*

  - helicopter

- *dump5.wav*

- horn
- some interesting noise and fragments of electronic music

Of course, we can convert kernel memory dumps to wave files and hear voices from kernel space too.

Crash Dump Analysis Card

I have been thinking for a while what kind of a useful marketing card I should have and finally came up with the following design:

Front

Backside

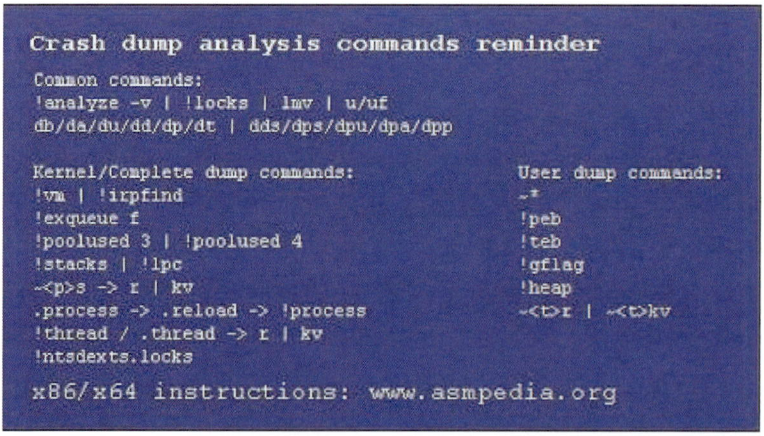

I put the most used commands (at least for me) and hope the backside of this card will be useful. If you see me in person, you have a chance to get this card (it is blue) in hardcopy.

Listening to Computer Memory

An alternative to converting memory dumps to sound files is to save a memory range to a binary file and then convert it to a wave file. The latter is better for complete memory dumps, which can be several Gb in size.

To save a memory range to a file, we can use WinDbg **.writemem** command:

```
.writemem d2w-range.bin 00400000 00433000
```

or

```
.writemem d2w-range.bin 00400000 L200
```

I wrote a WinDbg script that saves a specified memory range and then calls a shell script, which automatically converts the saved binary file to a wave file and then runs whatever sound program is registered for .wav extension. On many systems, it is Microsoft Media Player.

The WinDbg script code (*memsounds.txt*):

```
.writemem d2w-range.bin ${$arg1} ${$arg2}
.if (${/d:$arg5})
{
  .shell -i- memsounds.cmd d2w-range ${$arg3} ${$arg4} ${$arg5}
}
.elsif (${/d:$arg4})
{
  .shell -i- memsounds.cmd d2w-range ${$arg3} ${$arg4}
}
.elsif (${/d:$arg3})
{
  .shell -i- memsounds.cmd d2w-range ${$arg3}
}
.else
{
  .shell -i- memsounds.cmd d2w-range
}
```

The shell script (*memsounds.cmd*):

```
dump2wave %1.bin %1.wav %2 %3 %4
%1.wav
```

Because the WinDbg installation folder is assumed to be the default directory for both scripts and *Dump2Wave.exe,* they should be copied to the same folder where windbg.exe is located. On my system it is

```
C:\Program Files\Debugging Tools for Windows
```

Both scripts are included in Dump2Wave package available for free download at http://www.dumpanalysis.org/downloads/Dump2Wave.zip

To call the script from WinDbg we can use the following command:

```
$$>a< memsounds.txt Range [Freq] [Bits] [Channels]
```

where **Range** can be in *Address1 Address2* or *Address Lxxx* format, **Freq** can be 44100, 22050, 11025 or 8000, **Bits** can be 8 or 16, **Channels** can be 1 or 2. By default, it is 44100, 16, 2.

If we have a live debugging session or loaded a crash dump, we can listen to a memory range immediately. For example, the range of memory from 00400000 to 00433000 interpreted as 44.1KHz 16bit stereo:

```
0:000> $$>a< memsounds.txt 00400000 00433000
Writing 33001 bytes...

C:\Program Files\Debugging Tools for Windows>dump2wave d2w-range.bin d2w-
range.wav

Dump2Wave version 1.2.1
Written by Dmitry Vostokov, 2006

d2w-range.wav
d2w-range.bin
        1 file(s) copied.

C:\Program Files\Debugging Tools for Windows>d2w-range.wav
.shell: Process exited
0:000>
```

Or the same range interpreted as 8KHz 8bit mono:

```
0:000> $$>a< memsounds.txt 00400000 00433000 8000 8 1
Writing 33001 bytes...
```

```
C:\Program Files\Debugging Tools for Windows>dump2wave d2w-range.bin d2w-
range.wav 8000 8 1

Dump2Wave version 1.2.1
Written by Dmitry Vostokov, 2006

d2w-range.wav
d2w-range.bin
        1 file(s) copied.

C:\Program Files\Debugging Tools for Windows>d2w-range.wav
.shell: Process exited
0:000>
```

The script starts Windows Media Player on my system, and I only need to push the play button to start listening.

Visualizing Memory Dumps

As the first step towards **Memory Dump Tomography** (page 522), I created a small program that interprets a memory dump as a picture. We can visualize crash dumps with it. The tool is available for free download at:

http://www.dumpanalysis.org/downloads/Dump2Picture.zip

Simply run it from the command prompt and specify full paths to a dump file and an output BMP file. The memory dump file will be converted by default into true color, 32 bits-per-pixel bitmap. We can specify other values: 8, 16 and 24.

```
c:\Tools>Dump2Picture.exe

Dump2Picture version 2.2.3
Written by Dmitry Vostokov, Copyright (c) 2007 - 2018 Software Diagnostics
Institute.

Usage: Dump2Picture DumpFile BmpFile [8|16|24|32]

c:\Tools>
```

For example:

```
c:\Tools>Dump2Picture.exe MEMORY.DMP MEMORY.BMP 8

Dump2Picture version 2.2.3
Written by Dmitry Vostokov, Copyright (c) 2007 - 2018 Software Diagnostics
Institute.

MEMORY.BMP
MEMORY.DMP
        1 file(s) copied.
```

Below are some screenshots of bitmap files created by the tool. We can think about them as visualized kernel or user address spaces.

Vista kernel memory dump (8 bits-per-pixel):

Vista kernel memory dump (16 bits-per-pixel):

Vista kernel memory dump (24 bits-per-pixel):

Vista kernel memory dump (32 bits-per-pixel):

Notepad process user memory dump (8 bits-per-pixel):

Notepad process user memory dump (16 bits-per-pixel):

Notepad process user memory dump (24 bits-per-pixel):

Notepad process user memory dump (32 bits-per-pixel):

Paint process user memory dump (32 bits-per-pixel):

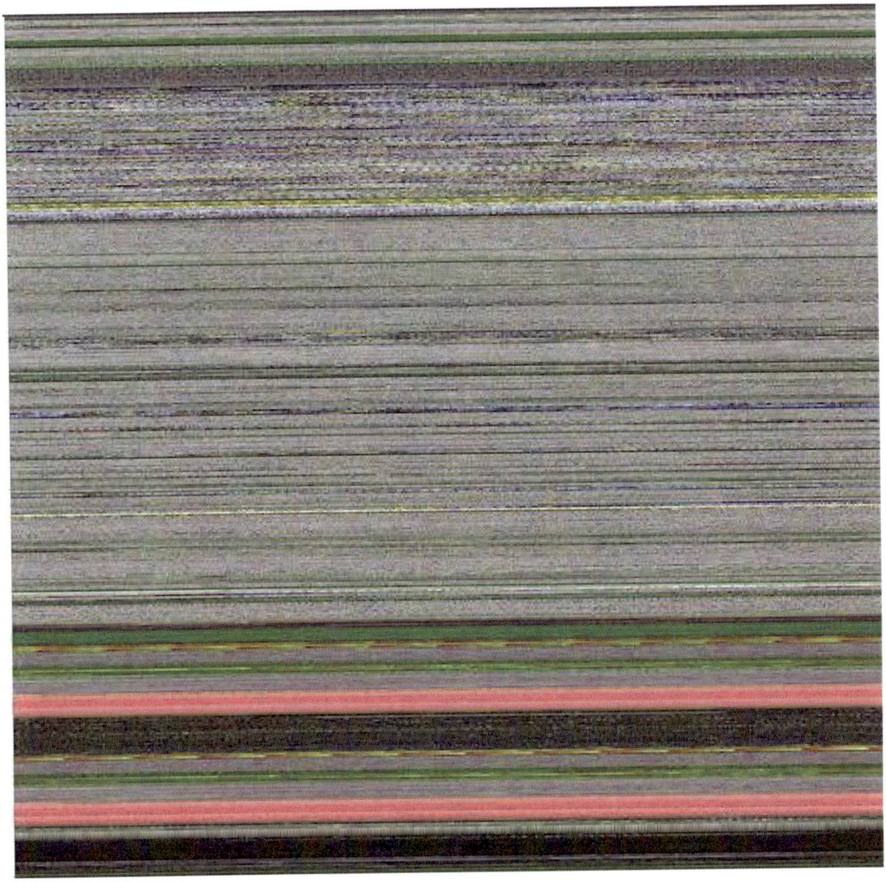

Paint process user memory dump after loading "*Toco Toucan.jpg*" from Vista Sample Pictures folder (32 bits-per-pixel):

Citrix ICA client process (*wfica32.exe*) user memory dump (32 bits-per-pixel):

Visualizing Memory Leaks

Dump2Picture (page 532) can be used to explore memory leaks visually. I created the following small program in Visual C++ that leaks 64Kb every second:

```
#include "stdafx.h"
#include <windows.h>

int _tmain(int argc, _TCHAR* argv[])
{
  while (true)
  {
    printf("%x\n", (UINT_PTR)malloc(0xFFFF));
    Sleep(1000);
  }

  return 0;
}
```

Then I sampled 3 dumps at 7Mb, 17Mb, and 32Mb process virtual memory size and converted them as 16 bits-per-pixel bitmaps. In the pictures below, we can see that the middle black memory area grows significantly. Obviously, *malloc* function allocates zeroed memory, and, therefore, we see black color.

7Mb process memory dump:

17Mb process memory dump:

32Mb process memory dump:

If we zoom in the black area we see the following pattern:

Colored lines inside are heap control structures that are created for every allocated block of memory. If this is correct, then allocating smaller memory blocks would create a hatched pattern. And this is true indeed. The following program leaks 256-byte memory blocks:

```
#include "stdafx.h"
#include <windows.h>

int _tmain(int argc, _TCHAR* argv[])
{
  while (true)
  {
    printf("%x\n", (UINT_PTR)malloc(0xFF));
    Sleep(1000/0xFF);
  }

  return 0;
}
```

The corresponding process memory picture and zoomed heap area are the following:

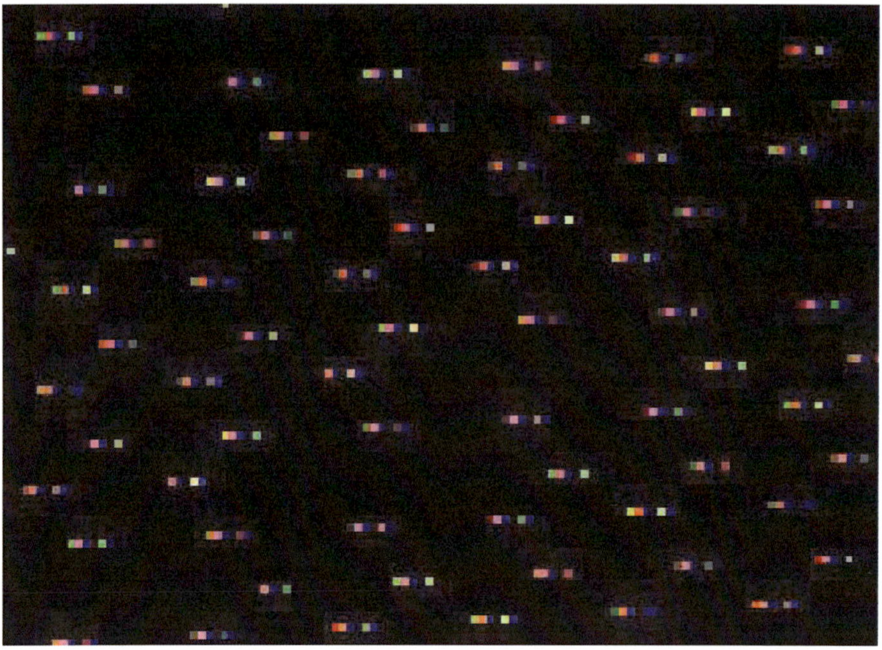

Making allocations 4 times smaller makes heap area to look hatched, and zoomed picture is more densely packed with heap control structures:

```
#include "stdafx.h"
#include <windows.h>

int _tmain(int argc, _TCHAR* argv[])
{
  while (true)
  {
    printf("%x\n", (UINT_PTR)malloc(0xFF/4));
    Sleep((1000/0xFF)/4);
  }

  return 0;
}
```

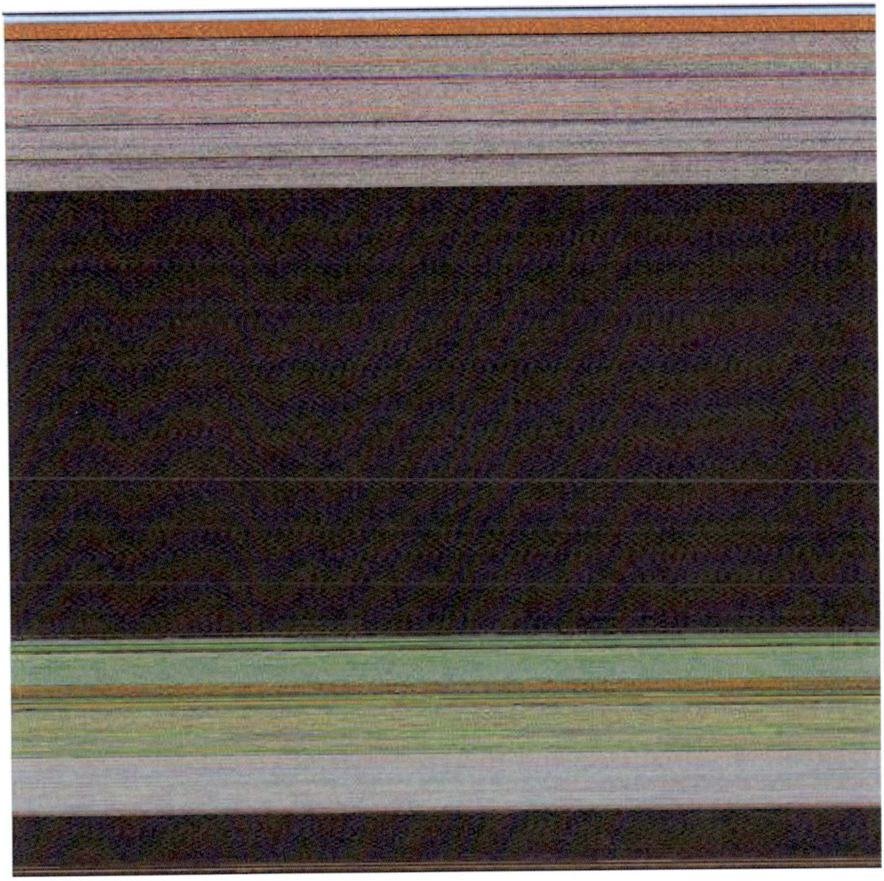

Here is another example. One service was increasing its memory steadily. The crash dump picture shows a huge hatched dark region in the middle:

And if we zoom in this region we get:

Because the pattern and allocation size look uniform, it could be the real heap memory leak for some operation that allocates constant size buffers. After opening the memory dump and looking at heap segments that had grown the most, we can see the same allocation size indeed:

```
0:000> !.\w2kfre\ntsdexts.heap -h 5
HEAPEXT: Unable to get address of NTDLL!NtGlobalFlag.
Index   Address  Name      Debugging options enabled
  1:   00140000
  2:   00240000
  3:   00310000
  4:   00330000
  5:   00370000
    Segment at 00370000 to 00380000 (00010000 bytes committed)
    Segment at 01680000 to 01780000 (00100000 bytes committed)
    Segment at 019C0000 to 01BC0000 (00200000 bytes committed)
    Segment at 01BC0000 to 01FC0000 (00400000 bytes committed)
    Segment at 01FC0000 to 027C0000 (00800000 bytes committed)
    Segment at 027C0000 to 037C0000 (01000000 bytes committed)
    Segment at 037C0000 to 057C0000 (02000000 bytes committed)
    Segment at 057C0000 to 097C0000 (00155000 bytes committed)
...
...
...
```

```
057B96E0: 01048 . 01048 [07] - busy (1030), tail fill
    057BA728: 01048 . 01048 [07] - busy (1030), tail fill
    057BB770: 01048 . 01048 [07] - busy (1030), tail fill
    057BC7B8: 01048 . 01048 [07] - busy (1030), tail fill
    057BD800: 01048 . 01048 [07] - busy (1030), tail fill
    057BE848: 01048 . 01048 [07] - busy (1030), tail fill
    057BF890: 01048 . 00770 [14] free fill
  Heap entries for Segment07 in Heap 370000
    057C0040: 00040 . 01048 [07] - busy (1030), tail fill
    057C1088: 01048 . 01048 [07] - busy (1030), tail fill
    057C20D0: 01048 . 01048 [07] - busy (1030), tail fill
    057C3118: 01048 . 01048 [07] - busy (1030), tail fill
    057C4160: 01048 . 01048 [07] - busy (1030), tail fill
    057C51A8: 01048 . 01048 [07] - busy (1030), tail fill
...
...
...
```

Picturing Computer Memory

An alternative to converting memory dumps to picture files is to save a memory range to a binary file and then convert it to a BMP file. Thus, we can view the particular DLL or driver mapped into the address space, heap or pool region.

To save a memory range to a file, we can use WinDbg **.writemem** command:

```
.writemem d2p-range.bin 00800000 0085e000
```

or

```
.writemem d2p-range.bin 00400000 L20000
```

I wrote a WinDbg script that saves a specified memory range and then calls a shell script, which automatically converts the saved binary file to a BMP file and then runs whatever picture viewer is registered for .bmp extension.

The WinDbg script code (*mempicture.txt*):

```
.writemem d2p-range.bin ${$arg1} ${$arg2}
.if (${/d:$arg3})
{
  .shell -i- mempicture.cmd d2p-range ${$arg3}
}
.else
{
  .shell -i- mempicture.cmd d2p-range
}
```

The shell script (*mempicture.cmd*):

```
dump2picture %1.bin %1.bmp %2
%1.bmp
```

Because the WinDbg installation folder is assumed to be the default directory for both scripts and *Dump2Picture.exe*, they should be copied to the same folder where windbg.exe is located. On my system it is

```
C:\Program Files\Debugging Tools for Windows
```

Both scripts are now included in Dump2Picture package available for free download at http://www.dumpanalysis.org/downloads/Dump2Picture.zip

To call the script from WinDbg, we use the following command:

```
$$>a< mempicture.txt Range [bits-per-pixel]
```

where **Range** can be in ADDRESS1 ADDRESS2 or ADDRESS LXXX format, **bits-per-pixel** can be 8, 16, 24 or 32. By default, it is 32.

For example, I loaded a complete Windows x64 memory dump and visualized HAL (hardware abstraction layer) module:

```
kd> lm
start             end               module name
fffff800`00800000 fffff800`0085e000   hal
fffff800`01000000 fffff800`0147b000   nt
fffff97f`ff000000 fffff97f`ff45d000   win32k
...
...
...

kd> $$>a< mempicture.txt fffff800`00800000 fffff800`0085e000
Writing 5e001 bytes...

C:\Program Files\Debugging Tools for Windows>dump2picture d2p-range.bin
d2p-range.bmp

Dump2Picture version 1.1
Written by Dmitry Vostokov, 2007

d2p-range.bmp
d2p-range.bin
        1 file(s) copied.

C:\Program Files\Debugging Tools for Windows>d2p-range.bmp
<.shell waiting 10 second(s) for process>
.shell: Process exited
kd>
```

Windows Picture and Fax Viewer application was launched and displayed the following picture:

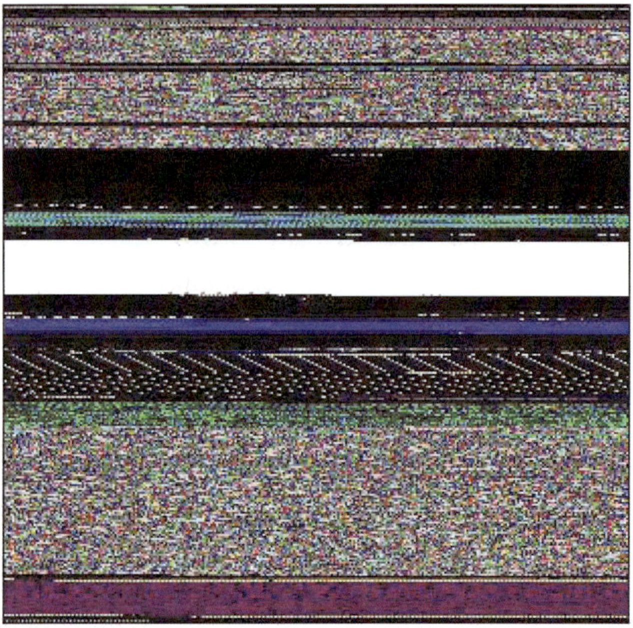

Unicode Illuminated

I generated a memory dump with plenty of Unicode and ASCII strings "Hello World!" to see how they look on a picture. Wide characters from Unicode (UTF-16))occupy two bytes:

```
0:000> db 008c7420 l20
008c7420  48 00 65 00 6c 00 6c 00-6f 00 20 00 57 00 6f 00  H.e.l.l.o.
.W.o.
008c7430  72 00 6c 00 64 00 21 00-00 00 00 00 00 00 00
00  r.l.d.!.........
```

Characters from ASCII encoding occupy one byte of memory:

```
0:000> db 008c72b4 l10
008c72b4  48 65 6c 6c 6f 20 57 6f-72 6c 64 21 00 00 00 00  Hello
World!....
```

We can see that the second byte for Unicode English characters is zero. I converted that memory dump into 8 bits-per-pixel bitmap using **Dump2Picture** (page 532). After zooming it sufficiently in Vista Photo Viewer until pixels become squares, I got the following picture that illustrates the difference between Unicode and ASCII strings:

Incidentally, the same memory dump converted to 32 bits-per-pixel bitmap shows Unicode "Hello World!" strings in green colors.

Teaching Binary to Decimal Conversion

Sometimes we have data in binary, and we want to convert it to decimal to lookup some constant in a header file, for example. I used to do it previously via calc.exe. Now I use **.formats** WinDbg command and **0y** binary prefix:

```
0:000> .formats 0y111010
Evaluate expression:
  Hex:      0000003a
  Decimal:  58
  Octal:    00000000072
  Binary:   00000000 00000000 00000000 00111010
  Chars:    ...:
  Time:     Thu Jan 01 00:00:58 1970
  Float:    low 8.12753e-044 high 0
  Double:   2.86558e-322
```

Once I was flying SWISS and found the binary watch in their duty-free catalog which I use now to guess time:

It has 6 binary digits for minutes. There are desktop binary clocks and other binary watches available if we google them, but they don't have 6 binary digits for minutes. They approximate them by using 2 rows or columns: tenths of minutes and minutes (2 + 4 binary digits) and we are all good in handling 4 binary digits because of our work with hexadecimal nibbles but not good in handling more binary digits like 5 or 6 when we see them in one row.

Crash Dumps and Global Conspiracy

There are Matrix-style conspiracy theories where we are like computer programs. Looking from crash dump analysis and debugging perspective, we ask a question of whether a process can detect its own past crash dumps? Obviously, yes, if the code was written with such intention. If the code was written without such intention but is complex enough to generate additional code or reuse the existing one to train itself in such procedure, then it can detect past crash dumps too. Therefore, if we can see our past crash dumps, then this is the proof that we live in a Matrix-type world.

More questions spring to conspiracy-savvy mind. Are there any secret software engineering societies (SSES)? Can we see patterns in memory dumps linking to alien code?

[This page is intentionally left blank]

PART 7: WinDbg For GDB Users and Vice Versa

AT&T and Intel Syntax

For Windows users, AT&T assembly language syntax might be uncomfortable. Source and destination operands are reversed, and negative offsets like -4 are represented in a hexadecimal format like 0xfffffffc. It is ok for small assembly language fragments but very confusing when looking at several pages of code. Here is an example of AT&T syntax:

```
C:\MinGW\bin>gdb a.exe
GNU gdb 5.2.1
Copyright 2002 Free Software Foundation, Inc.
GDB is free software, covered by the GNU General Public License, and you
are welcome to change it and/or distribute copies of it under certain
conditions.
Type "show copying" to see the conditions.
There is absolutely no warranty for GDB. Type "show warranty" for details.
This GDB was configured as "i686-pc-mingw32"...(no debugging symbols
found)...
(gdb) disas main
Dump of assembler code for function main:
0x4012f0 <main>:        push   %ebp
0x4012f1 <main+1>:      mov    %esp,%ebp
0x4012f3 <main+3>:      sub    $0x8,%esp
0x4012f6 <main+6>:      and    $0xfffffff0,%esp
0x4012f9 <main+9>:      mov    $0x0,%eax
0x4012fe <main+14>:     add    $0xf,%eax
0x401301 <main+17>:     add    $0xf,%eax
0x401304 <main+20>:     shr    $0x4,%eax
0x401307 <main+23>:     shl    $0x4,%eax
0x40130a <main+26>:     mov    %eax,0xfffffffc(%ebp)
0x40130d <main+29>:     mov    0xfffffffc(%ebp),%eax
0x401310 <main+32>:     call   0x401850 <_alloca>
0x401315 <main+37>:     call   0x4014f0 <__main>
0x40131a <main+42>:     leave
0x40131b <main+43>:     ret
0x40131c <main+44>:     nop
0x40131d <main+45>:     nop
0x40131e <main+46>:     nop
0x40131f <main+47>:     nop
End of assembler dump.
```

In GDB we can change AT&T flavor to Intel using the following command:

```
(gdb) set disassembly-flavor intel
```

The same function now looks more familiar:

```
(gdb) disas main
Dump of assembler code for function main:
0x4012f0 <main>:        push   ebp
0x4012f1 <main+1>:      mov    ebp,esp
0x4012f3 <main+3>:      sub    esp,0x8
0x4012f6 <main+6>:      and    esp,0xfffffff0
0x4012f9 <main+9>:      mov    eax,0x0
0x4012fe <main+14>:     add    eax,0xf
0x401301 <main+17>:     add    eax,0xf
0x401304 <main+20>:     shr    eax,0x4
0x401307 <main+23>:     shl    eax,0x4
0x40130a <main+26>:     mov    DWORD PTR [ebp-4],eax
0x40130d <main+29>:     mov    eax,DWORD PTR [ebp-4]
0x401310 <main+32>:     call   0x401850 <_alloca>
0x401315 <main+37>:     call   0x4014f0 <__main>
0x40131a <main+42>:     leave
0x40131b <main+43>:     ret
0x40131c <main+44>:     nop
0x40131d <main+45>:     nop
0x40131e <main+46>:     nop
0x40131f <main+47>:     nop
End of assembler dump.
```

Unfortunately, we cannot change Intel syntax to AT&T in WinDbg, so if you are accustomed to GDB and move to WinDbg, you have to get used to the new syntax flavor.

Installation

The primary motivation for this part is to help WinDbg users starting with FreeBSD or Linux core dump analysis (and vice versa) to quickly learn GDB debugger commands because most debugging and crash dump analysis principles and techniques are the same for both worlds. We need to disassemble, dump memory locations, list threads, and their stack traces and so on. GDB users starting with Windows crash dump analysis can learn WinDbg commands too. Here I start mapping WinDbg commands to GDB commands and vice versa.

Although GDB is primarily used on Unix systems, it is possible to use it on Windows. For this tutorial, I use MinGW (Minimalist GNU for Windows):

http://www.mingw.org/

At the time of this book revision GDB was included in Basic MinGW Installation package.

When installing MinGW package, we need to select Basic MinGW Installation and C++ compiler packages. This will download necessary components for GNU C/C++ environment.

Now we can create the first C program we use for learning GDB and WinDbg commands:

```
#include <stdio.h>
int main()
{
  puts("Hello World!");
  return 0;
}
```

We create *test.c* file, save it in *examples* folder, compile and link into *test.exe*:

```
C:\MinGW>mkdir examples

C:\MinGW\examples>..\bin\gcc -o test.exe test.c

C:\MinGW\examples>test
Hello World!
```

Now we can run it under GDB:

```
C:\MinGW\examples>..\bin\gdb test.exe
GNU gdb (GDB) 7.6.1
Copyright (C) 2013 Free Software Foundation, Inc.
License     GPLv3+:     GNU     GPL     version     3     or     later
<http://gnu.org/licenses/gpl.html>
This is free software: you are free to change and redistribute it.
There is NO WARRANTY, to the extent permitted by law.  Type "show copying"
and "show warranty" for details.
This GDB was configured as "mingw32".
For bug reporting instructions, please see:
<http://www.gnu.org/software/gdb/bugs/>...
Reading symbols from C:\MinGW\examples\test.exe...done.

(gdb) run
Starting program: C:\MinGW\examples/test.exe
[New Thread 33940.0xf68]
[New Thread 33940.0x8608]
Hello World!
[Inferior 1 (process 33940) exited normally]

(gdb) q

C:\MinGW\examples>
```

WinDbg equivalent to GDB **run** command is **g.**

Here is the command line on my machine to launch WinDbg and load the same program:

```
C:\MinGW\examples>"C:\Program Files (x86)\Windows
Kits\10\Debuggers\x86\WinDbg" test.exe
```

WinDbg will set the initial breakpoint, and we can execute the process with **g** command:

```
Microsoft (R) Windows Debugger Version 10.0.18362.1 X86
Copyright (c) Microsoft Corporation. All rights reserved.

CommandLine: test.exe
Symbol search path is: srv*
Executable search path is:
ModLoad: 00400000 00412000   image00400000
ModLoad: 77820000 779ba000   ntdll.dll
ModLoad: 75670000 75750000   C:\WINDOWS\SysWOW64\KERNEL32.DLL
ModLoad: 75f50000 7614e000   C:\WINDOWS\SysWOW64\KERNELBASE.dll
ModLoad: 77750000 7780f000   C:\WINDOWS\SysWOW64\msvcrt.dll
(2094.82e4): Break instruction exception - code 80000003 (first chance)
eax=00000000    ebx=0020f000    ecx=34620000    edx=00000000    esi=006d2b48
edi=7782688c
```

```
eip=778ce9e2 esp=0061fa20 ebp=0061fa4c iopl=0         nv up ei pl zr na pe
nc
cs=0023  ss=002b  ds=002b  es=002b  fs=0053  gs=002b             efl=00000246
ntdll!LdrpDoDebuggerBreak+0x2b:
778ce9e2 cc              int     3
```

q command to end a debugging session is the same for both debuggers.

Therefore, our first map between GDB and WinDbg commands contains the following entries:

```
Action                  GDB      | WinDbg
----------------------------------------
Start the process       run      | g
Exit                    (q)uit   | q
```

Disassembler

One of the common tasks in crash dump analysis is to disassemble various functions. In GDB, it can be done by using two different commands: **disassemble** and **x/i**.

The first command gets a function name, an address or a range of addresses and can be shortened to just **disas**:

```
(gdb) set disassembly-flavor intel

(gdb) disas main
Dump of assembler code for function main:
0x4012f0 <main>:        push   ebp
0x4012f1 <main+1>:      mov    ebp,esp
0x4012f3 <main+3>:      sub    esp,0x8
0x4012f6 <main+6>:      and    esp,0xfffffff0
0x4012f9 <main+9>:      mov    eax,0x0
0x4012fe <main+14>:     add    eax,0xf
0x401301 <main+17>:     add    eax,0xf
0x401304 <main+20>:     shr    eax,0x4
0x401307 <main+23>:     shl    eax,0x4
0x40130a <main+26>:     mov    DWORD PTR [ebp-4],eax
0x40130d <main+29>:     mov    eax,DWORD PTR [ebp-4]
0x401310 <main+32>:     call   0x401860 <_alloca>
0x401315 <main+37>:     call   0x401500 <__main>
0x40131a <main+42>:     mov    DWORD PTR [esp],0x403000
0x401321 <main+49>:     call   0x401950 <puts>
0x401326 <main+54>:     mov    eax,0x0
0x40132b <main+59>:     leave
0x40132c <main+60>:     ret
0x40132d <main+61>:     nop
0x40132e <main+62>:     nop
0x40132f <main+63>:     nop
End of assembler dump.

(gdb) disas 0x4012f0
Dump of assembler code for function main:
0x4012f0 <main>:        push   ebp
0x4012f1 <main+1>:      mov    ebp,esp
0x4012f3 <main+3>:      sub    esp,0x8
0x4012f6 <main+6>:      and    esp,0xfffffff0
0x4012f9 <main+9>:      mov    eax,0x0
0x4012fe <main+14>:     add    eax,0xf
0x401301 <main+17>:     add    eax,0xf
0x401304 <main+20>:     shr    eax,0x4
0x401307 <main+23>:     shl    eax,0x4
0x40130a <main+26>:     mov    DWORD PTR [ebp-4],eax
0x40130d <main+29>:     mov    eax,DWORD PTR [ebp-4]
0x401310 <main+32>:     call   0x401860 <_alloca>
0x401315 <main+37>:     call   0x401500 <__main>
```

```
0x40131a <main+42>:     mov    DWORD PTR [esp],0x403000
0x401321 <main+49>:     call   0x401950 <puts>
0x401326 <main+54>:     mov    eax,0x0
0x40132b <main+59>:     leave
0x40132c <main+60>:     ret
0x40132d <main+61>:     nop
0x40132e <main+62>:     nop
0x40132f <main+63>:     nop
End of assembler dump.

(gdb) disas 0x4012f0, 0x40132d
Dump of assembler code from 0x4012f0 to 0x40132d:
0x4012f0 <main>:        push   ebp
0x4012f1 <main+1>:      mov    ebp,esp
0x4012f3 <main+3>:      sub    esp,0x8
0x4012f6 <main+6>:      and    esp,0xfffffff0
0x4012f9 <main+9>:      mov    eax,0x0
0x4012fe <main+14>:     add    eax,0xf
0x401301 <main+17>:     add    eax,0xf
0x401304 <main+20>:     shr    eax,0x4
0x401307 <main+23>:     shl    eax,0x4
0x40130a <main+26>:     mov    DWORD PTR [ebp-4],eax
0x40130d <main+29>:     mov    eax,DWORD PTR [ebp-4]
0x401310 <main+32>:     call   0x401860 <_alloca>
0x401315 <main+37>:     call   0x401500 <__main>
0x40131a <main+42>:     mov    DWORD PTR [esp],0x403000
0x401321 <main+49>:     call   0x401950 <puts>
0x401326 <main+54>:     mov    eax,0x0
0x40132b <main+59>:     leave
0x40132c <main+60>:     ret
End of assembler dump.
(gdb)
```

Note: To see WinDbg in action, we need to compile and link our test program in Visual C++ because WinDbg doesn't understand MinGW symbolic information.

The equivalent command in WinDbg is **uf** (unassemble function) and **u** (unassemble):

```
0:000> .asm no_code_bytes
Assembly options: no_code_bytes

0:000> uf main
test!main [test.cpp @ 3]:
00401000 push    offset test!`string' (004020f4)
00401005 call    dword ptr [test!_imp__puts (004020a0)]
0040100b add     esp,4
0040100e xor     eax,eax
00401010 ret
```

```
0:000> uf 00401000
test!main [test.cpp @ 3]:
00401000 push    offset test!`string' (004020f4)
00401005 call    dword ptr [test!_imp__puts (004020a0)]
0040100b add     esp,4
0040100e xor     eax,eax
00401010 ret

0:000> u 00401000
test!main [c:\dmitri\test\test\test.cpp @ 3]:
00401000 push    offset test!`string' (004020f4)
00401005 call    dword ptr [test!_imp__puts (004020a0)]
0040100b add     esp,4
0040100e xor     eax,eax
00401010 ret
test!__security_check_cookie
[f:\sp\vctools\crt_bld\self_x86\crt\src\intel\secchk.c @ 52]:
00401011 cmp     ecx,dword ptr [test!__security_cookie (00403000)]
00401017 jne     test!__security_check_cookie+0xa (0040101b)
00401019 rep ret
0:000> u 00401000 00401011
test!main [test.cpp @ 3]:
00401000 push    offset test!`string' (004020f4)
00401005 call    dword ptr [test!_imp__puts (004020a0)]
0040100b add     esp,4
0040100e xor     eax,eax
00401010 ret

0:000> u
test!__security_check_cookie
[f:\sp\vctools\crt_bld\self_x86\crt\src\intel\secchk.c @ 52]:
00401011 cmp     ecx,dword ptr [test!__security_cookie (00403000)]
00401017 jne     test!__security_check_cookie+0xa (0040101b)
00401019 rep ret
0040101b jmp     test!__report_gsfailure (004012cd)
test!pre_cpp_init [f:\sp\vctools\crt_bld\self_x86\crt\src\crtexe.c @ 321]:
00401020 push    offset test!_RTC_Terminate (004014fd)
00401025 call    test!atexit (004014c7)
0040102a mov     eax,dword ptr [test!_newmode (00403364)]
0040102f mov     dword ptr [esp],offset test!startinfo (0040302c)

0:000> u eip
ntdll32!DbgBreakPoint:
7d61002d int     3
7d61002e ret
7d61002f nop
7d610030 mov     edi,edi
ntdll32!DbgUserBreakPoint:
7d610032 int     3
7d610033 ret
7d610034 mov     edi,edi
ntdll32!DbgBreakPointWithStatus:
7d610036 mov     eax,dword ptr [esp+4]
```

The second GDB command is **x/[N]i address** where N is the number of instructions to disassemble:

```
(gdb) x/i 0x4012f0
0x4012f0 <main>:        push   ebp

(gdb) x/2i 0x4012f0
0x4012f0 <main>:        push   ebp
0x4012f1 <main+1>:      mov    ebp,esp

(gdb) x/3i 0x4012f0
0x4012f0 <main>:        push   ebp
0x4012f1 <main+1>:      mov    ebp,esp
0x4012f3 <main+3>:      sub    esp,0x8

(gdb) x/4i $pc
0x4012f6 <main+6>:      and    esp,0xfffffff0
0x4012f9 <main+9>:      mov    eax,0x0
0x4012fe <main+14>:     add    eax,0xf
0x401301 <main+17>:     add    eax,0xf

(gdb)
```

It seems to be no way to disassemble just N instructions in WinDbg. However in WinDbg we can disassemble backward (**ub**). This is useful, for example, if we have a return address and we want to see the CALL instruction:

```
0:000> k
ChildEBP RetAddr
0012ff7c 0040117a test!main [test.cpp @ 3]
0012ffc0 7d4e992a test!__tmainCRTStartup+0x10f
[f:\sp\vctools\crt_bld\self_x86\crt\src\crtexe.c @ 597]
0012fff0 00000000 kernel32!BaseProcessStart+0x28

0:000> ub 7d4e992a
kernel32!BaseProcessStart+0x10:
7d4e9912 call    kernel32!BasepReport32bitAppLaunching (7d4e9949)
7d4e9917 push    4
7d4e9919 lea     eax,[ebp+8]
7d4e991c push    eax
7d4e991d push    9
7d4e991f push    0FFFFFFFEh
7d4e9921 call    dword ptr [kernel32!_imp__NtSetInformationThread
(7d4d032c)]
7d4e9927 call    dword ptr [ebp+8]
```

Our next version of the map contains these new commands:

Action	GDB	WinDbg
Start the process	run	g
Exit	(q)uit	q
Disassemble (forward)	(disas)semble	uf, u
Disassemble N instructions	x/i	-
Disassemble (backward)	-	ub

Stack Trace (Backtrace)

Displaying thread stack trace is the most used action in the crash or core dump analysis and debugging. To show various available GDB commands, I created the next version of the test program with the following source code:

```
#include <stdio.h>

void func_1(int param_1, char param_2, int *param_3, char *param_4);
void func_2(int param_1, char param_2, int *param_3, char *param_4);
void func_3(int param_1, char param_2, int *param_3, char *param_4);
void func_4();

int val_1;
char val_2;
int *pval_1 = &val_1;
char *pval_2 = &val_2;

int main()
{
  val_1 = 1;
  val_2 = '1';
  func_1(val_1, val_2, (int *)pval_1, (char *)pval_2);
  return 0;
}

void func_1(int param_1, char param_2, int *param_3, char *param_4)
{
  val_1 = 2;
  val_2 = '2';
  func_2(param_1, param_2, param_3, param_4);
}

void func_2(int param_1, char param_2, int *param_3, char *param_4)
{
  val_1 = 3;
  val_2 = '3';
  func_3(param_1, param_2, param_3, param_4);
}

void func_3(int param_1, char param_2, int *param_3, char *param_4)
{
  *pval_1 += param_1;
  *pval_2 += param_2;
  func_4();
}
```

```
void func_4()
{
  puts("Hello World!");
}
```

We need to compile it with **-g** gcc compiler option to generate symbolic debugging information. It is needed for GDB to display function arguments and local variables.

```
C:\MinGW\examples>..\bin\gcc -g -o test.exe test.c
```

If you have a crash in *func_4*, then we can examine the stack trace (backtrace) once we open a core dump. Because we don't have a core dump of our test program, we simulate the stack trace by putting a breakpoint on *func_4*. In GDB this can be done by **break** command:

```
C:\MinGW\examples>..\bin\gdb test.exe
...
...
...
(gdb) break func_4
Breakpoint 1 at 0x40141d

(gdb) run
Starting program: C:\MinGW\examples/test.exeBreakpoint 1, 0x0040141d in
func_4 ()

(gdb)
```

In WinDbg, the breakpoint command is **bp**:

```
CommandLine: C:\dmitri\test\release\test.exe
Symbol search path is:
SRV*c:\websymbols*http://msdl.microsoft.com/download/symbols
Executable search path is:
ModLoad: 00400000 0040f000   test.exe
ModLoad: 7d4c0000 7d5f0000   NOT_AN_IMAGE
ModLoad: 7d600000 7d6f0000   C:\W2K3\SysWOW64\ntdll32.dll
ModLoad: 7d4c0000 7d5f0000   C:\W2K3\syswow64\kernel32.dll
(103c.17d8): Break instruction exception - code 80000003 (first chance)
eax=7d600000 ebx=7efde000 ecx=00000005 edx=00000020 esi=7d6a01f4
edi=00221f38
eip=7d61002d esp=0012fb4c ebp=0012fcac iopl=0 nv up ei pl nz na po nc
cs=0023 ss=002b ds=002b es=002b fs=0053 gs=002b efl=00000202
ntdll32!DbgBreakPoint:
7d61002d cc               int     3

0:000> bp func_4
```

```
0:000> g
ModLoad: 71c20000 71c32000   C:\W2K3\SysWOW64\tsappcmp.dll
ModLoad: 77ba0000 77bfa000   C:\W2K3\syswow64\msvcrt.dll
ModLoad: 77f50000 77fec000   C:\W2K3\syswow64\ADVAPI32.dll
ModLoad: 7da20000 7db00000   C:\W2K3\syswow64\RPCRT4.dll
Breakpoint 0 hit
eax=0040c9d0 ebx=7d4d8dc9 ecx=0040c9d0 edx=00000064 esi=00000002
edi=00000ece
eip=00408be0 esp=0012ff24 ebp=0012ff28 iopl=0 nv up ei pl nz na po nc
cs=0023 ss=002b ds=002b es=002b fs=0053 gs=002b efl=00000202
test!func_4:
00408be0 55              push    ebp
```

We have to disable optimization in the project properties otherwise Visual C++ compiler optimizes away all function calls and produces the following short code:

```
0:000> uf main
00401000 push    offset test!`string' (004020f4)
00401005 mov     dword ptr [test!val_1 (0040337c)],4
0040100f mov     byte ptr [test!val_2 (00403378)],64h
00401016 call    dword ptr [test!_imp__puts (004020a0)]
0040101c add     esp,4
0040101f xor     eax,eax
00401021 ret
```

Now we are going to concentrate on commands that examine a call stack. **backtrace** or **bt** command shows the stack trace. **backtrace <N>** or **bt <N>** shows only the innermost N stack frames. **backtrace -<N>** or **bt -<N>** shows only the outermost N stack frames. **backtrace full** or **bt full** additionally shows local variables. There are also variants **backtrace full <N>** or **bt full <N>** and **backtrace full -<N>** or **bt full -<N>**:

```
(gdb) backtrace
#0  func_4 () at test.c:48
#1  0x00401414 in func_3 (param_1=1, param_2=49 '1', param_3=0x404080,
    param_4=0x404070 "d") at test.c:43
#2  0x004013da in func_2 (param_1=1, param_2=49 '1', param_3=0x404080,
    param_4=0x404070 "d") at test.c:35
#3  0x0040139a in func_1 (param_1=1, param_2=49 '1', param_3=0x404080,
    param_4=0x404070 "d") at test.c:27
#4  0x00401355 in main () at test.c:18
```

```
(gdb) bt
#0  func_4 () at test.c:48
#1  0x00401414 in func_3 (param_1=1, param_2=49 '1', param_3=0x404080,
    param_4=0x404070 "d") at test.c:43
#2  0x004013da in func_2 (param_1=1, param_2=49 '1', param_3=0x404080,
    param_4=0x404070 "d") at test.c:35
#3  0x0040139a in func_1 (param_1=1, param_2=49 '1', param_3=0x404080,
    param_4=0x404070 "d") at test.c:27
#4  0x00401355 in main () at test.c:18
```

```
(gdb) bt 2
#0  func_4 () at test.c:48
#1  0x00401414 in func_3 (param_1=1, param_2=49 '1', param_3=0x404080,
    param_4=0x404070 "d") at test.c:43
(More stack frames follow...)

(gdb) bt -2
#3  0x0040139a in func_1 (param_1=1, param_2=49 '1', param_3=0x404080,
    param_4=0x404070 "d") at test.c:27
#4  0x00401355 in main () at test.c:18

(gdb) bt full
#0  func_4 () at test.c:48
No locals.
#1  0x00401414 in func_3 (param_1=1, param_2=49 '1', param_3=0x404080,
    param_4=0x404070 "d") at test.c:43
        param_2 = 49 '1'
#2  0x004013da in func_2 (param_1=1, param_2=49 '1', param_3=0x404080,
    param_4=0x404070 "d") at test.c:35
        param_2 = 49 '1'
#3  0x0040139a in func_1 (param_1=1, param_2=49 '1', param_3=0x404080,
    param_4=0x404070 "d") at test.c:27
        param_2 = 49 '1'
#4  0x00401355 in main () at test.c:18
No locals.

(gdb) bt full 2
#0  func_4 () at test.c:48
No locals.
#1  0x00401414 in func_3 (param_1=1, param_2=49 '1', param_3=0x404080,
    param_4=0x404070 "d") at test.c:43
        param_2 = 49 '1'
(More stack frames follow...)

(gdb) bt full -2
#3  0x0040139a in func_1 (param_1=1, param_2=49 '1', param_3=0x404080,
    param_4=0x404070 "d") at test.c:27
        param_2 = 49 '1'
#4  0x00401355 in main () at test.c:18
No locals.

(gdb)
```

In WinDbg, there is only one **k** command, but it has many parameters, for example:

Default stack trace with source code lines:

```
0:000> k
ChildEBP RetAddr
0012ff20 00408c30 test!func_4 [c:\dmitri\test\test\test.cpp @ 47]
0012ff28 00408c69 test!func_3+0x30 [c:\dmitri\test\test\test.cpp @ 44]
0012ff40 00408c99 test!func_2+0x29 [c:\dmitri\test\test\test.cpp @ 35]
0012ff58 00408cd3 test!func_1+0x29 [c:\dmitri\test\test\test.cpp @ 27]
0012ff70 00401368 test!main+0x33 [c:\dmitri\test\test\test.cpp @ 18]
0012ffc0 7d4e992a test!__tmainCRTStartup+0x15f
[f:\sp\vctools\crt_bld\self_x86\crt\src\crt0.c @ 327]
0012fff0 00000000 kernel32!BaseProcessStart+0x28
```

Stack trace without source code lines:

```
0:000> kL
ChildEBP RetAddr
0012ff20 00408c30 test!func_4
0012ff28 00408c69 test!func_3+0x30
0012ff40 00408c99 test!func_2+0x29
0012ff58 00408cd3 test!func_1+0x29
0012ff70 00401368 test!main+0x33
0012ffc0 7d4e992a test!__tmainCRTStartup+0x15f
0012fff0 00000000 kernel32!BaseProcessStart+0x28
```

Full stack trace without source code lines showing 3 stack arguments for every stack frame, calling convention and optimization information:

```
0:000> kvL
ChildEBP RetAddr  Args to Child
0012ff20 00408c30 0012ff40 00408c69 00000001 test!func_4 (CONV: cdecl)
0012ff28 00408c69 00000001 00000031 0040c9d4 test!func_3+0x30 (CONV:
cdecl)
0012ff40 00408c99 00000001 00000031 0040c9d4 test!func_2+0x29 (CONV:
cdecl)
0012ff58 00408cd3 00000001 00000031 0040c9d4 test!func_1+0x29 (CONV:
cdecl)
0012ff70 00401368 00000001 004230e0 00423120 test!main+0x33 (CONV: cdecl)
0012ffc0 7d4e992a 00000000 00000000 7efde000 test!__tmainCRTStartup+0x15f
(FPO: [Non-Fpo]) (CONV: cdecl)
0012fff0 00000000 004013bf 00000000 00000000
kernel32!BaseProcessStart+0x28 (FPO: [Non-Fpo])
```

Stack trace without source code lines showing all function parameters:

```
0:000> kPL
ChildEBP RetAddr
0012ff20 00408c30 test!func_4(void)
0012ff28 00408c69 test!func_3(
   int param_1 = 1,
   char param_2 = 49 '1',
   int * param_3 = 0x0040c9d4,
   char * param_4 = 0x0040c9d0 "d")+0x30
0012ff40 00408c99 test!func_2(
   int param_1 = 1,
   char param_2 = 49 '1',
   int * param_3 = 0x0040c9d4,
   char * param_4 = 0x0040c9d0 "d")+0x29
0012ff58 00408cd3 test!func_1(
   int param_1 = 1,
   char param_2 = 49 '1',
   int * param_3 = 0x0040c9d4,
   char * param_4 = 0x0040c9d0 "d")+0x29
0012ff70 00401368 test!main(void)+0x33
0012ffc0 7d4e992a test!__tmainCRTStartup(void)+0x15f
0012fff0 00000000 kernel32!BaseProcessStart+0x28
```

Stack trace without source code lines showing stack frame numbers:

```
0:000> knL
 # ChildEBP RetAddr
00 0012ff20 00408c30 test!func_4
01 0012ff28 00408c69 test!func_3+0x30
02 0012ff40 00408c99 test!func_2+0x29
03 0012ff58 00408cd3 test!func_1+0x29
04 0012ff70 00401368 test!main+0x33
05 0012ffc0 7d4e992a test!__tmainCRTStartup+0x15f
06 0012fff0 00000000 kernel32!BaseProcessStart+0x28
```

Stack trace without source code lines showing the distance between stack frames in bytes:

```
0:000> knfL
 #   Memory  ChildEBP RetAddr
00           0012ff20 00408c30 test!func_4
01         8 0012ff28 00408c69 test!func_3+0x30
02        18 0012ff40 00408c99 test!func_2+0x29
03        18 0012ff58 00408cd3 test!func_1+0x29
04        18 0012ff70 00401368 test!main+0x33
05        50 0012ffc0 7d4e992a test!__tmainCRTStartup+0x15f
06        30 0012fff0 00000000 kernel32!BaseProcessStart+0x28
```

Stack trace without source code lines showing the innermost 2 frames:

```
0:000> kL 2
ChildEBP RetAddr
0012ff20 00408c30 test!func_4
0012ff28 00408c69 test!func_3+0x30
```

If we want to see stack traces from all threads in a process, we can use the following command:

```
(gdb) thread apply all bt

Thread 1 (thread 728.0xc0c):
#0  func_4 () at test.c:48
#1  0x00401414 in func_3 (param_1=1, param_2=49 '1', param_3=0x404080,
    param_4=0x404070 "d") at test.c:43
#2  0x004013da in func_2 (param_1=1, param_2=49 '1', param_3=0x404080,
    param_4=0x404070 "d") at test.c:35
#3  0x0040139a in func_1 (param_1=1, param_2=49 '1', param_3=0x404080,
    param_4=0x404070 "d") at test.c:27
#4  0x00401355 in main () at test.c:18
(gdb)
```

In WinDbg, it is **~*k.** Any parameter shown above can be used, for example:

```
0:000> ~*kL

.  0  Id: 103c.17d8 Suspend: 1 Teb: 7efdd000 Unfrozen
ChildEBP RetAddr
0012ff20 00408c30 test!func_4
0012ff28 00408c69 test!func_3+0x30
0012ff40 00408c99 test!func_2+0x29
0012ff58 00408cd3 test!func_1+0x29
0012ff70 00401368 test!main+0x33
0012ffc0 7d4e992a test!__tmainCRTStartup+0x15f
0012fff0 00000000 kernel32!BaseProcessStart+0x28
```

Therefore, the next version of the map contains these new commands:

```
Action                         | GDB                  | WinDbg
---------------------------------------------------------
Start the process              | run                  | g
Exit                           | (q)uit               | q
Disassemble (forward)          | (disas)semble        | uf, u
Disassemble N instructions     | x/<N>i               | -
Disassemble (backward)         | -                    | ub
Stack trace                    | backtrace (bt)       | k
Full stack trace               | bt full              | kv
Partial trace (innermost)      | bt <N>               | k <N>
Partial trace (outermost)      | bt -<N>              | -
Stack trace for all threads    | thread apply all bt  | ~*k
Breakpoint                     | break                | bp
```

Local Variables

Once we get a backtrace in GDB or stack trace in WinDbg, we are interested in concrete stack frames, their arguments, and local variables. I slightly modified the program used in the previous part to include some local variables:

```
#include <stdio.h>

void func_1(int param_1, char param_2, int *param_3, char *param_4);
void func_2(int param_1, char param_2, int *param_3, char *param_4);
void func_3(int param_1, char param_2, int *param_3, char *param_4);
void func_4();

int   g_val_1;
char  g_val_2;
int  *g_pval_1 = &g_val_1;
char *g_pval_2 = &g_val_2;

int main()
{
  int   local_0 = 0;
  char *hello = "Hello World!";

  g_val_1 = 1;
  g_val_2 = '1';

  func_1(g_val_1, g_val_2, (int *)g_pval_1, (char *)g_pval_2);
  return 0;
}

void func_1(int param_1, char param_2, int *param_3, char *param_4)
{
   int local_1 = 1;

   g_val_1 = 2;
   g_val_2 = '2';

   param_3 = &local_1;

   func_2(g_val_1, g_val_2, param_3, param_4);
}
```

```
void func_2(int param_1, char param_2, int *param_3, char *param_4)
{
   int local_2 = 2;

   g_val_1 = 3;
   g_val_2 = '3';


   param_3 = &local_2;

   func_3(g_val_1, g_val_2, param_3, param_4);
}

void func_3(int param_1, char param_2, int *param_3, char *param_4)
{
   int local_3 = 3;

   *g_pval_1 += param_1;
   *g_pval_2 += param_2;

   func_4();
}

void func_4()
{
   puts("Hello World!");
}
```

In GDB, the **frame** command is used to set the current stack frame. Then **info args** command can be used to list function arguments and **info locals** command can be used to list local variables:

```
(gdb) break func_4
Breakpoint 1 at 0x401455: file test.c, line 61.

(gdb) run
Starting program: C:\MinGW\examples/test.exe

Breakpoint 1, func_4 () at test.c:61
61          puts("Hello World!");

(gdb) bt
#0  func_4 () at test.c:61
#1  0x0040144d in func_3 (param_1=3, param_2=51 '3', param_3=0x22ff10,
    param_4=0x404070 "f") at test.c:56
#2  0x0040140c in func_2 (param_1=2, param_2=50 '2', param_3=0x22ff10,
    param_4=0x404070 "f") at test.c:46
```

```
#3  0x004013ba in func_1 (param_1=1, param_2=49 '1', param_3=0x22ff30,
    param_4=0x404070 "f") at test.c:34
#4  0x00401363 in main () at test.c:21

(gdb) frame
#0  func_4 () at test.c:61
61          puts("Hello World!");

(gdb) frame 0
#0  func_4 () at test.c:61
61          puts("Hello World!");

(gdb) info args
No arguments.

(gdb) info locals
No locals.

(gdb) frame 1
#1  0x0040144d in func_3 (param_1=3, param_2=51 '3', param_3=0x22ff10,
    param_4=0x404070 "f") at test.c:56
56          func_4();

(gdb) info args
param_1 = 3
param_2 = 51 '3'
param_3 = (int *) 0x22ff10
param_4 = 0x404070 "f"

(gdb) info locals
local_3 = 3
param_2 = 51 '3'

(gdb) frame 2
#2  0x0040140c in func_2 (param_1=2, param_2=50 '2', param_3=0x22ff10,
    param_4=0x404070 "f") at test.c:46
46          func_3(g_val_1, g_val_2, param_3, param_4);

(gdb) info args
param_1 = 2
param_2 = 50 '2'
param_3 = (int *) 0x22ff10
param_4 = 0x404070 "f"

(gdb) info locals
local_2 = 2
param_2 = 50 '2'
```

```
(gdb) frame 3
#3  0x004013ba in func_1 (param_1=1, param_2=49 '1', param_3=0x22ff30,
    param_4=0x404070 "f") at test.c:34
34          func_2(g_val_1, g_val_2, param_3, param_4);

(gdb) info args
param_1 = 1
param_2 = 49 '1'
param_3 = (int *) 0x22ff30
param_4 = 0x404070 "f"

(gdb) info locals
local_1 = 1
param_2 = 49 '1'

(gdb) frame 4
#4  0x00401363 in main () at test.c:21
21         func_1(g_val_1, g_val_2, (int *)g_pval_1, (char *)g_pval_2);

(gdb) info args
No arguments.

(gdb) info locals
local_0 = 0
hello = 0x403000 "Hello World!"

(gdb)
```

In WinDbg **kn** command shows stack trace with frame numbers, **knL** command additionally omits source code references, **.frame** command switches to particular stack frame, **dv** command shows parameters and local variables together, **dv /i** command classifies them into categories, parameters or locals, **dv /V** command shows their addresses and offsets for the relevant base frame register, usually EBP, **dv /t** command shows type information:

```
CommandLine: C:\dmitri\test\release\test.exe
Symbol search path is:
SRV*c:\websymbols*http://msdl.microsoft.com/download/symbols
Executable search path is:
ModLoad: 00400000 0040f000   test.exe
ModLoad: 7d4c0000 7d5f0000   NOT_AN_IMAGE
ModLoad: 7d600000 7d6f0000   C:\W2K3\SysWOW64\ntdll32.dll
ModLoad: 7d4c0000 7d5f0000   C:\W2K3\syswow64\kernel32.dll


(e38.ac0): Break instruction exception - code 80000003 (first chance)
eax=7d600000 ebx=7efde000 ecx=00000005 edx=00000020 esi=7d6a01f4
edi=00221f38
eip=7d61002d esp=0012fb4c ebp=0012fcac iopl=0 nv up ei pl nz na po nc
```

```
cs=0023 ss=002b ds=002b es=002b fs=0053 gs=002b efl=00000202
ntdll32!DbgBreakPoint:
7d61002d cc              int     3

0:000> bp func_4

0:000> g
ModLoad: 71c20000 71c32000   C:\W2K3\SysWOW64\tsappcmp.dll
ModLoad: 77ba0000 77bfa000   C:\W2K3\syswow64\msvcrt.dll
ModLoad: 00410000 004ab000   C:\W2K3\syswow64\ADVAPI32.dll
ModLoad: 7da20000 7db00000   C:\W2K3\syswow64\RPCRT4.dll
ModLoad: 7d8d0000 7d920000   C:\W2K3\syswow64\Secur32.dll
Breakpoint 0 hit
eax=0040c9d4 ebx=7d4d8df9 ecx=0040c9d4 edx=00000066 esi=00000002
edi=00000ece
eip=00408be0 esp=0012ff10 ebp=0012ff18 iopl=0 nv up ei pl nz na pe nc
cs=0023 ss=002b ds=002b es=002b fs=0053 gs=002b efl=00000206
test!func_4:
00408be0 55              push    ebp

0:000> knL
 # ChildEBP RetAddr
00 0012ff0c 00408c38 test!func_4
01 0012ff18 00408c7c test!func_3+0x38
02 0012ff34 00408ccc test!func_2+0x3c
03 0012ff50 00408d24 test!func_1+0x3c
04 0012ff70 00401368 test!main+0x44
05 0012ffc0 7d4e7d2a test!__tmainCRTStartup+0x15f
06 0012fff0 00000000 kernel32!BaseProcessStart+0x28

0:000> .frame
00 0012ff0c 00408c38 test!func_4 [c:\dmitri\test\test\test.cpp @ 60]

0:000> .frame 0
00 0012ff0c 00408c38 test!func_4 [c:\dmitri\test\test\test.cpp @ 60]

0:000> dv

0:000> .frame 1
01 0012ff18 00408c7c test!func_3+0x38 [c:\dmitri\test\test\test.cpp @ 57]

0:000> dv
        param_1 = 3
        param_2 = 51 '3'
        param_3 = 0x0012ff30
        param_4 = 0x0040c9d4 "f"
        local_3 = 3

0:000> dv /i
prv param  param_1 = 3
prv param  param_2 = 51 '3'
```

```
prv param  param_3 = 0x0012ff30
prv param  param_4 = 0x0040c9d4 "f"
prv local  local_3 = 3

0:000> dv /i /V
prv param  0012ff20 @ebp+0x08 param_1 = 3
prv param  0012ff24 @ebp+0x0c param_2 = 51 '3'
prv param  0012ff28 @ebp+0x10 param_3 = 0x0012ff30
prv param  0012ff2c @ebp+0x14 param_4 = 0x0040c9d4 "f"
prv local  0012ff14 @ebp-0x04 local_3 = 3

0:000> .frame 4
04 0012ff70 00401368 test!main+0x44 [c:\dmitri\test\test\test.cpp @ 21]

0:000> dv
        local_0 = 0
          hello = 0x0040a274 "Hello World!"

0:000> dv /i
prv local           local_0 = 0
prv local             hello = 0x0040a274 "Hello World!"

0:000> dv /i /V
prv local  0012ff68 @ebp-0x08          local_0 = 0
prv local  0012ff6c @ebp-0x04            hello = 0x0040a274 "Hello World!"

0:000> dv /t
int local_0 = 0
char * hello = 0x0040a274 "Hello World!"
```

Our comparison table has grown a bit:

Action	GDB	WinDbg
Start the process	run	g
Exit	(q)uit	q
Disassemble (forward)	(disas)semble	uf, u
Disassemble N instructions	x/<N>i	-
Disassemble (backward)	-	ub
Stack trace	backtrace (bt)	k
Full stack trace	bt full	kv
Stack trace with parameters	bt full	kP
Partial trace (innermost)	bt <N>	k <N>
Partial trace (outermost)	bt -<N>	-
Stack trace for all threads	thread apply all bt	~*k
Breakpoint	break	bp
Frame numbers	any bt command	kn
Select frame	frame	.frame
Display parameters	info args	dv /t /i /V
Display locals	info locals	dv /t /i /V

[This page is intentionally left blank]

PART 8: Software Troubleshooting

Four Pillars

They are (sorted alphabetically):

1. Crash Dump Analysis (also called Memory Dump Analysis or Core Dump Analysis)
2. Problem Reproduction
3. Trace and Log Analysis
4. Virtual Assistance (also called Remote Assistance)

Five Golden Rules

It is difficult to analyze a problem when we have crash dumps and traces from various tracing tools, and supporting information that we have is incomplete or missing. I came up with this easy to remember **4WS** questions to ask when sending or requesting traces and memory dumps:

- ***What*** - What had happened or had been observed? Crash or hang, for example?
- ***When*** - When did the problem happen if traces were recorded for hours?
- ***Where*** - What server or workstation had been used for tracing or where did memory dumps come from? For example, one trace is from a primary server, and two others are from backup servers, or one trace is from a client workstation, and the other is from a server.
- ***Why*** - Why did a customer or support engineer request a dump file or a trace? This could shed light on various hidden assumptions in the problem description.
- ***Supporting information*** - needed to find a needle in a haystack: for example, process id, thread id. Also, the answer to the following question is essential: how were memory dumps and traces created?

Every trace or memory dump shall be accompanied by **4WS** answers.

4WS rule can be applied to any troubleshooting because even the problem description itself is some kind of a trace.

Critical Thinking

Faulty thinking happens all the time in technical support environments, partly due to hectic and demanding business realities.

There is an interesting website that taxonomically organizes fallacies:

http://www.fallacyfiles.org/taxonomy.html

Take, for example, **False Cause** fallacy. Technical examples might include false causes inferred from trace analysis, customer problem description that includes steps to reproduce the problem. This also applies to debugging. The importance of critical thinking skills has been emphasized in the following book by Robert C. Metzger:

Debugging by Thinking: A Multidisciplinary Approach

Surface-level of basic crash dump analysis is less influenced by false cause fallacies because it doesn't have explicitly recorded a sequence of events. However, some caution should be exercised during the detailed analysis of thread waiting times and other historical information.

Troubleshooting as Debugging

This post is motivated by TRAFFIC steps introduced by Andreas Zeller in his book "Why Programs Fail?" that gives practical debugging skills coherent and solid systematical foundation.

However, these steps are for fixing defects in code, the traditional view of the software debugging process. Based on an analogy with systems theories where we have different levels of abstraction like psychology, biology, chemistry, and physics, I would say that debugging starts when we have a failure at the system level.

If we compare systems to applications, troubleshooting to source code debugging, the question we ask at the higher level is "Who caused the product to fail?" which also has a business and political flavor. Therefore I propose a different acronym: **VERSION**. If you always try to fix system problems at the code level, you get a huge "traffic" in all sense, but if you troubleshoot them first, you get a different system/subsystem/component version and get your problem solved faster. This is why we have technical support departments in organizations.

There are some parallels between TRAFFIC and VERSION steps:

```
Track                        View the problem
Reproduce                    Environment/repro steps
Automate (and simplify)      Relevant description
Find origins                 Subsystem/component
                                identification
Focus                        Identify the origin
                                (subsystem/component)
Isolate (defect in code)     Obtain the solution
                                (replace/eliminate
                                 subsystem/component)
Correct (defect in code)     New case study
                                (document,
                                 postmortem analysis)
```

Troubleshooting doesn't eliminate the need to look at the source code. In many cases, a support engineer has to be proficient in code reading skills to be able to map from traces to source code. This helps in component identification, especially if the product has an extensive tracing facility.

Pooltags

3rd-party drivers have their own pooltags. When we see the following or similar output from **!poolused** WinDbg command we can update *pooltag.txt* file located in Debugging Tools for Windows installation *triage* folder:

```
WD   UNKNOWN pooltag 'WD  ', please update pooltag.txt
```

A historical note: 'Ica' pooltag didn't belong to Citrix drivers, although it sounds like "ICA protocol." It came from Microsoft *termdd.sys* driver.

The List of Services

In the kernel or complete memory dumps coming from Windows servers running older versions of Citrix Presentation Server we could see the following processes running in session 0, for example:

```
2: kd> !process 0 0

PROCESS 895c7380  SessionId: 0  Cid: 03f0    Peb: 7ffdf000  ParentCid:
01a8
    DirBase: 0a43d220  ObjectTable: 895c7628  HandleCount: 684.
    Image: CpSvc.exe

PROCESS 892e3320  SessionId: 0  Cid: 060c    Peb: 7ffdf000  ParentCid:
01a8
    DirBase: 0a43d440  ObjectTable: 892e76c8  HandleCount:  93.
    Image: cdmsvc.exe

PROCESS 892ed4a0  SessionId: 0  Cid: 05f8    Peb: 7ffdf000  ParentCid:
01a8
    DirBase: 0a43d420  ObjectTable: 892f1268  HandleCount: 107.
    Image: CdfSvc.exe

PROCESS 89297020  SessionId: 0  Cid: 06ac    Peb: 7ffdf000  ParentCid:
01a8
    DirBase: 0a43d520  ObjectTable: 892991c8  HandleCount:  62.
    Image: encsvc.exe

PROCESS 892a4020  SessionId: 0  Cid: 06d4    Peb: 7ffdf000  ParentCid:
01a8
    DirBase: 0a43d540  ObjectTable: 892b9a48  HandleCount: 1088.
    Image: ImaSrv.exe

PROCESS 892a5020  SessionId: 0  Cid: 070c    Peb: 7ffdf000  ParentCid:
01a8
    DirBase: 0a43d560  ObjectTable: 8927b568  HandleCount: 188.
    Image: mfcom.exe

PROCESS 890e8620  SessionId: 0  Cid: 0cc4    Peb: 7ffdf000  ParentCid:
01a8
    DirBase: 0a43d6e0  ObjectTable: 890e8948  HandleCount: 691.
    Image: SmaService.exe

PROCESS 8901bd60  SessionId: 0  Cid: 0d80    Peb: 7ffdf000  ParentCid:
01a8
    DirBase: 0a43d880  ObjectTable: 89021e88  HandleCount: 148.
    Image: XTE.exe
```

```
PROCESS 88fce020  SessionId: 0  Cid: 1204    Peb: 7ffdf000  ParentCid: 01a8
    DirBase: 0a43d900  ObjectTable: 88fcfac8  HandleCount: 186.
    Image: ctxwmisvc.exe
```

The first step in reconstructing component dependencies is to find out the purpose of each high-level component, such as EXE, DLL, and SYS.

Reverse Engineering Component Dependencies

Crash dumps (and live debugging) can be very useful for reverse engineering component dependencies. Let's look at Microsoft Video Driver Architecture UML component diagram:

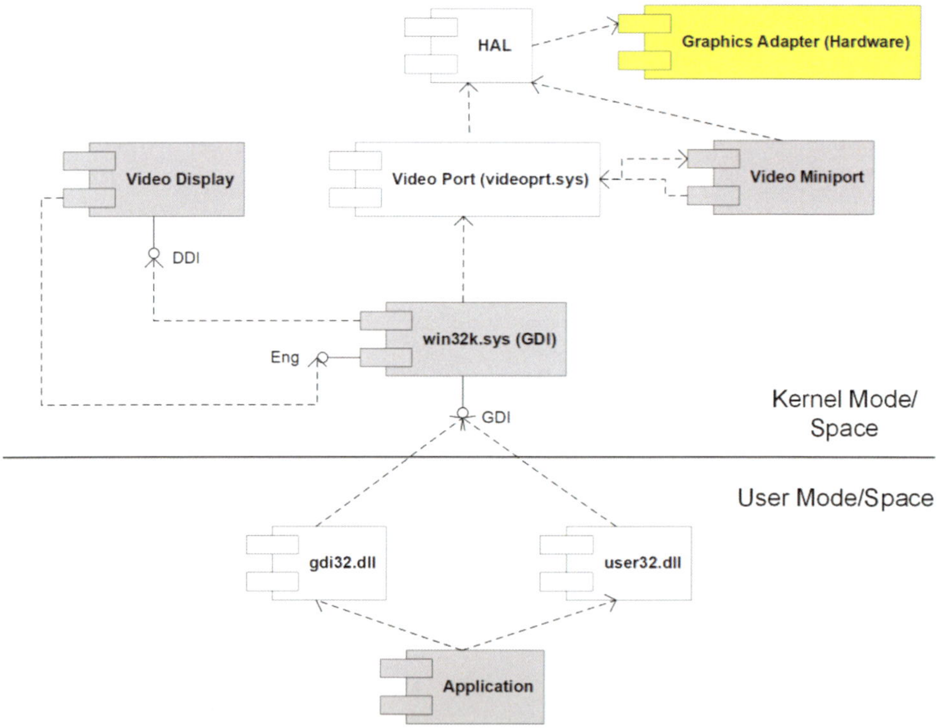

Coupled with this understanding and armed with Citrix symbol files (which are freely downloadable from Citrix support) I was able to transform this thread stack below and other similar stacks into the following UML component diagram (some functions are shown as *module!xxx* and offsets are removed for clarity):

```
nt!KiSwapContext
nt!KiSwapThread
nt!KeWaitForSingleObject
tcpip!xxx
tcpip!TCPDispatch
nt!IofCallDriver
nt!xxx
nt!xxx
TDTCP!xxx
TDTCP!xxx
```

```
TDTCP!TdIoctl
termdd!_IcaCallSd
termdd!IcaCallNextDriver
pdrframe!xxx
pdrframe!PdIoctl
termdd!_IcaCallSd
termdd!IcaCallNextDriver
pdcrypt1!xxx
pdcrypt1!PdIoctl
termdd!_IcaCallSd
termdd!IcaCallNextDriver
WDICA!xxx
WDICA!xxx
WDICA!xxx
WDICA!xxx
WDICA!xxx
WDICA!xxx
WDICA!WdIoctl
termdd!IcaCallStack
termdd!IcaCallDriver
termdd!IcaDeviceControlChannel
termdd!IcaDeviceControl
termdd!IcaDispatch
win32k!GreDeviceIoControl
win32k!EngDeviceIoControl
vdtw30!xxx
vdtw30!xxx
win32k!vMovePointer
win32k!GreMovePointer
win32k!xxxMoveEventAbsolute
win32k!ProcessMouseInput
win32k!InputApc
nt!KiDeliverApc
nt!KiSwapThread
nt!KeWaitForMultipleObjects
win32k!xxxMsgWaitForMultipleObjects
win32k!xxxDesktopThread
win32k!xxxCreateSystemThreads
win32k!NtUserCallOneParam
nt!KiSystemServiceCopyEnd
nt!KiSwapThread
nt!KeWaitForSingleObject
win32k!EngWaitForSingleObject
vdtw30!xxx
vdtw30!xxx
vdtw30!xxx
vdtw30!DrvTw2SaveScreenBits
win32k!GreSaveScreenBits
win32k!CreateSpb
win32k!zzzChangeStates
win32k!zzzBltValidBits
win32k!xxxEndDeferWindowPosEx
win32k!xxxSetWindowPos
win32k!xxxShowWindow
```

```
win32k!NtUserShowWindow
nt!KiSystemService
USER32!NtUserShowWindow
USER32!InternalDialogBox
USER32!DialogBoxIndirectParamAorW
USER32!DialogBoxParamW
```

Then we replace Microsoft components with Citrix ones:

- Video Display with *vdtw30.dll*
- Video Miniport with *icacdd.sys*
- Hardware and HAL with Terminal Services stack components (Microsoft *termdd.sys*, Citrix *wdica.sys*, etc.)

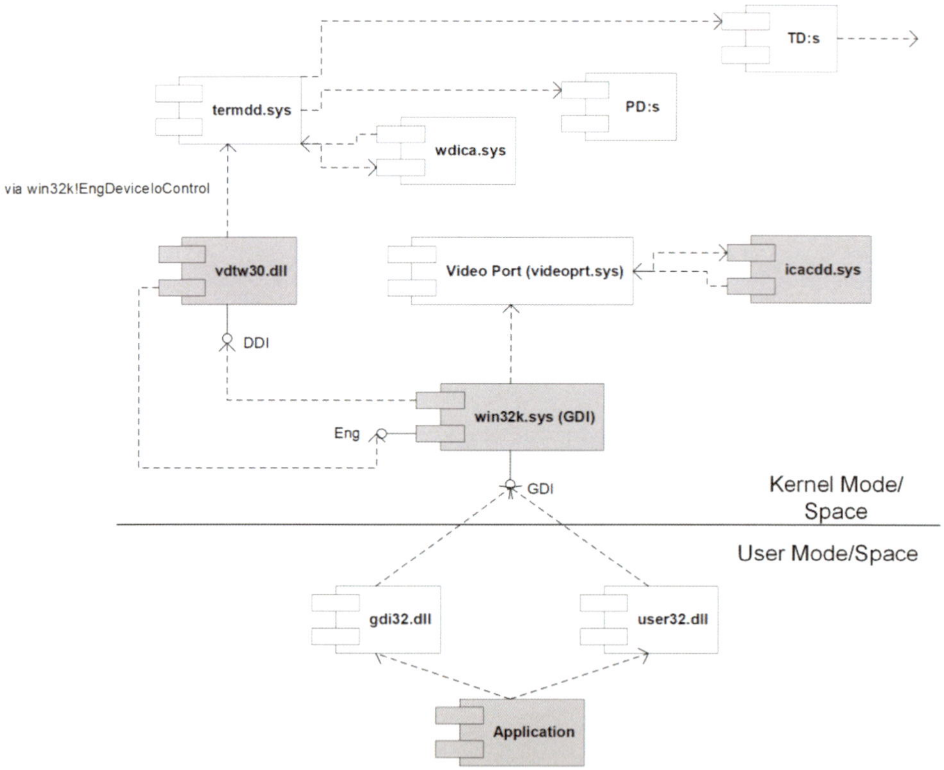

PART 10: Security

Memory Visualization

This security warning is related to sound files and pictures produced by **Dump2Wave** (page 521), **Dump2Picture** (page 532), and WinDbg scripts based on them.

> *These tools do not change computer memory data, and it is present in resulting WAV and BMP files unmodified. Do not publish these files on Internet. Otherwise, you might expose your private or sensitive data.*

If you use lossy compression afterward, like MP3 or JPEG, all original computer memory content is lost and becomes non-recoverable.

Therefore, if you create a piece of modern art using Dump2Picture and want to publish it electronically, then always transform it into JPEG, for example.

WinDbg is Privacy-Aware

WinDbg has two options for **.dump** command to remove the potentially sensitive user data (from WinDbg help):

- **r** - Deletes from the minidump those portions of the stack and store memory that are not useful for recreating the stack trace. Local variables and other data type values are deleted as well. This option does not make the minidump smaller (because these memory sections are simply zeroed), but it is useful if you want to protect the privacy of other applications.
- **R** - Deletes the full module paths from the minidump. Only the module names will be included. This is a useful option if you want to protect the privacy of the user's directory structure.

Therefore, it is possible to configure CDB or WinDbg as default postmortem debuggers and avoid process data to be included. Most of the stack is zeroed except frame data pointers and return addresses used to reconstruct stack trace. String constants like passwords are eliminated. I made the following test with CDB configured as the default postmortem debugger on my Windows x64 Server 2003:

```
HKEY_LOCAL_MACHINE\SOFTWARE\Wow6432Node\Microsoft\Windows
NT\CurrentVersion\AeDebug
Debugger="C:\Program Files (x86)\Debugging Tools for Windows\cdb.exe" -p
%ld -e %ld -g -c ".dump /o /mrR /u c:\temp\safedump.dmp; q"
```

I got the following stack trace from **TestDefaultDebugger** (page 641) where module names and function offsets are removed for visual clarity:

```
0:000> kvL 100
ChildEBP RetAddr  Args to Child
002df868 00403263 00425ae8 00000000 002df8a8 OnBnClickedButton1
002df878 00403470 002dfe90 00000000 00000000 _AfxDispatchCmdMsg
002df8a8 00402a27 00000000 00000000 00000000 OnCmdMsg
002df8cc 00408e69 00000000 00000000 00000000 OnCmdMsg
002df91c 004098d9 00000000 00580a9e 00000000 OnCommand
002df9b8 00406258 00000000 00000000 00580a9e OnWndMsg
002df9d8 0040836d 00000000 00000000 00580a9e WindowProc
002dfa40 004083f4 00000000 00000000 00000000 AfxCallWndProc
002dfa60 7d9472d8 00000000 00000000 00000000 AfxWndProc
002dfa8c 7d9475c3 004083c0 00000000 00000000 InternalCallWinProc
002dfb04 7d948626 00000000 004083c0 00000000 UserCallWinProcCheckWow
002dfb48 7d94868d 00000000 00000000 00000000 SendMessageWorker
002dfb6c 7dbf87b3 00000000 00000000 00000000 SendMessageW
002dfb8c 7dbf8895 00000000 00000000 00000000 Button_NotifyParent
002dfba8 7dbfab9a 00000000 00000000 002dfcb0 Button_ReleaseCapture
```

```
002dfc38 7d9472d8 00580a9e 00000000 00000000 Button_WndProc
002dfc64 7d9475c3 7dbfa313 00580a9e 00000000 InternalCallWinProc
002dfcdc 7d9477f6 00000000 7dbfa313 00580a9e UserCallWinProcCheckWow
002dfd54 7d947838 00000000 00000000 002dfd90 DispatchMessageWorker
002dfd64 7d956ca0 00000000 00000000 002dfe90 DispatchMessageW
002dfd90 0040568b 00000000 00000000 002dfe90 IsDialogMessageW
002dfda0 004065d8 00000000 00402a07 00000000 IsDialogMessageW
002dfda8 00402a07 00000000 00000000 00000000 PreTranslateInput
002dfdb8 00408041 00000000 00000000 002dfe90 PreTranslateMessage
002dfdc8 00403ae3 00000000 00000000 00000000 WalkPreTranslateTree
002dfddc 00403c1e 00000000 00403b29 00000000
AfxInternalPreTranslateMessage
002dfde4 00403b29 00000000 00403c68 00000000 PreTranslateMessage
002dfdec 00403c68 00000000 00000000 002dfe90 AfxPreTranslateMessage
002dfdfc 00407920 00000000 002dfe90 002dfe6c AfxInternalPumpMessage
002dfe20 004030a1 00000000 00000000 0042ec18 CWnd::RunModalLoop
002dfe6c 0040110d 00000000 0042ec18 0042ec18 CDialog::DoModal
002dff18 004206fb 00000000 00000000 00000000 InitInstance
002dff28 0040e852 00400000 00000000 00000000 AfxWinMain
002dffc0 7d4e992a 00000000 00000000 00000000 __tmainCRTStartup
002dfff0 00000000 0040e8bb 00000000 00000000 BaseProcessStart
```

We can see that most arguments are zeroes. Those that are not, either do not point to valid data or correspond to function return addresses and frame pointers. This can be seen from the raw stack data as well:

```
0:000> dds esp
002df86c  00403263 TestDefaultDebugger!_AfxDispatchCmdMsg+0x43
002df870  00425ae8
TestDefaultDebugger!CTestDefaultDebuggerApp::`vftable'+0x154
002df874  00000000
002df878  002df8a8
002df87c  00403470 TestDefaultDebugger!CCmdTarget::OnCmdMsg+0x118
002df880  002dfe90
002df884  00000000
002df888  00000000
002df88c  004014f0
TestDefaultDebugger!CTestDefaultDebuggerDlg::OnBnClickedButton1
002df890  00000000
002df894  00000000
002df898  00000000
002df89c  002dfe90
002df8a0  00000000
002df8a4  00000000
002df8a8  002df8cc
002df8ac  00402a27 TestDefaultDebugger!CDialog::OnCmdMsg+0x1b
002df8b0  00000000
002df8b4  00000000
002df8b8  00000000
002df8bc  00000000
002df8c0  00000000
002df8c4  002dfe90
```

```
002df8c8  00000000
002df8cc  002df91c
002df8d0  00408e69 TestDefaultDebugger!CWnd::OnCommand+0x90
002df8d4  00000000
002df8d8  00000000
002df8dc  00000000
002df8e0  00000000
002df8e4  002dfe90
002df8e8  002dfe90
```

We can compare it with the normal full or minidump saved with other **/m** options. The zeroed data when we used **/mr** option is shown in bold (module names and function offsets are removed for visual clarity):

```
0:000> kvL 100
ChildEBP RetAddr Args to Child
002df868 00403263 00425ae8 00000111 002df8a8 OnBnClickedButton1
002df878 00403470 002dfe90 000003e8 00000000 _AfxDispatchCmdMsg
002df8a8 00402a27 000003e8 00000000 00000000 OnCmdMsg
002df8cc 00408e69 000003e8 00000000 00000000 OnCmdMsg
002df91c 004098d9 00000000 00271876 d5b6c7f7 OnCommand
002df9b8 00406258 00000111 000003e8 00271876 OnWndMsg
002df9d8 0040836d 00000111 000003e8 00271876 WindowProc
002dfa40 004083f4 00000000 00561878 00000111 AfxCallWndProc
002dfa60 7d9472d8 00561878 00000111 000003e8 AfxWndProc
002dfa8c 7d9475c3 004083c0 00561878 00000111 InternalCallWinProc
002dfb04 7d948626 00000000 004083c0 00561878 UserCallWinProcCheckWow
002dfb48 7d94868d 00aec860 00000000 00000111 SendMessageWorker
002dfb6c 7dbf87b3 00561878 00000111 000003e8 SendMessageW
002dfb8c 7dbf8895 002ec9e0 00000000 0023002c Button_NotifyParent
002dfba8 7dbfab9a 002ec9e0 00000001 002dfcb0 Button_ReleaseCapture
002dfc38 7d9472d8 00271876 00000202 00000000 Button_WndProc
002dfc64 7d9475c3 7dbfa313 00271876 00000202 InternalCallWinProc
002dfcdc 7d9477f6 00000000 7dbfa313 00271876 UserCallWinProcCheckWow
002dfd54 7d947838 002e77f8 00000000 002dfd90 DispatchMessageWorker
002dfd64 7d956ca0 002e77f8 00000000 002dfe90 DispatchMessageW
002dfd90 0040568b 00561878 00000000 002dfe90 IsDialogMessageW
002dfda0 004065d8 002e77f8 00402a07 002e77f8 IsDialogMessageW
002dfda8 00402a07 002e77f8 002e77f8 00561878 PreTranslateInput
002dfdb8 00408041 002e77f8 002e77f8 002dfe90 PreTranslateMessage
002dfdc8 00403ae3 00561878 002e77f8 002e77f8 WalkPreTranslateTree
002dfddc 00403c1e 002e77f8 00403b29 002e77f8
AfxInternalPreTranslateMessage
002dfde4 00403b29 002e77f8 00403c68 002e77f8 PreTranslateMessage
002dfdec 00403c68 002e77f8 00000000 002dfe90 AfxPreTranslateMessage
002dfdfc 00407920 00000004 002dfe90 002dfe6c AfxInternalPumpMessage
002dfe20 004030a1 00000004 d5b6c023 0042ec18 RunModalLoop
002dfe6c 0040110d d5b6c037 0042ec18 0042ec18 DoModal
002dff18 004206fb 00000ece 00000002 00000001 InitInstance
002dff28 0040e852 00400000 00000000 001d083e AfxWinMain
002dffc0 7d4e992a 00000000 00000000 7efdf000 __tmainCRTStartup
002dfff0 00000000 0040e8bb 00000000 000000c8 BaseProcessStart
```

```
0:000> dds esp
002df86c 00403263 TestDefaultDebugger!_AfxDispatchCmdMsg+0x43
002df870 00425ae8
TestDefaultDebugger!CTestDefaultDebuggerApp::`vftable'+0x154
002df874 00000111
002df878 002df8a8
002df87c 00403470 TestDefaultDebugger!CCmdTarget::OnCmdMsg+0x118
002df880 002dfe90
002df884 000003e8
002df888 00000000
002df88c 004014f0
TestDefaultDebugger!CTestDefaultDebuggerDlg::OnBnClickedButton1
002df890 00000000
002df894 00000038
002df898 00000000
002df89c 002dfe90
002df8a0 000003e8
002df8a4 00000000
002df8a8 002df8cc
002df8ac 00402a27 TestDefaultDebugger!CDialog::OnCmdMsg+0x1b
002df8b0 000003e8
002df8b4 00000000
002df8b8 00000000
002df8bc 00000000
002df8c0 000003e8
002df8c4 002dfe90
002df8c8 00000000
002df8cc 002df91c
002df8d0 00408e69 TestDefaultDebugger!CWnd::OnCommand+0x90
002df8d4 000003e8
002df8d8 00000000
002df8dc 00000000
002df8e0 00000000
002df8e4 002dfe90
002df8e8 002dfe90
```

Crash Dumps and Security

Suppose you work in a banking industry or for any company that has sensitive information. Is it secure to send a crash dump outside for analysis? One semi-anonymous person asked this question on Crash Dump Analysis forum and here is my answer based on my experience in crash dump analysis and kernel level development:

```
"It depends on credit card transaction software design and architecture and what type of memory dump is configured in Control Panel\System\ Advanced\Startup and Recovery applet: Small, Kernel or Complete.

Software usually encrypts data before sending it down TCP/IP stack or other network protocol. If credit card transaction software doesn't have any kernel space encryption drivers and doesn't rely on any Microsoft or other third-party encryption API that might send data to kernel, communicate to KSECDD or to a user-space component like LSASS via LPC/RPC, we can safely assume that kernel memory dumps will not have unencrypted data. If encryption is done entirely in user space, Small memory dump and Kernel memory dump will only have encrypted fragments. Otherwise, there is a probability that BSOD happens just before encryption or after decryption or when a secure protocol is being handled. This exposure can even happen in Small memory dumps if BSOD happens in the thread that handles sensitive information in kernel mode.

The same applies if software stores credit data on any medium. If it stores only encrypted data and decrypts entirely in user space without any transition to kernel, it should be safe to enable kernel memory dump.

If our goal is the ultimate security, then even Small memory dump (64Kb) should not be allowed. But, in reality, when we consider probabilities, sending a small memory dump is equivalent to no more than exposing just one credit card number or just one password.

What we must avoid at any cost is to enable complete memory dump option in Control Panel. In this case, all credit card transaction software code and data including file system cache will be exposed.

Contrary to complete memory dump, kernel memory dump will not have much data even if some portion of it is being communicated during the crash time."
```

If you are interested too you can participate in that discussion: http://www.dumpanalysis.org/forum/viewtopic.php?t=56 or see the solution from WinDbg (page 600).

PART 11: The Origin of Crash Dumps

JIT Service Debugging

If we have services running under network service account (prior to Vista) and they crash we can use NTSD from recent Debugging Tools for Windows and **-noio** switch as described in the following article:

NTSD as a better Dr. Watson http://www.debuginfo.com/articles/ntsdwatson.html

We need to copy the latest *ntsd.exe*, *dbghelp.dll* and *dbgeng.dll* to some folder if we don't want to install Debugging Tools for Windows in a production environment.

The example of *AeDebug* key we can use for 64-bit JIT debugging is

```
C:\ntsd\ntsd -p %ld -e %ld -g -noio -c ".dump /ma /u c:\TEMP\new.dmp; q"
```

It is always good to double check these settings with **TestDefaultDebugger** tool (page 641).

Local Crash Dumps in Vista

It appears that Microsoft decided to help customers to save full user dumps locally for later postmortem analysis. According to MSDN, this can be done by using *LocalDumps* registry key starting from Vista SP1 and Windows Server 2008:

http://msdn2.microsoft.com/en-us/library/bb787181.aspx

This is a quote from the article above:

> *[...] Prior to application termination, the system will check the registry settings to determine whether a local dump is to be collected. The registry settings control whether a full dump is collected versus a minidump. The custom flags specified also determine which information is collected in the dump. [...] You can make use of the local dump collection even if WER is disabled. The local dumps are collected even if the user cancels WER reporting at any point. [...]*

From my understanding, it is independent of the default postmortem debugger mechanism via *AeDebug* registry key. If it works, then full user dump collection might be easier in production environments because of no need to install Debugging Tools for Windows to set up a postmortem debugger.

COM+ Crash Dumps

If we have problems with COM+ components we can configure Component Services in Control Panel to save a crash dump:

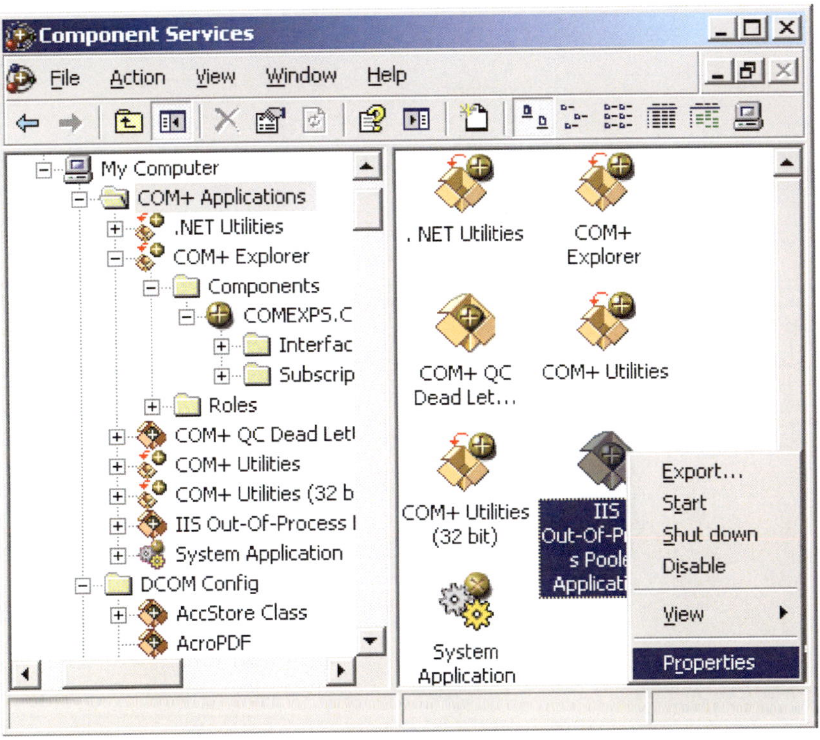

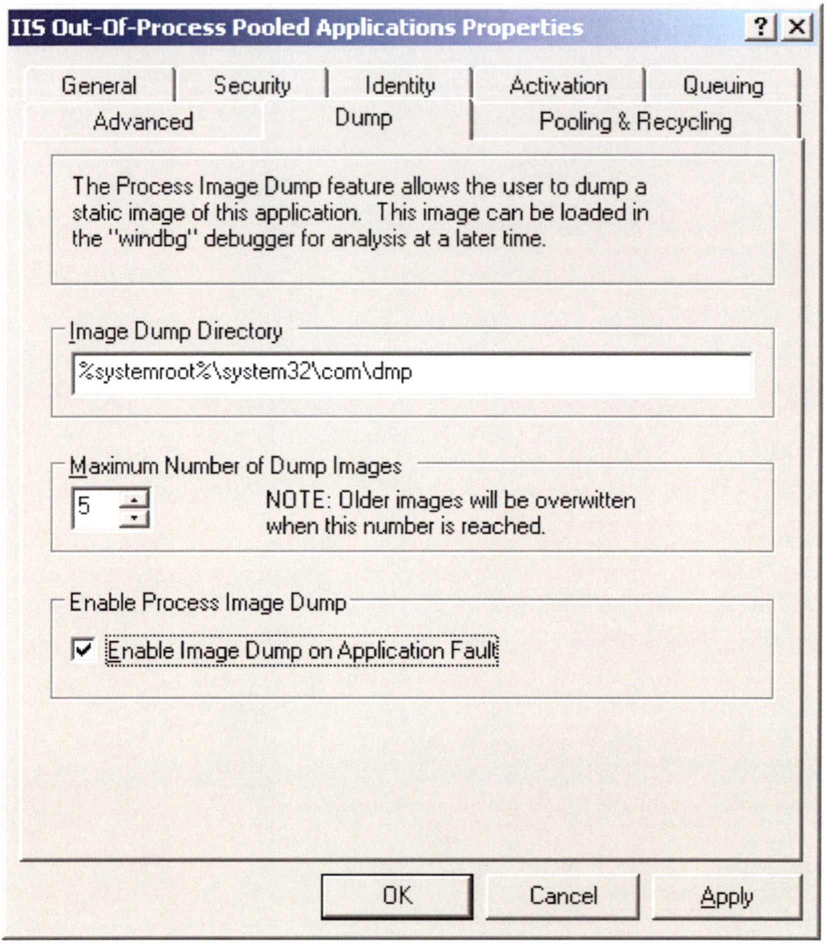

The following article explains how COM+ handles application faults:

Fault Isolation and Failfast Policy
http://msdn2.microsoft.com/en-us/library/ms679253.aspx

Now I show how to get an error message that was written to the event log when COM+ application was terminated due to a different error code than an access violation. If we get a crash dump from COM+ process we need to look at all threads and find the one that runs through *comsvcs.dll* (shown in a small font for visual clarity):

```
0:000> ~*kL
...
...
...
   6  Id: 8d4.1254 Suspend: 0 Teb: 7ffd9000 Unfrozen
ChildEBP RetAddr  Args to Child
0072ee30 7c822124 77e6baa8 00000394 00000000 ntdll!KiFastSystemCallRet
0072ee34 77e6baa8 00000394 00000000 00000000
ntdll!NtWaitForSingleObject+0xc
0072eea4 77e6ba12 00000394 ffffffff 00000000
kernel32!WaitForSingleObjectEx+0xac
0072eeb8 75c2b250 00000394 ffffffff 0072f640
kernel32!WaitForSingleObject+0x12
0072f340 75c2bb91 75b8e7fc 75b8e810 000008d4 comsvcs!FF_RunCmd+0xa2
0072f60c 75c2bc76 0072f640 75c6c5c0 0072fe44
comsvcs!FF_DumpProcess_MD+0x21a
0072f850 75c2be83 00000000 77ce21ce 0bd5f0f0 comsvcs!FF_DumpProcess+0x39
0072fdc0 75c2c351 75c6c5c0 75b8b008 00000142 comsvcs!FailFastStr+0x2ce
0072fe20 75bf31fa 0072fe44 75b8b008 00000142
comsvcs!CError::WriteToLog+0x198
0072fe8c 75bf3d48 0bcf5d0c 00000000 0bcf5cf8
comsvcs!CSurrogateServices::FireApplicationLaunch+0x13b
0072fee0 75bf3e19 75bf3e01 0072ff44 7c81a3c5
comsvcs!CApplication::AsyncApplicationLaunch+0x101
0072feec 7c81a3c5 0bcf5cf8 7c889880 0bcf5d50
comsvcs!CApplication::AppLaunchThreadProc+0x18
0072ff44 7c8200fc 75bf3e01 0bcf5cf8 00000000 ntdll!RtlpWorkerCallout+0x71
0072ff64 7c81a3fa 00000000 0bcf5cf8 0bcf5d50
ntdll!RtlpExecuteWorkerRequest+0x4f
0072ff78 7c82017f 7c8200bb 00000000 0bcf5cf8 ntdll!RtlpApcCallout+0x11
0072ffb8 77e66063 00000000 00000000 00000000 ntdll!RtlpWorkerThread+0x61
0072ffec 00000000 7c83ad38 00000000 00000000 kernel32!BaseThreadStart+0x34
...
...
...
```

FF_DumpProcess function is an indication that the process was being dumped. There is no *ComSvcsExceptionFilter* function in the thread stack trace, but we can still get an error message if we look at *FailFastStr* function arguments:

```
0:000> du 75c6c5c0 75c6c5c0+400
75c6c5c0  "{646F1874-46B6-4149-BD55-8C317FB"
75c6c600  "71CC0}....Server Application ID:"
75c6c640  " {646F1874-46B6-4149-BD55-8C317F"
75c6c680  "B71CC0}..Server Application Inst"
75c6c6c0  "ance ID:..{7A39BC48-78DA-4FBB-A7"
75c6c700  "46-EEA7E42CDAC7}..Server Applica"
75c6c740  "tion Name: My Server"
75c6c780  "..The serious nature of this err"
75c6c7c0  "or has caused the process to ter"
75c6c800  "minate...Error Code = 0x80131600"
75c6c840  " : ..COM+ Services Internals Inf"
75c6c880  "ormation:..File: d:\nt\com\compl"
75c6c8c0  "us\src\comsvcs\srgtapi\csrgtserv"
75c6c900  ".cpp, Line: 322..Comsvcs.dll fil"
75c6c940  "e version: ENU 2001.12.4720.2517"
75c6c980  " shp"
```

Also, if we examine parameters of *FF_RunCmd* call, we see what application was used to dump the process:

```
ChildEBP RetAddr Args to Child
0072f340 75c2bb91 75b8e7fc 75b8e810 000008d4
comsvcs!FF_RunCmd+0xa2

0:000> du 75b8e7fc
75b8e7fc  "%s %d %s"
0:000> du 75b8e810
75b8e810  "RunDll32 comsvcs.dll,MiniDump"
```

We can guess that the first parameter is a format string, the second one is a command line for a process dumper, the third one is PID, and the fourth one should be the name of a dump file to save. We can double-check this from the raw stack:

```
ChildEBP RetAddr Args to Child
0072f340 75c2bb91 75b8e7fc 75b8e810 000008d4
comsvcs!FF_RunCmd+0xa2

0:000> dd 0072f340
0072f340  0072f60c 75c2bb91 75b8e7fc 75b8e810
     ; saved EBP, return EIP, 1st param, 2nd param
0072f350  000008d4 0072f640 0072f84a 00000000
     ; 3rd param, 4th param
```

```
0:000> du 0072f640
0072f640  "C:\WINDOWS\system32\com\dmp\{646"
0072f680  "F1874-46B6-4149-BD55-8C317FB71CC"
0072f6c0  "0}_2007_07_16_12_05_08.dmp"
```

We can find the formatted command that was passed to *CreateProcess* call in the raw stack region:

```
0:006> du 0072ef2c
0072ef2c  "RunDll32 comsvcs.dll,MiniDump 22"
0072ef6c  "60 C:\WINDOWS\system32\com\dmp\{"
0072efac  "646F1874-46B6-4149-BD55-8C317FB7"
0072efec  "1CC0}_2007_07_16_12_05_08.dmp"
```

Correcting Microsoft Article about Userdump.exe

There is much confusion among Microsoft and Citrix customers on how to use userdump.exe to save a process dump. Microsoft published an article about this tool, and it has the following title:

How to use the Userdump.exe tool to create a dump file:
http://support.microsoft.com/kb/241215/

Unfortunately, all scenarios listed there start with:

> *1. Run the Setup.exe program for your processor.*

It also says:

> *<...> move to the version of Userdump.exe for your processor at the command prompt*

I would like to correct the article here. We don't need to run *setup.exe*; we just need to copy *userdump.exe* and *dbghelp.dll*. The latter is important because the version of that DLL in *system32* folder can be older and *userdump.exe* will not start:

```
C:\kktools\userdump8.1\x64>userdump.exe

!!!!!!!!!! Error !!!!!!!!!!
Unsupported DbgHelp.dll version.
Path   : C:\W2K3\system32\DbgHelp.dll
Version: 5.2.3790.1830

C:\kktools\userdump8.1\x64>
```

For most customers running *setup.exe* and configuring the default rules in Exception Monitor creates a significant amount of **False Positive Dumps** (page 259). If we want to dump a process manually, we don't need automatically generated memory dumps or fine-tune Exception Monitor rules to reduce the number of dump files.

Just an additional note: if we have an error dialog box showing that a program got an exception, we can find that process in Task Manager and use *userdump.exe* to save that process dump manually. Then inside the dump, it is possible to see that error. Therefore in the case when a default postmortem debugger wasn't configured in the registry, we can still get a memory dump for postmortem crash dump analysis.

Here is an example. I removed a postmortem debugger from

```
HKEY_LOCAL_MACHINE\SOFTWARE\Microsoft\Windows NT\CurrentVersion\AeDebug
Debugger=
```

Now if we run TestDefaultDebugger tool and hit the big crash button we get the following message box:

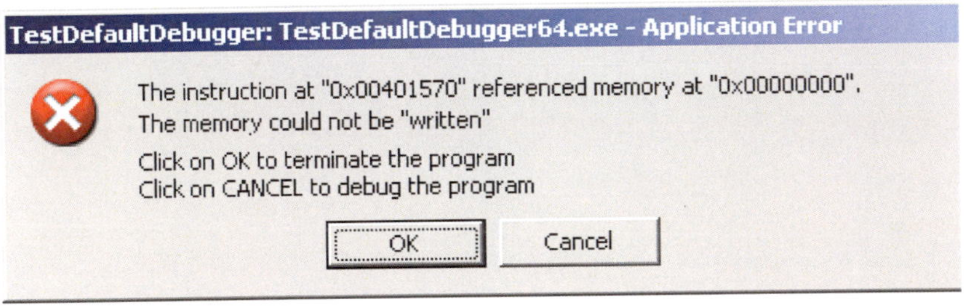

If we save TestDefaultDebugger process dump manually using *userdump.exe* when this message box is shown:

```
C:\kktools\userdump8.1\x64>userdump.exe 5264 c:\tdd.dmp
User Mode Process Dumper (Version 8.1.2929.4)
Copyright (c) Microsoft Corp. All rights reserved.
Dumping process 5264 (TestDefaultDebugger64.exe) to
c:\tdd.dmp...
The process was dumped successfully.
```

If we open it in WinDbg, we can see the problem thread there (shown in a small font for visual clarity):

```
0:000> kn
#  Child-SP          RetAddr           Call Site
00 00000000`0012dab8 00000000`77dbfb3b ntdll!ZwRaiseHardError+0xa
01 00000000`0012dac0 00000000`004148c6 kernel32!UnhandledExceptionFilter+0x6c8
02 00000000`0012e2f0 00000000`004165f6 TestDefaultDebugger64!__tmainCRTStartup$filt$0+0x16
03 00000000`0012e320 00000000`78ee4bdd TestDefaultDebugger64!__C_specific_handler+0xa6
04 00000000`0012e3b0 00000000`78ee685a ntdll!RtlpExecuteHandlerForException+0xd
05 00000000`0012e3e0 00000000`78ef3a5d ntdll!RtlDispatchException+0x1b4
06 00000000`0012ea90 00000000`00401570 ntdll!KiUserExceptionDispatch+0x2d
07 00000000`0012f028 00000000`00403d4d
TestDefaultDebugger64!CTestDefaultDebuggerDlg::OnBnClickedButton1
08 00000000`0012f030 00000000`00403f75 TestDefaultDebugger64!_AfxDispatchCmdMsg+0xc1
09 00000000`0012f070 00000000`004030cc TestDefaultDebugger64!CCmdTarget::OnCmdMsg+0x169
0a 00000000`0012f0f0 00000000`0040c18d TestDefaultDebugger64!CDialog::OnCmdMsg+0x28
0b 00000000`0012f150 00000000`0040cfbd TestDefaultDebugger64!CWnd::OnCommand+0xc9
0c 00000000`0012f200 00000000`0040818f TestDefaultDebugger64!CWnd::OnWndMsg+0x55
0d 00000000`0012f360 00000000`0040b2e5 TestDefaultDebugger64!CWnd::WindowProc+0x33
0e 00000000`0012f3c0 00000000`0040b3d2 TestDefaultDebugger64!AfxCallWndProc+0xf1
0f 00000000`0012f480 00000000`77c439fc TestDefaultDebugger64!AfxWndProc+0x4e
10 00000000`0012f4e0 00000000`77c432ba user32!UserCallWinProcCheckWow+0x1f9
11 00000000`0012f5b0 00000000`77c4335b user32!SendMessageWorker+0x68c
12 00000000`0012f650 000007ff`7f07c5af user32!SendMessageW+0x9d
13 00000000`0012f6a0 000007ff`7f07eb8e comctl32!Button_ReleaseCapture+0x14f
```

The second parameter to *RtlDispatchException* is the pointer to the exception context, so if we dump the stack trace verbosely we can get that pointer and pass it to **.cxr** command:

```
0:000> kv
Child-SP          RetAddr           : Args to Child
...
...
...
00000000`0012e3e0 00000000`78ef3a5d : 00000000`0040c9ec 00000000`0012ea90
00000000`00000001 00000000`00000111 : ntdll!RtlDispatchException+0x1b4
...
...
...

0:000> .cxr 00000000`0012ea90
rax=0000000000000000 rbx=0000000000000001 rcx=000000000012fd70
rdx=00000000000003e8 rsi=000000000012fd70 rdi=0000000000432e90
rip=0000000000401570 rsp=000000000012f028 rbp=0000000000000111
 r8=0000000000000000  r9=0000000000401570 r10=0000000000401570
r11=000000000015abb0 r12=0000000000000000 r13=00000000000003e8
r14=0000000000000110 r15=0000000000000001
iopl=0 nv up ei pl zr na po nc
cs=0033 ss=002b ds=002b es=002b fs=0053 gs=002b efl=00010246
TestDefaultDebugger64!CTestDefaultDebuggerDlg::OnBnClickedButton1:
00000000`00401570 c704250000000000000000 mov dword ptr [0],0
ds:00000000`00000000=????????
```

We see that it was NULL pointer dereference that caused the process termination. Now we can dump the full stack trace that led to our crash (shown in a small font for visual clarity):

```
0:000> kn 100
#  Child-SP          RetAddr           Call Site
00 00000000`0012f028 00000000`00403d4d
TestDefaultDebugger64!CTestDefaultDebuggerDlg::OnBnClickedButton1
01 00000000`0012f030 00000000`00403f75 TestDefaultDebugger64!_AfxDispatchCmdMsg+0xc1
02 00000000`0012f070 00000000`004030cc TestDefaultDebugger64!CCmdTarget::OnCmdMsg+0x169
03 00000000`0012f0f0 00000000`0040c18d TestDefaultDebugger64!CDialog::OnCmdMsg+0x28
04 00000000`0012f150 00000000`0040cfbd TestDefaultDebugger64!CWnd::OnCommand+0xc9
05 00000000`0012f200 00000000`0040818f TestDefaultDebugger64!CWnd::OnWndMsg+0x55
06 00000000`0012f360 00000000`0040b2e5 TestDefaultDebugger64!CWnd::WindowProc+0x33
07 00000000`0012f3c0 00000000`0040b3d2 TestDefaultDebugger64!AfxCallWndProc+0xf1
08 00000000`0012f480 00000000`77c439fc TestDefaultDebugger64!AfxWndProc+0x4e
09 00000000`0012f4e0 00000000`77c432ba user32!UserCallWinProcCheckWow+0x1f9
0a 00000000`0012f5b0 00000000`77c4335b user32!SendMessageWorker+0x68c
0b 00000000`0012f650 000007ff`7f07c5af user32!SendMessageW+0x9d
0c 00000000`0012f6a0 000007ff`7f07eb8e comctl32!Button_ReleaseCapture+0x14f
0d 00000000`0012f6d0 00000000`77c439fc comctl32!Button_WndProc+0x8ee
0e 00000000`0012f830 00000000`77c43e9c user32!UserCallWinProcCheckWow+0x1f9
0f 00000000`0012f900 00000000`77c3965a user32!DispatchMessageWorker+0x3af
10 00000000`0012f970 00000000`0040706d user32!IsDialogMessageW+0x256
11 00000000`0012fa40 00000000`0040868c TestDefaultDebugger64!CWnd::IsDialogMessageW+0x35
12 00000000`0012fa80 00000000`0040309c TestDefaultDebugger64!CWnd::PreTranslateInput+0x28
13 00000000`0012fab0 00000000`0040ae73 TestDefaultDebugger64!CDialog::PreTranslateMessage+0xc0
14 00000000`0012faf0 00000000`004047fc TestDefaultDebugger64!CWnd::WalkPreTranslateTree+0x33
```

```
15 00000000`0012fb30 00000000`00404857
TestDefaultDebugger64!AfxInternalPreTranslateMessage+0x64233]
16 00000000`0012fb70 00000000`00404a17 TestDefaultDebugger64!AfxPreTranslateMessage+0x23
17 00000000`0012fba0 00000000`00404a57 TestDefaultDebugger64!AfxInternalPumpMessage+0x37
18 00000000`0012fbe0 00000000`0040a419 TestDefaultDebugger64!AfxPumpMessage+0x1b
19 00000000`0012fc10 00000000`00403a3a TestDefaultDebugger64!CWnd::RunModalLoop+0xe5
1a 00000000`0012fc90 00000000`00401139 TestDefaultDebugger64!CDialog::DoModal+0x1ce
1b 00000000`0012fd40 00000000`0042bbbd
TestDefaultDebugger64!CTestDefaultDebuggerApp::InitInstance+0xe9
1c 00000000`0012fe70 00000000`00414848 TestDefaultDebugger64!AfxWinMain+0x69
1d 00000000`0012fed0 00000000`77d5966c TestDefaultDebugger64!__tmainCRTStartup+0x258
1e 00000000`0012ff80 00000000`00000000 kernel32!BaseProcessStart+0x29
```

The same technique can be used to dump a process when any kind of error message box appears, for example, when a .NET application displays a .NET exception message box, or a native application shows a run-time error dialog box.

Where did the Crash Dump Come from?

If our customer complains that the fix we sent yesterday doesn't work, we can check the computer name from the dump. It could be the case that our fix wasn't applied to all computers. Here is a summary of different dump types:

1. Complete/kernel memory dumps: **dS** *srv!srvcomputername* for Windows versions prior to 10:

```
1: kd> dS srv!srvcomputername
e17c9078 "COMPUTER-NAME"
```

For Windows 10:

```
1: kd> dS mrxsmb!SmbCeContext+10
ffffdb0d`dd910860 "COMPUTER-NAME"
```

2. User dumps: **!peb** and the subsequent search inside environment variables

```
0:000> !peb
PEB at 7ffde000
...
...
...
Environment: 0x10000
...

0:000> s-su 0x10000 0x20000
...
...
000123b2 "COMPUTERNAME=COMPUTER-NAME"
...
...
```

The **dS** command shown above interprets the address as a pointer to the UNICODE_STRING structure widely used inside the Windows kernel space:

```
1: kd> dt _UNICODE_STRING
+0x000 Length : Uint2B
+0x002 MaximumLength : Uint2B
+0x004 Buffer : Ptr32 Uint2B
```

Its DDK definition:

```
typedef struct _UNICODE_STRING {
    USHORT Length;
    USHORT MaximumLength;
    PWSTR Buffer;
} UNICODE_STRING *PUNICODE_STRING;
```

Let's **dd** the name:

```
1: kd> dd srv!srvcomputername l2
f5e8d1a0 0022001a e17c9078
```

Such a combination of short integers following by an address is usually an indication that we have a UNICODE_STRING structure:

```
1: kd> du e17c9078

e17c9078 "COMPUTER-NAME    "
```

We can double check it with **dt** command:

```
1: kd> dt _UNICODE_STRING f5e8d1a0
"COMPUTER-NAME"
+0x000 Length : 0x1a
+0x002 MaximumLength : 0x22
+0x004 Buffer : 0xe17c9078 "COMPUTER-NAME"
```

Custom Postmortem Debuggers in Vista

On the new Vista installation, we have neither *drwtsn32.exe* nor NTSD.

Despite that, any application that can attach to a process based on its PID and save its memory state in a dump file will do as a postmortem debugger. The first obvious candidate is *userdump.exe*, which actually can properly set up itself in the registry. Here are the detailed instructions. If we already have the latest version of *userdump.exe* we can skip the first two steps:

1. Download the latest User Mode Process Dumper from Microsoft. At the time of this writing, it has version 8.1
2. Run the downloaded executable file, and it will prompt to unzip. By default, the current version unzips to *c:\kktools\userdump8.1*. Do not run setup afterward because it is not needed for our purposes.
3. Create *kktools* folder in *system32* folder.
4. Create the folder where userdump will save our dump files. I use *c:\UserDumps* in my example.
5. Copy *dbghelp.dll* and *userdump.exe* from x86 or x64 folder depending on the version of Windows we use to *system32\kktools* folder created in step 3.
6. Run the elevated command prompt and enter the following command:

```
C:\Windows\System32\kktools>userdump -I -d c:\UserDumps
User Mode Process Dumper (Version 8.1.2929.5)
Copyright (c) Microsoft Corp. All rights reserved.
Userdump set up Aedebug registry key.
```

7. Check the following registry key:

```
HKEY_LOCAL_MACHINE\SOFTWARE\Microsoft\Windows NT\CurrentVersion\AeDebug
Debugger=C:\Windows\system32\kktools\userdump -E %ld %ld -D c:\UserDumps\
Auto=0
```

We can set Auto to 1 if we want to see the following dialog every time we have a crash:

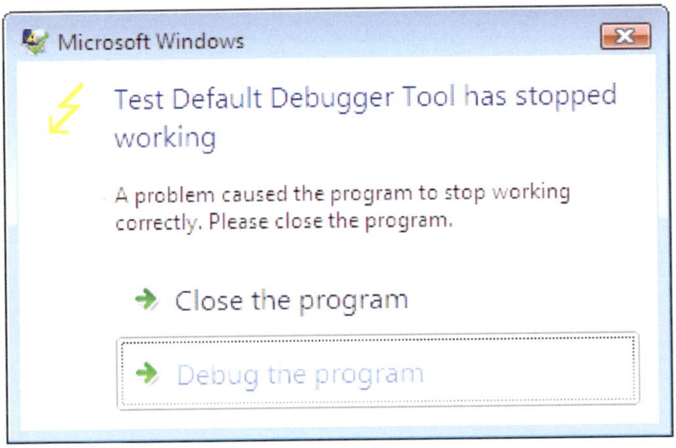

8. Test the new settings by using **TestDefaultDebugger** (page 641)
9. When we have a crash *userdump.exe* shows a window on top of our screen while saving the dump file:

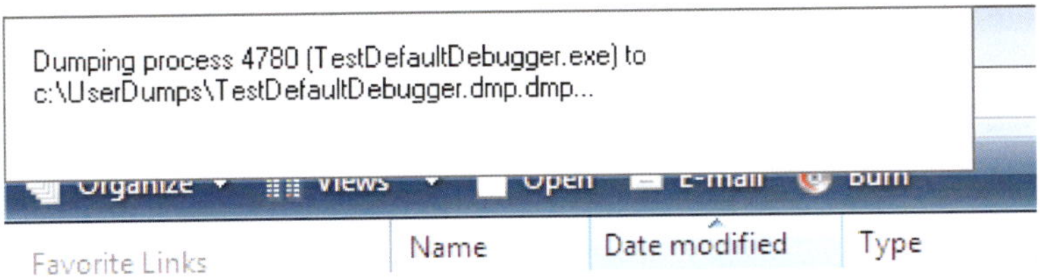

Of course, we can setup *userdump.exe* as a postmortem debugger on other Windows platforms. The problem with *userdump.exe* is that it overwrites the previous process dump file because it uses the module name for the file name, for example, *TestDefaultDebugger.dmp*, so we need to rename or save the dump file if we have multiple crashes for the same application.

Other programs can be set up instead of *userdump.exe*. One of them is WinDbg. Here is the registry key that I tested on Vista:

```
HKEY_LOCAL_MACHINE\SOFTWARE\Microsoft\Windows NT\CurrentVersion\AeDebug
Debugger="C:\Program Files\Debugging Tools for Windows\windbg.exe" -p %ld
-e %ld -g -c '.dump /o /ma /u c:\UserDumps\new.dmp; q' -Q -QS -QY -QSY
```

Finally, we can use the command line CDB user mode debugger from Debugging Tools for Windows. Here is the corresponding registry key:

```
HKEY_LOCAL_MACHINE\SOFTWARE\Microsoft\Windows NT\CurrentVersion\AeDebug
Debugger="C:\Program Files\Debugging Tools for Windows\cdb.exe" -p %ld -e
%ld -g -c ".dump /o /ma /u c:\UserDumps\new.dmp; q"
```

When we have a crash *cdb.exe* will be launched, and the following console window will appear:

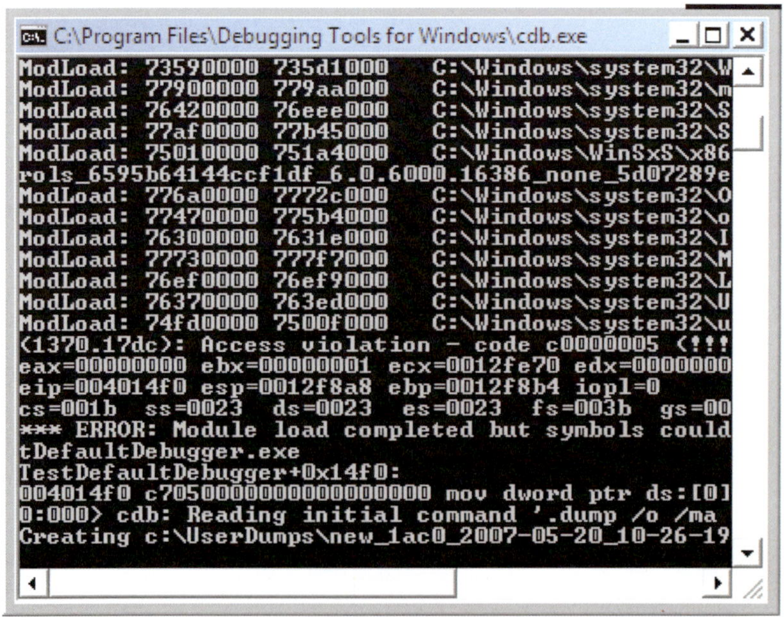

The advantage of using CDB or WinDbg is that we can omit **q** from the **-c** command line option and leave our debugger window open for further process inspection.

Note: We can also use Procdump Sysinternals tool instead of *userdump.exe*.

Resurrecting Dr. Watson in Vista

Feeling nostalgic about the pre-Vista time, I recalled that one month before upgrading my Windows XP to Vista, I saved the copy of Dr. Watson (*drwtsn32.exe*). Of course, during the upgrade, *drwtsn32.exe* was removed from the *system32* folder. Then I copied it back and set it as a default postmortem debugger from the elevated command prompt:

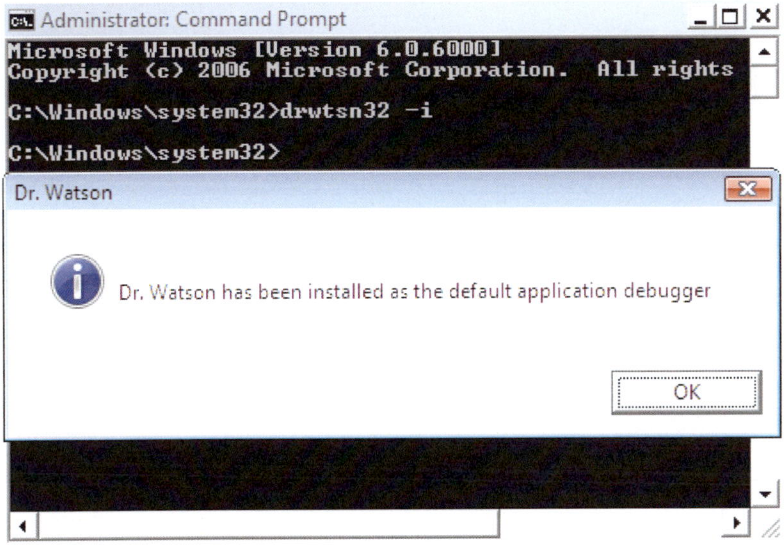

When I looked at the registry, I found the correctly set key values:

```
HKEY_LOCAL_MACHINE\SOFTWARE\Microsoft\Windows NT\CurrentVersion\AeDebug
Debugger=drwtsn32 -p %ld -e %ld -g
Auto=1
```

Auto=1 means do not show the error message box, just go ahead and dump a process. Actually, with *Auto=0*, Dr. Watson doesn't work on my Vista.

I also configured Dr. Watson to store the log and full user dump in *c:\DrWatson* folder by running *drwtsn32.exe* from the same elevated command prompt:

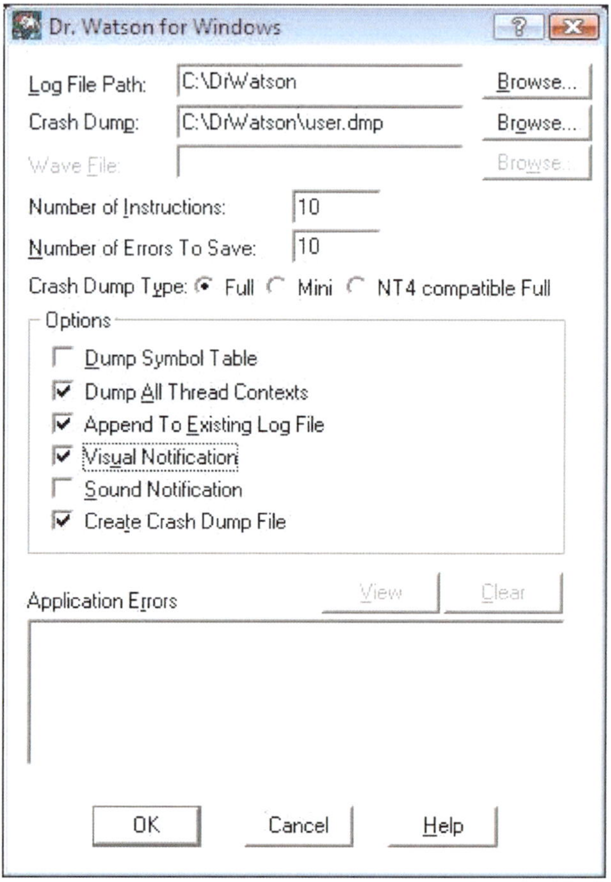

Next I launched **TestDefaultDebugger** (page 641) and hit the big crash button. Access violation happened, and I saw the familiar "Program Error" message box:

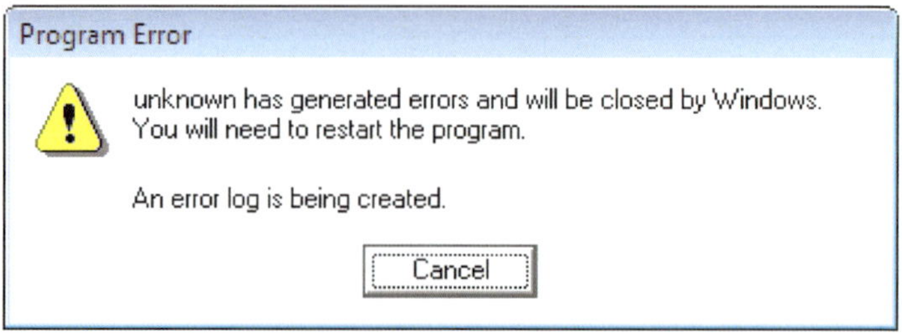

The log was created, and the user dump was saved in the specified folder. All subsequent crashes were appended to the log, and *user.dmp* was updated. When I opened the dump in WinDbg, I got the following output:

```
Loading Dump File [C:DrWatsonuser.dmp]
User Mini Dump File with Full Memory: Only application data is available
Comment: 'Dr. Watson generated MiniDump'
Symbol search path is:
SRV*c:\websymbols*http://msdl.microsoft.com/download/symbols
Executable search path is:
Windows Vista Version 6000 UP Free x86 compatible
Product: WinNt, suite: SingleUserTS
Debug session time: Sat May 19 20:52:23.000 2007 (GMT+1)
System Uptime: 5 days 20:00:04.062
Process Uptime: 0 days 0:00:03.000
This dump file has an exception of interest stored in it.
The stored exception information can be accessed via .ecxr.
(1f70.1e0c): Access violation - code c0000005 (first/second chance not
available)
eax=00000000 ebx=00000001 ecx=0012fe70 edx=00000000 esi=00425ae8
edi=0012fe70
eip=004014f0 esp=0012f8a8 ebp=0012f8b4 iopl=0 nv up ei ng nz ac pe cy
cs=001b ss=0023 ds=0023 es=0023 fs=003b gs=0000 efl=00010297
TestDefaultDebugger!CTestDefaultDebuggerDlg::OnBnClickedButton1:
004014f0 c70500000000000000000 mov dword ptr ds:[0],0
ds:0023:00000000=????????
```

Therefore, I believe that if I saved ntsd.exe before upgrading to Vista, I would have been able to set it as a default postmortem debugger too.

Process Crash - Getting the Dump Manually

Sometimes we have process crashes with exception dialogs, but no memory dumps are saved due to some reason. For example, Dr. Watson limitation or NTSD doesn't save dumps on Windows 2000. Then one solution is to dump the process manually while it displays an error message. Customers and support engineers can use Microsoft userdump.exe for this purpose. Then looking at the dump, we would see the exception because it is processed by an exception handler that either shows the error dialog or creates a Windows Error Reporting process. Non-interactive services usually call *NtRaiseHardError* to let *csrss.exe* display a message. The following stack trace is from IE memory dump saved when WER error dialog box was shown:

```
0:000> k
ChildEBP RetAddr
0012973c 7c59a072 NTDLL!ZwWaitForSingleObject+0xb
00129764 7c57b3e9 KERNEL32!WaitForSingleObjectEx+0x71
00129774 00401b2f KERNEL32!WaitForSingleObject+0xf
0012a238 7918cd0e IEXPLORE!DwExceptionFilter+0x284
0012a244 03a3f0c3 mscoree!__CxxUnhandledExceptionFilter+0x46
0012a250 7c59bf8d msvcr71!__CxxUnhandledExceptionFilter+0x46
0012a984 715206e0 KERNEL32!UnhandledExceptionFilter+0x140
0012ee74 71520957 BROWSEUI!BrowserProtectedThreadProc+0x64
0012fef0 71762a0a BROWSEUI!SHOpenFolderWindow+0x1ec
0012ff10 00401ecd SHDOCVW!IEWinMain+0x108
0012ff60 00401f7d IEXPLORE!WinMainT+0x2dc
0012ffc0 7c5989a5 IEXPLORE!ModuleEntry+0x97
0012fff0 00000000 KERNEL32!BaseProcessStart+0x3d
```

If we disassemble *DwExceptionFilter* function, we see *CreateProcess* call:

```
0:000> ub IEXPLORE!DwExceptionFilter+0x284
IEXPLORE!DwExceptionFilter+0x263:
00401b0e call dword ptr [IEXPLORE!_imp__CreateProcessA (00401050)]
00401b14 test eax,eax
00401b16 je   IEXPLORE!DwExceptionFilter+0x2f6 (00401ba1)
00401b1c mov  dword ptr [ebp+7Ch],edi
00401b1f mov  edi,dword ptr [IEXPLORE!_imp__WaitForSingleObject
(0040104c)]
00401b25 push 4E20h
00401b2a push dword ptr [ebp+68h]
00401b2d call edi
```

If we run **!analyze -v** command we are lucky because WinDbg finds the exception for us:

```
...
...
...
CONTEXT: 0012aa94 -- (.cxr 12aa94)
eax=00000000 ebx=00000000 ecx=00000000 edx=7283e058 esi=0271a60c
edi=00000000
eip=35c5f973 esp=0012ad60 ebp=0012ad7c iopl=0 nv up ei pl zr na pe nc
cs=001b ss=0023 ds=0023 es=0023 fs=0038 gs=0000 efl=00010246
componentA!InternalFoo+0x21:
35c5f973 8b01 mov eax,dword ptr [ecx] ds:0023:00000000=????????
...
...
...
STACK_TEXT:
0012ad7c 35c6042f 0012ae10 00000000 35c53390 componentA!InternalFoo+0x21
0012c350 779d7d5d 00000000 001ad114 00000000 componentA!InternalBar+0x157
0012c36c 77a2310e 02b23d5c 00000020 00000004 oleaut32!DispCallFunc+0x15d
0012c3fc 35cc8b60 024d2d94 02b23d5c 00000001
oleaut32!CTypeInfo2::Invoke+0x244
...
...
...
```

If we see several threads with *UnhandledExceptionFilter* - **Multiple Exceptions** pattern (page 255) - we can set the exception context individually based on the first parameter of *UnhandledExceptionFilter* which is a pointer to _EXCEPTION_POINTERS structure and then use **.cxr** command:

```
0:000> ~*kv
...
...
...
. 0 Id: 1568.68c Suspend: 1 Teb: 7ffde000 Unfrozen
ChildEBP RetAddr Args to Child
...
...
...
0012a984 715206e0 0012a9ac 7800bdb5 0012a9b4
KERNEL32!UnhandledExceptionFilter+0x140 (FPO: [Non-Fpo])
...
...
...
```

```
0:000> dt _EXCEPTION_POINTERS 0012a9ac
+0x000 ep_xrecord : 0x12aa78
+0x004 ep_context : 0x12aa94

0:000> .cxr 0012aa94
eax=00000000 ebx=00000000 ecx=00000000 edx=7283e058 esi=0271a60c
edi=00000000
eip=35c5f973 esp=0012ad60 ebp=0012ad7c iopl=0 nv up ei pl zr na pe nc
cs=001b ss=0023 ds=0023 es=0023 fs=0038 gs=0000 efl=00010246
componentA!InternalFoo+0x21:
35c5f973 8b01 mov eax,dword ptr [ecx] ds:0023:00000000=????????
```

Another stack fragment comes from a different Windows service, and it shows the thread calling *NtRaiseHardError* function:

```
0:000> ~*k
...
...
...
13 Id: 3624.16cc Suspend: 1 Teb: 7ffad000 Unfrozen
ChildEBP RetAddr
0148ed40 7c821b74 ntdll!KiFastSystemCallRet
0148ed44 77e99af9 ntdll!NtRaiseHardError+0xc
0148f3dc 77e84259 kernel32!UnhandledExceptionFilter+0x54b
0148f40c 7c82eeb2 kernel32!_except_handler3+0x61
0148f430 7c82ee84 ntdll!ExecuteHandler2+0x26
0148f4d8 7c82ecc6 ntdll!ExecuteHandler+0x24
0148f4d8 7c81e215 ntdll!KiUserExceptionDispatcher+0xe
0148f7e0 76133437 ntdll!RtlLengthSecurityDescriptor+0x2a
0148f80c 7613f33d serviceA!GetObjectSize+0x1c3
0148f8d0 77c70f3b serviceA!RpcGetObjectSize+0x1b
0148f8f8 77ce23f7 rpcrt4!Invoke+0x30
0148fcf8 77ce26ed rpcrt4!NdrStubCall2+0x299
0148fd14 77c709be rpcrt4!NdrServerCall2+0x19
0148fd48 77c7093f rpcrt4!DispatchToStubInCNoAvrf+0x38
0148fd9c 77c70865 rpcrt4!RPC_INTERFACE::DispatchToStubWorker+0x117
0148fdc0 77c734b1 rpcrt4!RPC_INTERFACE::DispatchToStub+0xa3
...
...
...
```

Upgrading Dr. Watson

I have been using NTSD as a default debugger on my laptop for a while and decided to revert it to Dr. Watson to get a couple of logs. Unfortunately, Dr. Watson itself crashed in *dbghelp.dll*. Loading *drwtsn32.exe* dump file reveals that it depends on both *dbghelp.dll* and *dbgeng.dll*. I tried to replace these DLLs with newer versions from the latest Debugging Tools for Windows and found that this change in *system32* folder is immediately reverted to original file versions. Instead of battling against Windows, I decided to create a completely separate Dr. Watson folder and copy *drwtsn32.exe*, the latest *dbghelp.dll* and *dbgeng.dll* from Debugging Tools for Windows there. Then I altered "Debugger" value under the following key to include the full path to *drwtsn32.exe*:

```
HKEY_LOCAL_MACHINE\SOFTWARE\Microsoft\Windows NT\CurrentVersion\AeDebug
Debugger=c:\drwatson\drwtsn32 -p %ld -e %ld -g
```

This solved the problem. Dr. Watson now uses the latest debugging engine to save dumps and logs.

Savedump.exe and Pagefile

I was curious about what *savedump.exe* does. And after some research, I found that in Windows 2000, it is a part of the logon process where it copies the crash dump section from the pagefile to a memory dump and also creates a minidump file.

On Windows 2003 and XP *savedump.exe* doesn't touch the pagefile. Session manager *smss.exe* truncates the pagefile and renames it to *dumpxxx.dmp* file (copying it to the boot volume if necessary). Then *savedump.exe* process copies that file to the correct location and then creates the minidump file.

I couldn't find *savedump.exe* in Vista. It looks like it was finally removed there.

Dumping Vista

32-bit Vista

If we need to dump a running 32-bit Vista system, we can do it with **SystemDump** tool (page 646). We just need to run it with elevated administrator rights:

- Right click *SystemDump.exe* in the appropriate Computer explorer folder and choose "Run as administrator."
- If we want to use command-line options, run *SystemDump.exe* from an elevated command prompt (Start -> All Programs -> Accessories, right-click Command Prompt and then select "Run as administrator").

Here is a screenshot before dumping my Vista system and WinDbg output from the saved kernel dump:

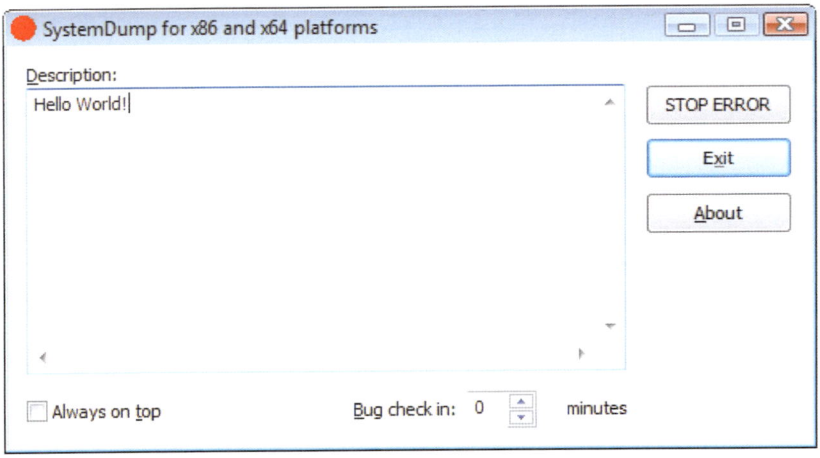

```
Loading Dump File [C:\Windows\MEMORY.DMP]
Kernel Summary Dump File: Only kernel address space is available
Windows Vista Kernel Version 6000 UP Free x86 compatible
Product: WinNt, suite: TerminalServer SingleUserTS
Built by: 6000.16386.x86fre.vista_rtm.061101-2205
Kernel base = 0x81800000 PsLoadedModuleList = 0x81908ab0
Debug session time: Sat Jan 27 20:13:10.917 2007 (GMT+0)
System Uptime: 0 days 1:33:13.589
Loading Kernel Symbols
Loading User Symbols
Loading unloaded module list
BugCheck E2, {cccccccc, 83286f08, 1a, 0}
Probably caused by : SystemDump.sys
```

64-bit Vista

Currently, to use 64-bit SystemDump, we have to disable "Driver Signature Enforcement" by any of these:

- F8 Advanced Boot Option.
- Command line tool BCDedit.
- Attaching an active kernel debugger.

Then we need to run *SystemDump64.exe* as administrator.

Dumping Processes without Breaking Them

We can do it on any Windows system after Windows 2000 without installing any additional tools like Userdump or WinDbg. And a process is not interrupted while its memory dump is being saved and continues to work. We can use the following command:

```
ntsd -pvr -p 'PID' -c ".dump /ma /u process.dmp; q"
```

PID is a decimal process ID we can get from Task Manager, for example.

Note: On x64 system to dump a 32-bit process (shown as *32 in Task Manager)we need to use NTSD from *\Windows\SysWOW64* folder (page 633). On Windows Vista, NTSD is no longer included but it can be found in Debugging Tools for Windows package.

Userdump.exe on x64

If we install the latest Microsoft user mode process dumper on x64 Windows, we see both x86 and x64 folders.

One advice here: do not dump 32-bit applications and services (shown as *32 in Task Manager) using *userdump.exe* from x64 folder: use *userdump.exe* from x86 folder. A 32-bit application runs in the WOW64 emulation layer in x64 Windows, and that emulation layer is itself native 64-bit process, so x64 *userdump.exe* saves that emulation layer and not the original 32-bit application. If we open that dump file in WinDbg, we see WOW64 thread stacks and not thread stacks from our original 32-bit application.

In summary, in x64 Windows, to save a memory dump file of a 64-bit application, we can use:

- *x64\userdump.exe*
- *\Windows\System32\ntsd.exe*
- 64-bit version of *WinDbg.exe*

To save a memory dump file of a 32-bit application we should use:

- *x86\userdump.exe*
- *\Windows\SysWOW64\ntsd.exe*
- 32-bit *WinDbg.exe*

Note: Now it is recommended to use Procdump Sysinternals tool or Task Manager.

NTSD on x64 Windows

If we need to attach NTSD to a process on x64 Windows and to save a memory dump file, we should remember that there are two versions of NTSD: x86 (32-bit) and x64. The former is located in *\Windows\SysWOW64* folder and should be used for attaching to 32-bit applications and services. For an explanation of why you need different versions of NTSD, please refer to the first picture in **Dumps, Debuggers, and Virtualization** (page 516).

If we use WinDbg for that purpose, we should install both 32-bit and 64-bit versions. If we want to install NTSD or WinDbg as a default postmortem debugger for 32-bit processes we should use *Wow6432Node* registry hive:

```
HKEY_LOCAL_MACHINE\SOFTWARE\Wow6432Node\Microsoft\Windows
NT\CurrentVersion\AeDebug

Debugger = ntsd -p %ld -e %ld -g -c ".dump /ma /u c:\TEMP\new.dmp; q"
```

Need a Dump? Common Use Cases

The most common scenarios technical support people encounter when facing the need to create a dump file are:

- Heap corruption

- CPU spikes

- No user dumps saved by Dr. Watson (or LocalDumps WER registry key after Windows Vista)

- Memory leak

  https://support.citrix.com/article/CTX106970

  The article applies to any process.

- Need a system dump from a remote session? Use NotMyFault tool (post-Windows Vista).

- Incorrect dump

  Use *dumpchk.exe* from Debugging Tools for Windows.

PART 12: Tools

Memory Dump Analysis Using Excel

Some WinDbg commands output data in a tabular format, so it is possible to save their output into a text file, import it into Excel and do sorting, filtering, and graph visualization. Some commands from WinDbg include:

- **!stacks 1** - Lists all threads with Ticks column so we can sort and filter threads that had been waiting for no more than 100 ticks, for example.
- **!irpfind** – Here, we can create various histograms, for example, IRP distribution based on [Driver] column.

The following graph depicts thread distribution in PID - TID coordinates on a busy multiprocessor system with 25 user sessions and more than 3,000 threads:

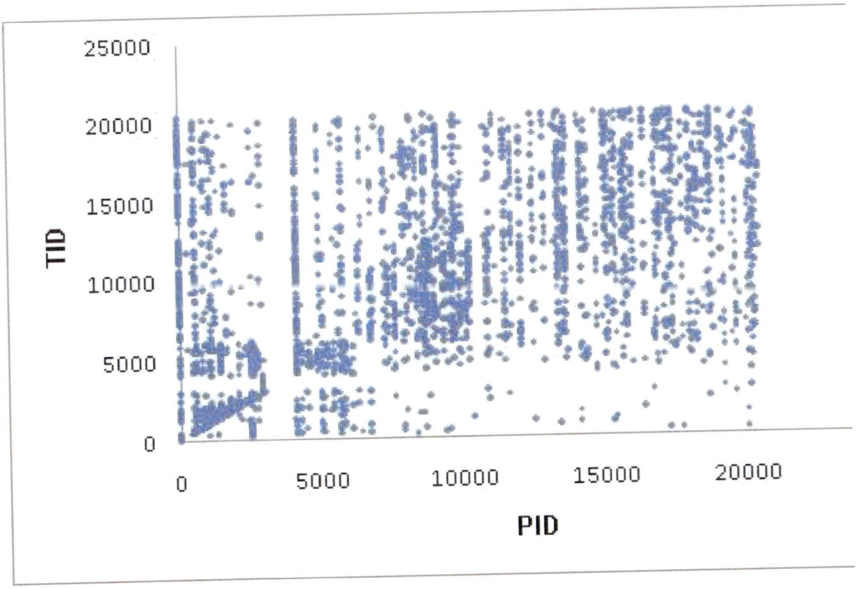

WinDbg scripts offer the possibility to output various tabulated data via **.printf**:

```
0:000> .printf "a\tb\tc"
a         b         c
```

TestDefaultDebugger.NET

Sometimes there are situations when we need to test exception handling to see whether it works and how to get dumps or logs from it. For example, a customer reports infrequent process crashes, but no crash dumps are saved. Then we can try some application that crashes immediately to see whether it results in error messages and saved crash dumps. That was the motivation behind TestDefaultDebugger package. Unfortunately, it contains only native applications, and we also needed to test .NET CLR exception handling and see what messages it shows in an environment. This is a simple program in C# that creates an empty Stack object and then calls its Pop method which triggers "Stack empty" exception:

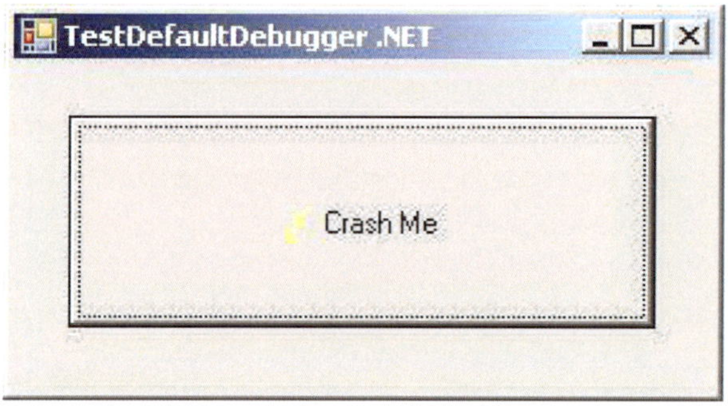

The updated package now includes *TestDefaultDebugger.NET.exe* and can be downloaded from Citrix support web site: http://support.citrix.com/article/CTX111901

Note: It is now a more improved version called TestWER.

Cons of Symbol Server

Symbol servers are great. However, I found that in crash dump analysis, the absence of automatically loaded symbols sometimes helps to identify a problem or at least gives some directions for further research. It also helps to see which hotfixes or service packs for a product were installed on a problem computer. The scenario I use sometimes when I analyze crash dumps from product A is the following:

1. Set up WinDbg to point to Microsoft Symbol Server
2. Load a crash dump and enter various commands based on the issue. Some OS or product A components become visible, and their symbols are unresolved.
3. From unresolved OS symbols, I'm aware of the latest fixes or privates from Microsoft
4. From unresolved symbols of product A and PDBFinder tool, I determine the base product level, and this already gives me some directions.
5. I add the base product A symbols to the symbol file path and continue my analysis.
6. If unresolved symbols of product A continue to come up, I use the PDBFinder tool again to find corresponding symbols and add them to the symbol file path. By doing that, I'm aware of the product A hot fix and service pack level.
7. Also, from the PDBFinder tool, I know whether there are any updates to the component in question.

Of course, all of this only works if we store all PDB files from all our fixes and service packs in some location(s) with easily identified names or abbreviations, for example, *PRODUCTA\VER20\SP31\FIX01*. Manually adding symbols helps to be focused on components, gives attention to some threads where they appear. We might think it is a waste of time, but it only takes very small percentage of the time, especially if we look at the memory dump for a couple of hours.

What is the PDBFinder tool? It is a program I developed to find the right symbol files (especially for minidumps). It scans all locations for PDB or DBG files and adds them to a binary database. Next time we run the PDBFinder tool, it loads that database, and we can find PDB or DBG file location by specifying the module name and its date. We can also do a fuzzy search by specifying a date interval. If we run it with *-update* command-line option, it builds the database automatically, useful for scheduling weekly updates.

StressPrinters: Stressing Printer Autocreation

Printer drivers are a great source of crash dumps, especially in Citrix and Microsoft terminal services environments. Bad printer drivers crash or hang spooler service (*spoolsv.exe*) when multiple users connect to a server.

Most of the bad drivers were designed and implemented for use in a single user environment without considering multithreading in mind. Some bad drivers display a dialog box every time the printer is created. Because this is done on a server-side, users cannot dismiss it unless spooler service is configured to interact with the desktop, and an administrator sees the dialog box. Some drivers are linked to a debug run-time library, and every exception brings up a dialog effectively hanging the thread and sometimes the whole spooler service if there was heap corruption, for example.

Therefore before allowing terminal services users to use certain printers, it is good to simulate multiple users trying to create particular printers to determine bad drivers and other printer components. Originally Citrix had a very popular command-line AddPrinter tool for this purpose. It has been replaced by **StressPrinters** tool where I designed and implemented GUI to set various options, coordination of multiple AddPrinter command-line tools launched simultaneously with different parameters, and overall log file management. We can even export settings to a file and import it on another server. The tool also has 64-bit executables to test printer auto-creation on x64 Windows.

The tool detects spooler crashes (if spoolsv.exe suddenly disappears from a process list), so we can check for crash dumps saved if we set up a default postmortem debugger (Dr. Watson or NTSD). If we see the progress bar hanging for a long time, then we can dump the spooler service using Microsoft userdump.exe to check for any stuck threads and resource contention.

You can read the documentation and download this tool from Citrix support:

StressPrinters for 32-bit and 64-bit platforms
http://support.citrix.com/article/CTX109374

InstantDump (JIT Process Dumper)

Techniques utilizing user mode process dumpers and debuggers like Microsoft userdump.exe, Procdump, NTSD, or WinDbg and CDB from Debugging Tools for Windows are too slow to pick up a process and dump it. We need either to attach a debugger manually or to run the command-line prompt or to switch to Task Manager. This deficiency was the primary motivation for me to use JIT (just-in-time) technology for process dumpers. The new tool, **InstantDump**, dumps a process instantly and non-invasively in a moment when we need it. How does it work? We point to any window and press a hotkey.

InstantDump could be useful to study hang GUI processes or to get several dumps of the same process during some period of time (CPU spiking case or memory leak, for example) or just dump the process for the sake of dumping it (for curiosity). The tool uses tooltips to dynamically display window information.

Here is the short user guide:

1. The program runs only on XP/W2K3/Vista (in fact, it does not load on Windows 2000).
2. Run *InstantDump.exe* on a 32-bit system or *InstantDump64.exe* on x64 Windows. If we attempt to run *InstantDump.exe* on x64 Windows it shows this message box and quits:

3. InstantDump puts itself into task bar icon notification area:

4. By default, when we move the mouse pointer over windows, the tooltip follows the cursor describing the process and thread id and process image path (we can disable tips in the Options dialog box):

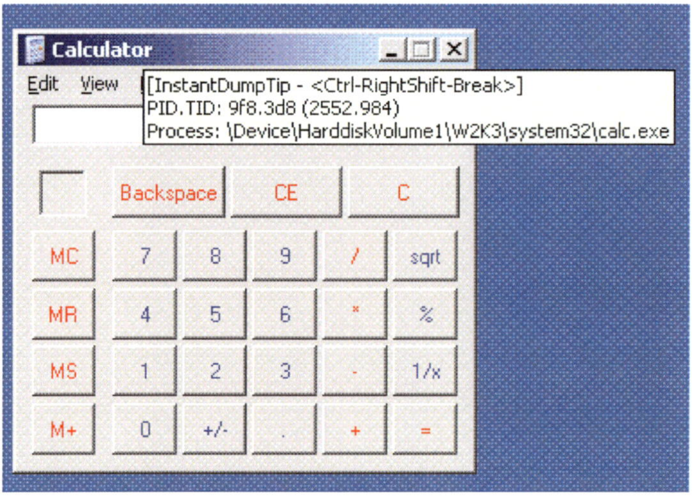

If we hold Ctrl-RightShift-Break for less than a second then the process (which window is under the cursor) is dumped according to the settings for external process dumper in the Options dialog (accessible via task bar icon right mouse click):

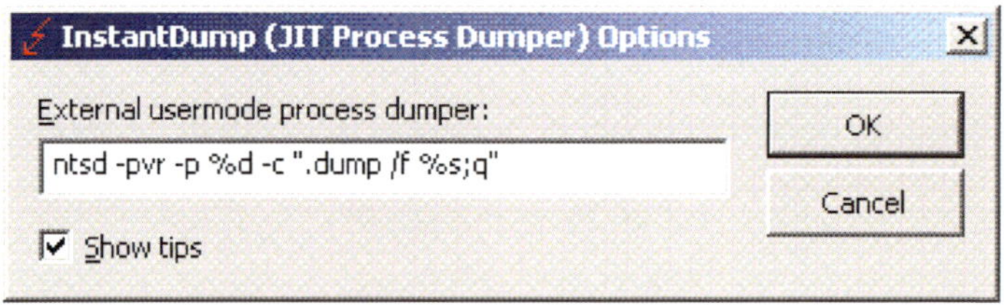

The saved dump name will be (in our Calculator window case): *calc.exe_9f8(2552)_22-17-56_18-Feb-2007.dmp*

There is no NTSD in Vista, so we have to use another user mode dumper, for example, install Microsoft *userdump.exe* and specify the following command line in Options dialog:

```
userdump.exe %d %s
```

Or resort to WinDbg or CDB command line, or Procdump Sysinternals tool.

Note: There is a replacement tool Window2Dump that does similar functionality:

https://bitbucket.org/softwarediagnostics/window2dump

TestDefaultDebugger

It often happens that support engineers advise customers to change their default postmortem debugger to NTSD. But there is no way to test new settings unless an application crashes again. And some customers come back saying that dump files are not saved despite the new settings and we don't know whether dump files were not saved because a crash hadn't yet happened, or default debugger hadn't been configured correctly, or something else had happened.

In addition, the arrival of 64-bit Windows brings another problem: there are two default postmortem debuggers on 64-bit Windows, one for 32-bit, and one for 64-bit applications respectively (page 633).

The new tool **TestDefaultDebugger** forces a crash on itself to test the presence and configuration of a default postmortem debugger (Dr. Watson, NTSD, or other). Then if the default postmortem debugger is configured correctly, OS launches it to save a memory dump of *TestDefaultDebugger.exe* process.

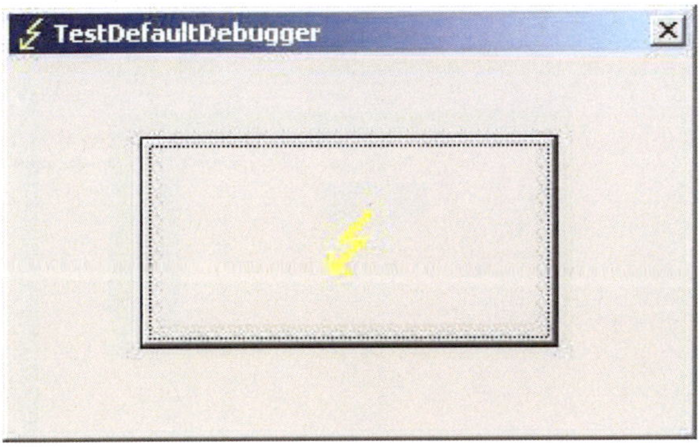

If we enabled NTSD as a default postmortem debugger the following console window would briefly appear:

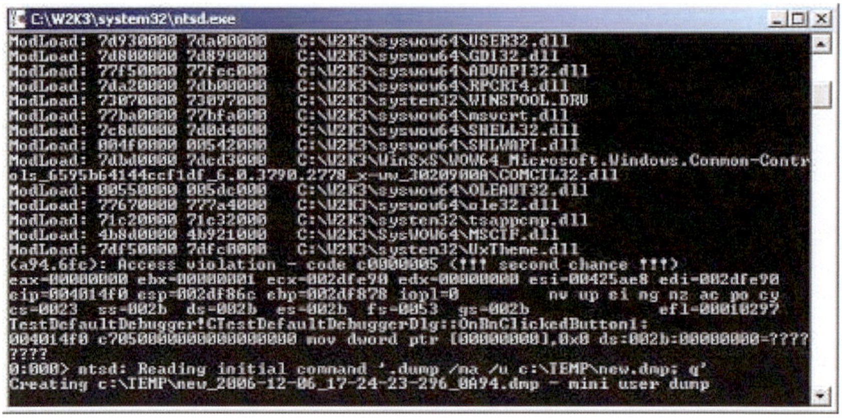

Postmortem debuggers are explained on page 28.

In 64-bit Windows, we can run both 32-bit *TestDefaultDebugger.exe* and 64-bit *TestDefaultDebugger64.exe* applications and then open crash dumps to see whether both postmortem debuggers have been configured properly. The tool also has a command-line interface so we can use it remotely:

```
c:\>TestDefaultDebugger.exe now
```

We can download the tool from Citrix support web site (it is now called TestWER):

TestWER (Test Windows Error Reporting)
http://support.citrix.com/article/CTX111901

DumpAlerts

The tool monitors folders where dumps can be saved, including Dr. Watson, a folder specified when NTSD is set as a default debugger. It then alerts a user, administrator, or software vendor whenever a new dump file is saved:

- The icon in System Tray changes its color from green to red
- Popup window appears until dismissed
- E-mail is sent to a specified address
- Sound is played
- The custom action is executed, for example, automatically launching WinDbg.exe with the latest memory dump file or copying it to an FTP server

All actions are fully configurable and can be enabled or disabled. Here is the screenshot of the main window:

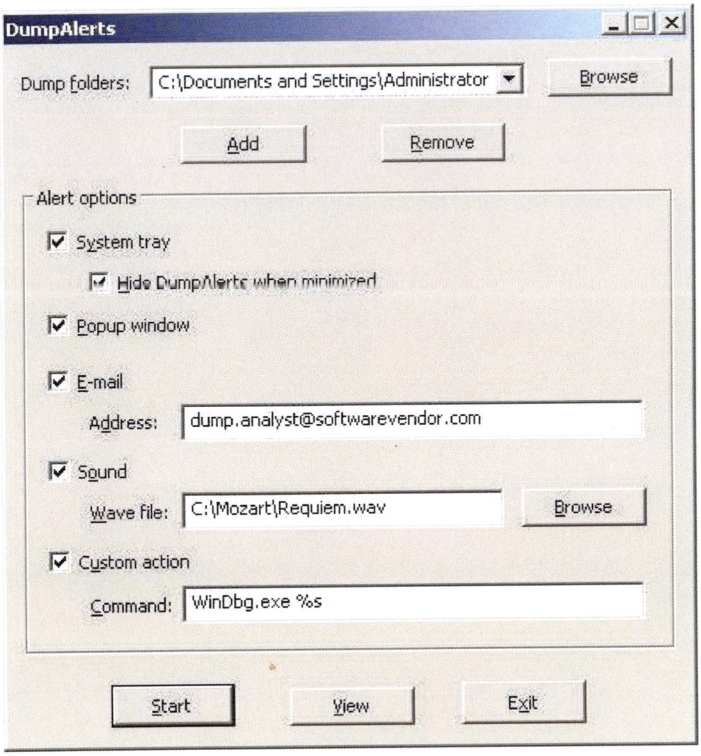

DumpDepends

There are many cases where we need to dump several processes simultaneously, and a complete memory dump is not an option. **DumpDepends** tool dumps processes and optionally packages them into a CAB file. There are several options:

- Dump all processes
- Dump essential services (Terminal, Printing, Spooler, *svchost.exe*)
- Dump all processes from the given session ID (additionally including children and necessary services if needed)
- Dump an individual process (optionally including children and necessary services)

The tool will use external process dumpers in a noninvasive manner (NTSD by default or any other specified, like *userdump.exe*). On x64, it distinguishes between 32-bit and 64-bit processes and dumps them accordingly. The command-line option is also available.

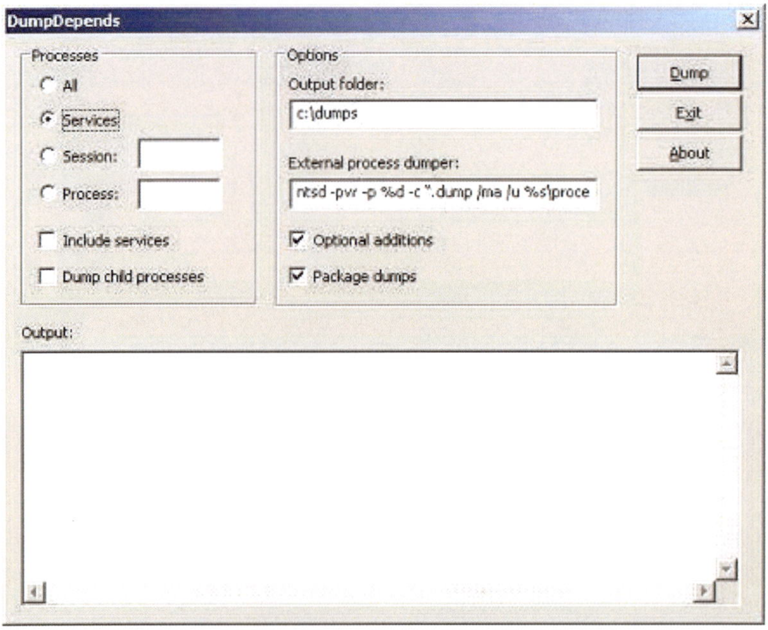

Dump Monitor Suite

Ramzy Mansour from Citrix Technical Support came up with a brilliant idea about **Dump Monitor Suite** and its two useful components for Citrix and Microsoft administrators:

DumpStats:

- Monitors and displays a graphical chart showing which services and processes crashed or hung on an individual server, their crash time and date, dump location, dump type, crash signature, and modules where crashes happened.
- Aggregates and displays statistics for the whole server farm.

DumpAlerts:

- Sends an e-mail alert and an SMS message to a cell phone when any crash or hang happens.
- Configures alerts based on the severity and specific processes.

Additionally, **Dump Monitor Suite** includes the following components (some of them already exist):

DumpChecks:

This is an enhanced and improved version of Citrix DumpCheck Explorer extension and its command-line version.

DumpProperties:

New Explorer extension (Properties dialog) which shows various data extracted from a dump, like process name, module list, whether heap checking was enabled and module name where crash happened.

DumpDepends:

This is an Integrated and enhanced version of SystemDump, which allows dumping dependent processes.

SystemDump

It was previously called CtxBSOD v2.1 but was renamed to show its purpose better. In addition to renaming, I added a command-line option to dump a system remotely or from a command line locally without using its GUI interface. The main motivation to write this tool was the absence of similar tools for 64-bit Windows at that time. SystemDump can dump a 64-bit server too!

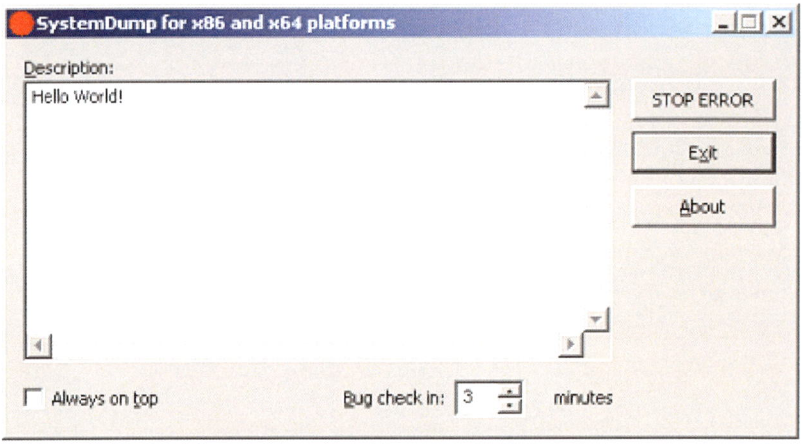

Main features:

- The tool has both GUI and command-line interfaces.
- We can type a message/text (or copy it from the clipboard) before forcing a memory dump. This message is saved in a dump file, and a support engineer can read it after loading the dump file in *WinDbg.exe*. This is implemented to encourage writing symptoms and conditions explaining why the dump has to be forced.
- The tool can stay on top of any window. We may need this to quickly dump the server after reproduction or during some activity.
- It is supplied with Program Database (PDB) symbols for the driver (32-bit and 64-bit), which is useful when we want to have all symbols to be present on the bug-check thread.
- The bugcheck clearly shows that the dump was manually generated.
- The tool can force a memory dump on both 32-bit and 64-bit platforms.
- Before forcing a fatal error on a server, the tool warns about potential damaging consequences: users are disconnected, and all the data which is not saved will be lost. It asks for confirmation.

- We can specify a period of time (in minutes) when to force a memory dump.

The latter feature is implemented entirely in kernel. The following command:

```
>SystemDump.exe abort
```

It allows us to abort the action if we ran the tool using command line options.

Here is the UML component diagram showing the architecture of this tool.

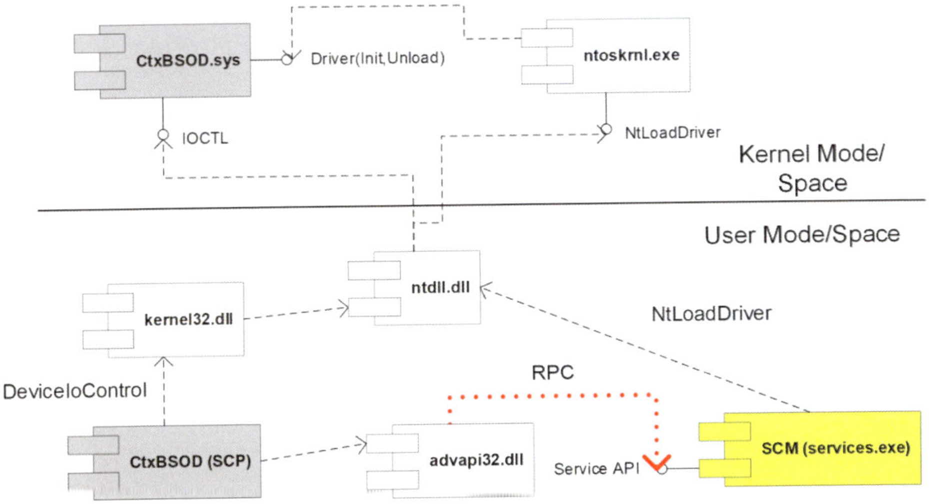

[This page is intentionally left blank]

PART 13: Miscellaneous

What is KiFastSystemCallRet?

This is a return function address for trap frames created for system calls on x86 post-W2K systems.

Since Pentium II, Microsoft changed OS call dispatching from an interrupt-driven INT /IRETD mechanism used in Windows NT and Windows 2000 to a faster optimized instruction sequence. This is SYSENTER / SYSEXIT pair on x86 32-bit Intel platforms and SYSCALL / SYSRET pair on x64 Intel and AMD platforms.

INT instruction saves a return address but SYSENTER doesn't. Let's look at a typical thread call stack a from complete memory dump coming from x86 Windows 2003 system:

```
1: kd> kL
ChildEBP RetAddr
a5a2ac64 80502d26 nt!KiSwapContext+0x2f
a5a2ac70 804faf20 nt!KiSwapThread+0x8a
a5a2ac98 805a4d6c nt!KeWaitForSingleObject+0x1c2
a5a2ad48 8054086c nt!NtReplyWaitReceivePortEx+0x3dc
a5a2ad48 7c91eb94 nt!KiFastCallEntry+0xfc
00a0fe18 7c91e399 ntdll!KiFastSystemCallRet
00a0fe1c 77e56703 ntdll!NtReplyWaitReceivePortEx+0xc
00a0ff80 77e56c22 RPCRT4!LRPC_ADDRESS::ReceiveLotsaCalls+0xf4
00a0ff88 77e56a3b RPCRT4!RecvLotsaCallsWrapper+0xd
00a0ffa8 77e56c0a RPCRT4!BaseCachedThreadRoutine+0x79
00a0ffb4 7c80b683 RPCRT4!ThreadStartRoutine+0x1a
00a0ffec 00000000 kernel32!BaseThreadStart+0x37
```

RPC module calls the native function to wait for a reply from an LPC port. Note that we disassemble the return address instead of the symbolic address because of OMAP Code Optimization:

```
1: kd> ub RPCRT4!LRPC_ADDRESS::ReceiveLotsaCalls+0xf4
                                                       ^ Unable to find valid
previous instruction for 'ub RPCRT4!LRPC_ADDRESS::ReceiveLotsaCalls+0xf4'
```

```
1: kd> ub 77e56703
RPCRT4!LRPC_ADDRESS::ReceiveLotsaCalls+0xd9:
77e566e8
e8edfeffff      call    RPCRT4!RpcpPurgeEEInfoFromThreadIfNecessary
(77e565da)
77e566ed ff75ec          push    dword ptr [ebp-14h]
77e566f0 8d45f0          lea     eax,[ebp-10h]
77e566f3 ff75f4          push    dword ptr [ebp-0Ch]
77e566f6 ff75fc          push    dword ptr [ebp-4]
77e566f9 50              push    eax
77e566fa ff7658          push    dword ptr [esi+58h]
77e566fd ff15b010e577    call    dword ptr
[RPCRT4!_imp__NtReplyWaitReceivePortEx (77e510b0)]

1: kd> dps 77e510b0 l1
77e510b0  7c91e38d ntdll!ZwReplyWaitReceivePortEx
```

NTDLL stub for the native function is small and transitions to level 0 via shared *SystemCallStub* immediately:

```
1: kd> uf ntdll!NtReplyWaitReceivePortEx
ntdll!ZwReplyWaitReceivePortEx:
7c91e38d mov     eax,0C4h
7c91e392 mov     edx,offset SharedUserData!SystemCallStub (7ffe0300)
7c91e397 call    dword ptr [edx]
7c91e399 ret     14h

1: kd> dps 7ffe0300 l3
7ffe0300  7c91eb8b ntdll!KiFastSystemCall
7ffe0304  7c91eb94 ntdll!KiFastSystemCallRet
7ffe0308  00000000

1: kd> uf ntdll!KiFastSystemCall
ntdll!KiFastSystemCall:
7c91eb8b mov     edx,esp
7c91eb8d sysenter
7c91eb8f nop
7c91eb90 nop
7c91eb91 nop
7c91eb92 nop
7c91eb93 nop
7c91eb94 ret
```

Before executing SYSENTER, ESP points to the following return address:

```
1: kd> u 7c91e399
ntdll!NtReplyWaitReceivePortEx+0xc:
7c91e399 ret     14h
```

SYSENTER instruction changes ESP and EIP to new values contained in machine-specific registers (MSR). As a result, EIP points to *nt!KiFastCallEntry*. After saving a trap frame and checking parameters, it calls *nt!NtReplyWaitReceivePortEx* address from the system function table. When the latter function returns KiFastCallEntry proceeds to *KiServiceExit* and *KiSystemCallExit2*:

```
1: kd> ub 8054086c
nt!KiFastCallEntry+0xe2:
80540852 mov     ebx,dword ptr [edi+eax*4]
80540855 sub     esp,ecx
80540857 shr     ecx,2
8054085a mov     edi,esp
8054085c cmp     esi,dword ptr [nt!MmUserProbeAddress (80561114)]
80540862 jae     nt!KiSystemCallExit2+0x9f (80540a10)
80540868 rep movs dword ptr es:[edi],dword ptr [esi]
8054086a call    ebx

1: kd> u
nt!KiFastCallEntry+0x105:
80540875 mov     edx,dword ptr [ebp+3Ch]
80540878 mov     dword ptr [ecx+134h],edx
nt!KiServiceExit:
8054087e cli
8054087f test    dword ptr [ebp+70h],20000h
80540886 jne     nt!KiServiceExit+0x10 (8054088e)
80540888 test    byte ptr [ebp+6Ch],1
8054088c je      nt!KiServiceExit+0x66 (805408e4)
8054088e mov     ebx,dword ptr fs:[124h]

1: kd> u
nt!KiSystemCallExit2+0x12:
80540983 sti
80540984 sysexit
```

Let's inspect the trap frame:

```
1: kd> kv5
ChildEBP RetAddr  Args to Child
a5a2ac64 80502d26 82ffc090 82ffc020 804faf20 nt!KiSwapContext+0x2f
a5a2ac70 804faf20 e12424b0 8055c0a0 e12424b0 nt!KiSwapThread+0x8a
a5a2ac98 805a4d6c 00000001 00000010 00000001
nt!KeWaitForSingleObject+0x1c2
a5a2ad48 8054086c 000000c8 00a0ff70 00000000
nt!NtReplyWaitReceivePortEx+0x3dc
a5a2ad48 7c91eb94 000000c8 00a0ff70 00000000 nt!KiFastCallEntry+0xfc
(TrapFrame @ a5a2ad64)
```

```
1: kd> .trap a5a2ad64
ErrCode = 00000000
eax=00000000 ebx=00000000 ecx=00a0fd6c edx=7c91eb94 esi=00159b38
edi=00000100
eip=7c91eb94 esp=00a0fe1c ebp=00a0ff80 iopl=0 nv up ei pl zr na pe nc
cs=001b ss=0023 ds=0023 es=0023 fs=003b gs=0000 efl=00000246
ntdll!KiFastSystemCallRet:
001b:7c91eb94 ret

1: kd> kL
  *** Stack trace for last set context - .thread/.cxr resets it
ChildEBP RetAddr
00a0fe18 7c91e399 ntdll!KiFastSystemCallRet
00a0fe1c 77e56703 ntdll!NtReplyWaitReceivePortEx+0xc
00a0ff80 77e56c22 RPCRT4!LRPC_ADDRESS::ReceiveLotsaCalls+0xf4
00a0ff88 77e56a3b RPCRT4!RecvLotsaCallsWrapper+0xd
00a0ffa8 77e56c0a RPCRT4!BaseCachedThreadRoutine+0x79
00a0ffb4 7c80b683 RPCRT4!ThreadStartRoutine+0x1a
00a0ffec 00000000 kernel32!BaseThreadStart+0x37
```

Therefore, it looks that the dummy *ntdll!KiFastSystemCallRet* function with one RET instruction is used to create a uniform trap frame across system calls. Otherwise, trap frames for different native API calls would have contained different return values.

Understanding I/O Completion Ports

Many articles and books explain Windows I/O completion ports from high-level design considerations arising when building high-performance server software. But it is hard to recall them later when someone asks to explain, and not everyone writes that software. Looking at complete memory dumps has an advantage of a bottom-up or reverse engineering approach where we see the internals of server software and can immediately grasp the implementation of certain architectural and design decisions.

Consider this thread stack trace we can find almost inside any service or network application process:

```
THREAD 86cf09c0  Cid 05cc.2030  Teb: 7ffd7000 Win32Thread: 00000000 WAIT:
(Unknown) UserMode Non-Alertable
    8a3bb970  QueueObject
    86cf0a38  NotificationTimer
Not impersonating
DeviceMap                 e15af5a8
Owning Process            8a3803d8       Image:         svchost.exe
Wait Start TickCount      2131621        Ticks: 1264 (0:00:00:19.750)
Context Switch Count      6
UserTime                  00:00:00.000
KernelTime                00:00:00.000
Win32 Start Address RPCRT4!ThreadStartRoutine (0x77c5de6d)
Start Address kernel32!BaseThreadStartThunk (0x77e6b5f3)
Stack Init ba276000 Current ba275c38 Base ba276000 Limit ba273000 Call 0
Priority 8 BasePriority 8 PriorityDecrement 0
ChildEBP RetAddr
ba275c50 8083d3b1 nt!KiSwapContext+0x26
ba275c7c 8083dea2 nt!KiSwapThread+0x2e5
ba275cc4 8092b205 nt!KeRemoveQueue+0x417
ba275d48 80833a6f nt!NtRemoveIoCompletion+0xdc
ba275d48 7c82ed54 nt!KiFastCallEntry+0xfc
0093feac 7c821bf4 ntdll!KiFastSystemCallRet
0093feb0 77e66142 ntdll!NtRemoveIoCompletion+0xc
0093fedc 77c604c3 kernel32!GetQueuedCompletionStatus+0x29
0093ff18 77c60655 RPCRT4!COMMON_ProcessCalls+0xa1
0093ff84 77c5f9f1 RPCRT4!LOADABLE_TRANSPORT::ProcessIOEvents+0x117
0093ff8c 77c5f7dd RPCRT4!ProcessIOEventsWrapper+0xd
0093ffac 77c5de88 RPCRT4!BaseCachedThreadRoutine+0x9d
0093ffb8 77e6608b RPCRT4!ThreadStartRoutine+0x1b
0093ffec 00000000 kernel32!BaseThreadStart+0x34
```

We see that I/O completion port is implemented via kernel queue object, so requests (work items, completion notifications) are stored in that queue for further processing by threads. The number of active threads processing requests is bound to some maximum value that usually corresponds to the number of processors:

```
0: kd> dt _KQUEUE 8a3bb970
ntdll!_KQUEUE
   +0x000 Header           : _DISPATCHER_HEADER
   +0x010 EntryListHead    : _LIST_ENTRY [ 0x8a3bb980 - 0x8a3bb980 ]
   +0x018 CurrentCount     : 0
   +0x01c MaximumCount     : 2
   +0x020 ThreadListHead   : _LIST_ENTRY [ 0x86cf0ac8 - 0x89ff9520 ]

0: kd> !smt
SMT Summary:
------------
   KeActiveProcessors: **------------------------------ (00000003)
        KiIdleSummary: **------------------------------ (00000003)
No PRCB     Set Master SMT Set                                     IAID
 0 ffdff120 Master     **—————————— (00000003)  00
 1 f772f120 ffdff120   **—————————— (00000003)  01
```

Kernel work queues are also implemented via the same queue object as we might have guessed already:

```
THREAD 8a777660  Cid 0004.00d0  Teb: 00000000 Win32Thread: 00000000 WAIT:
(Unknown) UserMode Non-Alertable
    808b707c  QueueObject
Not impersonating
DeviceMap                 e1000928
Owning Process            8a780818       Image:         System
Wait Start TickCount      2615           Ticks: 2130270 (0:09:14:45.468)
Context Switch Count      301
UserTime                  00:00:00.000
KernelTime                00:00:00.000
Start Address nt!ExpWorkerThread (0x8082d92b)
Stack Init f71e0000 Current f71dfcec Base f71e0000 Limit f71dd000 Call 0
Priority 12 BasePriority 12 PriorityDecrement 0
Kernel stack not resident.
ChildEBP RetAddr
f71dfd04 8083d3b1 nt!KiSwapContext+0x26
f71dfd30 8083dea2 nt!KiSwapThread+0x2e5
f71dfd78 8082d9c1 nt!KeRemoveQueue+0x417
f71dfdac 809208fc nt!ExpWorkerThread+0xc8
f71dfddc 8083fc9f nt!PspSystemThreadStartup+0x2e
00000000 00000000 nt!KiThreadStartup+0x16

0: kd> dt _KQUEUE 808b707c
ntdll!_KQUEUE
   +0x000 Header           : _DISPATCHER_HEADER
   +0x010 EntryListHead    : _LIST_ENTRY [ 0x808b708c - 0x808b708c ]
   +0x018 CurrentCount     : 0
   +0x01c MaximumCount     : 2
   +0x020 ThreadListHead   : _LIST_ENTRY [ 0x8a77a128 - 0x8a777768 ]
```

I've created the simple UML diagram showing a high-level relationship between various objects seen from crash dumps. Note that *Active Thread* object can process items from more than one completion port if its wait was satisfied for one port and then for another, but I have never seen this. *Waiting Thread* can wait only for one completion port.

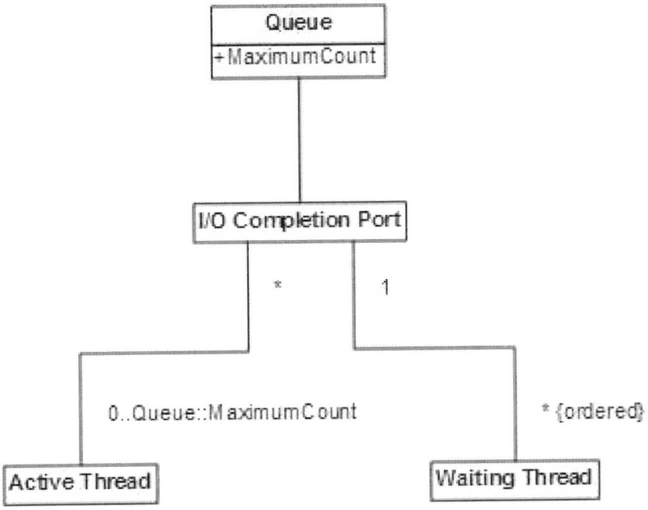

Symbol File Warnings

I started using new WinDbg 6.8.4.0 and found that it prints the following message twice when I open a process dump or a complete memory dump where the current context is from some user mode process:

```
0:000> !analyze -v
***
***    Your debugger is not using the correct symbols
***
***    In order for this command to work properly, your symbol path
***    must point to .pdb files that have full type information.
***
***    Certain .pdb files (such as the public OS symbols) do not
***    contain the required information.  Contact the group that
***    provided you with these symbols if you need this command to
***    work.
***
***    Type referenced: kernel32!pNlsUserInfo
***
```

Fortunately, *kernel32.dll* symbols were loaded correctly despite the warning:

```
0:000> lmv m kernel32
start    end        module name
77e40000 77f42000   kernel32   (pdb
symbols)          c:\mssymbols\kernel32.pdb\DF4F569C743446809ACD3DFD1E9FA2
AF2\kernel32.pdb
    Loaded symbol image file: kernel32.dll
    Image path: C:\WINDOWS\system32\kernel32.dll
    Image name: kernel32.dll
    Timestamp:        Tue Jul 25 13:31:53 2006 (44C60F39)
    CheckSum:         001059A9
    ImageSize:        00102000
    File version:     5.2.3790.2756
    Product version:  5.2.3790.2756
    File flags:       0 (Mask 3F)
    File OS:          40004 NT Win32
    File type:        2.0 Dll
    File date:        00000000.00000000
    Translations:     0409.04b0
    CompanyName:      Microsoft Corporation
    ProductName:      Microsoft® Windows® Operating System
    InternalName:     kernel32
    OriginalFilename: kernel32
    ProductVersion:   5.2.3790.2756
    FileVersion:      5.2.3790.2756 (srv03_sp1_gdr.060725-0040)
    FileDescription:  Windows NT BASE API Client DLL
    LegalCopyright:   © Microsoft Corporation. All rights reserved.
```

Double-checking return addresses on the stack trace shows that symbol mapping was correct:

```
kd> dpu kernel32!pNlsUserInfo l1
77ecb0a8  77ecb760 "ENU"

kd> kv
ChildEBP RetAddr  Args to Child
f552bbec f79e1743 000000e2 cccccccc 858a0470 nt!KeBugCheckEx+0x1b
WARNING: Stack unwind information not available. Following frames may be
wrong.
f552bc38 8081d39d 85699390 8596fe78 860515f8 SystemDump+0x743
f552bc4c 808ec789 8596fee8 860515f8 8596fe78 nt!IofCallDriver+0x45
f552bc60 808ed507 85699390 8596fe78 860515f8
nt!IopSynchronousServiceTail+0x10b
f552bd00 808e60be 00000090 00000000 00000000 nt!IopXxxControlFile+0x5db
f552bd34 80882fa8 00000090 00000000 00000000 nt!NtDeviceIoControlFile+0x2a
f552bd34 7c82ed54 00000090 00000000 00000000 nt!KiFastCallEntry+0xf8
0012efc4 7c8213e4 77e416f1 00000090 00000000 ntdll!KiFastSystemCallRet
0012efc8 77e416f1 00000090 00000000 00000000
ntdll!NtDeviceIoControlFile+0xc
0012f02c 00402208 00000090 9c400004 00947eb8
kernel32!DeviceIoControl+0x137
0012f884 00404f8e 0012fe80 00000001 00000000 SystemDump_400000+0x2208

kd> ub 77e416f1
kernel32!DeviceIoControl+0x11d:
77e416db lea     eax,[ebp-28h]
77e416de push    eax
77e416df push    ebx
77e416e0 push    ebx
77e416e1 push    ebx
77e416e2 push    dword ptr [ebp+8]
77e416e5 je      kernel32!DeviceIoControl+0x131 (77e417f3)
77e416eb call    dword ptr [kernel32!_imp__NtDeviceIoControlFile
(77e4103c)]
```

So everything is all right, and messages above shall be ignored.

Windows Service Crash Dumps in Vista

I was playing with Vista Platform SDK samples to create the minimal native Windows service that crashes to test various postmortem debugger configurations, Windows Error Reporting (WER) options and conditions under which crash dumps are available. Initially, I put a NULL pointer dereference into the service control handler, processing service stop command. Although the service crashed under WinDbg, I couldn't get CDB or NTSD configured as a default postmortem debugger to save the crash dump automatically. I tested under x64 Vista and Windows Server 2003 x64 both 32-bit and 64-bit versions of my service.

Here is the source code and stack trace from WinDbg when we attach it to the running service and then try to stop it:

```
//
// FUNCTION: service_ctrl
//
// PURPOSE: This function is called by the SCM whenever
// ControlService() is called on this service.
//
// PARAMETERS:
// dwCtrlCode - type of control requested
//
// RETURN VALUE:
// none
//
// COMMENTS:
//
VOID WINAPI service_ctrl(DWORD dwCtrlCode)
{
  // Handle the requested control code.
  //
  switch (dwCtrlCode)
  {
  case SERVICE_CONTROL_STOP:
    *(int *)NULL = 0;
    ReportStatusToSCMgr(SERVICE_STOP_PENDING, NO_ERROR, 0);
    ServiceStop();
    return;

  // Update the service status.
  //
  case SERVICE_CONTROL_INTERROGATE:
    break;
```

```
  // invalid control code
  //
  default:
    break;

  }

  ReportStatusToSCMgr(ssStatus.dwCurrentState, NO_ERROR, 0);
}

0:000> r
rax=0000000000000001 rbx=00000000001e36d0 rcx=0000000000000001
rdx=000000000a9ff32c rsi=0000000000000000 rdi=0000000000401aa0
rip=0000000000401ab9 rsp=000000000012fab0 rbp=00000000001e36d0
 r8=0000000000400000  r9=0000000077b3f990 r10=00000000004000d8
r11=00000000004000d8 r12=0000000000000000 r13=000000000a9ff32c
r14=00000000001e36e8 r15=000000000012fc20
iopl=0 nv up ei pl zr na po nc
cs=0033  ss=002b  ds=002b  es=002b  fs=0053  gs=002b  efl=00010246
simple!service_ctrl+0x19:
00000000`00401ab9 c704250000000000000000 mov dword ptr [0],0
ds:00000000`00000000=????????

0:000> k
Child-SP          RetAddr           Call Site
00000000`0012fab0 000007fe`fe276cee simple!service_ctrl+0x19
00000000`0012faf0 000007fe`fe2cea5d ADVAPI32!ScDispatcherLoop+0x54c
00000000`0012fbf0 00000000`004019f5
ADVAPI32!StartServiceCtrlDispatcherA+0x8d
00000000`0012fe70 00000000`00408b8c simple!main+0x155
00000000`0012fec0 00000000`0040895e simple!__tmainCRTStartup+0x21c
00000000`0012ff30 00000000`7792cdcd simple!mainCRTStartup+0xe
00000000`0012ff60 00000000`77a7c6e1 kernel32!BaseThreadInitThunk+0xd
00000000`0012ff90 00000000`00000000 ntdll!RtlUserThreadStart+0x1d
```

If we put *while(1);* code instead of NULL pointer dereference, the process is interrupted via the breakpoint and then terminated. There is no postmortem dump saved too. Therefore it looks like any fault inside the service main thread is not allowed to execute the potentially blocking operation of unhandled exception filter perhaps to avoid blocking the service control manager (SCM) communicating with service dispatcher code.

On Vista, if Windows Error Reporting service is running and WER is configured in Control Panel to allow a user to choose reporting settings we get the following familiar dialog but without Debug option to attach a postmortem debugger and save a crash dump:

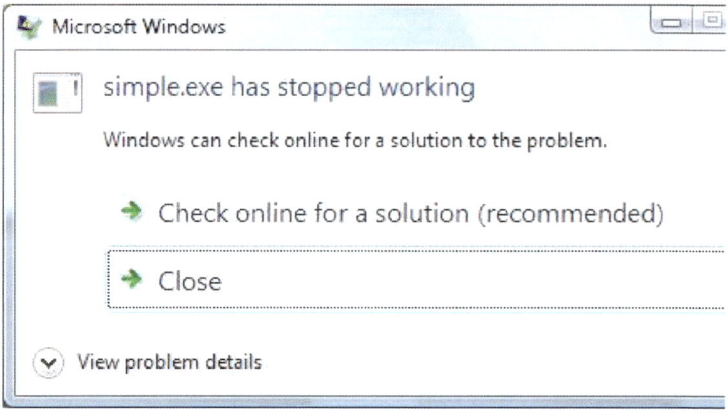

If we choose the recommended option, we get the following dialog showing the path where a minidump file was temporarily stored:

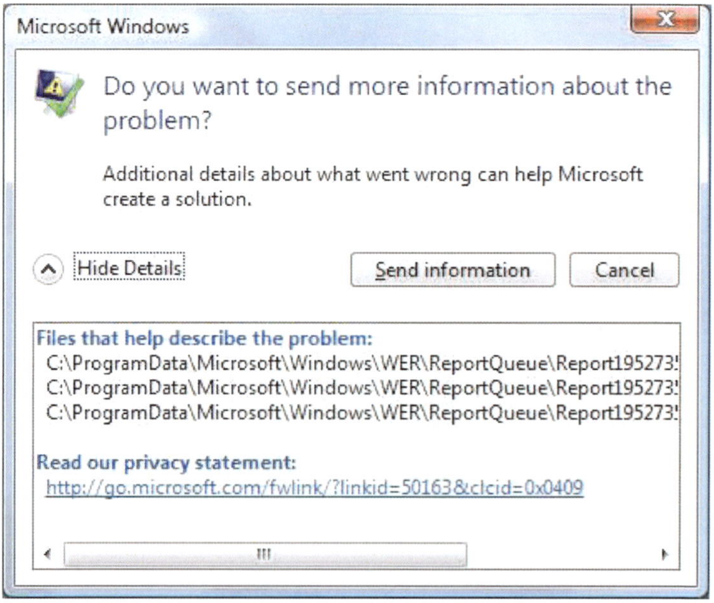

We need to leave this dialog open if we want to open the crash dump or copy it to another location; otherwise, report files are removed as soon as we dismiss the dialog box. They may be stored temporarily in another location. In the latter case, we can check this in *Problem Reports and Solutions\View Problem History* in Control Panel. If we open the crash dump using WinDbg we get the same stack trace that we got previously during live debugging:

```
Loading Dump File
[C:\ProgramData\Microsoft\Windows\WER\ReportQueue\Report19527353
\WER7346.tmp.mdmp]
User Mini Dump File: Only registers, stack and portions of memory are
available

Symbol search path is:
srv*c:\mss*http://msdl.microsoft.com/download/symbols
Executable search path is:
Windows Vista Version 6000 MP (2 procs) Free x64
Product: WinNt, suite: SingleUserTS
Debug session time: Fri Sep 28 16:36:38.000 2007 (GMT+1)
System Uptime: 2 days 1:42:22.810
Process Uptime: 0 days 0:00:10.000
.....
This dump file has an exception of interest stored in it.
The stored exception information can be accessed via .ecxr.
(13b0.d54): Access violation - code c0000005 (first/second chance not
available)
simple!service_ctrl+0x19:
00000000`00401ab9 c704250000000000000000 mov dword ptr [0],0
ds:00000000`00000000=????????

0:000> k
Child-SP          RetAddr           Call Site
00000000`0012fab0 000007fe`fe276cee simple!service_ctrl+0x19
00000000`0012faf0 000007fe`fe2cea5d advapi32!ScDispatcherLoop+0x54c
00000000`0012fbf0 00000000`004019f5
advapi32!StartServiceCtrlDispatcherA+0x8d
00000000`0012fe70 00000000`00408b8c simple!main+0x155
00000000`0012fec0 00000000`0040895e simple!__tmainCRTStartup+0x21c
00000000`0012ff30 00000000`7792cdcd simple!mainCRTStartup+0xe
00000000`0012ff60 00000000`77a7c6e1 kernel32!BaseThreadInitThunk+0xd
00000000`0012ff90 00000000`00000000 ntdll!RtlUserThreadStart+0x1d
```

Fault in any other service thread, for example, the one that SCM starts per every SERVICE_TABLE_ENTRY in dispatch table results in a default postmortem debugger saving a crash dump in Windows Server 2003 x64 but not in Vista x64 or Vista x86 (32-bit):

```
void __cdecl main(int argc, char **argv)
{
  SERVICE_TABLE_ENTRY dispatchTable[] =
  {
  { TEXT(SZSERVICENAME), (LPSERVICE_MAIN_FUNCTION)service_main},
  { NULL, NULL}
  };
  ...
  ...
  ...
  if (!StartServiceCtrlDispatcher(dispatchTable))
```

```
    AddToMessageLog(TEXT("StartServiceCtrlDispatcher failed."));
}

void WINAPI service_main(DWORD dwArgc, LPTSTR *lpszArgv)
{
  // register our service control handler:
  //
  sshStatusHandle = RegisterServiceCtrlHandler( TEXT(SZSERVICENAME),
service_ctrl);

  if (!sshStatusHandle)
    goto cleanup;

  // SERVICE_STATUS members that don't change in example
  //
  ssStatus.dwServiceType = SERVICE_WIN32_OWN_PROCESS;
  ssStatus.dwServiceSpecificExitCode = 0;

  // report the status to the service control manager.
  //
  if (!ReportStatusToSCMgr(
      SERVICE_START_PENDING, // service state
      NO_ERROR, // exit code
      3000)) // wait hint
    goto cleanup;
  *(int *)NULL = 0;
  ...
  ...
  ...
}
```

It seems the only way to get a crash minidump for analysis is to copy it from the report data as I explained above:

```
Loading Dump File
[C:\ProgramData\Microsoft\Windows\WER\ReportQueue\Report0fa05f9d
\WER5F42.tmp.mdmp]
User Mini Dump File: Only registers, stack and portions of memory are
available

Symbol search path is:
srv*c:\mss*http://msdl.microsoft.com/download/symbols
Executable search path is:
Windows Vista Version 6000 MP (2 procs) Free x64
Product: WinNt, suite: SingleUserTS
Debug session time: Fri Sep 28 17:50:06.000 2007 (GMT+1)
System Uptime: 0 days 0:30:59.495
Process Uptime: 0 days 0:00:04.000
.....
This dump file has an exception of interest stored in it.
The stored exception information can be accessed via .ecxr.
```

```
(d6c.fcc): Access violation - code c0000005 (first/second chance not
available)
simple!service_main+0x60:
00000000`00401aa0 c70425000000000000000000 mov dword ptr [0],0
ds:00000000`00000000=????????

0:001> ~*k

   0  Id: d6c.cf4 Suspend: 0 Teb: 000007ff`fffdd000 Unfrozen
Child-SP          RetAddr           Call Site
00000000`0012f978 00000000`777026da ntdll!NtReadFile+0xa
00000000`0012f980 000007fe`feb265aa kernel32!ReadFile+0x8a
00000000`0012fa10 000007fe`feb262e3 advapi32!ScGetPipeInput+0x4a
00000000`0012faf0 000007fe`feb7ea5d advapi32!ScDispatcherLoop+0x9a
00000000`0012fbf0 00000000`004019f5
advapi32!StartServiceCtrlDispatcherA+0x8d
00000000`0012fe70 00000000`00408bac simple!main+0x155
00000000`0012fec0 00000000`0040897e simple!__tmainCRTStartup+0x21c
00000000`0012ff30 00000000`7770cdcd simple!mainCRTStartup+0xe
00000000`0012ff60 00000000`7792c6e1 kernel32!BaseThreadInitThunk+0xd
00000000`0012ff90 00000000`00000000 ntdll!RtlUserThreadStart+0x1d

#  1  Id: d6c.fcc Suspend: 0 Teb: 000007ff`fffdb000 Unfrozen
Child-SP          RetAddr           Call Site
00000000`008eff00 000007fe`feb24bf5 simple!service_main+0x60
00000000`008eff30 00000000`7770cdcd advapi32!ScSvcctrlThreadW+0x25
00000000`008eff60 00000000`7792c6e1 kernel32!BaseThreadInitThunk+0xd
00000000`008eff90 00000000`00000000 ntdll!RtlUserThreadStart+0x1d
```

Spawning a custom thread with NULL pointer access violation doesn't result in a crash dump on my Vista x86 and x64 too. Therefore, it appears that there are no automatic postmortem crash dumps saved for native Window services in Vista unless there is some setting that I missed. This might create some problems for traditional 3rd party Technical Support procedures. However, it appears that there is a possible solution with Vista SP1 and Windows Server 2003 (page 606).

The Road to Kernel Space

If you are developing and debugging user space applications (or doing crash dump analysis in user space) and you want to understand Windows kernel dumps and device drivers better (and probably start writing your own kernel tools) here is the reading list I found the most effective:

0. Read and re-read Windows Internals book in parallel while reading all other books. It shows you the big picture and some useful WinDbg commands and techniques, but you need to read device driver books to fill the gaps and be confident in kernel space.

1. Start with "The Windows 2000 Device Driver Book: A Guide for Programmers (2nd Edition)." This short book shows the basics, and you can start writing drivers and kernel tools immediately.

2. Next, read the "Windows NT Device Driver Development" book to consolidate your knowledge.

3. Don't stop here. Read "Developing Windows NT Device Drivers: A Programmer's Handbook." This excellent book explains everything in great detail and good pictures.

4. Continue with WDM drivers and modern presentation: "Programming the Microsoft Windows Driver Model, Second Edition." A must-read, even if your drivers are not WDM.

5. Finally, read "Developing Drivers with the Windows Driver Foundation" book as this is the future, and it also covers ETW (event tracing for Windows), WinDbg extensions, PREfast, and static driver verifier.

Additional reading (not including DDK Help which you will use anyway) can be done in parallel after finishing "Windows NT Device Driver Development" book:

1. OSR NT Insider articles: http://www.osronline.com

2. "Windows NT File System Internals."

3. "Rootkits: Subverting the Windows Kernel" book shows Windows kernel from a hacker perspective.

Memory Dump Analysis Interview Questions

The following interview questions might be useful to assess the skill level of crash dump analysis on Windows platforms. These could be useful for debugging interviews as well.

1. What is FPO?
2. How many exceptions can be found in a crash dump?
3. You see the following message from WinDbg:

   ```
   WARNING: Stack unwind information not available. Following frames
   may be wrong.
   ```

   What would you do?

4. How would you find spinlock implementation if you have a kernel dump?
5. What is OMAP?
6. What is a full page heap?
7. The company name is missing from module information. How would you try to find it?
8. What is IDT?
9. How does a postmortem debugger work?
10. You've got a minidump of your application. How would you disassemble the code?
11. Memory consumption is growing for an application. How would you discover the leaking component?
12. What is IRQL?
13. When do you use TEB?
14. You've got 200 process dumps from a server. You need to find a deadlock. How would you do it?
15. You've got a complete memory dump from a server. You need to find a deadlock. How would you do it?
16. What is GC heap?
17. Your customer is reluctant to send a dump file due to security policies. What is your next step?
18. What is a first chance exception?

Music for Debugging

Debugging and understanding multithreaded programs is hard, and sometimes it requires running several execution paths mentally. Here listening to composers who use multithreading in music can help. My favorite is J.S. Bach. Virtuoso and heroic music helps me in live debugging too, and here my favorites are Chopin, Liszt, and Beethoven.

Many software engineers listen to music when writing code, and I'm not the exception. However, I have found that not all music suitable for programming helps me during debugging sessions.

Music for relaxation, quiet classical or modern music helps me to think about program design and write solid code. Music with several melodies played simultaneously, heroic, and virtuoso works help me to achieve a breakthrough and find a bug. The latter kind of music also suits me for listening when doing crash dump analysis or problem troubleshooting.

PDBFinder

Version 3.5 uses the new binary database format and achieves the following results compare to the previous version 3.0.1:

- 2 times smaller database size
- 5 times faster database load time on startup!

It is fully backward compatible with 3.0.1 and 2.x database formats and silently converts your old database to the new format on the first load.

Additionally, the new version fixes the bug in version 3.0.1, sometimes manifested when removing and then adding folders before building the new database which resulted in incorrectly built database.

The next version 4.0 is currently under development, and it will have the following features:

- The ability to open multiple databases
- The ability to exclude certain folders during build to avoid excessive search results output
- Fully configurable OS and language search options (which are currently disabled for the public version)

When a Process Dies Silently

There are cases when a default postmortem debugger doesn't save a dump file. This is because the default postmortem debugger is called from the crashed application thread on Windows before Vista, and if a thread stack is exhausted or critical thread data is corrupt, there is no user dump. On Vista, the default postmortem debugger is called from WER (Windows Error Reporting) process *WerFault.exe*, so there is a chance that it can save a user dump. During my experiments today on Windows 2003 (x64), I found that if we have a stack overflow inside a 64-bit process, then the process silently dies. This doesn't happen for 32-bit processes on the same server or on a native 32-bit OS. Here is the added code from the modified default Win32 API project created in Visual Studio 2005:

```
...
volatile DWORD dwSupressOptimization;
...
void SoFunction();
...
LRESULT CALLBACK WndProc(HWND hWnd, UINT message, WPARAM wParam, LPARAM
lParam)
{
...
  case WM_PAINT:
      hdc = BeginPaint(hWnd, &ps);
      SoFunction();
      EndPaint(hWnd, &ps);
      break;
...
}
...
void SoFunction()
{
  if (++dwSupressOptimization)
  {
      SoFunction();
      WndProc(0,0,0,0);
  }
}
```

Adding *WndProc* call to *SoFunction* is done to eliminate an optimization in Release build when a recursion call is transformed into a loop:

```
void SoFunction()
{
  if (++dwSupressOptimization)
  {
     SoFunction();
  }
}
```

```
0:001> uf SoFunction
00401300 mov     eax,1
00401305 jmp     StackOverflow!SoFunction+0x10 (00401310)
00401310 add     dword ptr [StackOverflow!dwSupressOptimization
(00403374)],eax
00401316 mov     ecx,dword ptr [StackOverflow!dwSupressOptimization
(00403374)]
0040131c jne     StackOverflow!SoFunction+0x10 (00401310)
0040131e ret
```

Therefore without *WndProc* added or more complicated *SoFunction* there is no stack overflow but a loop with 4294967295 (0xFFFFFFFF) iterations.

If we compile an x64 project with *WndProc* call included in *SoFunction* and run it, we never get a dump file from any default postmortem debugger, although **TestDefaultDebugger64** (page 641) tool crashes with a dump. We can also observe a strange behavior that the application disappears only during the second window repaint. However, it shall immediately crash when we launch it, and the main window is shown. What we see is when we launch the application, it is running, and the main window is visible. When we force it to repaint by minimizing and then maximizing, for example, only then it disappears from the screen and the process list. If we launch 64-bit WinDbg, load and run our application we would hit the first chance exception:

```
0:000> g
(159c.fc4): Stack overflow - code c00000fd (first chance)
First chance exceptions are reported before any exception handling.
This exception may be expected and handled.
StackOverflow!SoFunction+0x22:
00000001`40001322 e8d9ffffff call StackOverflow!SoFunction
(00000001`40001300)
```

Stack trace looks like a normal stack overflow:

```
0:000> k
Child-SP          RetAddr           Call Site
00000000`00033fe0 00000001`40001327 StackOverflow!SoFunction+0x22
00000000`00034020 00000001`40001327 StackOverflow!SoFunction+0x27
00000000`00034060 00000001`40001327 StackOverflow!SoFunction+0x27
00000000`000340a0 00000001`40001327 StackOverflow!SoFunction+0x27
00000000`000340e0 00000001`40001327 StackOverflow!SoFunction+0x27
```

```
00000000`00034120 00000001`40001327 StackOverflow!SoFunction+0x27
00000000`00034160 00000001`40001327 StackOverflow!SoFunction+0x27
00000000`000341a0 00000001`40001327 StackOverflow!SoFunction+0x27
00000000`000341e0 00000001`40001327 StackOverflow!SoFunction+0x27
00000000`00034220 00000001`40001327 StackOverflow!SoFunction+0x27
00000000`00034260 00000001`40001327 StackOverflow!SoFunction+0x27
00000000`000342a0 00000001`40001327 StackOverflow!SoFunction+0x27
00000000`000342e0 00000001`40001327 StackOverflow!SoFunction+0x27
00000000`00034320 00000001`40001327 StackOverflow!SoFunction+0x27
00000000`00034360 00000001`40001327 StackOverflow!SoFunction+0x27
00000000`000343a0 00000001`40001327 StackOverflow!SoFunction+0x27
00000000`000343e0 00000001`40001327 StackOverflow!SoFunction+0x27
00000000`00034420 00000001`40001327 StackOverflow!SoFunction+0x27
00000000`00034460 00000001`40001327 StackOverflow!SoFunction+0x27
00000000`000344a0 00000001`40001327 StackOverflow!SoFunction+0x27
```

RSP is inside stack guard page during the CALL instruction.

```
0:000> r
rax=0000000000003eed rbx=00000000000f26fe rcx=0000000077c4080a
rdx=0000000000000000 rsi=000000000000000f rdi=0000000000000000
rip=0000000140001322 rsp=0000000000033fe0 rbp=00000001400035f0
 r8=000000000012fb18 r9=00000001400035f0 r10=0000000000000000
r11=0000000000000246 r12=000000000012fdd8 r13=000000000012fd50
r14=00000000000f26fe r15=0000000000000000
iopl=0 nv up ei pl nz na po nc
cs=0033 ss=002b ds=002b es=002b fs=0053 gs=002b efl=00010206
StackOverflow!SoFunction+0x22:
00000001`40001322 e8d9ffffff call StackOverflow!SoFunction
(00000001`40001300)

0:000> uf StackOverflow!SoFunction
00000001`40001300 sub     rsp,38h
00000001`40001304 mov     rax,qword ptr [StackOverflow!__security_cookie
(00000001`40003000)]
00000001`4000130b xor     rax,rsp
00000001`4000130e mov     qword ptr [rsp+20h],rax
00000001`40001313 add     dword ptr [StackOverflow!dwSupressOptimization
(00000001`400035e4)],1
00000001`4000131a mov     eax,dword ptr
[StackOverflow!dwSupressOptimization (00000001`400035e4)]
00000001`40001320 je      StackOverflow!SoFunction+0x37
(00000001`40001337)
00000001`40001322 call    StackOverflow!SoFunction (00000001`40001300)
00000001`40001327 xor     r9d,r9d
00000001`4000132a xor     r8d,r8d
00000001`4000132d xor     edx,edx
00000001`4000132f xor     ecx,ecx
00000001`40001331 call    qword ptr [StackOverflow!_imp_DefWindowProcW
(00000001`40002198)]
00000001`40001337 mov     rcx,qword ptr [rsp+20h]
00000001`4000133c xor     rcx,rsp
```

```
00000001`4000133f call    StackOverflow!__security_check_cookie
(00000001`40001360)
00000001`40001344 add     rsp,38h
00000001`40001348 ret
```

However, this guard page is not the last stack page as can be seen from TEB and the current RSP address (0x33fe0):

```
0:000> !teb
TEB at 000007fffffde000
    ExceptionList:        0000000000000000
    StackBase:            0000000000130000
    StackLimit:           0000000000031000
    SubSystemTib:         0000000000000000
    FiberData:            0000000000001e00
    ArbitraryUserPointer: 0000000000000000
    Self:                 000007fffffde000
    EnvironmentPointer:   0000000000000000
    ClientId:             000000000000159c . 0000000000000fc4
    RpcHandle:            0000000000000000
    Tls Storage:          0000000000000000
    PEB Address:          000007fffffd5000
    LastErrorValue:       0
    LastStatusValue:      c0000135
    Count Owned Locks:    0
    HardErrorMode:        0
```

If we continue execution and force the main application window to invalidate (repaint) itself we get another first chance exception instead of the second chance:

```
0:000> g
(159c.fc4): Access violation - code c0000005 (first chance)
First chance exceptions are reported before any exception handling.
This exception may be expected and handled.
StackOverflow!SoFunction+0x22:
00000001`40001322 call StackOverflow!SoFunction (00000001`40001300)
```

What we see now is that RSP is outside the valid stack region (stack limit) 0x31000:

```
0:000> k
Child-SP          RetAddr           Call Site
00000000`00030ff0 00000001`40001327 StackOverflow!SoFunction+0x22
00000000`00031030 00000001`40001327 StackOverflow!SoFunction+0x27
00000000`00031070 00000001`40001327 StackOverflow!SoFunction+0x27
00000000`000310b0 00000001`40001327 StackOverflow!SoFunction+0x27
00000000`000310f0 00000001`40001327 StackOverflow!SoFunction+0x27
00000000`00031130 00000001`40001327 StackOverflow!SoFunction+0x27
00000000`00031170 00000001`40001327 StackOverflow!SoFunction+0x27
00000000`000311b0 00000001`40001327 StackOverflow!SoFunction+0x27
00000000`000311f0 00000001`40001327 StackOverflow!SoFunction+0x27
```

```
00000000`00031230 00000001`40001327 StackOverflow!SoFunction+0x27
00000000`00031270 00000001`40001327 StackOverflow!SoFunction+0x27
00000000`000312b0 00000001`40001327 StackOverflow!SoFunction+0x27
00000000`000312f0 00000001`40001327 StackOverflow!SoFunction+0x27
00000000`00031330 00000001`40001327 StackOverflow!SoFunction+0x27
00000000`00031370 00000001`40001327 StackOverflow!SoFunction+0x27
00000000`000313b0 00000001`40001327 StackOverflow!SoFunction+0x27
00000000`000313f0 00000001`40001327 StackOverflow!SoFunction+0x27
00000000`00031430 00000001`40001327 StackOverflow!SoFunction+0x27
00000000`00031470 00000001`40001327 StackOverflow!SoFunction+0x27
00000000`000314b0 00000001`40001327 StackOverflow!SoFunction+0x27
```

```
0:000> r
rax=0000000000007e98 rbx=00000000000f26fe rcx=0000000077c4080a
rdx=0000000000000000 rsi=000000000000000f rdi=0000000000000000
rip=0000000140001322 rsp=0000000000030ff0 rbp=00000001400035f0
 r8=000000000012faa8  r9=00000001400035f0 r10=0000000000000000
r11=0000000000000246 r12=000000000012fd68 r13=000000000012fce0
r14=00000000000f26fe r15=0000000000000000
iopl=0 nv up ei pl nz na pe nc
cs=0033 ss=002b ds=002b es=002b fs=0053 gs=002b efl=00010202
StackOverflow!SoFunction+0x22:
00000001`40001322 call    StackOverflow!SoFunction (00000001`40001300)
```

Therefore, we expect the second chance exception at the same address here, and we get it indeed when we continue execution:

```
0:000> g
(159c.fc4): Access violation - code c0000005 (!!! second chance !!!)
StackOverflow!SoFunction+0x22:
00000001`40001322 call    StackOverflow!SoFunction (00000001`40001300)
```

Now we see why the process died silently. There was no stack space left for exception dispatch handler functions and, therefore, for the default unhandled exception filter that launches the default postmortem debugger to save a process dump. So, it looks like in x64 Windows, when our process had first chance stack overflow exception, there was no second chance exception afterwards, and after handling the first chance stack overflow exception, process execution resumed, and finally hit its thread stack limit. This doesn't happen with 32-bit processes, even in x64 Windows, where unhandled first chance stack overflow exception results in the immediate second chance stack overflow exception at the same stack address and, therefore, there is a sufficient room for the local variables for exception handler and filter functions.

This is an example of what happened before exception handling changes in Vista.

ASLR: Address Space Layout Randomization

Vista has the new ASLR feature:

- Load address randomization (/dynamicbase linker option)
- Stack address randomization (/dynamicbase linker option)
- Heap randomization

The first randomization changes addresses across Vista reboots. The second randomization happens every time we launch an application linked with /dynamicbase option. The third randomization happens every time we launch an application linked with or without /dynamicbase option, as we see below.

Let's check ASLR feature by attaching WinDbg to calc, notepad, and pre-Vista application **TestDefaultDebugger** (page 641). Native Vista applications use ASLR.

Comparison between two *calc.exe* processes inspected separately before and after reboot shows that the main module and system DLLs have different load addresses:

```
0:000> lm
start    end      module name
009f0000 00a1e000 calc
74710000 748a4000 comctl32
75b10000 75bba000 msvcrt
...
...
76f00000 76fbf000 ADVAPI32
770d0000 771a8000 kernel32
771b0000 7724e000 USER32
77250000 7736e000 ntdll
0:000> lm
start    end      module name
00470000 0049e000 calc
...
...
743e0000 74574000 comctl32
...
75730000 757da000 msvcrt
757e0000 7589f000 ADVAPI32
...
75e20000 75ebe000 USER32
...
76cf0000 76dc8000 kernel32
76dd0000 76eee000 ntdll
...
```

Main module address has different third byte across reboots. I believe that 0x00 is not allowed otherwise we would have 0x00000000 load address. Therefore, we have 255 unique load addresses chosen randomly.

Stack addresses are different:

```
0:000> k
ChildEBP RetAddr
000ffc8c 771d199a ntdll!KiFastSystemCallRet
000ffc90 771d19cd USER32!NtUserGetMessage+0xc
000ffcac 009f24e8 USER32!GetMessageW+0x33
000ffd08 00a02588 calc!WinMain+0x278
000ffd98 77113833 calc!_initterm_e+0x1a1
000ffda4 7728a9bd kernel32!BaseThreadInitThunk+0xe
000ffde4 00000000 ntdll!_RtlUserThreadStart+0x23

0:000> k
ChildEBP RetAddr
0007fbe4 75e4199a ntdll!KiFastSystemCallRet
0007fbe8 75e419cd USER32!NtUserGetMessage+0xc
0007fc04 004724e8 USER32!GetMessageW+0x33
0007fc60 00482588 calc!WinMain+0x278
0007fcf0 76d33833 calc!_initterm_e+0x1a1
0007fcfc 76e0a9bd kernel32!BaseThreadInitThunk+0xe
0007fd3c 00000000 ntdll!_RtlUserThreadStart+0x23
```

Because module base addresses are different, return addresses in stack traces are different too.

Heap base addresses are different:

```
0:000> !heap
Index Address
1: 00120000
2: 00010000
3: 00760000
4: 00990000
5: 00700000
6: 00670000
7: 01320000
```

```
0:000> !heap
Index Address
1: 001b0000
2: 00010000
3: 00a00000
4: 009c0000
5: 00400000
6: 00900000
7: 01260000
```

PEB and environment addresses are different:

notepad.exe (PID 1248):

```
0:000> !peb
PEB at 7ffd4000
...
Environment: 000507e8
```

notepad.exe (PID 1370):

```
0:000> !peb
PEB at 7ffd9000
...
Environment: 003a07e8
```

If we look inside TEB we see that pointers to exception handler list are different and stack bases are different too:

notepad.exe (PID 1248):

```
TEB at 7ffdf000
    ExceptionList:        0023ff34
    StackBase:            00240000
    StackLimit:           0022f000
    SubSystemTib:         00000000
    FiberData:            00001e00
    ArbitraryUserPointer: 00000000
    Self:                 7ffdf000
    EnvironmentPointer:   00000000
    ClientId:             00001248 . 000004e0
    RpcHandle:            00000000
    Tls Storage:          7ffdf02c
    PEB Address:          7ffd4000
    LastErrorValue:       0
    LastStatusValue:      c0000034
    Count Owned Locks:    0
    HardErrorMode:        0
```

notepad.exe (PID 1370):

```
0:000> !teb
TEB at 7ffdf000
    ExceptionList:          001ffa00
    StackBase:              00200000
    StackLimit:             001ef000
    SubSystemTib:           00000000
    FiberData:              00001e00
    ArbitraryUserPointer:   00000000
    Self:                   7ffdf000
    EnvironmentPointer:     00000000
    ClientId:               00001370 . 00001454
    RpcHandle:              00000000
    Tls Storage:            7ffdf02c
    PEB Address:            7ffd9000
    LastErrorValue:         5
    LastStatusValue:        c0000008
    Count Owned Locks:      0
    HardErrorMode:          0
```

However, if we look at old applications that weren't linked with */dynamicbase* option, we see that the main module and old DLL base addresses are the same:

```
0:000> lm
start end module name
00400000 00435000 TestDefaultDebugger
20000000 2000d000 LvHook
```

To summarize different alternatives I created the following table where

"New" column - processes linked with /dynamicbase option, no reboot
"New/Reboot" column - processes linked with /dynamicbase option, reboot
"Old" column - old processes, no reboot
"Old/Reboot" column - old processes, reboot

```
Randomization   | New/Reboot | New | Old/Reboot | Old
-----------------------------------------------------
Module          |     +      |  -  |     -      |  -
-----------------------------------------------------
System DLLs     |     +      |  -  |     +      |  -
-----------------------------------------------------
Stack           |     +      |  +  |     -      |  -
-----------------------------------------------------
Heap            |     +      |  +  |     +      |  +
-----------------------------------------------------
PEB             |     +      |  +  |     +      |  +
-----------------------------------------------------
Environment     |     +      |  +  |     +      |  +
-----------------------------------------------------
ExceptionList   |     +      |  +  |     -      |  -
```

From PEB and process heap base addresses, we can see that environment addresses are always correlated with the heap:

```
0:000> !heap
Index   Address  Name      Debugging options enabled
  1:   005f0000
0:000> !peb
PEB at 7ffd7000
...
...
...
    ProcessHeap:         005f0000
    ProcessParameters: 005f1540
    Environment:         005f07e8
```

I think the reason why Microsoft didn't enable ASLR by default is to prevent instances of **Changed Environment** pattern (page 283).

Process and Thread Startup in Vista

If we looked at the process dumps from Vista or did live debugging, we might have noticed that there are no longer *kernel32* functions *BaseProcessStart* in the main thread stack trace and *BaseThreadStart* in the subsequent thread stack traces. In Vista, we have *ntdll!_RtlUserThreadStart*, which calls *kernel32!BaseThreadInitThunk* for both main and secondary threads:

```
0:002> ~*k

0 Id: 13e8.1348 Suspend: 1 Teb: 7ffdf000 Unfrozen
ChildEBP RetAddr
0009f8d8 77b7199a ntdll!KiFastSystemCallRet
0009f8dc 77b719cd USER32!NtUserGetMessage+0xc
0009f8f8 006b24e8 USER32!GetMessageW+0x33
0009f954 006c2588 calc!WinMain+0x278
0009f9e4 77603833 calc!_initterm_e+0x1a1
0009f9f0 779ea9bd kernel32!BaseThreadInitThunk+0xe
0009fa30 00000000 ntdll!_RtlUserThreadStart+0x23

1 Id: 13e8.534 Suspend: 1 Teb: 7ffde000 Unfrozen
ChildEBP RetAddr
0236f9d8 77a106a0 ntdll!KiFastSystemCallRet
0236f9dc 776077d4 ntdll!NtWaitForSingleObject+0xc
0236fa4c 77607742 kernel32!WaitForSingleObjectEx+0xbe
0236fa60 006b4958 kernel32!WaitForSingleObject+0x12
0236fa78 77603833 calc!WatchDogThread+0x21
0236fa84 779ea9bd kernel32!BaseThreadInitThunk+0xe
0236fac4 00000000 ntdll!_RtlUserThreadStart+0x23

# 2 Id: 13e8.1188 Suspend: 1 Teb: 7ffdd000 Unfrozen
ChildEBP RetAddr
0078fec8 77a3f0a9 ntdll!DbgBreakPoint
0078fef8 77603833 ntdll!DbgUiRemoteBreakin+0x3c
0078ff04 779ea9bd kernel32!BaseThreadInitThunk+0xe
0078ff44 00000000 ntdll!_RtlUserThreadStart+0x23

0:000> .asm no_code_bytes
Assembly options: no_code_bytes
0:000> uf ntdll!_RtlUserThreadStart
...
...
...
ntdll!_RtlUserThreadStart:
779ea996 push 14h
779ea998 push offset ntdll! ?? ::FNODOBFM::`string'+0xb6e (779ff108)
779ea99d call ntdll!_SEH_prolog4 (779f47d8)
779ea9a2 and  dword ptr [ebp-4],0
```

```
779ea9a6 mov  eax,dword ptr [ntdll!Kernel32ThreadInitThunkFunction
(77a752a0)]
779ea9ab push dword ptr [ebp+0Ch]
779ea9ae test eax,eax
779ea9b0 je   ntdll!_RtlUserThreadStart+0x32 (779c6326)
...
...
...
0:000> dds ntdll!Kernel32ThreadInitThunkFunction l1
77a752a0 77603821 kernel32!BaseThreadInitThunk
```

Race Conditions on a Uniprocessor Machine

It is a known fact that hidden race conditions in the code are manifested more frequently on a multiprocessor machine than on a uniprocessor machine. I was trying to create an example to illustrate this point and wrote the following code:

```
volatile bool b;
void thread_true(void *)
{
 while(true)
 {
  b = true;
 }
}
void thread_false(void *)
{
 while(true)
 {
  b = false;
 }
}
int _tmain(int argc, _TCHAR* argv[])
{
 _beginthread(thread_true, 0, NULL);
 _beginthread(thread_false, 0, NULL);
 while(true)
 {
  assert (b == false || b == true);
 }
 return 0;
}
```

The program has three threads. Two of them are trying to set the same Boolean variable b to different values, and the main thread checks that its value is either *true* or *false*. The assertion should fail in the following scenario: the first thread (*thread_true*) sets b variable to *true* value, so the first comparison in assertion fails. We expect the second comparison to succeed, but the main thread is preempted by the second thread (*thread_false*) that sets that value to *false* and, therefore, the second comparison fails too. We get an assertion dialog in debug build showing that Boolean variable b is neither *true* nor *false*!

I compiled and ran that program, and it wasn't failing for hours on my uniprocessor laptop. On a multiprocessor machine, it was failing in a couple of minutes. If we look at assertion assembly language code we see that it is very short so statistically speaking the chances that our main thread is preempted in the middle of the assertion are very low. This is because on a uniprocessor machine two threads are running not in parallel but until their quantum is expired. So we should make the assertion code longer to exceed the quantum. To simulate this, I added a call to *SwitchToThread* function. When the assertion code yields execution to another thread then, perhaps, that thread would be *thread_false*, and as soon as it is preempted by the main thread again we get the assertion failure:

```
volatile bool b;
bool SlowOp()
{
 SwitchToThread();
 return false;
}
void thread_true(void *)
{
 while(true)
 {
  b = true;
 }
}
void thread_false(void *)
{
 while(true)
 {
  b = false;
 }
}
int _tmain(int argc, _TCHAR* argv[])
{
 _beginthread(thread_true, 0, NULL);
 _beginthread(thread_false, 0, NULL);
 while(true)
 {
  assert (b == false || SlowOp() || b == true);
 }
 return 0;
}
```

I compiled and reran the program again, and I couldn't see any failure for a long time. It looks like *thread_false* is always running before the main thread, and when the main thread is running, then due to short-circuit operator || evaluation rule, we don't have a chance to execute *SlowOp()*. Then I added a fourth thread called *thread_true_2* to make the number of threads setting b variable to *true* value as twice as many as the number of threads setting b variable to *false* value (2 to 1), so we could have more chances to set b variable to *true* value before executing the assertion:

```
volatile bool b;
bool SlowOp()
{
 SwitchToThread();
 return false;
}
void thread_true(void *)
{
 while(true)
 {
  b = true;
 }
}
void thread_true_2(void *)
{
 while(true)
 {
  b = true;
 }
}
void thread_false(void *)
{
 while(true)
 {
  b = false;
 }
}
int _tmain(int argc, _TCHAR* argv[])
{
 _beginthread(thread_true, 0, NULL);
 _beginthread(thread_false, 0, NULL);
 _beginthread(thread_true_2, 0, NULL);
 while(true)
 {
  assert (b == false || SlowOp() || b == true);
 }
 return 0;
}
```

Now when I ran the new program, I got the assertion failure after a couple of minutes! It is hard to make race conditions manifest themselves on a uniprocessor machine.

Yet Another Look at Zw* and Nt* Functions

In one book I encountered the following macro definition to get function index in system service table:

```
#define HOOK_INDEX(func2hook) *(PULONG)((PUCHAR)func2hook+1)
```

I couldn't understand the code until I looked at the disassembly of a typical *ntdll!Zw* and *nt!Zw* function (x86 Windows Server 2003):

```
lkd> u ntdll!ZwCreateProcess
ntdll!NtCreateProcess:
7c821298 b831000000      mov     eax,31h
7c82129d ba0003fe7f      mov     edx,offset SharedUserData!SystemCallStub
(7ffe0300)
7c8212a2 ff12            call    dword ptr [edx]
7c8212a4 c22000          ret     20h
7c8212a7 90              nop
ntdll!ZwCreateProcessEx:
7c8212a8 b832000000      mov     eax,32h
7c8212ad ba0003fe7f      mov     edx,offset SharedUserData!SystemCallStub
(7ffe0300)
7c8212b2 ff12            call    dword ptr [edx]

lkd> u nt!ZwCreateProcess
nt!ZwCreateProcess:
8083c2a3 b831000000      mov     eax,31h
8083c2a8 8d542404        lea     edx,[esp+4]
8083c2ac 9c              pushfd
8083c2ad 6a08            push    8
8083c2af e8c688ffff      call    nt!KiSystemService (80834b7a)
8083c2b4 c22000          ret     20h
nt!ZwCreateProcessEx:
8083c2b7 b832000000      mov     eax,32h
8083c2bc 8d542404        lea     edx,[esp+4]
```

We can notice that user space *ntdll!Nt* and *ntdll!Zw* variants are the same. It is not the case in kernel space:

```
lkd> u nt!NtCreateProcess
nt!NtCreateProcess:
808f80ea 8bff            mov     edi,edi
808f80ec 55              push    ebp
808f80ed 8bec            mov     ebp,esp
808f80ef 33c0            xor     eax,eax
808f80f1 f6451c01        test    byte ptr [ebp+1Ch],1
808f80f5 0f8549d10600    jne     nt!NtCreateProcess+0xd (80965244)
```

```
808f80fb f6452001         test    byte ptr [ebp+20h],1
808f80ff 0f8545d10600     jne     nt!NtCreateProcess+0x14 (8096524a)
```

nt!Zw functions are dispatched through service table. *nt!Nt* functions are actual code. For completeness, let's look at AMD x64 Windows Server 2003. User space x64 call:

```
0:001> u ntdll!ZwCreateProcess
ntdll!NtCreateProcess:
00000000`78ef1ab0 4c8bd1          mov     r10,rcx
00000000`78ef1ab3 b882000000      mov     eax,82h
00000000`78ef1ab8 0f05            syscall
00000000`78ef1aba c3              ret
00000000`78ef1abb 666690          xchg    ax,ax
00000000`78ef1abe 6690            xchg    ax,ax
ntdll!NtCreateProfile:
00000000`78ef1ac0 4c8bd1          mov     r10,rcx
00000000`78ef1ac3 b883000000      mov     eax,83h
```

User space x86 call in x64 Windows Server 2003:

```
0:001> u ntdll!ZwCreateProcess
ntdll!ZwCreateProcess:
7d61d428 b882000000       mov     eax,82h
7d61d42d 33c9             xor     ecx,ecx
7d61d42f 8d542404         lea     edx,[esp+4]
7d61d433 64ff15c0000000   call    dword ptr fs:[0C0h]
7d61d43a c22000           ret     20h
7d61d43d 8d4900           lea     ecx,[ecx]
ntdll!ZwCreateProfile:
7d61d440 b883000000       mov     eax,83h
```

Kernel space call in x64 Windows Server 2003:

```
kd> u nt!ZwCreateProcess nt!ZwCreateProcess+20
nt!ZwCreateProcess:
fffff800`0103dd70 488bc4          mov     rax,rsp
fffff800`0103dd73 fa              cli
fffff800`0103dd74 4883ec10        sub     rsp,10h
fffff800`0103dd78 50              push    rax
fffff800`0103dd79 9c              pushfq
fffff800`0103dd7a 6a10            push    10h
fffff800`0103dd7c 488d057d380000  lea     rax,[nt!KiServiceLinkage
(fffff800`01041600)]
fffff800`0103dd83 50              push    rax
fffff800`0103dd84 b882000000      mov     eax,82h
fffff800`0103dd89 e972310000      jmp     nt!KiServiceInternal
(fffff800`01040f00)
fffff800`0103dd8e 6690            xchg    ax,ax
```

```
kd> u nt!NtCreateProcess
nt!NtCreateProcess:
fffff800`01245832 53               push    rbx
fffff800`01245833 4883ec50         sub     rsp,50h
fffff800`01245837 4c8b9c2488000000 mov     r11,qword ptr [rsp+88h]
fffff800`0124583f b801000000       mov     eax,1
fffff800`01245844 488bd9           mov     rbx,rcx
fffff800`01245847 488b8c2490000000 mov     rcx,qword ptr [rsp+90h]
fffff800`0124584f 41f6c301         test    r11b,1
fffff800`01245853 41ba00000000     mov     r10d,0
```

Here is the same code as in kernel x86: *Zw* functions are dispatched, but *Nt* functions are actual code. To remember which function variant is dispatched, and which is the actual code, I propose the mnemonic "**Z-dispatch.**"

Programmer Universalis

Just a short observation: it's very good to be able to understand and even write everything from GUI down to machine language instructions or up. Certainly understanding how software works at every level is very helpful in memory dump analysis. Seeing thread stacks in memory dumps helps in understanding software. The more we know, the better we are at dump analysis and debugging. Debugging is not about stepping through the code. This is a very narrow view of a specialist programmer. Programmer Universalis can do debugging at every possible level and, therefore, can write any possible software layer.

Dr. Watson Logs Analysis

The main problem with Dr. Watson logs is the lack of symbol information, but this can be alleviated by using WinDbg if we have the same binary that crashed and produced the log entry. I'm going to illustrate this point by using **TestDefaultDebugger** tool (page 641). Its main purpose is to crash itself. I use this tool here just to show how to reconstruct stack trace.

If we run it and Dr. Watson is our default postmortem debugger, we get this event recorded in Dr. Watson log:

```
*** ERROR: Module load completed but symbols could not be loaded for
C:\Work\TestDefaultDebugger.exe
function: TestDefaultDebugger
        004014e6 cc              int     3
        004014e7 cc              int     3
        004014e8 cc              int     3
        004014e9 cc              int     3
        004014ea cc              int     3
        004014eb cc              int     3
        004014ec cc              int     3
        004014ed cc              int     3
        004014ee cc              int     3
        004014ef cc              int     3
FAULT ->004014f0 c7050000000000000000 mov dword ptr
ds:[0],0  ds:0023:00000000=????????
        004014fa c3              ret
        004014fb cc              int     3
        004014fc cc              int     3
        004014fd cc              int     3
        004014fe cc              int     3
        004014ff cc              int     3
        00401500 0fb7542404      movzx   edx,word ptr [esp+4]
        00401505 89542404        mov     dword ptr [esp+4],edx
        00401509 e98e1c0000      jmp     TestDefaultDebugger+0x319c
(0040319c)
        0040150e cc              int     3
*--> Stack Back Trace <----*
*** ERROR: Symbol file could not be found.  Defaulted to export symbols
for C:\WINDOWS\system32\ntdll.dll -
ChildEBP RetAddr  Args to Child
WARNING: Stack unwind information not available. Following frames may be
wrong.
TestDefaultDebugger+0x14f0
TestDefaultDebugger+0x3470
TestDefaultDebugger+0x2a27
TestDefaultDebugger+0x8e69
TestDefaultDebugger+0x98d9
```

We see that when the log entry was saved, there were no symbols available, and this is the most common case. If we have such a log and no corresponding user dump (perhaps it was overwritten), then we can still reconstruct stack trace. To do this, we run WinDbg, set path to our application symbol files, and load our application as a crash dump:

```
Microsoft (R) Windows Debugger  Version 6.6.0007.5
Copyright (c) Microsoft Corporation. All rights reserved.
Loading Dump File [C:\Work\TestDefaultDebugger.exe]
Symbol search path is:
SRV*c:\websymbols*http://msdl.microsoft.com/download/symbols;c:\work
Executable search path is:
ModLoad: 00400000 00435000   C:\Work\TestDefaultDebugger.exe
eax=00000000 ebx=00000000 ecx=00000000 edx=00000000 esi=00000000
edi=00000000
eip=0040e8bb esp=00000000 ebp=00000000 iopl=0 nv up di pl nz na po nc
cs=0000  ss=0000  ds=0000  es=0000  fs=0000  gs=0000  efl=00000000
TestDefaultDebugger!wWinMainCRTStartup:
0040e8bb
e876440000      call    TestDefaultDebugger!__security_init_cookie
(00412d36)
```

Now we can use **ln** command to find the nearest symbol (shown in a small font for visual clarity):

```
0:000> ln TestDefaultDebugger+0x14f0
c:\testdefaultdebugger\testdefaultdebuggerdlg.cpp(155)
(004014f0)   TestDefaultDebugger!CTestDefaultDebuggerDlg::OnBnClickedButton1   |  (00401500)   Test
DefaultDebugger!CDialog::Create
Exact matches:
    TestDefaultDebugger!CTestDefaultDebuggerDlg::OnBnClickedButton1 (void)
0:000> ln TestDefaultDebugger+0x3470
f:\rtm\vctools\vc7libs\ship\atlmfc\src\mfc\cmdtarg.cpp(381)+0x18
(00403358)   TestDefaultDebugger!CCmdTarget::OnCmdMsg+0x118   |  (00403472)   TestDefaultDebugger!C
CmdTarget::IsInvokeAllowed
0:000> ln TestDefaultDebugger+0x2a27
f:\rtm\vctools\vc7libs\ship\atlmfc\src\mfc\dlgcore.cpp(85)+0x17
(00402a0c)   TestDefaultDebugger!CDialog::OnCmdMsg+0x1b   |  (00402a91)   TestDefaultDebugger!CDial
og::`scalar deleting destructor'
0:000> ln TestDefaultDebugger+0x8e69
f:\rtm\vctools\vc7libs\ship\atlmfc\src\mfc\wincore.cpp(2299)+0xd
(00408dd9)   TestDefaultDebugger!CWnd::OnCommand+0x90   |  (00408e70)   TestDefaultDebugger!CWnd::O
nNotify
0:000> ln TestDefaultDebugger+0x98d9
f:\rtm\vctools\vc7libs\ship\atlmfc\src\mfc\wincore.cpp(1755)+0xe
(004098a3)   TestDefaultDebugger!CWnd::OnWndMsg+0x36   |  (00409ecf)   TestDefaultDebugger!CWnd::Re
flectChildNotify
0:000> ln TestDefaultDebugger+0x6258
f:\rtm\vctools\vc7libs\ship\atlmfc\src\mfc\wincore.cpp(1741)+0x17
(00406236)   TestDefaultDebugger!CWnd::WindowProc+0x22   |  (0040627a)   TestDefaultDebugger!CTestC
mdUI::CTestCmdUI
0:000> ln TestDefaultDebugger+0x836d
f:\rtm\vctools\vc7libs\ship\atlmfc\src\mfc\wincore.cpp(243)
(004082d3)   TestDefaultDebugger!AfxCallWndProc+0x9a   |  (004083c0)   TestDefaultDebugger!AfxWndPr
oc
```

So we reconstructed the stack trace:

```
TestDefaultDebugger!CTestDefaultDebuggerDlg::OnBnClickedButton1
TestDefaultDebugger!CCmdTarget::OnCmdMsg+0x118
TestDefaultDebugger!CDialog::OnCmdMsg+0x1b
TestDefaultDebugger!CWnd::OnCommand+0x90
TestDefaultDebugger!CWnd::OnWndMsg+0x36
TestDefaultDebugger!CWnd::WindowProc+0x22
TestDefaultDebugger!AfxCallWndProc+0x9a
```

To check it, we disassemble the top and see that it corresponds to our crash point from Dr. Watson log:

```
0:000> u TestDefaultDebugger!CTestDefaultDebuggerDlg::OnBnClickedButton1
TestDefaultDebugger!CTestDefaultDebuggerDlg::OnBnClickedButton1
[c:\testdefaultdebugger\testdefaultdebuggerdlg.cpp @ 155]:
004014f0 c705000000000000000000 mov dword ptr ds:[0],0
004014fa c3             ret
004014fb cc             int     3
004014fc cc             int     3
004014fd cc             int     3
004014fe cc             int     3
004014ff cc             int     3
```

Post-Debugging Complications

The real story: suddenly, an application being developed started to leak memory very rapidly and in massive amounts, 100Mb per second. That application used a DLL that was known to have memory leaks, but those leaks were much smaller before. After spending the whole day debugging this problem, a developer renamed the application just to keep its current version and relaunched it. The same executable file, but under a different name, started to consume much less memory as before the problem. After renaming it back, the application started to consume huge amounts of memory again. Scratching his head, the developer recalled that he enabled full page heap (placing allocations at the end of full pages) 3 weeks ago.

The moral of this story is always to revert changes made for debugging purposes back, as soon as debugging session is finished, or to use new and separate debugging environment every time. The latter is much easier nowadays if we use VMWare, Virtual PC, or Xen.

The Elements of Crash Dump Analysis Style

After looking at the multitude of crash dump analysis reports from different companies and engineers, I would like to highlight several rules that make them good:

- Format your debugger output in a fixed size font (Courier New or Lucida Console). It is very important for readability.
- Bold and highlight (using different colors) important addresses or data.
- Keep the same color for the same address or data consistently.
- Use red color for bug manifestation points.
- If we refer to a dump file, we should put a link to it.

What is considered a bad crash dump analysis style? These are:

- Variable size font (you copy your debugger output to Outlook e-mail as is, and it is using the default font) there.
- Highlight the whole data set (for example, the stack trace) in red.
- Too much irrelevant information.

Crash Dump Analysis in Visual Studio

If we open a user crash dump as a solution/project, not as a file, then we can do crash dump analysis by using Visual Studio debug windows, for example, a powerful Watch window. As we can see from the picture below, I loaded a crash dump from my test application saved by NTSD, and it shows assembly code and source code nicely interleaved.

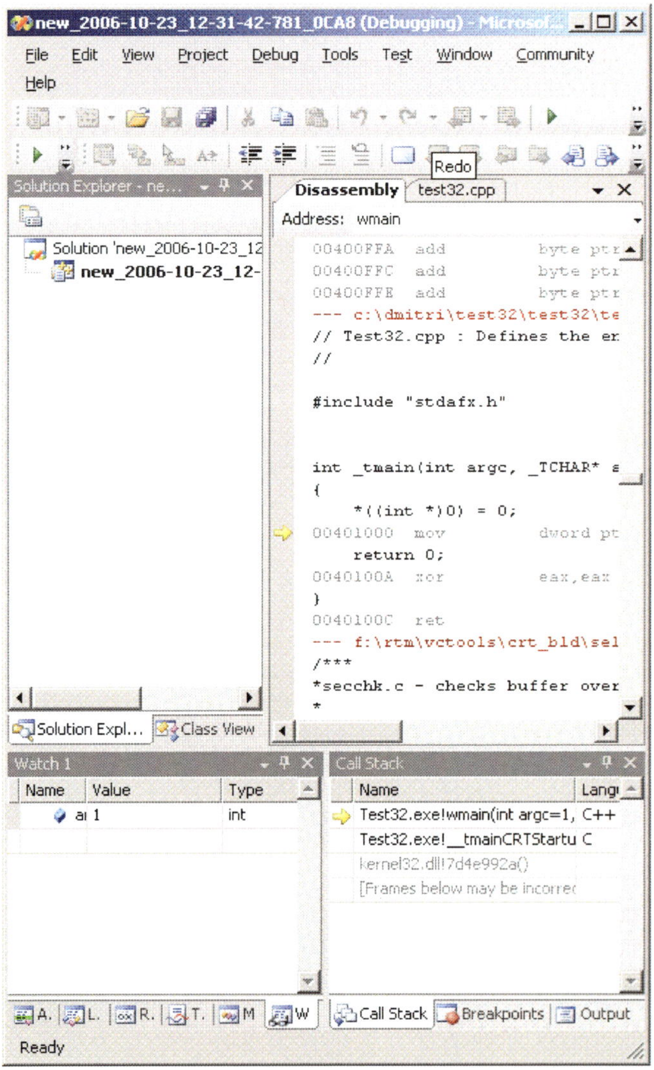

If we need to specify additional symbol paths or symbol server settings, we can do it in *Tools \ Options \ Debugging \ Symbols* dialog.

This might be good for engineers used to do live debugging in Visual Studio and having no experience in using WinDbg if they need to look at application crash dumps from customers.

32-bit Stack from 64-bit Dump

This is a short note that might be useful if we get a 64-bit dump of a 32-bit process from x64 Windows. I already wrote about separate dump types and tools for 32-bit and 64-bit processes (pages 632 - 633).

There is a simple solution when we get a 64-bit dump file, and we want to look at 32-bit thread stacks, etc. We need to use *wow64exts.dll* extension in 64-bit WinDbg.

The whole discussion and solution can be found on Crash Dump Analysis forum:

http://www.dumpanalysis.org/forum/viewtopic.php?t=39

Now if by accident a customer sends a 64-bit dump of a 32-bit process then we can look at threads without asking for a new dump and, therefore, avoid roundtrips and shorten time to problem resolution.

Asmpedia

As a part of my master's thesis, I founded Wintel assembly language encyclopedia where information was presented from dump analysis and reverse engineering perspective.

At that time, I created some entries to test and collect comments. Instruction description included:

- definition and examples
- x86 and x64 differences
- C-style pseudo-code
- annotated WinDbg disassembly
- C/C++ compiler translation examples

Opcodes and mnemonics were cross-referenced.

I used Intel and AMD manuals and disassembly output from WinDbg as a reference.

Finally, I could fulfill my desire to learn all x86 instructions. Further, plans were to start with ARM assembly language as soon as I finished most of the Wintel part because I did development for Windows Mobile, and I was interested in low-level stuff there.

Unfortunately, this project was later abandoned due to insufficient time, and even the domain was dropped. Fortunately, just before revising this volume, we found out that the domain was available again, so we took it back and plan to revive this encyclopedia.

How WINE Can Help in Crash Dump Analysis

You probably already know or have heard about the project WINE: Windows API on top of X and UNIX: winehq.com

I first heard about it when it started, more than 10 years ago, before I wrote this post. Then I rediscovered it again and was surprised. I was looking for one NT status code I couldn't find in Microsoft official documentation and found it there.

To run Win32 programs, WINE emulates all API calls including OLE32, USER32, GDI32, KERNEL32, ADVAPI32, and, of course, NTDLL. Plus hundreds of other components. All source code is available: https://source.winehq.org/git/

So if you want to see how a particular function or protocol might have been implemented hypothetically by Windows OS designers, it is an excellent place to start.

Horrors of Debugging Legacy Code

We all know that macro definitions in C and C++ are evil. They cause maintenance nightmares by introducing subtle bugs. I never took that seriously until I was debugging my old code written in the late mid-1990s, which uses macros written earlier mid-1990s.

My Windows Mobile 5.0 application was crashing when I was using POOM COM interfaces (Pocket Outlook Object Model). The crash never pointed to my code. It always happened after *pimstore.dll* and other Microsoft modules were loaded, and COM interfaces started to return errors. I first suspected that I was using POOM incorrectly, and rewrote all code several times and in different ways. No luck. Then I tried PoomMaster sample from Windows Mobile 5.0 SDK, and it worked well. So I rewrote my code in exactly the same way as in that sample. No luck.

My last hope was that moving code from my DLL to EXE (as in that sample SDK project) would eliminate crashes, but it didn't help too. Then I slowly started to realize that the problem might have been in my old code, and I also noticed that one old piece of code had never been used before. So I started debugging by elimination (commenting out less and less code) until I found a macro. I had to stare at it for a couple of minutes until I realized that one pair of brackets was missing, and that caused allocating less memory and worse: the returned pointer to allocated memory was multiplied by 2! So the net result was the pointer pointing to other modules, and subsequent string copy was effectively overwriting their memory and eventually causing crashes inside Microsoft DLLs.

Here is that legacy macro:

```
#define ALLOC(t, p, s)
((p)=(t)GlobalLock(GlobalAlloc(GHND, (s))))
```

It allocates memory and returns a pointer. It should have been called like this (size parameter is highlighted in bold):

```
if (ALLOC(LPWSTR,lpm->lpszEvents,(lstrlen(lpszMacro)+1)*sizeof(WCHAR)))
{
  lstrcpy(lpm->lpszEvents, lpszMacro);
  lpm->nEvents=lstrlen(lpm->lpszEvents)+1;
}
```

What I found is the missing bracket before *lstrlen* function and last enclosing bracket (size parameter is highlighted in bold):

```
if (ALLOC(LPWSTR,lpm->lpszEvents,lstrlen(lpszMacro)+1)*sizeof(WCHAR))
{
  lstrcpy(lpm->lpszEvents, lpszMacro);
  lpm->nEvents=lstrlen(lpm->lpszEvents)+1;
}
```

The resulted code after the macro expansion looks like this

```
if (lpm->lpszEvents=(LPWSTR)GlobalLock(GlobalAlloc(GHND,
  lstrlen(lpszMacro)+1))*sizeof(WCHAR))
```

We see that the pointer to allocated memory is multiplied by two, and the string copy is performed to a random place in the address space of other loaded DLLs corrupting their data and causing the process to crash later.

UML and Device Drivers

I got the impression after reading numerous books and articles about device drivers that UML is never used in describing kernel and device driver design and architecture. Everything is described either by words or using proprietary notations.

Recently I created some diagrams based on my past experience in using UML to describe and communicate the architecture and design:

0. Component diagram depicting major driver interfaces:

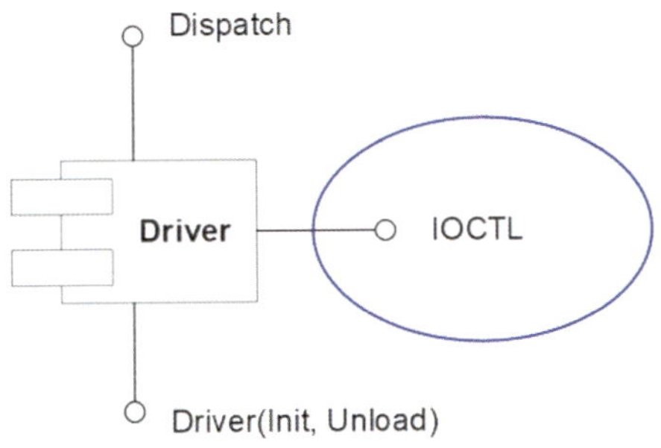

1. Class and object diagram depicting relationship between drivers and devices:

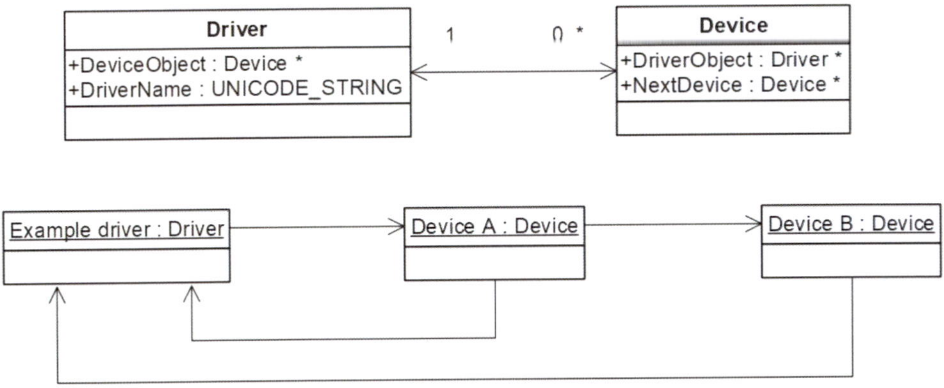

2. Component diagram showing dependencies and interfaces when calling Win32 API function *ReadFile*:

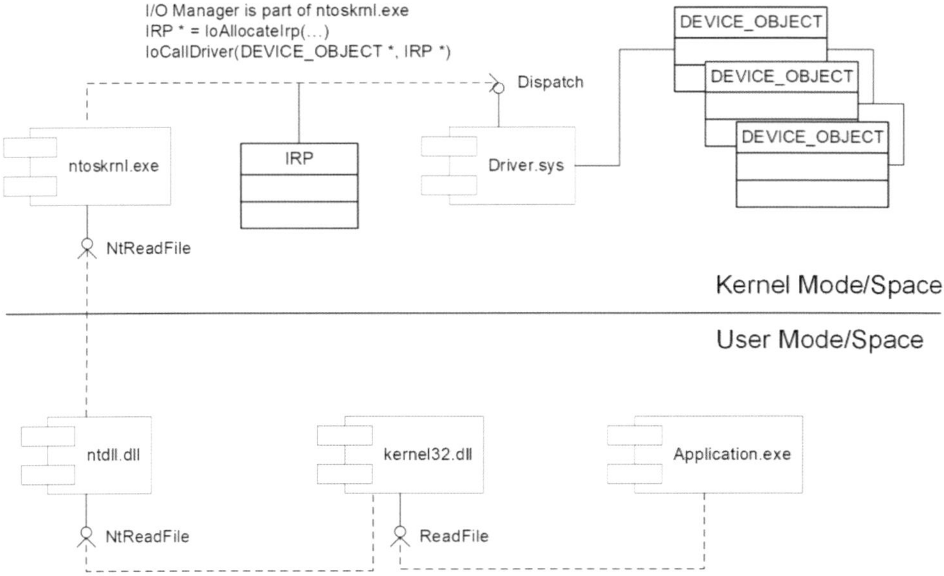

3. Component diagram showing IRP flow in a driver stack (driver-to-driver communication)

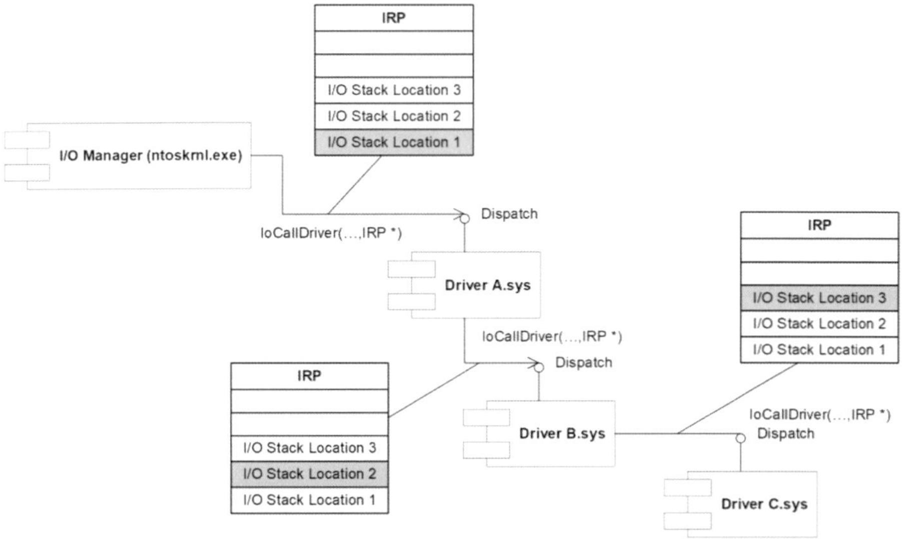

I found that some driver books incorrectly depict the ordering of I/O stack locations in IRP stack corresponding to driver or device stack. The correct layout is depicted above. IRP I/O stack locations grow down (to lower addresses) in memory like any other Wintel stack. We can see it from kernel dumps or the following macro from DDK header file *wdm.h* which shows that next IRP I/O stack location is down in memory (1 is subtracted from the current stack location pointer):

```
#define IoGetNextIrpStackLocation( Irp ) (\
    (Irp)->Tail.Overlay.CurrentStackLocation - 1 )
```

Memory dumps (and live debugging) are useful in studying component relationships and reconstructing sequence diagrams. For example, this edited fragment below is from a crash dump, and it shows who calls whom and component dependencies can be reconstructed from the call stack of Win32 API function *GetDriveType*: *SHELL32 (*calls it*) -> kernel32 -> ntdll -> nt (ntoskrnl.exe).* We can also see various Citrix hooks and filter drivers here (*CtxSbxXXX*):

```
kd> kL
CtxSbx!xxx
nt!IovCallDriver
nt!IofCallDriver
CtxAltStr!xxx
nt!IovCallDriver
nt!IofCallDriver
nt!IopParseDevice
nt!ObpLookupObjectName
nt!ObOpenObjectByName
nt!IopCreateFile
nt!IoCreateFile
nt!NtOpenFile
nt!KiSystemService
SharedUserData!SystemCallStub
ntdll!ZwOpenFile
CtxSbxHook!xxx
kernel32!GetDriveTypeW
SHELL32!CMountPoint::_EnumMountPoints
```

Statistics: 100% CPU Spread over all Processes

If this scenario happens after some event or user action, most likely, some notification hooks were involved. WinDbg **!thread** command for the current processor will most likely catch running thread than IdleLoop thread and **!process** command will show the current process context. Then from the thread stack, we can make an educated guess which components were likely responsible for that.

To change the current processor when looking at a memory dump file from a multiprocessor platform we can use **~"p"s** command where **"p"** is a zero-based processor number, for example, **~1s** changes the current processor to the second processor. Remember that every processor has its own thread and process context. If a processor has nothing to do, it is looping in the *KiIdleLoop* thread, which belongs to the Idle process.

Appendix

Crash Dump Analysis Portal

This all-in-one site features tight integration between:

- This book updates and errata
- Crash Dump Analysis blog
- Crash Dump Analysis forum
- Crash Dump Analysis patterns
- Reviews of debugging and software engineering books
- Links to various troubleshooting and debugging blogs, resources, and tools
- Information about current and forthcoming OpenTask titles
- Reference Stack Traces
- Asmpedia
- News
- Job advertisements
- WinDbg Quick Links
- Crash Dump Analysis checklist and poster
- E-zine

There is no registration unless you want to participate in various forums or subscribe to e-mail notifications.

This is how the portal looked like in 2008:

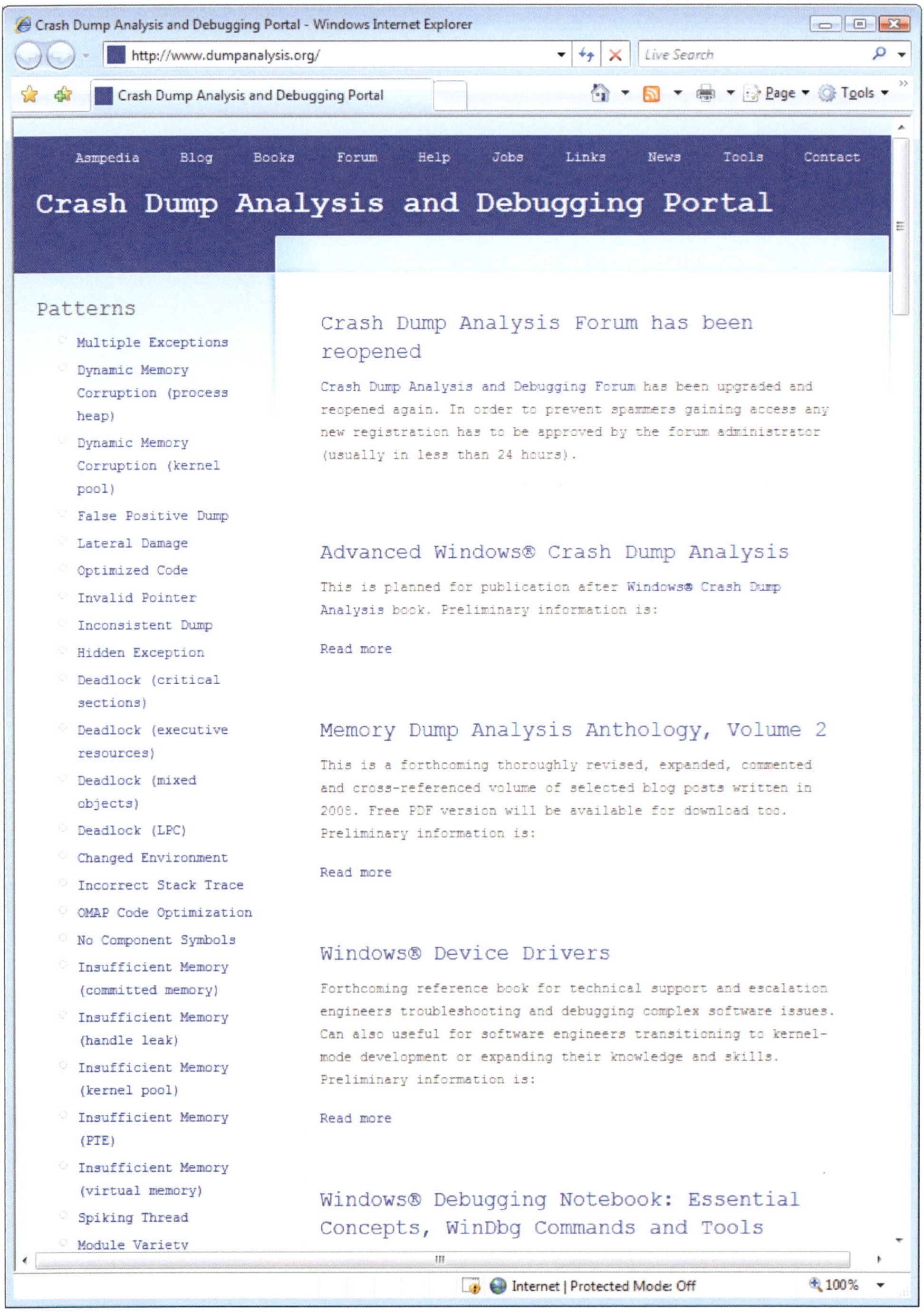

This is how it looks like in 2020 (renamed to Software Diagnostics Institute):

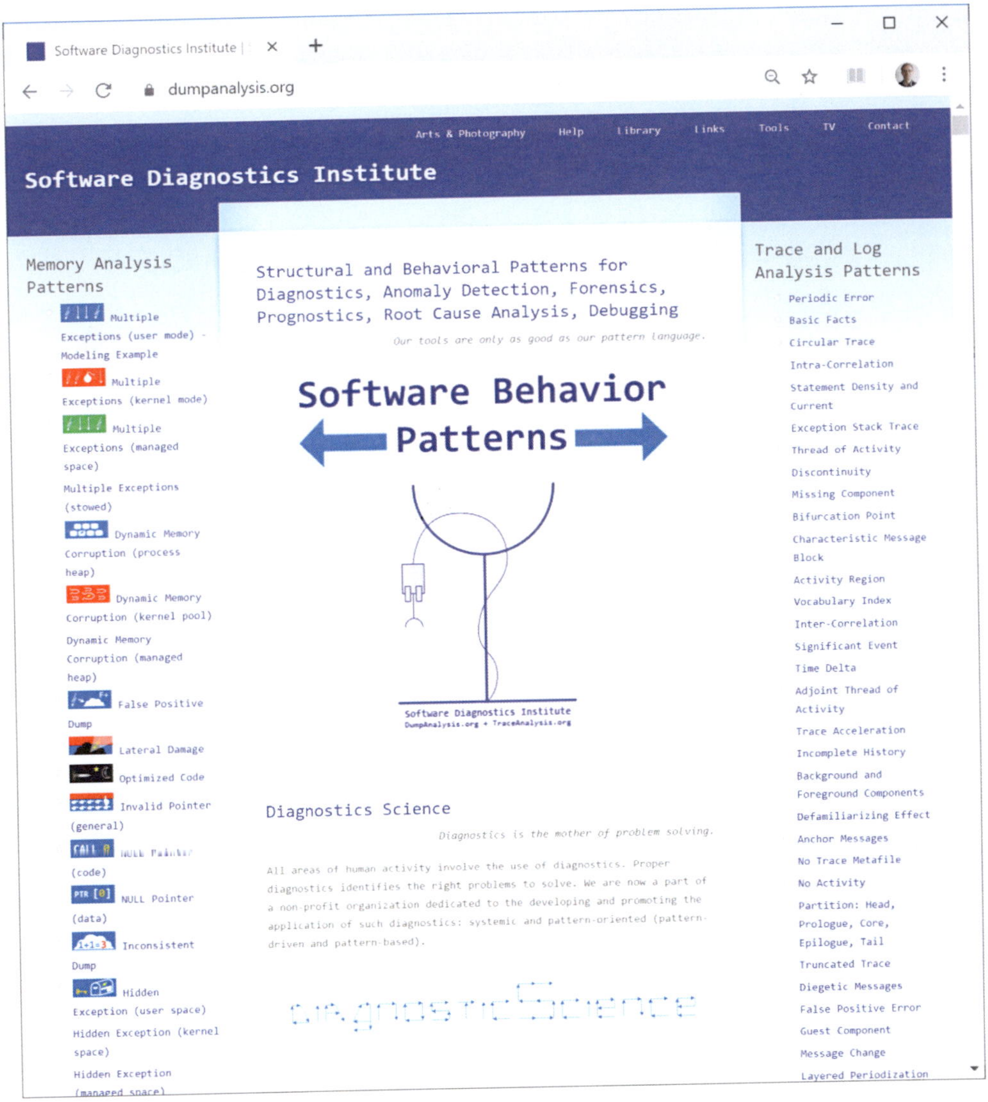

Reference Stack Traces

The following volumes contain typical thread stacks and other information from Windows complete memory dumps:

https://www.dumpanalysis.org/reference/ReferenceStackTraces_Vista_x86.pdf

https://www.dumpanalysis.org/reference/ReferenceStackTraces_Vista_x64.pdf

https://www.dumpanalysis.org/reference/ReferenceStackTraces_Windows2003_x86.pdf

Useful when trying to spot anomalies in the complete and kernel memory dumps coming from problem servers and workstations.

Index of WinDbg Commands

!

~

B

D

G

K

L

Cover Images

The front cover image is the picture of my book library, and the back cover image is visualized virtual process memory generated from a crash dump of **TestDefaultDebugger** (page 641) using **Dump2Picture** (page 532).

www.ingramcontent.com/pod-product-compliance
Ingram Content Group UK Ltd.
Pitfield, Milton Keynes, MK11 3LW, UK
UKRC031338111026
15625UKWH00052B/634